CENSUS OF INDIA 1911

D1878566

Census of India 1871-1951, 9 Sets In 384 Bindings (9788121258876) Rs. 700000

Census of India 1911, 23 Vols. In 41 Bindings (9788121271271) Rs. 69000

1. India - Report (9788121275071) Rs. 2475 (Vol. I, Pt. 1)
2. India - Tables (9788121275057) Rs. 2225 (Vol. I, Pt. 2)
3. Andaman and Nicobar Islands - Report & Tables (9788121275033) Rs. 900 (Vol. II, Pt. 1 & 2)
4. Assam - Report (9788121275019) Rs. 1000 (Vol. III, Pt. 1)
5. Assam - Tables (9788121274999) Rs. 1300 (Vol. III, Pt. 2)
6. Baluchistan - Report & Tables (9788121274975) Rs. 950 (Vol. IV, Pt. 1 & 2)
7. Bengal, Bihar And Orissa And Sikkim - Report (9788121274951) Rs. 3100 (Vol. V, Pt. 1)
8. Bengal - Tables (9788121274937) Rs. 2250 (Vol. V, Pt. 2)
9. Bihar And Orissa - Tables and Bengal And Sikkim - Chapter I of Administrative Volume (9788121274913) Rs. 1800 (Vol. V, Pt. 3 & 4)
10. City of Calcutta - Report and Tables and Administrative (9788121274876) Rs. 1300 (Vol. VI, Pt. 1 & 2 & 3)
11. Bombay - Report (9788121274814) Rs. 1950 (Vol. VII, Pt. 1)
12. Bombay - Imperial Tables and Administrative Report (9788121274791) Rs. 3300 (Vol. VII, Pt. 2 & 3)
13. Bombay (Town And Island) - Report And Tables (9788121274753) Rs. 1250 (Vol. VIII, Pt. 1 & 2)
14. Burma - Report (9788121274739) Rs. 2250 (Vol. IX, Pt. 1)
15. Burma - Tables (9788121274715) Rs. 1480 (Vol. IX, Pt. 2)
16. Central Provinces And Berar - Report (9788121274692) Rs. 1475 (Vol. X, Pt. 1)
17. Central Provinces And Berar - Tables (9788121274678) Rs. 1900 (Vol. X, Pt. 2)
18. Coorg - Report And Tables Madras - Report (9788121274630) Rs. 1740 (Vol. XI & Vol. XII, Pt. 1)
19. Madras - Imperial And Provincial Tables (9788121274616) Rs. 1500 (Vol. XII, Pt. 2)
20. Madras - Administrative Report and city of Madras (9788121274593) Rs. 630 (Vol. XII, Pt. 3 & 4)
21. North - West Frontier Province - Report & Tables (9788121274579) Rs. 2150 (Vol. XIII, Pt. 1 & 2)
22. Punjab - Report (9788121274555) Rs. 3000 (Vol. XIV, Pt. 1)
23. Punjab - Tables (9788121274531) Rs. 2200 (Vol. XIV, Pt. 2)
24. Punjab - Appendices To The - Imperial Tables (9788121274517) Rs. 950 (Vol. XIV, Pt. 3)
25. United Provinces of Agra And Oudh - Report (9788121274494) Rs. 2225 (Vol. XV, Pt. 1)
26. United Provinces of Agra And Oudh - Tables (9788121274470) Rs. 4000 (Vol. XV, Pt. 2)
27. United Provinces of Agra And Oudh - Provincial Tables And Appendices (9788121274456) Rs. 570 (Vol. XV, Pt. 3)
28. Baroda - Report (9788121274432) Rs. 2000 (Vol. XVI, Pt. 1)
29. Baroda State - The Imperial Tables (9788121274418) Rs. 850 (Vol. XVI, Pt. 2)
30. Central India Agency - Report And Tables (9788121274395) Rs. 1470 (Vol. XVII)
31. Cochin - Report And Imperial Tables (9788121274371) Rs. 1150 (Vol. XVIII, Pt. 1 & 2)
32. Hyderabad State - Report (9788121274357) Rs. 890 (Vol. XIX, Pt. 1)
33. Hyderabad State - Imperial And Provincial Tables (9788121274333) Rs. 1750 (Vol. XIX, Pt. 2)
34. Kashmir - Report (9788121274319) Rs. 950 (Vol. XX, Pt. 1)
35. Kashmir - Tables (9788121274296) Rs. 1170 (Vol. XX, Pt. 2)
36. Mysore - Report (9788121274272) Rs. 1200 (Vol. XXI, Pt. 1)
37. Mysore - Tables (9788121274258) Rs. 1500 (Vol. XXI, Pt. 2)
38. Rajputana And Ajmer-Merwara - Report (9788121274234) Rs. 1470 (Vol. XXII, Pt. 1)
39. Rajputana And Ajmer-Merwara - Tables (9788121274210) Rs. 1700 (Vol. XXII, Pt. 2)
40. Travancore - Report (9788121274197) Rs. 1870 (Vol. XXIII, Pt. 1)
41. Travancore - Imperial Tables (9788121274173) Rs. 870 (Vol. XXIII, Pt. 2)

Owing to the antiquity and rarity of this book, certain pages are regrettably absent, and readability is compromised due to the blurring of the original text. If you possess any insights regarding the availability of these missing sections, kindly inform us. Your assistance is crucial in ensuring the completion of this significant work for the benefit of future generations.

CENSUS OF INDIA, 1911

VOLUME - XVI

BARODA

PART I - REPORT

RAO BAHADUR
GOVINDBHAI H. DESAI

GYAN

Published by

GYAN

Gyan Publishing House
5, Ansari Road
Daryaganj, New Delhi-110002
Phone: 011-47034999, 9811692060
E-mail: books@gyanbooks.com

Distribution Network
gyanbooks.com
India, USA, Canada, UK, Australia

© Publisher
All rights reserved. No part of this work may be reproduced, stored, adapted, or transmitted in any form or by any means, electronic, mechanical, photocopying, micro-filming, recording or othrwise, or translated in any language, without the prior written permission of the copyright owner and the publisher.

ISBN: 978-81-212-7127-1 (Set) 23 Vols. In 41 Bindings

ISBN: 978-81-212-7443-2 (PB) Vol. XVI, Pt. I

First Published, 1911

2nd Impression 2024

Printed at: Gyan Press, Delhi.

The book is sold subject to the condition that it shall not, by way of trade or otherwise, be lent, resold, hired out, or otherwise circulated without the prior publisher's written consent.

CENSUS OF INDIA 1911

CENSUS OF INDIA, 1911.

VOLUME XVI.

BARODA.

PART I.

REPORT.

BY

RAO BAHADUR

GOVINDBHAI H. DESAI, B.A., LL.B.,

SUPERINTENDENT OF CENSUS OPERATIONS,

BARODA STATE.

Bombay:

PRINTED AT THE TIMES PRESS.

1911.

Price—Indian, Rs. 5 : English, 6s. 8d.

TABLE OF CONTENTS.

LIST OF DIAGRAMS AND MAPS.

LIST OF ILLUSTRATIONS.

INTRODUCTION.

Past Censuses.

The first Census of the territories of His Highness the Maharaja Gaekwad was taken on the 21st February 1872 along with the general Census in the Bombay Presidency. The results were tabulated partly in Baroda and partly in Bombay and the figures were published in the Census Report of the Bombay Presidency along with those of other States. The second Census was taken synchronously with that of the rest of India on the 17th February 1881. On this occasion, the results were extracted solely by the State agency and a Census Report—the first of its kind—was also prepared and published. Since then, Censuses are taken decennially and synchronously with the rest of India. The third Census was taken on the 26th of February 1891, and the fourth on the 1st of March 1901.

The present Census.

2. The present was the fifth Census of the State and was taken synchronously with that of the whole of India on the night of the 10th March 1911, that is, 10 years and 9 days after the preceding one. In fixing the date for taking the Census, days universally acknowledged as auspicious for marriages have to be avoided ; as also the greater festivals and important fairs which attract away people from their houses on a large scale. Again there ought to be enough moonlight on the date to be selected, so as to enable the Enumerators to complete the work of checking the schedules before midnight. The 10th of March 1911 complied with all these conditions and was agreed to by all Local Governments and Administrations.

Arrangement for the enumeration.

3. The present Census was taken on lines very similar to those of the previous ones, but more elaborate arrangements were made to ensure completeness and correct results. A full account of the procedure adopted in taking the Census and the compilation of the results has been given in a separate Administrative Report, but it may be interesting to note briefly in this introduction, a few of the more important facts connected with the operations. The Census office was opened on the 1st of May 1910. The villages and towns were first divided into convenient *Blocks,* each containing from 60 to 100 houses and placed in charge of an *Enumerator*, who was generally a village accountant (Talati), a school master or a clerk in some office. Over 10 to 15 Blocks was placed a *Supervisor* whose beat was called a *Circle* and who was a Police Naib-Foujdar (Head Constable) a Tajvijdar (Revenue Circle Inspector), or a Shirastedar or Head Clerk in some office. The taluka Vahivatdar (Tahsildar) was the *Charge Superintendent* for the Taluka, which had generally from 5 to 15 Supervisors and from 50 to 200 Enumerators. The Charge Superintendent for the City of Baroda was the Chief Officer of the Municipality and in Navsari, Patan, Amreli and such other Municipal and head-quarters towns, the Charge was held by the Chairman of the Municipality or the local Munsiff. The Charge Superintendents were in their turn subordinate to the Suba (District Magistrate) and his Sub-divisional Officers. There were in round numbers 92 Charge Superintendents, 1,273 Supervisors, and 10,893 Enumerators in the whole State. Census conferences were held in the head-quarters of all the districts ; instruction books were prepared for all the

stages of work ; written instructions were supplemented by oral teaching ; and, on the whole, everything possible was done to obtain correct entries in the different columns of the Census schedules.

House-numbering.

4. The first direct step towards the taking of the Census was the numbering of houses. The old definition of a house, *viz.*, a building with an independent entrance, was given up and a new one defining a house as the residence of a commensal family, that is, persons dining of food cooked on one *chula* or hearth, was adopted this time and each such house was given a separate number. In addition to the ordinary dwelling houses, care was taken to affix numbers to temples, *dharmshalas*, camping grounds, *bunders* and similar other places where any one was likely to sleep on the night of the Census. When all the houses had been numbered, a statement showing the number of houses and of the different grades of Census Officers was compiled and arrangements were made for supplying the necessary Census forms.

The Preliminary Enumeration.

5. Having been fully posted in their duties, the Enumerators took the next step of preparing the preliminary record, *i. e.*, the entry in the enumeration schedules of the necessary particulars regarding all persons ordinarily resident in each house. The information to be recorded included name, religion, sex, civil condition, age, caste, occupation, birth-place, parent tongue, literacy or illiteracy, knowledge of English and certain infirmities. The preliminary record was prepared in the mofussil between the 20th January and the 20th February. In towns, it was begun and finished ten days later. The period remaining before the 10th March was utilised in checking the entries. The closest supervision was exercised not only by the Supervisors and Charge Superintendents, but also by all other officers who could by any means be spared for the purpose, and special efforts were made to examine and correct the Enumerators' work.

The Final Census.

6. The final Census was the process of checking and correcting the record of the preliminary enumeration by striking out the entries relating to persons who had died or gone away and entering the necessary particulars of newly-born children and new-comers, so that it may correspond with the state of facts actually existing on the Census night. It commenced at about 7 p. m. on the evening of the 10th March and was completed by midnight.

In a few forest tracts in the Navsari District, where night Census was not possible owing to the houses being scattered over a large forest and mountainous area and danger from wild beasts, the final revision was commenced a few hours earlier, so that it might be completed by nightfall.

In order to secure reasonable expedition and to reduce the number of alterations to a minimum, a proclamation was issued some time beforehand, asking people to avoid that date for weddings and other social or religious gatherings and to stay awake at home with a light burning till the Enumerators had visited them.

The Provisional Totals.

7. Immediately after the final Census, the Enumerators repaired to a place previously fixed by their Supervisors and prepared an abstract showing the number of inhabited houses and of persons, male and female, in their Blocks. These abstracts after being

checked by a second Enumerator were posted by the Supervisor in a summary for his circle. The circle summaries were checked and posted in a charge summary, and the totals were wired to the head-quarters at Baroda where the Provisional Totals for the State were compiled. These summaries began to arrive on the morning of the 11th March, and continued to come in till the 12th idem. Considerable care and ingenuity were shown by the Taluka Officers in working out the scheme for getting in the totals as quickly as possible. The first to communicate its totals was Bhadran Peta Mahal. The totals of this charge were ready at 6 a.m. and were immediately telegraphed with the result that they reached me at 8-15 a.m. on March 11th. This reflects great credit on the Mahalkari, Mr. Hakumatrai Harrai, whose arrangements were excellent. The whole of the Census staff worked all night and the collection of circle summaries was effected by mounted men supplied by jamindars. Bhadran was followed by Sankheda, Dabhoi, Mehsana, Songhad, Vyara and other talukas. The totals for the State were reported to His Highness' Government and to the Census Commissioner for India within 48 hours after the taking of the Census. The total population as shown by those provisional figures differed by only 1,345 or ·066 per cent. from the figures arrived at after detailed tabulation—a result which the Census Commissioner for India considered as "most creditable to all concerned."

Preparation of Final Tables.

8. After the Census was over and the provisional totals were published, the schedules were collected together in the central office at Baroda and the next step was the preparation of the final tables. The books of the schedules containing the various particulars recorded by the Enumerators for each individual have been aptly described as the "raw material of the Census" and the final tables as the "manufactured product." The transformation of the one into the other involves three processes—abstraction, tabulation and compilation—of which the first is by far the most difficult and complicated.

The Slip System.

9. Previous to 1901, the figures for the final tables were obtained in India by means of what was known as the "tick" system. For every final table, there was a separate abstraction sheet, divided by rules into spaces corresponding to the headings of the table concerned. A separate sheet was used for each Enumerator's book and a tick was made in the appropriate column corresponding to each entry therein. When the whole book had been abstracted, the ticks were counted and the figures thus obtained were added up for the taluka, and the figures for the latter were compiled into a total for the district. This "clumsy, untrustworthy and antiquated" method was abandoned and the "slip" or card system invented by Herr Von Mayor, in connection with the Bavarian Census of 1872 and adopted in European countries, was introduced in the Indian Census by Sir Herbert Risley in 1901. This "slip" system, with such further improvements as were suggested by the experience of the last Census, was used in the present Census also. In the last Census, two separate slips—a coloured one and a white one—were prepared for each individual and the sexes were denoted by the difference in the length of the slips. In the present Census, only one slip, measuring two inches by four-and-a-half, was prepared for each individual. As a guide for the particulars that were required to be posted on to the slips, the

headings of the columns of the Census schedules were printed in brief on one side, and opposite each heading, the poster was ordered to write down the requisite information from the enumeration books given to him. In order to reduce writing work, slips of different colours were used for the different religions, and the following symbols were printed on them to indicate sex and civil condition :—

	Married.	Unmarried.	Widowed.
Male ...			
Female ...			

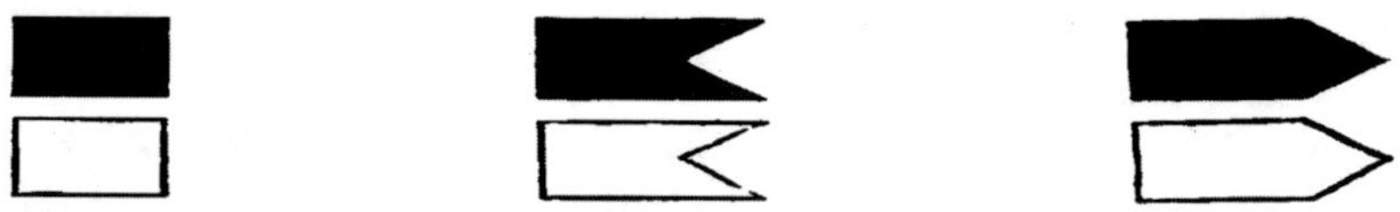

These devices obviated the necessity of making any entry on the slip for religion, sex and civil condition. Even in the heads for which entries had to be copied, the labour of copying was further reduced by the judicious use of abbreviations, *e. g.*, ગુ for Gujarati, મ for Marathi, ઇ for English, etc.

After the copying of the schedule entries on the slips was over, the slips were sorted for all the final tables in turn. Each Sorter was supplied with a set of pigeon-holes which were labelled to indicate their contents. For instance when sorting for education, one pigeon-hole would be labelled "literate," another "literate in English," and so on. All the slips on which "literate" was written were placed in the pigeon-hole labelled "literate" and all those for "literate in English" into the pigeon-hole labelled "literate in English." When the sorting for the table had been completed, the slips in each pigeon-hole were counted and the result was noted on a form called the "Sorter's Ticket." The figures in the sorter's tickets were then posted in the "Compilation Registers" and added up to obtain the taluka or district total.

Slip-copying.

10. The posting of the slips was done only in one central office at Baroda. It was begun on 16th March and finished on 30th April 1911. Excluding holidays it occupied 37 days. As soon as the posting of a book was completed, the book with the bundle of the slips was checked by the Supervisor in charge.

Sorting the slips.

11. The sorting of the slips was commenced on 1st May 1911 and finished within less than three months. There were in all 18 tables to be prepared, and some of them, such as those connected with caste and occupation, took up much time and involved correspondence with District Officers for further information on obscure or incorrect entries.

Compilation.

12. The sorting of slips was followed by compilation and tabulation, which took up about two months and was finished by the end of September. As soon as each table was ready, it was printed and copies were forwarded to the Census Commissioner for India for review, and when all the tables were passed as correct, they were finally reprinted in book-form. The Tables Volume was published early in November 1911, thus establishing a record for speed, not only for the State but for the whole of India. In this connection, I may be permitted to quote, with

pardonable pride, the following remarks of the Census Commissioner for India in his letter No. 1960, dated the 28th November 1911:—"I congratulate you on the extreme celerity with which your tables have been prepared and printed. They are the first which I have received in complete form; and so far as I can see no others are likely to reach me for the next six weeks or two months. At no previous Census has any Province or State completed its Imperial Tables so quickly as you have done on the present occasion."

The Report.

13. The writing of the report and the preparation of the diagrams were taken in hand when the tabulation work was well advanced, and the whole report was ready for the Press about the middle of December. Mr. Gait, the Census Commissioner for India, had intimated in his notes of inspection of the Census of Baroda that the report of the last Baroda Census was very bulky, mainly owing to the inclusion of unnecessary details, loose printing and the many full-page litho diagrams, and that on the present occasion, I should try to reduce its bulk as much as possible. Bearing in mind that the utility of a report is in inverse proportion to its bulk, I have tried my best to make this report as concise and handy as possible. Considerable space has been saved by solid printing and small scale inset diagrams in place of the old full-page lithographs. But before leaving out any details, I had to bear in mind what Mr. Gait himself wrote in 1901 in the introduction of his Bengal Census Report, *viz.*, that "completeness is more important than brevity, especially in India, where there is no body of professional statisticians ready and eager to pounce on the raw material provided for them at the Census and to make the required deductions, and, unless the Census Superintendent himself analyses the figures and points to the conclusions to be drawn from them, they are in danger of being left unnoticed altogether." With a view to make this report more interesting and intelligible, I have, with the approval of His Highness' Government and of the Census Commissioner for India, illustrated it with the photos of some typical people to be found within this State.

Cost of the Census.

14. I have done my utmost on the present occasion to complete the Census operations with as little cost and within as little time as possible. The whole time occupied from start to finish in the present Census is twenty-one months or about one year less than in 1901. The total expenditure of all kinds in the present Census will be about Rs. 56,000 or Rs. 26 per 1,000 of the population, compared with Rs. 1,25,000 or rather more than Rs. 60 per 1,000 of the population in 1901. This large reduction in cost was mainly due to strict economy under all the heads of charges and hard work throughout the operations.

Acknowledgments.

15. In conclusion, I must express my indebtedness to E. A. Gait, Esquire, C.I.E., I.C.S., Census Commissioner for India, for his cordial help and able guidance at all the stages of the work and to the authors of the various reports and works which I have freely consulted and sometimes merely copied. I am also indebted to all the District Officers who cordially co-operated with me. In my own office, my thanks are due to Mr. Manirai Trikamrai Joshipara, B.A., LL.B., who was my Assistant till Sorting work was over and to Mr. Maganlal N. Thakkar, B.A., LL.B., my Head

Clerk, and afterwards Personal Assistant, who laboured hard with me from start to finish, and whose high intelligence, devotion to duty and wide information, rendered his services extremely useful. In the subordinate staff all worked well, but the work of Messrs. Yadavrao Mahadev Vaidya and Vasudev Prabhashanker Trivedi was specially commendable. Lastly, I must express my acknowledgments to the *Times* Press, Bombay, for printing this Report, as also the Tables Volume, with a promptitude and neatness which reflect great credit on its organization and management.

G. H. DESAI,
Superintendent of Census Operations,
Baroda State.

BARODA, 25*th December* 1911.

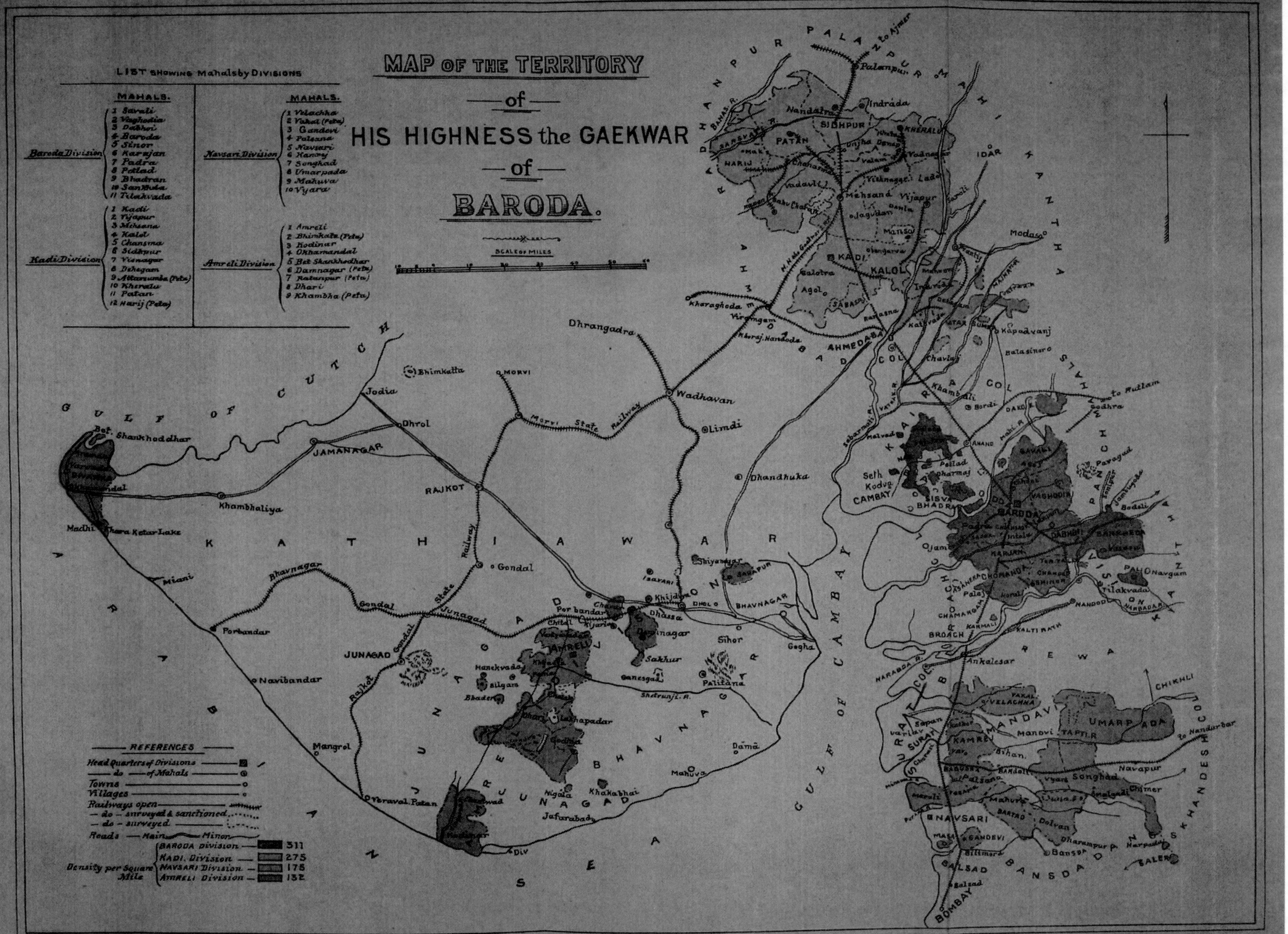

MAP OF THE TERRITORY
of
HIS HIGHNESS the GAEKWAR
of
BARODA.
SCALE OF MILES
LIST SHOWING Mahals by DIVISIONS
MAHALS.
Baroda Division
1 Savali
2 Vaghodia
3 Dabhoi
4 Baroda
5 Sinor
6 Karajan
7 Padra
8 Petlad
9 Bhadran
10 Sankheda
11 Tilakvada
Kadi Division
1 Kadi
2 Vijapur
3 Mehsana
4 Kalol
5 Chansma
6 Sidhpur
7 Visnagar
8 Dehegam
9 Attarsumba (Peta)
10 Kheralu
11 Patan
12 Harij (Peta)
MAHALS.
Navsari Division
1 Velachha
2 Vakal (Peta)
3 Gandevi
4 Palsana
5 Navsari
6 Kamrej
7 Songhad
8 Umarpada
9 Mahuva
10 Vyara
Amreli Division
1 Amreli
2 Bhimkatta (Peta)
3 Kodinar
4 Okhamandal
5 Bet Shankhodhar
6 Damnagar (Peta)
7 Ratanpur (Peta)
8 Dhari
9 Khambha (Peta)
REFERENCES
Head Quarters of Divisions
do of Mahals
Towns
Villages
Railways open
– do – surveyed & sanctioned
– do – surveyed
Roads — Main — Minor
Density per Square Mile
BARODA Division 311
KADI Division 275
NAVSARI Division 178
AMRELI Division 132
GULF OF CUTCH
KATHIAWAR
GULF OF CAMBAY
ARABIAN SEA
PALANPUR
MAHI KANTHA
REWA KANTHA
PANCH MAHALS
KHANDESH COL
BANSDA
AHMEDABAD
KAIRA COL
BROACH COL
SURAT COL
JUNAGAD
BHAVNAGAR
BARODA
NAVSARI
AMRELI
KALOL
KADI
PATAN
SIDHPUR
CAMBAY
RAJKOT
JAMANAGAR
Wadhavan
Dhrangadra
Limdi
Dhandhuka
Porbandar
Navibandar
Mangrol
Veraval Patan
Div
Jodia
Dhrol
Khambhaliya
Bhimkatta
Gondal
Gogha
Sihor
Palitana
Mahuva
Jafarabad
Bombay
Ankalesar
TIMES PRESS, BOMBAY.

REPORT

ON THE

CENSUS OF BARODA STATE, 1911.

Chapter I.

DISTRIBUTION OF THE POPULATION.

I.—GENERAL DESCRIPTION OF BARODA STATE.

Boundary.

1. The territories of His Highness the Maharaja Gaekwad lie between 20° 45′ and 21° 42′ N Latitude and between 70° 45′ and 71° 22′ E Longitude, excepting Okhamandal which lies between 22° and 22° 28′ N Latitude and between 68° 58′ and 69° 14′ E Longitude. Roughly speaking, from the Northern extremity of the Thana District to the South, to Palanpur to the North and from the Western limits of the Nasik District to the South-East to the extreme North-West of Kathiawad, there lie interspersed with British or other territory, tracts of land wherein His Highness the Gaekwad's sway is acknowledged.

History.

2. Baroda State has a very interesting history which stretches back through twelve centuries. When the famous Chinese traveller Houen Tsang visited India in the seventh century after Christ, he found the whole of Gujarat a very flourishing country, ruled by the Valabhis who had their capital at Valabhipur. In the following century, the power of the Valabhis was broken by the Chalukya Rajputs, who conquered the kingdom and established their capital at Anhilvar-Pattan, situated within the present limits of the Baroda State. When Mahmad of Gazni invaded Gujarat and attacked the famous temple of Somnath, the Prince of Anhilvar-Pattan marched against him with a large army and fought a decisive battle for his country and his religion. The Prince was defeated, but collected a fresh army to meet his foe again and Mahmad avoided a second encounter by retiring across the deserts of Sindh. A succeeding prince, Kumarpal, favoured the Jain religion and the Jains of Baroda assign many of their religious edifices and other public works and gifts to his reign. Altogether the Rajputs ruled for over five centuries, from the eighth to the close of the thirteenth, and some of the ruins of their temples, fortifications and edifices are still visible at Patan. Allaudin Khilji conquered the country from the Hindus, and the story of the beautiful Princesses Kalma Devi and Deval Devi, who became the wives of Allaudin and his son, is one of the romances of Indian history. For some centuries, Patan continued to be the capital of Gujarat under the Mahomedan rulers, but the seat of Government was eventually removed to Ahmedabad. Gujarat threw off the yoke of Delhi and became an independent Mahomedan kingdom in the fourteenth century, but was once more brought under Northern India by Akbar-the-Great in the sixteenth century. Aurangzeb's mad bigotry wrecked the Mogal empire which Akbar had built up, and in the eighteenth century, the Marathas spread over Gujarat, as over other parts of India. Pilajirao Gaekwad and his comrades in arms firmly established themselves in Baroda in 1723, and the present ruling family has therefore a dynastic record of nearly two centuries.

Administrative Districts.

3. For administrative purposes, Baroda State is divided into the four districts of Baroda, Kadi, Navsari and Amreli which are situated widely apart from each other and are separated, one from the other, by large tracts of British territory or of other Native States. None of these districts forms a continuous block of territory ; each is cut up by large tracts of intervening foreign territory. Each of the districts is sub-divided into Talukas, or Peta Talukas, which on the 10th of March 1911 were as under :—

Baroda District.	Kadi District.	Navsari District.	Amreli District.
Petlad.	Dehgam.	Navsari.	Amreli.
Bhadran.	Atarsumba.	Gandevi.	Damnagar.
Baroda (exclusive of Baroda City and Cantonment).	Kadi.	Palsana.	Dhari.
Padra.	Kalol.	Kamrej.	Khambha.
Karjan.	Vijapur.	Mahuva.	Kodinar.
Dabhoi.	Visnagar.	Velachha.	Okhamandal.
Sinore.	Mehsana.	Songhad.	Beyt.
Savli.	Sidhpur.	Vyara.	Ratanpur.
Vaghodia.	Kheralu.	Vakal.	Bhimkatta.
Sankheda.	Patan.	Umarpada.	
Tilakwada.	Chansma.		
	Harij.		

These divisions are the same as existed in 1901, with the exception that Vajpur, which was a separate peta taluka, is now joined to Songhad taluka, and Umarpada is carved out of it as a separate peta taluka. The talukas which were previously known by the names of Choranda and Vadavli are now known as Karjan and Chansma respectively ; and the peta talukas of Siswa and Shiyanagar are now officially known as Bhadran and Ratanpur respectively.

Physiography.

4. The greater part of the State lies within the area of the coastal band of alluvium which has been formed by the encroachment on the shallow gulf of Cambay, of the detrital deposits brought down by the many rivers, large and small, which drain the province of Gujarat, the western slopes of Malwa and the southern parts of Rajputana. The upward slope of the alluvial band, from the sea-board eastward is very gradual, so that, except where windblown accumulations of loam or sand make small local eminences, here and there, the surface of the country appears to be a dead flat. It is only as the eastern side of the alluvial flat is approached that it is interrupted by low hills, which rise up at intervals or bounded by yet lower downs dividing the different small river courses.

Hills and Ridges.

5. Though generally a flat country, Baroda territory both in Gujarat proper and Kathiawad is relieved by a few hills and ridges. In the Kadi District, the only eminences which diversify the general flat surface of the country are hillocks and ridges of blown sandy loam which rise on an average from 50 to 60 feet above the general level and only occasionally attain a height of about 100 feet. In the Baroda District even such hillocks are absent, except in the Sankheda taluka in the east, where they attain a height of about 500 feet above the sea level. The Navsari district is hilly and wooded in its eastern part. There the height of the hills ranges between 400 to 2,000 feet above the sea level, with the exception of one hill, *viz.*, Salher which attains a height of 5,263 feet and is the third highest point in the northern section of the Sahyadri range. In the Amreli district, it is only in the Dhari taluka that we meet with hills worth the name, ranging in height from 1,000 to 2,100 feet above the sea level. Kodinar taluka has small hills in its north, hardly rising over 400 feet ; while the flat places of Amreli and Damnagar talukas and the sandy level of Okhamandal are diversified by yet smaller eminences, some of which are flat topped, forming plateaux on the summit.

Hydrology.

6. The drainage of the Gujarat divisions of the Baroda State, all falls westward into the gulf of Cambay in the Arabian sea, which receives such a vast amount of silt brought down the larger rivers that it is rapidly being silted up as shown by the present condition of the harbours of Surat, Broach and Cambay. Not two centuries ago, these sea ports were visited by fleets of shipping of the ordinary

size of the traders of those days. Now they are with difficulty reached by vessels of as low a tonnage as about 30 tons.

Principal rivers.

7. The four principal rivers falling into the Gulf of Cambay are the Sabarmati, the Mahi, the Narbada and the Tapti, all large rivers and flowing in part of their course, comparatively a small one, through Baroda territory. Of much smaller size are the Dhadhar, between the Mahi and the Narbada, the Kim, between the Narbada and the Tapti, and to the south of the latter the Mindhola, the Purna and the Ambika. The only river of importance in the Amreli Division is the Shetrunji which rises in the highest part of the Gir forest and drains the central part of the division. The smaller ones are the Raval and the Dhantarwadi of the Dhari Taluka, the Singoara which divides the Kodinar Taluka into two unequal lobes and the Ranghola of the Damnagar Taluka.

Soil.

8. The soil in the whole of the State is alluvial, except in the hilly parts of the Navsari and Amreli Districts and in the south-east corner of the Baroda District, where it is mostly formed by disintegration of the underlying rocks. The alluvial soils of Baroda State may be roughly divided into (1) *Gorat* or sandy loam, (2) *Kali*, or black and (3) those formed by the intermixture of the two called "*Besar*." The rock-formed soils are for the most part black, but where they have come into contact with alluvial soils, they have formed a variety of *Besar*. The soils of the Navsari and Baroda Districts may principally be classed as *Gorat*, black and *Besar*. As a rule, the black soil of the Navsari District is far superior to the soil of similar kind found in the other districts. *Bhatha* lands or lands formed in the beds of rivers from alluvial deposits are often found in the Navsari District and are most productive. In the Kadi District, the soil is mostly of the light sandy kind. Black soil is met with, but only in patches, in parts of the district. The soils of Amreli District (Okhamandal excepted) may be classed under two main heads, black and *Gorat*, but the *Gorat* of this district is much inferior to the *Gorat* of Baroda and Navsari Districts. The black is also much inferior to the black of Baroda. In Okhamandal, the soil in the northern half is light red and along the whole of the coast line, it is sandy and unproductive, but inland it is fairly fertile.

Rainfall.

9. The average annual rainfall ranges from about 40 to 70 inches in the different parts of the Navsari District, from 30 to 50 inches in the Baroda District; from 15 to 35 in the Kadi District and from 13 to 30 in the Amreli District. Thus the fall is the heaviest in the southernmost district, and it goes on diminishing as the monsoon current travels from the south towards the north. It is considerably heavier in Gujarat proper, than in Kathiawad. The duration of rainfall is about 4½ months in the Navsari District commencing early in June and ending by the middle of October. It is four months in other divisions, commencing a little later, that is, about the end of June. The character of the *Kharif* crops and the good prospects of the *Rabi* depend entirely upon the regularity and seasonableness of rainfall from the middle of June or the beginning of July to the middle of October. The late showers of October help the spring crops also. Sufficient and timely rain in June, July and August in the Navsari District and in July and August in the other districts gives hopes of a good harvest ; but the full and satisfactory maturity of the crops depends upon the September and October showers.

Climate.

10. The climate of the Baroda State varies considerably in the different districts. But it may be said generally that it is dry and hot in the hot season, which commences in March and ends in June, the hottest months being May and June. The climate during the rainy season, that is from July to October is hot, moist and relaxing. During the cold season which commences in November and ends in February, the climate is dry and cool. The coldest months are generally December and January. In the months of September and October, the climate is more unwholesome than n any other time of the year, and the people suffer considerably from malarious fevers.

Temperature.

11. The mean yearly temperature ranges from 52°·5 at Baroda to 69°·4 at Mehsana. The minimum temperature during the cold weather months is about 40°·1 and the maximum during the hot weather 109°·5. The highest temperature recorded in 1910 was 114° in the month of June and the lowest 35° in the month of January at Mehsana (Kadi District). This shows that the climate of the Baroda State and adjoining parts of Gujarat is an extreme one especially in the northern parts when compared with that of the southern parts.

Health.

12. The general health of the Baroda District, including the Baroda City, is good during the hot and the early part of the rainy season; but during the later portion of the latter and the greater part of the cold season, there is a general prevalence of malarious fevers, bowel complaints and affections of the lungs. The general health in the Kadi District is much better than in the other districts. The most prevalent diseases are malarious fevers, diarrhœa, bronchitis, diseases of the elementary canal, rheumatic afflictions and skin diseases. The general health of the Navsari District is fair. Malarious fevers are extremely prevalent, especially in the Rani Mahals. At Songhad and Vyara, there is not a single individual who has not an enlarged spleen, which gives rise to a protuberant abdomen and in some cases to splenetic ascites, most fatal to those who are strangers in the land. The prevalent diseases in the Amreli district are generally fevers and bowel complaints. In Dhari and Khambha, people also suffer from diseases of the spleen, and in Okhamandal and Kodinar from guinea-worms due to drinking bad water.

Agriculture.

13. The inhabitants of the Baroda State are for the most part agriculturists. The principal crops are *juwar*, *bajri*, rice, pulse, cotton, tobacco and oil-seeds. The crops are generally thriving and plentiful in Kadi and the western half of the Baroda District; the coast line and the western talukas of the Navsari District are very fertile and yield garden produce, but the south-eastern parts are inferior in fertility and owing to rocks and mountains are hardly cultivable in some places. The Amreli district as a whole is much inferior in fertility, but there are very fertile tracts here and there, especially in the Amreli, Damnagar and Kodinar talukas.

Of the total culturable land in the State, 87·4 per cent. as against 86 per cent. in 1901 is under cultivation and 12·6 per cent. is available for further cultivation. On an average, each individual of the total population has 3 bighas of cultivated land and ·45 bighas of culturable land for further cultivation. Taking the districts separately, Baroda has 91·2 per cent., Kadi 84·5, Navsari 92·5 and Amreli 83·8 per cent. of its cultivable land under cultivation. Kadi and Amreli Districts have yet a large proportion of land that can be brought under cultivation.

Irrigation.

14. Small irrigation works are met with all over the Raj, especially what are called "Paddy tanks," whose duty is to protect rice, the chief of the monsoon crops by giving it water during a break in the rains and more especially giving it the last one or two waterings to mature it. The number of such tanks in each division or taluka varies with the nature of the staple crops, nature of the soil and the intelligence, skill and capacity of the cultivators. Navsari Division which has good and rich irrigable soil, intelligent cultivators, and high class crops grown, is singularly fortunate in the possession of a large number of paddy tanks, almost every village in each taluka possessing one or more. Baroda Division comes next to Navsari in point of their number, and the rice growing talukas of Vaghodia, Savli and to a certain extent, Baroda abound with them. Kadi Division has also a fairly large number of such tanks, especially the two sister talukas of Kadi and Kalol, where rice is extensively grown. Its cultivation is, however, falling off, owing to the scanty and ill-timed rainfall of late years, and the utter state of disrepair of all tanks. Hardly any rice is grown in the Amreli Division and so there are no paddy tanks worth the name. The division, however, like that of Navsari, possesses a few rivers and streams in which there is a flow throughout or nearly throughout the year. In both divisions, there are *bandharas* or weirs thrown

across such water-courses and the impounded water is led by channels to irrigate the fields. The Allidhar Vellar Bund near Harmadia, the Natalia Bund near Dhari, both in Amreli Division, and the Chikhli Bhandarpada and Tichakia (now broken) in Navsari Division, may be mentioned as instances of this form of irrigation. Besides the above, irrigation from wells is carried on in all divisions, chiefly for crops other than the monsoon ones. The sinking of new wells is encouraged by the State under a liberal and well-conceived system of taccavi advances. It was in the famine year of 1899-1900 that a great stimulus was given to the construction of irrigation works on systematic and scientific lines, providing on them, wherever possible, modern improvements. Irrigation works more than any other were generally adopted as famine works, for, consisting chiefly of storage tanks with earthen embankments, they were eminently suited for unskilled famine labour. And, secondly, the famine being due to the want of rains and water, the first idea naturally was to store and preserve water by all possible and practical means. The Karachia, Haripura, Lachara, Khokara, Kumbharia and Muval tanks, the Orsang works, all in Baroda Division, owe their inception as new tanks or their thorough repairs and enlargements to the great famine. Due to the same cause, the Chimnabai tank and Anawada works, the Thol tank, &c., in Kadi Division, and Pichvi and Bhimgaja works in Amreli Division, were undertaken. Irrigation works take years to produce their full economic effect. Most of the irrigation works in the State being new, have not had any appreciable effect in the increase of population in this decade, but they are expected to have far-reaching effects in the future.

Railways.

15. The B. B. and C. I. Railway with its auxiliary the Rajputana-Malwa Railway passes from south to north, almost in a straight line, through the Navsari, Baroda and Kadi Districts, and has many important stations like Bilimora, Navsari, Kosamba, Miyagam, Baroda, Kalol, Mehsana and Sidhpur in the State territory. In addition to this, there are several branch railways connecting important places in the interior of the State with the main line and serving as its feeders. The Tapty Valley Railway joining Khandesh with Gujarat at Surat, has stations at Vyara and Songhad, which are the headquarters of the forest talukas of the Navsari District. The Kosamba Zankvav branch line, which joins the main line at Kosamba in the same district opens out Velachha, Vakal and other fertile but backward talukas. In the Baroda and Kadi Districts, there is a regular network of railways, and there is hardly any important place which remains unconnected. From Miyagam in the Baroda District run two branches, one to Sinore on the Narbada, and another to Bodeli on the border of the Chhota Udepur State, both passing through a very fertile cotton district. From Baroda runs a line which connects it on one side with Dabhoi and Chandod, a very important place of pilgrimage, and on the other with Padra and Kanjat, near Jambusar in the Broach Collectorate. Another line connects Baroda with Godhra, Ratlam and Malwa; and a third one joins the town of Petlad with Anand Junction on the B. B. and C. I. Railway on one side and with the port of Cambay on the other. In the Kadi District, the Ahmedabad-Prantij Railway connects the Dehgam Taluka with Ahmedabad, and the Kalol-Kadi, Kalol-Vijapur, Mehsana-Patan, Mehsana-Viramgam, Mehsana-Dabhoda, Chansma-Bechraji and Chansma-Harij branch lines connect all the taluka stations of the district with Mehsana, the district headquarters in the centre, and with Ahmedabad, the capital of Gujarat and Baroda, the capital of the State. The remote district of Amreli in Kathiawad is awaiting the boon of railways. The attention of His Highness' Government had long been directed to the need of providing railways in that district, but the difficulties about the jurisdiction, &c., always brought matters to a stand-still. These have, however, now been overcome and a line from Dhasa to Lilia in Bhavnagar State, passing through the Damnagar Taluka of the State, is being laid, and one from Khijadia to Amreli and thence to Chalala and Velan Bunder on the sea-coast and another from Jamnagar to Dwarka are under projection. When completed, Amreli will have the same railway advantage which is enjoyed by the other districts of the State.

16. The statistics of the Census are grouped for administrative purposes according to the administrative units of a Province or State. But within

these, there are usually wide differences dependent for the most part on the aggregate of physical conditions commonly called environments. The Provincial figures are, therefore, also grouped under the chief Natural Divisions, so that some light may be thrown on the physical causes which affect the distributions of the people within the Province.

Natural Divisions. In the scheme of Natural Divisions, drawn up for the whole of India, Baroda State is included in the Natural Division Gujarat, which may be divided into two main blocks, namely (1) Kutch and Kathiawad, or Peninsular Gujarat, and (2) Main land Gujarat or Gujarat proper. Peninsular Gujarat in which the Amreli District of the Baroda State is situated, has, on account of its detached position and large sea-board, developed and preserved peculiar traits and characteristics in its population, which is stalwart and valorous and includes the brave Rajputs and Kathis, the sturdy Ahirs, Bharvads and Rabaris, the enterprising Bhatias, Luhanas, Memons and Khojas and the sea-faring Kolis, Vaghers and Kharvas, formerly notorious for their piracies in the Arabian Sea. Main land Gujarat, which includes the Gujarat Districts of Kadi, Baroda and Navsari, may be sub-divided into North, Central and South Gujarat, each of which has its own peculiarities. North Gujarat in which our District of Kadi and the town of Patan—the ancient capital of Gujarat—are situated, possesses the original settlements like Vadnagar, Modhera, etc., from which many of the Gujarat castes take their names, and differs in the manners, customs and civilization of its population from Central and South Gujarat. Good physique, wealth, business habits and thrift characterize North Gujarat, and a general softness, keen intellect and a taste for show, fashion and finery, are the distinguishing features of South Gujarat, in which our District of Navsari is situated. Central Gujarat, in which the capital of the State, and the Baroda District are situated, partakes of the peculiarities of both North and South Gujarat. Kadi District is noted for its hard working and skilful Kadwa Kanbi cultivators, Baroda for the Lewa Kanbi cultivators, and Navsari for the Anavala Brahman cultivators, and the early tribes, such as Dublas, Gamits, etc. From climatic point of view also, peninsular and main land Gujarat, as also the sub-divisions of the latter, differ from one another. Rainfall is the highest (50 inches) in Navsari, and goes on decreasing from Baroda (35 inches) to Kadi (25 inches) and thence to Amreli where it is the lowest (15 inches). Temperature which is the highest in Kadi (109°) goes on decreasing on one side towards Amreli (104°) and on the other towards Baroda (104°) and then to Navsari (108°). Each of the four districts of the State having thus its own peculiarity, and being detached from the rest, serves both as an administrative as also a Natural Division and has been taken as such for the purpose of this report.

17. Of the four districts, Kadi alone has no forests. Taking demarcated and undemarcated forests together, there were at the commencement of the decade, about 732,945 bighas or about 673 square miles of reserved forest in the Navsari, Baroda and Amreli Districts. About 31 miles of this have been deforested for the extension of cultivation mostly in the Songhad, Vyara and Mahuva Talukas of the Navsari District, Sankheda, Savli and Vaghodia Talukas of the Baroda District and Dhari and Kodinar Talukas of the Amreli District. The area noted in the margin measuring about 642 square miles continued as reserved forest at the end of the year 1910.

Forests.

Name of District.	Name of Taluka.	Reserved forest in bighas.		
Baroda	Savli	13,972	12	0
	Vaghodia	889	14	0
	Sankheda	11,577	18	0
		26,260	4	0
Navsari	Velachha	992	4	0
	Vakal	19,568	11	0
	Umarpada	106,850	0	0
	Mahuva	11,655	16	0
	Vyara	97,224	16	8
	Songhad	361,992	8	8
		598,303	15	16
Amreli	Dhari & Khambha ...	68,421	11	12
	Kodinar	5,479	1	0
		73,909	12	12
	Total ...	698,464	12	8

II.—AREA, POPULATION AND DENSITY.

Reference to Statistics.

18. The general statistics of the area and population of each district will be found in Imperial Table I. Provincial Table I. at the end of the Tables Volume, contains similar information for talukas; and at the end of this chapter, there are seven Subsidiary Tables showing—

(I)—Density, water supply and crops;
(II)—Distribution of population, classified according to density;
(III)—Distribution of the population between towns and villages;
(IV)—Number per mille, of the total population and of each main religion who live in towns;
(V)—Towns classified by population;
(VI)—Special statistics for the Baroda City; and
(VII)—Persons per house and houses per square mile.

The discussion in this chapter will be confined to the consideration of the population as it stood on the 10th March 1911, the day on which the Census was taken. The variations that are disclosed by a comparison with the results of the previous enumerations will be considered in the next chapter; and as from an administrative point of view, it will be the most important chapter in the whole report, such descriptive matter as may be necessary to elucidate the statistics will be held over for incorporation in that chapter.

Area of the State.

19. The area of the State as ascertained by the completion of Survey Operations in some of the talukas left unsurveyed at the time of the last Census, or re-surveyed during the decade is 8,182 square miles. It is not very extensive as compared with that of some of the other Native States; as for instance, Jodhpur and Bikaner in Rajputana, or Gwalior in Central India, but the population surpasses in number and density that of the more extensive States, as will be seen further on. Roughly speaking, the area equals that of the four British Zillas of Gujarat, *viz.*, Ahmedabad, Kaira, Broach and Surat, which are situated in close proximity with our Gujarat Districts. Compared with the larger States or groups of petty States that form the Gujarat feudatories, the State equals in extent the whole of the Palanpur Agency, surpasses Kutch and Reva Kantha, is more than double of Mahikantha and is about two-fifths of Kathiawad. It is nearly equal to Indore, is a little less than double of the total area of the Deccan group with Bhor and Satara Agency and exceeds the total Karnatic group, including Kolhapur and the Southern Maratha Jagirs. Compared with European countries, this State is larger than Wales by 700 square miles and greater than two-thirds of Belgium.

Area of the Divisions.

20. Of the four Divisions, Baroda, including the City of Baroda, has an area of 1,898 square miles, and Kadi, Navsari and Amreli have an area of 3,023, 1,914 and 1,347 square miles, respectively.

Total Population.

21. The population of the territories of His Highness the Maharaja Gaekwad, as ascertained in the present Census, was on the 10th March 1911, 2,032,798 souls (1,055,935 males and 976,863 females), as against 1,952,692 (1,008,634 males and 944,058 females) on 1st March 1901 (the date of the previous Census), thus showing an increase of 80,106 persons or 4 per cent.

Comparison with neighbouring districts, &c.

22. This population is *little more than one-tenth* of the population of the British districts of the Bombay Presidency, and is more than half of that of the entire group of its Northern Division. It falls short of the population of the neighbouring four British districts of Gujarat, namely, Ahmedabad, Kaira, Broach and Surat, only by less than one-fourth, or is more than three-fourths of the population of these districts. It comes up very nearly to the entire group of Gujarat Native States, excluding Kathiawad. Compared with other Native States of India, the population of Baroda is nearly equal to that of Marwar in Rajputana, and two-thirds of Gwalior in Central India. Compared with European

countries, Baroda has *one-twelfth* of the population of England and Wales together and nearly one-third of Belgium.

Population by districts.

Baroda	686,900
Kadi	832,162
Navsari	385,467
Amreli	178,269
Total ...	2,032,798

23. Having ascertained the total population, the first of our duties is to form a general conception of how that population is spread over the administrative divisions of the area within which it was enumerated to determine where it is dense and where it is sparse, to learn how the town-dwellers compare with the residents of the rural tracts and the like. The population of the State is distributed in the four districts as shown in the margin. Kadi District claims the largest number or 41 per cent. of the total population. Baroda comes next with 33·5 per cent., Navsari with 16 per cent. comes third, and lastly follows Amreli with the smallest percentage of 9·5. If the City of Baroda with its population of 99,345 is excluded, the population of the Baroda District is reduced from 33·5 per cent. to 23·5 per cent. of the total population, but it still maintains its second place.

Relation of area and population.

24. The diagram given in the margin illustrates graphically the relative area and population of the four districts in the State. Each white diamond therein represents 1 per cent. of the total area in each district and each black diamond 1 per cent. of the total population. A glance at the diagram shows the varying relations which prevail between the size of a district and the number of persons who inhabit it.

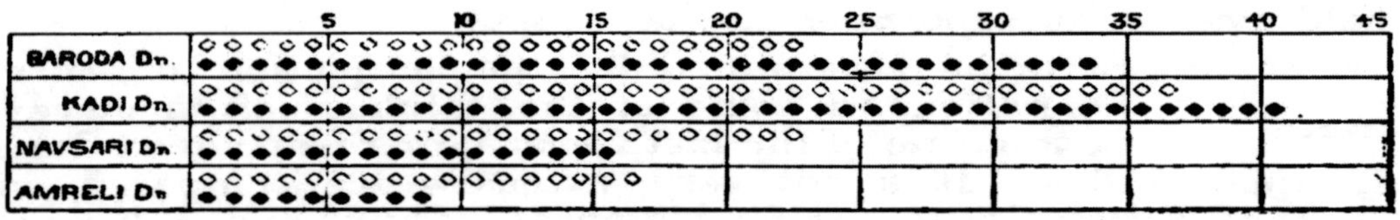

Kadi has relatively the largest area and population, Baroda comes next both in its relative area and population, while Navsari and Amreli have relatively more area but less population.

Density of the State.

25. Having already ascertained the total area in square miles and the total population, we can now ascertain for the whole State and for each of its districts the density, that is the average number of persons per square mile. For Baroda State, as a whole, the density is 248. This, compared with that of most of the European countries and the rest of India, is high. The mean density for the whole of India in the present census is 178 persons per square mile, which shows that the density of Baroda State is nearly half as much again as that of India.

Diagram showing the density of population in the State and other Provinces, etc.

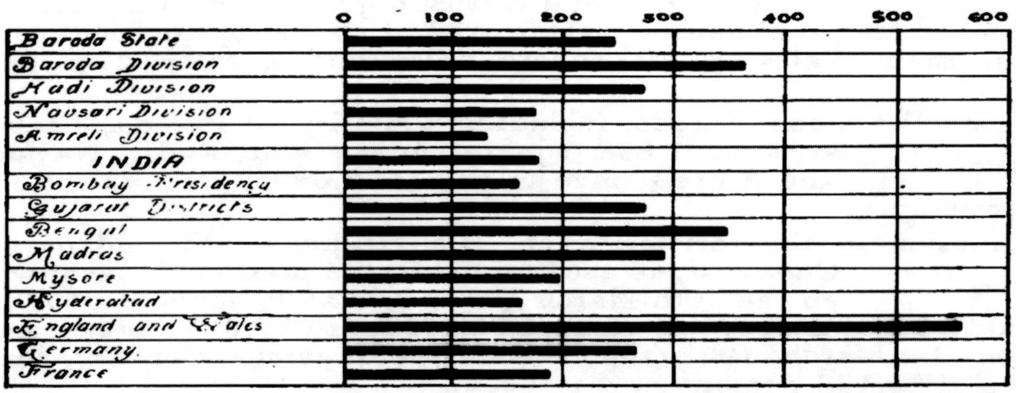

It is a little more than half as much again as that of the British Districts of Bombay, and a quarter as much again as that of the other leading Native State, Mysore; over 50 per cent. better than that of the premier State of Hyderabad and nearly more than double that of the other Native States in the Bombay Presidency. Compared with the densities of other Provinces in India, Baroda occupies the rank coming just below Madras and above the Punjab. Compared with the densities of European countries, Baroda occupies 8th rank, coming just below the German Empire and above Austria. The densest country Belgium, is nearly 2½ times as dense as

Baroda and England nearly 2 times. Baroda is inferior in density to Japan, Italy and the German Empire, but it heads Austria, France, Switzerland, Sweden and Norway, Russia and other European countries.

26. The pressure of the population on the soil of the State is far from uniform, and a reference to the map of Baroda at the commencement of this chapter will show that there are great variations between the different districts of the State. The density of the Natural Divisions (the districts) calculated by excluding the area and population of the City of Baroda from that of the Baroda District is given in the margin. Above the average State density of 248, there are two districts, Baroda and Kadi, with 311 and 275, respectively. Navasri with 175 and Amreli with 132 come next in the order of density. The density of Baroda District with City (362) is about twice that of Navsari and three times that of Amreli. The density of Kadi, though inferior to that of Baroda, is 57 per cent. higher than that of Navsari and more than double that of Amreli. The low density in Navsari is mainly due to the large forest area it contains, while the sparse population in Amreli is due to the inferior fertility in a hard tract of country. If we exclude the area occupied by reserved forests, 26 sq. miles in Baroda, 549 sq. miles in Navsari and 68 sq. miles in Amreli, the densities come to be 315 for Baroda, 246 for Navsari and 139 for Amreli.

Natural Divisions.	Density.
Baroda (ex. City) ...	311
Kadi	275
Navsari	175
Amreli	132

Comparison with British Zillas.

27. Arranging our districts with the neighbouring British Zillas of the Gujarat in the order of density, we get the following result :—Kaira 434, Surat 395, Baroda 311, Kadi 275, Ahmedabad 217, Broach 209, Panch Mahals 201 and Navsari 175. This shows that Baroda keeps very close to Surat, while Kadi still surpasses its neighbouring district of Ahmedabad and enjoys as much superiority over it as Baroda does over Kadi.

Density compared with that of the Native States.

28. Turning now to the surrounding Gujarat group of Native States, we find similarly that our districts surpass the neighbouring Native States in density. Kadi greatly surpasses her neighbours of Palanpur and Mahikantha, Baroda her neighbours of Cambay and Rewakantha. In 1901, Navsari preponderated over the neighbouring cluster of Native States under the Surat Agency in density and Amreli over her neighbouring Kathiawad States. Amreli still maintains that position but Navsari, in spite of the large increase in its population, has given place to the States in the Surat Agency. Comparing this State with Indore and Gwalior in Central India and Kolhapur in the Karnatic group, we find that, though Indore has an area equal to that of ours, it is nearly 1/6th in density ; Gwalior with a very large area of 25,041 is also far inferior, having only one-half the density of this State. Kolhapur with more than one-third area and less than half the population, has a density of 292, that is, higher than that of Baroda by 44.

Baroda Division.

29. The pressure of the population is not uniform even in the different parts of the same division. In the Baroda division, the density is the greatest in the Charottar talukas of Petlad (703) and Bhadran (520). The Charottar tract, as its name implies, is the best agricultural sub-division in the State. The soil in general is a sandy loam, suited to grow most crops, and the cultivators are intelligent and their culture intensive. Padra (391), known as Vakal tract, follows Charottar in density. Its lands are medium loams, resting on a clay subsoil, with plenty of fresh water underground. A large variety of crops is grown, but on account of high prices, cotton is steadily replacing others, of late. The talukas of Sinore (264), Dabhoi (256), Baroda (246), and Karjan (241), which follow Charottar in the order of density, form with the exception of a part of the Baroda Taluka which on account of its medium loams is grouped with Vakal, the black cotton soil district called *Kanam*. It is the district which grows the well known Broach cotton. The soil is a black loam, varying in depth from a few inches to 6 feet and resting on an impervious moory sub-soil. The high prices realised by cotton have added much to the prosperity of the people, and the

Kanam tract is expected to grow still further in population. Savli (236), Sankheda (239), and Tilakwada (222), where a large amount of culturable land has of late been brought under the plough, follow *Kanam* in density. Waghodia

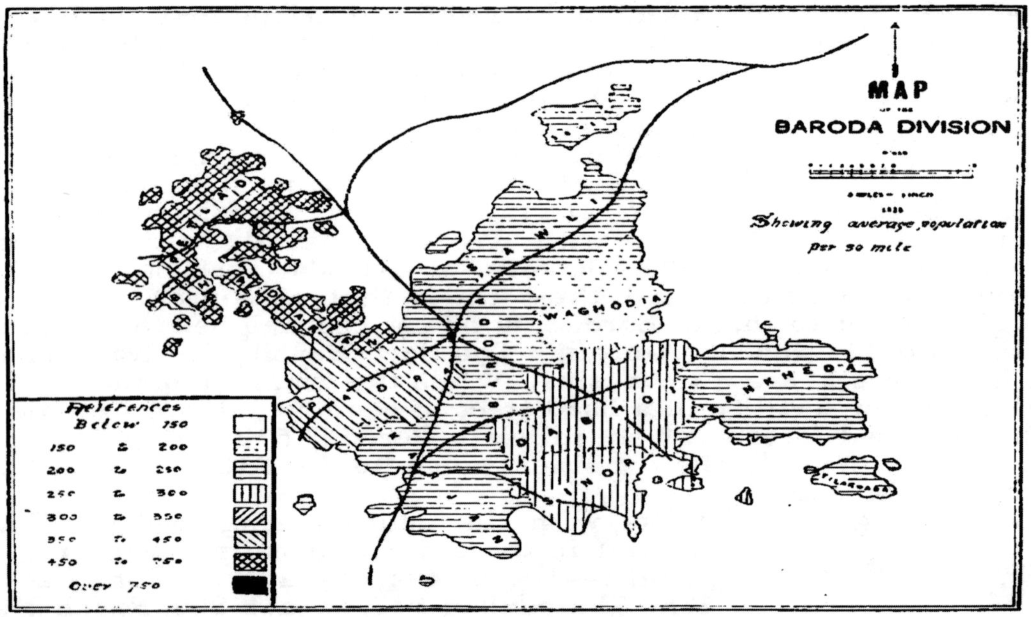

lags behind with the lowest density (171) in the district. But here also extension of cultivation and the gradual increase of area under cotton crop have made a beginning, and it is expected that this backward taluka will rise in density within the next few years.

Kadi Division.

30. In the Kadi Division, the pressure of the population is the greatest in the Mehsana (379), and Visnagar (367) talukas and then follow Sidhpur (348), Vijapur (321) and Kalol (304) talukas. The land in Visnagar and Mehsana is an alluvial free working loam, suited to grow most crops. The north-eastern portion has been water-logged and is known as *bheja* or wet lands and can grow wheat without irrigation. A part of this tract produces the well-known rape-seed which fetches the highest price of any rape in the

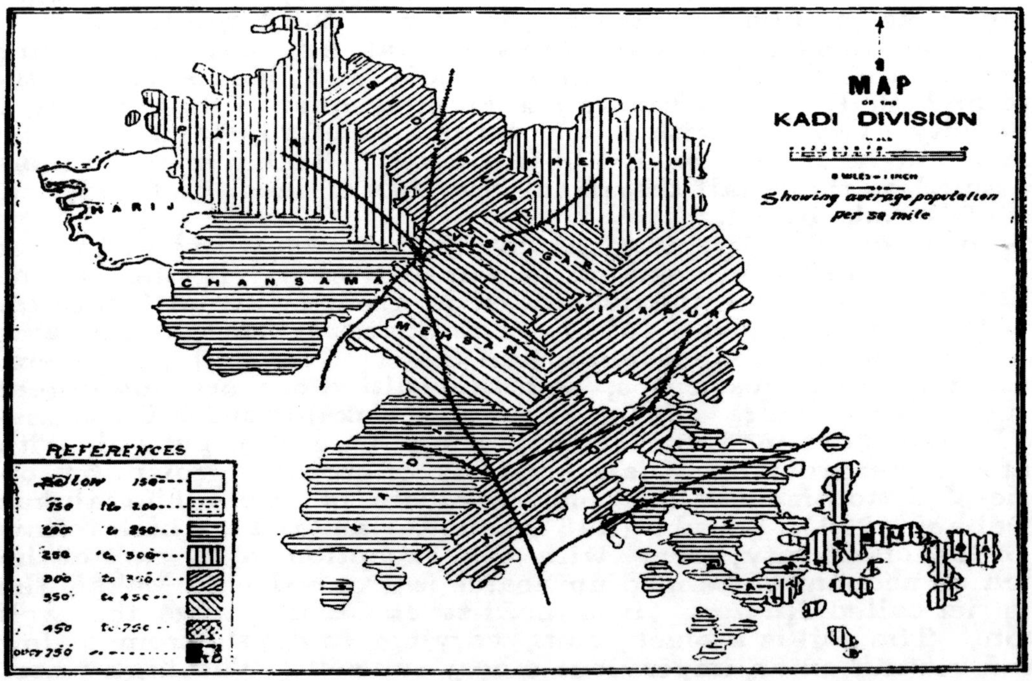

world and is exported mainly to England and Germany. Sidhpur, Mehsana and Kalol were the earliest to be blessed with the R. M. Railway; and their land is fertile. Vijapur, though only recently connected with Railway, has high density, mainly on account of the high fertility of its soil. Kheralu (287) is hilly and inferior to Visnagar in fertility. The Chimnabai irrigation tank recently constructed in this taluka will, in due course of time, greatly add to its fertility, and the population is sure to be denser than at present. Patan (262), which follows in order of density, is more sandy, the soil is thinner than in the Vijapur-Visnagar tract and well water is deeper. Kadi (230) has a large tract of poor soil called *Khakharia tappa*, and most of the able-bodied men from it, as also from Kalol and Dehgam, go to Ahmedabad, the centre of mill industry, which is close by, and which has of late much benefitted in population at the expense of our Kadi District. Chansma (207) like Patan has dry and inferior soil. In Dehgam (231), the surface soil is sandy, but here and there alluvial soil is met with. It is well-wooded, with the mango, *rayan* and *mahuda* fruit trees. Atarsumba (275) is hilly and wooded like Dehgam. The inhabitants are mostly Kolis, who are bad cultivators. Harij (102) is the most sparsely populated tract in the Kadi District. The land is poor and salt and so is the water underneath.

Navsari Division.

31. Navsari district is divided into three parts, the first of which is called *Rasti* and contains the populated and peaceful talukas of Navsari, Gandevi, Palsana and Kamrej. The soil of these is a calcarious black loam, resting on the retentive sub-soil. The population consists of skilful Anavala and Kanbi cultivators. Gandevi taluka has the highest density (719) on account of its having the best garden soil. Navsari comes next after it (442), and then follow Palsana (274) and Kamrej (267) in the order of the fertility of their soils. The second part of the Navsari District is called *Semi-Rasti*, or halfpopulated, and includes the talukas of Mahuva and Velachha. In the semi-Rasti tract, the population in Mahuva (278) is rapidly growing owing to extension of cultivation,

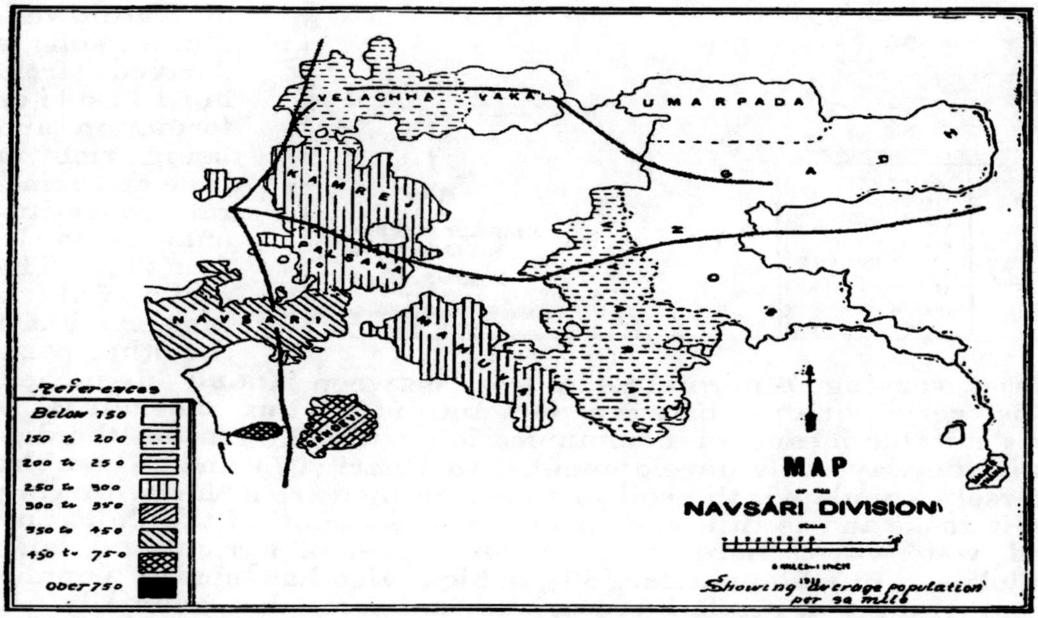

and so far as its density is concerned, it now equals any ordinary taluka in the Rasti Mahals. Velachha (184) has not improved so rapidly as Mahuva, but its density is superior to that of the third division of the Navsari District, which is called *Rani* or forest Mahals, and includes the talukas of Songhad (54) and Vyara (179) and the Peta Talukas of Vakal (139) and Umarpada (107). In these forest parts, the population is thin and consists mainly of the forest tribes. Owing to the low rates of assessment and the facilities given for taking up land, the population in these talukas is rapidly growing. Since the opening of the Tapty Valley Railway, most of the available land is taken up, and the density of the tract has risen from 72 to 94 (*i. e.* by 22), and will soon come up to the level of the semi-Rasti Mahals. Umarpada and Vakal are sparsely populated, but here also there is more demand for land than before. The unhealthiness of the climate and the want of good and easy means of communications deter people from the thickly populated Rasti Mahals from taking up the available land and settling in these talukas. Various measures of introducing *abadi* in these talukas have from time to time been adopted. Gradual removal of the forest has of late somewhat improved the climate, and when the roads, which are at present either under projection or construction, are completed, the Songhad taluka will certainly rise still more in its population.

Amreli Division.

32. In the Amreli Division, the density of population is the highest in Beyt (1,219), but it is a single town, though considered a Peta Mahal for administrative purposes. Then comes the Amreli Taluka (214). Excepting a belt of black soil on the northern bank of the Shetranji river, the soil of this part is a thin loam resting on a rock or moorum sub-soil. Damnagar (169) and Kodinar (167) follow Amreli. Kodinar Taluka forms the southern end of Kathiawad. The soil is derived from milliolite formation and being rich in lime and mineral constituents is fairly fertile. The rain-fall is higher than the other parts of the Amreli District, varying in normal years from between 20 and 30 inches. The temperature is very equable between 60° and 90°. But the taluka is isolated and without suitable means of communication with the rest of the district, which comes in the way of its development. In Dhari (97) and Khambha (77), which are sparsely populated, the soil has been formed from the withering and debris of the Gir rocks and is thin and poor. On account of the hills and many streams and waterways, there is no level stretch of agricultural land anywhere in the talukas. In Okhamandal (80), which also has sparse population, the soil is very thin, and rainfall precarious and irregular, generally not exceeding 5 or 6 inches. The two principal towns Dwarka and Beyt are renowned as places of Hindu pilgrimage and thousands of pilgrims from all parts of India visit them every year.

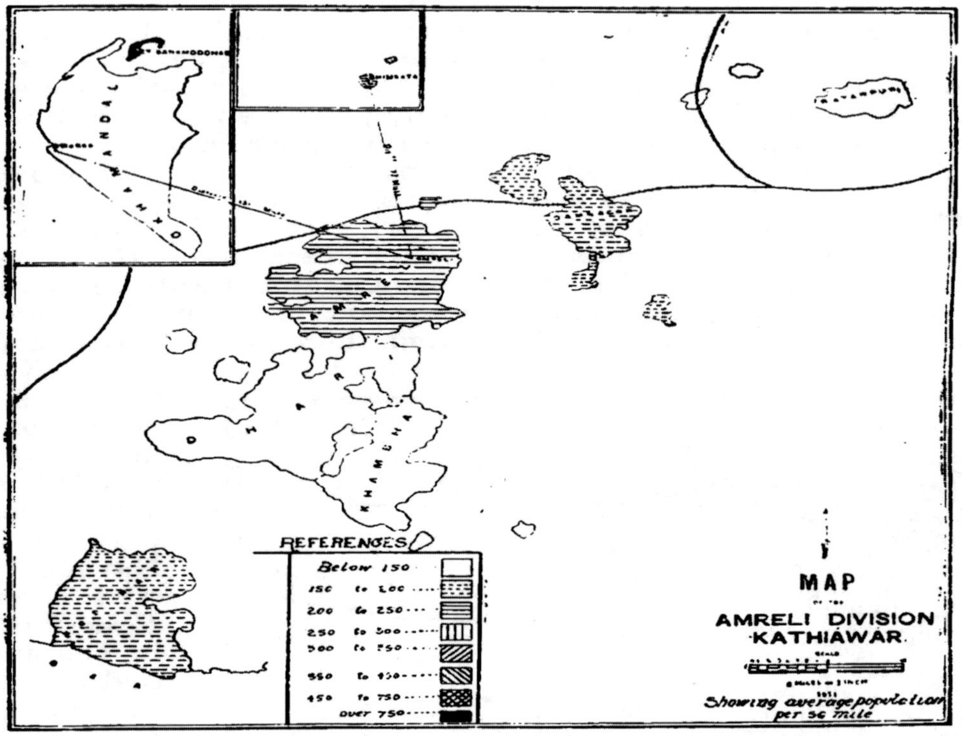

Causes of the variations of density.

33. The above examination of the density in the different parts of the districts of the State shows that the variations of density depend upon a number of causes, of which the principal are soil, rainfall and climate. Where all the elements co-exist, the density is the highest as in the Petlad Taluka of the Baroda District or the Gandevi Taluka of the Navsari District. In the Songhad Taluka of the Navsari District, the climate is malarious and unhealthy, and the density is therefore the least in the district as also in the State. Harij has less rain than the other talukas in the Kadi District, and the soil is also salt and

inferior. It has consequently the least density. The inferior density in Dhari and Khambha is due to bad climate, less rain, and the hilly nature of the country. Population decreases where the plain gives place to the mountain even though the rainfall is higher. Its tendency is to concentrate in the plains and not on the slopes and uplands. This is well illustrated by the inferior density in the Songhad, Dhari and other hilly talukas in the State.

Classification of the population according to density.

34. If we classify the population according to density, it appears that one-twentieth of the total population of the State is congregated on only 12 miles of the area, where there are 1,050 and more persons per square mile; one-twelfth on only 228 miles where the density is from 600 to 750 per square mile; 2 per cent. of the population on 1 per cent. of the area where the density is 450 to 600; more than a quarter of the population on less than one-fifth of the area at a density of 300 to 450 persons; nearly one-half on a little more than one-half of the area where the density is from 150 to 300 per square mile. Taking these figures together, we find that 93 per cent. of the population is living on 78 per cent. of the area, and the remaining 22 per cent. is still very sparsely inhabited and nowhere contains as many as 150 persons per square mile.

Taluka density.

35. The density of population in each taluka of the State is given in Provincial Table I at the end of the Tables Volume. The highest density, 719 persons per square mile, is in the Gandevi Taluka of the Navsari District. Then come in order Petlad Taluka with 703 persons, Bhadran Taluka with 520, and Navsari Taluka with 442. The lowest density, 54 persons, is in the Songhad Mahal of the Navsari District.

Taking into consideration the surrounding circumstances of geographical position, fertility of the soil, habits of the people and the general conditions of life in the Baroda State, the following standard of the different grades of density was adopted in the past Censuses:—

I.—Dense .. .. Over 500.
II.—Fairly dense ... ... Between 300 and 500.
III.—Average ... ... Between 200 and 300.
IV.—Thin ... ... Between 100 and 200.
V.—Sparse ... ... Below 100.

In accordance with this classification, the population of the State, as a whole, can be designated "average." Of the districts, Baroda is fairly dense, Kadi is average and Navsari and Amreli are thin. The talukas arrange themselves as below in accordance with their densities:—

Dense.	Fairly dense.	Average.	Thin.	Sparse.
Gandevi.	Navsari.	Kheralu.	Velachha.	Dhari.
Petlad.	Padra.	Mahuva.	Vyara.	Ratanpur.
Bhadran.	Mehsana.	Atarsumba.	Bhimkatta.	Okhamandal.
	Visnagar.	Palsana.	Vaghodia.	Khambha.
	Sidhpur.	Kamrej.	Damnagar.	Songhad.
	Vijapur.	Sinore.	Kodinar.	
	Kalol.	Patan.	Vakal.	
		Dabhoi.	Umarpada.	
		Baroda.	Harij.	
		Karjan.		
		Sankheda.		
		Savli.		
		Dehgam.		
		Kadi.		
		Tilakwada.		
		Chansma.		
		Amreli.		

Areality and proximity.

36. In addition to density, there are two other ways of expressing the relation of area to population. The one is to give the average area available for each individual. It is the converse of density and is called *areality*. The other is to calculate the

mean distance between two persons on the assumption that the total population is uniformly distributed over the entire surface of any given tract. This is the correlative of areality and is called *proximity*.

The average area per person for the State, as a whole, is 2·58 acres as against 2·68 acres in 1901. Looking to the districts, we find that the figures for Baroda (with City), Kadi, Navsari and Amreli 1·76, 2·32, 3·65 and 4·84 acres as against 1·89, 2·31, 4·7 and 4·97 respectively in 1901.

The average distance between any two persons on the supposition of equable distribution is approximately 112 yards as against 115 in 1901.

III.—TOWNS AND VILLAGES.

Statistics of towns and villages.

37. Having considered how the total population of the State is distributed in the four districts and the talukas, we now come to the distribution of the people between towns and villages. A *Dehzada* published in the Gujarati language gives the population and its distribution among the main religions for all the towns and villages in the State. The statistics regarding towns are contained in Imperial Tables IV. and V. The combined number of towns and villages and their distribution according to population will be found in Imperial Table III. The corresponding proportionate figures are given in the Subsidiary Tables III. and IV. at the end of this chapter.

Before discussing the statistics, it is first necessary to know what is meant by the terms "town" and "village."

A village described.

38. The land in the State is divided into portions varying in area from a few hundred to several thousand acres, each of which is apportioned to a single village. This revenue unit of area was taken as the Census village. "Parish" in the ordinary acceptation of the term denotes accurately enough one of these territorial divisions. The whole population of the parish live together in the village itself, which is generally situated near the centre of the area. The houses are closely packed together on a small site, usually about 5 per cent. of the total area, the rest of which is cultivated. There are sometimes hamlets subsidiary to large villages, but isolated dwellings are not met with except in the Rani Mahals of the Navsari District. The village is generally built beside a tank or a large embanked pond, shaded by trees among which is the temple of the local god or goddess. At the entrance are the huts of the Bhangis, one of whose duties is to guide travellers, and on the outskirts live, each in their separate quarters, the Dheds, Chamars and other low castes. In the middle of the village live the yeomen, the owners and cultivators of the land.

Types of villages.

39. There are various types of villages. Sometimes, as in Kathiawad, people reside in walled and fortified villages, a reminiscence of the troublous period which preceded British supremacy. Elsewhere, as in the Baroda and Kadi Districts, the fortifications disappear, but the houses are closely packed together within streets with no intervening spaces for orchards or gardens. Elsewhere, again, as in the greater part of the Navsari District, the houses, while still collected on a common site, are well separated, and most of them stand in their own ground. In the Rani Mahals of Songhad and Vyara, there is no regular village site at all, and each cultivator makes his dwelling place where it suits him best, either in the centre of his fields or on some adjacent patch of ground, such as the bank of a stream.

Town.

40. In the typical village, the community proper consists of husbandmen. But as civilization advances, the wants of the community gradually convert some of the villages into centres of trade and manufactures. In such places, in addition to the owners and cultivators of land, a large number of traders, artizans and others following non-agricultural professions form the principal part of the population. While a village with mostly agricultural population is called a *Mauza*, one with mostly non-agricultural population is called a *Kasba* (from *Kasab*, arts) or a town.

Social and economic conditions in villages and towns.

41. Social and economic conditions in villages differ materially from those in towns. The village community consists mainly of a few cultivating castes, such as Kanbis, Kolis, and Rajputs. Each caste lives as a compact body in its own *moholla* or street and follows its traditional occupation. A village is a self-supporting economic unit, and the occupations commonly followed satisfy all the ordinary requirements of its inhabitants. There are no strangers or foreigners on the village site. A close bond of sympathy and fellow-feeling unites all the inhabitants, who look upon each other as members of a family and are always ready to help each other. Town population, on the other hand, consists mainly of shopkeepers, traders, artizans and day-labourers. Most of them have come to reside there from different parts of the country and are strangers to each other. There is a spirit of competition, which makes each man care more for himself than for his neighbour. Nobody cares to know or has the time to enquire what others are doing. This engenders a spirit of freedom, which allows caste prejudices to be laid aside with impunity. Western arts, ideas and inventions, and above all spread of education have done much to break down caste prejudices in towns. The ever-increasing importation of Western products has deprived certain castes in towns of their traditional occupations, while new employments have been created, which draw people from all castes. In many cases, persons pursuing the same occupation belong to diverse castes, while persons of the same caste follow different occupations. The close bond which unites all the inhabitants of a village is thus wanting in towns, and leads to the weakening of caste restrictions.

Census definition of town and village.

42. A village was taken in the Census to mean a survey *Mauza* and included all hamlets within the boundary of the village lands. On the other hand, a town was defined, as in 1901, so as to include (1) every municipality of whatever size, (2) every Cantonment, (3) headquarters of talukas and (4) every other continuous collection of houses inhabited by not less than 5,000 persons, which it may be decided to treat as a town for census purposes.

Towns.	
Baroda	16
Kadi	14
Navsari	6
Amreli	6
Total ...	42

43. Including the City of Baroda, there are 42 places which may be called towns according to the Census definition. The number of such towns was 34 in 1881, 41 in 1891 and 47 in 1901. This shows that from 1881 to 1901, there was a growing increase of towns, but since 1901 there has been a reaction, and the number of towns in 1911 is less than the number in 1901 by 5. Valam, Umta, Balisana and Dhinoj in the Kadi District and Pihij, Mehelav and Dharmaj in the Baroda District, which were raised to the dignity of towns in 1901, owing to their having a population of 5,000 and above, have all declined in population in the present census; and there is nothing in the character of their population, which is mainly agricultural, to entitle them to be continued to be classed as towns. On the other hand, two new places, Vaghodia and Karjan, though having a population of less than 5,000 souls have been classed as towns; the first, besides being the headquarters of a taluka, has been provided with a municipality; and the second, though without a municipalitiy, is the headquarters of a taluka, and the junction of two Railway lines. Most of its population consists of traders and shopkeepers, and it has more than half a dozen ginning factories and cotton presses. Of the 42 towns, 26 have a population of more than 5,000 souls; of the remaining 13 are endowed with municipalities, 2 are the headquarters stations of talukas or important trade centres and 1 is a Military Cantonment.

Reasons for decrease in the number of towns in 1911.

44. The main cause for the increase in the number of towns in 1901 was the increase in the population of the larger villages like Valam, Dhinoj, Dharmaj, etc. Owing to the great famine of 1899-1900, there was a movement of the population from smaller to larger villages in search of food and employment. This swelled the population of some of the villages in 1901 to 5,000 or more and brought them within the Census definition of towns. When the famine was over, there was naturally a reaction and a move-back to the smaller

villages, which now resulted in the over-grown villages raised to township in 1901, assuming their old position of villages and thereby reducing the number of towns in the present census.

45. Following the Census classification, towns may conveniently be divided into (1) large towns of from 20,000 and over, (2) medium towns of from 10,000 to 20,000 and (3) small towns of less than 10,000 inhabitants. From the figures given in the margin, it will appear that most of our towns are small and they contribute the largest percentage to the urban population. 31 per cent. of the urban population live in large towns, 28 per cent. in towns of medium size, and 41 per cent. in small towns.

Town.	Number.	Population
Large	2	124,206
Medium	8	112,797
Small	32	168,014

Decay of towns.

46. The old native industries have ceased to be profitable and no new industries have taken their place. Trade which was formerly centred in towns is now shared to a large extent by the villages also. Thirty years ago, there were no shops to be seen in villages and the villagers had to go to the nearest town for the purchase of such articles as cloth, sugar, salt, etc. Now all the larger villages have their own shops which supply the local wants. The opening of new railways or the extension of old ones has also ruined the trade of some towns. When a place was unconnected with railway, goods for its market from Bombay, Ahmedabad or Surat were obtained through agents in the nearest town with a railway station. The agent not only ordered out but also received the goods, and forwarded them in carts to the indenters. When such a place itself becomes a railway station, goods are obtained direct, instead of through this agency, and the trade of the old railway towns thus suffers. For this, among other reasons, the town population in the State is in some places stationary and in others decadent. As will be seen from their brief notice in the following paras, most of the towns in all the districts have made no progress in population since 1872.

In the general account of towns which follows, it will be convenient to deal not only with their present condition but also with the progress that has been made in the past, instead of leaving the latter subject for discussion in a separate chapter, as has been done in the case of variations in the population generally.

Towns in the Baroda District.

47. In the Baroda District, next after the City of Baroda, Petlad, Dabhoi and Padra are the principal towns. Petlad was formerly the chief market of the rich Charottar tract, but the extension of railway to Cambay has brought forward a rival and the importance and trade of Petlad have, of late, much declined. The population has declined from 15,282 in 1901 to 14,863 in the present Census. Dabhoi was once a populous town. Forbes in 1780 estimated the population to be not less than 40,000. But it gradually declined and the population in 1872 was found to be only 14,898. It has since then remained stationary; the census of 1881, 1891 and 1901, returning almost the same population. The present census shows a heavy fall of 4,917 or 35 per cent. But this is due not to any permanent decrease in the population but to the fact of the town being plague-affected, and many of its inhabitants staying out on the census day. Padra was the market for the whole taluka, and also for the neighbouring Jambusar taluka of the Broach District. But the extension of the railway to Masar Road has deprived it within the decade of half its trade, and the town has declined in population from 8,289 in 1901 to 7,853 in the present census.

Towns in the Kadi District.

48. Kadi District has 14 towns. The largest is Patan with 28,339 inhabitants. In was the ancient capital of Gujarat and was founded by Vanraj Chavda in 745 A.D. In its palmy days, it was said to be twelve *kos* in extent and to possess magnificent palaces, parks, tanks, markets and offices. The old town was destroyed by Mahomedans and another, the modern Patan, sprang up on its ruins. It was famous for manufactures of swords, nut-crackers, silk cloth and *patolas* (variegated silken saris) for females. But all these industries have declined, and most of the artizans have migrated to Ahmedabad, Surat, Bombay and other places. Patan is a declining town, its population was 32,712 in 1881, 32,646 in 1891,

31,402 in 1901, and 28,339 (13,904 males and 14,435 females) in the present Census. The excess of females over males indicates that migration is at work, and the population is likely to show in the next Census a further decline. Vadnagar, Visnagar, Kadi, Unja, Vijapur, Kheralu and Ladol, all show a heavy decline in the population, mainly owing to plague, which was raging in the district throughout the decade. Sidhpur, where a cotton mill, the first of its kind, has lately been started, and which besides being a famous place of pilgrimage, is the headquarters of the rich and adventurous Daudi Vohoras, has grown in population by nearly 5 per cent. Mehsana, which has grown at the expense of Visnagar and Kadi, the former judicial and revenue headquarters of the district, is now the headquarters of the district and the centre of His Highness the Gaekwad's system of railways in the district. In spite of heavy loss from plague and famine in the past, it has maintained its slow but steady progress, and has grown from a population of 7,825 in 1872 to 10,141 in the present Census. Kalol and Dehgam have slightly declined, mainly on account of plague and the attraction of better wages in Ahmedabad, which is close by and affords an unlimited field for employment to those who want work.

Towns in the Navsari District.

49. Navsari possesses six towns of which all except Bilimora and Gandevi are decadent. The population of Navsari which is the headquarters of most of the Parsis in Western India, declined from 21,451 in 1901 to 17,982 in the present Census, mainly owing to plague from the grip of which fell disease, the town was not free even for a single year in the decade. Bilimora is a rising town. It possesses many brick factories giving employment to the labourers in the adjacent villages. The bricks are exported mainly to Bombay. The population which was 4,693 in 1901 has risen to 6,462 in the present Census. Gandevi was formerly the chief centre of trade, but the competition of Amalsad, a neighbouring British village, which possesses the advantage of being a railway station has lessened its importance as the principal market. Plague also has adversely affected the growth of the town. It therefore remains almost stationary, the growth in the population in the present Census from 5,927 to 6,482 souls being mainly due to a Jain religious gathering held on the Census day, which attracted to it people from the neighbouring villages.

Towns in the Amreli District.

50. Amreli District has no important towns except Amreli and Dwarka. Amreli besides being the headquarters of the district has several ginning factories, and its population steadily rose from 13,642 in 1881 to 15,653 in 1891 and 17,997 in 1901. In the present Census, the population is 17,443. Dwarka owes its importance to its being a place of pilgrimage and the presence or absence of pilgrims on the Census day determines its having more or less population at each successive Census. In the present Census, it shows a fall from 7,535 to 6,548, which is partly due to absence of pilgrims on the Census day and partly to the ravages of plague, which carried away according to vital statistics 465 persons between the years 1901-02 and 1910-11.

Density of different classes of towns.

51. The average density of towns, which possess a population below 5,000 is 31·2 per acre; that of those with a population between 5,000 and 10,000 is 68·1 per acre; and that of those with a population above 10,000 is 74·4. Generally speaking, density is in proportion to the population. But the town of Patan, though possessing a population larger than that of any other town, shows a density of 57·7 per acre which is much below the general average of the class. The reason is that, as stated before, it is an old capital of Gujarat, now lying waste and uninhabited in a greater part of its area. Some of its inhabitants emigrate to Bombay, Ahmedabad, Surat and other places in search of employment and many of the houses lie unoccupied all the year round.

Looking at density of towns from another point of view, we find that 37 towns with a Municipal Government have an average density of 58·3; two towns that are towns only because they happen to be the headquarter stations of talukas, have an average density of 47·4; and two that show a marked urban tendency have an average density of 76·1 per acre.

Variation in urban population.

52. The growth of the urban population since 1881 is obscured by changes in the list of places dealt with; some of those included in the tables of the past Censuses have been omitted in the subsequent ones, while others not previously treated as towns have been included in the present one. So far as they go, the figures show that while the total population of the State has increased by 4 per cent., that of the towns has decreased by 36,104 persons or nearly 8 per cent. In 1901, the general drift towards towns was accentuated by the famine of 1900, which drove some of the poorer sections of the rural population to seek a livelihood in some neighbouring town; after the famine there was gradually a move-back from the town to the village, resulting as the present Census shows, in a large decrease in urban population.

Religions in towns.

53. The extent to which towns attract persons of different religions is shown in subsidiary Table IV. It will be seen that while less than 20 per cent. of the inhabitants of the State, of all classes taken together, live in towns, 18 per cent. of the Hindus, 39 per cent. of the Jains, 42 per cent. of the Musalmans, 22 per cent. of the Christians and 80 per cent. of the Parsis do so. The proportions fluctuate in the different parts of the State. But on the whole, Musalmans, Jains and Parsis appear to show the greatest preference for town life. The percentage of Christians living in towns is small, on account of the Native Christians, who form the major part of the Christian population, and being agriculturists live in villages.

Sexes in towns.

54. In the population of the State as a whole, there are 92 females for every 100 males. In the population of towns, there are 93·5 females to every 100 males. If our towns had sufficient industrial activity, that is to say, if they were towns in the proper sense of the word, many immigrants, leaving their families in their native villages, would have come to them and the result would have been greater excess of males over females in towns than in the general population. But the reverse is the case. In some towns, like Patan, with a population from ten to fifty thousand, the females are actually in excess of males, showing that males are emigrating elsewhere in search of employment leaving their females at home.

55. The total number of villages in the State is 3,054. Of these, as shown in the margin, the largest number is in the Kadi District, and the least in the Amreli District. 1,921 or 62·9 per cent. of the villages as against 67·7 in 1901 contain a population of less than 500 souls; and 709, that is, 23·2 per cent. as against 19·8 in 1901, contain a population between 500 and 1,000 souls. Thus we see that 86·1 per cent. of the villages contain less than 1,000 souls; and only 13·9 per cent. of the villages have a population exceeding 1,000. Of the latter 10·6 per cent. as against 9·3 per cent. in 1901 have a population under 2,000, and the rest, that is, 3·3 per cent., as against 3·2 in 1901 have a population over 2,000. While the number of villages with a population under 500 has decreased, that of those with a population from 500 to 1,000 and from 1,000 to 2,000 has increased, showing thereby that the villages are growing in population and becoming larger. 16·7 per cent. of the rural population live in villages with a population exceeding 2,000; 56·7 per cent. in villages with a population of from 500 to 2,000 and 26·6 per cent. in villages with a population of less than 500.

Villages.	
Baroda	921
Kadi	1,076
Navsari	762
Amreli	295
Total ...	3,054

Inhabited villages.

56. In addition to the inhabited villages, there is often a large number of places which, though uninhabited, are designated as separate villages in the revenue lists. Sometimes a populated village site is abandoned by the inhabitants for one difficulty or another, and though the people may have migrated to another neighbouring spot, the old village continues as a separate entity. At other times, a large acreage of waste land is brought under the plough and designated by a certain name, though the cultivators may be all *uparvadias*, *i.e.*, dwellers of the villages

round about. But the Census is concerned with inhabited villages and no notice of such uninhabited places can be taken in this report.

Villages classified according to size.

57. There are considerable differences in the classification of villages according to size. Defining the terms as indicated in the margin, we find that in the whole State, 21 per cent. of the total population live in very small villages, 24 per cent. in small, 21 per cent. in large and only 13 per cent. in very large villages. The number of people living in very small and very large villages remains almost the same, but that in small villages has increased by about 3·3 per cent. and that in large villages by 1·6 per cent. of the total population.

Villages of.	Number.	Percentage of population.	
		1911.	1901.
Under 500 (very small) inhabitants...	1921	21·3	21·6
500 to 1,000 (small)	709	24·7	21·4
1,000 to 2,000 (large)	324	21·4	19·8
2,000 to 5,000 (very large)	100	13·3	15·2

Distribution of the population between towns and villages.

58. There exists a considerable difficulty in defining what population should be considered urban and what rural. Baroda State is a distinctly agricultural country and many of the so-called towns are merely overgrown villages. A large percentage of the people living in most of them is employed either in the production or distribution of agricultural produce. Industrial enterprise and manufactures on the Western model are confined only to the City of Baroda and four or five of the larger towns, like Petlad, Sidhpur, Dabhoi and Bilimora. Assuming, however, that the population of places classed as towns is urban, and the rest rural, we find that in the State as a whole, out of every 100 persons in the population, 20 live in towns and 80 in villages. Taking the districts separately, the urban population is considerable in Baroda Division where the inclusion of the City of Baroda, brings the proportion of urban population to 26·6 per cent. If it be excluded, it is only 14 per cent. After Baroda comes Amreli in which 23 per cent. of the people live in urban areas. Then follows Kadi with 16·7 per cent. and Navsari stands last with 12·6 per cent. as urban population.

Distribution of the population in	Towns.	Villages.
State	405,017	1,627,781
Baroda with City	182,713	504,187
Kadi	138,649	693,513
Navsari	42,221	293,246
Amreli	41,434	136,835

Diagram showing the total urban and rural population of the Baroda State in the different divisions.

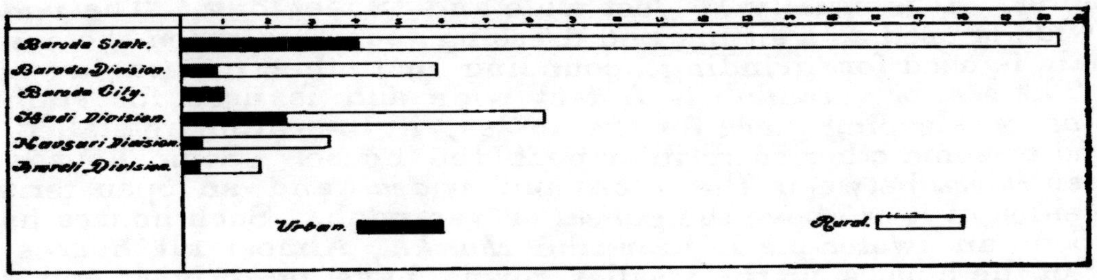

Areality of towns.

59. In the preceding paragraphs, we have compared the urban and rural population. Another way of showing the extent of towns is to mark the areality of towns. On the assumption that all the towns of the State are located at equal distances from each other, each would command an area of 195 miles. The areality of towns in the Navsari District is nearly double of this average (319 square miles), as it has comparatively fewer towns and larger area. The figures for Amreli and Kadi are a little more than the average, *viz.*, 224 and 216, respectively ; while the Baroda Division has a contracted town circle of 135 square miles. In the

Bombay Presidency, the town circle is as large as 755 miles including Sind, and 503 without it. This shows that Baroda State is about four times better off in being studded with towns than the Bombay Presidency. For British Gujarat the average areality of towns is about 338 to our 195 miles.

Proximity of towns in miles.

60. Roughly speaking the proximity of one towns to another on the assumption of equal distribution is 15 miles in the State as a whole. If the Baroda and Navsari Divisions were taken separately, each in respect of its own number of towns, a man in the former would have to walk 12½ miles in reaching from one town to another, and 21 miles in the latter. For Amreli and Kadi the distances are nearly the same as the average for the whole State. The proximity of towns in British Gujarat is about 20 to our 15 miles and for the Deccan about 25 miles.

Areality and proximity of villages.

61. In the same way, assuming villages to be placed at equal distances in each division, the average village areality for the State is 2·7 square miles; and in the different divisions it is 2·3 square miles in Baroda, 2·4 in Navsari, 2·9 in Kadi and 4 square miles in Amreli. The proximity of villages is about a mile and a half for the Baroda and Navsari Divisions, 1·8 miles for Kadi and 2·18 for Amreli. The average for the State is 1·7 miles.

IV.—HOUSES AND HOUSE-ROOM.

Types of Houses.

62. Houses are built within the State in various types which depend upon the locality and the stage of development and the race or caste of their inhabitants. In the outskirts of villages and towns, the houses of Bhils and other primitive classes consist of mud or wattle huts with a small single room measuring about 12 by 12 feet, circular in shape, covered up with thatch and having a small entrance in the front. The houses of Kolis, Dheds, Bhangis, Khalpas and similar other castes have generally an inner room called *ordo* and an outer room called *padsal* and occasionally *osri* or an open verandah in the front. The walls are made of mud, but the roof is tiled. The houses of Kanbis, Vanias, Brahmans and other higher castes and of artizans are made of bricks and have one or more storeys, but the arrangement of *ordo*, *padsal* and *osri* is the same. The *ordo* or inner room is used as a cooking and dining room and also as a retiring room for females, and for keeping the stores. It is usually 16 feet wide and 12 feet long. The *padsal* which is 12 feet wide is used as a sitting and dressing room and when the males are in the verandah, is used for grinding, pounding and other household work by the females. The *osri* or verandah is 8 feet wide and is used for stalling cattle or as a sitting or sleeping place for the males, if the cattle are stalled in the open compound or some other room in or near the house. Some houses in towns have an open *chowk* between the *ordo* and *padsal* and an open terrace either on the two sides of it or above the *padsal* or verandah. Such houses have a separate cook-room and water-place near the *chowk*. Almost all houses in villages and most of the houses in the smaller towns have no privies and the people go out to the fields to answer the call of nature. Windows are very sparingly placed and the few that exist being generally shut up, most of the houses are dark and ill-ventilated. In villages, houses though small, have open court-yards and the evil effects of the bad ventilation are to some extent mitigated by the fact that generally people sleep out whenever it is possible to do so. In towns the evil of bad ventilation is heightened owing to the want of open spaces near houses and to their being located close to each other in long, narrow and tortuous lanes. Education is, however, spreading among the people a better knowledge of sanitary principles and houses of a better kind are gradually coming into existence. There is a tendency to replace the old structures of mud and wood by structures of brick; and the sense of security afforded by efficient police *bandobast* is encouraging the opening of more doors and windows. The houses rebuilt in towns in recent years are generally far better in style and accommodation than those which they have replaced. The building of bungalows, more or less on the European model, by the wealthier classes in towns, is noticeable.

Census definition of house.

63. Circumstances vary so much in the different parts of India that a uniform Census definition of a house for the whole country is impossible. Discretion is, therefore, given to Provincial Superintendents to adopt a definition that would suit local conditions. In the Baroda Census of 1881 and 1891, a house was defined as the space within the external and party walls of each building or tenement having a separate and independent communication with a road. In 1901, it was defined as the dwelling place of one or more families having a separate entrance. These definitions enabled us to know the total number of houses of varying size from a hut to a palace in the State, but gave us no information about the number of families living in them. They gave us the structural but not the social information. It would be of great interest to ascertain the mean size of the family, as that may vary with the comparative prosperity of the locality, prevalence or scarcity of disease, the effect of migration and the comparative fertility of particular races or religious groups. It is more than interesting both in a political and social sense to learn how many families there are in these territories and in every district. Large families are a certain index of health and prosperity, whilst small ones are almost universally and equally clear index of poverty or disease.

A house was, therefore, defined in the present Census as consisting of "the buildings, one or many, inhabited by one family, that is, by a number of persons living and eating together of food cooked on one *chulah* or in one mess with their resident dependents such as mother, widowed sister, younger brothers, &c., and their servants who reside in the house." In other words a house was defined as the dwelling place of a family. This definition besides furnishing a means of ascertaining the normal size of the family, was easily grasped and accurately understood by the enumerators. It also accorded with the views of the people. In Gujarat, by the common understanding of the people, a *ghar* conveys the idea not of a homestead or enclosure but that of a place in which people living together have one common *chulah* (hearth). It is a custom in most of the Gujarat castes to make a present *lahani* of utensils, &c., on festive occasions, to the members of the caste. A *lota* or a *thali* is given to each *ghar* in the caste and for this purpose, those who have one *chulah*, *i.e.*, those who mess together, are taken to mean one *ghar*.

Accuracy of the return.

64. The return of houses may be taken as fairly accurate. There was occasionally a tendency in towns, where the question of the imposition of house-tax was pending, to conceal separate messes with a view to escape taxation, but such attempts were not successful to such an extent as to vitiate the statistics.

Comparability of the statistics of houses.

65. It might be thought that owing to change in definition, the statistics of houses in this Census are not quite comparable with those of the past ones. But except in the case of the comparatively well-to-do, the differences arising from the change do not seem to have any marked effect on house numbering. Amongst the lower classes who form an overwhelming majority of the population, the dwelling place with a separate entrance usually corresponds to the residence of a commensal family and the average population is therefore fairly uniform in all the Censuses as will be seen later on.

66. Houses have been divided for purposes of the Census into two classes: (*a*) occupied and (*b*) unoccupied. Those in which any person was residing on the Census night were taken as occupied and the rest as unoccupied. The unoccupied houses were either shops, warehouses, stables or houses shut up on account of their inmates residing elsewhere. The number of occupied houses in the State has risen from 489,955 in 1901 to 506,297 in 1911, an increase of 16,342 or 3·3 per cent., so that the rate of increase nearly equals that of the population. In the districts, houses have increased in Baroda and Navsari in keeping

Occupied houses in

District.	1911.	1901.
State	**506,297**	**489,955**
Baroda District ...	150,261	141,231
Baroda City	28,603	31,250
Kadi	219,976	218,300
Navsari	68,065	59,849
Amreli	39,392	39,325

with the increase in the population. In Amreli, while the population has increased by nearly 3 per cent., houses do not show any appreciable increase. Kadi shows a slight increase (·7) in the number of its occupied houses, in spite of its slight decrease (·31) in the population. This is due mainly to the tendency of the people to build houses away from the town or village site, as a means of safety against plague which was prevalent in the district throughout the decade. Baroda City has declined both in population and the number of its occupied houses, for reasons mentioned in the separate section devoted to it at the end of this chapter.

District.		Number of persons per house.
State	... ...	4·01
Baroda Division	...	3·91
Baroda City ..	...	3·47
Kadi	... ...	3·79
Navsari	... ...	4·93
Amreli	... ...	4·52

67. The average population per house in the State continues to decrease and is now only four as against 4·56 in 1881, and 4·48 in 1891. There is a great general uniformity between the average population per house in all the districts. The rather high average in Navsari and Amreli is probably due to a slightly greater tendency of families to remain joint and commensal. Throughout the State, the family, as a general rule, consists of the parents, sons, married and unmarried, and the unmarried daughters. It continues joint so long as living together in harmony is possible. But dissensions take place especially among the females and the grown up sons live apart as far as all domestic matters are concerned, though as regards property, there is, as a rule, no separation during the life-time of the father. There is slightly a greater tendency to hasten the breaking up of the joint family in towns than in villages ; among industrial and artizan classes than among agriculturists ; and among the educated than among the illiterate. But for all practical purposes, a house may be taken to represent a family. The total number of occupied houses returned in the Census is as mentioned before 506,297 which may be taken as representing the number of independent families in the State.

Houses in urban and rural areas.

68. The number of houses in urban areas has decreased by 12·5 per cent. only, while the decrease in the number of urban population has been about 13·6 per cent. On the other hand, while the increase in the rural population has been nearly 10 per cent., the increase in the number of houses in rural areas has been about 9 per cent. Thus in both urban and rural areas, the number of houses have kept pace with population, and there has been no noteworthy change in the housing of the people.

House-room.

69. The number of occupied houses per square mile is 80 in Baroda District, 72 in Kadi, 36 in Navsari and 29 in Amreli. The corresponding figures were 75, 72, 31 and 32 in 1901, showing that along with ths general increase in the population, the number of occupied houses have also increased or decreased, except in the Amreli District, where houses have not increased in the same proportion as the population.

V.—BARODA CITY.

Baroda City.

70. In Census phraseology, a town with at least 100,000 inhabitants is regarded as a City. Baroda City with the Cantonment fulfilled this condition in the past, but in the present Census, its population (99,345) is a little less than that standard. It has, however, been treated as a City on account of its local importance. It is the only City and contains five per cent. of the total population of the State. In the whole of India, there were in 1901 only 27 cities with a population of about two per cent. of the whole country. In England, nearly a third of the population is massed in cities, in Germany a sixth, and in France more than a seventh. But even in Europe the growth of cities is comparatively recent and due entirely to the development of trade and large industries. As we shall see in the next paragraph, the present decrease in the population of Baroda City is due to administrative reforms. And it is possible that the industrial awakening which is now apparent, may result at no very distant date in a marked increase in the population of the City.

Variation of population in the City proper.

71. Baroda City mainly owes its importance to the presence of a native court and its entourage. The luxuries and needs of the past Gaekwads and their Sardars and retainers attracted to it, jewellers, bankers, musicians, beggars, etc., who swelled its population which in 1872 numbered 112,057 exclusive of the Cantonment. The new regime established in 1875, brought on a change which naturally resulted in the efflux or emigration of that portion of the population, which was left without employment and brought on a decline in the population to 101,818 in the Census of 1881. There were in 1881, 53 jewellers less than in 1872. The number of concubines diminished by 144, that of songstresses by 46, that of perfume sellers by 40, that of goldsmiths by 354, that of cloth dealers by 173, and that of beggars by 4,042. The period 1881 to 1891 was one of general prosperity, and the population of the City increased by natural growth to 112,471. The next decade was affected by a virulent type of plague and the most severe famine within the memory of men and the population declined to 100,628 in the Census of 1901. The decade 1901-1911 was free from such marked distress but was not favourable to the growth of population owing to successive bad harvests and the consequent depression in trade. Moreover some administrative reforms operated to bring about a decline in the population of the City. The State Military was less in 1911 than what it was in 1901 by about 1,000 which at the rate of four in a family accounts for a loss of 4,000 persons. The criminal population in the Central Jail, which the great famine had swelled to the unusual figure of 1,200 in 1901, was in 1911 reduced to 500. The famine poor-houses in the City which increased the population by about 1,100 in 1901, were non-existent in 1911. In 1901 uncooked *khitchdi* was freely distributed to Dakshani Brahmans and cooked one to Musalmans as a charity from the State, but under the better regulation of this charity, brought about since then, it is now given only to the destitute and the deserving. A large number of idlers, dependent upon this charity, must have therefore migrated from a place where they could not earn their bread without resorting to the indignity of labour to which they were not accustomed.

Baroda Cantonment.

Baroda Cantonment which for Census purposes was taken as a part of Baroda City, had a population of 4,217 persons in 1872. In 1881 its population increased to 4,694, but declined to 3,949 in 1891 and to 3,162 in 1901. In the present Census, the Cantonment has a population of 3,478. The variations in the population of the Cantonment depend upon the strength of the British army stationed in it, the number of camp followers and immigrants from the City proper for better climate or for purposes of trade.

The area of the City.

72. The gross area of the whole city is nine square miles, of which the City proper occupies about eight and the Cantonment one. This gives a density of 11,983 persons per square mile to the City and 3,478 persons to the Cantonment. Excluding from the area of the City proper, the spaces occupied by extensive palace grounds, public gardens and wide roads which cover a greater portion of the city, the area comes to 1·66 square miles only.

Ward density.

73. The City is divided for municipal purposes into five wards, *viz.*, Wadi, City proper (portion within the four walls), Fatehpura, Raopura and Babajipura. The density of each ward calculated without deducting the superfluous areas comes to 28, 115, 24, 17 and 19 persons respectively per acre. The City ward shows here an inordinately high density, as compared with the other wards, because of the fact that it does not contain any open area lying waste or uninhabited. But if we apply the same process that we did, to the City, as a whole, the ward densities come to 116, 120, 53, 107 and 74 persons respectively per acre. These figures show that the City ward is the most congested part of the City and Fatehpura the least; next to the City ward in point of congestion are the Wadi, the Raopura and Babajipura wards in order. Compared with the various sections of the Bombay City, we find that the City and Wadi wards approximate to Girgam, Raopura approximates to Byculla, Babajipura to Tardev and Fatehpura to Chaupati or Parel.

Map of Baroda City showing density of the wards.

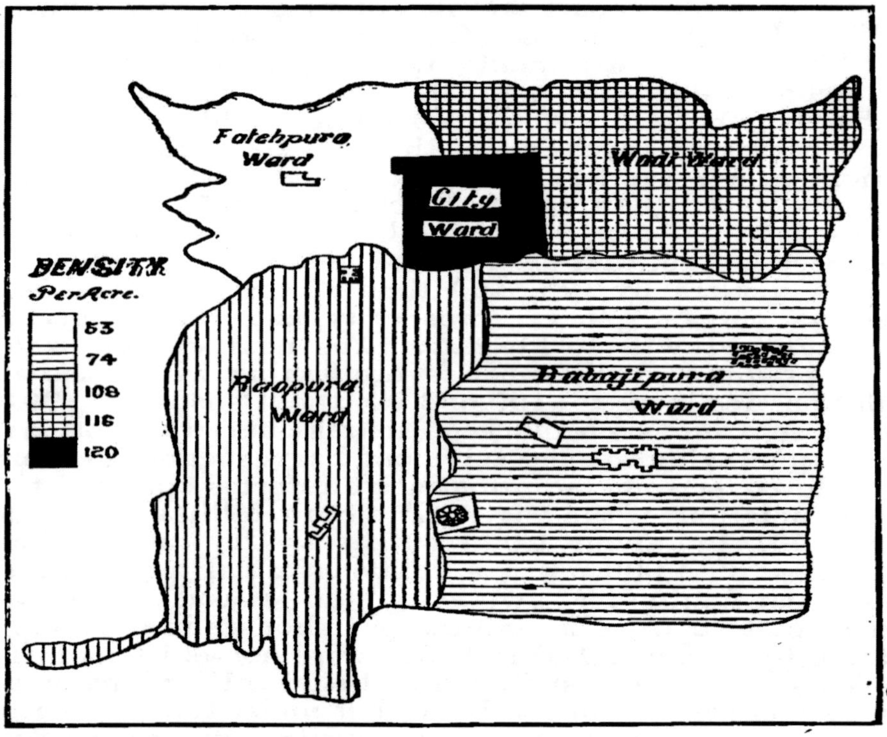

74. The total number of houses in the City with the Cantonment is 41,427, of which 28,603 as against 31,250 in 1911 were occupied on the Census night, and the rest unoccupied, owing to their being shops, stables, warehouses, etc. The decrease in the number of occupied houses is due to the decrease in the population and to the diminution in the total number of houses on account of the widening of the Raopura and Lahripura roads. A special inquiry shows that of the total number of houses 20 per cent. are built with earth and 80 with brick or stone. Again of the total number of houses 51 per cent. have only ground floor, 41 per cent. have one storey, 7 per cent. have two storeys, and 1 per cent. has more than two storeys. 59 per cent. of the houses are owned by those who live in them and 41 per cent. are rented by tenants. There are on an average 3·47 persons in each house and 2·25 persons on an average for each floor space.

Houses and House-room.

75. Of the total population of the City, only 65 per cent. were born within it and 35 born outside it. Of those born outside but enumerated in the City, fifteen in a hundred have come from the different talukas of the Baroda District, six from the Kadi District, one from the Navsari District, two from the Amreli District, and seventy-six from places outside the State. It thus appears that most of the immigrants in the City have come from places outside the State.

Those born in the City and immigrants.

76. According to the present Census, there are 85 females to every 100 males in the City. Considering the wards separately, we find that the proportion of females is highest in the City ward which is inhabited by the real local population of the City and is the lowest in Raopura which is largely inhabited by immigrants who generally come here for State service.

Sexes in the City.

Ward.	Proportion of females to 100 males.
Wadi	92
City	92
Fatehpura...	90
Raopusa	81
Babajipura...	83

77. Of the total population, 79 per cent. are Hindus, 17 per cent. Musalmans, 2 per cent. Jains, nearly 1 per cent. Christians and 1 per cent. "others."

Religions in the City.

SUBSIDIARY TABLE I.—Density, Water Supply and Crops.

District or Natural Division.	Mean density per square mile in 1911.	Percentage of total area.		Percentage to cultivable area of		Percentage of cultivated area which is irrigated.	Normal rainfall.	Percentage of gross cultivated area under							
		Cultivable.	Net cultivated.	Net cultivated.	Double cropped.			Wheat.	Rice.	Pulse.	Bajree.	Juwar.	Cotton.	Oilseed.	Others.
1	2	3	4	5	6	7	8	9	10	11	12	13	14	15	16
Baroda State	248	83	72·6	87·4	4·3	5	...	2·5	5·7	2·8	15·2	13·5	17·2	3·1	40
Baroda District	362	84·1	76·7	91·2	1·5	1·6	37·34	·3	12·9	4·3	8·2	6·2	27·5	0·9	39·7
Kadi do.	275	88·3	74·6	84·5	6·3	7·4	26·0	5·1	1·8	1·6	24·3	15·2	5·4	5·6	41
Navsari do.	175	72·6	67·2	92·5	·5	0·6	51·86	1	8·9	5·8	0·3	16·9	25·6	2·3	39·2
Amreli do.	132	80·9	67·9	83·8	3·8	4·5	21·21	1·6	0·3	...	19·7	17·3	21·2	1·3	38·6

SUBSIDIARY TABLE II.—Distribution of the population classified according to density.

District or Natural Division.	Talukas with a population per square mile of															
	Under 150.		150–300		300–450		450–600		600–750		750–900		900–1,050		1,050 and over.	
	Area.	Population.	Area.	Population.	Area.	Population.	Area.	Population.	Area.	Population.	Area.	Population.	Area.	Population.	Area.	Population.
1	2	3	4	5	6	7	8	9	10	11	12	13	14	15	16	17
Baroda State ...	,808 22·1	137,948 6·7	4,496 54·9	1,038,010 51·3	1,554 19	549,101 27	84 1	43,670 2·1	228 2·8	161,066 7·9	...	...	...	...	12 ·2	103,003 5
Baroda Division exclusive of City	...	...	1,428 75·6	339,625 57·8	195 10·3	76,252 13	84 4·5	43,670 7·4	182 9·6	128,008 21·8	...	...	...	...	...	...
City	...	...	...	...	...	...	...	...	...	...	...	...	...	...	9 100	99,345 100
Kadi District	157 5·2	15,947 1·9	1,632 54	398,636 47·9	1,234 40·8	417,579 50·2	...	...	...	...	...	.	..	...	...	...
Navsari District ...	882 46·1	55,613 16·6	861 45	191,526 57·1	125 6·5	55,270 16·5	...	...	46 2·4	33,058 9·8	...	...	...	...	...	...
Amreli District ...	769 57·1	66,388 37·2	575 42·7	108,223 60·7	...	...	...	...	...	...	...	..	...	...	3 ·2	3,658 2·1

Note:—The figures below the absolute ones represent the proportion per cent. which the area and population of each density group bear to the total area and population of the State.

SUBSIDIARY TABLE III.—Distribution of the population between towns and villages.

District or Natural Division.	Average population per		Number per mille residing in		Number per mille of urban population residing in towns with a population of				Number per mille of rural population residing in villages with a population of			
	Town.	Village.	Towns.	Villages.	20,000 and over.	10,000 to 20,000	5,000 to 10,000	Under 5,000	5,000 and over.	2,000 to 5,000	500 to 2,000	Under 500
1	2	3	4	5	6	7	8	9	10	11	12	13
Baroda State ...	9,643	533	199	801	307	278	276	139	......	167	567	266
Baroda Division (including City). ...	11,419	547	266	734	525	81	247	147	......	203	553	244
Kadi Division ...	9,903	644	167	833	204	451	296	49	......	207	584	209
Navsari Division ...	7,037	385	126	874	......	426	307	267	......	63	531	406
Amreli Division ...	6,906	464	232	768	......	421	305	274	......	55	612	333

SUBSIDIARY TABLE IV.—Number per mille of the total population and of each main religion who live in towns.

District or Natural Division.	Number per mille who live in towns.					
	Total population.	Hindu.	Musalman.	Christian.	Jain.	Parsi.
1	2	3	4	5	6	7
Baroda State	**199**	**181**	**423**	**216**	**388**	**799**
Baroda Division (including City)	266	250	462	205	478	933
Kadi Division	166	144	391	365	346	883
Navsari Division	125	119	311	516	471	785
Amreli Division	232	195	508	625	384	965

SUBSIDIARY TABLE V.—Towns classified by population.

Class of Town.	Number of towns of each class in 1911.	Proportion to total urban population.	Number of females per 1,000 males.	Increase per cent. in the population of towns as classed at previous Census.				Increase per cent. in urban population of each class from 1871 to 1911.	
				1901 to 1911	1891 to 1901	1881 to 1891	1871 to 1881	(a) in towns as classed in 1871.	(b) in the total of each class in 1911 as compared with the corresponding total in 1871.
1	2	3	4	5	6	7	8	9	10
Total ...	**42**	**100**	**934**	**— 7·7**	**— 6·7**	**+ 8**	**— 1·1**	**— 10·2**	**— 4·9**
I 100,000 and over...	...	...	...	— 4·7	— 10·5	+ 10·5	— 9·1	— 14·5	— 100
II 50,000–100,000 ...	1	23·7	867	...	...	...	...	...	+ 100
III 20,000– 50,000 ...	1	7	1,038	— 12·4	— 9·9	— 1·2	+ 3·8	— 10·1	— 10·1
IV 10,000– 20,000 ...	8	27·8	1,008	— 11·6	— 2·8	+ 6·7	— 2·7	— 13·5	— 23·5
V 5,000– 10,000 ...	16	27·6	926	— 8·4	— 10	+ 10	+ 3·8	— 5	— 4·9
VI Under– 5,000 ...	16	13·9	875	— 2·1	— ·7	+ 6	+ 22	+ 10·2	+ 222·3

SUBSIDIARY TABLE VI.—City.

City.	Population in 1911.	Number of persons per sq. mile.	Number of females to 1000 males.	Proportion of foreign born per mille.	Percentage of variation.				
					1901 to 1911	1891 to 1901	1881 to 1891	1871 to 1881	Total 1871 to 1911
1	2	3	4	5	6	7	8	9	10
Baroda City (with Cantonment).	99,345	11,038	853	263	—4·28	—10·84	+9·30	—8·39	—14·56

SUBSIDIARY TABLE VII.—Persons per house and houses per square mile.

District or Natural Division.	Average number of persons per house.				Average number of houses per square mile.			
	1911	1901	1891	1881	1911	1901	1891	1881
1	2	3	4	5	6	7	8	9
Baroda State	**4·01**	**3·98**	**4·48**	**4·56**	**61·88**	**60·49**	**65·52**	**55·97**
Baroda Division (exclusive of Baroda City and Cantonment)	3·91	3·82	4·31	4·30	79·54	75·21	82·92	76·27
Baroda City and Cantonment.	3·47	3·32	3·63	3·64	3,178·11	3,472·22	3,559·66	4,866·50
Kadi Division	3·79	3·82	4·40	4·50	72·76	72·40	79·42	69·41
Navsari Division	4·93	5·01	5·25	5·27	35·56	30·66	30·73	28·22
Amreli Division	4·52	4·41	4·68	4·73	29·17	31·59	32·39	19·95

Chapter II.

MOVEMENT OF POPULATION.

Reference to statistics.

78. The statistics showing the variations in the population of the State as a whole, as also in all its divisions, are contained in Imperial Table II. Similar information for talukas is given in Provincial Table I at the end in the Imperial Tables Volume. The proportional figures illustrating some of the more important features of the statistics will be found in the following Subsidiary Tables at the end of this chapter :—

Subsidiary Table I.—Variation in relation to density since 1872.

Subsidiary Table II.—Variation in natural population.

Subsidiary Table III.—Comparison with vital statistics.

Subsidiary Table IV.—(*a*) Variation by Talukas classified according to density (actual figures);

(*b*) Proportional variation, showing variation per cent.

Introductory remarks.

79. In the first chapter, the statistics of the population, as it stood on the 10th March 1911, have been considered. The present chapter will be devoted to a consideration of the changes that have taken place since the time of the first general Census which took place in 1872.

The information regarding the early population of the Baroda State is very scanty and unreliable. Estimates of the population were occasionally made for fiscal purposes, but none of them was based on an actual counting of the people. In 1849 Briggs (Cities of Gujarastra, p. 388) estimated the population of the State to be 2,250,000 by adopting a mean of different estimates supplied to him by different officials. The first regular Census taken in 1872 showed the population of the State to be 1,997,598, and it must therefore be considerably less when Briggs made his estimate about a quarter of a century before. The Census of 1872 included the population of Chandod and Deesa camp, and that of 1881 included the population of Manekwada contingent camp, and Prabhas and Prachi, which have not since then been censused in Baroda. Excluding the population of these places from the Censuses in which it was included, the population of the State from Census to Census stands as stated in the margin. The variations in the population between 1872 and 1881, 1881 and 1891 and 1891 and 1901 have already been dealt with in the reports of those Censuses. They will, therefore, be treated of very briefly and the discussion in this chapter will refer chiefly to the variations which have occurred during the last decade.

Year of Census.	Population.	Percentage of variations since previous Censuses.
1872	1,997,598	....
1881	2,182,158	+ 9·24
1891	2,415,396	+10·69
1901	1,952,692	—19·15
1911	2,032,798	+ 4·1

Variations since 1901.

80. As already stated, the population of the State now amounts to 2,032,798. The increase since 1901 is 80,106 or 4·1 per cent. This increase is neither general nor uniformly distributed over all the districts. Baroda (with city), Navsari and Amreli show an increase of 6·6, 11·6 and 2·7 per cent., respectively, while Kadi shows a decrease of ·31. The map on the next page illustrates the variations since 1901. It will be convenient first to examine the general conditions which cause variation in population and then to proceed to a consideration of the changes in each district and in the State as a whole.

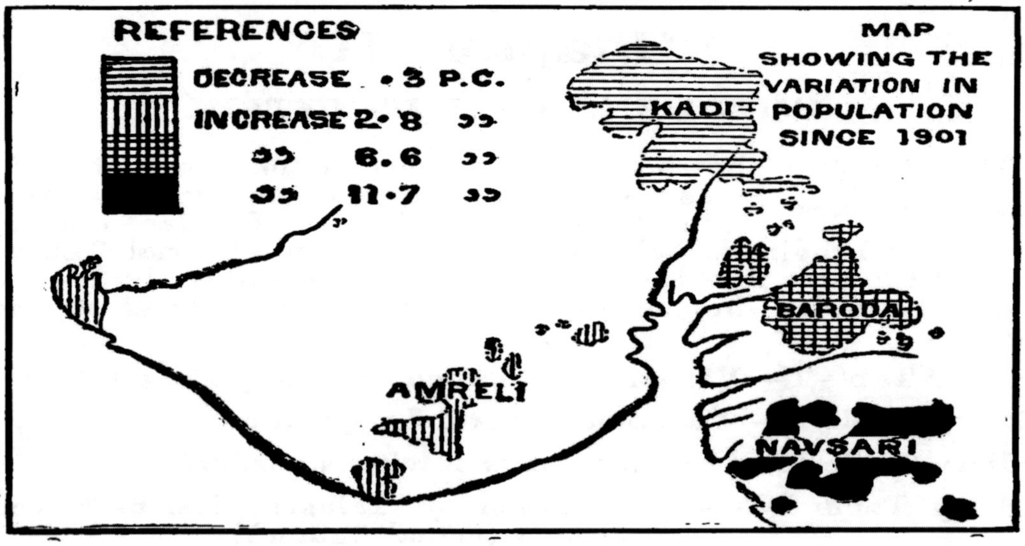

The forces causing variation in population.

81. Variation in population may be either *positive* showing an increase or *negative* showing a decrease, and is the net result of the operation of the forces that tend to its growth and those that retard it. Broadly speaking, the forces that cause the variation are (1) natural increase or decrease, that is, the difference between births and deaths, (2) famine, (3) epidemic diseases, (4) migration and (5) accuracy of enumeration. Of these, the last may now be said to be non-existing as this being the 5th Census of the State, a satisfactory degree of accuracy may now be assumed to have been reached. Famine and epidemics have their effects both on births and deaths and migration, and it may, therefore, be said briefly that variations in the population depend upon (1) excess or otherwise of births over deaths and (2) migration. Migration will be dealt with in the next Chapter and will be referred to here only so far as it is necessary to determine its effects on the variation in the population. Returns showing the number of births and deaths in each district are published in the annual reports of the Sanitary Commissioner for the State, and if they are correct, an estimate of the population based on them, with due allowance for migration, ought to approximate with the results of the Census.

Migration.

82. It will appear from the next Chapter, specially devoted to migration, that it does not play a very important part in the variation of the State population. The State gives only about 20,000 persons more to the rest of India than it receives from them. This works up to nearly one per cent. of the population. It refers only to persons who have migrated to other parts of India, and does not include those who have emigrated to South Africa, Zanzibar, Mauritius and other places beyond India.

Value of vital statistics.

83. Returns of vital statistics, if accurately maintained, would afford a fairly correct indication, not only of the variations that take place from time to time in the public health, but also of the actual growth or decadence of the population. Considerable attention has been paid, of recent years, to the improvement of the returns in this State, but as we shall see in the next para. they are yet so incomplete that the statistics returned are worthless in all matters in which exactness is required.

The vital statistics returns.

84. Previous to 1901, in villages, Mukhis and Patels (headmen) and in towns, the Police registered births and deaths and sent a monthly return from these registers to the Taluka Vahivatdar who tabulated a return for all the villages and towns of the Taluka and forwarded it to the Sanitary Commissioner, in whose office, births and deaths statistics for the whole State were compiled. The duty of reporting births or deaths was under this arrangement imposed upon the village watch-

men and not on the relations, and the result was always unsatisfactory. With a view to secure better registration, new rules were framed in June 1901 which are still in force. Under them in municipal towns, it is the duty of the municipality and elsewhere of the village headmen to keep a register of births and deaths. Vahivatdars, Naib Subas and Subas are required, while on their district tours, to inspect the registers and to see that they are properly maintained. It is only in the City of Baroda that the head of the family is bound within a fortnight of the event to send information about births and deaths in his family to the office of the Municipal Inspector of the ward and his failure to do so renders him liable to prosecution. Elsewhere there is no binding on the people to give information. As a matter of fact, the bulk of the people are yet unable to appreciate the utility of such information and are disposed even to resent inquiries into family matters as an unnecessary interference with the privacy of domestic life. With the provisions of law sitting so loosely on the shoulders of such ignorant people, the success of the system mainly depends on the efficiency of the staff employed and on the diligence with which their work is tested and checked.

Comparison o Census results with those indicated by birth and death returns.

85. An examination of the vital statistics of the decade as given in Subsidiary Table III reveals the fact that the work of registering them is very unsatisfactory. Except in the last three years, there is every year a consistent tale of high death-rate and low birth-rate and the average of ten years comes to an excess of nearly 10 deaths over births per 1,000 of the population per annum. At this rate the population of the State ought in the decade to be less than what it was in 1901 by more than 18[illegible],000 persons, but the actual counting in the Census has shown that as a matter of fact, the population has increased by 80,106. The registration of deaths is probably fairly accurate because information about them comes to the notice of the registrars easily owing to corpses being taken to the burning or burial grounds. But information about births cannot be had so easily and their registration is often neglected.

Year.	Rate per 1,000 of population in the decade reported.		
	Births.	Deaths.	Excess of births over deaths.
1900–01	6·8	59·6	—52·8
1901–02	21·5	29·6	— 8·1
1902–03	18·5	31·6	—13·1
1903–04	20·3	33·2	—12·9
1904–05	22·3	24·7	— 2·4
1905–06	21·9	23·7	— 1·8
1906–07	21·6	32·8	—11·2
1907–08	24·2	24·6	— 0·4
1908–09	24·9	22·0	+ 2·9
1909–10	24·7	23·4	+ 1·3
Average of ten years.	20·7	30·4	— 9·7

Reported causes of deaths.

86. As the agency recording deaths is untrained and consists of low-paid clerks, the registered causes of deaths are also unreliable. The first thing that strikes one is the high proportion of deaths ascribed to fever. More than sixty-eight per cent. of the total mortality is returned under this head. This is mainly due to the difficulty of diagnosing all but a few well defined diseases. Cholera, dysentery and small-pox are known, but most other complaints are classed indiscriminately as fever. The Sanitary Commissioner in his annual report for 1909-10 says: "No doubt several deaths, if not many, due to other causes, suchas from consumption, pneumonia, measles and whooping cough, etc., are wrongly returned as due to fever simply because that complaint is the most prominent feature of the diseases such as mentioned above and many others. As long as registration is in the hands of non-professional and untrained hands such as village Patels and Mukhis, this state of affairs will continue."

Conditions of the decade.

87. The record of vital statistics being thus useless for checking the Census statistics and accounting for the variation in population since 1901, we must turn to other available sources, and see if they throw any light on the subject. In a State like Baroda, where nearly seventy per cent. of the population are dependent on agriculture for their livelihood, the rate of growth of the population should naturally vary with the state of the harvest. When the crops are good, the

people would be prosperous and progressive, but when they fail, the pinch of scarcity would at once be felt and the rate of growth would be adversely affected. We may, therefore, enquire into the seasons and rainfall, general health, and other conditions likely to influence the growth of population.

Seasons and rainfall.

88. The following description of the seasons and rainfall, which has been extracted from the annual administration reports of the State, shows that the decade 1901-1911 did not witness such a widespread calamity as the great famine of 1899-1900, which occurred in the previous decade, but the seasons and rainfall were not favourable to the full growth of the population. Weakened and thinned by a great famine in the previous decade, the people had successive lean years during the present one. There was hardly any room for recuperation—hardly any breathing time or respite in this long series of lean years :—

1900-01.—Rainfall in all the divisions, except Amreli, was less than normal. It did not begin in time, and when it commenced, it fell continuously for some time and then held off. As a consequence of this, the paddy, *kodra, tuver* and gram crops were damaged. Wheat and tobacco crops were fair, so also was the cotton crop in the Kanam District. *Bajri* and *Juwar* crops were fair. No scarcity of grass was felt. Some damage was done by rats to cotton crops in Baroda Division. A disease called *geru* damaged the wheat crop in the Kadi and Amreli Divisions.

1901-02.—The rainfall in all the divisions was considerably less than normal. In Amreli it was abnormally low. As the rains held off in the latter part of the season, the paddy and *kodra* crops suffered a great deal in the Baroda and Kadi Divisions. In the Navsari Division the rainfall, though below normal, was seasonable in some parts. All the crops except paddy and sugarcane were fair. In the Amreli Division, all the crops failed. In the Baroda and Navsari Divisions, damage was done to the crops by rats. In the Amreli Division, rats destroyed crops in Shianagar and Damnagar ; in Kodinar crops were destroyed by some poisonous air coming from the sea.

1902-03 and 1903-04.—Rainfall was scanty everywhere in 1902-03 except in Navsari ; while in 1903-04 it was normal or copious everywhere except in Kadi. Crops suffered in many talukas; in Kadi on acccount of this scanty rainfall, while in some Talukas of Baroda and Amreli the rains were not seasonable. Locusts also appeared in all the four districts in 1903 and did damage to the crops. Cotton and sesamum crops in Kodinar Taluka in the Amreli District were considerably damaged by rats; otherwise the conditions were good.

1904-05.—The rainfall was scanty everywhere, and in many places it was badly distributed. The result was that in most parts of Amreli and Kadi Districts and in large portions of Baroda District, there was famine during the year, and relief operations had to be undertaken.

1905-06.—Rainfall during the year was less than the average of the preceding five years. In Kadi it was abnormal, and, being not evenly distributed, did more harm than good. In the Amreli District it was scanty and held off in the latter part of the season, and this brought about famine conditions.

1906-07.—The rainfall during the year was more than the average of the last five years and that of the previous year in all the divisions except Kadi, where it was a little less. It was also evenly distributed throughout the season. The average yield of staple crops in the various districts compared favourably with that of the previous year.

1907-08.—In all the districts except Kadi, the rainfall was less than that of the preceding year but more than the average of the last ten years. The rainy season commenced well, but, after a continuous fall during the month of July, it stopped at once in the middle of August. This sudden and untimely cessation of rains greatly reduced the yield of the *kharif* and *ravi* crops.

1908-09.—Rainfall in this year was above the average in all districts. Unfortunately, excepting in Navsari, it was not very timely nor very evenly distributed, and the cessation of rains in September affected the yield of the monsoon crops making it below average. The *ravi* crops, however, matured well and made up for the poorness of the *kharif*.

1909-10.—The rainfall during the year, though more than the average of the last ten, somewhat dry years, was a little less in Kadi and Baroda, and more in the other two districts than in the year preceding it. It was fairly and evenly distributed, and, though its cessation in September had some effect on crops, yet the outturn, on the whole, showed an improvement over that of the previous years.

Plague.

89. In addition to insufficient and unequally distributed rain and consequent bad seasons, there was another disturbing cause—plague—throughout the decade. Plague first appeared in the Baroda State in Bilimora (Navsari District) and spread over the whole State with varying force in 1899. From 1899 to 1910, 103,390 cases and 77,975 deaths have been reported; but, owing to a faulty system of registration, the totals reported are probably a good deal under the real figures. It is now endemic, regularly reappearing with varying severity in all the districts.

Railways.

90. Apart from the bad seasons and plague, the past decade was one of great progress. The State Railways, which in 1901 had an aggregate length of 184 miles, have in 1911 grown to 446 miles, or more than double in length.

Extension of Cultivation.

91. In 1901-02 the cultivated area in the State amounted to 5,815,095 bighas. In 1910-11 it was 6,074,321 bighas, an increase of 259,226 bighas or 4·5 per cent. The additional area brought under cultivation consisted mainly of fertile lands relinquished during the famine period.

District.	Cultivated area in	
	1901-02.	1910-11.
Baroda	1,559,219	1,600,338
Kadi	2,439,584	2,448,928
Navsari	946,157	1,039,328
Amreli	870,135	985,727
Total ...	5,815,095	6,074,321

Growth of factories and mills.

92. Weaving, dyeing, calico printing and other old industries, for which Baroda, Patan, Visnagar, Vadnagar, Petlad, Dabhoi, Amreli, Gandevi, Navsari, Kathor and other towns were famous, are mostly on the decline, and industries under new methods are gradually coming into existence. An important event in connection with the development of industries in the State was the creation, in 1905, of the office of an Economic Adviser, and the appointment thereto of Mr. R. C. Whitenack, an American gentleman, who soon justified his selection by manifestation of great energy and perseverance, quickness in comprehension of subjects and resourcefulness. The principal subjects that engaged the attention of the Economic Adviser, immediately after his appointment, were the organization of joint-stock banking, cotton-seed-oil industry, tanning and fibre industries, improvement of cotton staple, minerals and mining industries and technical education. The results were more than gratifying. In 1901, there was no bank even in the capital of the State, while in 1911 there are several with branches in the mofussil. In 1901, there was only one spinning and weaving mill in the City of Baroda and 44 ginning factories and presses in different parts of the State. In 1911, the number of spinning and weaving mills had increased to 4, that of ginning factories and presses to 83, and 7 dyeing factories, 5 oil factories and 42 factories of a miscellaneous nature had sprung up. Joint-stock companies have risen in number from 6 in 1901 to 39 and their capital has increased from Rs. 88,250 to Rs. 66,13,500. Everything seems to point to the fact that Baroda has entered upon an era of industrial development, which has brought a marked improvement in the material condition of the landless labourers and the poorer classes in general. The demand for labour far exceeds the supply, and it is confidently expected that, in the event of a crop failure in the future, the damage of loss of life is greatly diminished.

Improvement in public health.

93. In all the larger towns, the water supply and sanitary arrangements have been greatly improved. Much has been done in the smaller towns also and even in the villages. It is one of the duties of the village panchayats, established in every village in 1903-04, to look after the village sanitation and to keep in order the village roads, wells, tanks, etc. 37 towns have been endowed with municipalities, deriving their funds from octroi duty and other sources. Care is taken to guard against epidemic diseases at the fairs and festivals where the people assemble in large numbers. When cholera breaks out, efforts are made to eradicate it by the disinfection of wells and other sources of water supply. The protection of the people from small-pox by means of vaccination has made a great progress. When public health is found to be suffering from obstructed drainage, efforts are made to remove the defect by cutting artificial drainage channels. The number of dispensaries established by Government is rapidly increasing and medical relief is brought home to the people. Though there is yet much room for improvement, these and other measures cannot fail to have a beneficial effect upon the health of the people; and, apart from plague, against which as yet there has been no sure and satisfactory remedy, the general health of the people must be steadily improving.

Economic features of the decade.

94. The most marked economic features of the decade were the continued high prices, both of food and labour. Depopulation by famine and plague is the main cause, which has contributed to the rise in the value of labour. The causes of the rise in the prices of food stuffs are more complex, but there can be no doubt that less production, owing to bad seasons is one of the many. Curious, as it may seem, there has been a rise also in the price of land and extension in the area under cultivation. Whatever be the ultimate causes of the increased cost of labour, of food, and of acquiring culturable land, the immediate effects are quite clear in respect to the classes whose incomes are fixed. For them, the rise in the prices of food, fuel, land, service and rents has resulted in unmixed hardship accentuated by the correlated fact that the standard of living among all classes is rapidly rising. The effect of the high prices on the labouring classes is more than compensated by the enormous rise in their wages. The general impression is that the unskilled labourer, whether paid in cash or in kind, has greatly improved his economic position within recent years. Labour has become more mobile and the labourer more independent. The scarcity of labour seriously hampers agricultural operations and its increased cost impedes the execution of improvements. The position of the agriculturist under the changed conditions, coupled with the bad seasons, has been very hard. He has to pay more for labour and his produce is small. His cattle also cost him more now than before. The only relieving feature in his case is that his surplus produce repays him more handsomely than before, on account of the rise in the prices of food stuffs.

Abnormal increase possible after a famine.

95. When there has been a famine in the period between two censuses, the population is stationary or decadent according to the intensity of the famine; but when there has been no famine, it is progressive. The rate of growth is greatest during the period of good crops following close on the heels of a famine. The reason for this is partly that a calamity of this sort causes a high mortality, chiefly among the very old and the very young and other persons already of a feeble constitution, so that when it is over, the population contains an unusually high proportion of healthy persons at the reproductive ages ; and partly because by reducing the number of dependants to be supported, its ultimate effect is to improve the resources of the poorer classes, and so encourage them to have larger families. Thus Madras having suffered severely in the famine of 1876-77 added 15·1 per cent. to its population between 1881 and 1891, and Bombay which shared in the same calamity had an almost identical increment. Similarly our Amreli District lost nearly 9 per cent. of its population in the Census of 1881, owing to its having a famine in 1877, but added 25 per cent. to its population in the decade 1881-1891.

If the decade which followed the great famine had been one of uniformly good crops and free from plague and other disturbing causes, the increase in the population of this State in the present Census would have been more than normal. But as we have already seen, such was not the case, and no large increase in the population could be expected.

Normal rate of increase.

96. The Census of 1881 was taken exactly nine years after the first Census of 1872, and showed an increase of 9·24 per cent. in nine years. But, as has already been mentioned, in 1877, there was a partial famine in some parts of the Baroda District and total failure of crops in the Amreli District owing to failure of rain. Consequently, Baroda showed an increase of only about 4 per cent., while Amreli showed a decrease of nearly 9 per cent., in its population. In spite of a very high increase of 16 per cent. in the Kadi District and of 19 per cent. in the Navsari District, the general increase in the State was therefore reduced to 9 per cent. only. The Census of 1891, taken ten years after 1881, showed an increase of about 11 per cent. The Census of 1901, which showed a decrease of 19 per cent., was taken after one of the most terrible famines that ever visited the country and carried away hundreds of thousands from the population. The decade 1881-1891 was a normal one and the population was not materially affected by causes which may bring on an abnormal increase or decrease in the population, except in Amreli, which was affected by famine in the previous decade and showed an abnormal increase of nearly 25 per cent. Making due allowance for this, 10 per cent. in ten years, or 1 per cent. every year, may be taken as the normal rate of increase in the State.

Expected and actual variation.

97. Having regard to the successive bad seasons and some periods of actual scarcity and plague, which characterised the past decade, even a normal increase in the population could not, and as a matter of fact was not expected. The Suba of Kadi anticipated a large decrease (about 10 per cent.) in the population of his district, and though his estimate has been found to be too pessimistic, there has been some decrease (·31 per cent. of the population). The other Subas were not apprehensive of any decrease, but at the same time did not expect any large increase. Amreli which stood next after Kadi in the ill luck of having bad seasons, shows an increase of 2·7 only, while Baroda and Navsari, which were comparatively better off, show an increase of 8·7 and 11·6 respectively in the actual counting of the heads.

98. After these general remarks, we shall now take each district separately and briefly review the variations in its population as a whole and also in each of its talukas. Baroda Division is on the whole healthy and its soil fertile. It had in 1872, a population of 631,163. In the Census of 1881, it showed an increase of 3 per cent. Compared with Kadi and Navsari, this increase was very small. There was a partial famine in 1877 in most of the talukas and there was an epidemic of fever in 1881, which mainly accounted for the small increase in the population. The decade 1881-1891 was marked by good seasons and was free from epidemics of any kind, except fever and consequently showed an increase of 7 per cent. in the Census of 1891. Plague and the famine of 1899-1900 not only did not allow the population to show an increase in the Census of 1901, but there was a positive decline of about

Baroda Division.

Taluka.	Population in 1911.	Percentage of variation.				
		1901 to 1911.	1891 to 1901.	1881 to 1891.	1872 to 1881.	Net variation + or.—
District total ...	587,555	+ 9	—23	+ 7	+ 3	— 7
1. Petlad	128,008	— 5	—14	+ 7	} + 1	—12
2. Bhadran... ...	43,670	+ ·5	—19	+11		
3. Baroda	66,202	+10	—37	+ 7	+ 3	—24
4. Padra	76,252	+ 4	—20	+ 6	+ 1	—12
5. Karjan	56,334	+16	—22	+ 1	+ 5	— 4
6. Dabhoi	55,210	+12	—18	+ 6	+ 6	+ 4
7. Sinore	34,063	+15	—23	+ 1	+ 5	—10
8. Savli	44,339	+14	—15	+ 9	} + 7	+12
9. Vaghodia ...	24,467	+17	—24	+12		
10. Sankheda ...	51,471	+40	—36	+10	+15	+14
11. Tilakwada ...	7,539	+57	—48	+24	+ 9	+ 9

23 per cent. The present Census shows an increase of 8·75 per cent. The decade was not so prosperous as that of 1881-1891, but the increase is a little greater, mainly on account of the Census following the famine.

Looking to the variations in the talukas, we find that the increase in the present Census is not uniformly distributed over all the talukas. The greatest increase is shown by Savli, Vaghodia, Dabhoi, Sankheda, Karjan, Sinore and Tilakwada Talukas, which had lost from 15 to 48 per cent. of their population in 1901. The *Charottar* Taluka of Petlad, instead of any increase, shows a decrease of 5 per cent. and Bhadran is almost stationary. These talukas are now less populous than in 1872 by about 12 per cent. Long before 1881, all the available land in these talukas was brought under cultivation. The density of the population in 1881 was 726, and there was hardly any room for expansion. Those who do not find means of subsistence in the village of their birth generally emigrate to Bombay, Ahmedabad, Madras and of late to South Africa.

Map showing the Variation in Population by Mahals since 1901.

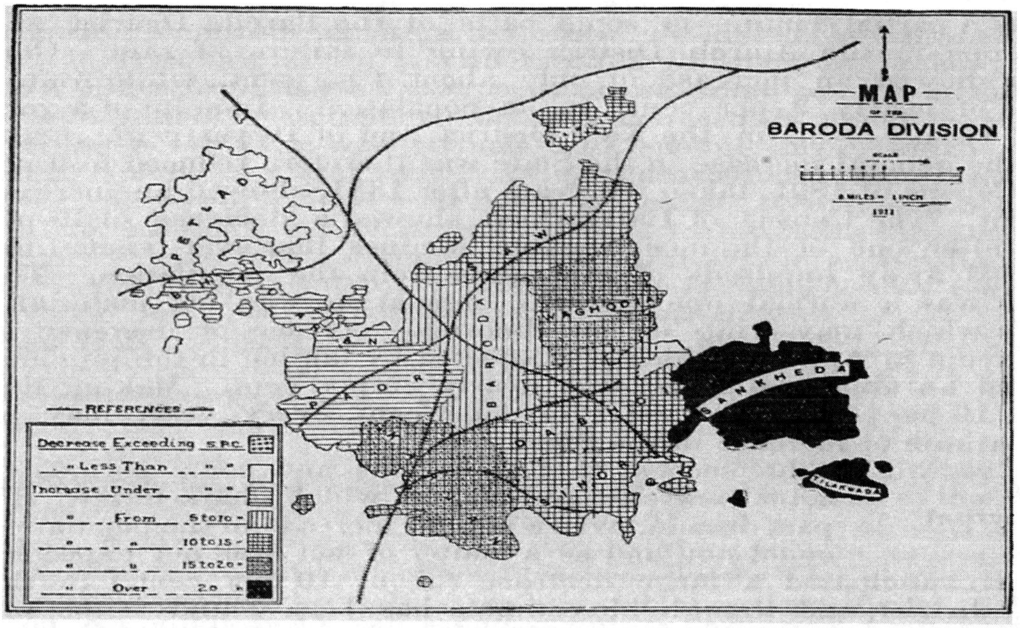

Similarly the *Vakal* Talukas of Baroda and Padra are now less populous than in 1872 by nearly 25 and 12 per cent. respectively. The *Kanam* Taluka of Dabhoi has gained nearly 4 per cent., while Karjan and Sinore have lost 4 and 10 per cent. respectively during the same period. The *Chorashi* Talukas of Savli and Vaghodia have improved from what they were in 1872 by about 12 per cent. Sankheda and Tilakwada are the only talukas which have been progressive and have at each Census, except that of 1901, added largely to their population. In 1901, these talukas showed a terrible decline of 36 and 48 per cent. respectively. But the increase shown by them in the present Census, *i.e.*, 40 and 57 per cent. is also remarkable. On the whole, Sankheda is now more populous than what it was in 1872 by 14 per cent. and Tilakwada by 9 per cent. Everywhere more land is brought under cultivation in these talukas. The new settlers are mostly people from the *Kanam* Talukas and also from the neighbouring petty states in the Sankheda Mewas.

99. The greater portion of the Kadi Division has rich alluvial soil except in the west where in parts of Kadi and Harij, there are tracts of poor salt land. The division is well-known for the healthiness of its climate. When there was no disturbing cause, such as famine or plague, the division always showed an increase in its population. The Census of 1881 showed an increase of 16 per cent. and that of 1891 an increase of 11 per cent. over the figures of the previous decades. Between 1891 and 1901 came the great famine of 1899 and cholera and other epidemics in its train, which carried away nearly one-fourth of the population. After the famine had carried away the weak and the infirm, the survivors would naturally be expected to be strong and to show a good increase in the present Census. But throughout the present decade, Kadi had to grapple with a new foe which in spite of all human attempts has carried away either by

death or by migration more than the number it would have shown as the natural increase in the decade. Till 1900-01, Kadi District was singularly free from plague. In the year 1902-03, the disease appeared in the Ahmedabad City and the infection thence proceeded to Kalol, and the village of Bahiyal in Dehgam taluka. The net-work of railways in the district, though a great boon to the people, was the chief cause for rapid spread of the epidemic and in 1903-04, there was no taluka in the district, which was not affected. Kheralu had 1,463 attacks and 1,061 deaths, Vijapur 1,310 attacks and 1,178 deaths, Visnagar 1,031 attacks and 780 deaths and Mehsana 565 attacks and 476 deaths and since then every year upto 1909-10, the Sanitary Commissioner chronicles the melancholy news that "the largest number of villages infected as well as of attacks and deaths was in the Kadi Prant." The total number of deaths reported as due to plague in the Kadi District during the eight years from 1902-03 was 4 per cent. of the population. But it is possible that many deaths due to plague must have been included under the head of fevers, to which, as already mentioned nearly 68 per cent. of the total deaths are annually ascribed. The Census has shown that the district instead of showing its normal increase shows a decrease of ·3 per cent. in its population. From this it can be inferred that the number carried away by plague, must be roughly speaking, equal to the extent of the expected growth in the population during the decade. This at 10 per cent. comes to 83,216 persons. While the district as a whole shows a slight decrease, some of its talukas which were sharply hit by famine in the previous decade, show good increase. Dehgam which had lost 29 per cent. of its population in 1901, now shows an increase of 12 per cent. Atarsumba which had lost 38 per cent. in the previous decade, now shows an increase of 11 per cent. Kadi which had lost 26 per cent., shows an increase of 6 per cent., while Harij which had lost 57 per cent. of its population in 1901, now shows an increase of 28 per cent.

Kadi Division.

Taluka.	Population in 1911.	Percentage of variation.				
		1901 to 1911.	1891 to 1901.	1881 to 1891.	1872 to 1881.	Net variation + or —
District Total ..	832,162	—·3	—24	+11	+16	—2·2
1. Dehgam ..	55,211	+12	—29	+ 7	+14	— 3
2. Atarsumba ...	20,922	+11	—38	+ 9	+ 5	—21
3. Kadi ...	76,198	+ 6	—26	+ 9	+16	—0·3
4. Kalol ...	81,187	+ ·8	—17	+ 9	+19	+ 8
5. Vijapur ...	110,913	— 5	—25	+ 9	+14	—12
6. Visnagar ...	63,053	—11	—23	+13	+10	—15
7. Mehsana ...	73,887	— 2	—10	+17	+17	+21
8. Sidhpur ...	88,539	— 2	—16	+13	+16	+ 8
9. Kheralu ...	70,641	— 8	—23	+13	+ 9	—12
10. Patan ...	107,003	+ 3	—23	+13	+23	+ 9
11. Chansma ...	68,661	+ 2	—34	+11	+19	—11
12. Harij ...	15,947	+28	—57	+11	+60	— 3

Map showing the Variation in Population by Mahals since 1901.

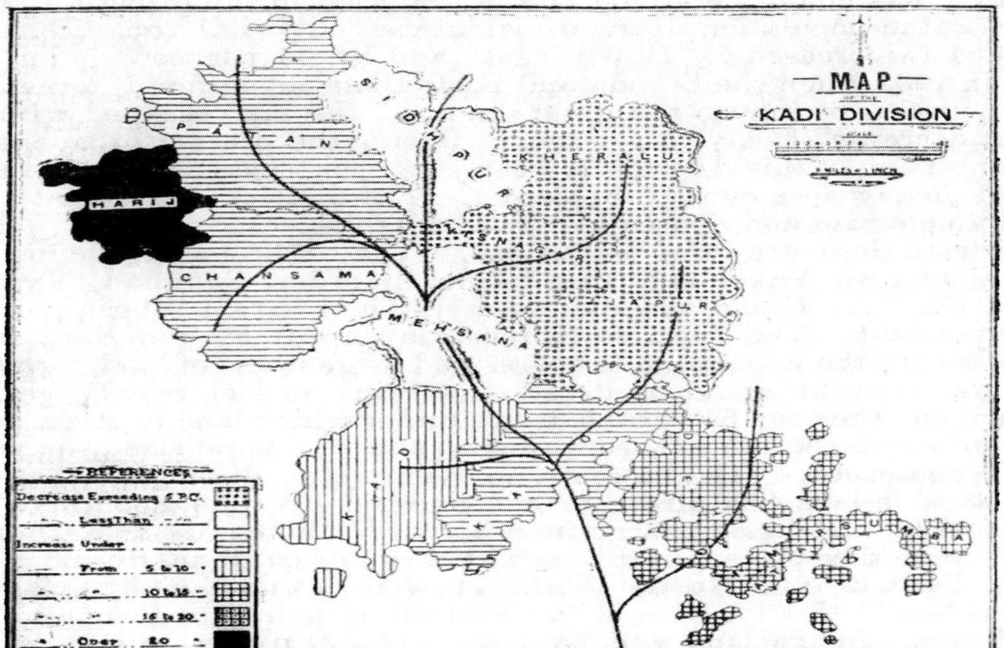

Vijapur, Visnagar, Sidhpur, Kheralu, and Mehsana show some slight decrease in their population mainly on account of plague ; while Patan, Kalol and Chansma which were also equally affected, show some slight increase. Kadi District will take long time to recover from its heavy loss in 1901. Its present population is now about 2 per cent. less than what it was in 1872, and 16 per cent. less than what it was in 1881. Mehsana, Sidhpur, Patan and Kalol are now somewhat better off than what they were in 1872 ; but Vijapur, Visnagar, Kheralu, Kadi, Chansma, Harij and Atarsumba have not yet recovered their loss and are far behind what they were forty years ago.

100. The Navsari Division has two classes of people, one of which is termed *Ujliparaj* or the white races, and the other *Kaliparaj* or dark races. As explained in the Chapter on Caste, the *Ujliparaj* include the Kanbis, Anavalas and other higher castes and the *Kaliparaj* comprise Bhils, Chodhras, Gamits, Dublas, &c. For the most part, the Ujliparaj abide in the *Rasti* or settled talukas and the Kaliparaj in the *Rani* or wild and uncultivated talukas. The soil is fertile, but before 1875, the division was poorly populated and most of the land lay uncultivated owing mainly to the very heavy rates of assessment and the bad climate of the Rani Mahals. In 1875, the total demand was greatly reduced, the reduction varying in the different talukas from 38 to 47 per cent. The industrious Anavalas and Kanbis and the poor Kaliparaj classes being thus relieved of their heavy burdens, the general condition of the cultivating classes, and it may be added, of the whole population has much improved and is reflected in the growth of the population. In 1872, the population of the division was only 241,255. During the decade 1872-1881 it increased by 19 per cent., and by 11 per cent. during the next decade. In 1901 when the Baroda and Kadi Districts suffered a heavy decline in their population owing to the great famine, Navsari escaped with a comparatively light decrease of only 6 per cent. During the present decade, the increase in the population of this district is nearly 12 per cent. or more than normal, in spite of heavy loss owing to plague. The district is fortunate in having timely and ample rain and consequent good seasons.

Navsari Division.

Taluka.	Population in 1911.	Percentage of variation.				
		1901 to 1911.	1891 to 1901.	1881 to 1891.	1872 to 1881.	Net variation + or —
District Total ...	**335,467**	**+12**	**— 6**	**+11**	**+19**	**+39**
1. Navsari ...	55,270	— 8	+12	+ 9	+ 7	+21
2. Gandevi ...	33,058	+ 7	— 6	+11	+ 7	+19
3. Palsana ...	24,908	— 1	+·09	+10	+ 6	+15
4. Kamrej ...	41,969	+ 1	— 7	+22	+12	+82
5. Mahuva ...	39,741	+18	— 5	+ 9	+22	+49
6. Velachha ...	27,431	+22	—11	+23	+56	+36
7. Songhad ...	42,446	+34	— 5	+ ·1	+31	+48
8. Vyara ...	57,477	+28	—17	+12	+58	+89
9. Vakal ...	10,812	+36	—26	+ 9	—37	......
10. Umarpada ...	2,355	+ 4	—27	......	......	......

Within the district, there are large variations. The highest increase in the present Census is shown by Vakal and then come in order, Songhad, Vyara, Velachha, Mahuva, Gandevi, Umarpada and Kamrej, the variation ranging from 1 per cent. to 37 per cent. The highest increase is shown by the Rani and semi-Rasti Mahals, where the population is sparse and large tracts of land, formerly lying waste, are brought under cultivation within the last twenty years. The light assessment and the very favourable terms under which land is given, has brought a large number of settlers to these talukas and the population, as was expected, has well increased. The increase in Kamrej is slight, but that is because all the cultivable land has already come under cultivation and there is no room for expansion. Besides, a large number of Vohoras from Kathore, Kholwad, Variav, and other places in this taluka has migrated to Burma and Africa. Navsari, Palsana and Gandevi talukas were badly hit by plague throughout the decade and this together with emigration mainly to Bombay has brought on the decrease in Palsana and Navsari. Gandevi also would have shown a decline, had it not been for the large increase in Bilimora due to the industrial activity which has already wonderfully developed. Besides being the centre of considerable trade in timber, cocoanut, &c., which are brought here in country crafts from Bombay and other places, Bilimora is also the market for Bansda, the Dangs and other districts in the interior. A branch railway from Bilimora to Sara, a village about 30 miles in the interior is under construction, and will, when completed, give further impetus to the trade of Bilimora.

Map showing the Variation in Population by Mahals since 1901.

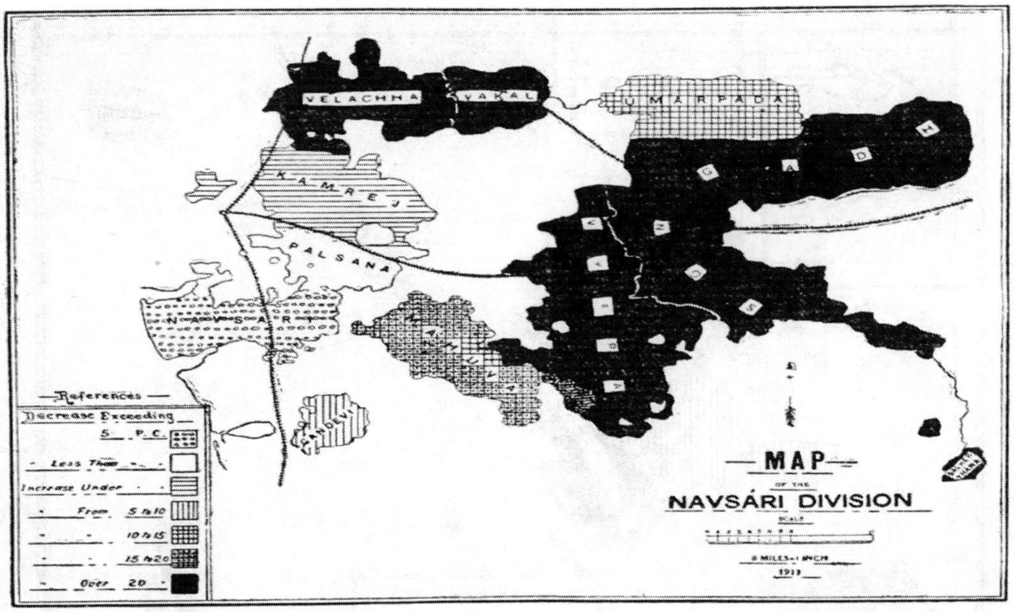

101. The soil of the Amreli Division is with a few exceptions inferior to that of the other divisions in productiveness, and the rainfall is scanty and unequally distributed. The Census of 1872 showed the population to be 158,581. In 1881 it was found to have lost 8 per cent. of its population owing to the famine of 1877, but during the next decade which was a prosperous one, it increased by 25 per cent. In the Census of 1901, while all other divisions showed a heavy decrease in their population, Amreli escaped with a loss of 3·74 per cent. only mainly owing to the special protective measures adopted against famine in this division. In the present decade, Amreli Division had not only lean years, but like Kadi had also plague, though in a less virulent form. Consequently the total population of the district shows an increase of only about 3 per cent. over the figures of 1901. The highest increase (38 per cent.) is shown by Khambha, which owing to famine had lost 21 per cent. of its population in the previous decade. Dhari, Ratanpur and Bhimkatta which were free from plague in this decade, but had lost heavily in the previous one, also show good increase. Kodinar had lost 16 per cent. of its population in the last decade. During this decade, there was hardly any year in which it was not affected by plague; and yet mainly owing to its having fertile land and ample and well distributed rain, it has somewhat made up its past loss, and added 3 per cent. to

Amreli Division.

Taluka.	Population in 1911.	Percentage of variation.				
		1901 to 1911.	1891 to 1901	1881 to 1891	1872 to 1881	Net variation + or —
District Total ...	**178,269**	+ 3	— 4	+ 25	— 8	+ 12
1. Amreli ...	54,679	— 1	+ 7	+ 24	— 16	+ 12
2. Damnagar ...	19,125	— 2	+ 4	+ 32	— 17	+ 12
3. Dhari ...	28,751	+ 11	— 6	+ 31	} — 14	+ 18
4. Khambha...	11,366	+ 38	— 21	+ 39		
5. Kodinar ...	33,471	+ 3	— 16	+ 24	— 7	— ·4
6. Okhamandal ...	21,740	— 4	+ 2	+ 11	+ 22	+ 33
7. Beyt ...	3,658	— 21	— ·2	+ 35	+ 24	+ 32
8. Ratanpur ..	4,531	+ 12	— 24	+ 6	+ ·2	— 10
9. Bhimkatta ...	1,048	+ 21	— 20	+ 9	......	......

its population. It is curious that Amreli, Damnagar and Okhamandal Talukas which show a decrease in this Census had shown an increase in the last one, when everywhere else, there was a decrease in the population owing to famine. It is just possible that this increase was not real but only apparent, having been

Map showing the Variation in Population by Mahals since 1901.

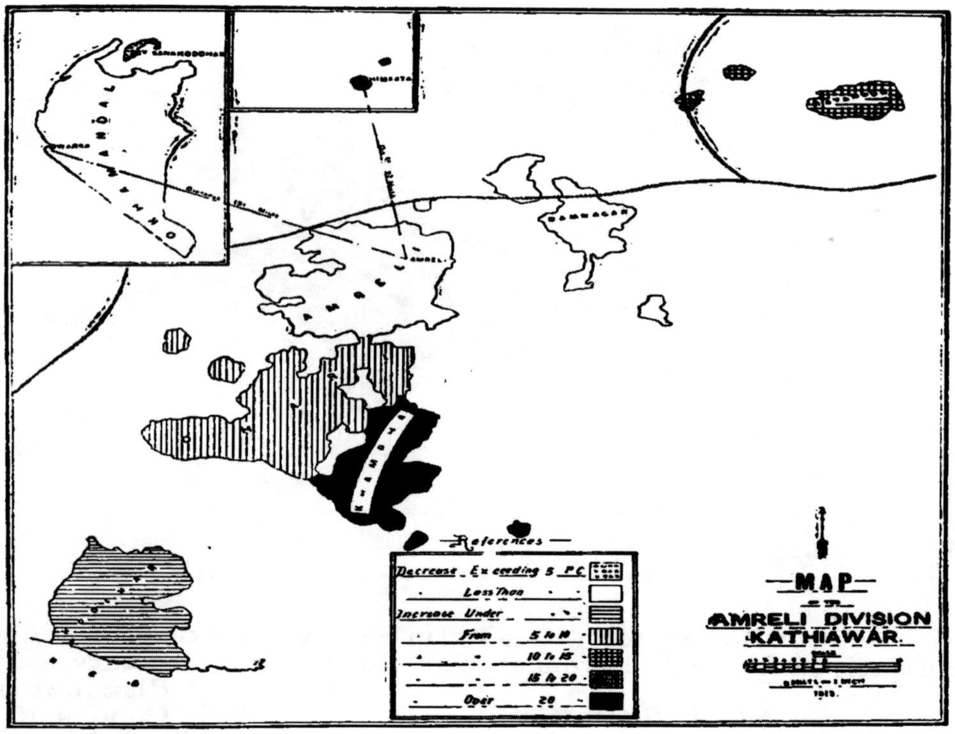

contributed by the temporary migration of people from the neighbouring foreign districts. The return of these people to their homes, after the calamity was over, may be one of the reasons for the decline in these talukas. Beyt and Dwarka are places of pilgrimage, and their population depends upon the presence or absence of pilgrims on the Census day. As the present Census came some days before the *Holi* holidays, the usual number of pilgrims were not present and this accounts for the large decrease which Beyt shows in its population.

Progress in each district compared.

102. In conclusion, we may briefly notice the progress in the State as a whole and in each of its Natural Divisions since 1872. The diagram on the next page shows the variations since 1872 in the population of the different Natural Divisions at each successive enumeration. Between 1872 and 1881 the total increase in the population of the State was 9·24 per cent. Navsari showed the greatest increase in its population (19·19 per cent.). Kadi which stood second also showed great increase (16·25 per cent.). Owing to some parts of it being partially affected by the famine of 1877, Baroda showed only a slight increase of 3·77 per cent. ; while Amreli which was much more affected, showed a decrease of nearly 9 per cent. The next period, 1881 to 1891, was one of general prosperity and good seasons, and the State increased by nearly 11 per cent. in its population. The greatest increase (24·59 per cent.) was shown by Amreli which had suffered a terrible loss of population owing to the famine of 1877 in the previous decade and its rapid growth was the natural reaction from that calamity during a period of renewed prosperity. Kadi and Navsari increased in their population by a little more than 11 per cent., but fever having carried away a large number of persons, the increase in the Baroda Division was limited to only about 7 per

cent. The decade 1891-1901 witnessed one of the greatest famines within the memory of men, and the appearance of a new and deadly disease in the form of plague and the State lost nearly 20 per cent. or one-fifth of its total population. The loss of life was the heaviest (over 24 per cent.) in the Kadi Division and nearly 22 per cent. in the Baroda Division. Navsari, owing to its more favoured situation with regard to rain, and Amreli, owing to the most lavish relief works opened within its limit, escaped with a comparatively smaller loss of nearly 6 and 4 per cent. respectively. Had the last decade been a prosperous one and free from plague, it would have shown a remarkable increase in population owing to its following the great famine, which had carried away the old and infirm from the population and left only the strong and productive. But as we have already seen, rain was generally precarious and the harvest poor, while plague was doing its evil work in all the parts of the State. In consequence of this, the increase in the population has been limited to only 4 per cent. The increase is the highest (11·66 per cent.) in the Navsari District. Baroda follows with nearly 9 per cent. and then comes Amreli with nearly 3 per cent. Kadi in which the battle of life was the hardest, shows a slight decline of ·31 per cent.

Diagram showing the Variation in Population since 1872.

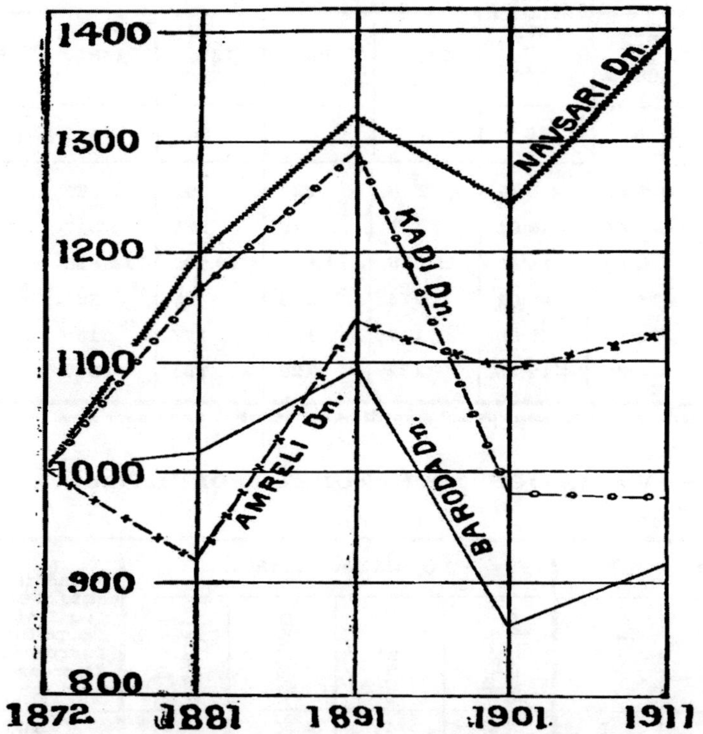

Summary.

103. Navsari and Amreli are the only districts, which passing through various vicissitudes during the last forty years, show an increase in their population compared with what it was in 1872. The population of Navsari is now 39 per cent. more than what it was forty years ago ; while Amreli has improved by 12·45 per cent. during the same period. But both Baroda and Kadi are now less populous than what they were forty years before by about 7 and 2 per cent. respectively. The net result of these gains and losses is that the State, as a whole, has now only 35,200 persons more in its population than it had in 1872. In other words the net increase of population during forty years has been only 1·76 per cent.

SUBSIDIARY TABLE I.—Variation in relation to density since 1872.

District or Natural Division.	Percentage of variation increase (+) decrease (—) 1901 to 1911	1891 to 1901	1881 to 1891	1872 to 1881	Net variation 1872 to 1911	Mean density per square mile. 1911	1901	1891	1881	1872
1	2	3	4	5	6	7	8	9	10	11
Baroda State ...	**+4·10**	**—19·15**	**+10·68**	**+9·24**	**+1·76**	**248**	**239**	**295**	**267**	**244**
Baroda Division ...	+8·74	—22·88	+6·96	+3·77	—6·91	311	286	371	347	334
Baroda City ...	—4·28	—10·84	+9·30	—8·39	—14·56	11,038	11,532	12,935	11,835	12,919
Kadi Division .	—·31	—24·02	+11·15	+16·25	—2·01	275	276	363	327	281
Navsari Division ...	+11·66	—5·94	+11·09	+19·19	+39·05	175	157	167	150	126
Amreli Division ...	+2·79	—3·74	+24·59	—8·80	+12·45	132	129	134	107	118

Note.—The figures of density for 1901 and previous censuses have been revised according to the latest figures for area.

SUBSIDIARY TABLE II.—Variation in natural population.

District or Natural Division.	Population in 1911. Actual population.	Immigrants.	Emigrants.	Natural population.	Population in 1901. Actual population.	Immigrants.	Emigrants.	Natural population.	Variation per cent.(1901-1911) in Natural population Increase (+) Decrease (—)
1	2	3	4	5	6	7	8	9	10
Baroda State ...	**2,032,798**	**222,957**	**242,033**	**2,051,874**	**1,952,692**	**172,931**	**202,270**	**1,982,031**	**+ 3·5**
Baroda Division ...	587,555	103,179			540,281	80,467			
Baroda City ...	99,345		District are not	figures available	103,790		District figures	are not available.	District figures are not available.
Kadi Division ..	832,162	45,158			834,744	28,629			
Navsari Division ...	335,467	50,229			300,441	43,288			
Amreli Division ...	178,269	34,931			173,436	32,423			

SUBSIDIARY TABLE III.—Comparison with vital statistics.

District or Natural Division.	1901-1910. Total number of Births.	Deaths.	Number per cent. of Population of 1901 of Births.	Deaths.	Excess (+) or Deficiency (—) of births over deaths.	Increase (+) or Decrease (—) of Population of 1911 compared with 1901. Natural Population.	Actual Population.
1	2	3	4	5	6	7	8
Baroda State ...	**404,377**	**594,374**	**20·7**	**30·4**	—189,997	927	**+4·1**
Baroda Division ...	117,695	164,653	21·8	30·5	—46,958	District figures not available.	+8·75
Baroda City ...	14,986	38,254	14·4	36·9	—23,268		—4·28
Kadi Division ..	143,103	253,473	17·1	30·4	—110,370		—·31
Navsari Division ...	86,874	86,236	28·9	28·7	+638		+11·66
Amreli Division ..	41,719	51,758	24·1	29·8	—10,039		+2·79

SUBSIDIARY TABLE IV.—VARIATION BY TALUKAS CLASSIFIED ACCORDING TO DENSITY.

(a)—*Actual variation.*

District or Natural Division.	Decade.	Variations in talukas with a population per square mile at commencement of decade of							
		Under 150	150 to 300.	300 to 450.	450 to 600.	600 to 750.	750 to 900.	900 to 1050.	Over 1050.
1	2	3	4	5	6	7	8	9	10
Baroda State ...	**1881-1891**	**+ 36,188**	**+ 77,679**	**+ 59,121**	**+ 30,329**	**+ 15,682**	**+ 1,201**	**+ 3,130**	**+ 9,908**
	1891-1901	**— 35,594**	**— 121,348**	**— 169,728**	**— 87,812**	**— 10,461**	**— 23,228**	......	**— 4,533**
	1901-1911	**+ 42,800**	**+ 71,124**	**— 11,672**	**— 12,332**	**— 4,412**	......	......	**— 5,402**
Baroda Division with City.	1881-1891	...	+ 24,309	......	+ 5,623	+ 15,682	......	......	+ 9,908
	1891-1901	..	— 61,115	— 46,585	— 18,933	— 10,461	— 23,228	......	— 12,630
	1901-1911	+ 6,311	+ 44,447	+ 2,857	+ 209	— 6,550	......	......	— 4,445
Kadi Division ...	1881-1891	+ 2,852	+ 28,985	+ 53,712	+ 24,706	......	......	......	......
	1891-1901	— 16,629	— 51,739	— 126,751	— 68,879	......	......	......	......
	1901-1911	+ 3,442	+ 16,441	— 14,529	— 7,936	......	......	......	......
Navsari Do. ...	1881-1891	— 647	+ 34,002	— 5,409	......	......	......	+ 3,130	......
	1891-1901	— 15,696	— 5,021	+ 3,608	......	......	......	......	— 1,893
	1901-1911	+ 26,496	+ 10,997	......	— 4,605	+ 2,138	......	......	......
Amreli Do. ...	1881-1891	+ 33,983	+ 383	......	......	......	+ 1,201	......	......
	1891-1901	— 3,269	— 3.473	......	......	......	......	......	— 10
	1901-1911	+ 6,551	— 761	......	......	......	......	......	— 957

SUBSIDIARY TABLE IV.—VARIATION BY TALUKAS CLASSIFIED ACCORDING TO DENSITY.

(b)—*Proportional variation.*

District or Natural Division.	Decade.	Variations in talukas with a population per square mile at commencement of decade of							
		Under 150.	150 to 300.	300 to 450.	450 to 600.	600 to 750.	750 to 900.	900 to 1050.	Over 1050.
1	2	3	4	5	6	7	8	9	10
Baroda State ...	**1881-1891**	**+ 13**	**+ 11·5**	**+ 10·5**	**+ 10**	**+ 8**	**+ 35·1**	**+ 10·5**	**+ 9·3**
	1891-1901	**— 17·3**	**— 18·2**	**— 20·1**	**— 26·4**	**— 19·4**	**— 14·7**	...	**— 9·4**
	1901-1911	**+ 19·6**	**+ 9·2**	**— 2·3**	**— 7·1**	**— 2·7**	...	...	**— 5**
Baroda Division with City	1881-1891	...	+ 6·5	...	+ 6·5	+ 8	...	...	+ 9·3
	1891-1901	...	— 25·4	— 29·8	— 20·5	— 19·4	— 14·7	...	— 10·8
	1901-1911	+ 24·6	+ 16·9	+ 3·9	+ 0·5	— 4·9	...	...	— 4·3
Kadi Division ...	1881-1891	+ 10·9	+ 11·9	+ 10·6	+ 11·5	...	...	...	...
	1891-1901	— 57·1	— 25·2	— 20·3	— 28·7	...	...	...	...
	1901-1911	+ 27·5	+ 5·3	— 3·3	— 11·2	...	...	...	...
Navsari Do. ...	1881-1891	— ·6	+ 29·4	+ 9·2	...	...	...	+ 10·5	...
	1891-1901	— 13·4	— 4·8	+ 5·6	...	...	...	...	— 5·8
	1901-1911	+ 30·6	+ 8·9	...	— 7·7	+ 6·9	...	...	...
Amreli Do. ...	1881-1891	+ 25·2	+ 6·4	...	...	...	+ 35·1	...	...
	1891-1901	— 5·4	— 3·0	...	...	...	...	...	— ·2
	1901-1911	+ 7·0	— 1·0	...	...	...	...	...	— 20·8

Chapter III.

BIRTH-PLACE.

Reference to statistics.

104. The statistics of birth-place are contained in Imperial Table XI. The following subsidiary tables, in which the prominent features of the statistics are given in brief, will be found at the end of this chapter.

Subsidiary Table I.—Showing the general distribution according to birth-place of the persons enumerated in each district.

Subsidiary Table II.—Showing the general distribution according to place of enumeration of the persons born in each district.

Subsidiary Table III.—Containing proportional figures of the migration to and from each district.

Subsidiary Table IV.—Showing the volume of migration between natural divisions at the present Census and in 1901.

Subsidiary Table V and V-A.—Showing the gain or loss by migration between the Baroda State and the other parts of India.

Object of discussion.

105. The movements of the people so far as they affect the total population of the State and of each of its districts have been considered in the last chapter. The present chapter will be devoted mainly to a consideration of the direction and character of the various streams of migration, the reasons that induce them and the extent to which they have grown or declined in volume, since the date of the previous Census.

Utility of the statistics.

106. Statistics recorded in Imperial Table XI tell us how many of the persons enumerated in this State on the 10th March 1911 were born within it, and how many were born in Provinces and States outside it. Similarly from Table XI of other Provinces and States in India, we can know how many persons born in this State were enumerated in those Provinces and States.

Immigration and Emigration.

107. All of those who were enumerated in this State, but recorded as born outside it, are not necessarily immigrants. Similarly all of those recorded as born in the State, but enumerated outside it, are not necessarily emigrants from it. The birth of many persons outside their real home is, in this country, often a casual event, owing to the practice of taking wives from outside, and young married women going to their parents' house for confinement. Moreover, those who have been regarded as immigrants or emigrants in a previous Census, from their birth district, will be similarly regarded in a subsequent Census also, if they continue to reside in the same place. Inference of migration based upon birth-place is thus likely to be erroneous. But as we have no other means of gauging the extent of immigration and emigration, we may use birth statistics as an approximation to the correct figures. It must, however, be remembered that Census statistics only furnish the condition of things as it exists at a certain moment, once in ten years and do not show what reciprocal movements occur from year to year or how these are affected by adverse seasons and similar casualties.

Types of migration.

108. Generally speaking, five different types of migration may be distinguished :—

(1) *Casual* or the accidental movement across the boundary line between contiguous districts. In all the districts of the State, people are constantly found moving short distances from their original home, for the purpose of marriage or other social functions. This is mainly due to the general feeling and custom among the Hindus that a wife cannot be taken from one's own village. This restriction which is less prevalent in towns than in villages is based on the old tribal distribution of the people and the primeval form of marriage by capture. The four districts of the State being detached blocks at a great distance from each other, there is very little of such movement

between them. But there is a great movement of this kind within the boundaries of each district and between the State districts and the foreign territory contiguous to them. When a man's wife is a native of another district, his children will usually be born there also, it being the usual practice for young married women to go to their parents' house for their confinement. This movement is reciprocal, and it is probable that as many real subjects of the State are returned as born outside it, as real foreign subjects are returned as born within it. In Subsidiary Tables I, II and III, migration between contiguous districts has been shown separately, and as there are no apparent reasons for a genuine permanent progression from one district to another, the whole or greater part of if may safely be taken as due to casual movement here described.

(2) *Temporary*—due to a temporary demand for labour on roads, railways, &c., and to journeys on business, pilgrimages and the like.

(3) *Periodic*—due to the changing seasons. Of this nature is the annual exodus, in the summer months, of Bharvads, Rabaris and Gaulis from their homes to places where they can find grazing pastures and water for their cattle. They generally return home when rainfall has filled the ponds and restored the herbage in their own district.

(4) *Semi-permanent.*—The natives of one place reside and earn their livelihood in another, but retain their connection with their own homes, where they leave their families, and to which they themselves return at more or less regular intervals and look forward to the time when they may again live there permanently. The settlement within the State of some of its servants from the Deccan and other parts of India is generally of this nature; so also is that of the Vohoras of Kathore and Sidhpur who have migrated to Rangoon and of the Vanias from Patan, Vadnagar and other places who are trading in Bombay.

(5) *Permanent, i. e.,* where overcrowding or distress on one hand or physical or political advantages on the other, drive away from one district and attract to another, people who settle down permanently on the land.

The ordinary course of permanent migration is as follows :—A family finds its ancestral land or business insufficient for its increasing numbers or is unable to obtain local employment for all its members and a son accompanied perhaps by a cousin or two goes off in search of land or work to places where he knows he can find them. He starts as a tenant or a clerk and after a time, becomes an owner, and sends for his wife to join him in his new home. Her brothers and cousins follow her on the same errand which brought her husband to the place, knowing that they will find friends. His sons look for wives and his daughters for husbands in the neighbourhood of the old home, and so a small colony is formed which serves as a nucleus for further migration. As time goes on, the colony expands, its numbers increase, migration ceases or assumes the reciprocal form, until at length, the ties connecting the colony with the people of the neighbourhood grow stronger and those with its original home relax and wives are no longer sought for at a distance. The instance of the Deccani castes, who have migrated to Baroda, is to the point. Formerly, they used to go to their original home for the weddings of their children ; but they have increased in Baroda to such an extent that they can manage their marriage affairs there, and have now practically severed all connection with their original home.

109. The Census figures do not distinguish between the different types of migration, but a clue to them may be obtained from the proportion of the sexes, the distance of the district of enumeration from the district of birth, the religions and castes to which the emigrants belong and the nature of the employment which attracts each group.

Clues to types of migration.

The character of the migration is to a great extent reflected in the proportion of the sexes. When it is casual, females will naturally be in excess as almost every woman changes her residence after marriage. When it is temporary or periodic, except when a pilgrimage is the object, the majority of migrants will be men. In the case of semi-permanent migration also, males are usually in excess. A man does not ordinarily take his wife and family with him until he is well established in the place of his migration. But when the movement is a permanent one, both the sexes are usually found in fairly equal numbers. Periodic migration often tends to become semi-permanent and semi-permanent migration, permanent.

Immigration.

110. An examination of our Table XI shows that out of our total population 1,809,841 persons or about 89 per cent. were born within the State and 222,957 or nearly 11 per cent. were born in other Provinces and States in India or in countries beyond India. 222,957 persons may, therefore, be taken as immigrants into the State. The number of such immigrants in 1901 was 172,931, showing an increase of 50,026 persons or about 2 per cent. of the total population, on the present occasion. The Census of 1901 was preceded by the great famine and the number of those born outside the State was comparatively smaller in the population owing to postponement of marriages, less attraction for outsiders and similar causes. Extension of railways in the present decade and the growing demand for labour appear to be the main causes for a larger number of foreigners within the State territory. We shall now analyse the figures of those born outside but enumerated in the State, and see how many of them are real immigrants, and how many have come into the State from the contiguous foreign districts mainly owing to marriage and other social customs.

Proportion of sexes among Immigrants.

111. The proportion of sexes among immigrants from contiguous foreign districts is 170 females to 100 males. Among those enumerated in non-contiguous districts of the Bombay Presidency and Bombay States and in other parts of India, the proportion is 73 females to 100 males. The relatively high proportion of females in the case of contiguous districts is due, as already explained, to marriage which usually means for a woman a move to a new home in another village, and not to migration properly so called.

Immigrants from contiguous foreign districts.

112. Of the total number of immigrants, 187,599 or 84 per cent. were born in the contiguous districts of the Bombay Presidency and the Native States under it. The four districts of the State being detached blocks, surrounded by foreign territory, there is a great movement of population between them and the contiguous foreign territory. These movements are, as a rule, only from one village to another in the neighbourhood across the border and are intended mainly for social purposes. There is an interchange of wives between the Baroda District and the British Districts of Kaira, Broach and Rewa Kantha Agency ; between the Navsari District and the British District of Surat and the Bansda, Dharampur and Sachin States ; between Kadi and the British District of Ahmedabad and the Palanpur and Mahi Kantha Agencies ; and between Amreli and the States of Kathiawad. If the State consisted of compact area, instead of the present detached blocks, these casual movements would not have received any prominence as migration.

Immigrants from non-contiguous districts in the Bombay Presidency.

113. Passing on to real migration, *i.e.*, movements to a distant place whether permanent or temporary, in search of employment, we find that 34,828 persons or 16 per cent. of the total number born outside the State have come to it from the non-contiguous foreign districts. Of these, 20,149 or 9 per cent. have come from the non-contiguous districts of the Bombay Presidency and the Bombay States, and the rest, *viz.*, 14,679 persons or 7 per cent. from other parts of India. Most of the immigrants from the non-contiguous districts of the Bombay Presidency and States have come from Kolaba, Ratnagiri and Poona Districts and the Kolhapur State, mainly for employment in the State service.

Immigrants from other Provinces.

114. We have already seen that the total number of immigrants from Provinces outside the Bombay Presidency is 14,679 or only 7 in 1,000 of the population of the State. Of these, the largest number, from a single Province is from Rajputana, which gives the State 6,239 persons mainly for labour

and trade. Then follow, the United Provinces which give the State 3,907 persons mainly for the recruitment of its Military and Police ; Central India Agency (Indore, Gwalior, &c.), which gives the State 1,413 persons, and the Punjab which sends 921 persons either as servants, traders or labourers. Immigrants from the rest of the Provinces are insignificant and call for no remarks.

Immigrants from countries beyond India.

115. The total number of immigrants from countries beyond India is only 530. Of these, 191 came from countries in Asia beyond India, 70 from European countries, 257 from countries in Africa and 12 from America. Those who came from countries in Asia were Afghan or Arab merchants or Nepalese pilgrims. Those who came from Africa were simply born there, being the children of emigrants from the State, to South Africa, Mauritius and Zanzibar.

Intermigration between the districts of the State.

116. The four districts of the State being widely apart from each other, there is no migration from contiguous districts of the State. But there is some small migration of a semi-permanent nature from one district of the State to another. This is due to people born in one district serving the State in another and to artizans, contractors and traders migrating from their home district in search of work to the other districts of the State. Thus Baroda receives 4,307 persons from Kadi, 1,060 from Navsari and 989 from Amreli. It gives them in return 1,406, 1,295 and 482 persons, respectively. Kadi receives 1,406 from Baroda, 130 from Navsari and 198 from Amreli, and gives them 4,307, 324 and 203 respectively in return. Navsari receives 1,295 persons from Baroda, 324 from Kadi and 105 from Amreli, and gives them 1,060, 130 and 41 respectively in return. Lastly, Amreli receives 482 persons from Baroda, 203 from Kadi and 41 from Navsari, and gives them in return 989, 198 and 105 respectively. These actual figures are given in Subsidiary Table IV, and compared with those for 1901. They show that Baroda District, which has the seat of the Central Government, and Kadi, which is the largest among the districts in area and population, exchange population to some slight extent, but in Navsari and Amreli, the interchange with the other districts is insignificant.

117. The diagram given in the margin illustrates the proportion in each district of immigrants from the other districts of the State and from foreign territory. The proportion of district-born is highest in the Kadi District and smallest in the Amreli District. The proportion of immigrants from contiguous foreign territory is highest (17 per cent.) in Amreli, and next to it in Navsari (12 per cent.), and then in Baroda (9 per cent.) owing to even their talukas being more or less detached from each other. Kadi being more compact

DIAGRAM
SHOWING THE PROPORTION OF IMMIGRANTS IN EACH DIVISION

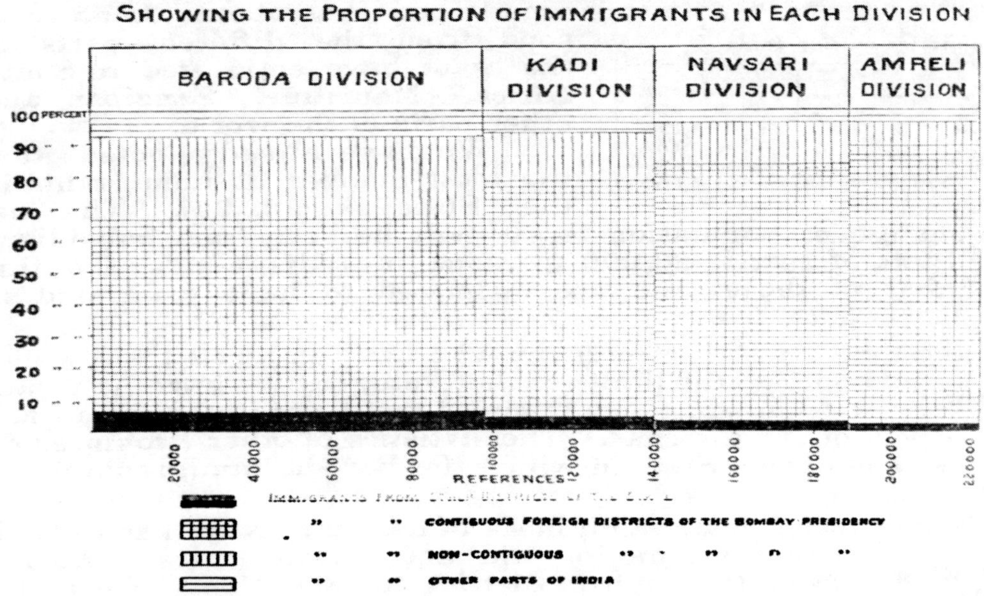

than the other districts has the lowest proportion of immigrants from non-contiguous districts. The proportion of immigrants from non-contiguous districts is the highest in the Baroda Division owing to its including the capital City of Baroda and the Cantonment which give employment to many immigrants from those districts.

Proportional figures of migration within the State.

118. On reducing the figures of immigration given in Subsidiary Table 1, to proportional parts, we find that out of every 1,000 persons in the population of the State, 890 were born in the districts of the State in which they were enumerated. Barely one was enumerated in one district, but born in some other district of the State, 92 were born in contiguous parts of other Provinces and States, and 17 in non-contiguous Provinces and States. As said before, the four districts of the State being detached blocks at a great distance from one another and surrounded by British and other foreign territory, there is no migration from "contiguous" districts within the State. But in its place, we have considerable migration of a casual type from the districts of the Bombay Presidency and Native States contiguous to the districts of this State. If the area of the State was compact, this casual migration would have come within the category of migration from contiguous districts of the State. The total amount of migration within the State (110 persons in 1,000 of the population) is small, and it would be still smaller and amount to only 18 in 1,000 of the population, if we exclude from consideration the casual migration across the borders from foreign contiguous districts. There are no industries on a large scale within the State to attract foreigners. State service is the main occupation which draws strangers from outside. Moreover, the natives of India are, as a rule, home-loving, and unless absolutely necessary are reluctant to leave their ancestral home. Even when they go abroad in search of a better livelihood than they can get in their own district, their exile is, as a rule, temporary. They return home from time to time and ultimately hope to retire to and die in the village of their birth.

Emigration.

119. The total number of persons born in Baroda but enumerated outside it in other Provinces and States in India is detailed in Subsidiary Table V. In addition to these emigrants, there are also to be reckoned those who migrate to countries beyond India and for whom the Census furnishes no data.

From a special inquiry made, through the taluka Vahivatdars, it is ascertained that about 3,555 persons from the different parts of the State have emigrated to South Africa, Mauritius, Zanzibar and other parts of the world.

Baroda subjects in countries outside India.	
Baroda District	94
Kadi District	810
Navsari District	2,499
Amreli District	152
Total	3,555

We have already noted that the total number of immigrants in the State is 222,957. The net outcome of the interchange of population is, as will be seen from Subsidiary Table V, a loss to the State of nearly 20,000 persons in India alone. To this may be added the number of those who are estimated to have emigrated to places outside India.

Emigration from the districts.

120. We know the total number of persons who have emigrated elsewhere outside the limits of the State, but we have no means of knowing how many of them emigrated from each of our districts. The statistics of other Provinces do not usually give the districts of this State in which the Baroda immigrants found by them, were born.

Change of ideas regarding migration of females.

121. About thirty or forty years ago, ideas of decorum as well as difficulties of locomotion did not permit males migrating from their birth district to take their wives with them. This feature was specially observable among Marathas, Rajputs, Lewa Kanbis and Mahomedans, among whom the *parda*

system is observed to a more or less extent. Those in State service at Baroda and other places lived alone and had to keep their wives in their native village. Those from the State who migrated to Ahmedabad, Bombay, and other places for trade or service, generally left their females at home. Western education and the convenience of easy locomotion afforded by railways have brought about a change in this custom, and now-a-days, there is a tendency among people who migrate from their home even temporarily to take their women with them.

Emigration and education.

122. Spread of education seems to be slowly but steadily encouraging emigration from the State. Most of the people in the State are so conservative that they would starve at home rather than go elsewhere for earning their livelihood. But these conservative ideas are disappearing under the influence of education, which is now both free and compulsory in this State. Young persons born and educated in Baroda are now to be found in Bombay and also in such distant places as Rangoon, Quetta and Madras, either serving as clerks and accountants or doing business on their own behalf.

Migration between Baroda State and the other Provinces and States in India.

123. A reference to the statistics of migration between Baroda and the Provinces and States in India given in Subsidiary Table V at the end of this chapter shows that the interchange of population between the State and the rest of India is small and insignificant, except in the case of the Bombay Presidency. Subsidiary Table V-A shows that in return for the 89 per cent. of its immigrant population which the State receives from the Bombay Presidency, it gives it 92 per cent. of its emigrant population. The net outcome of this interchange of population is a loss to the State of 21,559 persons. As in immigration so in emigration, the greatest amount of migration is to the districts of the Bombay Presidency and the Bombay States, which are contiguous to the State. But as already stated, this is for the most part a migration of a casual nature from across the boundary, for social purposes, such as marriage, &c. It is significant, however, that, while the Ahmedabad District gives the State only 18,309 persons (5,851 males and 12,458 females), it receives from it 58,704 persons (26,335 males and 32,369 females). The loss to the State amounts to 40,395 (20,484 males and 19,911 females) and indicates that there is considerable migration to Ahmedabad from the contiguous Kadi District of the State. There is a tendency among villagers to marry their daughters in the neighbouring towns, and it is probable that a small proportion of the loss sustained by the Kadi District may be due to Ahmedabad getting from it more wives than it gives it ; but there can be no doubt that a large proportion of the adverse balance to the State in connection with Ahmedabad must be due to the attraction of labourers in the cotton mills of that city. Similarly the British Broach and Panch Mahal Districts and the Cambay State receive from the State respectively 4,139, 2,517 and 1,187 persons more than they give it. On the other hand, the State receives 16,487 more persons from Kathiawad and 14,904 more persons from the Surat District than it gives to each of them.

Province or State.	Gives to Baroda.	Receives from Baroda.	Gain (+) or loss (—) to Baroda.
Bombay Presidency	207,748	229,307	— 21,559
British Districts of Bombay Presidency	128,412	143,636	— 15,224
Contiguous	114,359	135,498	— 15,224
Non-Contiguous	14,053	8,138	+ 5,915
Bombay States	73,686	81,228	— 7,542
Contiguous	73,240	80,844	— 7,604
Non-Contiguous	446	384	+ 62
Bombay Unspecified	5,650	4,443	+ 1,207

124. The statistics of migration from and to the State in the last three Censuses are given in the margin. It will be seen that the Census of 1891, which showed an increase of 10·69 per cent. in the State population indicated migration to the State to be in excess of migration from it by about 2·5 per cent. of the total population. The Census of 1901, preceded as it was by famine, showed a decline of 19·15 per cent. in the population. Of this decrease, loss of about 30,000 persons or 1·5 per cent. of the population by migration formed a part. The present Census also shows a loss of about one per cent. of the population by migration but compared with 1901 there is some improvement. Railways by reducing the difficulties of locomotion have encouraged people to more frequently migrate from their home. and, as already stated, education and spread of western ideas among the people, have also operated in the same direction. As its result, we find an increase in the volume of migration both from and to the State since 1901.

Comparison with previous Censuses.

	1891.	1901.	1911.
Immigration	311,922	172,931	222,957
Emigration	252,396	202,270	242,033
Gain (+) or loss (—) to the State.	+ 59,526	— 29,339	— 19,076

SUBSIDIARY TABLE I.—Immigration (Actual figures).

District or Natural Division where enumerated.	Born in: District (or Natural Division). Total.	Males.	Females.	Contiguous Districts in the State. Total.	Males.	Females.	Other parts of the State. Total.	Males.	Females.	Contiguous parts of other Provinces, &c. Total.	Males.	Females.	Non-contiguous parts of other Provinces, &c. Total.	Males.	Females.	Outside India. Total.	Males.	Females.
1	2	3	4	5	6	7	8	9	10	11	12	13	14	15	16	17	18	19
Baroda State ...	**1,809,841**	**965,918**	**843,923**	...	...	...	...	...	...	**187,599**	**69,593**	**118,006**	**34,828**	**20,120**	**14,708**	**530**	**304**	**226**
Baroda Division with City ...	583,721	325,045	258,676	...	...	...	6,356	3,527	2,829	62,191	19,752	42,439	34,471	19,053	15,418	161	109	52
Kadi Division ...	787,004	411,337	375,667	...	...	...	1,734	1,040	694	33,456	9,676	23,780	9,919	5,233	4,686	49	38	11
Navsari Division ...	285,238	145,856	139,382	...	...	...	1,724	1,062	662	40,174	17,357	22,817	8,049	4,825	3,224	282	125	157
Amreli Division ...	143,338	77,633	65,705	...	...	...	726	418	308	30,390	11,748	18,642	3,777	2,069	1,708	38	32	6

SUBSIDIARY TABLE II.—Emigration (Actual figures).

District or Natural Division of Birth.	Enumerated in: District (or Natural Division). Total.	Males.	Females.	Contiguous District in the State. Total.	Males.	Females.	Other parts of the State. Total.	Males.	Females.	Contiguous parts of other Provinces, &c. Total.	Males.	Females.	Non-contiguous parts of other Provinces, &c. Total.	Males.	Females.	Outside India. Total.	Males.	Females.
1	2	3	4	5	6	7	8	9	10	11	12	13	14	15	16	17	18	19
Baroda State ...	**1,809,841**	**965,918**	**843,923**	...	...	...	...	...	...	**216,342**	**84,599**	**131,743**	**25,691**	**15,297**	**10,394**	Figures not available.		
Baroda Division with City ...	583,721	325,045	258,676	...	...	...	3,183	1,906	1,277		District figures not available.							
Kadi Division ...	787,004	411,337	375,667	...	...	...	4,834	3,000	1,834									
Navsari Division ...	285,238	145,856	139,382	...	...	...	1,231	500	731									
Amreli Division ...	143,338	77,633	65,705	...	...	...	1,292	641	651									

SUBSIDIARY TABLE III.—Proportional migration to and from each district.

District or Natural Division.	Number per mille of actual population of Immigrants. Total.	Immigrants. From contiguous Districts.	Immigrants. From other places.	Emigrants. Total.	Emigrants. To contiguous Districts.	Emigrants. To other places.	Number of females to 100 males amongst Immigrants. From contiguous Districts.	Immigrants. From other places.	Emigrants. To contiguous Districts.	Emigrants. To other places.
1	2	3	4	5	6	7	8	9	10	11
Baroda State	**110**	92	18	**119**	**106**	**13**	**170**	**73**	**156**	68
Baroda Division with City	150	91	59	District figures not available.			215	81	District figures not available.	
Kadi Division	54	40	14	...	...	...	246	85	...	...
Navsari Division	150	120	30	...	...	...	181	67	...	...
Amreli Division	196	170	26	...	...	...	159	80	...	...

SUBSIDIARY TABLE IV.—Migration between Natural Divisions (actual figures) compared with 1901.

Natural Division in which born.		Number enumerated in Natural Division.			
		Baroda.	Kadi.	Navsari.	Amreli.
1		2	3	4	5
Baroda with City	1911	583,721	1,406	1,295	482
	1901	563,654	1,752	832	979
Kadi	1911	4,307	787,004	324	203
	1901	4,409	806,115	417	332
Navsari	1911	1,060	130	285,238	41
	1901	1,832	36	257,157	214
Amreli	1911	989	198	105	143,338
	1901	825	65	133	141,013

SUBSIDIARY TABLE V.—Migration between the Baroda State and the other Parts of India.

Province or State.	Immigrants to the Baroda State.			Emigrants from the Baroda State.			Excess (+) or deficiency (—) of immigration over emigration.		Remarks.
	1911.	1901.	Variation.	1911.	1901.	Variation.	1911.	1901.	
1	2	3	4	5	6	7	8	9	10
Bombay	207,748	161,153	+ 46,595	229,307	195,645	+33,662	—21,559	—34,492	Provinces and States from which statistics for column 5 have not been received are marked with an asterisk, and are assumed to take from the State the same number of persons as they give it.
Burma...	63	25	+38	136	......	+136	—73	+25	
Central Provinces and Berar.	321	141	+180	409	145	+264	—88	—4	
Madras	228	208	+20	320	306	+14	—92	—98	
Punjab	921	818	+103	225	105	+120	+696	+713	
North-West Frontier Province.	39	......	+39	11	......	+11	+28	......	
Baluchistan Agency...	41	12	+29	7	......	+7	+34	+12	
Central India Agency.	1,413	819	+594	4,554	4,452	+102	—3,141	—3,633	
Kashmir State ...	18	15	+3	4	6	—2	+14	+9	
Mysore State	32	22	+10	46	168	—122	—14	—146	
Travancore	......	......	......	4	......	+4	—4	......	
Cochin	......	......	......	......	......	......	......	......	
Ajmer-Merwara ...	179	60	+119	224	......	+224	—45	+60	
*Eastern Bengal and Assam.	6	6	......	......	......	......	......	+6	
*Bengal	482	915	—433	......	134	......	......	+781	
*United Provinces of Agra and Oudh.	3,907	3,200	+707	......	828	......	......	+2,372	
*Hyderabad State ...	164	223	—59	......	156	......	......	+67	
Rajputana Agency ...	6,239	4,139	+2,100	1,601	325	+1,276	+4,638	+3,814	
Foreign Settlements...	559	288	+271	......	......	......	......	+288	
India Unspecified ...	67	554	—487	......	......	......	......	+554	
Total ...	222,427	172,598	+49,829	242,033	202,270	+39,753	—19,606	—29,672	

SUBSIDIARY TABLE V-A.—SHOWING THE NUMBER OF IMMIGRANTS AND EMIGRANTS FROM AND TO THE BOMBAY PRESIDENCY.

District or State.	Gives to Baroda.		Receives from Baroda.		Gain (+) or loss (—) to Baroda.		
	Males.	Females.	Males.	Females.	Males.	Females.	Total.
Bombay Presidency	**79,778**	**127,970**	**91,800**	**137,507**	**— 12,022**	**— 9,537**	**— 21,559**
Bombay Districts	**48,992**	**79,420**	**60,793**	**82,843**	**— 11,801**	**— 3,423**	**— 15,224**
Contiguous Districts	*41,334*	*73,025*	*55,143*	*80,355*	*— 13,809*	*— 7,330*	*— 21,139*
Ahmedabad	5,851	12,458	26,335	32,369	— 20,484	— 19,911	— 40,395
Kaira	13,052	28,887	9,061	23,162	+ 3,991	+ 5,725	+ 9,716
Panch Mahals	1,258	2,688	3,193	3,270	— 1,935	— 582	— 2,517
Surat	15,720	20,000	9,545	11,271	+ 6,175	+ 8,729	+ 14,904
Broach	3,857	7,449	6,039	9,406	— 2,182	— 1,957	— 4,139
East Khandesh			74	40			
	1,126	1,134			+ 322	+ 398	+ 720
West „			730	696			
Nasik	470	409	166	141	+ 304	+ 268	+ 572
Non-Contiguous Districts...	*7,394*	*6,211*	*5,408*	*2,425*	*+ 1,986*	*+ 3,786*	*+ 5,772*
Thana	147	160	1,146	581	— 999	— 421	— 1,420
Colaba	723	298	288	67	+ 435	+ 231	+ 666
Ratnagiri	1,421	949	92	44	+ 1,329	+ 905	+ 2,234
Kanara	229	236	6	5	+ 223	+ 231	+ 454
Bombay City	2,927	3,054	3,255	1,246	— 328	+ 1,808	+ 1,480
Ahmednagar	176	140	89	70	+ 87	+ 70	+ 157
Poona	971	764	356	296	+ 615	+ 468	+ 1,083
Sholapur	113	118	44	28	+ 69	+ 90	+ 159
Satara	554	329	81	44	+ 473	+ 285	+ 758
Belgaum	21	17	24	15	— 3	+ 2	— 1
Dharwar	86	142	21	7	+ 65	+ 135	+ 200
Bijapur	26	4	6	22	+ 20	— 18	+ 2
Sind...	*259*	*181*	*182*	*55*	*+ 77*	*+ 126*	*+ 203*
Hydrabad	139	96	63	4	+ 76	+ 92	+ 168
Karachi	97	58	108	39	— 11	+ 19	+ 8
Shikarpur	23	27	......	......			
Larkhana	......	......	1	2			
Sukkar	......	......	......	......			
					+ 12	+ 15	+ 27
Khairpur	......	......	2	......			
Thar and Parkar	......	......	4	10			
Upper Sind Frontier	......	......	4	......			
Aden	*5*	*3*	*60*	*8*	*— 55*	*— 5*	*— 60*
Bombay States	**28,537**	**45,149**	**29,658**	**51,570**	**— 1,121**	**— 6,421**	**— 7,542**
Contiguous	*28,259*	*44,981*	*29,456*	*51,388*	*— 1,197*	*— 6,407*	*— 7,604*
Cutch	573	662	184	129	+ 389	+ 533	+ 922
Palanpur Agency...	3,947	5,795	3,627	6,345	+ 320	— 550	— 230
Mahikantha „	2,652	7,499	4,868	13,397	— 2,216	— 5,898	— 8,114
Kathiawad	16,199	22,727	8,677	13,762	+ 7,522	+ 8,965	+ 16,487
Rewakantha Agency	3,053	6,100	9,005	13,162	— 5,952	— 7,062	— 13,014
Cambay	1,131	1,412	1,386	2,344	— 255	— 932	— 1,187
Surat Agency	704	786	1,709	2,249	— 1,005	— 1,463	— 2,468
Non-Contiguous	*278*	*168*	*202*	*182*	*+ 76*	*— 14*	*+ 62*
Jawhar	1	......	4	2	— 3	— 2	— 5
Janjira	3	16	4	3	— 1	+ 13	+ 12
Savantvadi...	41	52	13	22	+ 28	+ 30	+ 58
Bijapur Agency (other Native States under Konkan.)	54	4	10	3	+ 44	+ 1	+ 45
Bhor	14	18	30	30	— 16	— 12	— 28
Akalkot	6	......	2	3	+ 4	— 3	+ 1
Satara Agency	......	1	......	4	......	— 3	— 3
Kolhapur	130	76	90	69	+ 40	+ 7	+ 47
Southern Marhatta Jaghirs ...	29	1	49	46	— 20	— 45	— 65
Bombay Districts—unspecified.	*2,249*	*3,401*	*1,349*	*3,094*	*+ 900*	*+ 307*	*+ 1,207*

Chapter IV.

RELIGION.

DISTRIBUTION AND VARIATIONS SINCE 1901.

Reference to Statistics.

125. Imperial Table VI gives the strength of all religions returned for the State as a whole, and its districts and Tables XVII and XVIII contain details of the sects, races and ages of Christians. The following subsidiary tables in which the most important features of the statistics are illustrated by means of proportional figures, will be found at the end of this chapter :—

Subsidiary Table I.—General distribution of the population by religion.
Subsidiary Table II.—Distribution by districts of the main religions at each of the last four Censuses.
Subsidiary Table III.—The variation in the number of Christians in each district.
Subsidiary Table IV.—Races and sects of Christians (actual numbers).
Subsidiary Table V.—The distribution per mille of (*a*) each race of Christians by sect and (*b*) of each sect by race.
Subsidiary Table VI.—Religions of urban and rural population.

The record of sects of religions other than Christianity was optional, but as they were recorded in this State, for all religions, their number is shown in an additional Subsidiary Table No. VII.

PART I—STATISTICAL.

126. The general distribution of the population by religion is noted in the margin.

Religion.	Number in.	
	1911.	1901.
Indo-Aryans—		
Hindus	1,697,146	1,546,936
Jains	43,462	48,290
Brahmos	6	6
Arya Samajis	598	50
Sikhs	90	38
Animists	115,411	176,250
Parsis	7,955	8,409
Musalmans	160,887	165,014
Christians	7,203	7,691
Jews	40	8
Total	2,032,798	1,952,692

It will be seen that more than four-fifths of the total population are Hindus, about 2 per cent. Jains, 8 per cent. Musalmans, 6 per cent. Animists, ·4 per cent. Parsis and ·4 per cent. Christians. The most noticeable feature in the figures is the rapid growth of the Hindus and Arya Samajis, as compared with the decadent condition of the Jains, Musalmans and Christians.

The distribution of the above religions varies greatly in the different parts of the State, and for this reason and also in order to ascertain the causes of the changes which have taken place, it is necessary to examine the statistics for individual districts. In this section, the discussion will therefore be mainly statistical, and all subjects of a general nature, which cannot be included in it, will be dealt with in a separate section headed "Descriptive."

Animism.

127. It will be convenient to begin with the Animists, the followers of the oldest religion. Animism is a term coined to express the various forms of belief of the aboriginal tribes like the Chodhras, Gamits, Bhils, &c., who have not yet come under the influence of Hinduism, Mahomedanism, Christianity or any other wellknown regular creed. The aboriginal tribes in this State worship two classes of beings : local or tribal divinities, and the spirits of their ancestors. Of the local or tribal divinities, *Khatridev*, a pillar of wood, is worshipped by most of the aboriginal tribes. The other gods are :—*Simadio Dev*, a red coloured stone placed under a *samdi* (*Prosopis spicigera*) tree and worshipped at marriage ; *Khetarpal*, the god of boundaries, a stone carved with the figure of a horse ; *Baba Dev*, a clay image of a horse and rider, worshipped chiefly by Bhils ; *Marli* and *Bharam Dev*, red stones set on hill tops, worshipped chiefly by Koknas : *Vetal Dev*, a round stone, about 4 feet high, also a hill god ;

Magaria and *Vagh Dev,* or the alligator and tiger deities, chiefly worshipped by Gamits; and *Samla Dev,* and *Haria Dev,* specially worshipped by Dhodias. Among all the tribes, the worship of their ancestors is the chief article of faith. A spot is set apart near each village as a *devasthan* or god-yard. Here are raised wooden pillars and seats, dome-shaped pots of clay and stones painted red in honour of their ancestors. With offerings of small clay horses and cows and with sacrifices of goats and fowls, they court and honour the spirits of their forefathers. They believe that, while all men of their class possess power over spirits, skill in this matter belongs to two sets of persons, unfriendly *dakins* or witches who stir spirits to work mischief and friendly *bhagats,* exorcists, who cast out evil spirits. The ill-natured *dakins,* who are supposed to have spirits at their back and to send them to trouble those against whom they bear ill-will, are generally old and ugly women. The well-disposed *bhagats* who cast out evil spirits and heal the sick, are religious recluses who worship some one of the many forms of the *devi* or mother and have in their huts a *dehru* or altar and on it an image of the goddess. When a man becomes ill or shows other signs of being possessed by a spirit, one of these *bhagats* or exorcists is called. He places some *urid* (*phaseotus mungo*) or grains of rice on a leaf and passes the leaf round the sick man's head. He then examines the grains and tells whether the patient is troubled by an evil spirit or by the spirit of his ancestors. If the cause of the evil is one of his forefathers, the sickness matters little, as by simply making an offering to his tomb, a cure will be effected. If the patient is troubled by an evil spirit, the holy man repeats some incantations, strikes the patient gently with the bough of a tree and continues the treatment for some days till the patient has recovered or is dead. The *bhagat* knows by whose power the spirit has been sent. In former times he used to name the *dakin* to the sick-man's friends, who would rush out and seize and torture her to death. Many Bhils have suffered in the past at the hand of law for their share in these murders, and the *bhagat* now wisely keeps his knowledge to himself.

Enumeration and strength of the Animists.

128. The Animists having no name for their religion, there is always a difficulty in obtaining a correct return of their number. The difficulty was got over by giving the following directions to the enumerators:—

" *Column 4 (Religion).*—[Enter here the religion which each person returns as Hindu, Musalman, Sikh, Jain, Christian, Parsi, etc. *In the case of the aboriginal tribes who do not say that they are Hindus, Musalmans, Christians, etc., the name of the tribe should be entered* in this column." The total of all the tribes thus recorded in the column for religion was taken as the strength of the Animists; and those of the tribemen, who expressly returned themselves as Hindus, etc., were included amongst the religion actually returned by them. From the note made on the title page of Table VI., it will appear that so many as 85,566 members of the aboriginal tribes have been classed as Hindus, simply because they said that they were Hindus. Their marriage and other relations are with the rest of their people, who did not claim to be Hindus, and were therefore returned by their tribe names and classed as Animists. The total strength of the Animists thus returned is **115,411** or nearly 6 per cent. of the total population of the State.

Where chiefly found.

129. The present Animistic tribes are apparently the descendants of those early tribes called *dasyus,* fiends, in the Vedas and *nishadas* or original settlers in the Ramayan. Before the advent of the Aryans, the original inhabitants of the hills and plains were closely allied. As successive streams of immigrants from the north-west and north-east poured in, upon the fertile plains and seaboard of Gujarat, those of the early occupants, who were on the plains, were either subjected and peaceably converted to Hinduism, like the Kolis, or driven back into the hills like the main body of the Bhils. The Animistic tribes are even now practically concentrated in the Songhad, Vyara, Mahuva and Velachha Talukas and Umarpada, Peta Mahal of the Navsari District and the Sankheda Taluka and Tilakwada Peta Mahal of the Baroda District, owing to the comparative non-accessibility and poverty of those tracts. With many minor clans, this aboriginal section includes fifteen chief tribes, *viz.*, Bhil, Chodhra, Dhanka, Dhodia, Dubla, Gamit,

Kathodia, Kokna, Kolgha, Kotwalia, Mavchi, Nayakda, Valvi, Vasava and Varli. The Kolis may be taken as an intermediate layer between the rest of the Hindu population, who are called *ujlivaran* or bright coloured as against the *kaliparaj* or dusky race, the general name of the early tribes.

Conversion to Hinduism.

130. Hinduism is gradually attracting the non-Aryan tribes within its fold. Education and closer contact with Hindus, due to improved means of communication, have created a tendency among some of the Animistic tribes to call themselves Hindus. They have begun to worship some of the gods and goddesses, who are reverenced by all followers of Brahmanism. Thus the Dublas worship Mahadev and Hanuman; the Chodhras worship Ram and Devi in her form of Durga, the destroyer Kakabalia is feared and courted by all. Some past students of the Songhad and Vyara Dhanka Boarding Schools have started a regular mission for the conversion of their people to Hinduism. Putting Hindu sect marks on the forehead, wearing *kanthis* on the neck, daily bathing and abstaining from drinking spirituous liquor, are extolled and encouraged, and I understand that the educated section of the people was instructed to return themselves as Hindus, in the present Census. When I was giving oral instructions in Census procedure to the Census staff of the Songhad Taluka, early in December 1910, a young Chodhra who was a student in the Songhad Dhanka Boarding School presented a petition, and requested me to issue orders that all the people of his tribe should be recorded as Hindus. He was informed that no such order could be issued, but that he and those of his people may return themselves as Hindus, if they really believed that they were Hindus and that their statement as to their religion would be accepted by the enumerators.

Distribution of Animists.

131. Nearly three-fourths of the Animistic population are to be found in the Navsari District and one-fourth in the Baroda District. There are no Animists in the Kadi and

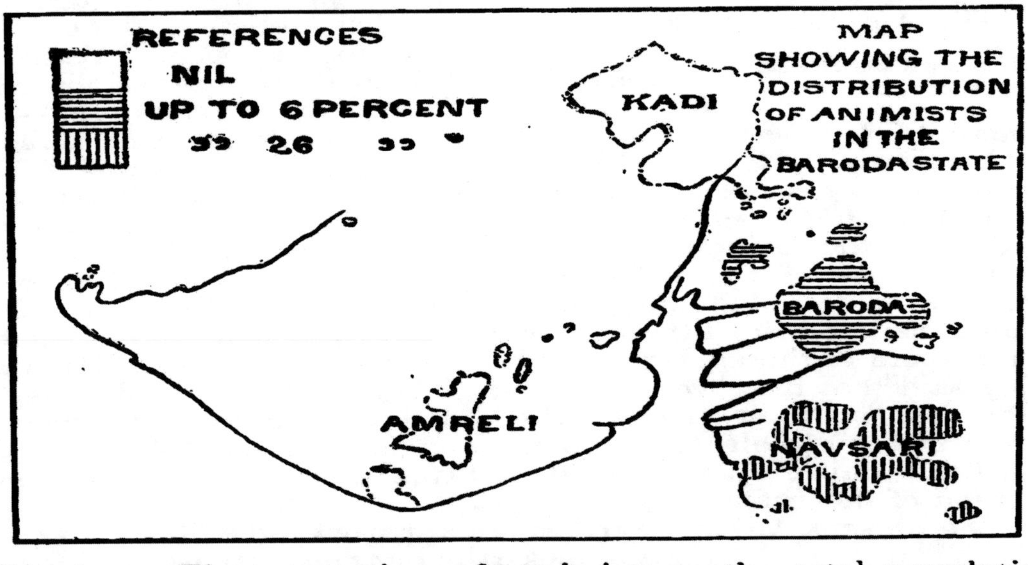

Amreli Districts. The proportion of Animists to the total population is 25·3 per cent. in the Navsari District and 5·2 per cent. in Baroda.

Comparison with 1901.

132. In the Census of 1872, no distinction was made between the Hindus and the members of the aboriginal tribes. In 1881, on the distinction being pointed out, a large number, though still less than a fourth of the real strength was returned, as aborigines, and in 1891 again tribal gods were mistaken for orthodox ones and almost all were returned as Hindus, a very small number only coming under "Castes in lieu of religion." The first approximately correct enumeration of the Animists was made in 1901, when their number was returned as 176,250 (89,423 males and 86,827 females). On that occasion all the members of the early tribes were classed as Animists, irrespective of their return either by their tribe

names or as Hindus. On the present occasion, the correct procedure was followed with the result that 115,411 persons (58,858 males and 56,553 females) were returned as Animists and 85,566 (43,625 males and 41,941 females) as Hindus. This has brought about a decrease of 34·5 per cent. in the Animistic population compared with 1901. There can be no doubt that a small portion of those who have returned themselves as Hindus, has, owing to contact with Hindus really accepted Hindu practices and worship Hindu gods, but the claim of a large portion of them to be Hindus is doubtful. From inquiry made after the Census, it appears that they follow their ancestral primitive beliefs and have returned themselves as Hindus, simply because their more enlightened brethren wished them to do so. When we examine the figures for the districts, we find that the decrease in the number of Animists is contributed to the extent of 38 per cent. of their population by the Navsari District and 16 per cent. by the Baroda District.

Who are the Hindus?

133. The question, what constitutes a Hindu, was mooted in the Census Commissioner's note, dated the 12th July 1911, where the feasibility was discussed of supplementing the statistics in Imperial Table VI by a note stating what classes of persons have been included in the figures for Hindus, who cannot strictly be regarded as such. Tests noted in the margin were laid down, and it was desired that a list should be prepared of the castes, &c., contributing more than one per mille to the total population of the State, who according to these tests cannot strictly be regarded as Hindus. It has already been mentioned that 85,566 members of the Animistic tribes have returned themselves as Hindus, but if these rigid tests are applied, they would have to be excluded from the category of Hindus. The untouchable and depressed classes contribute as noted in the margin, about 10 per cent. to the Hindu population. Except that orthodox Hindus do not touch them and good Brahmans do not serve them, they satisfy all other tests and are regarded as Hindus, both by them and the orthodox Hindus. How tenaciously these depressed classes cling to Hinduism is illustrated by the following story:—

(1) Deny the supremacy of the Brahmans.
This category includes two distinct groups :—
(a) certain sectarian groups which owe their origin to a revolt against the Brahmanical supremacy ; and
(b) the aboriginal tribes and also certain low castes who, being denied the ministrations of Brahmans, retaliate by professing to reject the Brahmans ;
(2) do not receive the *mantra* from a Brahman or other recognized Hindu Guru;
(3) deny the authority of the Vedas.
(4) are not served by good Brahmans as family priests.
(5) have no Brahman priests at all ;
(6) are denied access to the interior of ordinary Hindu temples ;
(7) cause pollution ; (a) by touch, (b) within a certain distance.
In southern India about half the population falls within this category.
(8) bury their dead.
Here again there are two groups, *viz* : (a) castes derived from ascetics and (b) low castes imperfectly Hinduised,
(9) eat beef and do not reverence the cow.

1.	Bhangi ...	26,397
2.	Dhed ...	99,798
3.	Garoda ...	6,281
4.	Chamar or Khalpa ...	32,210
5.	Shenva ...	7,587
6.	Others ...	921
	Total ...	173,194

" A Mohummedan sovereign asked his Hindu Minister, which was the lowest caste of all. The minister begged for leisure to consider his reply, and having obtained it, went to where the Dheds lived and said to them " You have given offence to the Padishah. It is his intention to deprive you of caste, and make you Mohummedans." The Dheds, in the greatest terror, posted off in a body to the sovereign's palace, and standing at a respectful distance, shouted at the top of their lungs, " If we have offended Your Majesty, punish us in some other way than that. Beat us, fine us, hang us if you like, but don't make us Mohummedans." The Padishah smiled, and turning to his minister, who sat by, affecting to hear nothing of the matter, said, " So the lowest caste is that to which I belong !" (Rasmala, p. 538).

Distribution of Hindus.

134. We have seen that more than four-fifths of the total population are Hindus. They are most numerous in the Kadi District, where 91 persons out of a 100 are Hindus. After Kadi, comes Amreli with 88 Hindus in a 100 of the population. Then follow

Baroda Division with 84 and Baroda City with 79 in a 100 who are Hindus. The Navsari District stands last with only 65 Hindus in a 100 of the whole population. The lowest proportion of Hindus in this district is due to its having a large population of the primitive tribes whose Animistic forms of belief have already been described.

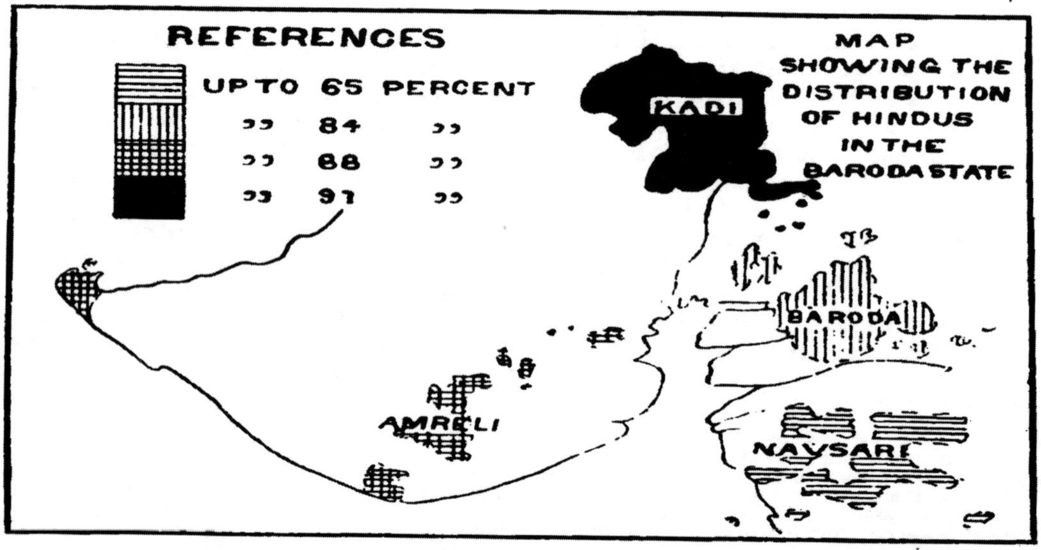

Variations in Hindus.

135. In the State as a whole, the Hindus have increased by nearly 9·7 per cent. during the decade. The changes in the strength of any religion depend on three causes, *viz.*, (1) the reproductive power of its adherents, (2) migration and (3) conversion. Migration does not seem to have materially affected the number of Hindus in the State, for the gain by immigration is counterbalanced by the loss by emigration. The productive power of the Hindus does not seem to be superior to that of the followers of the other religions. Conversion therefore is the main cause which accounts for the large increase in the Hindu population of the State. We have already seen that 85,566 Animists have in this Census returned themselves as Hindus. In addition to this, the half-Hindu—half-Musalman Matias and Shaikhdas who as followers of the Pirana sect founded by Saiyad Imamshah, previously returned themselves as Musalmans, have on the present occasion returned themselves (401 Matias and 51 Shaikhdas) as Hindus. In 1901, the Pirana sect was shown to have only 3,655 Musalman followers. On the present occasion, there is a return of 3,630 Hindus and 2,102 Musalmans as its followers. Thus, the total gain of Hindus by conversion amounts to 86,018 persons. In 1901, there were only 50 Arya Samajists in the State. In the present Census, their number has increased to 598, mostly owing to conversion from Hinduism which has thus lost 548 persons. Subtracting the loss from the gain, the net gain to Hinduism is of 85,470 persons or 5 per cent. of its population. If this gain is not taken into consideration, the natural increase of the Hindus amounts to 4·2 per cent. of their population which is just equal to the general increase during the decade.

Conversion to Hinduism.

136. It has often been said that Hinduism never openly takes in new converts, and that when they are admitted that is done on the fiction that they have been Hindus all along. Until recently, there were no known cases of the admission into Hinduism of persons who had previously been Musalmans or Christians. It is understood, however, that the Arya Samajists are now endeavouring to secure the re-admission of such persons. Not long ago, nearly 400 Musalman Rajputs are said to have been taken back into Hinduism at Banthra in the Ethwa District of the United Provinces. At the Arya Samaj Conference held in January 1911 at the village of Ranoli in the Baroda District, nearly a dozen of persons converted to Christianity were re-admitted to Hinduism and were forthwith treated as Hindus

by all concerned. Matias and Shaikhdas, who were originally Hindu Kanbis, and accepted Islam about 300 years ago, owing to the preaching of the Ismalia Saiyad, Imam Shah, had been previously returning themselves as Musalmans of the Pirana sect. They have lately reverted to Brahmanism, worship Hindu gods, go on pilgrimages to Benares, Dwarka, Dakorji, etc., and employ Brahmans for the performance of marriage ceremonies, and have also returned themselves as Hindus in the present Census. Upon further inquiry, I learn that they are recognised as Hindus and have been re-admitted into the Vaishnava sects founded by Ramanand and Swaminarayan.

Hindu sects.

137. Nearly one-half of the Hindus returned themselves as Vaishnavas under one name or another ; one-fifth as Shaivas or Smartas, and one-sixth as Shaktas or *Devi Upasaks*. Only 53 per mille of the total Hindu population did not return any sect. Details about these main and other minor sects will be found in the descriptive section of this chapter.

138. The followers of Shaivism and Shaktism did not return any sub-sect. But about 96 per cent. of the followers of Vaishnavism returned minor sub-sects named after their principal religious preceptors. All of these, with the number of their followers have been detailed in Subsidiary Table VII at the end of this chapter, and the most important of them have been shown in the margin. It will appear from it that the Ramanandi sub-sect is the most popular among the Vaishnava Hindus of the State. More than one-half of the Vaishnava Hindus are Ramanandis and one-fifth are followers of Vallabhacharya. One out of eight Vaishnavas is a Ramanuji and one out of 16 is a follower of Swaminarayan.

Vaishnava sub-sects.

Name of the sect.	Number of followers.
Ramanuji	104,987
Ramanandi	434,679
Vallabhachari	171,460
Swaminarayan	53,721

Sect Marks.

139. Hindu males paint on their foreheads white or coloured marks indicative of their sects. Some of these *tilaks* or sect marks are illustrated in the margin. *Tripundra* or three traverse streaks, painted with *vibhuti* (sacred ashes) or sandal paste with a round mark in the middle, or merely two round white marks distinguishes the Shaiva or worshipper of Shiv. Each Vaishnav sub-sect has its own distinguishing mark. Ramanujis paint on their foreheads the *trifala*, three lines drawn upwards from near the meeting of the eyebrows, the central line red and the outer ones white, made with *gopichandan* or white clay, procured from a tank near Dwarka in which, according to legend the *gopis* (milkmaids), drowned themselves on hearing of the death of their divine lover Shri Krishna. The Vallabhachari sect-mark consists of two red perpendicular lines converging in a semi-circle at the root of the nose. The followers of Swaminarayan

Diagram illustrating sect marks.

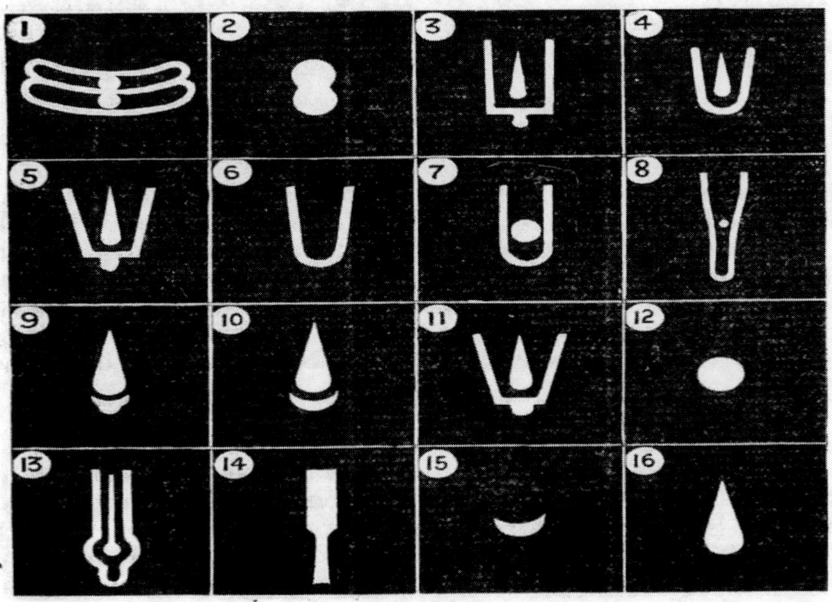

(1—2) Shaiva ; (3) Ramanuji (tengali) ; (4) Ramanuji (vadagali) ; (5) Ramanandi ; (6) Vallabhachari ; (7) Swaminarayan ; (8) Pranami ; (9) Bijpanthi ; (10) Ramde Pir ; (11) Gopinath ; (12-16) Jain; (13) Madhvachari ; (14) Kabirpanthi ; (15) Shakta.

have a similar sect-mark, made with *gopichandan* and with a round red powder mark in the middle. Irrespective of sects, Hindu females mark their foreheads with a *chanlla*, a round red powder mark, which indicates that they are *saubhagyavati* or with good luck, *i. e.*, have their husbands alive.

Distribution of Jains.

140. One person out of 50 in the total population of the State is a Jain. Jains are most numerous in the Kadi District, which contains more than one-half of their total population. Next to the Kadi District, comes Baroda City in having a comparatively large Jain population. Out of a thousand in the population, those who are Jains are 20 in the Amreli District and 13 in the Baroda District. Navsari District has only 83 Jains in 10,000 of its population.

More than nine-tenths of the Jains belong to the Vania castes and only about one-tenth belongs to other castes, such as Bhavsar, Bhojak, Kanbi, etc.

Comparison with 1901.

141. Compared with 1901, Jains show a decrease of 10 per cent. in their total population. The districts responsible for this decrease are Kadi and Baroda; Navsari and Amreli show an increase of 3 and 8 per cent., respectively, in their Jain population. The decrease is heavy in the Kadi District and amounts to 14 per cent., while in the Baroda District without the city, it is 7 per cent., and in the Baroda City alone it is 3 per cent. Considering their general prosperity, it is not likely that Jains could have suffered from scarcity, plague or any like cause to a greater or even the same extent as the general population. After the recent Jain Conferences, Jains in Gujarat are so tenacious about their religion that the decrease cannot be ascribed to any tendency among them to describe themselves as Hindus. Migration is probably the main cause, which is responsible for such a surprisingly large decrease in the Jain population of the State. Most of the Jains in the Kadi District emigrate to Bombay and other places for trade purposes. Their business trait is so developed that they do not now hesitate even to go to Europe or America. Several Jains from the Kadi District are said to have recently established themselves as jewellers in Paris. It is, therefore, not improbable that migration could have taken away a large number of their population from their homes.

Jain Sects.

142. The Jains are divided into two principal sects called *Swetambaris* or white-clad and *Digambaris* or sky-clad. A later schism among the Swetambaris led to a section of them being called Sthanakvasi Swetambaris or Dhundias (see para. 237.) The Swetambari sect is the most numerous, 84 out of 100 Jains being its followers. One in ten Jains is a Digambari and one in seventeen is a Dhundia or Sthanakvasi Swetambari as these people now choose to call themselves. Jains have no distinguishing sect marks. They make, however, *tilaks* like Hindus, but use saffron and sandal paste instead of red powder. (See Nos. 12-16 diagram, para. 139.)

Distribution of Mahomedans.

143. Mahomedans form only 8 per cent. of the total population of the State. Their proportion is the largest in the Baroda City where they form 17 per cent. of the population. After the City comes the Amreli District with 11 per cent., and then Baroda District with only 10 per cent. of its population who are Mahomedans. The proportion of Mahomedans to the total population is the smallest, *viz.*, 6·3 and 6·9 per cent. in the Kadi and Navsari Districts respectively. Nearly one-third of the total Mahomedan population in the State is in the Kadi District, nearly one-fourth in the Baroda District and the rest in the Amreli and Navsari Districts and Baroda City.

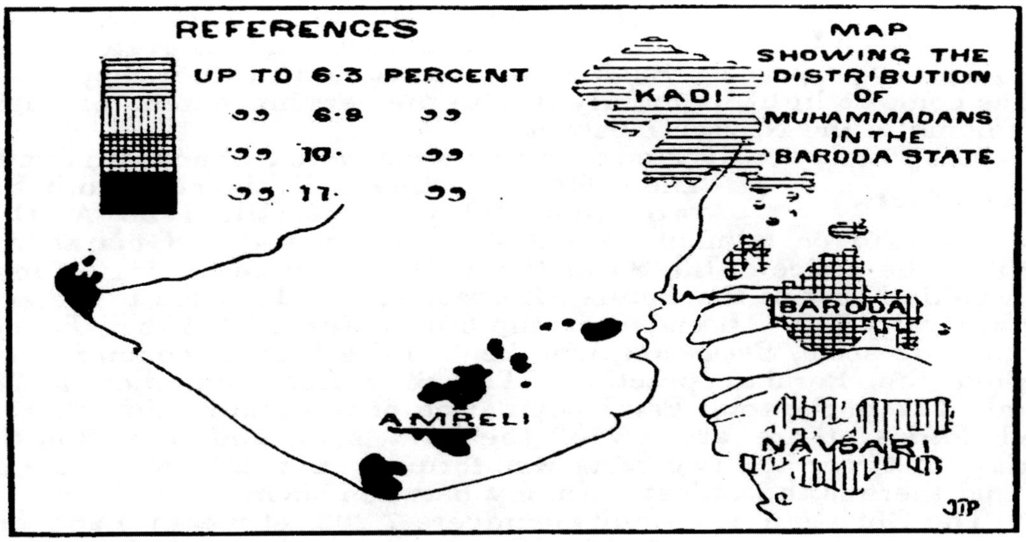

Variation since 1901.

144. In the State as a whole, Mahomedans have decreased by 2·5 per cent. during the last decade. Only in the Baroda District, they show an increase of about 8 per cent., but elsewhere they show a decrease of from 5 to 8 per cent. The decrease is heavy (8 per cent.) in the City of Baroda and the Navsari District. It amounts to nearly 5 per cent. in the Amreli and Kadi Districts. Some Matias (401) of the Navsari District and Shaikhdas (51) of the Baroda District, who previously returned themselves as Musalmans, have, on the present occasion, returned themselves as Hindus ; but this loss is trifling, and does not materially affect the proportion of the Mahomedans in the State. The decrease in their number can only be explained by migration and plague. An ever-increasing number of Mahomedans has been migrating from the Navsari District to South Africa, Mauritius, Burma and other places for trade and other purposes. Similarly Khojas and Memons from the Amreli District and Vohoras from Sidhpur and the Baroda City migrate to Bombay, Madras and other parts of India and to Singapore. Kadi Mahomedans migrate to Ahmedabad, Surat, Mahikantha and Palanpur Agencies for service as constables, sepoys and sowars. Plague, which was raging in one place or another, in the whole State throughout the decade, must also be responsible to some extent for the diminution of the Mahomedan population. The Mahomedans are great fatalists, and this, together with their zenana system, makes them very reluctant to leave their quarters even when severely affected by plague, with the result that they lose largely in their numerical strength.

Musalman Sects.

145. Most of the Musalmans in the State are Sunnis. Out of every 100 followers of Islam, 85 are Sunnis, 14 are Shias and 1 is a follower of the Imamshahi or Pirana sect, an account of which will be found in the descriptive section of this chapter. The followers of the Shia sect are mostly trading Vohoras, Khojas and Arabs, while the followers of the Pirana sect are known as Momnas and Shaikhdas whom Imamshah of Pirana, near Ahmedabad, and his kinsmen converted from Hinduism in the 15th century.

Distribution of Parsis.

146. The total Parsi population in the State consists of 7,955 persons, of whom 7,179, or nearly 90 per cent., are in the Navsari District, and 561 or 7 per cent. in the Baroda City. Elsewhere Parsi population is only nominal, there being only 109 persons in Baroda District, 77 in Kadi and only 29 in the Amreli District. Navsari is the head-quarters not only of the Parsis in the State, but also of many others living in Bombay and elsewhere for trade and other purposes.

147. Compared with 1901, the Parsi population in the State has decreased by about 5 per cent. The Parsis are an energetic and adventurous race and migrate to all parts of India for business purposes. Such a slight variation in their population in the State as has come to light, is mainly due to the varying extent of their absence from their home in the Navsari District.

Comparison with 1901.

148. The Parsis are divided into two sects called Shenshahis and Kadmis. The agitation which split the community into these two sects did not arise till 1736 A. D., when a Zoroastrian *behedin* or layman named Jamsed arrived in Gujarat from Persia. He brought to the notice of the Surat Parsis that their reckoning of months was one month behind that of the Persian Zoroastrians. This led to a dispute which lasted for several years. It ended on the 6th of June 1745 by the community splitting into two sects, *Shenshahi*, who kept to the Indian reckoning, and *Kadmi* who adopted the Persian practice. The Shenshahis number 7,778 and the Kadmis only 177 in the total Parsi population of the State. In other words, in a hundred Parsis, there are 98 of the first sect, and only 2 of the second. Intermarriage between the two sects was formerly not allowed, but now it is common, and there is the fullest harmony between them.

Parsi Sects.

149. The Christian community numbers 7,203, of whom 6,962 are Natives and 241 Europeans and Anglo-Indians (formerly called Eurasians). Of the Native Christians, 4,833 or nearly two-thirds are Methodists, 189 Presbyterians, 400 Roman Catholics and 1,540 or a little more than one-fifth are Salvationists. Of the Europeans and Anglo-Indians, 139 belong to Anglican Communion, 4 are Baptists, 7 Lutherans, 17 Methodists, 4 Presbyterians and 68 Roman Catholics. Two European males returned themselves as Agnostic, and are therefore classed under the head " Indefinite beliefs." As the return of Christian sects was vitiated in the past Censuses, owing to the ignorance of the Native Christians regarding their sects, special measures were taken on the present occasion to ensure a correct return. The heads of missions working within the State were addressed shortly before the Census, with a view to securing their co-operation ; and they all readily responded and agreed to supply their converts with slips on which the correct name of their sect was printed. The enumerators were instructed to call for the sect slip from each Native Christian enumerated by them and to copy out the entry thereon, in the sect column of the Census schedule.

Christians.

150. Five-sixths of the total number of Europeans and Anglo-Indian Christians are in the City of Baroda (with the Cantonment) and the rest who are mostly employed on Railways, are distributed in the districts of the State. Of the Native Christians 84 per cent. are in the Baroda District, 10 per cent. in the Baroda City and 5 per cent. in the Kadi District. Christianity is not yet spread to any appreciable extent in the Navsari and Amreli Districts.

Distribution of Christians.

151. The number of Christians in the State increased from 313 in 1872 to 771 in 1881, but declined to 646 in 1891. It rose to the remarkable figure of 7,691 in 1901 owing mainly to the humane efforts of the missionaries in giving shelter to the destitute poor, during the great famine of 1899-1900. After the famine was over, many of the destitute sheltered by the missionaries returned to their home and probably reverted to their own religion , and new conversions are rare. This has resulted in the decline of the Christians by 488 persons or 6·35 per cent. in the present Census.

Variation since 1872.

152. The classes most receptive of Christianity are those who are outside the Hindu system or whom Hinduism regards as degraded and untouchable and treats unjustly. It is for this reason that missions generally succeed in having converts from Dheds and similar castes. Amongst the higher Hindu castes, there are serious obstacles in the way of conversion, of which family influence and the caste system are the greatest. By accepting Christianity, a man at once cuts himself off from all his old associations and is regarded even by his family as an outcaste. Moreover, the prospect of such an occurrence is

Classes receptive of Christianity.

viewed with the greatest dread, and when any one is suspected of an intention to become a Christian, the greatest possible pressure is brought to bear on him by all his relations and friends, in order to make him change his mind.

Methodist Episcopal Church Mission.

153. The missions working in the State are :—(1) the Methodist Episcopal Church Mission, (2) the Salvation Army and (3) the Irish Presbyterian Mission. Of these, the Methodist Mission is the most important and has secured the largest number of followers within the last thirty years. The first Christian missionary who came to Baroda was a representative of the London Missionary Society and arrived in that City in the year 1844. Two years later, the work was taken over by the Irish Presbyterian Mission and that Mission carried on work in the City for some years. In the year 1870, representatives of the Methodist Episcopal Church Mission came to Baroda for work among the English-speaking people and commenced work for all classes in the year 1881. This mission is working in many parts of the Baroda and Kadi Districts with headquarters at Baroda. In the year 1880, a small Church was erected in the Cantonment. A boarding-school for boys and another for girls were soon opened and both of them were in a flourishing condition before the great famine. They were thrown open to receive destitute children and during the time of the great famine of 1899-1900, three thousand children were cared for. After the close of the famine, the majority of the children, who had gone in the boarding-schools, returned to their native villages.

At present there are in the Baroda Cantonment separate boarding-schools for boys and girls. 369 boys and girls are students in these schools. In connection with the boarding institutions, there are a Primary Girls' School, a Boys' School of the primary grade and a Co-educational Anglo-Vernacular School and High School. In the Boys' Boarding School, there is a Manual Training Department and lads showing proficiency in that Department are transferred to the Industrial School of this Mission situated at Nadiad, while boys of that institution, who are especially promising, are transferred to the Baroda Mission High School. The girls of the boarding-school are taught domestic work and useful industries, such as weaving, lace-making, sewing, &c. The Florence Nicholson School of Theology at Baroda occupies commodious quarters. To this institution, young men with their wives come for training to prepare them for the work of the Christian ministry. The buildings are a memorial to the lady whose name the institution bears and were erected by her husband. The Theological course covers a period of three years, and there are ninety students in the school. The Mission has a large Hospital for women and children located near the Cantonment. It is well equipped and is in charge of an American lady physician, who is assisted by a competent staff of nurses. Medical work is also carried on throughout the district in the villages where the Christians live.

In addition to this institutional work, there are upwards of 150 preachers who are working in the Baroda District, and the converts are now nearly 5,000 in number.

Arya Samajis.

154. The total number of Arya Samajis in the whole State is 598. Of these, 169 are in the City of Baroda, 185 in the Baroda District, 25 in the Kadi District, 153 in the Navsari District and 66 in the Amreli District.

Comparison with 1901.

155. The Census of 1901, for the first time, returned 50 followers of the Arya Samaj within this State. During the present decade, their number has shown a remarkable increase as detailed in the above para. The increase is mainly due to the preachings of missionaries from the United Provinces and to the two Arya Samaj Conferences held at Itola and Ranoli villages of the Baroda District in 1910 and 1911. Most of the Arya Samajis belong to the Lewa Kanbi or Anavala and Audich Brahman castes, and respect their caste restrictions. In the Census, many of them returned "Hindu" as their religion and "Arya Samaji" as a name of their sect.

Brahmo.

156. There are only six Brahmos (four males and two females) in the whole State. They are immigrants from Bengal, the mother-land of this new form of religion.

Sikhs and their distribution.

157. Sikhs number 90, who are mostly immigrants engaged in the army; 65 of them are in the Amreli District, 13 in the Baroda City, nine in the Baroda District, two in Kadi and one in Navsari.

Sikhism.

Sikhism was founded in the Punjab by Guru Nanak (1469-1538 A. D) and was further developed by succeeding *Gurus*, notably by Guru Govind Singh (1675-1708 A. D.) The Sikh creed involves belief in one God condemning the worship of other deities; it prohibits idolatry, pilgrimage to the great shrines of Hinduism, faith in omens, charms or witchcraft; and does not recognise ceremonial impurity at birth and death. As a social system, it abolishes caste distinctions and Brahmanic supremacy in all ceremonies at birth, marriage and death. Sikhs are permitted to eat flesh, though not beef, but are prohibited from using tobacco in any form. Every Sikh is required to bear foremarks known as five *ka*, the hair uncut (*kesh*), the short drawers (*kachh*), the *kara* or iron bangle, the *khanda* or steel knife and *kangha* or comb. The main object of the early Gurus was to distinguish their disciples from the Hindus among whom they lived. Now, however, many shades of opinion prevail among the Sikhs and many Hindu practices, *e. g.*, going on a pilgrimage to Hardwar, find favour amongst large portion of the brotherhood.

Sikhism has given rise to several mendicant orders, of which the principal are Udasi, Nirmali and Akali.

Jews.

158. Jews number 40 only in the whole State and are mostly immigrants for State service. 17 of them are in the City of Baroda, 12 in Amreli, 6 in Navsari, 2 in Kadi and 3 in Baroda District.

PART II—DESCRIPTIVE.

1.—Hindu religious beliefs and practices.

Comprehensiveness of Hinduism.

159. Hinduism includes such a variety of creeds that it has been called an "Encyclopædia of Religions." It is not one homogeneous growth of religious thought. Starting from the Veda, Hinduism has ended in embracing something from all religions and in presenting phases suited to all minds. It is all tolerant, all comprehensive, all absorbing. "It has its spiritual and material aspect, its esoteric and exoteric, its subjective and objective, its rational and irrational, its pure and impure. It may be compared to a huge polygon or irregular multilateral figure. It has one side for the practical, another for the severely moral, another for the devotional and imaginative, another for the sensuous and sensual and another for the philosophical and the speculative. Those who rest in ceremonial observances find it all sufficient; those who deny the efficacy of works and make faith the one requisite, need not wander from its pale; those who are addicted to sensual objects may have their tastes gratified; those who delight in meditating, on the nature of god and man, the relation of matter and spirit, the mystery of separate existence and the origin of evil may here indulge in their love of speculation; and this capacity for almost endless expansion causes almost endless sectarian divisions even among the followers of any particular line of doctrine." (Hinduism by Professor Monier Williams, p. 12).

Definition of Hinduism.

160. Such being the comprehensiveness of this great religion, it is difficult to define it in precise terms. Several definitions given by various writers on the subject were considered in the last India Census Report, p. 356. In the Punjab Census Report of 1881, Sir Denzil Ibbetson described it as :—

"A hereditary sacerdotalism with Brahmans for its Levites, the vitality of which is preserved by the social institution of caste, and which may include all shades and diversities of religion native to India, as distinct from the foreign importation of Christianity and Islam, and from the later outgrowths of Buddhism, more doubtfully of Sikhism, and still more doubtfully of Jainism."

Mr. Baines, who was Census Commissioner in 1891 proceeded by the method of exclusion, and defined Hinduism as "the large residuum that is not Sikh, or Jain, or Buddhist, or professedly Animistic, or included in one of the foreign religions, such as Islam, Mazdaism, Christianity, or Hebraism." Sir Alfred Lyall described Hinduism as "The religion of all people who accept the Brahmanic scriptures." He went on to speak of it as "a tangled jungle of disorderly superstitions." Finally he called it the collection of rites, worships, beliefs, traditions and mythologies that are sanctioned by the sacred books and ordinances of the Brahmans and are propagated by Brahmanic teaching. While accepting the general accuracy of this definition, Sir Herbert Risley, with a view to give an idea of the elements out of which popular Hinduism has been evolved, and of the conflicting elements which it has absorbed described it as "Animism more or less transformed by philosophy or magic tempered by metaphysics." "Within the enormous range of beliefs and practices, which are included in the term Hinduism, there are comprised two entirely different sets of ideas ; at one end, at the lower end, of the series is Animism, an essentially materialistic theory of things which seeks by means of magic to ward off or to forestall physical disasters, which looks no further than the world of sense and seeks to make that as tolerable as possible, as the conditions will permit. At the other end is Pantheism, combined with a system of transcendental metaphysics." The same idea is expressed by a modern Hindu writer on the subject, who has tersely summarised the main features of Hinduism in the following Sanskrit couplet :—

प्रामाण्य बुद्धिर्वेदेषु साधनानामनेकता ।
उपास्यानामनियमः एतद्धर्मस्य लक्षणम् ॥

i.e., "The religion which has implicit faith in the Vedas, recognises diverse ways of attaining the (spiritual) goal and has unlimited objects of adoration."

Brahmanism.

161. In Hinduism we have at the top of the ladder, Brahmanism represented by a few known as *Vedantists*, whose leading dogma, *Ekam eva adwitiyam*, 'There is but one being, without a second' summarises their whole creed. According to them nothing really exists, but the one Universal Spirit called Brahma or *Parmatma* and whatever appears to exist separately from that Spirit is a mere illusion ; *Jivatma* or individual soul is identical with *Parmatma* or Supreme Soul, as microcosm with macrocosm ; it is restrained from consciousness of its unity, and hence from union with it by the resultants of its previous *karma* or actions. So long as there remains attached to the soul a resultant of its previous actions, it is doomed to wander in repeated incarnations, from body to body. Only those souls in which the resultant finally vanishes attain *moksha*, or emancipation. They lose all sense of individual personality by complete absorption (*sayujya*) into the only really existing Being who is wholly unfettered by action and without qualities of any kind (*nirguna*) and called *satchidanand* because he is pure life, pure thought, pure joy.

Popular Hinduism.

162. Popular Hinduism, though supposed to accept this creed, called *Gnyana Marga* or the way of true knowledge, adds to it two other inferior ways :—(1) *Karma Margo*, or 'path of religious rites', *i. e.*, the belief in the efficiency of sacrifices, rites, lustral washings and austerities ; and (2) *Bhakti Marga* or 'path of love and devotion' to personal deities. Popular Hinduism supposes that the one Universal Being amuses himself by illusionary appearances ; and that all visible and material objects, good and bad, including gods, demons, demi-gods, good and evil spirits, human beings and animals are emanations from Him and are ultimately to be re-absorbed into His essence. Popular Hinduism is represented by the complicated system of polytheistic doctrines and caste-usages which have gradually resulted out of the mixture of Brahmanism with Buddhism, with the non-Aryan creeds of Dravidians and Aborigines. Popular Hinduism is something very different from Brahmanism, though the one is derived from the other. It is like a huge

irregular structure which has spread itself over an immense surface by continual additions and accretions. It has adopted much of the Fetishism of the Negrito inhabitants of India; it has stooped to the practices of various hill tribes and not scrupled to encourage the adoration of serpents, rocks, stones and trees.

Every day religion.

163. A Gujarat Hindu attaches the greatest importance to bathing. As a rule, he does not take his morning meal before having a bath which consists in pouring a few *lotas* of water on his person. After bath, he worships his family gods or goddesses, or goes to the temple of his sect for the same purpose. The *darsan* in the temple consists simply of getting a glimpse of the idol and saying *je, je, je*, chanting *bhajans*, hymns and leaving a few coppers or a handful of grain in the dish kept for the purpose. On holidays, he offers flowers to the idols. The temple is visited also in the afternoon by those who are very devout. Whenever he is at leisure, or in a contemplative mood, he mutters the name of Shri Ram or Shri Krishna, either alone or in company with their respective consorts, *i.e.*, Rama Rama or Sita Rama, or Radha Krishna. He gives alms in the shape of a handful of rice, pulse or flour to Brahmans and Sadhus. He either sets apart a portion of his food or uses the remainder at his table for dogs and cows which wander about in the streets. He observes a fast on every Monday, Saturday or on every eleventh day in a fortnight. He feeds Brahmans or Sadhus, whenever he is inclined to accumulate extra merit. He goes on a pilgrimage to Dakorji, Narmadaji, Kalka Mata, Amba Mata and other places when he has taken a vow to do so, or whenever it pleases him to do so. He believes in heaven, hell and transmigration of soul. His next life and his going to heaven or hell depends upon his actions in present life. He hopes to better his position in this and the life to come by his devotion to his god, his *dan*, charity to Brahmans, and his *daya*, kindness to men, cows, etc.

Observance of caste rules.

164. So great is the influence exerted by caste-rules on the daily life of the Hindus that the whole of their religion may be said to be centered in caste observances and Hinduism and caste have become convertible terms. Strictness in the maintenance of caste is the only real test of Hinduism exacted by the Brahmans of the present day. In matters of mere faith, Hinduism is all tolerant and all receptive. No person who is not born a Brahman can become one, but any person can be admitted into the lower ranks of Hinduism, who will acknowledge the supremacy of the Brahmans and obey the rules of caste. So long as a man observes the rules of his caste, he is at liberty to hold any religious opinion he likes.

Religious belief and practice of the different castes.

165. All Gujarati Brahmans, except a few, who belong to the Swaminarayan sect are followers of Shiva, and almost all have household gods, whose worship some member of the family performs. The family gods are either some or all of the Hindu *panchayatan* or the group of five, *viz.*, a stone *ling* for Mahadev, a stone *shaligram* or a picture of Shri Nathji for Vishnu, a picture or metal image of Shakti, Bhavani or Mata, typifying divine energy; Ganpati and Surya or the Sun, or Hanuman, the Monkey-god. Their social and religious customs are chiefly ruled by the Mayukh, the Mitakshara and the Dharma and Nirnaya Sindhu. They perform *sandhya* or twilight prayer at least once a day in the morning, count their beads and repeat the *gayatri* or sun-hymn. Priests and beggars are almost the only men who observe the regular fasts. As a rule, on Mondays and on the first and fifteenth of each month and on the great religious festivals, men visit Shiva's temple for worship. Women are more careful than men to observe fasts, but are less regular in visiting the temples. Family and village priests learn by rote the ritual required at the different everyday ceremonies, but with a few exceptions, have no claim to learning.

Like Gujarati Brahmans, most of the Dakshani Brahmans are Shaivas or Smarts. But they are more ceremonious, more scrupulous in observing ceremonial purity and keep more closely to religious rules than Gujarati Brahmans.

Brahma-Kshatris keep the rules laid down for Brahmans-reading the sacred books, worshipping, meditating, repeating prayers, making offerings to the Sun and at meals putting on a silk sacred cloth. Kayasthas mostly belong to the Vallabhachari sect, but some of them are Ramanuji and some Shaiva. Vanias are very religious and as a class are staunch adherents of the Vallabhachari sect to which they were converted about four hundred years ago. In South Gujarat, each house has a separate god-room. They worship daily at the Vallabhachari temples and in their houses. Instead of the sacred thread, both men and women wear round their neck a *kanthi* (basil thread necklace). They mark their brows with two upright lines of *kanku*, (red powder), rub their eyelids and forehead with *gopichandan*, the yellow clay found near Dwarka, Gokul and Mathura, and imprint a seal dipped in sandal dust between the sectarian lines and on the temples, neck and arms. Bhatias are Vaishnav of the Vallabhachari sect and are very observant of religious rites. Like Vanias, they visit Vaishnav temples and worship in their houses the image of Vishnu in the form of Ranchhodji and Radha Krishna. Luhanas are Vaishnavas of the Vallabhachari and Ramanuji sects. Their family goddess is Randel Mata and they are devout worshippers of Darya Pir, the spirit of the Indus. Rajputs do not differ from other Hindus in their religious observances and practices. Though many are followers of the Vallabhachari, Swaminarayan and Ramanuji sects, Rajputs from remote ages have been partial to the worship of Shiva. At the same time, they worship all Hindu gods and goddesses and their house shrines contain their images of Shiva, Vishnu, Ganpati and of the tutelary goddess of the clan. The Kathis worship the Sun and the Parajia Sonis worship fire. Among other castes, such as Kanbis, Kolis, Kachhias, and the agricultural and artizan castes, generally a striking feature is the great hold which comparatively modern cults called *marga* or *panth*, ways, have taken upon them. Of these, the chief are Ramanandi, Swaminarayan, Kabirpanthi, Bijmargi, Pranami, or Meherajpanthi, Ramsanehi, Dadupanthi, Radha Vallabhi, Santarampanthi, and Shakta or Vammargi. Some time when they are between seven and eleven, both boys and girls are taken to the religious head or *guru*, who binds round the neck of the novice a rosary of beads made of the stem of the basil plant. Besides a day's food, the *guru* receives about Rs. 2 as the initiation fee. If they fall sick, they take vows to feed a certain number of Brahmans or not to eat milk, ghee or any other dainty or to put on a turban, till they have been on a pilgrimage to the shrine of their favourite deity. The untouchable and depressed classes, such as Dheds, Bhangis, &c., are very religious and honour most of the Brahmanic gods, but chiefly Hanuman, Ganpati, Rama, and Devi and above all, they revere the sacred basil or *tulsi* plant. As they are not allowed to enter them, people of these classes seldom worship at the regular village temples or shrines. In some hut near their dwellings, they have an image of Hanuman or of Meheldi Mata where, on holidays, they light a lamp or offer flowers. In front of their houses most of them keep a plant of basil or *tulsi* and inside some of them have an image of Mata, Hanuman or Ganpati. Those who can afford it, are fond of going on pilgrimage for worshipping Krishna at Dakore and the Mata at Pavagadh and Ambaji. They do not pass into the building but stand in the portico, bow as they catch a glance of the image and present a few coppers to the temple servants.

A belief in demonology, sorcery, witchcraft, the evil eye and omens is found more or less in almost all castes. Among religious practices, worship of ancestors, the elements, planets, the sea, rivers, animals, and plants is common to all.

Offerings.

166. All the gods and goddesses have offerings made to them, either daily or on special days. Offerings are either bloody or bloodless. Blood offerings are made to goddesses by Ahirs, Bharvads, Bhils, Charans, Dheds and other low castes. Blood offerings are sometimes made even by high caste Hindus in fulfilment of a vow taken to avert or cure some family sickness or secure the favour of some goddess. Blood offerings are also made for general good health and agricultural prosperity by the villagers as a body, or by some wealthy villager. Some high caste Hindus, who scruple to kill an animal, simply lay before the

goddess a live cock, sometimes with one of its legs cut off or an ear-bored goat and allow the animal to roam at large. With a sword, they cut a pumpkin or sprinkle on the goddess the blood that oozes out by having the animal's ear lopped off or its body scratched with a knife.

Bloodless offerings consist of grain, fruit, flowers and tree leaves. They are made both in every-day worship and on special days and differ for different gods. To the stone image of Shiva are offered the leaves of the *bili* tree (*aegle marmelos*). To Devi or Mata, Shiva's consort, all red flowers are offered, especially the *karena*, (oleander). The flowers of *akdo*, swallow wort, cannot be offered to any god except Hanuman. To Vishnu in his form of Krishna are offered white flowers.

Rain worship.

167. If the rain holds off till late in June or July and a drought is imminent, efforts are made to induce Indra, the rain-god, to favour the earth with showers. Wealthy men engage Brahmans to repeat prayers to the rain-god in a Shiva or Mata temple. Sometimes the outlet through which the water passes from the basin in which Shiva's *linga* is set is closed, and the women of the village keep pouring water on the *linga* till it is deep sunk in water. This pouring of water, intended to please Shiva, is repeated for eight days unless it rains in the meantime. Sometimes the people of a village quit the place in a body for a few days and leave it *ujjad* or uninhabited and cook their food outside. This is done, because by holding off rain, Indra wishes to lay waste the land, and by voluntarily doing it, people believe that finding his wish fulfilled, he would send rain. Sometimes a party of Koli, Vaghari or Bhil women walk in the street singing the praise of *Mehulo*, the rain-god. One of the party bears on her head a basket containing a clay frog with three twigs of *nimb* tree stuck in it. The party stops at every house where the women pour a potful of water over the frog drenching the bearer and presenting them with doles of grain.

Sea worship.

168. The sea is worshipped by all high caste Hindus on every *Amavasya* day, particularly when it falls on Monday. Bathing in the sea is considered specially cleansing, because on that day the water of 999 rivers is believed to be brought into the sea by the spring tides. During the whole of the intercalary month, sea bathing is also held cleansing.

River worship.

169. On Sundays, Tuesdays and on the 12ths and dark 15ths of every Hindu month and during the whole of the intercalary month, people bathe in the rivers in the hope of their sins being washed away. The rivers which are considered particularly sacred in Gujarat, are the Tapti, the Narbada, the Mahi and the Saraswati. The Kolis of Mahikantha call it a Mata and the feeling of awe for the Mahi Mata is so great that, if made to swear by its name, no man will dare tell an untruth. The bones of the dead are thrown after cremation into the nearest river and in the case of the well-to-do are taken to the Narbada, the Saraswati or the Ganges. The Saraswati at Sidhpur is held very sacred and is much sought after by persons wishing to perform after-death ceremonies for women. The water of the Jumna is stored by most Vaishnavas who sip it after the daily worship is over. The water of the Ganges is dropped into the mouth of the dying in the hope that it will wash away all sins.

The moon.

170. According to the Hindus, the moon is a male deity and is respected by all lunar Rajputs who daily worship a representation of it. Non-moon days or *Amas* of each month is unlucky for all undertakings and is observed as a day of rest by traders, shopkeepers and craftsmen. If it falls on a Monday, the day is sacred and people bathe in a river or pool and make gifts to Brahmans. On the bright second day of a month, *bij*, the moon is hailed by most high caste Hindus, particularly by traders and shop-keepers. After seeing the new moon, people take care that the first person they look at is good and lucky. If their neighbours are not such, they look at a silver coin. The new moon, *bij*, is held particularly sacred by all who belong to the Bijmargi sect which has many followers among Ahirs, Bhavsars, Bhangis, Darjis, Dheds, Golas, Kathis, Kolis, Luhars, Mochis, Rabaris, Rajputs and Sathawaras. Some Kolis bow to the new moon and ask three

blessings thus: *bij mavdi, chule tavdi, be godha ne ek gavdi, i. e.,* "Mother Bij, give a cooking pan (that is daily bread), two bullocks and a cow." The bright fourths are called *Ganesh Chaturthi* or Ganpati's fourth and the dark fourths are called *Sankashta Chaturthi* or trouble clearing fourth. The sight of the moon on the bright fourths is considered unlucky and specially so, in the month of *Bhadarvo.* It is believed that any one who sees the moon on that day will be falsely charged. After sunset, people shut all windows. If by chance any one happens to see the moon, he throws stones on his neighbours' roofs till some one in the neighbour's house gets angry enough to abuse the stone-thrower, when the risk of the false charge of theft passes away. From this stone-throwing, the day is called *dagdâ choth* or "stone fourth". The bright fifteenths or full moon, *punam,* are sacred to all Matas or goddesses. On particular full moons, such as the *Kartik, Paush, Chaitra and Ashwin,* the temples of the different gods and goddesses as also the sacred places on the river banks are thronged by pilgrims. The Aso full moon is called *Manekthari punam* or the pearl-making full moon, for, it is believed, that if a rain-drop on this night falls into the mouth of an oyster, it is turned into a pearl.

Persons to whom the moon is unfriendly, wear a white diamond or a pearl ring or engage a Brahman to repeat a special prayer in his honour eleven thousand times to ward off his evil influence.

Eclipse.

171. For twelve hours before a sun eclipse begins and for eight hours before a moon eclipse begins, no cooked food is eaten. Before the eclipse begins, all water jars are emptied and the store of pickles and *papad* is carefully locked. All including the household gods are held to be impure so long as the eclipse lasts. The people explain this impurity by saying that *Rahu* was a Bhangi or sweeper and that his touch defiles the sun and the moon. During the eclipse, gifts are made to Bhangis who go from door to door shouting *karo dharm chhutê grahan,* that is 'Give gifts and the seizure will be loosened.' When the eclipse is over, every one bathes either at home or in a river or in the sea. They fetch fresh drinking water, purify the house-gods by going through the regular daily worship, and present grain or copper and silver coins to the family priests.

Animal Worship.

172. Among the Hindus the cow is particularly sacred. Her tail with the help of which they hope to cross the hell river (*Vaitarni*), is applied by people to their eyes or instead of the tail, they put their right hand on the cow's haunches and apply their hand to the eye. The gift of the cow, *gaudan,* is the noblest of gifts. It is generally made during the intercalary month or before a person's death. The cow to be given is decorated and the donor holding her tail in his right hand gives her to a Brahman. After the dead body is burnt, a cow is milked on the funeral pile or her milk is poured over the ashes. High caste Hindu women perform *gautrat, i. e.,* cow worship for their husband's long life and if a widow, to exchange her lot in the next birth.

The bull called *sandhio, akhalo* or *godho* is Shiva's carrier and is held sacred. In a Shiva temple, there is always an image of a bull which is worshipped along with Shiva. On the *Dasara* festival, owners get their horses washed, mark their head with a *tila* and put garlands of flowers on their neck. Similarly bullocks are worshipped by Kanbis and other agriculturists.

Serpent Worship.

173. The serpent, generally the *nag* or cobra is much dreaded and worshipped by almost all classes. In spite of its destructive nature, a cobra is never killed. When a cobra appears in the house, the people bow to it and pray it not to harm the inmates. At the most, it is caught, put in an earthen jar, and the jar is laid in a lonely spot. The day held most sacred to serpent-worship is the bright or dark fifth of Shravan, called *nagpanchmi.* On that day women worship the cobra or its image. When a person is bitten by a snake, an adept in curing snake bites is called. He gives charmed cow-dung ashes to be rubbed on the bitten part or while repeating some charm, ties, knot after knot on a thread. If the person is still restless, the adept dashes seven handfuls of water on the eyes of the sick and otherwise tries to force the snake to leave the body. Under the influence of the water or charm, the snake, through the person bitten, tells why he bit the man.

If the injury which prompted the snake to bite was slight, the snake agrees to leave his body ; if the injury done was heavy, the snake persists in not leaving the body and the patient dies. In the City of Baroda, there is a Nagar Brahman family, all the members of which are deemed to be adepts in curing snake bite by charms and their services are more readily requisitioned than those of the expert medical officers.

Tree Worship.

174. The trees and plants held in high reverence are *darbha, daro, piplo, shami, tulsi* and *bili*. *Darbha* is used in all religious ceremonies, both lucky and unlucky. A blade of *darbha* grass is held by the bride and bridegroom just before their hands are joined ; and a blade of it represents the dead in the *shradha* ceremony.

The *daro* (cynodon daclyton) grass is Ganpati's favourite offering. The day sacred to it is the bright 8th of Bhâdrapad when men and women drop water, flowers, red powder (*kanku*) and rice on it.

The *piplo* (ficus religiosa) is believed to be the emblem of Vishnu and the haunt of *Munja*, the spirit of a thread-girt and unmarried Brahman lad.

The *shami* (prosopis spicigera) is regarded as Shiva's wife and is called *Vijayadevi*. The tree is held sacred by all Hindus but chiefly by Rajputs, because on it the Pandwas hung their arms when they were banished. The arms were turned into snakes and remained untouched till the owners came back to take them. By worshipping this tree on the Dasara day, Rama conquered Ravan, Vàli conquered Sugriva and the Pandwas conquered the Kauravas. In worshipping this tree, people walk round it and while walking, repeat verses telling how the tree purifies from sin, destroys enemies, cures diseases and ensures success.

All Vaishnavas keep the *tulsi* plant in their houses. Dheds also hold it sacred and keep it in front of their houses. To get rid of barrenness, women walk 108 times around the *tulsi* and *piplo* planted together. *Tulsi* leaves are believed to have great sin-cleansing power and a *tulsi* leaf is therefore put in the mouth of the dying.

The *bili* (ægle marmelos) is planted near shrines and other holy places and is believed to be the home of Parvati, after whom it is called *Shivaraksha*. Brahmans gain merit by repeating prayers sitting under its shade. The leaves of the tree are the favourite offerings to Shiva.

Fire worship.

175. Fire is held in high veneration. It is used in burning the dead and in all sin-cleansing rites. Offerings are made to fire in thread, marriage and pregnancy ceremonies. When a lamp is lighted in the evening and brought into a room, those sitting in it, make a bow to it and to each other. Sonis, Luhars, Kansaras and all other artizans who use fire in their calling, make offerings of clarified butter and rice to their fire-place. The followers of the Kabir and the Bijmargi sects who profess not to worship idols, hold the flame of a lighted lamp sacred, and make offerings to it, just as others do to their idols.

Book worship.

176. In the evening of the last day of the year, bankers and merchants perform *vahi-pujan* or book worship. New books for the coming year are piled on a wooden stool, generally in front of an image of Lakshmi, the goddess of wealth, lighted lamps are placed round them and flowers are strewn on the books. The priest repeats a prayer for the favour of the goddess on the next year's business and dipping his fingers in *kanku* makes round marks on the first page of each book. The worship ends by writing on the walls of the room, the words *Shri Ganeshayanamah, Lakshmi matani madat, Bhandar bharpur*, "salutation to Ganesh ; mother Lakshmi, help us ; overflow our treasure chests."

Stone-worship.

177. Consecrated stones are held sacred by almost all classes of Gujarat Hindus. Most gods and goddesses are made of stone and when consecrated by prayers and offerings, become the dwelling place of some guardian spirit. Bhils, Kolis, Vagharis, Dublas and other wild tribes have no elaborate rites for making a stone fit to be the house of a guardian. With them, the mere rubbing of a stone with red lead makes it an object of reverence. A red lead trident is painted on the

trunk of a *nimb* or *piplo* tree and a heap of stones is piled at its root. Believing the place to be the dwelling of some god or goddess, passers-by show their reverence for it by adding a stone or two to the heap.

Tomb worship.

178. Among Hindus in Gujarat, tomb worship is not common. The few tombs that are worshipped are those raised over the remains of a *sati*, that is a woman who burnt herself with her dead husband, of ascetics and of Mahomedan saints. Over the spot where a woman was burnt, a *devdi* or masonry platform was used to be erected by the ruler of the land or by the members of her family. A stone is set on the platform which is sometimes canopied and on the stone are carved the Sun and the Moon and the figure of a woman with her right hand uplifted. The members of the woman's family visit the Sati's *devdi* generally on the dark fourteenth of *Aso* (October), daub it with red lead, lay a lighted lamp near it and offer a cocoanut and a robe to it. Sati's tomb is worshipped by barren women and by fever-striken people.

Masonry platforms raised over the remains of a Hindu ascetic are called *samadhi*, because the ascetic is believed at the time of death to be in a state of mental absorption or *samadh*. A stone is set on the platform and on the stone a pair of footprints is carved. These *samadhis* are worshipped by disciples, daily or at least on Sundays, Tuesdays and Thursdays, *Ashad* full moon or on the anniversary of the ascetic's death.

The *takiyo* or tombs of Musalman *Pirs* or *Saints* are worshipped by middle and low class Hindus, when a vow taken in the saint's honour is to be fulfilled. The intercession and help of these Pirs are asked when a man's life is in danger, when a lost article is to be recovered, when the milk-yielding power of milch cattle is to be restored, when punishment is to be avoided, and when epidemics, cholera, cattle plague, snake-bite, woman's barrenness, &c., are to be cured. When by the saint's help the object is gained, offerings are made to the tombs. During the *Mohorram*, the *taboots* or *tazias* which are models of the tombs of Hassan and Hussain are held sacred by Marathas, Rajputs, Vagharis, Kolis, Dheds and other low class Hindus. Brahman, Vania and some other high caste Hindu boys are dressed by their parents as *fakirs* and made to live on gifts made by friends and relations. In fulfilment of a vow, some pour water, throw themselves on the road and with a cocoanut in their hands roll in front of the *taboots*; some pass and repass under them, some walk a considerable distance with their faces turned towards the *tazia* and some paint themselves as tigers and bears.

Epidemic scaring.

179. Epidemics are believed to be caused by a goddess or *Mata* whose wrath requires to be appeased by offerings. The ceremony with which these offerings are made is called *shanti* or quieting rite. It is performed by a whole caste or by the people of a street or village, near a goddess's temple, in the market where four roads cross or in a street. Shanti ceremonies are also performed when the rainfall is scanty, when the fields are attacked by locusts, when a child is born under an unlucky star and when an unlucky occasion, such as marriage is beset with obstacles. After the offerings are made, the ends of the street or of the market are festooned with cocoanuts and *nimb*, *asopalo* and mango leaves with, at each end of the festoon, two earthen pots one over the other.

Disease worship.

180. Disease both in its milder endemic form in which it is generally present and in its fiercer epidemic form which breaks out from time to time, is believed to be due to spirit possession. Endemic diseases are believed to be caused by the unfriendly influence of some planet or of some god or goddess or of some evil spirit. Epidemic diseases are believed to be caused by the anger of some goddess. If a disease is caused by the unfriendly influence of some particular planet, a Brahman is engaged to offer prayers to it and articles sacred to it are used or are given away in charity. If it is caused by some god or goddess, prayers are repeated in their name and their favourite offerings are made to them. If it is caused by the influence of some spirit, offerings are made to the tombs of Musalman saints and charmed articles are worn on the arms or neck. The shrines usually frequented by the sick are at Behecharaji in the Chansma

taluka of the State, Miradatar near Unja, Ambaji in the Danta State and Kalka Mata in the Panch Mahals. Epidemic small-pox is believed to be presided over by a goddess called *Shitala Mata* and endemic small-pox by a god called *Saiyyad Kaka*. Both are propitiated by parents, especially by mothers, once in a year to protect their children.

Spirits.

181. There is a widespread belief in spirits, *bhuts*, and spirit possession, *valgan*. Spirits are of two kinds, *gharna bhut* or family spirits and *baharna bhut* or outside spirits. The influence of the family spirit is confined to the house or family to which it belongs. It does not trouble outsiders. A family spirit is generally the ghost of a member of the family who died with some desire unfulfilled or whose after-death ceremonies were neglected or improperly performed. Married women are very liable to be possessed by the spirit of a husband's former wife. To guard against it, a second wife always wears round her neck a gold ornament called *shokyapaglu*, the former wife's footprint which is sometimes marked with mystic letters or figures. Family spirits are quieted by performing special after-death rites. The chief outside spirits are (males) *Jhand, Jin, Khavas, Shikotar* and *Vir* and (females) *Chudel, Jhampadi, Jogni, Meldi, Pari, Shikotari,* and *Vantri*. Of these female spirits, *Jhampadi, Meldi* and *Shikotri* are the favourite goddesses of most of the low-caste Hindus, like Bhangis, Dheds, &c., who avert their evil influence by offerings. The favourite haunts of these spirits are burning grounds, *pipal* or *babul* trees, wells, empty houses, &c. They are said to enter the bodies of those who annoy them by committing a nuisance in, or otherwise defiling, their abodes, and by leaping over the circle within which offerings are laid for them, at the crossings of the four roads. The days most favourable for spirits entering human bodies are all Tuesdays and Sundays, the *navratra* festival which lasts for nine days in *Aso Sud* and the dark fourteenth of *Aso*; the hours of the day when they are most likely to enter are sunset and midnight.

Exorcism.

182. When a person is believed to be spirit possessed, a little of cowdung, chillies, mustard, an iron nail and live charcoal are placed on a bell-metal plate. Over these articles, a bell metal cup is turned with its rim down and over the bottom of the cup, a mixture of cowdung and water is poured. The plate is then waved over the head of the sick seven times by a woman. If after some time, the cup sticks to the plate, the spirit is believed to have left the person and to have gone inside the cup. Sometimes charmed threads supplied by some exorcists are tied to the wrist or the neck. Sometimes Brahmans are engaged to repeat sacred verses in a goddess temple. If the spirit is a weak one, it gets frightened by one or more of these processes and leaves the victim. If it is a strong spirit and cannot easily be got rid of, an exorcist is sent for. He is called a *bhuvo* and may be a Brahman, Khatri, Rabari, Bharvad, Vaghari, Koli or a Bhil. He may be a Jain Gorji or a Musalman Fakir or Molvi. Exorcists are said to gain their power of scaring spirits by mastering spells, *mantra*, which force spirits to become their servants and obey their orders. An exorcist goes to a burial-ground alone at midnight on the dark fourteenth of *Aso* every year and unearthing the body of a low-caste Hindu, mutters the *mantras*, sitting on the corpse. When he is consulted, the exorcist's first care is to ascertain whether the sick person suffers from spirit possession or from some other disease. This is done either by the Hindu method of counting grain or the Musalman method called *hajrat* of examining the reflection of a lighted lamp in a liquid. The Hindu exorcist gives a member of the sick person's family some rice, wheat, *juvar*, or *adad*, a nail, a piece of charcoal, seven clods of earth, seven particles of salt and a copper coin. These are wrapped in a piece of cloth, waved seven times over the head of the sick and the bundle is tied to his sleeping cot. On the next day which must be a Sunday, or a Tuesday, the bundle is opened and the exorcist takes a pinch of the grain from the bundle. The grains are arranged in twos and if one grain remains over, it is called *vadhavo* and shows that the spirit is in the sick man's body; if no single grain remains, there is no spirit in the sick man. If by this process the sick man is found to be possessed by a spirit, the exorcist first tries mild measures, and if they fail, harsh measures to

dislodge the spirit. He drives an iron nail into the threshold of the house and gently brushes the sick man's face with a peacock's feather or a *nimb* twig, all the while exhorting him to speak out. He forces the sick man to swing his body from side to side and to speak out the name of the spirit which has possessed him. Sometimes a whole night passes without any result, and the operation is repeated on the next night. A fire is lighted, a few chillies, mustard, and cumin seeds, salt, dung of a dog, monkey or donkey and a piece of leather are dropped into the fire and the fumes blown through the sick man's nostrils. To impress the sick man with his superhuman powers, the exorcist beats his own back with an iron chain. When the sick man is thus teased and annoyed, he replies to every question put by the exorcist, gives his name, explains why and how he entered the sick man's body, and after a solemn promise from the sick man's friends and relations to satisfy his demands, agrees to return to his old haunts.

Western education has weakened the belief of high caste Hindus in evil spirits. But among the low castes, such as Golas, Ghanchis, Kolis, Dheds, Bhangis, &c., who are still very ignorant, it is yet as strong as ever.

Omens.

183. Almost all classes of Gujarat Hindus believe that the result of every undertaking is foreshadowed by certain signs and hints. The business of the day will prosper or fail according to the nature of the object first seen after waking. The objects which the people are most anxious to begin the day by looking at, are the household gods, the *pipal* tree, the basil plant, a Brahman or a cow. Unless the signs are favourable, no new work is undertaken. If the first signs are unfavourable, people sit down and await the appearance of favourable signs. Kolis, Bhils, and others of the depredatory classes wait for the appearance of good omens on the village outskirts, and if they do not appear, put off their starting on a plundering raid from day to day. The goodness or badness of signs is determined by the appearance of certain living and lifeless objects in a particular form, in a particular way and in a particular state. An armed man, a cavalier, a mace-bearer, a school boy, a cultivator returning from his fields with his plough, a barber with his bag, a musician with his instruments, a mali or gardener with a basket of flowers, a woman with two water pots filled with water on her head, a cow on the left, a horse neighing to the right, &c., are considered good signs. Eating of curds before going on a journey is considered lucky. A journey is avoided to the north on a Sunday, to the north-west on a Monday, to the west on a Tuesday, to the south-west on a Wednesday, to the south on a Thursday, to the south-east on a Friday and to the east on a Saturday. Among bad signs are a physician, a goldsmith, a blacksmith, a pregnant woman, a widow, a buffalo, a camel, a goat, a cat, a woman carrying three earthen pots, sneezing, &c. A man who is cat-eyed or who has no hair on the breast or upper lip is considered unlucky. The popular saying is : *makadmuchho ne manjro, jene haide nahi val, te nar jo samo male, to nishche jage kal, i. e.*, it is a sure sign of ruin if on the way you meet one who has reddish moustaches, who is cat-eyed and who has no hair on the chest.

Pilgrimage.

184. Places of pilgrimage owe their sanctity to their possessing the shrines of the objects worshipped and as being places mentioned in the legendery lore. Such places are many, both within the State, such as Sidhpur, Modhera, Behecharaji, Dwarka, Chandod, Unai, and outside it, such as Shrinathji, Dakorji, Pavaghad, Ambaji, Gokul Mathura, Benares, &c. Of the places of pilgrimage connected with this State, Dwarka (Amreli District), Sidhpur (Kadi District) and Chandod (Baroda District) are well-known throughout India. Dwarka is looked upon as a very holy place on account of its once being the capital of Shri Krishna and at present possessing the shrine of Shri Ranchhodji. Sidhpur is looked upon as the only place in the whole of India where *shradha* can be performed, for the propitiation of the manes of the deceased mother. What Gaya is for the father, Sidhpur is for the mother. Chandod is situated on the sacred Narbada, ablutions in whose water are believed to cause the purification of sins. Large number of pilgrims from within and without the State, constantly visit these holy places, thus providing a livelihood for the local Brahman priests who administer to them the necessary rituals.

The Jains have their own places of pilgrimage, such as Mount Abu, Shatrunjaya and Girnar. People have great faith in the merit to be attained by going on a pilgrimage and thousands flock to places of pilgrimage several times in a year, if they are near and once in their life, if they are very distant. In the old unsettled times, pilgrims used to go in bands called *sanghs* with hereditary leaders called *sanghavis*. Railways have made pilgrimages easier, safer and less costly; but devout Hindus, especially Jains, still go on foot, expecting thereby to gain more religious merit.

Death-rites.

185. A Hindu on his death-bed gives a Brahman, the *gaudan*, that is the gift of a cow or of a cow's worth, not less than one rupee and four annas. With the help of her tail, he hopes to cross the hell river *Vaitarni*. He is then made to pour some water on the ground saying "so much (naming the sum) will be given in charity after my death." When the end draws near, he is bathed and with his head to the north is laid on the ground, which has been cleansed with fresh cowdung wash. While he lies on the ground, he is told to remember Rama and drops of Ganges water and *tulsi* leaves are laid in his mouth and a lamp is lighted. When life is gone, the body is covered with a sheet and the relations raise a loud cry. A bier of bamboo poles is prepared, the dead body is bound on it and borne, head first out of the house. The bier is carried on the shoulders of four near relations, the chief mourner going a little in front, carrying slung in a string, an earthen jar holding lighted cow-dung cakes. The female mourners follow the funeral party for some distance and then stop, beat their breasts and go to the village pond or river to bathe and then return home weeping. About halfway to the burning ground, the bier is turned round and set on the ground and rice, betel-nuts and coppers are laid on the spot where the bier was rested. From this spot to the burning ground, the body is carried feet first instead of head first. On the way the bearers chant to each other "*Ram bolo bhai Rama*"—"Say Rama, brother, say Rama." At the burning ground the body is unbound, bathed and laid on the funeral pile. The chief mourner takes out a lighted cow-dung cake from the earthen jar and after dipping it in clarified butter lays the cake on the mouth of the corpse. He fills the jar with water standing at the head of the corpse. He next walks round the pile and lights it at the head. When the body is consumed, the fire is put out either on the same or next day and the ashes are thrown into the sea or into a river. A few bones are collected and sent to some sacred river and the place where the body was burnt is washed with water. An earthen pot of water is set on the spot and broken with a stone thrown by the chief mourner. The funeral party raise a loud cry, leave the burning ground, bathe and return home.

Post-death rites.

186. On the next or third day after a death, a cow is brought and milked, so that the milk may fall on the spot where the body was burned. Letters called *chithis* announcing the death are sent to friends and relations by post or by a special carrier. For ten days relations and friends, especially females, come and weep morning and evening. Milk and water are set on the *tolla* or wooden peg in front of the house on the first day by a Brahman and on the succeeding three days by some member of the household. The nearest relations remain impure for ten days during which they touch no one, do not approach the house-gods, do not visit the temples and do not shave. If the deceased has left a widow, her head is shaved on the tenth day after his death and the heads of the male members of the family are also shaved. Near relations also shave their moustaches.

The *shradha* ceremony is performed by the chief mourner from the tenth to the thirteenth day; on the eleventh day it is performed with the help of a Kayatia Brahman and on the other three days with the help of the family priest. During the four days of the *shradha* ceremony, the chief mourner, instead of a turban, wears a *saniyu* or silk cloth wound round his head. The *saniyu* is removed on the thirteenth day when his father-in-law presents him with a new turban. Near relations are feasted from the tenth to the thirteenth day and the caste people on the twelfth. On the thirteenth day the family priest is presented with *sajja* or a sleeping cot with bedding, brass and copper vessels and various kinds of fruits and vegetables for the use of the departed soul. During the first year, monthly, half-yearly and yearly (*masiso, chhamasi,* and *varshi*) *shradhas* are performed. A yearly *shradha* is performed in all subsequent years and an additional one during the latter half of the month of *Bhadarvo.*

Common philosophical beliefs.

187. Apart from the all-pervading physiolatry and superstitious beliefs briefly described in the preceding paragraphs, some essential doctrines of Hindu philosophy are well-known to almost all the Hindus and passing like a rich heritage from father to son, have reached even the illiterate and ignorant masses. They promote virtuous living, discourage worldliness and teach resignation in their existing troubles. The first and the foremost among these is the belief in *lakshachorasi avatar* or the transmigration of soul. (It is a general understanding that while earthly desires remain unextinguished and while earthly passions continue to exist, the human soul is subject to be reincarnated again and again until finally emancipated from all mundane hopes and affections. The second belief is that the circumstances of each embodied existence are the result of the works done in the previous existence; and that souls, according to their actions, may enjoy happiness in this world or the heaven of god, or on the other hand suffer punishment on this earth or in hell reserved for evil doers. *Karyan karma bhogavavana chhe* or "as you will sow, so you will reap," is an axiom which even a rustic, believes to be applicable to this life and the one to come. Consequently, he believes that he must bear his miseries in life with patience and it is to his present and future welfare to live rightly, and to free himself from all carnal desires so as to ensure his early release from rebirth and to effect his union with god.)

2.—Hindu Sects.

Sects recorded.

188. The record of sects at the Census was optional with Local Governments. It was attempted in this State in 1901 as also on the present occasion, with a view to ascertain, as far as possible, the sectarian distribution of the people.

Accuracy of the return.

189. Most of the higher castes, such as Brahmans, Vanias, Kanbis, Bhats, Rajputs and the artizan classes know the name of the *panth* or sect to which they belong. Even those of them who have no clear idea of the distinctive tenets of their faith, have an intuitive knowledge as to whether they are Shaivas, Shaktas or Vaishnavas, and if the last, whether they belong to the Ramanuj, Ramanand, Vallabhacharya or Swaminarayan *sampradaya.* Such, however, is not the case with the members of the lower castes, such as Kolis, Vagharis, etc. Only a few of them know the name of their sect. The majority of their number who are illiterate and ignorant, know, only generally, the name of Parmeshwar, Rama, Shivaji, Amba, Bahuchara or Kalka Mata, but have no idea of sectarian differences or of sect names and are generally content with saying that they are Hindus. In spite of this in 1901, sects were returned for the whole Hindu population; and on the present occasion, there are only 53 in 1,000 for whom no sect is returned. This leads to the suspicion that many of the persons for whom sects have been entered, especially among the lower classes, owe them to the fact that names of sects were given in the instructions to the enumerators as illustrations of the kind of entry required, and it is probable that the most likely of them were entered by the enumerators when the enumerated themselves could not name any. Being thus vitiated no accuracy can be claimed for, and no implicit reliance can be placed on the Census return of sects. It can, however, be used to form an estimate of the followers of the various forms of religious beliefs which exist in the State.

Main division of sects.

190. All the Hindu sects returned at the Census fall into two main categories: (1) those who advocate the rival claims of one or other of the great Vedic deities or of Pauranic accretions to the orthodox pantheon such as Durga, etc., and (2) those who deny the regular deities and prohibit idol worship. To the former class belong (*a*) the Shaivas or Smartas, (*b*) Shaktas or Devi Bhaktas, (*c*) Vaishnavas and (*d*) the followers of minor deities, such as Sauryas, Ganpatyas, etc. To the latter class belong the followers of Kabir, Dadu, Santram, Ravisaheb and many others.

191. Of the total Hindu population, 1,454,660 persons or 85·7 per cent. belong to the sects which reverence Vedic and Pauranic deities; and 229,963 persons or 13·5 per cent. are the followers of Kabir and others, who do not reverence Vedic deities, but believe in one impersonal God. The rest are merely Hindus without partiality for any sect. Compared with 1901 the followers of Shaivism and Shaktism have increased by 26·8 and 10·5 per cent. respectively, while Vaishnavism shows a decline of 2 per cent. in its votaries. It is difficult to account for these variations. The statistics being not quite reliable, any inference drawn only from the apparent variations disclosed by the figures, is likely to be misleading. But having regard to the present tendency among the people, a conjecture may be ventured to the effect that the increase in Shaivism may be due to the growing popularity of Shankar's *adwait* philosophy; the increase in the number of Shaktas is doubtless due to the inclusion among Hindus of the members of the early tribes, most of whom are returned as *devi bhaktas* or votaries of Devi, a dubious term which may equally apply to the Pauranic deities as also to their tribal goddesses. The decrease in the number of Vaishnavas is only apparent and due to the coming into existence of new sects which, though really Vaishnavite in belief and practices, are known by the name of new *gurus* or preceptors, who by their fascinating practices and preaching draw around them a large number of people looking upon them as god-incarnate and distinguishing them as their followers. Such was, within the last few years, Kuberdas of Sarsa, whose followers, though really Vaishnavas, are known as Kuberpanthi.

Sect Statistics.

Name of Sect.	Number of followers in 1911.	Number of followers in 1901.	Increase + or Decrease —	Percentage.
I—Believers in Vedic and Pauranic deities...	1,454,660	1,367,957	+ 86,703	+ 6·3
1. Shaiva or Smarta	350,495	276,489	+ 74,006	+ 26·8
2. Shakta	287,547	260,096	+ 27,451	+ 10·5
3. Vaishnav	816,618	831,372	— 14,754	— 1·8
(1) Ramanuji	104,987	18,060	+ 86,927	+ 481·3
(2) Ramanandi	434,679	506,320	— 71,641	— 14·2
(3) Vallabhachari	171,460	183,015	— 11,555	— 6·3
(4) Swaminarayan	53,721	90,871	— 37,150	— 40·8
(5) Miscellaneous & unspecified ...	51,771	33,106	+ 18,665	+ 56·4
II—Non-believers in Vedic and other deities...	229,963	178,979	+ 50,984	+ 28
4. Kabir Panth	34,954	42,626	— 7,672	— 18·5
5. Bij Panth	170,645	119,847	+ 50,798	+ 42·4
6. Parnami	6,854	8,148	— 1,294	— 15·9
7. Dadu Panthi	2,401	...	+ 2,401	...
8. Ramde Pir	8,409	6,098	+ 2,311	+ 38
9. Miscellaneous...	6,700	2,260	+ 4,440	+ 196·5
III—Worshippers of Musalman saints ...	3,630	...	+ 3,630	...
10. Pirana	3,630	...	+ 3,630	...
IV—Sect not returned	8,893	...	+ 8,893	...
Total ...	1,697,146	1,546,936	+ 150,210	+ 9·7

No sectaranism among Hindu Sects.

192. The division of the Gujarat Hindus into sects is not a division into so many water-tight compartments between which no communion is possible. There is no doubt a certain amount of hostility is felt by the leaders and the inner circle of devotees of some sects against the adherents of their rival sects. It is due to this that devout Vaishnavas of the Vallabhachari sect are careful that they do not pronounce the Gujarati word *shivavun*, to sew, lest they may thereby indirectly utter the name of Shiva and show him reverence. The head of the Shaiva sect, the Shankaracharya of Dwarka similarly shows hostility to the Swaminarayan and other Vaishnav leaders and the brawls between them sometimes result in legal notices, apologies and even criminal proceedings. But beyond these, lies the great mass of the people who, while showing special reverence to the god of their sect, their *ishta devta*, worship also all the gods of the Hindu pantheon. A Shaiva Brahman, for instance, visits Shiva's temples and also Vishnu *mandirs* and Mata temples. A Vaishnav makes obeisance to the Rama or Krishna idols of his sect and also visits Mahadev and Mata temples; and similarly *Devi-upasaks* have no objection to reverence Mahadev or Krishna. The Gujarat Hindu is very religious and very tolerant. He worships not only his own and his people's gods, but also shows reverence to Musalman Pirs and

Christian *padris*. He abstains from insulting the religious feelings of others and avoids anything that may bring upon him the wrath of any deity.

No religious preacher of note produced by Gujarat.

193. It is noteworthy that Gujarat has not produced any religious leader of note. *Acharyas* from the south like Shankar, Ramanuja and Vallabh and from the north, like Sahajanand Swami and Kabir have spread their faith in Gujarat. Before Mahomed of Ghazni's invasion on Somnath Patan, Brahmanism as represented by Shankaracharya was supreme in Gujarat. Jainism was confined only to a few Vania castes. The faith of the people in Shaivism was, however, shaken when Mahomed could with impunity break to pieces the famous idol of Somnath Mahadev and carry away its treasures. This was the opportunity, first for Ramanuj and then for each successive Vaishnav preacher from the south or the north. The local sect makers like Kuberdas, Santram, Bhabharam are simply copyists and have been able to secure followers on account of their personal high character. They were exponents of the non-idolatrous principle laid down by Kabir, but their beliefs and practices were tinged with Vaishnavism in one form or another.

Shaivas.

194. The Shaivas or worshippers of Shiva number 350,495 or 21 per cent. of the total Hindu population of the State. They are mostly Brahmans and Gosains, but a large number of Rajputs, Kadwa Kanbis, Bhats and Sutars also belong to this sect. They worship the deity under the name of Rudra, Shiva, Sadashiv, Shankar, Shambhu and Mahadev in their own houses as the family god, as also in the temples, which are to be found in almost every village. Shiva is a god whose anger is dreaded and whose favour is propitiated. His heaven is supposed to be the *Kailasa* where he dwells with his wife Parvati (also called Durga, Kali, Uma, Bhavani, etc.), and his countless troops of servants (*ganas*). Shiva is sometimes represented in sculptures and paintings with five faces, (*Panchanana*), sometimes with one face and with three eyes. He is commonly represented with a moon's crescent on his fore-head, a serpent round his neck, and a second necklace of skulls, with numerous other serpents above his person. On the top of his knotted hair he bears the Ganges, the rush of which he intercepted in its descent from Vishnu's foot, that the earth might not be crushed by the weight of the falling stream. His complexion is sometimes white from the reflection of the snows of Kailasa, sometimes dark from his identification with the dark destroyer, time (*Kâla*). His throat is blue from the stain of the deadly poison which would have destroyed the world, had not Shiva, in compassion for the human race undertaken to drink it up, upon its production from the churning of the ocean. He rides on a white bull, called *Nandi*, stone or plaster images of which are often placed outside his shrines. As Shiva is constantly engaged in battle with mighty demons, he carries a three-pronged trident (*trishul*), a bow, a thunder-bolt (*vajra*), etc. He holds in his hands a noose for binding his enemies and a kind of drum called *damaru* which he uses as a musical instrument to keep time in dancing. But, though, Shiva is thus depicted in sculptures and paintings, in Shaiva shrines he is worshipped under the impersonal symbol of the phallus or *lingum*, for he is supposed to reproduce after destruction, and as such is worshipped as if he were the creator. The *ling* or *bana* is of stone, pyramidal in shape and from three inches to several feet high. The chief of these emblems are called *svayambhu* or self-created and *jyotir* or luminous. The essential doctrine of Shaivism is the existence of a personal deity, the one existent and universal soul without a second or *adwait* and the unity of the divine or universal soul *Parmatma* with the individual soul or *Jivatma*. All nature is but a manifestation of the universal soul, takes its origin from that soul, and is eventually absorbed therein. In order to impress this doctrine upon his mind the Shivite is required by his religion to mutter every now and then, *Shivoham*, that is 'I am Shiva'. The daily worship is simple and consists in offering *chandan*, water and the leaves of bili (Aegle marmelos) to the *ling*. But on *Shivratris*, dark fourteenth of each month, and especially on that of Magh, called *Maha Shivratri*, the god is invested with a brass or silver mask and in winter the *ling* is decked with refrigerated clarified butter in ornamental shapes called *ghina kamal*. In cases of anxiety

or of serious illness and evil planetary influence prayers called *rudri* and *mritunjay jap* (death conquering prayer) are offered to Shiva in his temples. This consists in Brahmans pouring water over his *ling* and reciting the *Rudradhyaya*, or panegyric in honour of *Rudra*. It is recited 11 times in *Rudri*, 121 times in *Laghu Rudra*, 131 times in the *Maha Rudra* and 14,641 times in the *Ati Rudra*.

Shiva worship has continued from the earliest times to be the cult of the Brahmans. Towards the close of the eighth century, it was extended and adopted by Shankaracharya to popular worship. Shiva's terrible aspects as *Rudra, Bhairav, Ugra* and *Aghor* easily adapted him to the religion of fear and propitiation prevalent among the non-Aryan races. He thus became the deity of the highest and the lowest of castes.

Shankaracharya established in India four seats where he installed his pupils as *acharyas* or religious heads and their successive pupils still occupy the *gadis*. One of these called *sharda pith*, or throne of learning, is situated at Dwarka in this State and is endowed by His Highness the Gaekwad who sanctions the appointment of every new pontiff, called Shankaracharya. The chief duty of the Shankaracharya is to preach and disseminate the doctrines of the Vedic religion. He is an authority in religious questions for the followers of Shaivism in Gujarat.

Shaivas use a traverse streak on their fore-head as a religious mark. They also put on a necklace of *rudraksha* (Elaecarpus ganitris) berry, and use *rudraksha* hand rosaries.

Shâktâs.

195. 287,547 Hindus or 17 per cent. of the total Hindu population returned themselves as Shâktâs or Devi *bhakts*. They are found in all the Prants. The Shaktas give prominence to the worship of the female counterpart of Shiva, the goddesses Devi, Durga and Kali, all consorts of Shiva. This worship of *shakti* or energy is inculcated in the Tantras and in the Brahma Vaivart, Skand and Kalika Purans. A section of the Markandeya Puran called the Devi Mahatmya or Chandipath is devoted to the praise of Durga. It is read in Mata temples to avert the wrath of the goddess as also to secure happiness and prosperity even by those who call themselves Shaivas or Vaishnavas. Songs in honour of the *Matas* are also sung throughout Gujarat, especially during the *navratra* or nine nights sacred to Matas in the bright half of Aso.

Though not so returned in the Census, Shaktas are said to be divided into two classes *Dakshinachari* or right-hand worshippers and *Vamachari* or left-hand worshippers. The *Dakshinacharis* worship their goddess publicly and with the usual Vedic or Pauranic ritual. They do not allow blood sacrifices. Worship is restricted to Shiva's consort and to Shiva only as identified with her. The *Vamacharis* make the Tantras their Veda, and adopt a ritual which holds the Vedas, Smritis and Purans in contempt. Besides Shiva's wife, they worship Matrikas, Yoginis, the evil doing Dakinis and Sakinis and Shiva in his form of Bhairav. At their chief ceremony which is performed secretly at night, a circle is formed composed of men and women without respect to caste or relationship. The five *makars* or *ms* are required., viz., *madya* wine, *mansa* flesh, *matsya* fish, *mudra* parched grain and *maithun* sexual union. The goddess is represented by a woman in the flesh. Wine and flesh are first offered to the woman goddess and then distributed among the votaries, orgies follow, and the ceremony called *shrichakra* or *purnabhishek* or full initiation ends the rite. A branch of *vammargis* found in North Gujarat and Kathiawad is called *Kanchalipanth* or bodice sect which holds that promiscuous intercourse between the sexes on certain days confers religious merit.

Shaktas generally make two perpendicular vermillion marks on their forehead or a red streak upto the middle of the forehead, with a round red *chanla* at the root of the nose. The division of the sect into *Dakshinachari* and *Vamachari* and of the latter into *Kanchalipanth* has not been returned in the census but there can be no doubt that they have many secret votaries who join the faith in the high hopes held out in the Tantric texts.

196. 104,987 persons are followers of the Ramanuji sect, so called from the name of the founder Ramanuj, a Tamil Brahman, who flourished in the twelfth century. Against Shankaracharya's *adwait* or strict "monism", Ramanuj set up a theory called *Vishishtadwaita* or 'qualified monism' maintaining (1) that individual souls are not essentially one with the supreme soul though he is their source, and hence the soul after salvation enters into a relation of perfect heavenly service to him and (2) that the supreme is not purely abstract being, but possesses real *qualities* of goodness and the like, infinite in degree. The Ramanujis worship Vishnu as Narayan and his bride Laxmi or Shri.) The special marks of a Ramanuji are a close-shaven mustache, a *tulsi* or sweet basil rosary, and two vertical or slanting lines on the forehead of white clay, a perpendicular red streak for Laxmi in the middle with a horizontal white clay line connecting the three across the root of the nose, the whole from one to two inches wide and representing Vishnu's throne. (There are two main divisions of the sect, *Ten-gala* or southern school and *Vadagala* or northern school which differ chiefly in externals. The northern school accepts the Sanskrit Veda. The southern has compiled a Veda of its own called *Nalayira* or "The four thousand verses written in Tamil.")

Ramanuji sect.

An important difference of doctrine, caused by different views of the nature of the soul's dependence on Vishnu, separates the two parties. The view taken by the Vadagalas is called the "monkey theory." The soul, say they, lays hold of the Supreme Being by its own free will, act, and effort, just as the young monkey clings to its mother. The Tengalas hold what is called the "cat-hold theory." The human soul remains helpless until acted on by the Supreme Being, just as the kitten remains helpless until transported by the mother cat.

The two divisions are distinguished by different marks on the forehead, to which they attach great importance. The Vadagalas contend that the mark on the forehead ought to represent the right foot of Vishnu, while the Tengalas contend that equal reverence is due to both feet. The Tengalas draw the whole line half down the nose to represent the lotus throne of Vishnu. Both divisions agree in branding the emblems of Vishnu—the disc and conch shell on their breasts, shoulders and arms. Both are noted for the strict privacy with which they eat and even prepare their meals.

197. The Ramanandi sect has 434,679 followers mostly of the lower castes. It was founded by Ramanand, a disciple of Ramanuj who flourished at Benares about the beginning of the 14th century. The only point on which Ramanandis differ from Ramanujis is that they do not observe privacy in preparing and taking food, on which Ramanuj laid great stress. It is said that Ramanand having travelled extensively over India returned to one of the monasteries of his sect, where some priest raised the objection that in his wanderings he could not possibly have observed the rule of the Ramanuj sect requiring meals to be strictly private. On these grounds, Ramanand was required to eat apart from the rest of the brethren. In resentment he founded a new sect and to show his contempt for caste distinctions freely admitted into it men of all castes, even the lowest. It is for this reason that even Dheds, Bhangis and Chamars are followers of this sect, along with Brahmans, Vanias and artizan classes. Ramanand inculcated the worship of Vishnu as Rama with Sita and Laxman. The initiatory verse is ***Shri Rama*** and the salutation *Jaya Sita **Rama***. The forehead mark is like that of Ramanujis made of ***gopichandan***, but the red vertical streak is narrower.

Ramanandi sect.

198. Another strong current of Vishnuism arose from Vallabhacharya, a Tailanga Brahman born in 1478. In theory he had much affinity with Ramanuja but in practical religion, he laid far more stress upon the myths of Krishna's childhood and amours, narrated in the tenth Chapter of the Bhagwat Puran, in which he is represented as Bala Gopala, the cowherd boy who indulged in amorous dalliance with the frail milkmaids of Brindraban. Philosophically, Vallabha held that the human soul (***Jivatma***) was a spark from the divine essence (***Parmatma***) and though separated from, was yet identical with it. Unlike his sect-forming

Vallabhachari sect.

predecessors, Vallabh discountenanced all mortifications of the flesh, maintaining that the body should be reverenced and not ill-used. Building on this philosophical basis, Vallabh introduced elements of pleasure and enjoyment in divine worship rejecting the austerity and hardship of the other sects and called his cult *pushtimarga* or creed of spiritual nourishment. He found many adherents especially among the Brahman, Kanbi and other middle classes in Gujarat. In this State, the followers of the Vallabhachari sect number 171,460, or 10 per cent. of the total Hindu population, or 21 per cent. of the total number of Vaishnavas of all sects. Vallabha married and enjoined marriage and worldly life to his successors who are now known as Gosaiji Maharaj or Gosaiji Vallabhakul. There are seven seats or *gadis* of this sect each of which is presided over by the lineal descendants of the founder. They are at Ahmedabad and Surat in Gujarat, Gokul, Mathura and Kankroli in the United Provinces, and Kotah and Nathadwara in Rajputana. There are subordinate establishments in Bombay, Baroda, and most of the larger towns, where they are called *haveli* or palace.

Both mental and physical worship are prescribed for the followers of this creed. Mentally the image of Krishna is to be imagined as existing before the mind's eye and to be worshipped without rites or ceremonies. Physically the actual human image of Krishna is to be worshipped with pomp and ceremony. In their *mandirs*, temples, which are built like ordinary houses, without porch or spire, images of Shrikrishna in various forms are set on raised platforms and homage is paid by devotees at fixed hours every day. On holidays, the image is profusely decorated seated on a richly carved dais or swung in fancy cradles of glass, ivory, or wood decked with flowers. Seven daily services or *darsans* are held. Thousands of devotees, males and females, flock to the Gosaiji temples and there are many who do not take their food if they have not been able to get a glimpse, *jhanki*, of the Thakorji. The first darsan is called *mangala* and takes place at about six or half past six in the morning when the image is shown as rising from bed. The rest are :—(2) *sangar* at 8 A. M. when the image is richly attired ; (3) *rajbhoga* at noon when the image is shown as taking a meal after returning from cattle tending ; (4) *utthapan* at 3 in the afternoon, when the image is shown as rising from repose ; (5) *bhogasun* at 4 P. M. the afternoon luncheon ; (6) *sandhya* or *arti* at about sun-down ; and (7) *sen* or repose for the night after lamp light.

Initiation of a novice begins in childhood. The first instruction begins between the second and fifth year. The novice is taken to the Maharaja who repeats the formula *Shrikrishna Sharanam Mama*, *i. e.*, Shri Krishna is my refuge. After the child is made to repeat the initiatory prayer, the Maharaja passes round his neck a basil (*tulsi*) *kanthi* or rosary. A later and more important initiation, takes place after the eleventh or twelfth year and at or before marriage for females. After the second initiation, the votary is supposed to consecrate his *tan* (body), *man* (mind) and *dhan* (property) to the deity. The ceremony is called *Brahma sambandha* or union with the supreme being and enjoying a total surrender of self to the deity. In practice, this principle sometimes degenerates into great depravity, the worshippers regarding the Gosaiji Maharajas as incarnations of the god, pay to them the service which they believe to be due to him, including sometimes the *jus primæ noctis.*

The Vallabhachari brow-mark consists of two red perpendicular lines converging in a semi-circle at the root of the nose. Though the sect has no sadhus, some of the followers take the *samarpan* or dedicatory vow and do not eat food cooked for them by others. They are called *marjadi*. They do not ordinarily eat in metal vessels but use leaf-plates and obtain their drinking water in canvass covered receptacles.

Swaminarayan sect.

199. The epicurean principles of the Vallabhachari sect led to the reform of the Vaishnav church early in the nineteenth century by Sahajanand Swami, a man of deep religious feeling and high morality whose sect known as the Swaminarayan sect, is at present of great importance in Gujarat and has a large number of

followers among Brahman, Kanbi, Bhavsar, Charan, Darji, Ghanchi, Gola, Kachhia, Kathi, Koli, Luhar, Mali, Rajput, Salat, Sathawara, Soni and Sutar castes. Sahajanand was born in A. D. 1780 at the village of Chhapai, eight miles from Ayodhya in the United Provinces. His parents dying when he was 11 years old, he became a recluse and knew the Bhagwatgita and Vishnu Sahasra Nama by heart. In 1799 he began to associate with a body of Ramanandi Sadhus and in 1800 was initiated with the name of Sahajanand. He began to preach the Vishishtadwait faith of Ramanuja with such effect that the then head of the Ramanuja body appointed him his successor. During his rambles, he visited Gujarat several times, and being offended at some of the practices of the Vallabhachari sect, preached chastity and purity of soul to be the key-note of his religion. By his preaching and his own exemplary life, he succeeded in making many converts, chiefly among the lower classes. When he knew that he had gained a sufficient ground, he boldly asserted that he himself was an incarnation of Krishna, born to restore the Vaishnav faith to its former purity. He died in 1830 at Gadhada in Kathiawad where his *padukas*, footmarks, are worshipped. Being a celibate, he adopted two of his nephews, one of whom was installed at Ahmedabad and the other at Vadtal. These descendants are the hereditary Acharyas of the sect. Though the Acharyaship is hereditary, it requires a confirmation by a council of four Brahmacharis, four Sadhus, and four laymen, *satsangis* before accession. If the Acharya does not behave properly he may at any time be deposed. Such a course had to be taken at the Vadtal *gadi* about four years ago, for the first time in the history of the sect.

The tenets of the Swaminarayan sect are embodied in a book called *Vachanamrit*, nectar of precepts, which is a treatise on all branches of religious philosophy. Their authoritative works are the Vedas ; the Vedanta Sutra of Vyasa, as interpreted by Ramanuja ; the Bhagwat Purana ; three chapters of Mahabharat, *viz.*, Vishnu Sahasra Nama, Bhagwatgita and Vidur Niti ; and Vasudeva Mahatmya, a chapter of the Skanda Puran. The book which is usually read by the followers of the sect in their daily prayers is called *Shikshapatrika*, or book of precepts embodying practical ethics. It prohibits the destruction of animal life, promiscuous intercourse with the other sex, use of animal food and intoxicating drinks and drugs, theft and robbery, blasphemy, false accusation, caste pollution, &c.

The ceremony of initiation begins with the novice offering a palmful of water near the feet of Acharya saying, " I give over to Swaminarayan my mind, body, wealth and sins of (all) births (*man, tan, dhan ane janamna pap*)." He is then given the sacred formula, *Shri Krishna twam gatir mam, i. e.*, " Shri Krishna, thou art my refuge." The novice then pays at least half a rupee to the Acharya. ordinarily every follower is expected to present to his Acharya a twentieth of his yearly income, while the more devout is expected to pay a tenth. Before taking his food, he is enjoined to worship an image of Sahajanand Swami which he keeps in his house along with the *Shiksha Patrika*. He also worships his footprints on a piece of cloth and tells his rosary beads repeating his name. There is a Swaminarayan temple in almost every important village which is attended either in the morning or in the evening, or at both times, by all the followers. There are separate passages in the temples for women and also separate reading and preaching halls for them.

The distinguishing mark which followers of the sect make on their forehead consists in a vertical streak of *gopichandan* clay or sandal with a round red powder mark in the middle. They also wear a necklace of basil beads.

Minor Vaishnav sub-sects.

200. Among the minor Vaishnav sub-sects may be mentioned Radhavallabhi founded in the sixteenth century by one Haribansh of Bindraban near Gokul. The Radhavallabhis give more importance to Krishna's mistress than other Vaishnavas, and worship her with Krishna as her *vallabh* or lover. Another minor Vaishnav sub-sect, with followers chiefly in the Kadi District, is Gopinath Panth, founded by one Gopinath, a Ramanuji Visnagara Nagar, in the fifteenth or sixteenth century. Gopinath was a great devotee of Shri Rama, a tendency for whose worship he

manifested from his early childhood. He used to keep images of Shri Rama and Sita at his house, and there used to offer prayers and sing songs to them every day. He showed many miracles to the people of Visnagar, where he had a large *mandir* built for him by the Babi, the then reigning chief at Visnagar. The Babi was once imprisoned by the Raja of Patan and was being removed there by the Raja's men bound in chains, when Gopinath is reported to have said to those men: "Why are you taking him in this way? He deserves to be and will be taken there with great pomp, seated in a *myana* (or palanquin), and attended by a great number of followers." The bearers did not mind his words but took away the Babi forcibly. When they were a *kos* from Patan, they were astonished to find a large body of armed men, with a palanquin and tom toms and such other pomp, sent from Patan to receive the Babi with honour and dignity. The Babi on his return to Visnagar inquired after Gopinath, who lived at Lalpur, and sent for him from there. The Babi then ordered a temple to be built at Visnagar for Gopinath, where he afterwards stayed for the remainder of his life. He was greatly respected by many who took him to be an incarnation of Rama and thus his followers began to style themselves Gopinath Panthis; and the creed was named Gopinath Panth.

Nearly three thousand persons reported that they were worshippers of *tulsi*, the basil plant, sacred to Vishnu. On inquiry they appear to be some Dheds and Bhangis in the Baroda and Navsari Districts, who not being allowed to enter Vaishnu's temples, worship at home his emblem and call themselves followers of *tulsi panth* by which of course they mean that they are Vaishnavas.

Surya Upasak.

201. The Surya Upasakas are the worshippers of the Sun (*Surya Narayan*). Their manner of worship is as follows:—Every morning after taking a bath, the devotee stands facing the sun and, looking up towards him, pours out a potful of water on the ground, supposing that the water thus poured out reaches the sun as his humble offering. He then throws up a little red powder (*kanku*) or sandalwood paste towards the sky; and, in the end, takes a few rounds bowing to the sun every time when a round is finished.

There are no special observances or religious holidays among this sect, and they have also no preceptor (*guru*). Its followers are principally the Suryavanshi Rajputs, Kathis and the like. Some of them eat flesh and drink spirituous liquors. They adore the Tulsi plant and the *pipal* tree sometimes and hold the cow in reverence.

Non-idolatrous sects.

202. All the sect-makers from Shankaracharya to Swaminarayan were Brahmans and men of learning. In Kabir and others of his type, we have men from the lower castes, unacquainted with Sanscrit showing a repulsion for caste and idol worship, seceding from Vaishnavism, and founding non-idolatrous sects on a basis of equality between man and man. They were greatly affected by the example of Islam in their disregard for caste and idol worship. They also promulgated a high moral code, declaring that life was a sacred gift of God and that the blood of men or animals ought never to be shed by his creatures. Great stress is laid on truthfulness and adoration is allowed to be paid to Vishnu or Rama, not as idols, but as names of one God.

Kabir Panthi Sect.

203. The Kabir Panthi Sect which has 34,954 followers in the State is a branch of the Ramanandis, and was founded in about 1380-1420 A. D. by Kabir, (Arabic, the great) a low caste Hindu or Musalman of Upper India who by force of genius, earnest faith and sincerity of conviction rose to be one of the greatest religious reformers of India. Kabir's birth and parentage are shrouded in mystery. It is said in the *Bhakta Mala* that he was the son of a Brahman virgin widow who was unconsciously blessed with a son by Ramanand. She exposed the child which was taken and adopted by a Musalman weaver or *Jhulaiya* which is the name by which Kabir calls himself in his *bhajans*. He was a disciple of Ramanand and is said to have originally been a worshipper of the deity endowed with form

and attributes as Rama Krishna. Subsequently he rose a step higher, and under the influence of Islam preached the doctrine of a god-without form and attributes. He tried to unite, in one common faith, both Hindus and Musalmans alike, discarding the worship of all forms of the deity and the observance of Hindu or Musalman rites and ceremonies. His faith prescribes no initiatory *mantra*, no fixed form of sectarian salutation, no distinctive forehead mark and no rosary. As a sample of his teaching, the following translation may be quoted from Prof. Campbell Oman's book, p. 124 :—

"To Ali and Rama, we owe our existence and should therefore show similar tenderness to all that live : of what avail is it to shave your head, prostrate yourself on the ground or immerse your body in the stream ? Whilst you shed blood, you call yourself pure and boast of virtues that you never display. Of what benefit is cleaning your mouth, counting your beads, performing ablutions and vowing yourself in temples, when whilst you mutter your prayers or journey to Macca or Madina, deceitfulness is in your heart ? The Hindu fasts every eleventh day, the Musalman during the Ramazan ; who formed the remaining months and days that you should venerate but one ? If the creator dwells in tabernacles, whose residence is the universe ? Who has beheld Rama seated amongst the images or found him at the shrine to which the pilgrim has directed his steps ? The City of Hara is to the east, that of Ali to the west, but explore your own heart, for there are both Rama and Karim."

The tenets of the faith are embodied in voluminous works which are mostly in dialogues in different languages, the authors being Kabir and his immediate disciples. They are collectively called the *khas grantha* and consist of some twenty volumes which are preserved at the head-quarters of the sect, the Kabir Chaura at Benares.

The followers of Kabir in this State belong mostly to the Luhana, Kanbi, Soni, Sutar, Kumbhar, Luhar, Darji, Khatri, Kachhia, Ghanchi, Bhavsar, Hajam, Dhobi and Koli castes. The sect has temples in most of the important towns where the devotees adore Kabir's *gadi* and offer flowers to his books. On full moon nights, they sit beside these books, singing *bhajans* or devotional songs till dawn.

Bij Panth or Margi Sect.

204. The Bij Panth or Margi sect is said to have been founded about 500 years ago by one Ugamsi at Benares. Bij Panthis believe in an impersonal god holding that the human and the eternal soul are one. The object of worship is the flame of a lamp as an emblem of the formless but all intelligent essence. Their principal temples in Gujarat are at Dudhrej near Wadhwan in Kathiawad, at Tarabh in the Visnagar Mahal, and at Chaveli and Pipal in the Chansma Mahal of the Kadi Division in this State. Their *gurus* or preceptors are generally monks of the *Atit* order. At present the Atit Bava who presides in the temple at Tarabh is their chief leader and preceptor, and makes new *chelas* or followers. Potters, Barbers, Atits, Rajputs, Rabaris, Charans, Bhats, and such other low castes are members of this creed and altogether number 170,645 in this State. No people from the higher castes or from the degraded and unclean ones join it. Their principal religious holiday is the 2nd day of the first half of every month, on which they join together and sing *bhajans* or hymns. The Rabari followers do not sell milk on that day, nor do they prepare curds out of it ; but either use it themselves or give it away in charity. The special and peculiar custom among the followers of this creed is that of calling a meeting of their members for the *Patha*. This meeting is generally held at the house of one of the followers in the dead of night, with closed doors ; and those only who have been served with previous invitations are allowed to attend it. A *Kotwal*, or guard, is placed outside the door of the room in which the meeting is held to watch and take care that no stranger or intruder gets in. In a spacious room or hall, persons of both sexes are gathered together. In its centre a *bajath* or *patla* (square wooden seat) is placed and covered with red cloth. Four small heaps of corn of different kinds, such as wheat, rice, *bajri* and pulse, are arranged on the four corners of it having images of Ramde's horse, Ganpati, Hanuman, a *ling* and an image of Shakti in the centre. Five lamps fed with ghee are then placed over these heaps and ignited by the Atit Bava or Guru, after repeating certain incantations over them. The votaries sit round the blaze, feed it with ghee and sing *bhajans* or hymns. At midnight an offering of sweets is made to the flame and a lighted lamp waved round it. If a stranger wishes to be admitted as a member of

this creed, he is first asked to stay out of the room, where the *Patha* meeting is held, by the Kotwal, who announces him first to the Atit Bava or *guru*, who in his turn inquires of the persons sitting round about him as to the character of the stranger; and when some one from the meeting or company stands security for him or recognizes him properly, the Bava asks him some questions from the inside. If the stranger answers them satisfactorily from out of the room, the Kotwal is told to bring him in, blindfolded. Then the stranger is made to take an oath that he would dutifully keep the pledge taken by him then for life; and when he promises to do so in the presence of all gathered there, by sitting before the central burning lamp on the *patla* and vowing in its name, the covering over his eyes is removed and he is given the *kanthi* or necklace and made a *chela*. Afterwards, he gives the Bava or *guru* some *bhet* or present, generally in cash, and distributes sweetmeats to the company after offering it first to the lamp, as *prasad*. It is strictly conditional among these people to admit that man or woman only, among their followers, who can afford to leave money enough for holding a meeting of the *Patha* for inviting all the members at the time of his or her funeral obsequies.

Ramde Pir Sect.

205. The followers of Ramde Pir (8,409) worship the image of a horse called Ramde Pir. The legend about Ramde Pir is that Ajmalsing Tuar, a Marwar Rajput, went to the temple of Dwarka to solicit a son. The deity gave him a son who was named Ramde Pir. As enjoined by the deity, the favourite charger of Ramde Pir is the horse now being worshipped along with his *padukas* or foot impressions. The principal temple belonging to this creed is at Ranuja in Marwar, which is, in consequence, considered to be a very sacred place. There are in this temple the *paglas* (foot-impressions) of Ramde Pir and four horses of metal representing the four principal *yugas*, or cycles. There are no particular forms or ceremonies in this sect. Their worship consists in simply burning incense and keeping a lamp fed with either ghee or oil burning before their deity for some time every day. A person wishing to be admitted into this creed has first to attend the big fair held in the temple of Ramdevji at Ranuja, on the *Bhadrapad Sud Agiarash*, and there pay Rs. 1-4-0, as his humble offering to the deity; he then gets in return one of the many horses of rags lying there, as the pious offer of the devotees. He has also to buy a silver pair of *paglas* of Ramdevji which are sold in the shops at the fair. Both of these articles he takes home and worships them daily. Hindus of all castes, high and low, including the depressed classes are admitted into this creed.

Paranami Sect.

206. The Paranami sect which has 6,854 followers among Kanbi, Vania, Rajput, Bhat, Sutar, Darji, Gola, Koli and other castes is said to have been founded by one Devchand (A. D. 1582) of Amarkot in Sindh, who was much devoted to the study of the Bhagvat—Puran and travelled to Jamnagar where he consecrated a temple to Radha Krishna. Devchand's chief disciple was Meheraj Thakore, after whom the sect is also called Meheraj Panth. Meheraj then instituted a seat at Surat, and after travelling to Delhi and other places finally settled at Jharna Parna. The chief feature of this sect is that no idol or image should be worshipped, but only Meheraj's Book of Faith. In spite of this canon, devout Paranamis now worship Krishna as Bal Gopal. In some temples, ornaments are so arranged as to look like an idol from a distance, while in others, images of Radhâkrishna are now-a-days kept and worshipped.

Ravi Panth.

207. The Ravi Panth was founded by one Bhow or Ravi Saheb, a follower of Kabir, about 1750 A. D. Except that they adore Ravi Saheb as their spiritual lord, the Ravi Panthis are now Vaishnavas to all intents and purposes. The founder is said to have worked miracles in Baroda and was therefore looked upon as an incarnation of god. He died at Serkhi, in the Baroda Taluka, where his descendants have built a *mandir* over his tomb and have placed therein images of Rama, Laxman and Sita whom they worship every day. Some members of the Luhana, Bhatia, Koli, and Soni castes are followers of this sect. The sect has *âchâryâs* who invest their followers with *kanthis* or necklets.

208. The Uda Panth was founded by one Gopaldas about 300 years ago. He preached the possibility of final emancipation by *jap* or devout contemplation of the all-pervading spirit and held that future births were necessary for fulfilling unaccomplished desires. Its followers are called *Uda* who are mostly of the Kanbi caste. They mark a part of their forehead and nose with white clay, pour water on the *tulsi* plant and worship their sacred Book of Faith. In the evening they bow to the cushion on which the book is kept, wave a lighted lamp and chant hymns. They are very scrupulous about their food which they cook with their own hands. The *Mahant* of their sect is selected by a council of five. He ties a *tulsi* necklet to the novice, fixes days for marriage and funeral feasts, and punishes disobedience by expulsion. He also officiates at marriages. Udas do not perform funeral obsequies. They carry their dead with tom-tom and music.

Uda Panth.

209. The Santaram Panth, founded about a hundred years ago, prescribes no distinctive marks and no necklet. It admits within its fold people of all castes, creeds and persuasions, who are asked to conform to a few simple rules of every-day morality. Its head-quarters are at Nadiad in the Kaira District, and it has temples at Baroda and Padra in this State. The devotees hold the *gadi* of the founder in great respect and keep a butter-fed lamp burning near it. In memory of the founder, a fair is held at the head-quarters every year on the full moon of *Magh* and the day is passed in chanting *bhajans* or hymns in his praise. The mode of salutation is *je maharaj*. Each pontiff nominates his successor from among the Sadhus, who are not allowed begging and are only a few in number. Any person who has severed his connection with the world can become a Sadhu.

Santaram Panth.

210. Dadu Panth was founded about the close of the 16th century by one Dadu, a cotton-cleaner of Ahmedabad. The doctrines of the sect are the same as those of Shankaracharya's Vedant School, but Dadu, finding them too abstract for his followers, preached a sort of non-idolatrous sect of Ram worshippers.

Dadu Panth.

211. The brief account of the non-idolatrous sects given in the preceding paras shows that Hindu sects have a tendency to relapse into orthodoxy as soon as the zeal which inspired their earlier adherents has grown cold. At first, idolatry is altogether discarded. Then a beginning is made with the worship of the *guru's gadi* or *pothi*; then worship of Krishna as Bal Gopal is at first tolerated and afterwards actively preached. And, finally, images of Radha Krishna are installed, as at Serkhi, by the followers of Ravi Saheb; or ornaments are so arranged as to look like an idol, from a distance, as with the Paranamis.

Tendency to relapse into Orthodoxy.

212. Just as after the advent of the Musalmans, Hindu religious reformers like Kabir were greatly influenced by the monotheistic ideas of that religion, so in more recent times two movements known as Brahmo Samaj and Arya Samaj have been formed under the inspiration of Western education and Western thought. Many people belong to one or other of the great religions of the world, such as Hinduism, Muhammedanism, Christianity, etc. But there are a few who frame for themselves what are called *eclectic* systems. They do not attach themselves to any particular sect but select from the opinions and principles of each what they think to be true and good. Such is the Brahmo Samaj of Bengal which has only 6 followers in this State. And the same may be said to a certain extent about the Arya Samaj which had only 50 followers in 1901, but now claims no less than 598. As these movements are likely to attract more persons in the near future, especially from the educated class, a brief account of their rise and progress may be found interesting.

Recent theistic movement.

213. The Brahmo Samaj is a theistic movement founded by Raja Rama Mohan Roy about eighty years ago. It aims at purging Hinduism of its idolatrous and superstitious practices and provides a reformed religion for educated Hindus. At present it is divided into three sections, the *Adi* or "original," the *Navavidhan* or "New Dispensation,"

Brahmo Samaj.

and the *Sadharan* or "common" Samaj, but all alike believe in the unity of the Godhead, the brotherhood of men and direct communion with God in spirit without the intervention of any mediator. The differences which exist are ritualistic and social rather than religious. The Adi Samaj or the oldest section is the most conservative. While discarding idolatrous forms, it follows as closely as possible the rites of Hinduism and draws its inspiration solely from the religious books of the Hindus, especially the Upnishadas and not from the Bible or Koran. Inter-caste marriages are not allowed. In other respects, the restrictions of the caste system sit lightly on the members of the Samaj, but they are particular to style themselves Hindus ; and before the Census of 1891, they had submitted a memorial intimating their desire to be entered as Theistic Hindus and not as Brahmos.

The *Navavidhan* Samaj, or church of the New Dispensation, is also known as the *Bharatvarshya.* Brahmo Samaj was founded by Keshav Chandra Sen. It is more eclectic and has assimilated what it considers just, not only in the Shastras, but also in the religious teachings of Christianity, Budhism and Islam. Inter-caste marriages, though not generally disapproved of, are rare.

The *Sadharan* Brahmo Samaj is the most advanced of all the three. It relies, like the Navavidhan, on the teachings of all religious systems, but is more uncompromising in its disapproval of ritual and set forms of worship. It rejects altogether the system of caste. It is strongly opposed to the *parda* system, gives women a liberal education and allows them an equal voice in all matters of Church Government. It freely permits inter-caste marriages.

Arya Samaj.

214. Like Brahmo Samaj, Arya Samaj is a form of Theistic Hinduism founded by Swami Dayanand Saraswati about the year 1875. On finishing his Vedic studies, he was struck to find that the Vedas do not sanction idol worship, man worship, incarnation of god in man, animal sacrifice, child marriage enforced widowhood, caste system based on birth, sole monopoly of the Vedic study by the born Brahmans, showy and meaningless ceremonials, miracles, ***mritak shradha***, blind faith and many other superstitions which are generally known among the Hindus by the name of Dharma. He set in right earnest to preach the monotheism of the Vedas taking as his motto "*Ekam eva adwitiyam*" (there is but one Being without a second). He wrote his well-known discourses in a book-form called the "Satyarth Prakash" (Light of Truth). He never divorced reason from religion but preached that what is irrational is not religion but superstition.

He framed the 10 principles of the Arya Samaj, in which he inculcated on his followers the mental worship of the One All-pervading, Intelligent cause of the Universe and the importance of the study of the Vedas. He made the Arya Samaj not only the "Vedic Church" for the Hindus but for all human beings, as is evident from his sixth principle, which says that the primary object of the Arya Samaj is to do good to the world.

The theology of the Arya Samaj is based on the Vedas and the Upanishadas. It upholds the performance of *hom,* on the scientific grounds of the purification of the atmosphere. In their *homs,* Arya Samajists burn in strong fire sweet-scented vegetable disinfectants with clarified butter and saffron. It preaches the *karmic* theory or in the words of Mr. Herbert Spencer, the law of "Action and Reaction" and asserts the supremacy of self-exertion over fate. Sanyasis, Mahatma Sadhus, preachers, teachers, donors and unselfish workers are held in respect, but no man can be the special favourite, messenger or incarnation of God according to the Arya Samaj.

The Arya Samaj holds merits or demerits of a person as the only constituting element of his or her social position or "*varna,*" but not his or her birth. It does not believe in caste or its divisions. But its followers in this State do in practice follow their caste restrictions.

One of the best service rendered by the Arya Samaj is in directing charity to its right course. It has been able by utilizing public charity to establish nearly 200 important educational and philanthropic institutions in India. It is a strong advocate of female education and has started nearly 100 girls' schools, including one female college, in various parts of the country. For encouraging the study of Sanskrit, Hindi and modern sciences, the Arya Samaj has established over India eight *gurukuls,* one college for males, six high and seven secondary schools and a number of Sanskrit *patha shalas.* There are ten orphanages started by the Samaj for feeding and educating helpless boys and girls. There are six Widows' Homes which are doing good service in relieving the wretched lot of widows in this country. It has established many Sanskrit, Hindi, and English libraries. It has got good many *upadeshakas* (missionaries) to carry on its mission, which is social and religious and has nothing to do with politics.

The members of the Arya Samaj are divided into three groups. To the first group belong the Sanyasis and the Sadhus who have taken a vow of renunciation and are working for the cause of the Samaj. To the second group belong the Pandits, *upadeshakas,* lecturers, authors, donors, heads of various provincial educational institutions and members of the Pratinidhi Sabhas who are generally *grahasthas* or *brahmacharis.* To the third group belong the office holders of the various local Samajis, the heads of the local institutions and local donors in each Province.

3.—Hindu Sadhus or Ascetics.

Ascetic worship.

215. No account of the religious life and beliefs of the Hindus would be complete without even a brief description of the *Sadhus* or ascetics whose *seva* or service forms an important part of their daily devotion. Sadhus under various names and in the guise of one or other of the existing sects are to be found not only in the local monasteries at Dwarka, Sidhpur, Karnali and other sacred places and the temples of the various sects in all the towns, but are also to be found roaming about in villages, either singly or in large parties under their respective leaders. Except during the four months of the rainy season, they are on a move either in their own district or on a pilgrimage to the innumerable sacred places. Sadhus command the respect and even the superstitious veneration of the people, who believe that they are possessed of supernatural power for good or evil. Pious Hindus desirous of securing the blessing of heaven have, in most of the towns and larger villages, established *sadavrats* or charity houses, where any *Sadhu* can get some food. To the *Maharaj or Bapji,* as Sadhus are called, coming as mendicant near their door, Hindu females readily give a handful of *lot* (flour) or cooked food if it can be acceptable to him. Those who can afford show a willingness to minister to Sadhus' wants under the belief that it secures great religious merit. Many humbly invite them to partake of a meal at their place or offer to provide *sidha* for the whole of their *jund* or body, when they are passing through their village. So great is the implicit faith placed by the people in Sadhus, that Vagharis and other criminal tribes find a Sadhu's garb a good means of carrying out their depradatory designs ; police detectives, disguised as Sadhus, often obtain valuable information in tracing out crimes ; and lastly political agitators are also said to occasionally conceal their identity under a Sadhu's disguise.

Reasons which lead to Asceticism.

216. In his admirable Treatise on the Mystics, Ascetics and Saints of India (p. 16), Professor Omen summarises the reasons which prompt men to ascetic practices as under:—(1) a desire which is intensified by all personal or national troubles to propitiate the unseen powers, (2) a longing on the part of the intensively religious to follow in the footsteps of their *master,* almost invariably an ascetic, (3) a wish to work one's own *future* salvation or emancipation by conquering the evil inherent in human nature, *i. e.,* flesh, (4) a yearning to prepare oneself by purification of mind and body for entering into *present* communion with the Divine Being, (5) despair arising from disillusionment and from defeat in the battle of life, and lastly (6) mere vanity, stimulated by the admiration which the multitude bestow upon the ascetic. The first three reasons are most operative in the case of the true ascetics, but there are many

who have been Sadhus, simply because they were neglected orphans or were abducted by other Sadhus from the lawful guardianship of their parents or had no desire to fight the battle of life. A saying common in Gujarat reflects the views of the people on the subject :—*Topimahe tran gun; nahi vero nahi veth; bavo bavo sau kahe, sukhe bhare pet, i. e.,* 'a Sadhu's garb confers three benefits : you have neither to pay taxes nor to labour, every one calls you Bava (that is father), and you get your food easily'.

General description of Sadhus.

217. As a rule, ordinary Sadhus adopt a life of easy, irresponsible indolence and mendicancy. They know well how to time their wanderings so as to make them fit in with the festal event of each locality within their annual round. They are generally attired most scantily, and for protection from the sun's rays and insect pests, have their skin rubbed over with ashes. Most of them have on their foreheads and noses *tilaks* or neatly painted white or coloured sect marks. Irrespective of sect some called *Juttadharis* have their hair braided and coiled upon the anterior part of the crown of the head ; some called *Bhoureeahs* wear their hair falling in disorder about the face ; while others have shaven pates. Most Sadhus wear strings of beads about their necks or carry rosaries in their hands. From the nature of the beads it is easy to distinguish between the followers of Vishnu or Shiva, according as they favour beads of the holy basil wood (*Ocynum sanctum*) or the rough berries of the *rudraksha* tree (*Elaecarpus ganitrus*). The Shiva rosary or *japmala* consists of 84 *rudraksha* beads and the Vaishnava one of 108 beads of *tulsi* (basil) wood. Some Sadhus wear phallic emblems suspending from the neck by woollen threads ; some wear great wood or metal ear-rings ; and others wear armlets of iron, brass or copper which are well-known as badges of visits to the lofty Himalayan monasteries of Pasupatinath, Kedarnath and Badrinath. Some have a white conch tied on to their wrist, indicating a pilgrimage to Rameshwar and some have symbolical marks branded conspicuously upon the arm as evidence of a pilgrimage to Dwarka. Most of the Sadhus keep in their hand a pair of big iron fire-tongs. They use a wooden staff, called *bairagun* as a chin-rest or arm-rest and earthen pipes called *chillums* for smoking *ganja*. Some Sadhus keep with them miniature chapels with miniature stone or metal idols or pictorial representations of the deities, which are set up when they make a halt at any place.

As a part of their *tapascharya* or austerities, some Sadhus undergo many inconveniences, pains and sometimes even terrible tortures. Some called *Panch Dhuni* sit under the open sky girt about with five small fires ; sometimes only four fires are lighted, the sun overhead being regarded as the fifth one. Some sit and sleep on a bed of spikes, called *kanak saiya* ; some called, *tharashri*, stand leaning on some kind of rest for days or weeks together. Sadhus known as *Urdhvamukhi* hang head downwards suspended from the bough of a tree for half an hour or more. Those known as *Urdhvabahu* keep one or both of their arms erect over head till they are reduced to a shrunken and rigid condition. Some practise *Ashtangdandvata*, that is, applying the eight parts of the body—the forehead, breast, hands, knees and insteps—to the ground and thus measuring the ground, go on a long pilgrimage by slow and laborious marches. Some called *Jalshai* sit a whole night immersed in water. Some called *Falahari*, live upon fruits, others called *Dudhahari* subsist on milk alone, while those known as *Aluna* never eat salt with their food. As aids to meditation, a great number of *asans* or postures, *e. g.*, *padmasan* or lotus posture, have been devised. Some Sadhus perform purificatory rites known as *neti karma*, drawing a thread through the mouth and one of the nostrils with the object of cleansing the nasal fossæ ; *dhoti karma* swallowing a long strip of cloth and after it has reached the stomach drawing it out again with the object of cleansing out the stomach ; *Brahma datan* cleansing the throat with a long and thin green stick used as a brush ; *brajote karma* and *ganesh kriya*, for flushing the colon without instrumental aid.

A Sadhu's anger and displeasure are much dreaded and avoided as far as possible. Some Sadhus are believed to have magic powers by which they can work wonders and cause calamities. Some are believed to be proficient in alchemy by which they can turn the baser metals into gold ; while some affect to be fortune-tellers, palmists, and expert medicine men and conversant with hidden treasures. Many a credulous or greedy devotee has lost his all and come to grief in seeking to become rich with the help of Sadhus.

Number of Sadhus.

218. Sadhus have not been separately classified but there can be no doubt, there must be a large number of them in this State, having regard to the fact that it has in its population 6,464 persons returned as Bavas, 3,515 Gosains, 15,871 priests and ministers, 1,558 religious mendicants and inmates of monasteries, and 8,457 beggars and vagrants.

Shaiv and Vaishnav Sadhus.

219. The Sadhus usually met with in this State are: (1)—Shaiva :—(*a*) Brahmachari, (*b*) Sanyasi, (*c*) Dandi, (*d*) Yogi and (*e*) Paramhansa ; and (2)—Vaishnav :—(*a*) Ramanuji or Shri Vaishnav, (*b*) Ramanandi, (*c*) Ramasanehi and (*d*) Swaminarayan. Shaiva Sadhus while paying special honour to Shiva do not, as a rule, reject the other gods of the Hindu Pantheon. In the same way, Vaishnava Sadhus while specially adoring Vishnu in his human incarnations as Ramachandra or Krishna, either with or without their consorts, do not disregard Shiva altogether.

Brahmacharis.

220. Brahmacharis or celibates belong to an inferior ministering order. This order is said to have been created by Shankaracharya to serve as helps and companions to Sanyasis and Paramhansas. Brahmacharis also generally serve as worshippers in Mahadev or Mata temples, put on a red fisher-like cap on their head, and a necklace of *rudraksha* beads on their neck.

Sanyasi.

221. All Hindus, even Shudras and out-castes may become Sanyasis. When after a period of probation the postulant wishes to be received as a *chela*, he has to bring an offering including a *linga* and a *rudraksha* berry to the Sanyasi whose disciple he wishes to become. Four Sanyasis are required for the initiatory ceremony. The chief of the four, the selected guru, whispers into his ear the *mantra* of the order ; another confers a new name upon him, which generally ends in one of the following ten suffixes :—Giri, Puri, Bharti, Ban, Auran, Parvat, Sagar, Tirth, Ashram and Saraswati ; the third rubs him over with ashes, and the fourth breaks his sacred thread if he have one, and cuts off his *shikha* or scalp-lock. After initiation, the *chela* is expected to serve his *guru* for a time in order to learn wisdom from him. When the period of probation is over, more ceremonies are performed including *shradh* or post funeral rites of the new *Sanyasi*. When a Sanyasi dies, he is buried in a sitting posture facing east or north-east, with arms supported on a wooden rest called *bairagun*. As the followers of Shankar, though paying special honour to Shiva, do not reject the other gods of the Hindu Pantheon, the order of Sanyasi is a mixed one and has many Vaishnavas and even Tantries among its members. All Sanyasis may eat together and accept food from any Hindu. They rub ashes over their bodies, wear salmon coloured robes and a tiger skin if they can get one. They make sect marks on their forehead, wear a necklace of *rudraksha* berries or at least one such berry. The hair of their head and beard is allowed to grow freely. In their hands they carry a pair of iron tongs. Whenever they are seated, they light a fire and smoke *ganja*.

Dandi.

222. The Dandis, so called from the *danda*, or staff, which every member is required to carry, were originally recruited exclusively from the twice-born or sacred thread-bearing castes, but now any Hindu is allowed to join the order. He who wishes to become a Dandi fasts for three days. On the fourth day, there is a *havan* (sacrifice) after which he is shaved, head and all. He is then taken to a river or tank in which he is made to stand waist deep in water, and take out his sacred thread. While in water, he receives the *mantra* of the order from his guru and also a new name which has for its suffix, *ashram*, *tirth*, *bharati* or *swami*,

when he steps out of water, he is given the ***dand***, a bamboo with six knots, and a piece of salmon coloured cloth attached to it and a gourd and is robed in five pieces of salmon colored cotton cloth, one piece being wrapped round the head. Rules for his guidance in life are explained to him. They are to the effect that he must not touch fire, must take one meal a day, must get his food from the houses of Brahmans only and so on. He is further enjoined to preach to the people and to practise virtue. Dandis shave their head, upper lip and beard. As a distinctive feature, they bear the Shaiva mark on their forehead, *viz.*, the *tripundra*, a triple transverse line made with ashes obtained from the fire of an Agnihotri Brahman. A Dandi is not required to worship any god, but some worship Shiva and also Vishnu as Narayan. They repeat initiatory mantras. *Om Namah Shivaya*, salutation to Shiva and *Namo Narayan*, salutation to Narayan. Some Dandis worship the deity *Nirgun Niranjaya*, that is, devoid of attributes, or passion. Dandis are either buried or thrown into some river when they die.

Yogi.

223. Yogi or Jogi, as they are called in the vernacular properly means one who practises *Yoga* with the object of uniting his soul with the Divine Spirit. The word *Yoga* means union and *Yoga Vidya* is the complex system of philosophical doctrines and practical exercises for promoting union between the individual soul and the divine spirit. The *Yoga* philosophy founded by Patanjali teaches that by certain practices a man is able to obtain complete mastery over matter. These practices are *pranayams* or long continued suppression of breath and 84 different ways of fixing the eyes on the tip of the nose. It has recently attracted much attention in the west and the United States of America. Yoga is not confined at present to Yogis alone, nor is it practised by all who are known as Yogis. Many a religiously-disposed layman and follower of other sects resorts to it when so inclined. Yogis regard one Gorakhnath as the founder of their order. They pay special respect to Shiva, a demi-god called Bhairava and nine *Nathas* or immortal saints. They also hold in special veneration 84 *Siddhas* or perfect Yogis, some of whom are believed to be still living upon the earth. Members of all castes may become Yogis. They are divided into several sub-orders, of which the two more prominent are *Kanfati* and *Oghar*. They wear rosaries of *rudraksha* beads and put on *langotis*, or loin cloth only and sometimes salmon coloured garments. They wear their hair plaited with threads of black wool and coiled on the top of the head. They mark their forehead with a traverse line of ashes and also smear the body with ashes. They live in monasteries and often move about the country in groups or singly. They bury their dead in a sitting posture facing the north. The *Kanfatis* wear huge wooden ear-rings (*mudra*) and their sect names end in *Nath*. The *Oghars* have names ending in *das* and are recruited from the lowest of castes. They do not wear ear-rings but keep a small wooden pipe, called *nath* suspending from the neck by a black thread.

Some Yogis are earnest men of high character, but many of those who move about the country in the guise of ascetics are ignorant and worthless impostors and even dangerous characters.

Yogis returned to a worldly life have formed castes in Gujarat which are known as Jogi, Ravalia, or Bharathari. They live as itinerant beggars, common carriers, tape weavers and day labourers. Those of them who are beggars carry a small fiddle with them and sing religious songs and verses in the streets.

Paramahansa.

224. Paramahansa, derived from Sanskrit *param*, great and *hansa*, a swan which can separate water from milk, means one who can distinguish truth from falsehood. The order of *Paramahansa* ranks higher than that of Sanyasi or Dandi. Only those Dandis or Sanyasis who have undergone a probation for not less than twelve years can be admitted to it. Paramahansas occupy themselves solely with the investigation of the supreme Brahma, without regard to pleasure or pain, heat or cold satiety or want. In proof of their having attained this ideal perfection, they move about in all weathers and sometimes do not speak even to indicate any natural want. Some members of this order even go about naked or affect

to live without food, or eat only when fed by others. Some refuse food unless they are fed by a *kumarika* with her own hand. Paramahansas are buried when dead or floated in a running stream.

Aghori.

225. Shiva ascetics called *Aghori* or Aghor panthi are seldom seen in towns and villages, but a few are said to be living on the Abu, Girnar and Pavagadh hills. The Aghoris seem originally to have been worshippers of Devi and to have required even human victims for their rites. They are hideous in appearance and their habits are very repulsive. They eat human flesh which they procure secretly from the graves in the villages they pass through. They push in pantheistic doctrines of the Vedant philosophy to its logical conclusion by arguing that if anything in existence is only a manifestation of the Universal soul, nothing can be unclean. Aghoris are much dreaded by the people, and sometimes impostors succeed in extracting alms from them by threatening to eat in their presence disgusting offal or foul carrion.

Vaishnav Sadhus.

226. All Sadhus of the Vaishnav sect devote themselves especially to the worship of Vishnu and differ from one another mainly in paying adoration to him in his human incarnations either as Ramchandra or as Krishna. Rama worshippers may or may not associate Sita with their God. Krishna worshippers usually adore his consorts Laxmi and Radha or his mistress Radha alone along with the deity.

Shri Vaishnava.

227. Ascetics of the Ramanuji sect are called *Shri Vaishnavas* because they worship Laxmi as the consort of Vishnu. They have monasteries in the Deccan, but occasionally reside in the Ramanuj temples at Baroda, Dabhoi, Dwarka, Sidhpur and other places in the State. They wear silk or wool garments and are scrupulous in keeping caste distinctions and in the preparation and privacy of their meals. Their necklaces and rosaries are made of *tulsi* wood or of lotus *seeds.* A novice is initiated with the name of Narayan or Vishnu. The special marks of the Ramanuja sect are a close shaven mustache, and Jai Sita Rama, as the salutation phrase; the disc or *chakra* and the conch or *shankh*, emblems of Vishnu, and vertical or slanting lines on the forehead of white clay, a perpendicular red streak for Laxmi in the middle, with a horizontal white clay line connecting the three across the root of the nose, the whole from one to two inches wide and representing Vishnu's throne.

Ramanandi.

228. Ramanandi Sadhus bear on their foreheads the distinguishing Vishnu sect mark, the *trifala*, which consists of three upright lines: the centre one red and the side ones white. They also wear necklaces and rosaries of *tulsi* wood. Marriage is allowed among a division called *sanjogi* but forbidden to the division called *naga* or naked. The head guru who resides at Kheda in Jodhpur is enjoined celibacy. The Nagas are divided into (1) Achari, (2) Sanyasi, (3) Khakhi, and (4) Vairagi. The Acharis wear silken and woollen garments, the Sanyasis salmon colored cotton clothes, the Khakhis only a loin cloth with their bodies besmeared with ashes and their hair and nails unclipped. Some of them perform severe austerities such as standing on the head, sitting amidst fire and smoke, keeping their heads erect for hours together believing that the greater the self-inflicted severity, the greater the salvation. The name Vairagi derived from *vi*, without, and *rag*, passion, *i. e.*, without attachment to the world, is commonly applied to all Vaishnavite Sadhus. Vairagis do not wear coloured clothes but put on *janoi* or sacred thread, whether originally of the twice-born caste or not. They keep a tuft of hair on the crown of the head and as a head covering use a white cotton *safa*. Ramanandi Sadhus salute each other with the words *Jaya Sita Rama.*

Ramsanehi Sadhus.

229. Sadhus of the Ramsanehi sect live in their monasteries in Marwad and in their subordinate establishments in Baroda, Visnagar and other places. Among their rules of conduct, truthfulness, control over the passions, a solitary residence and begging readymade food from lay followers are enjoined. The use of fire or even a

lamp at night is strictly forbidden and even the touch of a coin is held sinful. They rise and bathe at early dawn and wear an ochre coloured piece of cloth. Their forehead mark is of white *gopichandan* clay in shape like the flame of a lamp emblematic of divine light. They use a rosary of *ratanjal* or red sandal.

Kabir Panthis.

230. Kabir Panthi Sadhus have no distinctive dress or ceremonies. As far as they affect peculiarities of any kind, they follow those of *bairagis* wearing *tulsi* beads and having the *trifala* painted on their foreheads.

Swaminarayan ascetics.

231. Swaminarayan ascetics are of three orders: *Brahmachari, Sadhu* and *Palo.* Brahmacharis rank the highest, after them come Sadhus, while the Palas who rank the lowest are mere attendants on the Acharya or head guru, or temple servants.

Brahmachari.

A Brahman follower of the sect who is prepared to lead a celibate life and dedicate himself to the service of the faith can be a *Brahmachari* after the probation of about a year. A Brahmachari wears a white *dhoti,* wraps an ochre coloured cloth round the upper part of his body and puts on a red woollen cap or *phenta* on his head. His duty is to read the Purans and other religious books, and to preach to those who visit the temples. Brahmacharis are allowed to use metal vessels for eating and drinking. They can also keep hair on the head and wear moustache and beard.

Sadhu.

Satsangis or followers of the sect who are lower in rank than Brahmans, but not lower than Kanbis, can be Sadhus. A Sadhu must lead a celibate life and devote his full time to the service of the faith. He is required to shave his head, beard and moustache. He must put on an ochre coloured *dhoti,* wrap round his person another similarly coloured cloth, and put on a *falia* or head dress of the same colour. Brahmacharis and Sadhus are prohibited from wearing coats, jackets or other tailor-made garments. A Sadhu must use a wooden dish (*patra*) and a wooden jug (*kamandal*). He should on no account use metal vessels. Like the Brahmachari, he reads or preaches to the people. Swaminarayan Sadhus and Brahmacharis are not allowed to go out of the temples singly. They always move about in pairs or groups. At the head-quarters, they live in the monasteries; while moving in the district they live in the temples of the sect which are to be found in almost every village.

Palas.

Like Brahmacharis and Sadhus, Palas also must lead a celibate life and devote themselves to the service of the faith. They are recruited from the Koli, Rabari and other low castes. They are allowed to put on white garments and also to use shoes, and tailor-made coats. They serve as menials waiting upon the Acharya or as servants and managers of the temples. They are quite necessary in the organization of the sacerdotal order of the sect, for only they can touch money or make the necessary purchases.

Daily life.

Brahmacharis, Sadhus and Palas rise early, offer prayers and attend the six o'clock meeting where the head Brahmachari or Sadhu delivers a sermon or reads from the Purans. They retire at nine o'clock and read or study till dinner time at eleven. They then meet at the temple, take a recess at two, reassemble at three and hold religious discourses till six in the evening. At night supper is served only to the weak or infirm and to those who wish to have it. The rest read sacred books and retire at eleven o'clock. Brahmacharis and Sadhus are forbidden to indulge in the pleasures of the palate. They are required to mix up the different viands together before eating. A Brahmachari or Sadhu may not even look at a woman. Should he touch one, even accidentally, he has to expiate for the sin by a whole day fast.

The distinguishing forehead mark of this sect is a vertical streak of *gopichandan* clay or sandal paste with a round red powder mark in the middle and a necklet of sweet basil beads.

4.—JAINISM.

232. Jainism was founded by Parsvanath about two hundred years before Buddha. It was reformed and firmly established by a Kshatriya Prince named Vardhaman or Mahavir who was born at Vansali near Patna about 599 B.C. He is said to have been originally an erring man who by his own power attained to omniscience and freedom and out of pity for suffering mankind, preached the way of salvation which he had found. Because he conquered the *manus* in the human heart he became known as *Jina*, the victor, from which the term Jainism is derived. He is also called *Jineshwar*, Chief of the Jinas ; *Arhat*, the venerable Tirthankar, the sage who has made the passage of the world ; *Sarvagna*, omnicient, and *Bhagavat*, holy one. His followers were mainly Kshatriyas and Vaishyas. The artizan classes were but little affected by his propaganda. The characteristic feature of this religion is that it rejects the authority of the Vedas and denies the spiritual supremacy of the Brahmans. It also declares its object to be, to lead all men to salvation, and to open its arms, not only to the noble Aryan, but also to the low born Sudra and even to the alien, *mlechha*. The Jains like Buddhists, deny the existence of a great creator and pay reverence to twenty-four Jinas or perfect saints raised to the rank of gods. Parsvanath and Mahavir are considered to be the last two of these saints for the present Yuga. The disciples are divided into ecclesiastics and laity. At the head stands an order of ascetics called *yatis* or sadhus, and under them the general community of *upasaka*, "the worshippers" or the *Shravak*, the "hearers." The highest goal of Jainism is *Nirvana* or *Moksha*, the setting free of the individual from the *sanskara*, the revolution of birth and death. The means of reaching it are, as in Buddhism, the three jewels, the Right Knowledge (*Sat-gnyana*), the Right Belief (*Sat-darshan*) and the Right Conduct (*Sat-charitra*). The first jewel, Right Knowledge, is the correct comprehension of the philosophical system which the *Jina* taught. According to the Jain doctrine, soul exists not only in organic structures, but also in apparently dead masses, in stones, in lumps of earth, in drops of water, in fire, and in wind. Virtue leads to the heavens of the gods or to birth among men in pure and noble races. Sin consigns the souls to the lower regions, in the bodies of animals, in plants or even into masses of lifeless matter. The bondage of souls if they inhabit a human body, can be abolished by the suppression of the causes which led to their confinement and by the destruction of the *Karman* merit and sin. The final state is the attainment to a knowledge which penetrates the Universe to *keval gnyana* and *nirvan* or *moksha* : full deliverance from all bonds. The second jewel, the Right Belief, requires the full surrender to the teacher, the *Jina*, and the firm conviction that he alone has found the way to salvation and only with him is protection and refuge to be found. The third jewel, the Right Conduct, which contains the Jain ethics, may be summarised in the words : not to hurt, not to speak untruth, to appropriate nothing to one's self without permission, to preserve chastity and to practise self-sacrifice, in special relation to thoughts, words and deeds.

Jainism.

233. Jainism was formerly supposed to be an outcome of Buddhism on the ground of similarity of principles, but materials have since been discovered in the Budha *suttras* themselves, which show that it is quite as ancient as Buddhism. Jains hold the same tenets as the Buddhists regarding the sacredness of life, but differ from them in accepting the orthodox Hindu view of self-mortification by bodily penances. They believe in the separate existence of the soul which the Buddhists deny. Souls according to the Jains may exist in stocks, stones, lumps of earth, drops of water, particles of fire, etc. Jainism also differed from Buddhism in that it admitted its lay adherents into communion with the order and held devotional services for them. Buddhism on the other hand gave its lay adherents no share in the monastic organisation and held no services for their benefit. Consequently when the Brahmanic revival of Shankaracharya came and was followed by Mahomedan persecution and the destruction of monasteries, Buddhism in India simply disappeared and became merged in the various Vaishnav sects which grew into prominence about the 12th and 13th

Jainism compared with Buddhism.

centuries, while Jainism still survives as the religion of many of the Vania castes who represent the ancient Vaishyas.

Hindu beliefs and practices.

234. Jainism is gradually drifting back into the current of Brahmanism which everywhere surrounds it and attracts it. Jains observe Hindu holidays like *Diwali, Holi* and *Akhatrij* and have a sort of modified belief in the Hindu gods, especially Brahma, Vishnu, Shiva and Ganesh with their consorts as being subordinated to the Jinas. Representatives of these deities are sometimes observable in the precincts of their temples. They observe the caste system and sometimes claim to be regarded as Hindus, though rejecting the Hindu Veda. In actual practice, they celebrate most of the purificatory rites prescribed by the Brahmanical Shastras and employ Brahmans as priests for the performance of these as well as for offering worship to their Tirthankaras. Jains also mark their foreheads with saffron a small spot as a sect-mark in imitation of the Hindus. The schism from Hinduism does not operate as a bar to marriage or commensality any more than do differences which are admittedly only sectarian. Jain Shrimalis intermarry with those of their community who belong to the Vaishnava sect of Hindus. If a Hindu girl marries a man who is a Jain, she attends the Jain ceremonies when in her husband's house and worships the Brahmanical gods when she goes to visit her parents.

Effect on Hinduism.

235. Jain beliefs and practices have largely affected the Hindus especially in kindness towards animal life. *Ahinsa parmo dharma*, non-killing is the highest religion, is now as much a Hindu as a Jain belief. Animal sacrifice which was once very common with the Hindus is now practically non-existing in Gujarat; white pumpkins are cut instead of goats and oblations are made of rice. Hindus as well as Jains join in maintaining the *panjarapole*, or animal hospitals, which are established in most of the towns. The killing of street dogs and the catching of fish from ponds are opposed both by the Hindus and Jains as a common cause. *Parbudis* or pigeon-houses in street corners are built by the followers of both the religions.

236. As already mentioned, Jains are divided into two leading sects, Digambaras or sky-clad and Swetambaris or white-clad. This distinction is now mainly observed in images.

Swetambaris.

Swetambaris adorn their images with jewellery and insert crystals in their eyes. Their images are represented as clothed; and on seated statues, the left hand rests upon the right. They admit idols of Hindu gods into their temples and Brahmans often officiate. They believe in 12 heavens. Their *yatis* go about in clean white clothes (Swetambars) and eat out of dishes. They allow that women can attain eternal bliss. They do not as a rule wear the *janoi*, but when worshipping, they throw the *rumal* across the shoulder in the position in which the *janoi* rests. This they call *uttarasana*. Their authorities are the 45 *Angamas*.

Digambaras.

Which of the two sects represents the original and oldest followers of Mahavir, is yet undecided. Both persist in claiming the honour. Digambaras appear to be the orthodox sect as Anandgiri, who was a contemporary of Shankaracharya, mentions no other sects in his treatise. They revere the 24 Tirthankaras, but do not worship them. They worship the Deva, Gurus and Dharm, looking on the Tirthankaras as models and meditators, and not in themselves objects of worship. The laity are at first taught to worship the Tirthankaras; as they rise in knowledge and religious standing, they cease to do so. Gurus (yatis) only look on the Tirthankaras as examples to be followed. Digambaras do not adorn their images or fill their eyes with crystals, etc. In the case of seated images, the right hand rests on the left. Hindu gods are not found in their temples, except Indra occasionally; and they do not employ Brahmans to officiate. They believe in 16 heavens. Their gurus go naked, and only eat from the hands of a disciple. They deny that women can attain eternal bliss.

237. About four hundred years ago, a section of the Swetambaris formed themselves into a separate sect, called Dhundia. One Lonkashah of Ahmedabad, who lived in 1643 A. D., and was employed in copying Jain manuscripts, found that there was no sanction for idol worship in the *sutras*, which contained doctrines quite different from those that were practised by the monks of the time. After having studied the *sutras* thoroughly, he cast off idol worship and proclaimed to the Jain community that the priests, who taught image worship, were hypocrites; and that it had no place in the Sutras. He soon got a small number of followers. In spite of the opposition and persecution of the priests, Lonkashah succeeded in starting a new sect, which was nick-named by their idolatrous enemies as Dhundias.

Dhundias.

This name is said to have been derived from their having had to search (*dhundvu*), their religious books for true knowledge, or from the fact that they always seek (*dhundha*), carefully to remove all animal life from their path for fear of accidentally killing it. They have no images or temples at all, but worship the abstract ideal only of Dharm, and follow men who have overcome their passions. They admit the good example of the Tirthankaras, but pay them no special respect. Their gurus are dressed in dirty white. They always carry on small broom of cotton fibre, with which to sweep all animal life out of their path and wear over the mouth a pad to prevent themselves from swallowing any small insect. They live in monasteries (*Thanak*). Women are treated on an equality with men as regards the *sidh* condition. These women (*sadhwis*) are celibates, dress in white, wear the pad and carry the broom, just as the *sadhus* do. They accept only 32 out of the 45 Angamas, and reject the commentaries (Bhashya charitra).

In order to distinguish themselves from the idolators—Swetambaris and Digambaras, the followers of Lonkashah are lately calling themselves Sthanakvasi Swetambaras. They strenuously resent the appellation of Dhundia, which they assert, has been given by outsiders as a term of reproach.

238. There are three classes of ascetics—Sadhus, Sadhwis and Gorjis. Any person may become a Sadhu. The Sadhu wears only two pieces of *bhagava* or ochre coloured cotton cloth but no head-dress. He does not allow the hair of his head, moustaches or beard to grow. Except when enfeebled by age he does not shave, but after allowing his hair to grow for about six months, tears it out with his fingers or gets it clipped. He always carries his staff (*dand*) and (*ogho*) brush, and before he sits down, sweeps the ground to push insects away. He sleeps on a blanket and owns no property. He never kindles fire or cooks food for fear of killing any living thing, but begs cooked food from Shravaks. He enters those houses, only whose doors are open and on entering repeats the words *Dharma Labha* (fruits of religion). The owner of the house lays before him *bhiksha* or cooked food. When he has gathered enough for a meal from the different houses, the Sadhu returns and eats at home. Drinking water is collected in the same way. During the fair season, Sadhus are forbidden to stay more than five days in the same village and more than a month in the same town. But they are allowed to pass at one place the rainy season, that is, the four months from Ashadh Sudi 14th to Kartik Sudi 14th. The Sadhu's chief duties are to study and teach the Jain Shastras and to keep the *panch maha vratas* or five main vows. They are: to refrain from *pranatipat*, life-taking, *murkhavad*, lying, *adattadan*, receiving anything without the knowledge of the owner, *maithun*, sexual intercourse, and *parigraha*, taking gifts not allowed by religious rules.

Jain Ascetics.

239. Sadhwis or nuns are recruited from religious Shravak women. A Sadhwi wears one robe round the waist and another on the upper part of the body. Like the Sadhu, she tears out the hair of her head once in six months, carries *dand* and *ogho* and begs her meal and water.

Sadhwis.

240. A Gorji differs from a Sadhu in wearing white instead of red ochre clothes. Gorjis grow the moustache and hair of the head. Unlike Sadhus, Gorjis have no order of female Gorjis. Except a few who break the rules and cook rich food in their monasteries, Gorjis never cook but beg *bhiksha* like Sadhus. Any person may become a Gorji. At present most of them are sons of low-caste Hindus, or illegitimate children, who are brought up by *Gorjis*. For this reason, they have sunk in estimation. Gorjis practise sorcery and magic and prescribe medicine.

Gorjis.

241. Sadhus and Sadhwis belong to no *gachha*. Gorjis and Shravaks are divided into *gachhas* or bodies. Each *gachha* has a spiritual head, called Shripujya, who is chosen from among the Gorjis of the same *gachha*, provided he was originally a Shravak or a Brahman. Shripujyas wear their hair and dress and beg in the same way as Gorjis, except that a Gorji sometimes brings his food and water for him with his own.

Shripujya.

242. There is little difference in the entrance ceremonies for Sadhus, Sadhwis or Gorjis. The person who wishes to become a Sadhu goes to a learned Sadhu, and bowing at his feet humbly asks him to take him as his pupil or chela. The Sadhu finds out that the parents and relations of the youth are willing that he should become a Sadhu, and that he has sufficient strength of body and mind to stand the fasting and other discipline laid down in the Jain scriptures. A lucky day is chosen for the initiatory ceremony. When the disciple is a man of means, the ceremony is performed at his expense. In other cases, the cost is contributed by the Shravak community, who are always pleased when additions are made to the number of their religious class. The ceremony is celebrated with the same pomp as a marriage. A procession starts from the house of the disciple, who is seated in a palanquin, with a cocoanut in his hand and passing through the principal streets. A female relation of the person to be initiated carries in her hand a *chhab* or bamboo basket with the articles required for the intended Sadhu. The procession passes outside of the town and stops below an *asopalo* (*Polyalthia longifolia*) tree, where the *guru*, who is awaiting the arrival of the procession performs the initiatory ceremony. The Sadhus form a circle round the novice, and the laity stand behind. The novice puts off his old clothes except the waist cloth. He then plucks out the hair of his head or gets some one to do so, and puts on his new garments as a Sadhu. He is then given a new name, containing at least one letter of his original name. Camphor, musk, sandal, saffron and sugar are applied to his bare head, while the initiator reapeats texts calling on him to observe with care the five prescribed vows, *panch maha vratas*. He is then supplied with the articles allowed to an ascetic by the Jain scriptures. They include five wooden pots or *patra* in the shape of deep dishes, a *dand*, about five feet long, a *ogho* or brush, which, while walking is carried under the left armpit and is used to sweep the ground. The ceremony is completed by the guru throwing *vas khep* or fragrant powder on the head of the new ascetic as he passes. He does not return to the town, but passes the night in the neighbouring village or in a rest-house outside the town. He comes back next morning and stays in the *apasara* or monastery.

Initiation.

243. The religious temples of the Jains are of two classes, *apasaras*, monasteries and *dehras*, temples. They are built either by a single wealthy Shravak or by subscription. Shravaks are very liberal in the sums they spend on temples. A Shravak temple is always called after one of the twenty-four *Tirthankaras* or patron saints. The image of the chosen Tirthankar called *Mulnayak* is set on a raised seat and on both of his sides, images of one or more of the other *Tirthankaras* are placed and all are worshipped with equal respect. Below the idol of the *Mulnayak* or in other nitches or upper storeys, images of Hindu goddesses are placed and worshipped with offerings of cocoanuts, betel nuts and rice. Sadhus, Sadhwis and Gorjis rarely visit the temple and do not perform the daily *puja*, which is left to paid servants called pujaris who are generally Shrimali Brahmans, Tapodhans, Malis or Kanbis. They live in

Temples, idols and monasteries.

apasaras which are quite distinct from temples. Apasaras are buildings with large halls without bath or cooking rooms. The Shripujyas and Gorjis live in one apasara and Sadhus and Sadhwis in separate apasaras. In the Sadhu apasaras, Jain scriptures are daily read from 7 to 9 in the morning. Sadhwis like Shravaks come to hear the scriptures, but sit separate from the men and listen at a distance. Sadhwis give instruction to Shravak women in their apasaras, but a Gorji or Shripujya seldom lectures or preaches.

Temple service.

244. Any Hindu who is not a flesh eater or spirit drinker is considered a fit temple servant. As mentioned before ministrants in Shravak temples are Tapodhan Brahmans, Bhojaks or Malis. A Shravak ministrant is never paid in money. Ministrants of other castes are paid upto Rs. 100 a year, in addition to the right of using fruit and other presents laid before the image by votaries. Jain temples are always closed during the night and as a rule, a lamp is not kept burning in them. Except in big temples where other servants are employed, the ministrant sweeps the temple, keeps charge of the temple vessels and performs the worship of the idol. With a piece of cloth tied round his mouth the ministrant first washes the idol with water mixed with curds and then with plain water, and dries it with a soft cloth. He lays flowers before and over it and applies fragrant substances to its toe, ankle, navel, brow, heart, palm, shoulders, neck and crown; aloe-sticks are burnt, and lamps are waved as *arti.* He then draws on a footstool, a *sathio* or half square with grains of rice and as sacred food places on it almonds, sesame and sweetmeats brought from a Shravak family. After this he unties his mouth and sits in the hall chanting prayers. The temples are closed at noon and re-opened again an hour or two before sunset. Shravaks both males and females visit their temples both in the morning and evening. Some males bathe in the temple and go through the same ritual as the ministrant. Women rarely do so, though they are not forbidden to do so. Shravaks set in front of the idol rice, flowers, etc. They do not take anything in their pocket when visiting a temple, as on returning home, they cannot use it for any other purpose. Taxes or fixed payments are sometimes levied for the maintenance of Jain temples. Whatever money is laid before the idol is credited in an account book and spent in repairing the temple, paying the *pujari* and buying saffron, aloe-sticks and other articles required for the daily worship. Temple management is entrusted to one or more trustees who are chosen from the *gachha* to which the builder of the temple belongs.

Food and drink.

245. Jains are not only strict vegetarians, but also avoid eating vegetables which are many-seeded such as brinjals, or such bulbous and tuberous plants as potatoes, yams, &c. On certain days called *parva*, the use of green vegetables is forbidden. Every family has a large supply of brass plates and wooden stools. The plate is set on the stool and two or three persons eat together from the same plate. Water is believed to be full of insect life. On ordinary days, it is carefully strained through a fine cloth and the sediment called *sankharo* is thrown into the well or river from which the water was taken. On fast days, Jains drink water that has been boiled within eight hours of the time of drinking.

Fasts.

246. Some Shravaks keep five and others twelve monthly fasts. The five fast days are the two-eighths, the two-fourteenths and the fifth of the bright half of every Hindu month; the twelve fast days are the two-seconds, the two-fifths, the two-eighths, the two-elevenths, the two-fourteenths and the bright and dark fifteenths of every Hindu month. Jains ought to fast during the whole week of their *pachusan* holidays, but the rule is observed by a few; but almost all however fast on the last day. Sometimes, but rarely, a Jain Sadhu takes the vow of fasting to death. This is called *santharo* or sleeping. After fasting for some days, the Sadhu's body is constantly rubbed with a wet cloth. When he dies he is placed in a litter in a sitting posture and carried in procession with music to the burning ground. Now-a-days the vow of *santharo* is taken a day or two previous to death when all hopes of life are given up.

Holidays.

247. The most important of the Jain holidays are the Pachusan or Paryusan, meaning the sacred season. The Swetambaris observe it on from the twelfth of the dark half of *Shravan* to the fifth of the bright half of Bhadrapad. The Digambaris observe it for fifteen days from the fifth of the bright half of Bhadrapad to the fifth of the dark half of the same month. During these holidays, Shravaks observe fasts and visit all their temples in the village or town several times during the day. They also visit the *apasaras* where Sadhus read and explain the *kalpa sutra*, one of their forty-five religious books. *Padikamna* or more correctly *parikraman* ceremony which is like a confession, is also performed by a body of persons together. A Shravak wishing to perform the ceremony goes to the apasara of his *gachha* with a *katasan* or seat of woollen cloth eighteen inches square, a *mohopali*, or mouth fillet, a *chavlo* or brush. He sits on the woollen seat and holds the *mohopali* before the mouth with the right hand and puts the brush by his side. The brush is used to brush the seat and his person whenever he has occasion to stand up or sit down. When all have taken their seats, an oath called *samayak* binding each person to be attentive is given. The Sadhu of the monastery then recites certain verses praying that all sins as regards animal life committed knowingly or unknowingly by the congregation may be pardoned. The ceremony ordinarily lasts for an hour, but on the last day of the Pachusan, it lasts for three hours. Before it breaks up, the meeting is daily served with *patasas*, and with *ladus* on the last day. On the day following the Pachusan, images of the Tirthankaras are taken in procession round the town. During these holidays, fishermen and butchers are sometimes induced by money payments to give up fishing and slaughtering animals.

5.—Gujarat Muhammadans.

Muhammadanism in Gujarat.

248. The earliest existence of Muhammadans in Gujarat is traced to the 7th century. From the middle of the seventh to the end of the eighteenth century, foreign Musalmans continued to find their way into Gujarat. The first to arrive were the Arabs, the sailors and soldiers of the Bagdad fleets, who came to plunder and conquer the Gujarat coasts. The next comers were traders from the Persian Gulf, who were encouraged by the Rajput kings of Anhilwad to settle in the country. There was thus a small Muhammadan population in Gujarat, especially in the coast towns, when it was conquered by Alif Khan in 1297 A. D. After its conquest to the end of the 18th century, foreign Musalman soldiers, traders, missionaries and refugees kept flocking into Gujarat both by land and sea. From time to time Muhammadan missionaries and men of learning coming either of their own accord or invited by the rulers of Gujarat, succeeded in winning to their faith large bodies of Hindus. Of these missionaries, the most important was Abdulla who founded in the eleventh century the sect of the Shiah Vohoras. Among other distinguished missionaries may be mentioned Imam Shah of Pirana who made many converts from the Kanbi and other castes. His descendants still continue to enjoy the spiritual headship of the Momna, Matia and Shaikhda castes whom he converted. But most of the converts were forced to adopt Islam. Alif Khan (A. D. 1297-1317) introduced Muhammadan faith by force from Anhilwad to Broach. Of the Ahmedabad kings Sultan Ahmed (A. D. 1411-1441), Mahmod Begda (A. D. 1459-1513); and Mahmod II (A. D. 1536-1547), specially exerted themselves to spread Islam, and of the Mughal emperors Jahangir in A. D. 1618 and Aurangzeb in A. D. 1646 attempted by persecution to force the Hindus to become Muhammadans. It was only from the high castes that Muhammadan converts were forcibly made. The Rajputs who submitted were called Molesalams and the Vanias, Brahmans and Kanbis joined the sect of Vohoras.

Conversion in modern time.

249. There is at present no attempt to spread Islam. Now and then a Hindu from worldly or other motives changes his religion. But cases of conversion from the preaching of religious men are almost unknown. When a Hindu agrees to embrace Islam, a party of Musalmans is called together and in

their presence he repeats the creed. Then sugared water is drunk and the convert is set on a horse and led in state through the town. On his return, he is circumcised and a Musalman name, generally Abdullah (slave of Allah) or Din Mahamad (he who has entered the faith of Mahamad), is given to him.

Estimate of the proportion of foreign blood among the Muhammadans of Baroda.

250. The Musalmans in the State may be divided into two main sections : (1) those with a foreign strain, and (2) descendants of local Hindu converts. Those with a foreign strain include the four regular classes of Shaikh, Saiyad, Mughal and Pathan and a few others, such as Afghans, Arabs and Baluchis, who are wholly or partly of foreign descent. The local converts are the Vohora, Khoja, Memon, Molesalam, Ghanchi, Tai, Pinjara, Momna, Matia, Shaikhda and similar other groups who still keep up their old caste associations. It is impossible to form an exact estimate of the relative strength of these two elements, the Indian and the foreign. Many of those who assume the high names of Shaikh or Pathan are really descended from Hindus. Assuming, however, that those who have returned themselves by these names are of foreign descent, the strength of the foreign element among the Muhammadans of Baroda, is about one-third of the total number of persons who profess the faith of Islam.

Race.	Number.
Shaikh	31,510
Saiyad	8,772
Mughal	1,054
Pathan	16,307
Afghan	113
Arab	316
Baluch	951
Total ...	59,023

Mahomedanism.

251. The essential doctrine in Mahomedanism is the absolute unity and supremacy of God as opposed to the old Arab Polytheism on the one hand and the Christian Trinity on the other. It however admits of angels and genii. The Koran also teaches the doctrine of eternal decrees or absolute predestination of an intermediate state after death, and of the resurrection and judgment. Stress is laid on prayer, ablution, fasting, almsgiving and the pilgrimage to Mecca. Wine and gambling are forbidden. Moslem worship consists of a number of bows and prostrations accompanied with prayers and verses from the Koran. A Mahomedan should pray five times a day, if he is a Sunni, before sunrise, *fazar*, at noon, *zuhr*, between noon and sunset, *asar*, at sunset, *magrib*, and from 8 to 12 P. M., *isha*. The Shiah prays three times—before sunrise, *fazar*, at noon when he repeats both the *zuhr* and the *asar* prayers, and at sunset when he says the *magrib* and *isha* prayers.

Practice.

252. Though not very zealous, Gujarat Musalmans are on the whole careful to observe the chief rules of their faith. Few of them go to the daily public prayers, but the Friday service is well attended. Both Shiahs and Sunnis observe the month of fasting and attend services on the Ramzan and Bakr-Id feasts. All who can afford it, give alms freely and few, except those of Hindu origin, lend money at interest or drink spirits. They reverence the name of the Prophet and the Koran. The irregular classes of Shiahs and most of the Sunnis become *murids* or disciples, the former to their *mullahs* and the latter to some religious person called their *pirzada*. Among the women, a few are well taught in the Koran and other religious books. They do not appear at places of public worship, but repeat at home their daily prayers, and keep fasts and other religious observances.

Musalman Sects.

253. The Moslem sects are as numerous as those of the Hindus or Christians. The Dubistân mentions 73. The two main sects are Shiah and Sunni. The original question in dispute between them whether, as the Sunnis hold, Abubakur, Umar and Uthman were the lawful successors of the Prophet, or were, as the Shiahs contend, usurpers, defrauding Ali of his right to the Khilafat, has given rise to several differences in belief and practice. The chief of the differences are that the Shiahs leave out of the Koran certain passages which they say, were written by Uthman ; they add a chapter in praise of Ali, which, they say, Uthman kept back ; and to other parts they give a different meaning from that accepted by

the Sunnis. The Shiahs do not believe in saints, and follow the precepts of the twelve instead of the four Imams. They claim for their head doctors in Persia, the *Mujtahids* or religious superiors, the power of altering the spiritual and temporal law; the Sunnis say that the time for change ceased with four Imams—Shafai, Abu Hanifah, Malik and Hambal. In practice some sects of Shiahs differ from Sunnis, chiefly by counting the month from the fading of the old moon and not as the Sunnis do from the shining of the new moon. They pray thrice instead of five times a day, and in praying hold their hands open by their sides instead of folding them below the breast. Except these and a few other particulars, the beliefs and customs of the rival sects are the same.

Pirana Sect.

254. A peculiar sect called *Pirana* has its followers both among the Hindus and Musalmans. It has got its name from the village of Pirana, ten miles south-east of Ahmedabad. It is said that Imam Shah, a Shiah Ismalia Saiyad, converted many Hindus of the Kanbi caste early in the 16th century by showing them the miraculous powers of his faith. One story is to the effect that bringing rain after two seasons of scarcity, Imam Shah was able to convert a large body of Hindu cultivators. Another story is that a band of Hindu pilgrims, while passing by Pirana on their way to Benares, were told by Imam Shah that, if they would carefully listen to his doctrines, they would visit Benares without the trouble of going there. Some of the pilgrims paid no attention to what he said and went to Benares. Others, who trusted in Imam Shah, saw in a trice Benares, bathed in the Ganges and paid their vows. Astonished with this miracle, they adopted Imam Shah as their spiritual head. Those who were actually converted came to be known as *Momna* from *momin*, believers, while those not actually converted but following a half-Hindu and half-Musalman faith came to be known as *Matia* from *mat*, opinion. Another group of half-converted Hindus came to be known as *Shaikh* or *Shaikhda*. The Momnas, Matias and Shaikhs call themselves Pirana Panthis, *i. e.*, followers of the Pirana sect. They read Imam Shah's book of religious rules in which the Atharva Veda is also mentioned; and as a prayer repeat their saint's name. All bury their dead and the Momnas also perform circumcision. They keep Ramzan fast and observe as holidays the *uras* or saint's day. Besides Musalman holidays, they observe the Hindu holidays of Holi, Akhatrij, Divaso, Balev and Divali. During the last thirty or forty years, there has been a tendency among the Matias and Shaikhs to revert to Hinduism. In addition to the Musalman *nika* ceremony, they call a Brahman and go through the Hindu marriage ceremony. A Ramanandi Sadhu, named Nirmaldas, preached to the Matias in 1880 that they were originally Kanbis and should abandon their Musalman practices. Since then some calling themselves Vaishnav Matias, separated themselves from the rest who were known as Pirana Matias. In the Census of 1901, 137 Matias returned themselves as Hindus and 251 as Musalmans. In the present Census, all (401) the Matias have returned themselves as Hindus. No Hindu Shaikhs were returned in 1901. On the present occasion, 51 have returned themselves as Hindus. Shaikhs who have abandoned the Pirana sect make Hindu brow-marks and follow the Swaminarayan sect.

In addition to the Momnas, Shaikhs and Matias, many Rabaris, Sonis and Vanias, while worshipping their Hindu gods and continuing as Hindus, worship the Pirana saints, and call themselves Pirana Panthis. In 1901, they were not distinguished from the Musalmans and 3,655 persons in all were returned as Musalman followers of the Pirana sect. In the present Census, 3,630 Hindus and only 2,102 Musalmans have returned themselves as followers of this sect.

Priests.

255. In addition to the *Mujawar* (beadle) and the *Mutavalli* (mosque-guardian), *Mulla* (the priest), *Khatib* (preacher), *Molvi* (doctor of divinity) and *Kazi* (civil judge) are entrusted with religious duties. Of these the *Mulla* is the lowest. His duties are calling to prayers five times a day, acting as Imam or leader of the prayer, and where there is no Mujawar, keeping the mosque clean. Besides these duties, a Mulla acts as a schoolmaster and dealer in charms. He often does not understand the Koran, but he can read it and teach his pupils to spell through it. As a dealer in charms, he writes verses of the Koran to be bound

round the arm, or hung on the neck, to ward off or cure diseases or to ward off evil spirits or the influence of the evil eye and dreams. For fever, he gives a black string with ten or fifteen knots to be worn round the neck. Sometimes he reads verses from the Koran, breathes them on a jar of water and gives the water for the patient to drink. For bad eyes, he gives an amulet (*tawiz*). The *Molvi* is generally intelligent and well-read. On certain occasions, he preaches in private dwellings a sermon (*waaz*), on the text of a verse from the Koran. Sometimes he knows the whole Koran by heart and has the title of Hafiz placed before his name. A Molvi, who follows the profession of a spiritual guide, spends several months of the year in touring in the villages where his followers live. He takes up his quarters in the mosque or with the richest of his disciples. Here he preaches, teaches and visits from house to house, prescribing for those who are sick. As a curer of diseases, he, like the Mulla, writes the text from the Koran to be used as a charm in amulets For a sick patient, he gives a knotted string necklace or writes a charm in sacred characters on paper or with saffron-water on a china plate. The ink or saffron is washed off and the water is drunk.

Except in towns, where the *kazi* or judge does the duty on Fridays and fast days, the sermon, *khutbah*, is read by the *khatib* or preacher. The office is hereditary, and the holder of it follows some calling or profession.

Under Mahomedan rule, the *kazi* was the civil and criminal judge. Now, except that he leads the public prayers on the days of *Ramzan* and *Bakr* feasts, he is a little more than a registrar of marriages and divorces.

Pir Muridi.

256. The profession called *pir muridi* is practised by Saiyads, and a few Shaikhs. They call their followers *murids*, and their followers call them *pirs* or *pirzadahs*. Each class, especially among the converts from Hinduism, has its *pir* or *murshid*. The necessity of having a *pir* is carried so far that *bepir* or *pir*-less is a term of scorn. Thus the Bukharis have the Memons and Chhipas as their *murids*; the Pirana Saiyads have the Momnas and Kakas, and some Saiyads claim Gandhraps or musicians as their *murids*. The *pir* first initiates his Murid by inculcating on him the tenets of the faith and by exhorting him to eschew the ways of evil. He sips a little *sherbat* out of a cup, and makes his disciple drink a little of it. This is said to be taking the *lab* or lip-saliva of the *pir*. The ceremony is performed either at the age of initiation, *i. e.*, four years, four months and four days (see para. 384) of life. The *pir* does not impose on his disciples a regular tax, but he is always paid either in cash or grain so as to maintain himself in decent comfort. He visits his congregation once in every four years, when his followers raise subscriptions to supply him with money. The *pir* is sometimes invited by one of his people to bless the dying, the bride and bridegroom or a new house. On these occasions also he is paid handsomely in cash or kind.

Some *pirzadahs* have followers only in a few villages, some in all parts of Gujarat, and some not only in Gujarat, but in places far distant like Mauritius and Natal, in Burma and in Singapur. When a *pirzadah* dies, his sons distribute among themselves their father's people, assigning to each son, a certain number of households. It sometimes happens that for a sum of money or other consideration one *pirzadah* makes over to another the spiritual charge and the income derived from a certain number of families.

Religious buildings.

257. Musalmans have three kinds of religious buildings : *masjid* or mosque, *idgha* where *id* or festival prayers are said and *imambadas* or private mourning chapels for Shiahs. There are many old mosques but few new ones are built, owing mainly to want of funds. To meet the cost of repairs, lighting, muzavar's pay, etc., most mosques have some small endowments, the rent of lands, houses or shops. These funds are entrusted to a few men of family and position, known as *Mutavalli*. If there is no endowment, the charges are met by congregation The Idgah used only by Sunnis is generally built outside of a town. It consists of a pavement of stone or cement raised three or four feet above the level of the ground. Along the west facing east is a wall with a small turret at each end.

At the middle 3 to 5 steps rise from the pavement and form the pulpit, from which on the *Ramzan-Id* and *Bakr-Id* festivals, sermons are preached after the prayers are over.

Vows.

258. Vows are allowed by the Mahomedan faith, and are largely practised by the people in Gujarat. They are of three kinds: vows made to saints, vows made to Tabuts and vows made to genii or spirits. Among the shrines of saints in the Baroda State, the principal are (1) Miradatar at Unawa near Unja in the Kadi district, (2) Pirana near Ahmedabad, (3) Ganj Pir inthe village of Vasravi in the Velachha taluka of the Navsari district, (4) Saiyad Sadat Saheb, in the town of Navsari and (5) Pir Salar Bahadur in Kamrej. Of these the most famous is that of Miradatar, which has come into special importance, owing to the faith reposed in the saint by His Highness the late Khanderao Gaekwad, who, as a thank-offering, presented it a railing of solid silver. The reputation which this shrine enjoys as an exorciser of spirits is not equalled by any other in Gujarat. As soon as a spirit-afflicted person arrives at the shrine, the Mujawar allots him quarters befitting his station in life in one of the out-houses of the shrine. In the evening the patient sits with other votaries near the railing of the saint's grave. He is given a cup of water from the shrine well, on drinking which, if he is spirit-possessed, begins to nod his body backward and forward, or if a woman, to toss her hair and roll her eyes. If after one or two repetitions of the draught, no effect is produced, the ailment is concluded to be constitutional. In that case, the remedy is the internal or external use of the leaves of a tree growing near the grave of the saint. The tree is said to have grown out of a *datan*, which after using, the saint thrust into the soft ground near him. It put out shoots and gave forth leaves which are believed to cure the most obstinate and chronic diseases. Sometimes the leaf remedy is dispensed with. The patient or one of his party or one of the Mujavars is warned in a dream that the patient is well and should go. If the first warning is disregarded, a second one follows accompanied by the threat of evil if the patient does not leave. The spirit-expelling element at Miradatar is more interesting than the medical. It often happens that a spirit is obstinate, and in spite of frequent punishment, it does not leave. Then the further punishments inflicted are sometimes as terrible as they are degrading. The man possessed by one of these stubborn spirits is seen being dragged unwillingly as if by an unseen agent to a post where without any visible cord, his hands seem to be bound and he to writhe and rave as if under severe corporal punishment. Sometimes the possessed seems to be dragged towards the latrines of the shrine, all the while entering and praying the Miran and promising future obedience and abject submission to his invisible master. His mode of progression has all the appearance of being forced and reluctant. Seeming to be dragged to the urinaries or latrines, he is immersed into the impurities and made to wallow in them. At last when he gives a faithful promise of future good conduct, and when the fit is exhausted, he removes himself from the place often with a shoe between his teeth as a sign of abject admission of defeat, and runs from the shrine enclosure and drops as if dead. About an hour after, he wakes from his trance an entirely changed man. He is now in his proper senses, the wild and fagged look in his face during the days of his possession has disappeared, the dazed expression with the snake-like fixedness of the eyeballs is gone. He regains his usual spirits and after the performance of his vow is sent back to his home.

Some people vow that, if they gain their desire, they shall on the tenth of every Mohoram roll on the ground for a certain distance before the Tazia while it is on its way to its final immersion. Others vow that, if they get a son or if a sick child recovers, that child up to a certain age shall be made to go about at each Mohoram in the guise of a tiger or a bear or a Hindu ascetic. The vows made to genii are called *hazrats* (literally presences). Hazrats are generally held by women. Dinners are cooked and musicians are hired to sing songs in praise of the particular *ginn* whose vow is to be performed. On such occasions, the lady who is possessed by the *ginn* is believed to be completely under the influence of the spirit, and is called the *asardanni*. Those who want to consult her ask questions and in reply she directs them to do or abstain from certain acts or to present certain dishes as a thanksgiving, if they want to gain their object.

Magic.

259. The Koran, though forbidding its practice, enjoins its belief in the existence of magic. The magic is often resorted to, especially by women, to win another's affection, to cause a strife between rivals and to get rid of a foe. To gain the first two ends, love or hate potions are given, and to gain the third an image of the victim is made in dough and pricked to pieces with needles. Belief in the evil eye is so strong, that a Mahomedan will seldom eat a meal in the sight of a stranger, and before taking his infant into the street, will blot its face with collyrium or lamp-black.

Hindu practices.

260. Most of the lower and uneducated classes of converts from Hinduism are deeply infected with Hindu superstitions; their knowledge of the faith they profess, does not extend beyond the three cardinal doctrines of the Unity of God, the mission of Mahomed and the truth of the Koran; and they have a faint idea of the differences between their religion and that of the Hindus. The Khojas, Memons and others follow the Hindu succession law. Among Khojas on the sixth day after birth, the goddess *chhathi* is worshipped as among the Hindus. Most of the peasant Vohoras still keep some Hindu practices. Some of them call their children by Hindu names, *e g.*, Akhuji, Bajibhai. Two or three days before marriage in honour of a special deity, *Wanudev*, they distribute dishes of two kinds of pulse, *lang* and *val*, boiled together. At death their women beat the breast and wail like Hindus. The Hindu practice of celebrating marriage, pregnancy and death by large caste entertainments is followed by Vohoras, Tais, Momnas, Pinjaras, Shaikhs and others. *Ladu*, *kansar*, *pakvan* and other Hindu dishes are prepared on such occasions. Molesalams, Kasbatis and other converted Rajputs marry Hindu wives and at such marriages occasionally a Brahman officiates. The Matia Kanbis call Brahmans to all their chief ceremonies and except that the Pirana saint is their spiritual guide, that they help to support and go to visit his tomb, and that they bury their dead, their customs are Hindu. Among Rathods, when the bride is a Hindu, both Brahman and Musalman ceremonies are performed. The Shaikhs or Shaikhdas, the followers of Bala Mahamud Shah, one of the minor Pirana saints, bury their dead, but except for this observance and for their name, their customs are Hindu. They are not circumcised and do not eat with Musalmans. They wear *tila*, forehead mark, and at the time of marriage, both a Musalman and a Hindu priest attend. The Musalman ceremony is performed by a *fakir* and the Hindu rite of *chori* or altar worship by a Brahman. Among the Musalman Ghanchis women go singing with the bridegroom to the bride's house, as among the Hindus, and at marriage feasts they have generally Hindu dishes.

Hindu superstitions.

261. Many Hindu superstitious beliefs are respected and followed. Omens are drawn from the cry of birds and animals. The cooing of a dove foretells ruin and the cawing of a crow, the arrival of some member of the family or of a friend. A death follows the lonely midnight howl of the dog. A cat crossing the path is a bad omen. But it is lucky to see a child at play or a woman fetching water or carrying milk or whey. Creeping feelings in the skin of the face are a favourite source of omens. They are lucky, if felt on the right corner of the right eyelid, and unlucky if felt on the left corner of the left eyelid. A sudden fit of hiccup is a sign of being affectionately remembered by absent friends as the itching of the right palm foretells gain of money. The same feeling in the sole of the right foot prognosticates a journey. Each day of the week is believed to be fitted for certain acts and unsuited for others. Sunday is a good day for naming a child, eating a new dish, wearing new clothes, learning a new lesson, beginning a service and tilling land. It is a bad day to buy a horse or to set out on a journey. Monday is good for taking the first bath after recovery from illness, for sending a bride to her husband's house, for laying the foundation of a house, for entrusting anything to a person, for bartering an animal, and for travelling east. Tuesday is good for eating a new dish, taking a recovery bath, giving

any business in charge and buying an animal. It is an ill day for travelling north and for buying a cow. Wednesday is good for sending a bride to her husband's house, naming an infant, putting on new clothes, shaving, eating a new dish, learning a new lesson, tilling the ground, laying the foundation of a house, and changing a residence. It is bad for travelling north and for buying a cow. Thursday is good for the same works as Wednesday, but is bad for travelling south and for buying an elephant. Friday is good for the same works as Wednesday and bad for buying goats. Saturday is good for the same works as Wednesday and bad for travelling east or for buying a camel. And certain days of the month, depending on direction in which the traveller is going, are good for starting on a journey.

FAKIRS.

Origin of Fakirs and Dervishes.

262. The natural disposition of the Arabs for a solitary and contemplative life led them soon to forget the command of the Prophet "no monks in Islamism." Another expression in the Koran "poverty is my pride" was the argument which, thirty years after the death of the Prophet, was used by his sectarians to found numerous monasteries in imitation of the Hindus and the Greeks; since then the order of Fakirs (poor) and of dervishes (sills of the door) so multiplied in Arabia, Turkey and Persia that they reached the number of seventy-two, exclusive of an equal number of heretic sects (Brown's Dervishes, p. 76).

Gujarat Fakirs.

263. Fakirs in Gujarat lead a roving life and include in their ranks men from all parts of India and of every variety of descent. They move from house to house gathering money, grain and cooked food. The money they keep and the grain and broken food they sell to potters as provender for their asses. Others reciting praises of the generous and abuse of the stingy, ask for a copper in the name of Allah to be repaid tenfold in this world and a hundredfold at the day of judgment. Fakirs belong to two main classes; *beshara, i.e.*, those beyond the Mahomedan law or celibates and *bashara, i.e.*, those within the law or those who marry and have families. Those beyond the law have no homes and neither fast nor pray, nor rule their passions. Those under the law have wives and houses and pray, fast and keep all Mahomedan rules. There are many kinds of Fakirs, but those commonly met with are :—*Abdali*, also called Dafali or Fadali, players on the tambourine *daf*; *Nakshaband*, or mark-makers; *Benawa* or the penniless, also called *Alifshai*; *Kalandar* or monks; *Madari*; *Musa Suhag*, who put on women's dress; *Rafai*, also called Munhphoda or Munhchira; and *Rasulshahi* also called Mastan or madmen. The first two brotherhoods belong to the bashara order and the last six to the beshara or lawless order.

Abdali, also called Dafali or Fadali, players on the tambourine, *daf*, are found wandering in small numbers. They speak Hindustani and beg in the name of Allah, beating their one-end drum, *danka*, and singing religious songs. In north Gujarat, they have a fixed due or tax upon the houses of Musalmans in towns and villages.

Nakshaband—literally mark-makers—are found all over Gujarat. They speak Hindustani, keep the head bare and wear the hair and beard long and well combed. With a lantern in hand, they move about singly chanting their saint's praises. In return for alms, they mark children on the brow with oil from their lamps. They are quiet and well behaved and have homes and families.

Benawas are fakirs of the *beshara* order. They are also called Alifshahi from wearing a black Alif-like (first letter of the Persian alphabet) line down the brow and nose. They wear Persian-like woollen hat, sleeveless shirt and round the neck long rosaries of beads of *selis*. They move about in bands of five or ten begging in the name of God. In each town, they have a headman called *bhandari* or treasurer, who receives their earnings and after giving back for expenses, forwards the surplus amount to the *murshid* or spiritual head of the order.

Kalandar, from an Arabic word meaning monk, are Fakirs who wander over the country for begging and are troublesome in their demands. They shave the whole body including the eye-brows, and are Sunnis in faith.

Madari fakirs are mostly converted Hindus of the *nat* or tumbler class. They take their name from Badi-ud-din Madar Shah, the celibate saint of Syria, and belong to the *beshara* order of Sunnis. They beg alone or in bands of two or three. Some move about dragging a chain or lashing their legs with a whip to force people to give them alms. Others are snake-charmers, tumblers, monkey dancers and trainers, tricksters and rope-dancers. They honour Hindu Gods and follow Hindu customs. They marry only among themselves and form a separate community with a headman.

Musa Suhag are Musalman fakirs, who are so called after their patron saint Musa, who lived at the close of the 15th century and used to dress as a woman to indicate that he was devoted to God as a wife to her husband. In memory of their saint, fakirs of this order dress like married women in a red scarf, a gown and trousers. They do not shave the beard, but put on bracelets, anklets and other garments. They are Sunnis in religion and never marry.

Rafai fakirs are also called *Munphoda* or *Munhchira,* that is, face lashers or face splitters. They are found in small numbers all over the State. They hold in their right hand a twelve-inch iron spike called *gurz,* sharp-pointed and having near the top many small iron chains. While begging, they rattle the chains, and if people are slow in giving them alms, strike at their cheek or eye with the sharp iron point, which however causes no wound. They are Sunnis; some are celibates, while some are married.

Rasulshahi fakirs are also known as *mastan* or madmen. They put on only a shirt and a waist cloth. They are Sunnis of the *beshara* or celibate order and beg with a wooden club in their hands.

Sidi.

Sidi or *Habshi* fakirs are the descendants of African negroes brought to India. Their chief object of worship is Babaghor, an Abyssinian saint, whose tomb stands on the hill near Ratanpur in the Rajpipla State. Sidi fakirs move about in small bands. While begging they play upon a peculiarly shaped fiddle ornamented with a bunch of peacock feathers and sing in a peculiar strain in praise of their patron saint.

Organization.

264. Each brotherhood has generally three office-bearers. Of these, the principal is called *sarguroh* or head teacher. He controls the whole body and receives a share of all earnings. The other two are *izni* or *nakib,* who calls the members to all entrance, marriage and death feasts, and the *bhandari* or treasurer, who sees that pipe and water are ready at the Fakir's meeting place. Among the members, there are two orders: the *murshid* or teachers and the *khadim* or *chela.* Every newcomer joins as the disciple of some particular teacher.

Initiation.

265. The teacher sees that the entrance ceremony is properly performed; that the disciple is shaved and bathed; that he learns the names of the heads of the order; that he promises to reverence them; that he receives certain articles of dress; that he gets a new name; that he learns the new salutation; that he swears not to steal, not to lie, not to commit adultery; to work hard as a beggar or in any other calling and to eat things lawful; and finally that the entrance feast is duly given. At the close of each day, the newcomer lays his earnings before the head teacher, *sarguroh.* Taking out something for himself and a share to meet the treasurer's charges, the head teacher gives back the rest. This the beggar takes to his teacher, who giving him a little as pocket money, keeps the rest for himself. So long as the teacher lives, a beggar continues to be his disciple. When a teacher dies, the oldest disciple succeeds, or if the teacher has a son, the son and the senior disciple share the other disciples between them.

6—Parsism.

Zoroastrianism.

266. The religion of the Parsis, originally the people of Pars or Fars, a south-west province of Persia, is known as Zoroastrianism from their prophet Zoroaster, who flourished about 2500 B. C. The present Parsis of India are descendants of those who about 1300 years ago left their mother-country to escape from the oppression of the Mahomedans who had conquered it. They are said to have landed first at Diu, in Kathiawad, and then at Sanjan near Daman. The Hindu Raja of the place gave them shelter and allowed them liberty to follow their own religion, which with its rituals, they have preserved intact. The sacred books of the Zoroastrians are known as the Zand Avasta or the translations of the Avasta or sacred texts. According to tradition in Zoroaster's time, these books included twenty-one *nusks* or parts, of which only a few fragments now remain. In addition to these fragments the sacred books of the present Parsis include modern commentaries. The language of the early fragments is known as Zend and that of the commentaries as Pehlvi. In addition to these, the Parsis have a collection of writings in Persian called *ravayets*, meaning customs, which are the results of references by Indian Parsis to Persian Zoroastrians on doubtful points chiefly of ritual. The leading beliefs which as a Zoroastrian, the ordinary Parsi holds are the existence of one God, Ahurmazd, the creator of the universe, the giver of good, the hearer and answerer of prayer. Next to Ahurmazd, the name most familiar to a Parsi is that of Ahirman, or satan, to whom he traces every evil and misfortune that happens to him and every evil thought and evil passion that rises in his mind. He believes that every man has an immortal soul, which after death passes either to a place of reward, *behesht* or of punishment, *duzak*. The reward or punishment of the soul depends on its conduct during life. He believes in good angels who carry out the wishes of God and watch over fire, water and earth. He venerates fire and water and the sun, moon and stars which Ahurmazd has made. He believes in Zoroaster or Zarathustra as the prophet who brought the true religion from Ahurmazd. His code of morals is contained in two sets of three words, the one set "*Humata, hukhta, huvrasta,*" holy mind, holy speech, holy deeds, to be praised and practised, pleasing to God, the path to heaven; the other set *dushmata, duzukhta, duzuvarata*, evil mind, evil speech, evil deeds to be blamed and shunned, hateful to God, the path to hell. Fire, *atesh*, is the chief object of Parsi veneration and the fire-temple (Atesh Behram and Agiari) is the public place of Parsi worship. Religious Parsis visit the fire-temple almost daily and on four days in each month, the 3rd, 9th, 17th and 20th, which are sacred to fire, almost all Parsis go there and offer prayers.

Priests and laity.

267. Among the Parsis also there is a sort of hierarchy, though not on the rigid method of the Hindus, but there are no castes. The *Mobeds* are to them what the Brahmans are to the Hindus. The stronghold of the Mobeds is our town of Navsari, and it has been so for some centuries, because the Parsis early migrated to it from Sanjan, and have thrived and flourished there ever since. No religious ceremony can be performed, no marriage tie can be knit, no prayer after the dead can be recited, and no funeral service can be held, except by the Mobeds. These services are not at all optional, but compulsory, and fees are paid for each and all of them. Before the Mobed is engaged in services in the fire temples, or in religious services at the houses of his *Behdins* (persons belonging to the laity, for whom and for whose deceased relatives he recites prayers), he has to perform ceremonies exclusively for nine days and nights during which time no one can touch him. He also cannot dine with a Behdin or eat food cooked by a Behdin, while he is actually officiating as a priest.

Initiation.

268. Children are initiated into the Parsi religion between the age of seven and nine. The ceremony is called *navzot* or making a new believer. It consists in clothing the child with a sacred muslin shirt called *sadra* and tying round its waste a sacred cord called *kasti*. The *kasti* is made by the wives and daughters of Parsi priests by

the inter-twinings of 72 strong threads spun out of wool, and woven in a special way, on a sort of loom. It is sufficiently long to go thrice round the waist and to allow of its being tied up in certain ways, which the child is taught to do. From the day on which the investiture takes place to the day of death, a Parsi, male or female, cannot part with the *kasti*; parting with it is an overt act of abandoning the Parsi religion. It is daily untied and retied for prayers and changed for a new when it gets old.

Death.

269. When a Parsi dies, his body is washed, dressed in clean white cotton clothes and laid with the feet towards the north in a corner of the front hall. A lamp fed with ghee is kept burning near the head and a priest repeats prayers and burns sandalwood in a censer in front of the body. Two priests stand at the threshold opposite the body and recite prayers called *gehsarna*. Before the body is put on the bier, which is a plain iron cot, a dog is brought to look on the face of the dead and drive away evil spirits. The bier-bearers known as *nasesalar* are Parsis, specially paid and set apart by the community for the purpose. Four of them, dressed in white, carry the bier with the feet foremost. Priests and friends of the dead walk behind the bier, each couple holding the ends of a handkerchief. At the Tower of Silence, the bier is set down at a little distance from the door. When all have bowed to the dead, the bier is taken into the tower where the body is lifted from it and laid on the inner terrace of the tower. The clothes are torn off and the body is left to the vultures. In places where there are no Towers of Silence close at hand, Parsis bury their dead. Every morning for three days after a death, rice is cooked and laid in the verandah for dogs to eat. The ceremony of *uthamna* or rising from mourning takes place in the afternoon of the third day. On the fourth day a feast is held especially for priests. A little of the food cooked on this day is sent to all relations, who must eat at least a little of it. On the tenth and thirtieth day after a death, the death-day in each month for the first year and every yearly death-day, ceremonies in honour of the dead are performed.

Observances.

270. Besides the leading rites and ceremonies, the Parsis have many minor practices and observances to which more or less of a religious sanction is supposed to attach. A Parsi must always keep his head and feet covered, he must be never without the sacred shirt (*sadra*) and cord (*kasti*), must never smoke and must wash his hands if he ever puts his fingers in his mouth. In practice, however, many of these rules are neglected, more especially by the educated. Contact with Hindus and Musalmans has introduced among the Parsis many of their superstitious beliefs and practices. Some Parsis of the old type make offerings to the Hindu Holi, offer vows and sacrifice goats to the small-pox goddess and a few carry oil to the Hindu Hanuman god on Saturdays. Some offer vows and make presents to the Mohoram *tabuts* and at the tombs of Musalman saints. The faith in ghosts, magic, astrology and witchcraft is strong and widespread, especially among the females. Children have soot or lamp black rubbed on their eyes, cheeks and brows to keep off the evil eye.

7.—External characteristics of main religions.

271. The above notes briefly indicate only the main features of the religions of the people. Religion is a wide and debatable subject, and it would be impossible to deal fully with all the questions involved in it in a Census Report. In conclusion it may be interesting to note a few external characteristics by which the followers of the main religions may be recognised.

External characteristics of the main religions.

Hindus and Jains pray facing the east, while Musalmans pray facing the west, that is, towards Mecca. Hindus and Jains worship in temples while Musalmans pray in mosques. Hindus have Brahman priests, while Musalman and Jain ministrants are drawn from their own congregation. The Hindu venerates the cow, will not, as a rule, kill animals, and most of them abstain from meat.

The Jain scrupulously protects animal life and never touches meat. The Musalman loathes the pig and the dog but has no prejudice against any other animal. Hindus, Jains and the Musalmans use tobacco, but most of them reject narcotics and ardent spirits. Hindus and Jains shave their heads leaving a scalp-lock. Musalmans shave their head, but keep no scalp-lock and generally do not shave the beard. Hindus and Jains button their coats to the right, while Musalmans to the left. Hindus and Jains wear ***dhotis*** while Masalmans usually put on long trousers and only occasionally a ***dhoti,*** but without *kacchadi* or back-piece. Hindus and Jains prefer red and saffron colours and dislike black, while Musalmans prefer green to all others. Hindus and Jains use brass vessels, while Musalman vessels are usually of copper. Hindus and Jains may cook in, but may not eat out of, an earthen vessel, which has already been used for the purpose ; a Musalman may use an earthen vessel over and over again to eat from. Musalmans, and to some extent, even Jains eat together from a common dish, while Hindus use separate dishes for each person. Hindus and Jains marry in circumambulation of the sacred fire, but among Musalmans formal consent of the parties is asked and given before witnesses. Musalmans practise circumcision, but Hindus and Jains do not. Musalmans bury their dead, while Hindus and Jains, as a general rule, burn them. A Musulman will eat and drink without scruple from the hand of a Hindu or a Jain, but no Hindu or Jain will take either food or water from a Musalman. Musalman converts from Hinduism retain many of the customs and prejudices of the castes from which they have originated, and form an exception to this general rule.

ILLUSTRATIONS.

HINDU SADHUS.

(*For descriptive matter, see paras.* 215 *to* 231.)

BRAHMACHARI (*Shaiva*).

DANDI (*Shaiva*).

PARAMAHANSA (*Shaiva*).

SADHU (*Ramanuji*).

HINDU SADHUS—*contd.*

ACHARI (*Ramanandi*).

KHAKHI (*Ramanandi*).

BRAHMACHARI (*Swaminarayan*).

SADHU (*Swaminarayan*).

PALO (*Swaminarayan*).

JAIN SADHUS.

(For descriptive matter, see paras. 238 to 242.)

SADHU.

GORJI.

MUSALMAN FAKIRS.

(For descriptive matter, see paras. 262 to 265.)

NAKSHABAND.

BENAWA.

MUSALMAN FAKIRS.—*contd.*

MADARI.

MUSA SUHAG.

RAFAI.

MUSALMAN FAKIRS—*contd.*

Rasulshahi.

Sidi.

PARSI PRIEST.

(*For descriptive matter, see para.* 267.)

Mobed (*Parsi Priest*).

SUBSIDIARY TABLE I.—General Distribution of the Population by Religion.

Religion and Locality.	Actual Number in 1911.	Proportion per 10,000 of the Population. 1911	1901	1891	1881	Variation per cent. increase (+) or decrease (—). 1901-1911	1891-1901	1881-1891	Net variation 1881-1911.
1	2	3	4	5	6	7	8	9	10
Hindu.									
Baroda State	1,697,146	8,349	7,922	8,850	8,480	+ 9·71	— 27·63	+ 15·37	— 8·40
Baroda Division	493,906	8,406	8,202	8,879	8,926	+ 11·45	— 28·76	+ 6·40	— 15·52
Baroda City	78,218	7,878	7,783	7,897	7,890	— 3·17	— 12·13	+ [illegible]·39	— 6·93
Kadi Division	752,157	9,039	8,939	9,055	9,034	+ 0·81	— 25·01	+ 11·41	— 15·77
Navsari Division	217,195	6,474	4,215	8,518	5,707	+ 71·53	— 53·47	+ 65·82	+ 3·31
Amreli Division	155,670	8,732	8,662	8,686	[illegible],621	+ 3·63	— 4·06	+ 23·17	+ 22·45
Musalman.									
Baroda State	160,887	791	845	781	801	— 2·50	— 12·57	+ 7·86	— 8·05
Baroda Division	48,982	834	840	774	791	+ 7·94	— 16·29	+ 4·65	— 5·44
Baroda City	17,206	1,732	1,809	1,793	1,798	— 8·33	— 10·11	+ 9·03	— 10·15
Kadi Division	52,587	632	667	625	639	— 5·49	— 18·95	— 8·62	— 16·81
Navsari Division	23,207	692	847	759	800	— 8·82	+ 4·93	+ 5·44	+ 0·86
Amreli Division	18,905	1,061	1,140	1,151	1,208	— 4·68	— 4·68	+ 16·42	+ 6·11
Animist.									
Baroda State	115,411	568	903	124	465	— 34·52	+ 490·37	— 70·59	+ 13·68
Baroda Division	80,317	516	670	217	154	— 16·21	+ 137·6[illegible]	+ 50·48	+ 199·69
Baroda City	199	20	51	1	...	— 62·45	+5,788·89	+ 125	+ 48·75
Kadi Division	1	...	17	11	1	— 99·93	+ 19·21	+1,290·59	— 98·82
Navsari Division	84,894	3,530	4,595	431	3,176	— 38·50	+ 927·04	— 85·28	— 7·03
Amreli Division	......	...	5	...	...	— 100	......	...	......
Jain.									
Baroda State	43,462	214	247	208	214	— 10	— 4·06	+ 7·74	— 6·97
Baroda Division	8,005	136	160	127	126	— 7·46	— 3·11	+ 8·35	— 2·85
Baroda City	2,208	222	218	213	203	— 2·56	— 8·44	+ 11·94	— 0·14
Kadi Division	26,963	324	[illegible]76	309	325	— 14·19	— 7·33	+ 5·51	— 16·07
Navsari Division	2,772	83	89	62	58	+ 3·24	+ 23·05	+ 30·90	+ 66·29
Amreli Division	3,514	1[illegible]7	188	158	168	+ 7·56	+ 15·04	+ 14·70	+ 42·04
Parsi.									
Baroda State	7,955	39	43	34	37	— 5·40	+ 2·47	+ 1·08	— 2·01
Baroda Division	109	2	2	2	2	+ 3·81	— 23·91	+ 12·20	— 11·38
Baroda City	561	56	57	50	46	— 5·87	+ 2·11	+ 18·78	+ 14·49
Kadi Division	77	1	1	...	1	— 22·22	+ 167·57	— 31·49	+ 57·14
Navsari Division	7,17[illegible]	214	252	233	259	— 5·40	+ 2·04	— 0·05	— 3·52
Amreli Division	39	2	1	1	1	+ 45	+ 66·67	— 26	+ 93·33
Christian.									
Baroda State	7,203	35	39	3	3	— 6·35	+ 1,090·56	— 16·21	+ 834·24
Baroda Division	6,039	103	126	1	1	— 11·06	+11,812·28	— 25·97	+7,743·86
Baroda City	718	7[illegible]	75	43	58	— 3·36	+ 53·57	— 17·78	+ 23·02
Kadi Division	348	4	...	...	...	+ 1[illegible]50	— 50	+ 9·09	+ 690·91
Navsari Division	60	2	1	1	...	+ 39·53	+ 79·17	+ 84·62	+ 361·54
Amreli Division	8	...	4	1	1	— 86·67	+ 361·54	— 45·83	— 66·67
Others.									
Baroda State	734	4	1	...	...	+ 619·61	+ 82·14	+ 100	+2,521·43
Baroda Division	197	3	...	...	...	+ 1870	+ 100	+ 400	+ 19,600
Baroda City	205	21	7	3	...	+ 184·72	+ 84·62	+ 1,200	+6,733·33
Kadi Division	29	...	...	...	...	+ 866·67	— 75	+ 140	+ 480
Navsari Division	160	5	1	...	...	+ 841·18	......	— 100	+ 1,900
Amreli Division	143	8	...	...	1	......	......	— 100	+ 1,200

SUBSIDIARY TABLE II.—Showing the proportional strength of main religions.

District or Natural Division.	Hindu. Proportion per 10,000 of the population.				Musalman. Proportion per 10,000 of the population.				Animist. Proportion per 10,000 of the population.			
	1911.	1901.	1891.	1881.	1911.	1901.	1891.	1881.	1911.	1901.	1891.	1881.
1	2	3	4	5	6	7	8	9	10	11	12	13
Baroda State ...	**8,349**	**7,922**	**8,850**	**8,480**	**791**	**845**	**781**	**801**	**568**	**903**	**124**	**465**
Baroda Division ...	8,406	8,202	8,879	8,926	834	840	774	791	516	670	217	154
Baroda City ...	7,873	7,783	7,897	7,890	1.732	1,809	1,793	1,798	20	51	1	...
Kadi Division ...	9,039	8,939	9,055	9,034	632	667	625	639	...	17	11	1
Navsari Do. ..	6,474	4,215	8,518	5,707	692	647	759	800	2,530	4,595	421	3,176
Amreli Do. ...	8,732	8,662	8.689	8,621	1,061	1,140	1,151	1,208	...	5	...	...

District or Natural Division.	Jain. Proportion per 10,000 of the population.				Parsi. Proportion per 10,000 of the population.				Christian. Proportion per 10,000 of the population.				Others. Proportion per 10,000 of the population.			
	1911.	1901.	1891.	1881.	1911.	1901.	1891.	1881.	1911.	1901.	1891.	1881.	1911.	1901.	1891.	1881.
1	14	15	16	17	18	19	20	21	22	23	24	25	26	27	28	29
Baroda State ...	**214**	**247**	**208**	**214**	**39**	**43**	**34**	**3**	**35**	**39**	**3**	**3**	**4**		...	...
Baroda Division ...	136	160	127	126	2	2	2	2	103	126	1	1	3	...	...	...
Baroda City ..	222	218	213	208	56	57	50	46	76	75	43	58	21	7	3	...
Kadi Division ...	324	376	309	325	1	1	..	1	4	...	...	...	...	...	...	...
Navsari Do. ...	83	89	68	58	214	252	233	259	2	1	1	...	5	1	...	...
Amreli Do. ..	197	188	158	168	2	1	1	1	...	4	1	1	8	...	...	1

SUBSIDIARY TABLE III.—Christians. Number and variations.

District or Natural Division.	Actual number of Christians in				Variation per cent.			
	1911.	1901.	1891.	1881.	1901 to 1911.	1891–1901.	1881–1891.	1881–1911.
1	2	3	4	5	6	7	8	9
Baroda State ...	**7,203**	**7,691**	**646**	**771**	**— 6·35**	**+ 1,090·56**	**— 16·21**	**+ 834·24**
Baroda Division ...	6,039	6,790	57	77	— 11·06	+ 11,812·28	— 25·97	+ 7,742·86
Baroda City	748	774	504	613	— 3·36	+ 53·57	— 17·78	+ 22·02
Kadi Division	348	24	48	44	+ 1,350	— 50	+ 9·09	+ 690·90
Navsari Do.	60	43	24	13	+ 39·53	+ 79·17	+ 84·62	+ 361·54
Amreli Do.	8	60	13	24	— 86·67	+ 361·54	— 45·83	— 66·67

SUBSIDIARY TABLE IV.—Races and sects of Christians (actual numbers).

Sect.	European.		Anglo-Indian.		Native.		Total.		Variation. + or —
	Male.	Female.	Male.	Female.	Male.	Female.	1911.	1901.	
1	2	3	4	5	6	7	8	9	10
Anglican Communion ...	52	45	16	26	...	...	139	7,074	— 6,935
Baptist	1	3	...	...	...	...	4	5	— 1
Lutheran	3	...	2	2	...	...	7	14	— 7
Methodist	8	7	2	...	2,548	2,285	4,850	157	+ 4,693
Presbyterian	4	...	...	...	105	84	193	15	+ 178
Roman Catholic	20	14	14	20	266	134	468	404	+ 64
Salvationist	...	...	...	...	812	728	1,540	...	+ 1,540
Indefinite belief	2	...	...	...	...	...	2	...	+ 2
Sect not returned	...	...	...	...	...	...	...	22	— 22
Total ...	90	69	34	48	3,731	3,231	7,203	7,691	— 488

SUBSIDIARY TABLE V.—Distribution of Christians per mille (*a*) races by sect and (*b*) sects by race.

Sect.	Races distributed by Sect.				Sects distributed by Race.			
	European.	Anglo-Indian.	Native.	Total.	European.	Anglo-Indian.	Native.	Total.
1	2	3	4	5	6	7	8	9
Anglican Communion.	610	512	...	19	698	302	...	1,000
Baptist	25	...	...	·5	1,000	...	...	1,000
Lutheran	19	49	...	1	429	571	...	1,000
Methodist	94	24	694	673·3	3	·4	996·6	1,000
Presbyterian... ...	25	...	27	27	21	...	979	1,000
Roman Catholic ...	214	415	58	65	73	73	854	1,000
Salvationist	...	...	221	214	...	...	1,000	1,000
Indefinite belief ...	13	...	...	·2	1,000	...	...	1,000
	1,000	1,000	1,000	1,000	...	...	...	...

SUBSIDIARY TABLE VI.—Religion of urban and rural population.

District or Natural Division.	Number per 10,000 of urban population who are							Number per 10,000 of rural population who are						
	Hindus.	Musalmans.	Animists.	Jains.	Parsis.	Christians.	Others.	Hindus.	Musalmans.	Animists.	Jains.	Parsis.	Christians.	Others.
1	2	3	4	5	6	7	8	9	10	11	12	13	14	15
Baroda State ...	7,599	1,681	100	417	157	38	8	8,535	570	684	164	9	35	3
Baroda Division with City	7,829	1,676	105	268	35	73	14	8,511	706	567	105	1	107	3
Kadi Division ...	7,826	1,485	...	673	5	9	2	9 281	461	...	255	...	3	...
Navsari Division ...	6,126	1,716	504	310	1,335	8	1	6,525	545	2,822	50	53	1	4
Amreli Division ...	7,336	2,321	...	326	7	1	9	9,155	679	...	158	...	...	8

SUBSIDIARY TABLE VII.—

Sect.	Per cent.	Baroda State.			Baroda Division.		
		Persons.	Males.	Females.	Persons.	Males.	Females.
1	2	3	4	5	6	7	8
Hindu	**100**	**1,697,146**	**884,474**	**812,672**	**493,906**	**264,700**	**229,206**
I—Believers in Vedic and Pauranic deities.	85·71	1,454,660	757,710	696,950	449,535	240,943	208,592
1. Shaiva or Smarta	20·65	350,495	182,377	168,118	47,077	24,741	22,336
2. Shakta	16·94	287,547	148,267	139,280	61,341	32,027	29,314
3. Vaishnav	48·12	816,618	427,066	389,552	341,117	184,175	156,942
(1) Ramanuji	6·19	104,987	52,760	52,227	36,881	17,823	19,058
(2) Ramanandi	25·61	434,679	228,371	206,308	229,291	124,467	104,824
(3) Vallabhachari	10·10	171,460	90,124	81,336	53,165	29,549	23,616
(4) Swaminarayan	3·17	53,721	28,681	25,040	21,558	12,177	9,381
(5) Haribava	·59	9,990	4,749	5,241	...	...	...
(6) Tulsi Upasak	·17	2,948	1,599	1,349	162	127	35
(7) Radha Vallabhi	·09	1,566	865	701	...	...	...
(8) Gopinath	·04	629	346	283	...	...	...
(9) Kuber Panth	·03	437	222	215	...	...	...
(10) Vishwa Karma	·03	424	240	184	60	32	28
(11) Surya Upasak	·02	408	207	201	...	...	...
(12) Madhvacharya	...	71	46	25	...	...	...
(13) Nrisinhacharya	...	68	35	33	...		...
(14) Ganesh Panth	...	38	23	15	...	...	..
(15) Unspecified	2·08	35,192	18,798	16,394	...	...	...
II—Non-believers in Vedic and other deities.	13·55	229,963	120,084	109,879	43,304	23,157	20,147
4. Kabir Panth	2·06	34,954	18,067	16,887	19,049	9,882	9,167
5. Bij Panth	10·05	170,645	89,312	81,333	15,086	8,365	6,721
6. Parnami	·40	6,854	3,559	3,295	3,586	1,917	1,669
7. Dadu Panth	·14	2,401	1,242	1,159	2,314	1,191	1,123
8. Ramde Pir	·50	8,409	4,324	4,085	83	58	25
9. Naya Kaka	·12	2,084	1,046	1,038	913	480	433
10. Santram	·07	1,148	648	500	1,148	648	500
11. Bhabharam	·07	1,092	583	509	1,092	583	509
12. Uda Panth	·03	511	309	202	...	...	...
13. Khijdia Panth	·02	358	169	189	...	...	...
14. Saji Savai	·02	334	176	158	...	...	...
15. Patvala	·03	429	225	204	...	...	...
16. Vadvala	·01	144	85	59	...	...	...
17. Ajepal	·01	185	99	86	...	...	...
18. Ravi Saheb	...	51	42	9	33	33	...
19. Nakalank	...	47	25	22	...	...	...
20. Satyakeval	·01	135	69	66	...	...	...
21. Mota Panth	·01	123	75	48	...	...	...
22. Nirat Panth	...	59	29	30	...	...	...
III—Worshippers of Musalman Pirs and Saints	·21	3,630	1,912	1,718	643	331	312
IV—Sect not returned	·53	8,893	4,768	4,125	424	269	155
Jain	**100**	**43,462**	**21,875**	**21,587**	**8,005**	**4,195**	**3,810**
1. Swetambari	83·89	36,460	18,240	18,220	5,907	3,081	2,826
2. Digambari	10·10	4,389	2,267	2,122	1,705	883	822
3. Swetambar Sthanakvasi	6·01	2,613	1,368	1,245	393	231	162
Musalman	**100**	**160,887**	**82,986**	**77,901**	**48,982**	**26,244**	**22,738**
1. Sunni	85·02	136,792	70,766	66,026	43,897	23,808	20,089
2. Shiah	13·67	21,993	11,156	10,837	3,193	1,472	1,721
3. Imamshai or Pirana	1·31	2,102	1,064	1,038	1,392	964	928
Parsi	**100**	**7,955**	**3,420**	**4,535**	**109**	**75**	**34**
1. Shehenshai	97·78	7,778	3,370	4,408	108	74	34
2. Kadmi	2·22	177	50	127	1	1	...

SECTS BY DIVISIONS.

Baroda City.			Kadi Division.			Navsari Division.			Amreli Division.		
Persons.	Males.	Females.	Persons.	Males.	Females.	Persons.	Males.	Females.	Persons.	Males.	Females
9	10	11	12	13	14	15	16	17	18	19	20
78,218	42,103	36,115	752,157	387,162	364,995	217,195	110,070	107,125	155,670	80,439	75,231
71,213	38,519	32,694	578,443	296,773	281,670	210,995	106,864	104,131	144,474	74,611	69,863
27,064	14,924	12,140	235,090	120,996	114,094	20,551	11,085	9,466	20,713	10,631	10,082
8,306	4,335	3,971	66,546	35,043	31,503	116,977	59,085	57,892	34,377	17,777	16,600
35,843	19,260	16,583	276,807	140,734	136,073	73,467	36,694	36,773	89,384	46,203	43,181
1,856	973	883	46,622	23,391	23,231	5,502	2,984	2,518	14,126	7,589	6,537
11,579	6,186	5,393	139,695	71,052	68,643	44,839	22,225	22,614	9,275	4,441	4,834
16,341	8,698	7,643	39,698	19,984	19,714	7,312	3,687	3,625	54,944	28,206	26,738
2,248	1,257	991	20,493	10,303	10,190	1,227	598	629	8,195	4,346	3,849
...	...	...	...	...	...	9,990	4,749	5,241	...	...	...
...	...	...	2,764	1,464	1,300	22	8	14	...	...	...
11	8	3	1,555	857	698	...	...	...	...	...	...
..	...	...	629	346	283	...	...	...	...	...	...
34	12	22	106	59	47	297	151	146	...	...	...
16	9	7	304	174	130	44	25	19	...	...	...
...	...	...	...	...	...	...	...	...	408	207	201
51	29	22	...	...	...	20	17	3	...	...	...
53	27	26	11	4	7	4	4	...	...	...	...
34	19	15	4	4	...	...	...	...	...	...	...
3,620	2,042	1,578	24,926	13,096	11,830	4,210	2,246	1,964	2,436	1,414	1,022
5,734	2,899	2,835	165,893	86,316	79,577	4,106	2,062	2,044	10,926	5,650	5,276
4,448	2,180	2,268	8,313	4,389	3,924	2,426	1,260	1,166	718	356	362
329	183	146	150,832	78,436	72,396	217	128	89	4,181	2,200	1,981
192	89	103	1,494	809	685	911	411	500	671	333	338
3	2	1	75	44	31	9	5	4	...	...	...
174	98	76	4,366	2,232	2,134	50	29	21	3,736	1,907	1,829
...	...	...	712	357	355	459	209	250	...	...	...
...	...	...	...	...	...	...	...	...	...	...	...
...	...	...	...	...	...	...	...	...	...	...	...
511	309	202	...	...	...	...	...	...	...	...	...
...	...	...	...	...	...	...	...	...	358	169	189
...	...	...	...	...	...	...	...	...	334	176	158
...	...	...	...	...	...	...	...	...	429	225	204
...	...	...	...	...	...	...	...	...	144	85	59
...	...	...	...	...	...	...	...	...	185	99	86
18	9	9	...	...	...	...	...	...	...	...	...
...	...	...	...	...	...	...	...	...	47	25	22
...	...	...	101	49	52	34	20	14	...	...	...
...	...	...	...	...	...	..	...	...	123	75	48
59	29	30	...	...	...	...	...	...	...	...	...
53	28	25	2,911	1,548	1,363	23	5	18	...	...	...
1,218	657	561	4,910	2,525	2,385	2,071	1,139	932	270	178	92
2,208	1,153	1,055	26,963	13,147	13,816	2,772	1,559	1,213	3,514	1,821	1,693
1,846	964	882	24,776	12,040	12,736	2,388	1,342	1,046	1,543	813	730
240	124	116	1,415	726	689	331	191	140	698	343	355
122	65	57	772	381	391	53	26	27	1,273	665	608
17,206	9,250	7,956	52,587	26,750	25,837	23,207	11,206	12,001	18,905	9,536	9,369
12,839	7,039	5,800	41,885	21,220	20,665	22,916	11,044	11,872	15,255	7,655	7,600
4,367	2,211	2,156	10,492	5,430	5,062	291	162	129	3,650	1,881	1,769
...	..	...	210	100	110	...	...	...	...	...	...
561	319	242	77	46	31	7,179	2,965	4,214	29	15	14
539	310	229	73	44	29	7,029	2,927	4,102	29	15	14
22	9	13	4	2	2	150	38	112	...	...	...

Chapter V.

AGE.

Reference to statistics.

272. The age distribution of the population for each age year of life up to 5 and then for quinquennial periods up to 70, with a single head for persons aged 70 and over is given in Imperial Table VII. Persons returned as suffering from the four infirmities dealt with at the Census are classified according to the same age periods in Table XII. In Table XIV the ages of certain selected castes are exhibited in connection with the statistics of civil condition ; and in Table VIII the prevalence of literacy is shown for the total population and for each religion, but the age periods selected for these two tables are somewhat less elaborate than those for Table VII. The age statistics, so far as they tend to throw light on the proportions of the sexes, the marriage customs of the people, the degree of education they enjoy and their liabilities at different ages to the infirmities above referred to have been dealt with in separate chapters devoted to these subjects ; and in the present chapter, the discussion will be confined to a consideration of the information to be derived from them regarding the longevity and fecundity of the people and of the changes which have occurred in their age distribution since the previous Census with the reasons for the same. The following Subsidiary Tables at the end of this chapter illustrate the more important points in the statistics by means of proportional figures :—

Subsidiary Table I.—Age distribution of 100,000 persons of each sex by annual periods.

Subsidiary Table II.—Age distribution of 10,000 of each sex in the State and each Natural Division.

Subsidiary Table III.—Age distribution of 10,000 of each sex in each main religion.

Subsidiary Table IV.—Age distribution of 1,000 of each sex in certain castes.

Subsidiary Table V.—Proportion of children under 10 and of persons over 50 to those aged 15-40 ; as also of married females aged 15-40 per 100 females.

Subsidiary Table VI.—Variation of population at certain age periods.

Subsidiary Table VII.—Reported birth-rate by sex and Natural Divisions.

Subsidiary Table VIII.—Reported death-rate by sex and Natural Divisions.

Subsidiary Table IX.—Reported death-rate by sex and age in decade and in selected years per mille living at same age according to the Census of 1901.

Subsidiary Table X.—Reported deaths from certain diseases per mille of each sex.

Instructions to the enumerators.

273. The instructions given to the enumerators were :—"Column 7 (Age).—Enter the age as it will be on the 10th March 1911. Note that the number of years actually completed are to be entered and not the current year of age. For infants less than one year old, enter the word 'infant' and not the number of months since birth."

Ignorance of age.

274. Most of the people in this country do not know their precise age and when asked what it is, give such vague replies as *panch sat* 'five seven,' *das bar* 'ten twelve,' *pandar vis* 'fifteen twenty', *pachis tis* 'twenty-five thirty,' *tis chalis* 'thirty forty', and so on. Even when they are precise in their reply, there is a tendency to select certain round numbers which are exact multiples of 5 or 10. It is a matter of

everyday experience in our courts that Kolis, Bhils and other illiterate people, when asked to state their age, either say that they do not know it, or give ridiculous replies. With a view to secure as correct an age return as possible, the enumerators were further instructed that, when the reply given appeared grossly absurd from the appearance of the person enumerated, they should consult one or two sensible persons in the locality and put down the age which may be deemed to be the most likely.

Inaccuracy of the age return.

275. In spite of these precautions, the age return does not seem to be very reliable. In a progressive or stationary population, the greatest number should be at the age "under 1 year" and it should steadily decrease from year to year. It will be seen from Subsidiary Table 1 and from the diagram in the margin, which has been prepared from a special table showing the actual ages as returned by the people of this State that children shown as 5 years of age are more numerous than those of 1 year, but they are, in their turn, exceeded by the number of males returned at the ages 20, 25, 30, 35, 40 and 50. This is due mainly to the tendency already alluded to, to return certain favourite numbers which are for the most part multiples of five; the most popular numbers of all are apparently 20, 25, 30, 35, 40 and 50.

Diagram showing the actual number of males returned at each age per 100,000.

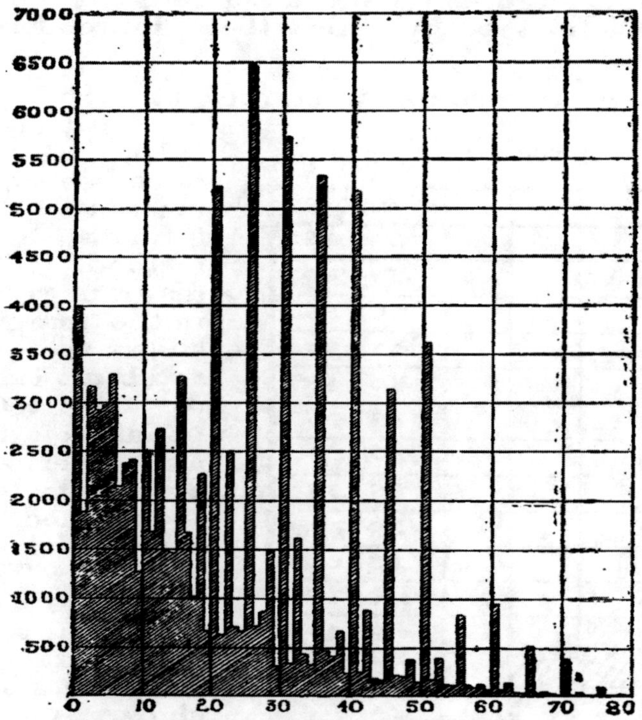

The number returned as between 1 and 2 years of age is less than half of that under 1 year. The very small number returned as between 1 and 2 years of age appears to be due to the rule that children under 1 year of age should be entered as "infants." The object of this provision was to avoid the confusion between months and years which would arise if the ages of such children were stated in months. Many children over 1 year of age who were still unweaned and were therefore popularly regarded as infants were shown as such in the census schedules and were accordingly classed as "under 1 year of age" in the course of tabulation. The number of males and females at the ages 20-25 and 25-30 is comparatively greater than what it should be, and shows that amongst both sexes, there is a general desire to be considered young, and many aged 40 or thereabout must have described themselves as 25 or 30 years of age. Amongst old people of both sexes, but especially in the case of females, exaggeration in the matter of age is very common. The number of both sexes aged 60-65 is far greater than their number in the age-period 55-60. The same phenomena are observed when the numbers in the age periods 65-70 and '70 and over' are compared. Females aged '70 and over' are nearly double of those aged 65-70.

These are the main causes of error. They are neither new nor confined to this State. They are common to all Provinces in India, both at the present and all previous enumerations.

Its utility.

276. In spite of the above irregularities and errors in the age return, it need not be set aside as useless. The degree of error from census to census may be assumed to be constant and the collation of the results for successive enumerations may

bring to light the alteration in the age distribution of the people, which may have taken place owing to famine, plague or other disturbing causes. Again the registration of vital statistics in the State is still very imperfect, and we cannot therefore afford to neglect any other source from which a fair approximation to actual facts regarding the mean duration of life and the birth and death-rates may be deduced. In a large population, errors due to over and under statement tend to cancel each other, while the plumping on certain favourite numbers can be eliminated by a process known as "smoothing by Bloxam's method," which was described on pages 391 to 395 of the India Administrative Volume for 1901.

Mean age.

277. The most important use to which the age return can be put, is the light which it throws on the question of the relative longevity of the people of different religions and localities and at different times. The mean age of the people in each natural division and at each of the last four censuses has been shown in Subsidiary Table II and the corresponding figures for the main religions have been given in Subsidiary Table III. The method by which these figures have been arrived at is as follows :—

In the first place the irregularities in the numbers returned at each age-period (0-5, 5-10, etc.) have been eliminated by "Bloxam's method." The diagram given in the margin shows the distribution of the total population by age-periods according to the method of smoothing adopted. The mean age has been calculated from the number shown as living at each age-period in the manner described in para. 756 of the last India Census Report. The totals showing the number of persons at the end of each quinquennial period have been multiplied by 5 and raised by $2\frac{1}{2}$ times the total number of persons dealt with, and the sum thus obtained has then been divided by the number of persons.

Diagram showing adjusted age-periods.

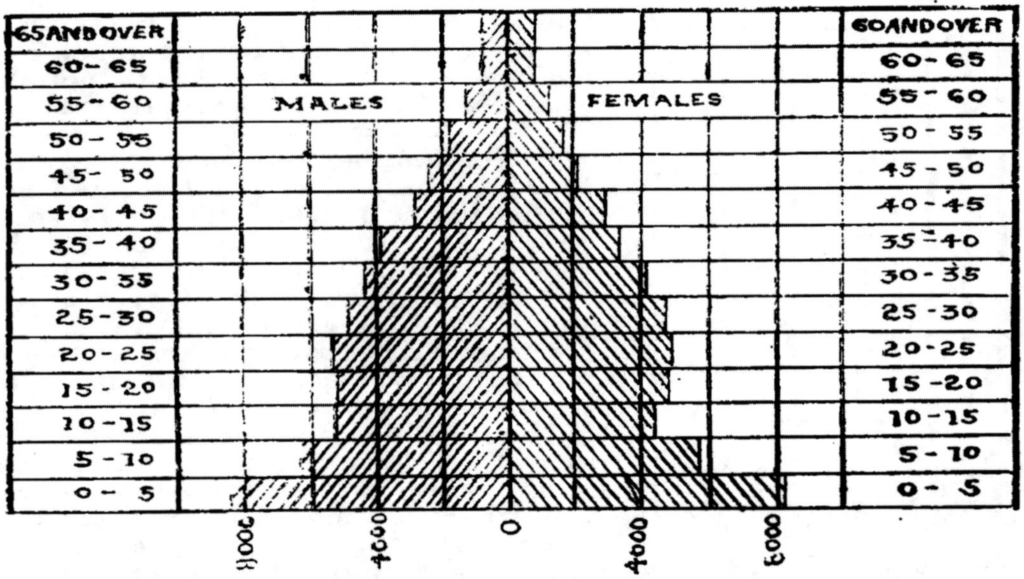

It should be clearly understood that no pretence is made to absolute accuracy and no attempt has been made to allow for errors other than fondness for round numbers, *e. g.*, to a tendency to understate or overstate age ; but it is believed that whatever error may attach to the method is uniform for all the figures dealt with and will not therefore vitiate comparison between districts, religions and censuses.

Meaning of mean age.

278. Before discussing the figures, it is necessary to bear in mind the precise import of the expression 'mean age.' As here calculated, 'mean age' refers to the average age of the persons enumerated at the census, *i.e.*, of the living, and does not coincide with the mean duration of life or the expectation of life at birth, except in the exceptional case, when the population has been stationary for at least a genera-

tion. The figure largely depends on the relation between the birth and death-rates, and in a growing population, *i. e.*, where the births exceed the deaths, there will be an excess of young persons and the mean age of the living will be less than in a decadent one, where the children are few in number, even though there is no difference in the average longevity of the individuals, who compose the two communities. Variations in the mean age as calculated in Subsidiary Tables II and III may, therefore, be due to a change either in the proportion of births or in the rate of mortality.

279. In discussing variations in mean age, it seems desirable to consider only the figures for males, as it is believed that there is less inaccuracy in the return of their ages than is the case with females. From the figures given in the margin it will be noticed that in the State as a whole, the mean age of males rose slightly during the decade 1891-1901, owing to lesser proportion of children in the population on account of the great famine. Since 1901, the proportion of children is comparatively larger, and consequently there has been a fall in the mean age of the living. Calculated separately, the mean age of males in the City of Baroda is the highest in the whole State owing to the large number of immigrants of adult age.

Variations in mean age.

Division.	Mean age of males in 1911.	1901.	1891.
State	22·7	23·6	23·2
Baroda	23·6	25·1	24·8
Kadi	22·1	23·7	23·2
Navsari	23·3	23·5	23·2
Amreli	22·1	24·5	23·7
Baroda City	24·6	27·1	27·7

The figures for natural divisions show that the mean age is the highest in the Baroda district, where (owing to its including Baroda City) the proportion of adult immigrants is the greatest. On the other hand, Kadi has the lowest mean age on account of the large number of emigrants of adult age that it sends out.

280. Among religions, Jains have the highest mean age, owing to their being the least prolific. The Animists, on the other hand, have the lowest mean age, owing to greater fecundity and a shorter span of life. The Hindus have a lower mean age than the Mahomedans, because they are comparatively more prolific.

Religion.	Mean age of males.
Hindu	22·9
Jain	24·7
Musalman	23·4
Animist	20·6

Death and birth-rates.

281. We learn from the Sanitary Commissioner's report for 1909-10 that, excluding the years 1899-1900 and 1900-01, when abnormal deaths occurred as the result of the famine, the decennial mean death-rate in the State comes to 27·0 and the birth-rate to 21·6. If these figures were correct, that is, if the death-rate was really higher than the birth-rate, the population of the State, instead of showing as it has done in the census, an increase of four per cent. would have shown a very large decrease. The record of vital statistics in the State being imperfect, the birth and death ratios, based on it, are obviously incorrect; and we must look to some other data from which a fair approximation to the actual facts may be deduced. This is afforded by the mean age referred to in paragraph 277 above. An average age of 22·8 in a stationary population would indicate a death-rate per 1,000 of $\frac{1000}{22 \cdot 8}$ or about 44. As the population is not stationary but growing, the death-rate, calculated on this basis, would be somewhat less than 44. The average yearly increase in the population is 4 per 1,000 and a death-rate of 44 per 1,000 would therefore give a birth-rate of about 48 per 1,000. The death and birth-rates thus disclosed appear highly probable, having regard to the sanitary conditions and plague and other epidemics prevailing in the State. The birth-rate also should be high in a growing population in which marriage is universal.

282. The age distribution of the people shows great variations in the State as a whole, as also in its natural divisions at different enumerations (Subsidiary Table II). In the State as a whole, for example, the proportion of male children under 5 rose from 1,231 in 1881 to 1,321 in 1891, fell to 963 in 1901 and has again risen to 1,489 in the present Census. These proportions depend upon the normal birth and death-rates and the occurrence or otherwise of special calamities, such as famine, plague, &c., which disturb the normal age distribution. The birth and death-rates are determined by various factors not easily gauged and they change but slowly. The marked difference in the age distribution occurring within short intervals of ten years must be due to the influence of some special calamity such as famine, plague, etc. The effect of a calamity like the famine of 1899-1900 is far-reaching and may be described in the words of the India Census Report for 1901 (p. 474) as under :—

Age distribution.

District.	Number of males under 5 per 10,000.			
	1911.	1901.	1891.	1881.
Baroda State	**1,489**	**963**	**1,321**	**1,231**
Baroda	1,397	846	1,219	1,056
Kadi	1,543	959	1,366	1,369
Navsari	1,611	1,302	1,491	1,493
Amreli	1,567	931	1,430	1,047

"When a tract is afflicted by famine the mortality rises in a greater or less degree according to the severity and duration of the calamity and the effectiveness of the measures taken to mitigate it. All sections of the population, however, are not equally affected ; the very old and the very young suffer most, while those in prime of life sustain only a comparatively small diminution in their numbers. * * * Consequently at the close of the famine the population consists of an unusually small proportion of children and old persons and of a very large proportion of persons in the prime of life, *i.e.*, at the reproductive ages. For some years, therefore, in the absence of any fresh calamity, the growth of the population is very rapid. The number of persons capable of adding to the population not having been affected, the actual number of births is very little less than before the famine, but the proportion calculated on the diminished population is much greater and so too is the excess of births over deaths, as the latter are much below the average in a population consisting of an unusually large proportion of healthy persons in their prime, and of a comparatively small proportion of persons who by reason of youth, old age, or infirmity have a relatively short expectation of life. This more rapid rate of growth continues for some time, but then, as the persons who, at the time of the famine, were in their prime, pass into old age and their place is taken by the generation born shortly before the famine with its numbers greatly reduced by the mortality which then occurred, the birth-rate falls, not only below that of the years following the famine, but also below the average. The disturbance of normal conditions is still not ended and the pendulum continues to swing backwards and forwards between periods of high and low birth-rate, but its oscillations gradually become fainter until they cease from natural causes to be apparent or, as more often happens, until some fresh calamity obliterates them."

In accordance with the general principles laid down in the above extract, we find that in the Baroda and Amreli Districts, which suffered from the famine of 1876-77, the number of children under 5 years of age per 1,000 males was in 1881 only 1,056 and 1,047 respectively, but in 1891, *i.e.*, after a period of recovery, it had risen to 1,219 and 1,430 respectively. The Census of 1901 was preceded by the great famine which affected the whole State and caused appreciable increase in the mortality, and it is, therefore, that we find in all the districts a sharp decline in the proportion of children. The conditions of the decade which has just been over were not quite satisfactory. We had in the midst of it two or three years of deficient rainfall and more or less plague throughout. But the number of persons adding to the population not having been much affected, the number of births, after the great famine, has been unusually large, and we have now in all the districts a much larger proportion of children than ever before.

The proportion of males below 5 being the lowest in 1901, the number of those aged 10-15 should be less in this Census than ten years previously. A reference to Subsidiary Table II shows that it is so. The proportion of males aged 10-15 to 1,000 persons in the population in the whole State is now 935 against 1,357 in 1901, 1,108 in 1891 and 1,208 in 1881.

Variations by age-periods.

283. In Subsidiary Table VI are given the variations in the population at certain age-periods. During the decade 1881-1891, although the total population of the State increased by 10·5 per cent. only, the increase in the age-period 0-10 was 14·6 per cent.

which was mainly contributed by the large increase of 44·6 per cent. in the number of children below 10 in the Amreli Division, which had suffered hard from the famine of 1877. The famine of 1899-1900, which preceded the Census of 1901, brought about a heavy decline of 35·6 per cent. in the number of children below 10; and though the present Census shows an increase of about 4 per cent. in the total population, the age-period 10-15 which corresponds with the inflated age-period 0-5 of 1901 shows a decline of about 28 per cent., while the age-period 0-10 shows a marked increase of about 22 per cent. The famine having removed the old, the age-period 60 and over showed in 1901 a heavy decline of about 40 per cent., while the general decline in the population was about 19 per cent. The present Census shows an increase of about 20 per cent. in the number of old people aged 60 and over, as those in the previous age-period who suffered the least from the famine, have attained this age.

Age distribution of different castes.

284. The proportional age distribution of some of the main castes will be found in Subsidiary Table IV. It would occupy too much space to discuss the figures at length, but taking males only a few interesting results may be briefly noticed. As a general rule, castes, which are considered high, have the largest number of males over 40 per 1,000, *viz.*, Brahman Anavala (239), Brahman Audich (238), Brahman Deshastha (315), Brahman Nagar (275), Vania Disaval (313), Vania Shrimali Hindu (254), Saiyad (241) and Parsi (276). Conversely, castes and tribes considered low have the smallest proportion of persons of this age, *viz.*, Ahir (197), Bharvad (190), Chamar (170), Ghanchi (191), Gola (174), Kumbhar (177), Talavia (181), Vaghari (182), Bhil (175), Chodhra (171), Dhanka (191), Dhodia (159), Gamit (167), Nayakda (189) and Momna (171). These proportions are determined as already explained, not only by the relative longevity of these groups but also by their fecundity. When the proportion of children is large, that of the adults must necessarily be smaller and the average age of the community will be less, even if the actual duration of life be the same. Figures given in the margin will show that amongst the high castes, the proportion of children is much smaller than it is amongst the aboriginal tribes. It can, therefore, be said that on the whole the higher castes have less fecundity, but they enjoy a longer span of life than those of lower status.

Caste or Tribe.	Number of male children under 5 per 1,000 of population.
Brahman Anavala	120
" Audich	116
" Deshastha	97
" Modh	109
Vania Disaval	105
" Shrimali	105
Chamar	170
Gola	166
Bhil	204
Chodhra	179
Dhanka	180
Dhodia	184
Gamit	175
Nayakda...	174

General increase in the birth-rate.

285. There appears to have been a general and progressive increase in the birth-rate since 1881. Out of 10,000 of each sex in the State as a whole, there were 253 boys and 274 girls aged 0-1 in 1881, 314 boys and 343 girls in 1891, 145 boys and 156 girls in 1901 and 394 boys and 416 girls in 1911. The low proportion in 1901 was due to the effects of the famine which preceded the Census, and if that abnormal period be left out of account, it is clear that there has been a steady rise in the proportion of children from Census to Census. Figures given in Subsidiary Table II show that, even in the different districts, the same phenomena are to be observed.

It may be said, however, that five years is too short a period from which to draw any general conclusion, and that we should, therefore, compare the proportion of children under ten years of age. The figures given on the next page refer to the Natural Divisions only, but a more detailed comparison of the figures for the last three Censuses will be found in Subsidiary Table V at the end of this Chapter. "It must be remembered that the variations in the proportion borne by children to the total population depend not only on the changes in the birth-rate but also on the deaths which occur. If owing to the prevalence of epidemics or general unhealthiness, the mortality amongst adults is high, the proportion of children will be greater, even though the number of births remain the same as before. On the other hand, a general increase in the longevity of the people, due to an improvement in their material condition, would tend to reduce the proportion which children bear to the total population. Similarly, if there are any causes of mortality, especially in the life of children, the proportion of the latter will be reduced accordingly." (Bengal Report 1901, p. 216).

District.	Number of children under 10 per 1,000 of the population.							
	Male.				Female.			
	1911.	1901.	1891.	1881.	1911.	1901.	1891.	1881.
Baroda State ...	**137**	**115**	**140**	**130**	**128**	**111**	**140**	**113**
Baroda District... ...	128	107	129	120	115	98	123	105
Kadi "	140	113	150	133	131	110	149	110
Navsari "	144	134	152	148	141	141	155	141
Amreli "	136	114	146	122	133	111	145	117

It is very difficult to ascertain how far the proportions have been affected in the different parts of the State by considerations such as these; but taking the figures as they stand, it may be observed that as compared with 1881 the proportion of children aged 10 in 1891 was higher. Famine and plague combined to bring about a heavy fall in the proportion in 1901, but the figures for 1911, exceed those for 1881, nearly approach those of 1891, and would have exceeded the latter, had it not been for the disturbing cause of plague, which was prevalent throughout the decade in all the districts and to the infection of which children and females staying in the house are more liable than males. Measles, mainly in its epidemic form, also carried away a large number of children in the years 1903 and 1904. If the next decade is free from such disturbing causes, the proportion of children in the next Census is sure to exceed that of 1891.

286. The proportion of children of both sexes aged 10 per 100 married females aged 15-40 is highest in the Navsari District, where the population is growing, especially among the Animistic tribes. Then follow Kadi, Amreli and Baroda Districts in order; and Baroda City stands last with only 119 children. The number of births depends on the number of married women of child-bearing ages and the proportion of such women in the City is much smaller than elsewhere, owing to immigrants coming to it without their women folk.

Relative fecundity in different natural divisions.

Division.	Proportion of children aged10 of both sexes per 100 married females aged 15-40.
Baroda State	**145**
Baroda Division	135
Baroda City	119
Kadi Division.	148
Navsari Division.	155
Amreli Division.	146

287. Turning to the proportion of children amongst the different religions, we notice that it is highest among the Animistic tribes and lowest among the Musalmans. The Hindus occupy a middle place approaching more nearly the Musalmans than the Animists. There is no marked difference in the relative longevity of Hindus and Musalmans, and the excess of children amongst the former is in all probability due to a higher birth-rate. In the Navsari (2,882) and Amreli (2,994) Districts, Musalmans have a higher proportion of children than Hindus and it is only due to their having lower proportion of children in the Baroda and Kadi Districts, that they lag behind the Hindus in the State as a whole. The

Relative fecundity in different religions.

Religion.	Proportion of children under 10 per 10,000.	
	Male.	Female.
Hindu...	2,604	2,630
Musalman	2,545	2,576
Animist	3,287	3,334

aboriginal tribes are known to be comparatively short-lived, and though they are very prolific, the greater number of children among them as compared with the Hindus and Musalmans may also be due in part to the fact that there are fewer old people amongst them. The inferior prolificness of Musalmans as indeed of the Hindus may be explained by the inactive and secluded life which their females, and more especially those of the former, live in their *zananas*.

Reproductive forces when most active.

288. Some curious information about the months most favourable for conception is deducible from the annual reports of the Sanitary Commissioner. An examination of the statements in the annual reports for the last ten years shows that the largest number of births is registered either in the month of October or November and the least in the month of February or March. Calculating the probable time of conception, *i.e.*, nine months earlier, we find that the months most favourable to conception are the winter months of December and January. The extent to which conception takes place shows a steady decline from February to April. In the very hot months of May and June, the fecundity of the people remains at a minimum and then again rises slowly and reaches the maximum in the cold weather.

Months for maximum and minimum mortality.

289. A similar study of the Sanitary Commissioner's reports for the last decade shows that in the whole State, mortality is the heaviest in the month of March and the lowest in the month of June. This, as explained by the Sanitary Commissioner, is probably due to the month of March being unhealthy in the State on account of the high incidence of malaria in the cold season after the monsoon ; and June is healthy on account of the excessive heat destroying disease germs.

SUBSIDIARY TABLE I.—Age distribution of 100,000 of each sex by annual periods.

Age.	Males.			Females.		
	Hindu.	Muhammadan.	Both religions.	Hindu.	Muhammadan.	Both religions.
1	2	3	4	5	6	7
Total	**100,000**	**100,000**	**100,000**	**100,000**	**100,000**	**100,000**
0	3,918	3,703	3,899	4,173	3,788	4,139
1	1,874	1,682	1,858	2,106	1,761	2,076
2	3,157	3,054	3,148	3,435	3,363	3,429
3	2,871	2,882	2,872	3,370	3,219	3,357
4	2,937	2,996	2,942	2,954	3,142	2,971
5	3,109	2,653	3,070	2,779	3,010	2,799
6	2,097	2,217	2,107	2,021	2,040	2,023
7	2,385	2,464	2,392	2,196	2,064	2,185
8	2,441	2,590	2,454	2,092	2,054	2,089
9	1,257	1,209	1,253	1,173	1,318	1,186
10	2,424	2,670	2,445	1,877	2,162	1,902
11	1,132	1,144	1,132	961	1,213	983
12	2,765	3,007	2,786	2,346	2,661	2,374
13	1,463	1,586	1,473	1,592	1,263	1,563
14	1,512	1,117	1,478	1,340	1,266	1,334
15	3,280	3,139	3,268	2,939	2,816	2,928
16	1,685	1,641	1,681	1,538	1,628	1,546
17	1,005	1,070	1,010	941	1,112	956
18	2,326	2,341	2,328	2,218	2,180	2,215
19	665	553	656	542	467	535
20	5,380	5,231	5,367	6,038	6,153	6,048
21	624	708	631	495	501	496
22	2,559	2,187	2,527	2,487	2,531	2,490
23	691	665	688	645	709	650
24	593	1,102	637	641	715	647
25	6,622	6,589	6,620	7,020	6,878	7,007
26	685	680	685	582	540	578
27	837	772	832	717	710	716
28	1,519	1,198	1,491	1,588	1,354	1,568
29	273	196	266	249	223	246
30	5,842	5,871	5,845	6,725	6,804	6,732
31	292	248	288	199	253	204
32	1,616	1,454	1,602	1,570	1,421	1,558
33	400	211	384	281	267	280
34	311	225	304	198	176	196
35	5,417	5,210	5,400	5,222	4,911	5,194
36	437	411	434	307	327	309
37	364	305	359	271	277	271
38	671	404	648	641	426	621
39	223	270	227	176	164	175
40	5,347	5,580	5,367	6,062	6,254	6,079
41	211	206	210	156	105	151
42	888	764	877	704	566	692
43	149	119	147	120	105	119
44	119	260	131	113	86	111
45	3,167	3,566	3,201	3,008	2,961	3,004
46	178	183	179	106	96	105
47	182	176	182	135	95	132
48	357	351	356	324	225	315
49	122	116	122	102	76	100
50	3,690	4,170	3,731	3,903	4,418	3,948

SUBSIDIARY TABLE I.—AGE DISTRIBUTION OF 100,000 OF EACH SEX BY ANNUAL PERIODS—*contd.*

AGE.	MALES.			FEMALES.		
	Hindu.	Muham-madan.	Both religions.	Hindu.	Muham-madan.	Both religions.
1	2	3	4	5	6	7
51	147	145	147	163	86	156
52	390	399	391	373	276	365
53	101	105	101	138	48	130
54	91	117	93	133	67	127
55	1,341	1,491	1,354	1,187	1,270	1,194
56	94	116	96	89	90	89
57	74	64	73	50	54	51
58	121	76	117	108	86	106
59	46	28	44	41	40	41
60	1,870	2,235	1,901	2,535	2,816	2,560
61	54	46	53	45	39	44
62	117	157	121	115	87	112
63	23	34	24	23	24	23
64	28	25	27	14	24	15
65	512	593	519	530	585	535
66	27	35	28	22	16	22
67	32	59	35	24	28	24
68	26	24	26	28	27	28
69	11	30	12	12	16	12
70	375	480	384	455	581	466
71	18	13	17	11	13	11
72	42	36	42	29	45	30
73	8	17	9	7	18	8
74	8	5	8	3	1	2
75	137	211	144	175	307	186
76	8	5	8	8	8	8
77	6	5	7	7	6	7
78	9	11	9	7	8	7
79	3	6	4	3	24	5
80	131	153	133	188	280	196
81	5	5	5	4	5	4
82	5	10	5	6	6	6
83	4	1	3	3	5	4
84	2	......	2	1	......	1
85	22	34	23	23	32	25
86	1	1	1	2	1	2
87	2	......	2	1	......	1
88	1	2	1	1	3	1
89	1	2	1	......	......	......
90	20	41	21	27	59	30
91	1	2	1	3	......	2
92	1	2	2	1	3	2
93	......	1	......	......	4	1
94	1	......	1	2	3	2
95	5	11	5	10	16	10
96	1	2	1	2	......	2
97	......	......	......	1	3	1
98	1	1	1	2	5	2
99	1	1	1	1	1	1
100 and over	7	17	7	9	30	11

SUBSIDIARY TABLE II—Age Distribution of 10,000 of each sex in the State and each Natural Division.

Age.	1911. Male.	1911. Female.	1901. Male.	1901. Female.	1891. Male.	1891. Female.	1881. Male.	1881. Female.
1	2	3	4	5	6	7	8	9
Baroda State.								
0—1 ...	394	416	145	156	314	343	253	274
1—2 ...	188	208	133	139	164	186	183	202
2—3 ...	316	343	205	226	272	316	241	277
3—4 ...	292	340	220	249	282	340	273	312
4—5 ...	299	302	260	286	289	324	281	304
Total ... 0—5 ...	1,489	1,609	963	1,056	1,321	1,509	1,231	1,369
5—10 ...	1,141	1,044	1,254	1,236	1,424	1,407	1,435	1,424
10—15 ...	935	825	1,357	1,200	1,108	932	1,208	1,067
15—20 ...	887	818	1,036	941	865	772	856	768
20—25 ...	970	1,026	998	1,007	921	995	898	939
25—30 ...	986	1,006	978	959	916	909	916	894
30—35 ...	840	895	869	831	865	850	867	853
35—40 ...	712	656	679	653	609	559	637	603
40—45 ...	666	705	632	693	649	675	934	944
45—50 ...	406	364	380	399	327	301		
50—55 ...	439	462	419	461	465	480	481	503
55—60 ...	170	150	167	190	142	127	173	173
60—65 ...	211	272						
65—70 ...	64	64	268	374	388	484	364	463
70 & over ...	84	104						
Mean Age ...	22·71	22·77	23·56	23·76	23·19	23·47	23·92	24·34
Baroda City.								
0—1 ...	278	323	147	160	284	333	163	182
1—2 ...	147	171	87	121	118	158	130	164
2—3 ...	224	260	154	183	168	214	152	183
3—4 ...	205	257	166	196	165	210	155	180
4—5 ...	224	244	179	217	184	210	157	188
Total ... 0—5 ...	1,078	1,255	733	877	919	1,125	757	897
5—10 ...	859	902	1,020	1,038	880	981	883	989
10—15 ...	889	787	1,091	881	828	751	975	923
15—20 ...	935	909	946	824	880	863	785	822
20—25 ...	1,177	1,105	1,057	877	1,156	1,126	1,070	1,057
25—30 ...	1,093	959	1,074	1,082	1,103	965	1,100	1,009
30—35 ...	921	849	930	867	1,035	914	1,137	992
35—40 ...	669	618	782	787	712	570	758	652
40—45 ...	766	783	782	761	872	844	1,279	1,196
45—50 ...	430	379	450	522	377	340		
50—55 ...	508	573	551	585	562	620	587	625
55—60 ...	201	196	209	291	168	169	183	189
60—65 ...	271	393						
65—70 ...	83	94	375	608	508	732	486	649
70 & over ...	120	198						
Mean Age ...	24·55	25·65	27·15	28·52	27·72	27·76	28·36	28·36
Baroda Division.								
0—1 ...	374	410	126	126	310	338	219	238
1—2 ...	170	193	119	119	165	185	143	157
2—3 ...	299	321	184	205	246	290	202	234
3—4 ...	278	322	196	222	250	314	238	290
4—5 ...	276	289	221	220	248	284	254	283
Total ... 0—5 ...	1,397	1,535	846	892	1,219	1,411	1,056	1,202
5—10 ...	1,084	992	1,232	1,228	1,299	1,299	1.401	1,447
10—15 ...	869	746	1,303	1,082	1,047	833	1,227	1,058
15—20 ...	847	768	945	830	876	790	857	755
20—25 ...	988	987	979	1,061	960	1,056	908	953
25—30 ...	1,003	1,023	1,080	1,058	972	948	963	938
30—35 ...	842	922	946	911	868	852	902	888
35—40 ...	·787	738	729	720	658	620	701	668
40—45 ...	712	732	667	746	694	723	1,018	1,027
45—50 ...	460	435	405	431	374	354		
50—55 ...	444	476	439	475	500	504	472	471
55—60 ...	194	170	168	199	161	146	162	154
60—65 ...	220	290						
65—70 ...	69	76	261	367	372	464	333	439
70 & over ...	84	110						
Mean Age ...	23·61	23·77	25·06	26·05	24·84	24·97	24·44	24·71

N. B.—Mean age for 1901 and 1891 (for Districts) has been calculated from the figures of age-periods without any process of smoothing. Figures for 1881 have been taken from that Report.

SUBSIDIARY TABLE II—Age distribution of 10,000 of each sex in the State and each Natural Division—*contd.*

Age.	1911.		1901.		1891.		1881.	
	Male.	Female.	Male.	Female.	Male.	Female.	Male.	Female.
1	2	3	4	5	6	7	8	9
Kadi Division.								
0—1	414	433	137	147	312	346	276	294
1—2	196	216	130	129	161	182	214	234
2—3	331	363	208	223	289	332	274	312
3—4	289	349	217	242	290	345	289	321
4—5	313	300	267	271	314	350	306	324
Total ... 0—5	1,543	1,661	959	1,012	1,366	1,555	1,359	1,485
5—10	1,192	1,032	1,259	1,237	1,547	1,494	1,513	1,451
10—15	931	798	1,407	1,259	1,191	1,007	1,219	1,080
15—20	901	810	1,156	1,044	891	760	885	773
20—25	977	1,060	1,029	1,042	875	942	875	921
25—30	1,006	1,033	984	954	850	878	859	846
30—35	867	931	838	836	845	846	806	814
35—40	658	627	622	600	546	521	565	558
40—45	670	737	633	714	627	669	853	889
45—50	348	321	347	375	282	263		
50—55	455	496	384	459	466	485	504	533
55—60	142	122	143	144	124	109	182	185
60—65	195	258						
65—70 ...	42	40	239	324	390	471	380	465
70 & over ...	73	74						
Mean Age	22·10	22·74	23·71	24·60	23·25	23·54	23·33	23·94
Navsari Division.								
0—1 ...	416	412	218	231	331	340	264	290
1—2	204	209	186	187	173	190	228	243
2—3	320	335	259	283	297	337	297	325
3—4	340	362	304	336	355	403	366	404
4—5	331	342	335	426	335	354	338	351
Total ... 0—5	1,611	1,660	1,302	1,463	1,491	1,624	1,493	1,613
5—10	1,247	1,184	1,360	1,358	1,520	1,492	1,505	1,459
10—15	1,097	1,039	1,327	1,172	1,134	996	1,145	997
15—20	834	853	964	916	767	771	718	701
20—25	833	972	943	876	841	948	830	888
25—30	898	942	791	826	895	886	893	883
30—35	774	835	766	696	823	830	848	862
35—40	762	637	711	682	695	583	720	625
40—45	538	558	519	550	560	552	905	880
45—50	460	359	413	412	383	337		
50—55	361	335	374	382	362	390	408	442
55—60	195	179	202	215	161	151	189	197
60—65	193	226						
65—70	96	90	328	452	368	440	346	453
70 & over ...	101	131						
Mean Age	22·25	22·09	23·49	23·88	23·23	23·19	23·27	23·65
Amreli Division.								
0—1	397	407	120	149	332	364	308	325
1—2	204	234	134	170	186	221	119	135
2—3	354	373	204	222	304	348	161	190
3—4	319	359	199	239	314	369	229	250
4—5	293	301	274	356	294	331	230	255
Total ... 0—5	1,567	1,677	931	1,136	1,430	1,633	1,047	1,155
5—10	1,077	1,062	1,273	1,149	1,372	1,388	1,330	1,385
10—15	904	806	1,498	1,502	1,001	851	1,348	1,251
15—20	1,015	900	936	897	827	728	976	883
20—25 ...	1,011	1,059	961	979	1,020	1,095	1,002	1,024
25—30	936	965	880	951	1,001	960	988	963
30—35	781	775	914	784	935	868	945	851
35—40	642	604	673	579	579	506	592	545
40—45	669	709	618	647	606	645	887	916
45—50	388	340	358	333	282	232		
50—55	456	471	516	496	435	439	425	469
55—60	156	133	189	281	115	99	126	118
60—65	246	329						
65—70	64	59	258	366	397	556	334	440
70 & over ...	88	111						
Mean Age	22·06	22.87	24·50	24·69	23·69	23·80	23·71	24·05

N. B.—Mean age for 1901 and 1891 (for Districts) has been calculated from the figures of age-periods without any process of smoothing. Figures for 1881 have been taken from that Report.

SUBSIDIARY TABLE III.—Age distribution of 10,000 of each sex in Main Religions.

Age.	1911.		1901.		1891.		1881.	
	Male.	Female.	Male.	Female.	Male.	Female.	Male.	Female.
1	2	3	4	5	6	7	8	9
All Religions.								
0—1	394	416	145	156	314	343	253	274
1—2	188	208	133	139	163	186	183	202
2—3	316	343	205	226	272	316	241	277
3—4	292	340	220	249	282	340	273	312
4—5	299	302	260	286	289	324	281	304
Total ... 0—5	1,489	1,609	963	1,056	1,320	1,609	1,251	1,369
5—10	1,141	1,044	1,254	1,236	1,424	1,407	1,435	1,424
10—15	935	825	1,357	1,200	1,108	932	1,208	1,067
15—20	887	818	1,026	941	865	772	856	768
20—25	970	1,026	998	1,007	922	995	898	939
25—30	986	1,006	978	959	916	909	916	894
30—35	840	895	869	831	865	850	867	853
35—40	712	656	679	653	609	559	637	603
40—45	666	705	632	693	649	675	934	944
45—50	406	364	380	399	327	301		
50—55	439	462	419	461	465	480	481	503
55—60	170	150	167	190	142	127	173	173
60—65	211	272						
65—70	64	64	268	374	388	484	364	463
70 & over ...	84	104						
Mean Age	22·71	22·77	23·56	23·76	23·19	23·47	23·92	24·34
Hindus.								
0—1	391	417	136	144	315	345	252	274
1—2	187	211	122	125	164	189	179	191
2—3	315	344	197	215	275	322	228	275
3—4	287	337	208	237	285	346	268	310
4—5	293	295	247	272	299	328	277	303
Total ... 0—5	1,473	1,604	910	993	1,358	1,520	1,214	1,353
5—10	1,128	1,026	1,268	1,239	1,438	1,422	1,439	1 432
10—15	929	812	1,372	1,215	1,111	926	1,217	1,080
15—20	896	818	1,045	948	868	773	876	781
20—25	984	1,020	994	1,009	919	993	904	943
25—30	994	1,016	1,004	973	918	909	[illegible]	888
30—35	847	897	869	848	861	845	863	847
35—40	711	662	688	660	603	557	628	600
40—45	671	716	637	706	642	668	490	484
45—50	406	367	378	398	322	299	459	459
50—55	441	471	426	473	462	475	482	499
55—60	167	148	156	186	138	121	171	173
60—65	209	273						
65—70	61	62	253	352	380	472	361	461
70 & over ...	83	98						
Mean Age	22·86	22·94	23·70	24·66	23·85	23·86	23·26	23·61
Jains.								
0—1	334	322	159	182	304	353	279	280
1—2	144	162	117	148	129	147	177	179
2—3	259	254	180	220	207	254	208	219
3—4	234	252	194	221	193	253	192	237
4—5	224	228	223	271	222	252	216	222
Total ... 0—5	1,195	1 218	873	1,042	1,065	1,199	1,072	1,137
5—10	1,116	993	1,019	993	1,161	1,181	1,173	1,188
10—15	1,022	933	1,182	1,066	1,048	952	1,108	974
15—20	888	766	999	839	885	720	819	646
20—25	952	1,020	1,101	1,080	917	977	910	886
25—30	958	958	1,049	928	891	859	978	921
30—35	831	880	902	[illegible]	877	870	862	879
35—40	895	679	715	700	691	616	703	715
40—45	687	800	689	761	751	784	1,071	1,118
45—50	472	413	468	463	444	377		
50—55	502	517	461	566	584	599	569	624
55—60	214	203	229	258	223	194	288	293
60—65	243	261						
65—70	104	96	313	489	533	692	447	619
70 & over ...	94	120						
Mean Age	24·65	25·31	25·34	26·33	26·58	27·02	25·48	26·40

N. B.—Mean age figures for 1901 have been taken from the last report and those for 1891 and 1881 have been calculated on the figures for age-periods without the process of adjustment (smoothing).

SUBSIDIARY TABLE III.—AGE DISTRIBUTION OF 10,000 OF EACH SEX IN MAIN RELIGIONS—*contd.*

AGE.	1911.		1901.		1891.		1881.	
	Male.	Female.	Male.	Female.	Male.	Female.	Male.	Female.
1	2	3	4	5	6	7	8	9
Animists.								
0—1	488	507	186	223	358	372	288	3:6
1—2	238	239	220	246	203	217	294	302
2—3	366	397	288	341	321	406	340	407
3—4	404	455	345	388	399	499	451	472
4—5	406	425	394	439	368	435	426	452
Total ... 0—5	1,902	2,023	1,433	1,637	1,649	1,929	1,799	1,949
5—10	1,385	1,310	1,252	1,304	1,712	1,653	1,733	1,669
10—15	914	909	1,295	1,172	1,13.	891	1,065	906
15—20	724	817	1,028	946	779	818	620	652
20—25	738	938	1,027	972	842	1,025	761	863
25—30	970	955	777	851	936	944	858	928
30—35	819	885	792	698	795	829	843	867
35—40	821	645	644	608	690	520	729	584
40—45	548	516	524	550	527	496	} 838	783
45—50	436	316	373	369	316	274		
50—55	304	250	304	288	320	278	343	355
55—60	167	147	226	205	107	107	155	150
60—65	160	166						
65—70	63	57	} 325	400	196	236	256	294
70 & over ...	49	66						
Mean Age	20·59	19·92	22·54	22·12	21·37	20.79	21·28	21·01
Musalmans.								
0—1	370	379	176	178	299	333	244	249
1—2	168	176	147	149	156	172	163	179
2—3	305	337	207	203	251	280	229	247
3—4	288	322	201	216	248	278	237	259
4—5	299	314	254	270	276	290	262	266
Total ... 0—5	1,430	1,528	985	1,016	1,230	1,353	1,136	1,200
5—10	1,120	1,049	1,182	1,197	1,288	1,287	1,291	1,286
10—15	952	856	1,310	1,141	1,082	907	1,216	1,056
15—20	874	820	967	916	829	765	801	735
20—25	989	1,061	981	1015	957	1,018	898	969
25—30	943	970	947	948	896	922	936	930
30—35	800	892	945	830	923	920	928	913
35—40	659	611	630	623	639	566	676	613
40—45	693	712	684	713	720	739	584	504
45—50	439	345	389	429	346	293	422	511
50—55	494	489	470	494	503	536	523	584
55—60	177	154	190	192	144	123	171	176
60—65	249	299						
65—70	74	67	} 320	486	443	571	419	523
70 & over ...	107	147						
Mean Age	23·42	23·47	23·80	25·26	25·03	25·34	24·38	24·88

N. B.—Mean age figures for 1901 have been taken from the last report and those for 1891 and 1881 have been calculated on the figures for age-periods without the process of adjustment (smoothing).

SUBSIDIARY TABLE III.—Age distribution of 10,000 of each sex in Main Religions—*contd.*

Age.	1911.		1901.		1891.		1881.	
	Male.	Female.	Male.	Female.	Male.	Female.	Male.	Female.
1	2	3	4	5	6	7	8	9
Parsis.								
0—1	319	240	275	249	304	262	248	288
1—2	155	106	194	96	131	108	229	142
2—3	222	177	215	151	223	164	183	155
3—4	296	212	272	224	293	229	308	234
4—5	249	216	275	221	226	228	272	196
Total ... 0—5	1,241	951	1,231	941	1,177	991	1,240	1,015
5—10	1,228	1,026	1,285	1,005	1,439	1,098	1,348	1,084
10—15	1,133	1,014	1,420	1,007	1,398	1,010	1,406	1,028
15—20	1,006	915	1,153	1,001	903	825	730	702
20—25	719	920	851	828	711	894	779	753
25—30	564	798	577	864	647	738	703	879
30—35	570	721	577	739	611	725	703	823
35—40	483	596	663	647	583	677	657	745
40—45	535	730	493	630	644	799	921	1,068
45—50	526	498	458	469	430	391		
50—55	549	518	382	649	388	601	540	702
55—60	342	359	277	334	237	238	316	306
60—65	334	429						
65—70	175	183	633	886	832	1.013	657	895
70 and over ...	295	342						
Mean Age	25·26	28·67	21·35	28·84	25·63	28·82	24·71	27·78
Christians.								
0—1	381	355	144	121	163	324	84	346
1—2	1[illegible]5	173	92	153	70	324	67	173
2—3	301	218	227	269	210	185	67	520
3—4	262	361	211	279	257	231	117	462
4—5	272	158	215	255	187	463	67	231
Total ... 0—5	1,411	1,265	889	1,077	887	1,527	402	1,732
5—10	965	1,144	1,566	1,657	628	1,157	619	1,830
10—15	1,061	998	1,689	1,256	442	741	284	1,040
15—20	1,169	1,138	993	739	1,046	972	418	867
20—25	1,149	1,024	944	1,002	1,675	1,482	2,659	1,040
25—30	908	947	960	1,138	1,373	1,157	1,839	1,213
30—35	851	854	932	751	838	926	1,421	757
35—40	690	576	459	563	1,140	741	987	693
40—45	672	642	643	684	558	602	920	635
45—50	309	296	244	283	761	231		
50—55	405	678	383	413	419	...	284	347
55—60	122	101	92	119	163	93	67	173
60—65	174	209						
65—70	39	32	206	318	70	371	100	173
70 and over ...	75	96						
Mean Age	22	23·08	21·58	22·84	27·20	22·69	27·20	21·23

N. B.—Mean age figures for 1901 have been taken from the last report and those for 1891 and 1881 have been calculated on the figures for age-periods without the process of adjustment (smoothing).

SUBSIDIARY TABLE IV.—Age Distribution of 1,000 of each sex in certain castes.

Caste.	Males. Number per mille aged.					Females. Number per mille aged.				
	0–5	5–12	12–15	15–40	40 and over.	0–5	5–12	12–15	15–40	40 and over.
1	2	3	4	5	6	7	8	9	10	11
Hindus.										
Ahir ...	151	112	49	491	197	186	112	37	441	224
Bahrot ...	130	142	55	426	247	131	119	46	425	279
Bava ...	101	101	55	443	300	87	82	38	505	288
Bhangi ...	157	160	71	434	178	175	141	57	456	171
Bharvad ...	144	135	73	458	190	166	144	64	422	204
Bhavsar ...	143	150	62	417	228	124	135	63	446	232
Bhoi ...	135	146	66	460	193	167	126	47	440	220
Brahman Anavala ...	120	136	74	431	239	126	167	68	398	241
„ Audich ...	116	138	64	444	238	125	119	45	417	294
„ Deshastha ...	97	116	60	412	315	124	131	54	391	300
„ Mewada ...	112	128	67	448	245	98	113	65	462	262
„ Modh ...	109	134	70	450	237	115	124	57	445	259
„ Nagar ...	115	137	70	403	275	107	128	60	430	275
„ Tapodhan ...	133	150	67	457	193	142	129	61	446	222
Chamar ...	170	158	70	432	170	180	127	52	424	217
Darji...	159	155	59	405	222	157	128	50	445	220
Dhed ...	163	146	68	438	195	171	131	61	432	205
Garoda ...	170	178	73	406	173	193	127	50	440	190
Ghanchi ...	147	168	67	427	191	145	138	66	432	219
Gola (rice-pounders) ...	166	165	71	434	174	151	126	80	427	216
Gosain ...	137	118	50	442	253	136	116	42	447	259
Hajam...	160	153	62	411	214	150	121	46	454	229
Kachhia ...	150	128	68	407	247	122	124	63	413	278
Kanbi, Anjana ...	135	152	60	462	191	149	112	60	454	225
„ Kadwa ...	140	133	47	491	189	165	144	68	444	179
„ Karadia ...	188	120	60	455	177	190	120	46	427	217
„ Lewa ...	128	143	68	435	226	140	132	54	434	240
Koli ...	161	140	64	450	185	172	103	55	431	239
Kumbhar ...	168	148	68	439	177	159	124	56	430	231
Luhana ...	140	156	64	423	217	172	142	52	411	223
Luhar ...	155	159	72	431	192	160	128	55	450	207
Machhi ...	163	149	62	413	213	174	143	63	426	194
Maratha ...	109	121	73	497	200	123	134	48	436	259
Mochi ...	145	159	66	419	211	162	139	54	439	206
Rabari ...	149	132	58	453	208	149	159	50	432	210
Rajput ...	129	132	62	460	217	137	117	52	452	242
Ravalia ...	169	141	59	444	187	175	133	51	452	189
Sathawara ...	156	154	63	442	185	164	126	46	469	195
Shenva ...	195	156	52	433	164	193	135	44	464	164
Soni ...	159	141	64	400	236	137	134	60	421	248
Sutar ...	144	151	65	433	207	146	124	53	453	224
Talavia ...	160	124	147	388	181	169	139	67	439	186
Targala ...	175	128	51	396	250	95	98	38	482	287
Vagher ...	142	137	67	434	220	118	151	47	424	260
Vaghari ...	182	152	61	423	182	197	139	51	440	173
Vania Disaval ...	105	109	77	396	313	115	121	53	436	275
„ Lad ...	138	119	66	431	246	114	119	53	430	284
„ Shrimali ...	105	134	63	444	254	169	123	61	402	245
Jains.										
Vania Shrimali ...	165	132	74	410	219	133	139	53	436	239
Animists.										
Bhil ...	204	174	47	400	175	160	165	78	452	145
Chodhra ...	179	171	59	420	171	197	157	73	418	155
Dhanka ...	180	173	85	371	191	216	163	45	423	153
Dhodia ...	184	175	71	411	159	192	145	88	413	162
Gamatda ...	175	182	62	414	167	172	167	66	416	179
Nayakda ...	174	173	78	381	189	214	137	71	427	151
Musalmans.										
Fakir ...	133	134	54	440	239	145	146	56	431	222
Ghanchi ...	137	123	51	463	226	153	134	58	428	237
Malek ...	139	137	53	469	202	141	133	49	442	235
Memon ...	159	170	60	405	206	147	166	72	370	245
Molesalam ...	146	123	48	440	243	150	121	44	447	238
Momna ...	176	143	60	450	171	162	124	58	459	197
Pathan ...	135	120	53	468	224	142	129	48	449	232
Pinjara ...	151	157	64	411	217	161	130	57	410	222
Saiyad ...	136	130	58	435	241	134	126	60	452	228
Shaikh ...	144	131	52	449	224	143	126	51	489	191
Vohora ...	166	164	60	361	249	144	136	65	422	233
Parsis.										
Parsis ...	124	176	90	334	276	95	137	68	394	306
Christians.										
Native ...	143	133	72	476	176	128	135	81	452	204

SUBSIDIARY TABLE V.—Proportion of children under 10 and of persons over 50 to those aged 15-40; also of married females aged 15-40 per 100 females.

District or Natural Division.	Proportion of children both sexes per 100.						Proportion of persons over 50 per 100 aged 15-40.						Number of married females aged 15-40 per 100 females of all ages.		
	Persons aged 15-40.			Married females aged 15-40.			1911		1901		1891				
	1911	1901	1891	1911	1901	1891	Male.	Female.	Male.	Female.	Male.	Female.	1911	1901	1891
1	2	3	4	5	6	7	8	9	10	11	12	13	14	15	16
Baroda State ...	**60**	**50**	**68**	**145**	**135**	**162**	**44**	**47**	**39**	**44**	**48**	**52**	**37**	**34**	**36**
Baroda Division ...	56	45	60	135	122	144	44	51	38	43	46	53	39	36	38
Baroda City ...	44	39	41	119	117	111	50	63	50	63	51	67	35	33	37
Kadi Division ...	61	49	74	148	129	174	41	48	35	38	45	53	37	35	35
Navsari Division ...	68	67	76	158	171	177	46	45	46	49	70	80	36	32	34
Amreli Division ...	61	53	68	146	161	163	46	50	46	53	44	51	37	29	37

SUBSIDIARY TABLE VI.—Variation in Population at certain Age-Periods.

District or Natural Division.	Period.	Variation per cent. in Population (Increase + and Decrease —).					
		All ages.	0-10	10-15	15-40	40-60	60 and over.
1	2	3	4	5	6	7	8
Baroda State	**1881—1891**	**+ 10·5**	**+ 14·6**	**+ 0·8**	**+ 10·9**	**+ 9·1**	**+ 16·7**
	1891—1901	**— 19·2**	**— 35·6**	**+ 1·1**	**— 12·4**	**— 14·7**	**— 40·6**
	1901—1911	**+ 4·1**	**+ 22**	**— 28·4**	**+ 2·2**	**+ 4·9**	**+ 20·9**
Baroda Division	1881—1891	+ 6·9	+ 9·6	— 11·9	+ 7·7	+ 11·8	+ 16
	1891—1901	— 22·9	— 38	— 2·3	— 17	+ 3·3	— 42·4
	1901—1911	+ 8·75	+ 29·6	— 26·4	+ 4·5	— 14·9	+ 47·4
Baroda City	1881—1891	+ 9·3	+ 20·8	— 8·9	+ 8·7	+ 6·3	+ 18
	1891—1901	— 10·9	— 16	+ 11·6	— 11·9	— 6·7	— 29·7
	1901—1911	— 4·3	+ 6·9	— 19	— 4·2	— 11·4	+ 12·9
Kadi Division	1881—1891	+ 11·1	+ 14·1	+ 6·2	+ 11·8	+ 9·4	+ 13·3
	1891—1901	— 24·1	— 48·1	— 7·9	— 13·1	— 11·7	— 51·9
	1901—1911	— 0·3	+ 21·3	— 35·4	— 2·9	+ 2·5	+ 19·7
Navsari Division	1881—1891	+ 11·1	+ 12·1	+ 10·3	+ 6·8	+ 6·5	+ 12·6
	1891—1901	— 6	— 19·6	+ 10·3	+ 0·2	— 0·5	— 9·2
	1901—1911	+ 11·6	+ 16·1	— 4·6	+ 18·8	+ 8·7	+ 19·9
Amreli Division	1881—1891	+ 22·1	+ 44·6	— 12·9	+ 18·6	+ 18·6	+ 51·4
	1891—1901	— 3·8	— 25·8	+ 55·2	— 4·5	+ 15·8	— 36·9
	1901—1911	+ 2·79	+ 23·0	— 41·3	+ 5·6	— 0·5	+ 48·1

SUBSIDIARY TABLE VII.—Reported Birth-rate by sex and Natural Divisions.

Year.	Number of Births per 1,000 of Total Population (Census of 1901).									
	Baroda State.		Baroda Division.		Kadi Division.		Navsari Division.		Amreli Division.	
	Male.	Female.	Male.	Female.	Male.	Female.	Male.	Female.	Male.	Female.
1	2	3	4	5	6	7	8	9	10	11
1900—01	7·2	6·4	6·1	5·4	5·3	4·4	14·4	12·9	8·8	8·2
1901—02	22·2	20·8	22·8	21·8	19·6	17·7	30·3	28·1	19·3	18·4
1902—03	19·0	17·9	17·1	16·3	17·6	15·9	26·0	25·0	21·6	20·1
1903—04	20·8	19·8	19·3	19·1	17·9	16·4	28·8	28·0	27·0	24·6
1904—05	22·8	21·8	22·2	21·8	19·4	17·6	32·4	31·0	24·9	25·9
1905—06	23·5	21·3	22·9	22·4	18·5	16·6	33·5	31·9	22·1	20·9
1906—07	22·2	20·9	23·6	22·8	16·6	15·0	30·4	28·5	29·9	28·9
1907—08	24·8	23·7	24·3	23·5	20·8	19·0	35·8	32·6	30·7	30·6
1908—09	25·7	24·0	25·9	24·9	22·6	20·0	33·6	30·5	29·4	28·7
1909—10	25·6	24·0	25·4	25·0	21·9	19·3	34·1	31·7	30·2	29·3

SUBSIDIARY TABLE VIII.—Reported Death-rate by sex and Natural Divisions.

Year.	Number of Deaths per 1,000 of Total Population (Census 1901).									
	Baroda State.		Baroda Division.		Kadi Division.		Navsari Division.		Amreli Division.	
	Male.	Female.	Male.	Female.	Male.	Female.	Male.	Female.	Male.	Female.
1	2	3	4	5	6	7	8	9	10	11
1900—01	64·7	54·0	60·3	49·9	73·8	59·4	44·8	39·1	74·0	69·4
1901—02	30·4	28·8	36·5	37·0	28·0	24·1	27·2	27·7	24·0	24·2
1902—03	31·3	31·9	42·5	49·0	22·8	19·7	30·9	32·0	30·0	30·3
1903—04	33·0	33·5	32·0	32·0	32·0	32·2	32·1	31·6	42·8	48·9
1904—05	24·5	24·9	25·9	26·5	22·1	22·2	30·3	30·9	20·8	21·6
1905—06	24·5	23·1	23·9	23·1	24·5	23·1	25·5	25·0	21·4	19·9
1906—07	32·7	32·9	26·5	28·1	41·8	41·1	26·6	26·3	23·3	22·3
1907—08	25·2	23·6	24·1	23·6	26·4	23·6	25·1	23·8	24·1	22·7
1908—09	22·5	21·2	21·2	20·3	24·0	21·9	22·9	22·4	19·1	18·8
1909—10	23·5	22·0	24·9	24·5	22·6	20·3	25·7	23·7	19·5	18·6

SUBSIDIARY TABLE IX.—Reported Death-rate by sex and age in decade and in selected years per mille living at same age according to the Census of 1901.

Age.	Average of Decade.		1903.		1905.		1907.		1909.	
	Male.	Female.	Male.	Female.	Male.	Female.	Male.	Female.	Male.	Female.
1	2	3	4	5	6	7	8	9	10	11
All Ages	31,481	27,955	31·3	31·9	24·5	24·9	32·7	32·9	22·5	21·2
Under 1 year ...	4,029	3,396	3·8	3·4	3·8	3·6	4·2	3·8	4·4	3·9
1—5 ...	3,905	3,336	3·0	2·9	3·0	2·6	4·2	4·1	3·3	3·4
5—10 ...	1,877	1,699	1·7	2·0	1.2	1·3	1·8	1·8	1·0	0·9
10—15 ...	1,655	1,532	1·9	2·0	1·4	1·5	2.0	2·2	0·8	0·7
15—20 ...	1,688	1,456	1·7	1·6	1·3	1·4	2·2	2·2	0·9	0·8
20—30 ...	3,851	3,737	4·2	4·8	3·1	3·5	4·7	4·9	2·5	2·7
30—40 ...	4,138	3,698	4·4	4·5	3·2	3·2	4·4	4·5	2·5	2·4
40—50 ...	3,846	3,007	4·0	3·6	2·9	2·6	3·9	3·5	2·4	1·0
50—60 ...	3,228	2,571	3·4	3·1	2·2	2·1	2·9	2·6	2·1	1·7
60 and over...	3,001	3,145	2·9	3·6	2·1	2·3	2·3	2·8	2·0	2·3

SUBSIDIARY TABLE X.—Reported Deaths from certain diseases per mille of each sex.

Year.	Whole Province.					Cholera.				
	Actual number of deaths.			Ratio per mille of each sex.		Actual number of deaths.			Ratio per mille of each sex.	
	Total.	Male.	Female.	Male.	Female.	Total.	Male.	Female.	Male.	Female.
1	2	3	4	5	6	7	8	9	10	11
1900—01 ...	116,337	65,361	50,976	64·7	54·0	3,631	1,783	1,848	1·8	1·9
1901—02 ...	57,898	30,684	27,214	30·4	28·8	72	36	36	0·03	0·04
1902—03 ...	61,718	31,556	30,162	31·3	31·9	145	73	72	0·07	0·07
1903—04 ...	64,892	33,262	31,630	33·0	33·5	151	76	75	0·07	0·08
1904—05 ...	48,227	24,724	23,503	24·5	24·9	141	58	83	0·06	0·08
1905—06 ...	46,221	24,352	21,869	24·5	23·1	145	68	77	0·07	0·08
1906—07 ...	64,112	33,013	31,099	32·7	32·9	413	207	206	0·2	0·2
1907—08 ...	47,730	25,455	22,275	25·2	23·6	83	44	39	0·04	0·04
1908—09 ...	42,703	22,666	20,037	22·5	21·2	492	251	241	0·3	0·2
1909—10 ...	44,536	23,742	20,794	23·5	22·0	208	104	104	0·1	0·1

Year.	Small-Pox.					Fever.				
	Actual number of deaths.			Ratio per mille of each sex.		Actual number of deaths.			Ratio per mille of each sex.	
	Total.	Male.	Female.	Male.	Female.	Total.	Male.	Female.	Male.	Female.
1	12	13	14	15	16	17	18	19	20	21
1900—01 ...	326	170	156	0·1	0·2	91,216	51,322	39,894	50·9	42·3
1901—02 ...	121	77	44	0·07	0·04	44,734	24,115	20,619	24·0	21·8
1902—03 ...	124	79	45	0·08	0·03	43,157	22,670	20.487	22·5	21·6
1903—04 ...	601	327	274	0·3	0·3	36,397	19,280	17,117	19·23	18·12
1904—05 ...	1,002	541	461	0·5	0·5	29,428	15,580	13,848	15·5	14·7
1905—06 ...	1.986	1 052	934	1·1	1·0	31,096	16,711	14,385	16·6	15·2
1906—07 ...	175	96	79	0·09	0·08	37,681	19,964	17,717	19·8	18·8
1907—08 ...	537	332	205	0·3	0·2	31,937	17.192	14,745	17·07	15·6
1908—09 ...	296	146	150	0·2	0·14	30,461	16.307	14,154	16·2	15·01.
1909—10 ...	1.119	593	526	0·6	0·6	31.253	16,821	14,132	16·7	15·3

SUBSIDIARY TABLE X.—Reported Deaths from certain diseases per mille of each sex.—*contd.*

Year.		Dysentery and Diarrhœa.					Injuries.				
		Actual number of deaths.			Ratio per mille of each sex.		Actual number of deaths.			Ratio per mille of each sex.	
		Total.	Male.	Female.	Male.	Female.	Total.	Male.	Female.	Male.	Female.
1		22	23	24	25	26	27	28	29	30	31
1900—01	...	6,559	3,907	2,652	3·9	2·8	376	205	171	0·2	0·2
1901—02	...	1,375	752	623	0·7	0·7	426	235	191	0·2	0·2
1902—03	...	1,226	689	537	0·75	0·6	425	227	198	0·2	0·2
1903—04	...	1,050	577	473	0·5	0·5	411	218	193	0·2	0·2
1904—05	...	958	557	401	0·54	0·4	376	204	172	0·2	0·2
1905—06	...	951	545	406	0·5	0·4	310	188	122	0·18	0·14
1906—07	...	916	489	427	0·5	0·42	380	188	192	0·18	0·2
1907—08	...	1,067	601	466	0·6	0·5	465	243	222	0·2	0·2
1908—09	...	992	548	444	0·5	0·5	508	240	268	0·2	0·3
1909—10	...	900	520	380	0·5	0·4	455	228	227	0·2	0·2

Year.		Plague.					Respiratory Diseases.					All other Causes.				
		Actual number of deaths.			Ratio per mille of each sex.		Actual number of deaths.			Ratio per mille of each sex.		Actual number of deaths			Ratio per mille of each sex.	
		Total.	Male.	Female.	Male.	Female.	Total.	Male.	Female.	Male.	Female.	Total.	Male.	Female.	Male.	Female.
1		32	33	34	35	36	37	38	39	40	41	42	43	44	45	46
1900—01	...	...	Figures for plague are not available.	...	...	...	...	...	...	...	...	14,229	7,974	6,255	7·8	6·6
1901—02	...	...		...	...	...	...	...	...	...	...	11,170	5,469	5,701	5·4	6·04
1902—03	...	...		...	...	...	...	...	...	...	...	16,641	7,818	8,823	7·7	9·4
1903—04	...	...		...	...	...	...	...	...	...	...	26,282	12,784	13,498	12·7	14·3
1904—05	...	...		...	...	...	...	...	...	...	...	16,322	7,784	8,538	7·7	9·02
1905—06	...	...		...	...	...	...	...	...	...	...	11,633	5,788	5,845	5·75	6·28
1906—07	...	...		...	...	...	...	...	...	...	...	24,547	12,069	12,478	11·93	13·2
1907—08	...	6,416	3,251	3,165	3·2	3·4	119	66	53	0·06	0·06	7,106	3,726	3,380	3·73	3·6
1908—09	...	3,880	1,941	1,939	1·9	2·05	467	280	187	0·3	0·2	5,607	2,953	2,654	2·9	2·8
1909—10	...	4,381	2,191	2,190	2·2	2·3	862	504	358	0·5	0·4	5,358	2,781	2,577	2·7	2·7

Chapter VI.

SEX.

Reference to statistics.

290. Imperial Table VII shows the distribution of the sexes for the State as a whole and for each district and religion by age-periods. The following Subsidiary Tables at the end of this chapter exhibit the main features of the statistics in proportionate parts and also furnish further information relating to sexes from the vital statistics :—

Subsidiary Table I.—General proportion of the sexes by natural divisions and districts.

Subsidiary Table II.—Number of females per 1,000 males at different age-periods by religions at each of the last three Censuses.

Subsidiary Table III.—Number of females per 1,000 males at different age-periods by religions and natural divisions.

Subsidiary Table IV.—Number of females per 1,000 males for certain selected castes.

Subsidiary Table V.—Actual number of births and deaths reported for each sex during the decades 1891-1900 and 1901-1910.

Subsidiary Table VI.—Number of deaths of each sex at different ages.

Accuracy of the return.

291. The return of females is likely to be less accurate than that of males in India, owing to the peculiar customs and habits of the people. It is possible that some portion of unmarried girls, who have passed the age of puberty while still unmarried, and young married women living in *pardah*, may not be reported. But in Gujarat, except in the upper groups in a few castes like Rajputs, Marathas and Lewa Kanbis and some high class Mahomedan families, *pardah* is not observed and no special stigma attaches to those who do not marry their girls before the age of puberty. There is, therefore, no motive to conceal females from enumeration. Precautionary measures were, however, taken to see that females were not left out of the count. Influential members from the castes in which concealment of females was likely, accompanied the Enumerators and satisfied themselves that no one was left out. In testing the work of the Enumerators, Supervisors and Charge Superintendents specially tested the entries of females in such quarters, but failed to detect any tendency towards concealment. So far as this State is concerned, I have therefore no reason to suppose that the return of females is less accurate than that of males.

General proportion of the sexes in actual population.

292. In all European countries, except Bulgaria, Greece and a few others, the females outnumber the males. The excess of females is 68 per 1,000 males in England and Wales and 61 in Denmark. In India, on the other hand, the male population is generally in excess and in the whole country taken together, there are only 953 females to 1,000 males. The only exception to the general rule is furnished by Madras, Central Provinces States, Bengal and the Cochin State. In the Bombay Presidency there are 920 females to 1,000 males. From Imperial Table VII, we find that there were 1,055,935 males and 976,863 females in this State on the 10th March 1911. The males are thus numerically in excess of the females by 79,072, or in other words, in the State as a whole, there are only 925 females to 1,000 males.

Proportions in different parts of the State.

293. The diversity which exists in the different parts of the State is nowhere more clearly illustrated than in the proportion of the sexes. From the figures given on the next page, it will be seen that the pro-

portions of the sexes approach an equality in the Navsari District. Then follow Kadi, Amreli and Baroda Districts in order and Baroda City stands last with only 853 females to 1,000 males.

Divisions.	No. of females to 1,000 males.
Baroda State	**925**
Baroda Division exclusive of City	872
Baroda City	853
Kadi Division	947
Navsari Division	982
Amreli Division	940

294. The above observations refer to the actual population or the persons enumerated in the State, irrespective of the place where they were born. The proportion of the sexes is affected by migration from or to the State. In order to ascertain the proportions in the natural population, *i.e.*, the persons born in the State, we must discount the effect of migration by deducting the persons who have come into the State from outside and adding those born in it who have gone elsewhere. Thus calculated, the proportion of females to 1,000 males for the whole State is 927, which shows that in the State as a whole, migration does not much disturb the sex proportions. We have no means for exactly determining similar proportions for the districts; for though we know how many persons have immigrated into each district from other parts of India and also how many have emigrated from the State to other parts of India, we do not know how many of the latter have emigrated from each of the districts. The figures supplied by the other provinces refer to the Baroda State as a whole and not to its districts. But as immigration and emigration vary almost equally in the State as a whole, as also in its component parts, the proportions of sexes in the actual, as also in the natural population, remain almost the same.

Proportion in natural population.

295. If there was any concealment of females, it might naturally be expected that the Mahomedans with their greater reticence in all matters which concern their females, would have a smaller proportion of women in the Census than the Hindus, but this is not the case. In the State as a whole, they have 939 females to 1,000 males, while the Hindus have only 918. If the figures for the different parts of the State are examined, it will be found that except in the Baroda District, where the proportions of the two religions are equal, in every district the proportion of females is higher than amongst the Hindus. In the Navsari District, Mahomedan females outnumber their males, owing mainly to the males going abroad to Africa, Burma, etc., for employment, leaving their females at home. The Animistic tribes, among whom early marriages are rare, have a relatively larger number of women than Hindus or Mahomedans. Jains also show higher ratio than Hindus in the State as a whole; but when we consider the districts separately, we find that in the Navsari and Amreli Districts, the ratio of females amongst them is smaller than amongst the Hindus, whilst in the Kadi and Baroda Districts it is higher. The higher ratio is explained by the fact that many Jains from these districts have emigrated to Bombay and other places leaving their females at home. Our Kadi District, the home of more than half of our Jain population, is well-known for sending out Jain emigrants to Bombay, Poona and other places in the Deccan. This explains the actual excess of Jain females over Jain males in the Kadi District. The Parsis

Proportions of females to 1,000 males in different religions.

Religion.	Baroda State.	Baroda District (ex. of City)	Baroda City.	Kadi District	Navsari District.	Amreli District.
All religions	**925**	**872**	**853**	**947**	**982**	**939**
Hindu	918	866	857	942	973	935
Jain	987	908	915	1,051	778	929
Mahomedan	939	866	860	965	1,071	982
Parsi	1,326	458	759	67	1,421	933
Christian	867	955	433	731	622	142
Animistic	960	963	...	...	960	...

in the Navsari District show a remarkably high proportion of females, mainly because there is absence of early marriage among them and many of the males go to Bombay and other places in search of employment. The Native Christian community in Baroda is small, and mainly drawn from the Hindus, and it is for this reason that the proportion of females amongst them approximates that of the Hindus.

Proportions in different castes.

296. The proportions of sexes in the different castes (Subsidiary Table IV) are so diverse that it is difficult to draw from them any inference of a general application. The proportion of females to males is higher in some of the lower castes, such as Bhavsar, Chamar, Darji, Dhobi, Garoda, Gola, Luhar, Sutar and Targala, while it is lower in some of the higher castes, such as Brahman, Vania, Rajput, Maratha and Kanbi. Nagar Brahmans as a whole community seem to have more females than males, but if its different sections are viewed separately, we find that there is a paucity of girls among Vadnagara and other Nagars, and it is only the Visnagaras who have an excess of females which is partly due to the migration of the males of this community to Bombay and other places. Similarly the apparent excess of females amongst Disaval and Lad Vanias is also due to migration. The proportion of females among the Bhils, Nayakdas, Gamits and other primitive people is higher than among most of the Hindu castes. There seems to be some correspondence between sex and race. It may be said that, as a general rule, women are less numerous among the Rajputs and other high castes in which there is some strain of Aryan blood, while they are more numerous in the Dravidian tribes and the lower castes which have been recruited mainly from them.

Comparison with previous Censuses.

297. There has been a rise in the number of females per 1,000 males from 891 in 1872 to 917 in 1881, and from 928 in 1891 to 936 in 1901, but in the present Census, it has fallen from 936 to 925 mainly on account of plague which was more or less prevalent in all the districts and to which infection females were more liable from their reluctance to leave affected areas. All the divisions, except Amreli, contribute to the decrease. In the City of Baroda, the number of females per 1,000 males has remained stationary; but in the Baroda District (exclusive of City), it has fallen from 891 to 872; in Kadi, from 956 to 947 and in Navsari, 992 to 982. In Amreli, the proportion of females has risen from 920 in 1891 to 939 in 1901 and to 940 in the present Census. The increase in Amreli is mainly due to the increasing number of Khojas, Memons, Kapols and others emigrating from that district to Bombay in search of employment, leaving their families behind them. The decrease in Baroda, Navsari, and Kadi is mainly due to greater mortality among females during plague and to the growing practice of emigrants taking their wives with them.

Diagram showing the number of females to 1,000 males at each age-period.

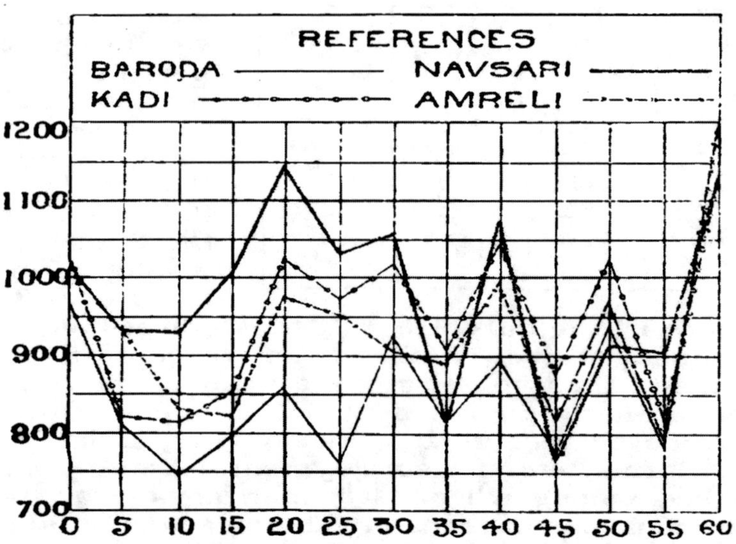

Proportions at different ages.

298. Subsidiary Table II. at the end of this Chapter shows that in the first year of life, the proportion of females to 1,000 males is 977 for all religions. Taking the religions separately, the corresponding proportion is 978 amongst Hindus, 960 amongst Musalmans, 954 amongst Jains and 999 amongst

the Animistic tribes. This would show that in all the main religions, the number of males born exceeds that of females in the general ratio of 1,023 to 1,000. Elsewhere in India also, males are in excess of females at birth. But in spite of the larger number of boys at birth, they are fewer in number than girls in the second, third and the fourth year, in the general population. At age 5, females are actually in excess of males amongst Musalmans, Jains, Parsis and the Animistic tribes, while among Hindus, their proportion is slightly lower. The general average for both the sexes in all religious is equal and the advantage which males had over females at birth, disappears within the first five years of life. The proportion of females declines from age 5 onwards to age 20 in all religions except among the Parsis and the Animistic tribes and again rises in the age-period 20-25, with the result that though females still continue to be in defect among Hindus, Jains, Musalmans, Parsis and the Animistic tribes, they are somewhat in excess of males at age 25-30 ; the previous excess of females over males continues only among the Parsis. In the age-period 30-40 and 40-50, females are in defect of males in all religions except among Jains and Parsis, while in the age-period 60 and over, females are in excess of males in all religions.

299. Having regard to the fact that in the population as a whole, the proportion of males is greater than that of females in the earliest years of life, their larger proportion at birth is naturally to be expected. I have already stated in the chapter on Movement of Population that the record of vital statistics in the State is not accurate ; but as there is no reason to suppose that vital occurrences relating to females are less reported than those relating to males, the record of statistics, such as it is, may be looked into to give an indication of the relatively greater or less proportion of births and deaths among males and females. Subsidiary Tables V. and VI., which have been prepared from vital statistics furnished by the Sanitary Commissioner, show that the vital statistics also, like the Census, show that at birth, males are more numerous than females. As regards mortality also, like the Census, the vital statistics show that it is higher amongst males than amongst females in the first few years of life. There is no correspondence between the results of the two records in the higher age-periods. The vital statistics show greater mortality amongst males in all age-periods except 20-30 and 60 and over, while the Census indicates greater mortality amongst females in most of the higher ages.

Excess of males per 1,000 females at birth.

According to census.	According to vital statistics.
23	125

Comparison with European countries.

300. As in India, so in European countries also there is an excess of males over females at birth (about 29 per 1,000). But in spite of the general excess of males at birth in European countries, there is an excess of females in the general population, the excess varying from 5 females in the case of France to 91 in Portugal. But as already mentioned, we have here an excess of 75 males over females per 1,000. Similarly in India as a whole (47), in the Bombay Presidency (80) and in the British Gujarat Districts also (72), the male population is in excess of females. The question naturally arises, how is it that while males are in excess at birth both here and in Europe, females eventually preponderate over males in the latter, while they are in defect in this country. Regarding Europe, it is said that the excess of males at birth disappears at the age of 15 or earlier owing to the relatively greater mortality among males. At the higher ages, the proportion of females to males continues to grow owing partly to greater mortality amongst males, and partly to migration. The reason for the greater mortality of males is that in early life, they are more delicate than females, while later on, they are exposed to various occupations to risks from which the females are immune. In this State also in spite of the fact that boys are more liked and cared for than girls, there is a greater mortality among them than among females, in the earliest years of life. Males come on a par with females at about the age of 5, but afterwards, and especially from 10 to 20,

females die in greater number than males owing to the peculiar marriage and other social customs of this country. This explains why females are in defect of males in the population of the State.

Causes of higher female mortality.

301. Among the possible causes of higher female mortality in this State may be mentioned :—(1) Female infanticide; (2) Neglect of female infant; (3) Infant marriage and premature sexual intercourse and child-bearing; (4) A very high birth-rate; (5) Unskilful midwifery; (6) Abortion; (7) Confinement and bad feeding of women at puberty; (8) The hard life of widows; and (9) The hard labour which women have to perform.

I shall take these causes one after another in order and consider how far they operate to increase female mortality in this State :—

(1) *Female infanticide* was once practised in Gujarat by the Jadeja Rajputs and *kulin* Kanbis. The necessity, among these people, of marrying girls in higher social groups and the extravagant expenditure to be incurred on their wedding, had brought about the evil custom of killing girls by plunging them into a pot of milk, immediately after birth. This custom was known as *dudh piti* or making (the child) drink milk. It was due to the benevolent and persistent efforts of the Hon. Mr. Jonathan Duncan, Governor of Bombay, and Major Alexander Walker, Resident at the Court of Baroda, that a beginning was made early in the nineteenth century to suppress the wicked practice which was found upon inquiry to be prevalent in Gujarat, Kathiawad and Kutch. The humane work started by these officers was continued by their successors Lord Mountstuart Elphinstone, Captain Carnac and Mr. Willoughby. Both coercive and persuasive measures were taken and infanticide was believed to have been stamped out of Gujarat. In 1871, however, information collected in connection with the Infanticide Act (VIII of 1870) showed among the Kanbis a startling excess in the number of males over females. Enquiries were made and the result seemed so suspicious that in April 1871, the provisions of the Infanticide Act were applied both to the Lewa and Kadwa Kanbis. The result of more complete information showed that the fears of Government were excessive and the operation of the Act was withdrawn. The question was again revived in British Gujarat in 1888 by Mr. G. F. Shephard, Commissioner, Northern Division. Under the suspicion that extravagant marriage expenditure might lead to the destruction of female life in the Lewa Kanbi caste, rules restricting expenditure at marriage were applied to the 13 *kulin* Lewa Kanbi villages of *Charottar*. Of these 5 are in British territory, 1 is under Cambay and 7 under Baroda State. The rules framed by the State for the reduction of marriage expenditure among the *kulin* Lewa Kanbis, in conjunction with the Bombay Government, are still in force, and have, by reducing marriage expenditure, removed the cause which once led to the destruction of female life. The attitude of the Lewa Kanbis towards their females has much improved within the last 20 years, owing to the spread of education; and the difficulty of securing brides for their sons which most of them have of late been experiencing

Proportion of females amongst the Kulin Lewa Kanbis of Charottar.

Name of village.	Proportion of females to 1,000 males.
Savli	722
Dharmaj	647
Pihij	638
Bhadran	696
Sojitra	690
Vaso	849
Nar	539

on account of a split among themselves, separating 5 villages (Nar and Pihij under Baroda and Uttarsanda, Sunav and Ode under British territory) from the rest and the *ekdas* or solemn agreements passed by the Lewas of non-*kulin* villages, binding them not to give their daughters in marriage to the *kulins*. The result has been that the sons of the *kulins*, for whose hand offers were made while they were babies rocking in the cradle, now remain bachelors, though over 20 years old. It is mainly due to this changed circumstance which makes it difficult to get brides for their boys from outside, and not to female infanticide, that the proportion of females among the Lewa Kanbis is at present so very low.

(2) *Neglect of female infants.*—In all castes as a general rule, male children are desired and the birth of a female child is unwelcome. When a son is born, sweetmeats are distributed and *vadhamani* or good news is sent to friends and relations. On the other hand, nothing of the sort is done when a daughter is born. A girl is spoken of as a *patharo* or stone, and receives less attention than a boy. This is specially so amongst castes, where the procuring of a bridegroom is a matter of considerable expense. This difference of treatment must doubtless be exercising some adverse effect on female life. But the ideas of the people on the subject have of late much improved and in most of the castes, sons and daughters receive equal treatment. Neglect of female life does not now seem to be a factor of any great importance ; and as a matter of fact, the Census shows that in spite of greater attention paid to boys, their mortality in the earlier years of life is greater than that of girls.

(3) *Infant marriage and premature sexual intercourse and child-bearing* are the principal causes of the great mortality in the female sex, especially among the Hindus. As mentioned in paragraph 326, cohabitation does not generally take place immediately after marriage, but when once a girl is married, it does take place as soon as physical circumstances permit ; and a large proportion of early marriages means a correspondingly high percentage of early consummations and of early births from immature mothers. This circumstance might naturally be expected to exercise a very prejudicial effect upon the longevity and vitality of the female sex and even to be the cause of a considerable number of deaths among them, and statistics go to show that this in fact is actually so, especially during the ages 15 to 20.

(4) *High birth-rate.*—Early marriage leads to high birth-rate, and prematurely breaks down the constitution of the mother thereby producing greater relative mortality among females than in the other sex.

(5) *Unskilful midwifery* is one of the main causes of high female mortality. The wife of the village barber is generally employed as a midwife and her bungling and blundering often entails permanent injury and in many cases diseases hard to cure.

(6) *Abortion, etc.*—Young females living under enforced widowhood are exposed to temptations and sometimes undergo operations at the hand of quacks for abortion to conceal their shame, and thus meet with an untimely death.

(7) *Confinement and bad feeding.*—There is no evidence of deliberate bad feeding of females unless when poverty necessitates it, but confinement in the house is a factor of great importance affecting female mortality. Females of the higher classes live confined in their houses, which are generally dark and ill-ventilated. They scarcely go out to enjoy fresh air, and thus fall victim to consumption and other diseases which carry them away in youth.

(8) *The lot of Hindu widows* is very hard. They have to live confined in a corner in the house and forego most of the pleasures of life, which tells greatly upon their health.

(9) *Hard labour.*—Women, especially in the lower classes, have to perform very hard labour in the house. Except in a few well-to-do families, servants are generally not employed and the females have to do all the household pounding, grinding and sweeping work. They have not only to cook, but also to cleanse the kitchen, and wash the pots in the scullery. They are required to draw water from the village well and bring it home in water pots on their heads. While on one hand, want of work spoils the health of females in the higher castes, on the other, in the lower castes, it is too much of work which ruins their constitution and prematurely sends them to the grave.

Marriage of grown-up males with very young females.

302. In addition to the above causes a great loss of female life is caused in Gujarat by the marriage of grown-up males with very young girls. It is a matter of every-day experience that a connection between a girl of thirteen or fourteen years and a man of thirty-five or above, proves fatal to the life of the girl. A widowed man marrying a girl of twelve after he has lost his first wife, soon loses her and another is brought into the house ; this also meets with the same fate and a fourth is married when the man is past fifty and she is left a widow before she has arrived at womanhood or soon after. Sometimes negotiations for the new connection are entered into on the burning ground, while the dead body of the old wife is being consumed by fire.

Effect of paucity of females on marriage.

303. Owing to the deficiency of females in some castes such as Kanbis, Vanias, etc., wives are brought from Kathiawad. Necessity leads to laxity in inquiring into the status of the proposed bride and to a willingness to accept on trust the statements made regarding her by her guardians or vendors. It sometimes happens that a Kathiawadi bride subsequently turns out to be a widow or to be really of the Kumbhar, Vaghari or other low caste. She is turned out and the husband after remaining outcaste for some time regains admission into his caste on payment of fine in addition to a caste dinner.

Proportion of females in towns.

304. Females are generally less numerous in urban than in rural tracts. The deficiency is more marked in large towns than in small ones. In this State, the paucity of females is noticeable only in the City of Baroda, where their proportion is the lowest in the whole State. In all other important towns except Petlad, the proportion of females is higher than in the State as a whole. This shows that instead of receiving, our towns are sending out emigrants. Patan and Navsari have an excess of females over males, owing to Vanias and artizans from the former and Parsis from the latter migrating to Bombay and other places for employment. Our towns are merely overgrown villages and have few attractions for the foreigner. The inhabitants of true urban areas are to a great extent merely temporary residents whose permanent homes are elsewhere and who frequently leave their females at home, when they come to seek a livelihood in towns.

Name of town.	No of females per 1,000 males.
Baroda City	853
Patan	1,038
Amreli	961
Petlad	893
Navsari	1,069
Dabhoi	946

European theories regarding causes influencing sex.

305. Various theories have been put forward at different times, regarding the causation of sex. Ever since Aristotle's days, inquirers have sought to discover the causes which determine the sex of the offspring. As soon as one of them puts forward his theory with a certain amount of plausibility, there is another prepared to upset it by arraying the figures of other tribes or localities. An account of modern European theories on the subject is given in Westermarck's *History of Human marriage* and in Geddes and Thomson's *Evolution of Sex.*

But no conclusion commanding general assent has yet been arrived at. The various theories as collected by Westermarck are :—

(1) More boys are born, if the husband is older than the wife and more girls, if the wife is older.
(2) The less the difference of age between the parents, the greater is the probability of boys being born.
(3) Polygamy leads to the birth of a greater proportion of female children.
(4) Organisms when unusually well nourished produce comparatively more female offsprings ; in the opposite case, more male.
(5) The male births are in greater excess in country districts, the population of which is badly fed than in towns where the conditions of life are more luxurious.
(6) A similar excess is found among poor people as compared with well-off classes.
(7) In the highlands comparatively more boys are born than in the lowlands.
(8) The mixture of races produces an excess of female births.
(9) The temporarily superior parent produces the opposite sex, and
(10) Unions between related individuals or generally between individuals who are very like each other produce more male offsprings.

The Census statistics do not furnish means to test all these theories. They seem however to favour the 5th and 7th and to disprove the 10th. Mahomedans and Parsis who favour cousin marriages, have more females than Hindus who do not.

In an article on "The Hereditary Tendency towards Twin-bearing and the Influences aiding in the determination of Sex," in the *Lancet* of August 19, 1911, Dr. James Oliver, M. D., Physician to the Hospital for Women, London, after reviewing the principal theories regarding the causation of sex, says :—"In the case of the human race and the higher animal kingdom, we are nevertheless driven to the conclusion that there must be some force or forces at work which tend to balance the relationship of male to female births. For more than 2,000 years, philosophers and physicians alike have diligently endeavoured to seek out and elucidate these forces, but so far, their efforts have been attended with practically no success. . . . . . The question of the causation of sex is, in fact, to us as great a mystery as it has ever been."

Indian theories.

306. Several theories regarding the causes which influence sex, are also current among the people of this country. The author of a work called *Koka Shastra* has propounded several theories of which the principal is that sex is determined by the preponderance of the male over the female principle or the reverse, at the time of conception. The female principle is supposed to be weaker on certain days than on others, and it is believed therefore that conception on even days following the commencement of the menses tends to result in male and on other days in female children. These general tendencies however might be counteracted and a strong and healthy woman is advised to fast or reduce her diet at the time when she expects to conceive if she wishes to have a male offspring.

Ceremonies for male children.

307. Male children are greatly desired by Hindus as indeed by Jains, Musalmans and Parsis. If a married pair is not blessed with a male issue within a few years of married life, many expedients are resorted to in order to secure it. Charms given by Sadhus, Yatis and Fakirs are worn and vows are offered to goddesses (*Mata*) and saints (*Pir*). Among Hindus a special ceremony called *punsavan* or male making which was once performed soon after conception is now performed in the seventh month of the pregnancy. It consists of certain rites with offerings and spells of which the principal consists in dropping into the right nostril of the pregnant woman, a little juice extracted from a piece of the root of the bunyan tree (*ficus indica*).

SUBSIDIARY TABLE I—General proportions of the Sexes by Natural Divisions or Districts.

Districts or Natural Divisions.	Number of Females to 1,000 Males.					
	1911.		1901.		1891.	
	Actual Population.	Natural Population.	Actual Population.	Natural Population.	Actual Population.	Natural Population.
1	2	3	4	5	6	7
Baroda State	**925**	**927**	**936**	**970**	**928**	**929**
Baroda Division, Ex. of City ...	872	Not available.	891	Not available.	883	Not available.
Baroda City	853		853		852	
Kadi Division	947		956		950	
Navsari Division	982		992		985	
Amreli Division	940		939		920	

SUBSIDIARY TABLE II—Number of Females per 1,000 Males at different Age-periods by Religion at each of the last three Censuses.

Age.	All religions.			Hindus.			Musalmans.			Animists.			Jains.		
	1891.	1901.	1911.	1891.	1901.	1911.	1891.	1901.	1911.	1891.	1901.	1911.	1891.	1901.	1911.
0—1	1,015	1,004	977	1,010	982	978	1,049	966	960	1,004	1,163	999	1,113	1,092	954
1—2	1,057	976	1,025	1,059	951	1,033	1,040	963	983	1,082	1,086	969	1,003	1,203	1,186
2—3	1,077	1,028	1,003	1,078	1,016	1,000	1,047	935	1,034	1,224	1,110	1,041	1,083	1,161	970
3—4	1,118	1,060	1,077	1,121	1,056	1,079	1,059	1,030	1,048	1,212	1,093	1,085	1,151	1,083	1,060
4—5	1,039	1,032	936	1,042	1,021	924	990	1,027	985	1,141	1,081	1,004	997	1,152	1,005
Total 0—5	1,060	1,026	1,000	1,060	1,013	999	1,036	988	1,002	1,131	1,109	1,023	1,075	1,135	1,009
5—10	917	922	846	913	908	835	942	968	884	935	1,012	909	932	926	878
10—15	781	828	817	778	822	802	790	833	844	763	879	955	849	857	899
15—20	828	855	854	822	842	839	870	906	881	1,015	893	1,053	777	799	852
20—25	1,002	945	979	998	942	962	1,003	990	1,007	1,177	921	1,221	1,017	932	1,059
25—30	921	918	944	914	901	939	970	959	966	976	1,063	947	921	841	988
Total 0—30	924	909	914	920	898	904	938	936	936	996	981	1,007	939	908	948
30—40	887	897	925	884	899	920	898	883	966	879	883	896	905	891	1,009
40—50	927	1,010	922	926	1,009	928	913	1,017	876	886	995	812	944	1,006	1,033
50—60	929	1,040	939	922	1,053	932	961	994	900	879	898	809	1,000	1,137	998
60 and over	1,156	1,307	1,152	1,144	1,293	1,031	1,215	1,452	1,116	1,161	1,194	1,026	1,241	1,481	1,316
Total 30 and over	936	990	945	952	987	945	951	993	944	900	949	870	979	1,020	1,048
Total all ages (actual population)	925	936	925	924	929	919	943	956	939	968	971	961	955	951	987

SUBSIDIARY TABLE III—Number of Females per 1,000 Males at different Age-periods by Religions and Natural Divisions. Census of 1911.

AGE.	Baroda Division.						Baroda City.				Kadi Division.			
	All religions.	Hindus.	Musalmans.	Jains.	Animists.	Christians.	All religions.	Hindus.	Musalmans.	Jains.	All religions.	Hindus.	Musalmans.	Jains.
1	2	3	4	5	6	7	8	9	10	11	12	13	14	15
0—1	955	951	983	707	1,051	763	989	978	1,108	641	996	997	951	1,046
1—2	990	999	845	1,164	1,069	687	987	950	1,103	1,571	1,046	1,046	994	1,140
2—3	937	912	1,118	1,010	1,069	598	992	997	968	1,034	1,040	1,039	1,072	1,015
3—4	1,010	985	1,088	1,186	1,140	1,264	1,065	1,062	1,074	1,400	1,144	1,152	1,091	988
4—5	912	916	897	823	941	536	925	922	996	808	910	893	1,145	1,020
Total 0—5	*958*	*949*	*994*	*932*	*1,053*	*769*	*990*	*982*	*1,043*	*984*	*1,022*	*1,020*	*1,049*	*1,034*
5—10	798	780	839	961	898	1,175	907	916	910	800	820	817	864	842
10—15	749	738	751	775	834	1,013	754	757	826	899	813	804	882	934
15—20	790	779	716	774	1,223	1,027	829	833	897	809	852	846	909	929
20—25	871	850	934	962	1,212	844	801	802	812	811	1,028	1,024	1,016	1,187
25—30	890	895	829	868	908	1,022	749	746	790	836	974	967	1,047	1,064
Total 0—30	*851*	*841*	*856*	*882*	*1,009*	*955*	*838*	*838*	*881*	*857*	*926*	*921*	*967*	*993*
30—40	888	883	921	843	954	857	786	791	776	794	969	961	998	1,181
40—50	868	880	789	903	796	860	827	841	743	1,079	986	986	922	1,112
50—60	883	889	836	968	740	1,371	923	963	794	888	973	975	919	1,034
60 and over	1,113	1,112	1,135	1,448	961	1,031	1,229	1,215	1,290	1,692	1,122	1,120	1,036	1,300
Total 30 and over	*903*	*906*	*884*	*945*	*875*	*958*	*876*	*888*	*830*	*1,000*	*989*	*985*	*964*	*1,144*
Total all ages (actual population).	*872*	*866*	*866*	*908*	*963*	*956*	*853*	*858*	*860*	*915*	*947*	*943*	*966*	*1,051*
Total all ages (Natural population)						Figures not available.								

AGE.	Navsari Division.						Amreli Division.			
	All religions.	Hindus.	Musalmans.	Jains.	Parsis.	Animists.	All religions.	Hindus.	Musalmans.	Jains.
1	16	17	18	19	20	21	22	23	24	25
0—1	975	972	956	1,000	990	981	961	976	840	1,000
1—2	1,009	1,046	1,046	1,091	840	931	1,076	1,074	1,133	903
2—3	1,032	1,047	973	564	1,087	1,023	991	1,005	902	883
3—4	1,046	1,050	943	1,194	989	1,060	1,056	1,066	975	1,096
4—5	1,018	1,019	919	1,034	1,127	1,032	973	978	881	1,386
Total 0—5	*1,015*	*1,023*	*960*	*947*	*1,015*	*1,010*	*1,004*	*1,014*	*923*	*1,047*
5—10	933	935	948	931	1,106	913	932	930	947	978
10—15	931	915	934	879	962	976	838	832	864	908
15—20	1,004	971	1,151	645	1,306	1,047	833	823	957	756
20—25	1,147	1,093	1,330	822	1,918	1,226	964	975	1,101	871
25—30	1,031	1,032	1,189	661	2,228	966	968	952	1,105	1,174
Total 0—30	*1,003*	*992*	*1,054*	*812*	*1,258*	*1,007*	*934*	*930*	*970*	*954*
30—40	937	937	1,115	587	1,874	876	911	900	1,051	787
40—50	903	900	1,063	758	1,691	819	933	927	979	945
50—60	909	891	1,091	844	1,506	834	926	924	942	901
60 and over	1,129	1,116	1,162	1,000	1,710	1,050	1,173	1,199	1,027	1,074
Total 30 and over	*944*	*939*	*1,103*	*717*	*1,702*	*868*	*950*	*945*	*1,006*	*886*
Total all ages (actual population).	*982*	*973*	*1,071*	*778*	*1,421*	*961*	*940*	*935*	*982*	*930*
Total all ages (Natural population)					Figures not available.					

SUBSIDIARY TABLE IV—NUMBER OF FEMALES PER 1,000 MALES FOR CERTAIN SELECTED CASTES.

CASTE.	NUMBER OF FEMALES PER 1,000 MALES.						
	All ages.	0–5	5–12	12–15	15–20	20–40	40 and over.
1	2	3	4	5	6	7	8
Hindus.							
Ahir	895	1,104	898	679	736	822	1,013
Bahrot	944	953	787	794	918	949	1,067
Bava	503	433	412	351	441	604	482
Bhangi	970	1,079	851	782	929	1,043	930
Bharvad	941	1,089	1,002	816	713	920	1,012
Bhavsar	1,059	915	958	1,073	1,201	1,115	1,077
Bhoi	868	1,074	749	614	733	858	988
Brahman—Anavala	862	904	1,055	794	666	834	869
„ Audich	946	1,016	817	672	814	908	1,166
„ Deshastha	846	1,089	956	788	836	793	807
„ Mewada	821	720	721	792	1,004	808	880
„ Modh	956	1,010	878	786	882	963	1,044
„ Nagar	1,048	969	979	901	1,016	1,150	1,049
„ Tapodhan	858	919	737	776	747	864	987
Chamar	1,029	1,089	827	768	762	1,096	131
Darji	1,091	1,075	906	925	1,020	1,249	1,083
Dhed	975	1,022	876	948	886	997	1,024
Garoda	1,011	1,146	727	685	880	1,179	1,111
Ghanchi	964	950	796	940	869	1,006	1,104
Gola (rice-pounders)	1,013	922	775	1,147	1,028	1,015	1,254
Gosain	810	804	800	676	846	810	831
Hajam	986	921	780	738	873	1,144	1,056
Kachhia	886	717	862	829	841	917	993
Kanbi-Anjana	989	1,091	729	997	825	1,015	1,164
„ Kadwa	940	1,106	1,015	1,360	884	842	894
„ Karadia	982	989	988	761	691	1,003	1,204
„ Lewa	833	909	767	664	645	890	886
Koli	904	961	668	773	782	890	1,169
Kumbhar	981	931	819	812	927	970	1,280
Luhana	936	1,160	865	758	801	957	967
Luhar	1,027	1,059	875	782	1,055	1,076	1,111
Machhi	911	973	877	926	1,034	898	829
Maratha	838	943	930	548	905	699	1,086
Mochi	887	987	776	734	728	996	867
Rabari	899	899	1,086	775	790	875	907
Rajput	859	904	761	722	679	898	960
Ravalia	918	947	867	805	862	980	926
Sathawara	1,005	1,057	826	732	714	1,163	1,067
Shenva	936	925	814	785	840	1,046	936
Soni	1,009	869	954	950	1,024	1,074	1,059
Sutar	914	928	752	749	822	995	988
Talavia	829	873	924	381	844	985	854
Targala	1,210	660	927	893	1,020	1,620	1,385
Vagher	921	766	1,019	647	743	1,024	1,088
Vaghari	913	987	841	764	806	993	866
Vania-Disaval	1,172	1,289	1,298	802	965	1,397	1,029
„ Lad	1,041	859	1,036	839	745	1,138	1,204
„ Shrimali	868	1,049	801	847	625	831	836
Jains.							
Vania Shrimali	1,043	841	1,097	723	1,026	1,133	1,654
Animists.							
Bhil	967	757	919	1,603	1,180	1,078	795
Chodhra	962	1,058	878	1,202	1,127	922	873
Dhanka	967	1,162	911	507	1,252	1,077	773
Dhodia	962	1,004	799	1,188	1,014	994	980
Gamit	947	931	871	1,001	1,071	925	1,017
Nayakda	991	1,220	762	900	1,213	1,084	794
Musalmans.							
Fakir	877	954	955	917	973	837	815
Ghanchi	924	1,036	932	1,048	632	948	970
Malek	893	904	865	833	763	859	1,039
Memon	1,105	1,025	1,080	1,317	832	1,061	1,315
Molesalam	861	882	846	803	871	876	837
Momna	778	713	676	756	818	788	899
Pathan	881	927	950	802	838	844	914
Pinjara	757	995	897	832	708	1,008	965
Saiyad	916	906	888	940	895	970	806
Shaikh	907	809	871	898	956	994	775
Vohora	1,074	925	881	1,152	1,092	1,281	995
Parsis.							
Parsis	1,326	1,017	1,028	993	1,206	1,722	1,472
Christians.							
Native	866	772	879	970	801	831	1,005

SUBSIDIARY TABLE V—Actual number of Births and Deaths reported for each sex during the Decades 1891—1900 and 1901—1910.

Years.	Number of Births.			Number of Deaths.			Difference between columns 2 and 3. Excess of latter over former + Defect —	Difference between columns 5 and 6. Excess of latter over former + Defect —	Difference between columns 4 and 7. Excess of former over latter + Defect —	Number of female births per 1,000 male births.	Number of female deaths per 1,000 male deaths.
	Male.	Female.	Total.	Male.	Female.	Total.					
1	2	3	4	5	6	7	8	9	10	11	12
1891 ...	17,425	14,612	82,037	15,301	12,032	27,333	— 2,813	— 3,269	+ 4,704	839	786
1892 ...	17,059	14,502	31,561	19,364	15,997	35,361	— 2,557	— 3,367	— 3,800	850	826
1893 ...	14,152	12,081	26,232	26,558	22,807	49,365	— 2,071	— 3,751	— 23,132	854	859
1894 ...	20,022	17,326	37,348	27,997	22,354	50,351	— 2,696	— 5,643	— 13,003	865	798
1895 ...	19,558	16,718	36,276	22,814	18,352	41,166	— 2,840	— 4,462	— 4,890	855	804
1896 ...	22,138	19,749	41,887	24,978	19,703	44,681	— 2,389	— 5,275	— 2,794	892	789
1897 ...	21,088	17,871	38,909	20,098	16,268	36,366	— 3,167	— 3,830	+ 2,543	849	809
1898 ...	19,340	16,641	35,981	23,233	19,285	42,518	— 2,699	— 3,948	— 6,537	860	830
1899 ...	22,553	19,487	42,040	26,076	22,962	49,038	— 3,066	— 3,114	— 6,998	864	881
1900 ...	16,846	14,557	31,403	75,763	55,498	131,261	— 2,289	— 20,265	— 99,858	864	733
Total 1891—1900	*190,131*	*163,544*	*353,675*	*282,182*	*225,258*	*507,440*	*— 26,587*	*— 56,924*	*— 153,765*	*860*	*798*
1901 ...	7,330	6,091	13,421	65,361	50,976	116,337	— 1,239	— 14,385	— 102,916	881	780
1902 ...	22,422	19,598	42,020	30,684	27,214	57,898	— 2,824	— 3,470	— 15,878	874	887
1903 ...	19,219	16,876	36,095	31,556	30,162	61,718	— 2,343	— 1,394	— 25,623	878	956
1904 ...	20,994	18,736	39,730	33,262	31,630	64,892	— 2,258	— 1,632	— 25,162	892	951
1905 ...	22,967	20,617	43,584	24,724	23,503	48,227	— 2,350	— 1,221	— 4,643	898	951
1906 ...	22,782	20,101	42,883	24,352	21,869	46,221	— 2,681	— 2,483	— 3,338	882	898
1907 ...	22,434	19,766	42,200	33,013	31,099	64,112	— 2,668	— 1,914	— 21,912	881	942
1908 ..	24,986	22,347	47,333	25,455	22,275	47,730	— 2,639	— 3,180	— 397	894	875
1909 ...	25,937	22,666	48,603	22,666	20,037	42,703	— 3,271	— 2,629	+ 5,900	874	884
1910 ...	25,860	22,648	48,508	23,742	20,794	44,536	— 3,212	— 2,948	+ 3,972	876	876
Total 1901—1910	*214,931*	*189,446*	*404,377*	*314,815*	*279,559*	*594,374*	*— 25,485*	*— 35,256*	*— 189,997*	*881*	*888*

SUBSIDIARY TABLE VI.—Number of Deaths of each sex at different ages.

Age.	1905.		1906.		1907.		1908.		1909.		Total.		Average number of female deaths per 1,000 male deaths.
	Male.	Female.	Male.	Female.	Male.	Female.	Male.	Female.	Male.	Female.	Male.	Female.	
1	2	3	4	5	6	7	8	9	10	11	12	13	14
0—1	3,897	3,305	4,710	4,051	4,223	3,581	4,661	3,937	4,454	3,741	21,945	18,615	849
1—5	3,072	2,573	3,994	3,509	4,251	3,781	4,363	3,545	3,862	3,265	19,542	16,683	854
5—10	1,245	1,254	1,146	1,105	1,840	1,767	1,224	1,072	1,015	911	6,470	6,109	944
10—15	1,496	1,472	1,121	1,114	2,098	2,134	1,184	1,188	807	732	6,706	6,590	983
15—20	1,348	1,405	1,178	1,107	2,253	2,076	1,243	1,062	924	815	6,946	6,465	931
20—30	3,156	3,491	2,785	2,784	4,701	4,683	2,995	2,787	2,500	2,554	16,137	16,299	1,010
30—40	3,241	3,186	2,791	2,545	4,409	4,399	2,938	2,664	2,508	2,328	15,887	15,122	952
40—50	2,968	2,487	2,584	2,000	3,938	3,368	2,582	2,024	2,409	1,835	14,481	11,714	809
50—60	2,236	2,047	2,145	1,669	2,920	2,578	2,152	1,757	2,140	1,630	11,593	9,681	852
60 and over ...	2,065	2,283	1,898	1,985	2,380	2,722	2,113	2,289	2,047	2,226	10,503	11,505	1,095

Chapter VII.

CIVIL CONDITION.

Reference to statistics.

308. The statistics regarding civil condition are given in Imperial Tables VII and XIV. In the former, civil condition is shown in combination with age and religion and in the latter with age and caste. The more important features of the statistics are exhibited in the following subsidiary tables at the end of this chapter :—

Subsidiary Table I.—Distribution by civil condition of 1,000 of each sex, religion and main age-period at each of the last four Censuses.

Subsidiary Table II.—Distribution by civil condition of 1,000 of each sex at certain ages in each religion and natural division.

Subsidiary Table III.—Distribution by main age-periods and civil condition of 10,000 of each sex and religion.

Subsidiary Table IV.—Proportion of sexes by civil condition at certain ages for religions and natural divisions.

Subsidiary Table V.—Distribution by civil condition of 1,000 of each sex at certain ages for selected castes.

Contrast between India and Europe.

309. There is a wide contrast between the marriage customs of Europe and India. The most striking fact one notices in India is the universal prevalence of the married state. "In Europe sentiment and prudence hold divided sway, and the tendency on the whole is rather towards a decline in the number of marriages. In India neither of these motives comes into play. Religion on the other hand, which in the west makes in the main for celibacy, throws its weight in India almost wholly into the other scale." (Risley's People of India, p. 148). A Hindu must marry and beget a son (*putra*) to save him from hell (*put*). He must also see that his daughters are not left unmarried at puberty, for to do so would not only bring social obloquy on his family but subject him and his ancestors to damnation. While marriage is obligatory it is hampered by numerous restrictions. In Europe the field from which a man can choose his wife is practically unlimited. The restrictions based on consanguinity are few and marriages are generally determined by the free choice of the marrying parties. There is no restriction on widow-marriage. The later period of life at which the people enter into wedlock coupled with the greater equality of age on the part of husband and wife reduces the period by which the wife on the average survives the husband, and there are no child-widows. In India a Hindu must marry within his own caste and outside the circle of those who are related to him within seven degrees. Most of the children are married by their parents in their infancy, and they make their first acquaintance when they are already husband and wife. Widows, except in certain lower castes, are prohibited from remarrying, though widowers are not only allowed to remarry but even to marry more than one wife. The Mahomedans, and especially those of them who are converts from Hinduism, have been affected in various degrees by the example of Hindu marriage usage ; and Indian Christians also have not always escaped the same pervading influence.

General features of the statistics.

310. This difference in customs shows a striking difference in statistics. In England from three-fifths to two-thirds of both the sexes are single and about a third are married. The proportion of the widowed is only 1 in 30 in the case of males and 1 in 13 in the case of females. In the Baroda State, however, the Census shows that of the total male population only two-fifths (43 per cent.) are unmarried. A reference to the age details shows that nearly three-fourths of the unmarried males (73 per cent.) are under 15 years of age. Of the males enumerated at the ages 15 to 30, only ⅓, and of those enumerated at

the ages 30 to 40 only 8 per cent. are unmarried; between 40 and 60 the number of bachelors is less than 5 per cent. and at the higher ages it is just 5 per cent. Amongst females the figures are even more striking. Less than a third (28 per cent.) of the total number of females of all ages is unmarried, and of these more than four-fifths (83 per cent.) are under 10 and three-fourths of the remainder are under 15 only. Only 5 per cent. of the total number of single females are over 15 years of age. The Hindu females, who are returned as spinsters at the age of 20 and upwards are mostly either prostitutes or persons suffering from some bodily affliction such as leprosy and the like. The number of genuine old maids is very small and belongs to the Rajput, Maratha and other high caste Hindus among whom girls remain unmarried to an older age owing to the difficulty of procuring for them suitable husbands.

Diagram showing the proportion of the married, single and widowed. at each age-period.

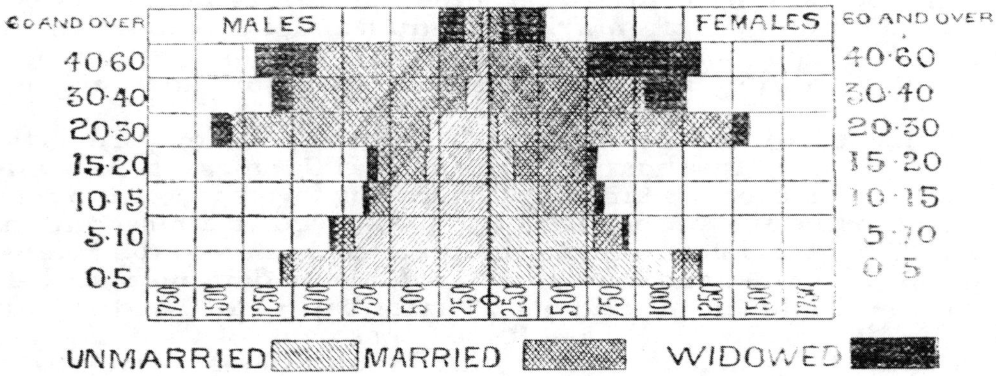

Comparatively few males (about 8 per cent.) were returned as widowed and most of these were fairly advanced in life. Amongst females, on the other hand, nearly a sixth of the total number are widows; and, although in their case also the majority is of the age of 40 and upwards, their number at the lower ages is by no means inconsiderable. There were 26 widows less than a year old, 225 of the age-period 1 to 5, 532 of 5 to 10, 1,723 of 10 to 15 and 2,628 of the ages between 15 to 20. Of the females enumerated between the ages 20 and 30 nearly one-fourteenth was returned as widows.

Local variations.

311. The above proportions are based on the returns of the State as a whole, but there are great local variations. 51 per cent. of the males are married in the Baroda as well as in the Kadi District and Baroda City, 47 per cent. in the Navsari District, and 46 per cent. in the Amreli District. 57 per cent. of the females are married in the Baroda District, 55 per cent. in the Kadi District, 51 per cent. in the Navsari District and the City of Baroda and only 50 per cent. in the Amreli District.

Variations by religions.

312. Subsidiary Table II. shows that the differences are equally well marked if we take religion instead of locality as the dividing line.

Hindus.

Universality of marriage, early marriage and enforced widowbood are the three prominent features of marriage customs among Hindus who form 83·4 per cent. of the population; and the rest of the people are more or less affected by their example. Among Hindus, marriage is not a civil contract but a religious sacrament, essential and irrevocable. As already said, a man must marry in orderto beget a son who may perform his funeral ceremonies and rescue his soul and the souls of his ancestors from hell. It is equally obligatory for a father to obtain a husband for his daughter and the most awful penalties are prescribed in the Shastras, if a girl should attain puberty while yet unmarried. Parashara, for instance, says "the mother, the father and the elder brother of a girl go to hell on seeing her menstruate while yet unmarried." We may find perhaps a few males, who, owing to some deformity or scarcity of girls in their caste, have not been able to marry, but we will very rarely find a female who has grown old without being married. The proverb says: *Doso kunvaro mare, pan dosi kai mare nahi, i.e.,* an old man may die unmarried but an old woman would never.

The Hindus bulk so largely in the total population that the difference between the figures for them and for all religions together, is not very striking. In 100 males, they have 50 married, 42 single and 8 widowed as compared with 49, 43 and 8 respectively in the general population. In 100 females, they have 55 married, 27 single and 18 widowed as compared with 54 married, 28 single and 18 widowed in the total population of the State. Both sexes marry earlier and of the unmarried females only one-twenty-fifth are over the age of 15, as compared with one-twentieth in the figures for all religions together. 16 per cent. of the total number of married Hindu females are under 15 years of age, as compared with 14 per cent. in all religions. The proportion of the married at 15-40 and later in life is almost identical with that in the general population.

Mahomedans.

313. There are marked differences between the corresponding proportions for Musalmans. In every 100 males, there are four more who are single, and four fewer who have wives, than among the Hindus, while the proportion of the widowed is almost the same in both the religions. The deficiency among the married is due to the comparatively later age at which Mahomedans marry. One Mahomedan marries before the age of 10, while three Hindus do so, and one marries between 10 and 15, while two Hindus do so. In the age-period 15—40, 31 per cent. of the total Hindu males are married against 27 per cent. among the Mahomedans ; from 40 and after, there is an excess of married Mahomedan males owing to Mahomedan widowers marrying much more readily than those who are Hindus. Widow marriage being allowed, a grown-up widowed Mahomedan has no difficulty in securing a suitable wife, while most of the high caste Hindus have to elect between not marrying at all or marrying a child-wife.

The differences are even more marked in the case of females. As compared with Hindus, in every 100 Mahomedan females, there are seven more spinsters, five wives less and two fewer widows. The smaller proportion of the married is due entirely to the relatively small number of child-wives amongst Mahomedan girls below the age of 10. Only a little more than 1 per cent. of the total number of females is married as compared with nearly 4 per cent. among the Hindus ; and at 10-15 only 3 per cent. compared with 4·5 per cent. On the other hand at the child-bearing ages, *i. e.*, from 15 to 40 the married women amongst Mahomedans are almost equal to those amongst Hindus. Those who lose their first husband while still young, find it easier to enter the married state with the result that whereas 5 per cent. of the Hindu women enumerated at the ages 15 to 40 were returned as widowed, the corresponding proportion for Mahomedans is 4·5. The difference is of course not very striking, as a very large proportion of those who profess the faith of Islam, are the descendants of converts from Hinduism and there is amongst many sections of them a lingering sentiment against the re-marriage of widows.

Animistic tribes.

314. The distribution of the Animistic males by civil condition shows a general resemblance to that prevailing among Mahomedans. In comparison with the latter, there is in every 100 an excess of four bachelors, one fewer married, and three fewer widowed. The excess of bachelors is attributable to the less prevalence of early marriages.

In the case of females, the Animists have in every 100, thirteen more spinsters, three fewer wives and ten fewer widows. Marriage of girls is much later than even among Mahomedans. Only three girls in 1,000 are married before the age of 10, compared with 13 amongst Mahomedans, and only 13 in the age-period 10 to 15 compared with 30. There are only 14 widows in 1,000 females of the ages 15 to 40 as compared with 46 among the Mahomedans, and only 57 in "40 and after" as compared with 132.

Jains.

315. The Jains of both sexes marry even later than the Mahomedans and the result is that they have amongst them more single persons and fewer who are married. Of every 100 males, 49 are single, 42 married and 9 widowed. Very few males are married before the age of 10 and only 11 in 100 before the age of 15. Nearly one-fourth are married at 15-40 and one-seventh at 40 and after. There are practically no

widowers before the age of 15 and only 1 in 42 of the ages 15 to 40, and 1 in 15 of the ages 40 and after.

As regards females 29 per cent. are single, 43 per cent. are married and 28 per cent. widowed. The proportion of widows is the largest, amongst all the religions because Jains are mostly of the Vania castes all of which enforced widowhood. Under the age of 10 marriage is practically unknown, and of those between 10 and 15 only 2 per cent. are married; and nearly two-fifths are married after 15. The usual age for the marriage of Jain girls seems to lie between 15 and 20. There are practically no widows before the age of 15 and in the age-period 15-40, as also in 40 and after, the number of widows is much larger than in the case of any other religion.

Christians.

316. Owing to the fact that most of the Christians are natives and the ranks of the Christians are being augmented by new accessions from persons already married or widowed, from the lower castes of Hindus, among whom infant marriages are most prevalent, the distribution of Christians by civil condition according to the return of the Census does not afford a very reliable reflex of the customs existing amongst converts of long standing. So far as figures go, they are in some respect higher even than those of Hindus. In 100 males, nine more are married, eight fewer are single and one fewer is widowed, as compared with Hindus. Similarly in the case of females, there are seven more married, two fewer single and five fewer widows. A larger number of both males and females marries while still of immature age, but there is a smaller proportion of widows, as widow-marriage is not only allowed but is freely practised.

Parsis.

317. As compared with the Hindus, the Parsis have, in one hundred males, 12 fewer married, 16 more unmarried and four fewer widowed. In 100 females, they have 15 fewer married, 18 more spinsters and three fewer widowed. Both males and females marry after the age of puberty. Widow-marriage though allowed is not practised by those who are well-to-do and grown-up and have children.

EARLY MARRIAGE.

Origin of early marriage among Hindus.

318. The Aryan Society of the Vedic or more properly speaking the Grihya Sutra period presents the institution of marriage in a form which recognized female liberty and the dignity of womanhood in full, slight traces of which are seen in the old Sanskrit ritual, which is still recited and in the ceremonies which are blindly performed. Woman's freedom and dignity were vindicated and in the Kshatriya caste especially, liberty to choose her husband in the form of *swayamvara*, or marriage by free choice, so well illustrated in the stories of Sita, Damyanti, Rukmini and Draupadi, was widely allowed. Marriage took place in *all* castes at a comparatively mature

Map showing the number per 1,000 Hindu females aged 0—10 who are married.

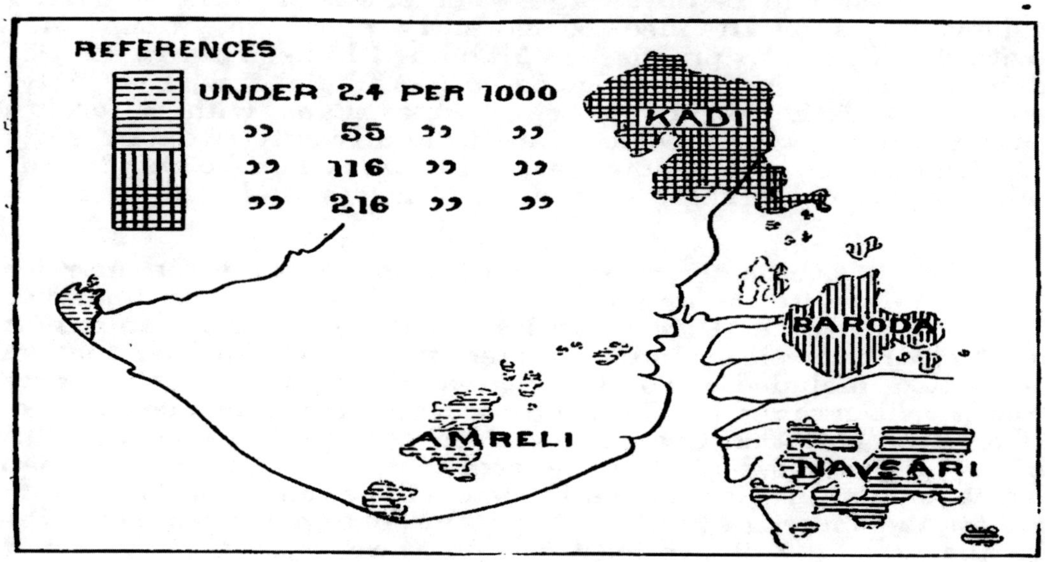

age, and the re-marriage of widows was not looked upon as disreputable. Later on owing to causes which it is not possible to trace fully, there was a revulsion of feeling and the Vedic institutions were practically abandoned or ignored and in their place usages grew up which brought on infant marriages and enforced widowhood. The Shastras explain the revulsion of feeling by ascribing it to be the result of the change of *Yuga* that is the setting in of the Kali Yuga. But it was probably the reflex action of the rise of Buddhism with its horror of female society joined with the confusion caused by the invasions of barbarous hordes such as the Shakas, Hunas and Jats from outside and the rise of non-Aryan tribes to power in the country which deluged the land with bloodshed and extinguished the spirit of chivalry, learning and independence and reduced the nation to the subjection of people with a lower type of civilization about the commencement of the Christian era (Ranade's Religious and Social Reforms, p.32). The growth of the institution of caste must have also brought about a change in the customs of the people and encouraged early marriages. The commands of the Shastras for early marriages based as they must have been on the necessity created by this peculiar institution, must have also powerfully affected the bent of the people. It being essential among the Hindus that a girl should marry within the narrow circle of the caste or sub-caste, it is obviously desirable at least among the families of higher status that the matter should be settled before a girl is old enough to form an attachment with some one with whom she cannot be married. The earlier the matter is taken in hand, the larger is the field of choice. If the father defers the arrangement for a husband, he may find that all the eligible boys of the proper age have already been appropriated and that he must put up with one who for his daughter is either considerably older or younger or her inferior in social position. When the custom of infant marriage had once been started under the pressure of social necessity by the families of the higher groups in a caste, a sort of fashion would have been set up and blindly followed through all the grades. The gradual lowering of the position of women from the ideal of Vedic times, and the distrust of their virtue induced by the example of prematrimonial license set by the Dravidian races must also have its effect and a girl would thus be married as a child in order to avert the possibility of a scandal later on (Risley's People of India, p. 182).

Among the followers of other religions:

Among the Animistic tribes, both males and females are fully mature before they enter the bonds of matrimony.

Among Mahomedans.

Marriage, among the Mahomedans, being a civil contract rather than a religious sacrament, in theory at least, the girl should be of an age when she is capable of giving her consent. This, however, is not attended to, and early marriage, though far less common than with the Hindus, is practised. Mahomed himself married a girl of 7, Ayesha, the daughter of his immediate successor, Abdullah, who is better known as Abu Bakr or the father of the virgin. Musalmans with a foreign strain, generally marry their boys between sixteen and twenty-two and girls at ten to eighteen. Hindu converts, however, who generally belong to the functional groups, adhere to their Hindu customs and marry their children at a very early age.

Among Parsis.

According to the law of Zoroaster, a boy or girl ought not to be married before the age of fifteen and this rule was observed by the Parsis while in Persia. But among a number of customs which the Parsis in India adopted from the Hindus, that of early marriages was also included. To those unacquainted with the early history of the Parsis, it will perhaps be startling to learn that instances are not wanting among them of the betrothal of a boy of three years of age to a girl of two. It may seem very ridiculous, but it is nevertheless a fact, that less than fifty years ago it was a custom in Navsari and some of the cities of Gujarat to arrange or negotiate for the marriage of children who had not even seen the light of this world ; that is to say, if two lady friends were *enceinte* they would conclude an arrangement that if one should bear a son and the other a girl, the infants would be united in marriage. A great change has taken place within the last fifty or sixty years. As a rule, Parsis have now adult marriages, although there are now and then a few instances of early marriages.

Early marriage : (1) By locality.

319. These diverse customs are reflected in the statistics of civil condition. In the State as a whole, 39 boys and 83 girls aged 0-4 are married per thousand of each sex. The corresponding proportions for the age-period 5-9 are 111 boys and 188 girls and for the age period 9-14, 236 boys and 515 girls per 1,000 of each sex. But this is the result of very uneven proportions in the different districts and in the different religions. 16 boys and 57 girls are married in one thousand of each sex aged 0-4 in the Baroda District. The corresponding proportions for the other districts are 75 boys and 147 girls in Kadi, 10 girls and 14 boys in Navsari, 15 boys and 16 girls in Amreli, and 14

Diagram showing the proportion of the married per 1,000 of each age-period by districts.

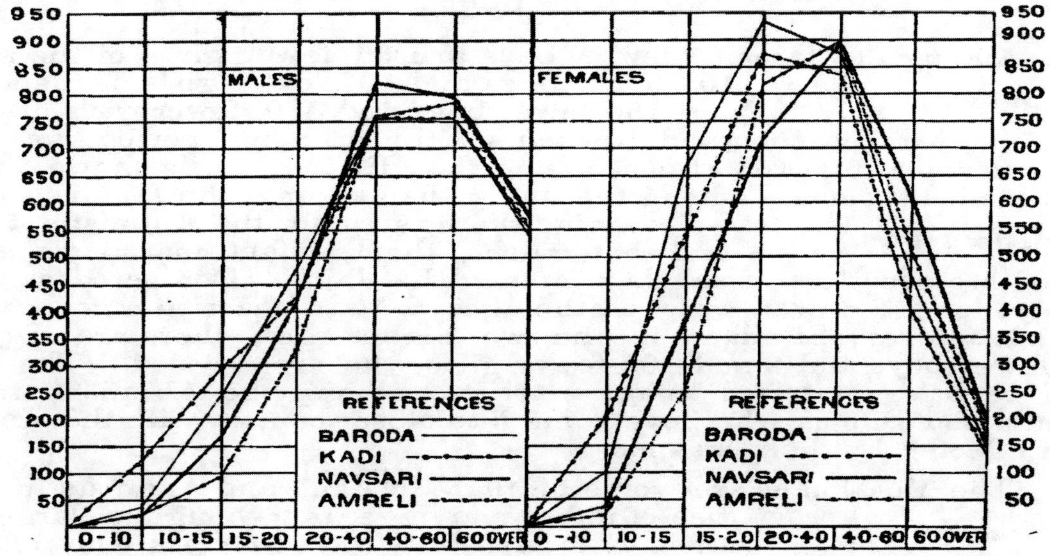

boys and 25 girls in the Baroda City. 69 boys and 178 girls are married in one thousand of each sex aged 5-9 in the Baroda District, the corresponding proportions for the other districts being 186 boys and 288 girls in Kadi, 38 boys and 74 girls in Navsari, 30 boys and 33 girls in Amreli and 74 boys and 133 girls in the City of Baroda. Similarly in the age-period 9-14, 257 boys and 687 girls in Baroda, 292 boys and 538 girls in Kadi, 169 boys and 366 girls in Navsari, 93 boys and 248 girls in Amreli, and 170 boys and 568 girls in the City are married in one thousand of each sex. This shows that early marriages of both males and females are most prevalent in the Kadi District, mostly owing to the large number of Kadwa Kanbis who as stated in para. 365 have in that district peculiar marriage customs which compel them to marry their children at a very early age. Early marriages are the least prevalent in the Amreli District. Girls in that district are kept unmarried till 16 or even 20, and it is for this reason that widowers or grown-up bachelors of Gujarat who can afford to pay a large bride-price, usually bring their wives from Kathiawad. In the Navsari District the proportion of married girls before 10 years of age is lower than in Baroda and Kadi, owing to the large Animistic population, among whom girls are not married before puberty.

(2) By religion : Hindus.

320. Taking the figures for the different religions separately, there are among the Hindus 6 more boys and 13 more girls aged 0-5 who are married per thousand each of that age than in the corresponding figures for all religions. Similarly in the

next two age-periods also, there are respectively 15 and 27 more boys and 30 and 55 more girls who are married than in the general average.

Diagram showing the number per 1,000 aged 0-10 who are married.

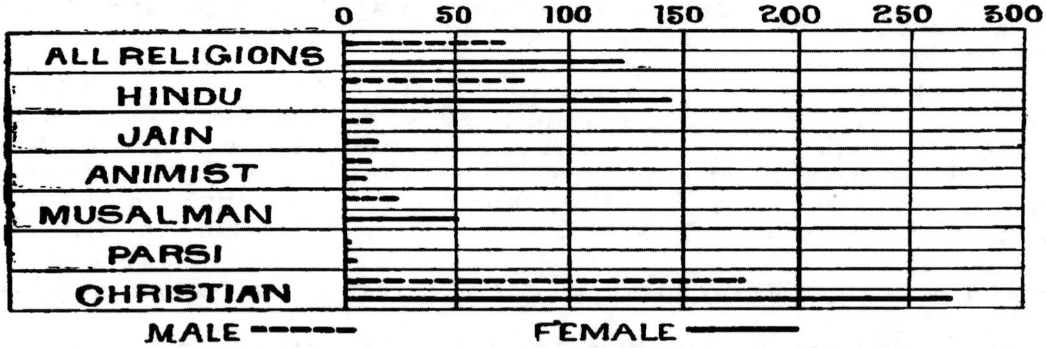

Jains.

321. Among the Jains 37 fewer boys and 86 fewer girls of the ages 0-5, 107 fewer boys and 197 fewer girls of the ages 5-10 and 156 fewer boys and 320 fewer girls of the ages 10-15 are married per thousand of each sex in each age-period, as compared with the corresponding proportions among the Hindus. This shows that infant marriages are less common among the Jains than among the Hindus, but when we examine the figures for the Animistic tribes, we find that among them, infant marriages, as might be expected are even less usual than among the Jains. Compared with Jains, 4 fewer boys and 8 fewer girls of the ages 0-5 are married among them per thousand of each sex. Similarly in the two higher ages, there are respectively 1 and 55 fewer boys and 2 and 102 fewer girls who are married. The few who are found to have practised infant marriage among the Animistic tribes are mostly Bhils and Dublas who have come into closer contact with the Hindus and have been affected by their customs.

Animistic tribes.

Musalmans.

322. The Musalmans are worse off than the Jains and Animists in the practice of infant marriage, but though a large part of them is formed by Hindu converts who follow their old Hindu customs, compared with Hindus, they have 32 fewer boys and 66 fewer girls who are married in one thousand of each sex aged 0-5 and in the age-periods 5-10 and 10-15, they have respectively 84 and 135 fewer boys and 135 and 214 fewer girls who are similarly married.

Parsis.

323. There are no boys or girls below 5 who are married among the Parsis. In the age-period 5-10, they have only 5 boys and 11 girls who are married in one thousand of each sex and the number of married children in the next higher age is also equally insignificant.

Native Christians.

324. Most of the Native Christians are drawn from the Dhed and other low castes among whom infant marriages are most prevalent. Most of the new converts are already married before accepting Christianity. It is for this reason that we find among the Christians a proportion of married infants which in some respects exceeds even that among the Hindus. Compared with Hindus, they have 8 fewer boys, but 36 more girls in one thousand of each sex, who are married before 5 years of age. Similarly in the age-periods, 5-10 and 10-15, they have respectively 254 and 150 more boys and 200 and 92 more girls who are married than among the Hindus.

Infant marriage in selected castes.

325. Imperial Table XIV gives the actual numbers of the married, unmarried and widowed of both sexes for selected castes at each of the assigned age-periods, while Subsidiary Table V, which is worked out from it, gives the proportional figures for each condition at the same age-periods. The

proportions of the married, unmarried and widowed among the **Bavas** and **Gosains** are naturally abnormal, owing to a large portion of their number living a celibate life and they must therefore be left out of consideration when comparing the statistics of civil condition of the different castes. As might be expected from their peculiar marriage customs, infant marriages are the most prevalent among the Kadwa Kanbis. They have 336 married males and 625 married females out of every 1,000 of each sex aged 0-5, and 626 married males and 894 married females out of every 1,000 of each sex aged 5-12. Next to the Kadwas come the Golas (rice-pounders) in the performance of early marriages, they having 70 boys and 99 girls aged 0-5 and 516 boys and 702 girls aged 5-12, who are married out of 1,000 of each sex in each period. Comparatively a larger proportion of infants of both sexes aged 0-5 and 5-12 are married among Dhed, Dhobi, Ghanchi, Koli, Kachhia, Anjana Kanbi, Kumbhar, Mali, Rabari, Ravalia, Sathawara and other low castes, and a smaller one among Brahman, Vania and Rajput castes. It is their blind persistence in the evil custom of infant marriage that has made these low castes more liable for prosecution under our early Marriage Prevention Act. The better practice of the higher castes is reflected in the lesser number of prosecutions to which they have made themseves liable. (*See* para. 332.) Kapol Vanias, Kayasthas, Brahma-Kshatris, and Shenavi Brahmans are the most reformed with regard to age in the marriage of their children. Among them boys are not married before 20 and girls before 15. Marathas, Prabhus, Deshastha Brahmans and several other high castes marry their sons at puberty, but their daughters are married much earlier and the result is that among them a bridegroom is always senior to the bride by 5 to 10 or even 15 years. Among Jains, infant marriages are performed to some extent by Shrimalis, but not by Oswals. Ghanchi, Molesalam, Momna, Pinjara, Tai, Vohora and similar Hindu converts to Islam practise infant marriage like low-caste Hindus, but to a smaller extent. For instance, the Musalman Ghanchi caste which seems to favour infant marriages the most, among Musalmans, has 55 boys and 44 girls aged 0-5 who are married in 1,000 of each sex; and 112 boys and 236 girls aged 5-12, who are married in 1,000 of each sex of that age. Infant marriages are not unknown among the Memons, Khojas and other converts less affected by Hindu customs, and among the Shaikhs, Saiyads and Pathans, but they are less common. The greater proportion of females are married in the age-period 12-20, and males in the age period 20-40. Infant marriages are rare among the members of the Animistic tribes. Most of the males and females are married after 15 or 20 years of age. Imitation of Hindu customs has introduced infant marriages to some extent, especially among the Bhils, Dhankas and Dublas, and we find some boys and girls married even in the age-period 0-5.

Cohabitation.

326. Although marriage is performed at a very early age, cohabitation generally does not take place before sexual maturity. The newly married girl is sent to her father-in-law's house, just to become acquainted with her new relations; but, unless she has reached maturity or her husband is a widower, she is not allowed to meet him. Within a few days she is taken back to her father's house and stays there till she is fully grown-up and her father is able to provide her with the ornaments, clothes and cash customary in the caste. No ceremony is necessary before the girl is sent to her husband's except among the Deccani Brahmans, who perform the *rutu shanti*, or menses quieting ceremony, when the girl begins to menstruate, after which she is considered to be fit for cohabitation with her husband.

Changes in the early marriage practice since 1881.

327. In Subsidiary Table I, the number of each sex per mille in each age-period, who were returned as married at each of the last four Censuses, has been compared. For 1881, the proportion of males married at 0-5 per mille is not available, but it was 41 in 1891, 24 in 1901 and 39 in the present Census, which shows that, though the number of boys married below the age of 5 is now less by 2 per 1,000 than what it was in 1891, it is more by 15 than what it was in 1901. But the figures of 1901 were abnormal. They were affected by the great famine which discouraged

marriages. A period of 10 years is besides too short a one to disclose any real and far-reaching change, particularly at present when the decade preceding the Census had at both its ends two marriage seasons of the Kadwa Kanbis among whom infant marriages are most in vogue. The total number of infants married before the age of 5 is 19,240 in the whole State, of which 12,818 or nearly two-thirds belong to the Kadwa Kanbis. If the Kadwa Kanbis were left out of account, the figures of the present Census would show a marked improvement on those of 1901 also. It cannot therefore be said that because the present Census shows more infant marriages than that of 1901, there has been no change in the attitude of the people towards this evil custom. The figures for 1901 being abnormal, it would be best to leave them aside and institute a comparison between those of 1891 and 1911. 92 females out of 1,000, aged 0-5, were married in 1891, while the corresponding proportion in 1911 is 83, that is, less by 1 per cent. 117 boys and 234 girls, aged 5-10, were married per mille of each sex in 1891 against 111 and 188 respectively in the present Census. Similarly in the age-period 10-15, the proportion of married boys and girls was 272 and 542 in 1891 against 236 and 515 in the present Census, thus showing that infant marriage is gradually becoming less prevalent.

Present day tendencies against early marriage.

328. Weddings are legitimate occasions of rejoicings and festivities, and the ignorant masses are glad to have the opportunities they afford, for the display of their wealth in giving caste dinners as early as possible. The females in the house are particularly anxious to marry their children as early as possible so that they may get a daughter-in-law to domineer over in the house or a son-in-law to pour out their affection on. The occasion of a marriage also gives them an opportunity to display their jewellery and rich dresses, and so they urge on the males to bring about an early consummation of their wish. Moreover the uneducated and especially those of the Gola-Ghanchi classes who allow their widows to remarry, seem to think that early marriage gives them a higher social status. Among them, therefore, there is perhaps a more extended resort to the practice of infant marriage. The Animistic tribes, who in the seclusion of their homes in the forest, favour adult marriage, have, owing to greater intercourse with Hindus, begun to imitate their custom of early marriages. There is, however, a general feeling amongst Brahman-Vanias and educated Hindus of all castes who are influenced by Western ideas against marrying their children while they are yet infants. Those of them among whom widow marriage is prohibited, are specially careful to defer the marriage of their daughters to as late a date as possible, and thus to minimise the danger of a lifelong misery. They allow their girls to grow up from 12 to 15 and their boys from 14 to 20 before they are married. They are not liable to any penalty beyond being censured or spoken of lightly by their ignorant caste fellows, which they can afford to ignore. Their number is slowly but steadily increasing. The disastrous consequences both to the individual and to the race from the evil custom of early marriage are every now and then brought home to the people by the Social Reform Conferences, which are now yearly institutions in connection with the Indian National Congress and are also held at certain intervals in most of the higher castes. Monthly or quarterly periodicals published by the Audich, Modh, Anavala, Luhana, Kadwa and Lewa Kanbi castes are also devoted to the same subject. Considerations of economy in marriage expenditure, *e. g.*, by marrying several girls at one and the same time, or securing a good alliance, *e. g.*, by marrying a child in a respectable family is sometimes said to impel even those who understand the evil to resort to it, but such cases are now rare, and so far as the upper classes are concerned, infant marriage may be said to be on the decline.

Social Reform by legislation.

329. In 1884 Mr. Malbari convulsed the Hindu society with his celebrated notes on Early Marriage and Enforced Widowhood. He denounced the customs with his usual vigour and earnestness and succeeded in creating a lively and permanent interest in the subject. This resulted in the Government of India Act on the Age of Consent under which sexual intercourse by a man with his own

wife under 12 years of age is an offence. About 20 years ago, Mr. Manmohan Ghose, a Bengali gentleman, put forward a proposal that a general law should be passed for British India declaring that no marriage shall be valid if either of the contracting parties at the time of celebrating their marriage is below twelve years. The main argument put forward by him in support of his proposal was that so eminent a Sanskrit scholar as Dr. Bhandarker had held that there was nothing in the Hindu scriptures to make it obligatory upon a Hindu to marry his daughter before she is twelve; but it was not supported and nothing came out of it. Unless the matter complained of comes within the pale of the criminal law, the British Government follows the policy of non-interference. In their celebrated Resolution of 1886 they have declared: "When caste or custom lays down a rule which is by its nature enforceable in the Civil Courts, but is clearly opposed to morality or public policy, the State will decline to enforce it. When caste or custom lays down a rule which deals with such matters as are usually left to the option of citizens, and which does not need the aid of Civil or Criminal Courts for its enforcement, State interference is not considered either desirable or expedient." This view of its position, laid down by the British Government, was not approved by the late Mr. Justice Ranade and other ardent advocates of social reform. In one of his speeches Justice Ranade said:—"The State in its collective capacity, represents the power, the wisdom, the mercy and charity of its best citizens. What a single man, or a combination of men, can best do on their own account that the State may not do; but it cannot shirk its duty if it sees its way to remedy evils, which no private combination of men can check adequately, or which it can deal with more speedily and effectively than any private combination of men can do. In these latter cases, the State's regulating action has its sphere of duty marked out clearly. On this and on this principle alone can State action be justified in many important departments of its activity, such as the enforcement of education, sanitation, factory legislation and of State undertakings like the postal service, or subsidies given to private effort in the way of railway extension and commercial development. The regulation of marriageable age has in all countries, like the regulation of the age of minority, or the fit age of making contracts, been a part of its national jurisprudence, and it cannot be said with justice that this question (infant marriage) lies out of its sphere. The same observation holds true of the condition of the widow rendered miserable in early life and thrown helpless on the world. More legitimately than minors, the widows are the wards of the nation's humanity, and to the extent that the evil they suffer is remediable by man, it cannot be said that this remedy may not be considered by the State as fully within its proper function."

The Mysore Act.

330. In pursuance of the above views, the Mysore State was the first to introduce a regulation to prevent infant marriages in its territory. Under its provision any person who causes the marriage of an infant girl or aids or abets such marriage and any man above eighteen years of age who marries an infant girl is liable to be punished with simple imprisonment upto six months. No restriction is placed upon infant marriages between the age eight or fourteen. The law is mainly intended to stop the practice of aged widowers marrying child-wives. Any man who having completed fifty years of age marries a girl, who has not completed fourteen years of age, is liable to be punished with fine or imprisonment which may extend to two years or with both.

Social legislation in Baroda.

331. But the most remarkable activity in social legislation has been displayed during the past decade by the Government of His Highness the Maharaja Gaekwad. The first important enactment of the kind, the Widow Remarriage Act, was passed in August 1901. Following the Government of India Act of 1856 and some of the older Smritis, it aims at legalising and thus indirectly encouraging the marriages of widows. Another measure passed about the same time is called the Liberty of Conscience Act, which was designed to remove the disabilities of those persons who adopt a religious faith that is in consonance with their conscientious beliefs but foreign to the religion of the

caste to which they belonged. Another object was to take out the sting of excommunication by depriving it of its effect on the proprietory or other rights of the person excommunicated. Then followed the most important social enactment, the Infant Marriage Prevention Act, which for a time ruffled the thought of the people of the State. It was passed in July 1904. The avowed object of the Act was to ameliorate the physical condition of the people, especially of the future generations, by raising the standard of marriageable age. The evils of child-marriages are patent to all, but few dare go against the current of the prevalent popular opinion. To such persons this measure would serve as a buoy to swim across the torrent of public opinion, which in itself is sure to ultimately lose much of its force and thus render the help of this buoy quite unnecessary. The draft of the Act, when published, strongly agitated the public mind in the State, and it was also widely criticised even outside its limits. The opposition, however, appeared to centre round the question of marriageable age, which in the draft was fixed at 14 for girls and 18 for boys. In deference to this opposition His Highness the Maharaja was pleased to reduce these ages by two years and agreed to make such other modifications in the original Bill so as to make it less obnoxious to orthodox communities. As finally passed, the Act defines a minor girl as one who has not completed her twelfth year and a minor boy as one who has not completed his sixteenth year. If the guardians of a minor girl, whose age is above nine, desire to get her married, they must apply to a tribunal consisting of the local sub-judge and three assessors of the petitioners' caste. If the tribunal is satisfied that in the event of the marriage not taking place on the date proposed, it will probably not take place at all or not within one year of the bride attaining her majority, or that the parents and the guardians of the girl are not likely, owing to old age and infirmity to survive until she comes of age, and that she has no other guardian, or that inevitable difficulties of a similar nature are likely to occur, they may grant permission for the marriage to take place. If the sub-judge disagrees with the assessors the case is referred to the District Judge whose decision is final.

Working of the Infant Marriage Prevention Act.

332. Judged by the light of the statistics furnished by the Census, the Infant Marriage Prevention Act does not appear to have succeeded in achieving any marvellous result. The slight decrease in the number of Infant Marriages noticed in para. 327 may be attributed to the progress of education and enlightened ideas. The Legal Remembrancer has, among other duties, to watch the operation of the Act and to report the results from time to time. From the statistics furnished by that office, it appears that the freedom to contract marriages within the prohibited limits of age, has been freely availed of. No less than 22,218 applications were made for seeking exemption under the Act. The circumstance that such permission was accorded in 95 per cent. of such petitions and refused in 5 per cent. only, shows that the Courts are very indulgent in their treatment of applications for exemption which may be said to be practically given for the asking. Possibly the Courts are led away by misplaced sympathy and forget the real object of the enactment. In addition to the large number of licences granted for performing infant marriages, over twenty-three thousand have been performed in violation of the provisions of the Act. And though the parties at fault have been prosecuted, it is believed that there must have been an equally large number who escaped punishment owing to the negligence of the Village Registrars (ordinary village patels) in reporting them. Most of those prosecuted were fined from a few to a hundred rupees, but those bent upon celebrating an infant marriage, do not regard such a punishment as

Year.	Applications for permission to marry infants.		No. of persons charged with infringement of the Act.	
	Filed.	Rejected.	Convicted.	Not convicted.
1904	695	...	718	...
1905	499	140	1,441	333
1906	583	100	1,858	709
1907	1,001	39	2,967	483
1908	190	48	1,506	211
1909	17,336	579	5,461	1,010
1910	1,914	198	9,437	1,200
Total ...	22,218	1,104	23,388	3,946

deterrent but count it as an additional item of expenditure to be incurred on marriage occasions.. Probably it is yet too premature to judge of the salutary effects of this beneficent enactment. It has been in force only for about six years in this decade. District Officers with whom I had conversation on the subject said that when the bill which subsequently ripened into law was published, it created an alarm among the ignorant people who form the bulk of the population, and there was an unusual activity in hurrying up marriages before the expected restraint was imposed. Those who could not afford to celebrate them immediately made formal contracts to do so as one of the sections of the proposed law purported to exempt such previously made contracts from its operation. Then again as mentioned in para. 327 two marriage seasons of the Kadwa Kanbis fell in during the decade, greatly increasing the number of infant marriages. The coming Census, before which the Act will have operated for a sufficiently long period, may be expected to furnish sufficient materials to properly judge of its effects.

WIDOW MARRIAGE.

Widow marriage among Hindus.

333. The practice regarding marriage of widows is different among the followers of the different religions. Widow marriage is prohibited in Gujarat among the Brahmans and Vanias and allowed in most of all other Hindu castes. Even some Brahman castes, such as Tapodhan, Vyas, Sarswat, Rajgor, Bhojak, Targala and Koligor allow it, but they are looked upon as degraded. Among the Kshatriyas, also Kathis, Marathas, Rajputs, Lewa Kanbis, Vagharis and Vadhels allow it. The castes which do not allow widow marriage, form only 15 per cent. of the total Hindu population of the State. But the higher families among castes which allow remarriage of widows do not, as a rule, have recourse to it, as such marriages are considered undignified. It is this feeling and a desire to raise their social status by adopting Brahmanical practices which have led some castes, such as a section of Marathas, Lewa Kanbis, Sonis, Sutars and others to put a stop to widow marriage within the last forty or fifty years. Infant marriage and enforced widowhood are looked upon among the lower classes as the two hallmarks of good birth and high standing, and their attitude is towards extending both the evil practices.

Among Jains.

The Jains are mostly of the Vania castes, who strictly prohibit widow marriage.

Among Animistic tribes.

Among the Animistic tribes a male or a female remarries soon after the death of his or her partner, and this accounts for the surprisingly small number of widows and widowers among the primitive people. Among the Dhodias, a woman marries again when her husband's funeral ceremonies are over and a dinner has been given in his honour. If she has any children by her first husband, they are left in charge of his relations.

Among Musalmans.

The marriage of widows is enjoined by Mahomedan law and the Prophet himself married several widows, including his first wife Khadija. But in India the example of the Hindus created a prejudice in the other direction and at the present day, it is seldom that a man takes a widow as his first wife. Widows who marry again usually become the wives of widowers or of men who have already got another wife.

Among Parsis.

The Parsis have not copied the Hindus in the cruel custom of prohibiting their widows from remarrying. But, notwithstanding the permission, there are very few Parsi widows who marry again, and if they do so it is generally before they have arrived at the age of forty. Those who have reached this age, retain, as a general rule, their state of widowhood, particularly if they are blessed with children and have sufficient means to provide for them.

Causes of prohibition against widow marriage among Hindus.

334. Prohibition of widow marriage was unknown in Vedic times. The Mahabharat furnishes several instances of widow marriage. Ulupi, the widowed daughter of a patriarch of the Naga tribe, was given in marriage by her father to Arjun. Another instance is furnished by the story of Nala and Damayanti. After having been abandoned by her husband in the forest, Damayanti found her way to her father's house, and after long waiting for him in vain, contrived a plan for finding him out. With the help of learned Brahmans and the consent of her father, she advertised that in consequence of the disappearance and probable death of Nala, she was going to make a second choice of a husband for herself. The third illustration is furnished by the Padma Puran and refers to the unfortunate daughter of a king of Benares, who was married no less than twenty times, it being her peculiar misfortune that as soon as the marriage rites were performed, the husband so married died. But though this happened over and over again, her father with the consent of the Brahmans of his Court solemnly gave her in marriage as often as she became a widow. What motives induced the Brahmans of a later age to prohibit widow marriage, it is difficult to trace. The causes which favoured the growth of the modern custom which forbids the widows of the highest castes to marry again, have thus been summarised by Sir Herbert Risley in the last India Census Report, page 428 :—

"In the first place the anxiety of the early Hindu law-givers to circumscribe a woman's rights to property would unquestionably tend to forbid her to join her lot to a man whose interest it would be to assert and extend those rights as against the members of her husband's family. At the same time the growth of the doctrine of spiritual benefit would require her to devote her life to the annual performance of her husband's *shradha*. Technical obstacles to her remarriage also arise from the Brahmanical theory of marriage itself. The ceremony being regarded as a sacrament ordained for the purification of women and its essential portion being the gift of the woman by her father to her husband, the effect of the gift is to transfer her own *gotra* or exogamous group into that of her husband's." * * * * *

"Some influence must also have been exerted in the same direction by the competition for husbands resulting from the action of hypergamy. Widows certainly would be the first to be excluded from the marriage market, for in their case the interest of the individual families would be identical with those of the group. The family would already have paid a bridegroom-price to get their daughter or sister married, and would naturally be indisposed to pay a second, and probably higher price to get her married again. The group, in its turn, would be equally adverse to an arrangement which tended to increase the number of marriageable women."

The widowed : (1) by Locality.

335. In the State as a whole, of every thousand persons of each sex 76 males and 176 females are returned as widowed. In other words nearly every fifth female in the State is a widow, while only one in fourteen of the males is a widower. Taking the divisions separately, we find that the corresponding proportions are 78 males and 176 females in Baroda, 82 males and 196 females in Kadi, 59 males and 119 females in Navsari, 64 males and 156 females in Amreli and 85 males and 244 females in the City of Baroda. Everywhere the proportion of widows is more than double or treble that of widowers ; for, while the widowers are free to marry again in all castes and creeds, widows are prohibited to do so among the higher Hindu and Jain castes ; and even in the castes and communities which allow widow marriage, it is considered less decorous for her to do, if she is grown up and has children. Baroda City has the highest proportion of the widowed, both among males and females, owing to its possessing a higher proportion of high caste Hindu and Jain population, while Navsari has the least owing to the large porportion of the Animistic tribes in its population. After Baroda City stands the Kadi District where the Kadwa Kanbis are noted for their infant marriages and for their curious custom of marrying little girls with bunches of flowers and declaring them widowed after

throwing the flowers into a well, so that they can afterwards be married in the *natra* form with a suitable bridegroom whenever convenient. Then comes Baroda District where the *kulin* Lewa Kanbis, Marathas and even Kolis, in imitation of the Brahman-Vanias, forbid their widows to remarry, and then follows Amreli where both infant and unequal marriages are less common, and so there is a smaller proportion of the widowed.

(2) By Religion.

336. Among Hindus 78 males and 181 girls are widowed in 1,000 of each sex of all ages. The corresponding proportions are 88 males and 278 females among Jains, 39 males and 71 females among the Animistic tribes, 73 males and 179 females among Musalmans, 47 males and 153 females among Parsis and 67 males and 138 females among the Native Christians. These varying proportions are due to the differences in customs with respect to widow marriage as described in para. 333. Of all religions, the Jains have the highest proportion of widows, as they mostly belong to the Vania castes all of which prohibit widow marriage, while the Animistic tribes have the lowest proportion, as among them there is no prohibition either of custom or sentiment, and as a rule widows marry soon after being widowed. Among Musalmans, though there is no prohibition against widow marriage, the Hindu prejudice against the marriage of widows affects most strongly those of them who are converts from that religion and are relatively the more numerous.

Widows at child-bearing ages.

337. In one thousand females of the child-bearing ages, *viz.*, 15-40, in each religion, Hindus have 112 widows, Jains 231, Animistic tribes 33, Musalmans 106, Parsis 57 and Christians 50. These figures alone are sufficient to give an idea of the incalculable harm, Hindus and Jains cause to those poor creatures, to themselves and to the society at large. In spite of the existence of women fit for marriage in their castes, many a grown-up male has to remain a bachelor or widowed or to take a child-wife. It often happens that a man marries a girl at the most of 12 or 13 after he has lost his first wife ; she dies after a time and another is married. This also meets with the same fate and a fourth is married when probably the man is 50, and she is left a widow before she has arrived at womanhood or soon after. In some of the Brahman-Vania castes, negotiations for a new wife are carried on in the burning ground, while the dead body of the late wife is being consumed by fire. How cruel and selfish it is that these very people, who are themselves so eager to contract a second marriage, enforce their unlucky daughters and sisters to undergo life-long widowhood!

Diagram showing the number per 1,000 aged 15-40 who are widowed (by religions).

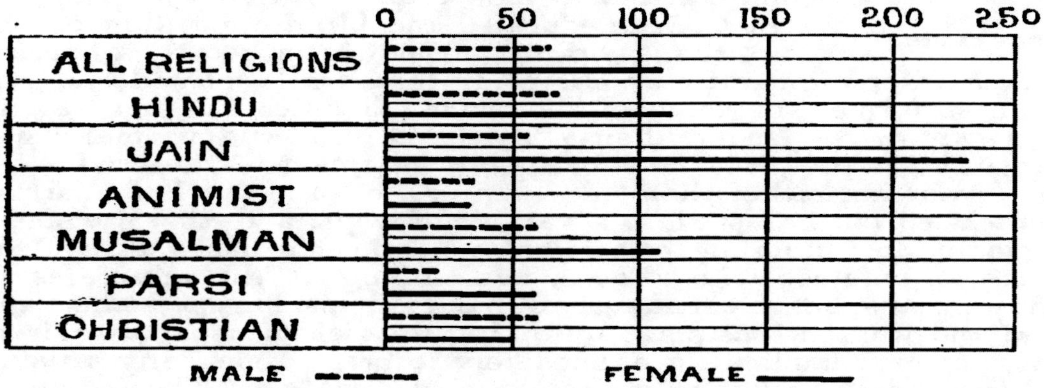

Child-widows.

338. Infant marriages result in the sickening spectacle of child-widows. In the State as a whole, 2 girls per mille aged 0-5, 5 per mille aged 5-10, and 25 per mille aged 10-15 are returned as widows among the Hindus. The corresponding figures among Jains are 1, 1 and 11, and among Musalmans 1, 3 and 9, respectively. There are practically no child-widows among the Parsis and the Animistic tribes. The widowhood of Musalman girls, and of girls belonging to the castes which allow

widow marriage is only nominal, but the lot of those belonging to Hindu and Jain castes forbidding their marriages is miserable and can best be imagined than described.

339. Statistics given in the margin, which have been extracted from Subsidiary Table I, show that compared with the figures of 1901, the proportion of Hindu widows of all ages is now considerably less than what it was ten years ago.. But the return of 1901 was abnormal, owing to the heavy mortality which occurred during the great famine which preceded it. Similarly the Census of 1881 also followed a period of scarcity. In considering the varying prevalence of widowhood, so far as it is due to social causes, it is better to look to the results of 1891 rather than to those of 1901 and 1881. It will appear that the proportion of widows at all ages is now higher than what it was 20 years before. This increase is not due to any change in the social customs of the people, but to the effects of famine and plague in the years following the Census of 1891. No caste, which was formerly known as allowing widow marriage, has prohibited the practice during the last twenty years. Infant marriages are now no doubt less common than before, at least among the higher castes ; and had it not been for famine and plague, which preceded this decade and the two Kadwa Kanbi marriage seasons which came in its midst, the proportion of widows, both at the early and higher ages, would no doubt have been smaller now than ten or twenty years ago.

Comparison with past Censuses.

Proportion of widows in 1,000 Hindu females at

Age-period.	Census of			
	1911.	1901.	1891.	1881.
0—5	2	4	1	3
5—10	5	12	4	
10—15	25	44	13	17
15—20	35	95	22	33
20—40	129	206	93	117
40—60	539	528	461	459
60 and over ...	847	775	834	802

340. The present day attitude of the people towards widow marriage may be summarised in the words "passive sympathy on the part of the educated and blind opposition on the part of the ignorant." Eloquent speeches are made at all the annual Social Conferences for ameliorating the hard lot of widows, and Associations have been formed in some of the principal cities for encouraging the remarriage of widows. Under their auspices a few widow marriages have been performed in the past, but the subsequent treatment of those who led the way serves as a warning rather than an example to others. The married pair is not only outcasted but harassed, in a variety of ways, and the promoters of the marriage remain aloof clinging to their caste. No caste has yet resolved to give up its custom of enforced widowhood ; and so long as the advocates of the cause of widows have not the courage to band themselves together and defy their ignorant and illiterate castemen by taking the risk of separating from them, their efforts, however laudable, are not likely to bring about any satisfactory result. A distinguished student of sociology has said :—"The Indian is distinguished from the European by his lack of personal independence. He is afraid to stand alone or to do anything of which his society disapproves." This is one of the reasons why even the advocates of social reform sometimes fail to put their views into practice.

Present day attitude towards widow-marriage.

341. The question of widow marriage has now become a question of necessity. The number of females being smaller than that of males, and there being a prohibition against widow marriage, many persons in some castes have perforce to remain without wives. Some widow remarriages have taken place in Gujarat as a result of this necessity. In the year 1907-08 a number of petitions were received by His Highness the Maharaja Gaekwad from Sinore, Savli, Baroda, Patan and Navsari, praying that widow-remarriage should be made compulsory, and that those widows, who did not remarry, should be fined heavily. The petitioners recounted the hardships widows have to suffer, and, in addition, their own hardships in having

Widow marriage, a social necessity in some castes.

to remain bachelors, owing to the paucity of virgin brides in their castes. The applicants from Sinore regretted why His Highness' Government did not make widow-remarriage compulsory when they had made such a thing as education compulsory. These petitions show that a strong feeling in favour of widow-marriage is awakened in the hearts of some of the people. His Highness the Maharaja, to whom the cause of social reform owes much for its advancement, could not, of course, make widow-marriage compulsory as desired by these people, but he has made it permissive by passing the Widow-remarriage Act. Under its provision any girl, who has become a widow, can remarry with the consent of her guardian, if she is under 16, and of her own free will, if above 16. Such a remarriage is no bar to her acquiring rights of inheritance as widow or mother in her new husband's family.

WIDOW REMARRIAGE CEREMONIES.

Widow remarriage ceremonies.

342. The ceremony relating to the performance of a widow marriage is not so elaborate as that of a first marriage. Remarriage (*natra*) is generally performed at night. Lewa Kanbi and such other comparatively higher castes employ Brahmans who perform some short ceremony, while Kolis and such other lower castes neither employ Brahmans nor perform any ceremony. It is sufficient among the latter, for the widow intending to marry to put on clothes and bangles given to her by her future husband and then enter his house with a pot of water on her head. Rice is sprinkled over the newly-married couple, who in company with a few friends, partake of sweetmeats. Among the higher castes, the future husband goes to the widow's house with his friends and relations, gives a sum of money to the father of the widow as bride-price and returns home after the ceremony is performed. Here also rice is sprinkled over the newly-united pair. On the completion of the ceremony, a feast is generally given to the caste people by the parents of the widow-bride. A Tuesday or a Sunday is generally selected for solemnising a widow's marriage.

No ceremonies are performed among the Animistic tribes when a widow marries. The husband presents her with a new petticoat, bodice and robe. He comes to her house and takes her away with him. Among the Nayakdas this must be done at night, for it is the common belief that if a widow is remarried in day-time, the village will be burnt.

Among the Bhils, marriage with a widow generally takes the form of an elopement, the bride and bridegroom being generally received back after the bridegroom has made the bride's friends and the headman a present. The couple pass the day after the wedding in some solitary place, three or four miles from the village from which they must not return till dusk.

Among Musalmans, the same ceremonies that are performed on the first marriage are performed on the marriage of a widow. Among Parsis a widow marriage differs from a maiden marriage in that it is performed at midnight instead of in the evening; and while the blessings are repeated the rice is thrown from below instead of from above as in a maiden marriage. The marriage of a bachelor and a spinster and the marriage of a widower and a spinster are called *shahzan* or royal marriage. The remarriage of a widow either with a bachelor or a widower is called *chakarzan* marriage or *natra*.

Treatment of widows.

343. On the day of her husband's death, the widow has to break her bracelets in all Hindu castes and on the tenth day, after the funeral, she has to cause her head to be shaved in all Gujarati castes in which remarriage of widows is prohibited. Among Deccani castes a widow's head is shaved even on the first day. If she is very young or pregnant or has a suckling child, she is allowed to wear her bracelets and her hair until she is about 20 to 30 years old, when on the occurrence of a death among her near relations or on a visit to a place of pilgrimage, her bracelets are broken and her head is shaved. A widow cannot make the usual red powder mark, *chanlla*, on her forehead. She must put on plain dark garments and live on coarse food. Among Deccanis red or white

garments are allowed. For one year after the death of her husband, she has to mourn sitting in a corner of the house. Then she goes to her father's house to leave off mourning. After this she is allowed to move about and go out of the house. But, so long as she lives, she takes no part in caste dinners or other happy gatherings, for a widow's shadow is deemed unlucky. She generally passes her time in working as a household drudge in her father-in-law's house and in hearing *kathas*, visiting temples and performing pilgrimages. If she wishes to live apart, she is given a room in the house and an allowance in cash or kind sufficient for the bare necessaries of life.

Among Musalmans the mourning laid down by the Mahomedan Law for a widow is four months and ten days. During that period the widow does not leave the house. Besides this strictly Mahomedan observance, other customs have been adopted from the Hindus. As soon as life is gone, the mother and the widow of the dead break their bangles. The mother may put on new bangles, but the widow never again wears bracelets or a nose ring.

DIVORCE.

Divorce.

344. As a general rule, *chhuta chhedo* or divorce is allowed among castes which practise widow-remarriage. Adultery and disagreement are the usual grounds of divorce. Though allowed, divorces are rare, except among the lowest castes. A divorced wife is in the position of a widow and can contract a second marriage, but the children by her first husband remain with him. Among Bahrots, Kanbis and other higher castes, a husband may divorce his wife, but the wife is not allowed to divorce her husband. Among Kachhias, Ghanchis and other artizan castes, permission of the caste *panchayat* is necessary before a divorce, either by the husband or wife can be granted. Among Kolis a husband can divorce his wife simply by making a formal declaration to that effect. A Koli woman can also divorce her husband, but she has to return the *palla* or dowry settled on her at the time of marriage. Marriage ties are broken among the depressed classes on the slightest grounds. Among Dheds divorce can be obtained to an indefinite extent. Before they settle to wedded life, most couples have more than once changed their partners. But before the change takes place, there must be formal divorce recognised by the caste. Among the Animistic tribes, husband and wife divorce each other even merely from fancy. Among Naikdas, if a woman deserts her husband and goes to live with another man, he has to pay her first husband Rs. 16. If the husband consents to give up his wife, he is paid nothing. Among Koknas, a woman may leave her husband and go to live with another man on his agreeing to pay her husband the amount he spent as dowry. Similarly, a married Bhil woman, taking fancy to a man, may go and live with him, if he is willing to pay her husband's marriage expenses.

Among Musalmans divorce is at the option of the husband. But in Gujarat it is rarely practised. A divorcer finds it difficult to marry suitably a second time, and a woman once divorced tries as far as she can to shun matrimony for the rest of her life on the ground of the proverb "*sej badlane se karma nahi badalate*," *i.e.*, by changing the bed, fate cannot be altered. After divorce a woman cannot marry for three months called *iddat* or term during which her husband is bound to maintain her.

Among Parsis divorces are regulated by Parsi Marriage and Divorce Act (XXV) of 1865.

POLYGAMY.

Hindus.

345. Among Hindus, though the Shastras permit polygamy, Brahmans and Vanias are, as a rule, monogamous. But some Brahman castes, such as Audich, Anavala, Tapodhan, etc., and some Vania castes, such as Deshavals allow polygamy. In all other castes polygamy is allowed and practised. As a general rule, however,

a second wife is not taken, unless the first is barren, gives birth to daughters only or is afflicted with some incurable disease. In a few castes, such as Ghanchis, etc., permission from caste panchayat is necessary before a second wife can be married in the life-time of the first. But in most of the castes no such permission is necessary and a second wife is taken merely at the caprice of the husband or on such flimsy grounds as the father of the wife delaying sending her to her husband or not providing her with sufficient clothes and ornaments. Sometimes it is the first wife who goads her husband to marry a second one when she herself is barren, or when her children do not live. Among Anavala and Audich Brahmans and Lewa Kanbis polygamy was once practised, simply because each new wife meant getting a good dowry from her father. In the State as a whole, the Census shows that there are 1,007 married women to every 1,000 married men. The apparent excess of wives is probably due to the large number of emigrants, many of whom are married and leave their wives at home, but allowing for this, it is clear that monogamy is the general rule and polygamy the exception.

Animistic tribes.

346. Polygamy is allowed among all the Animistic tribes. A man marries a second or third wife if the first does not bear children or if she cannot get on well with him or if he does not like her or if he has a large number of children and the work of the house-hold is heavy. Cases of polygamy are, however, getting rare, and generally when a new wife is brought, the old one leaves the house and joins some one else in matrimony. There are thus only 1,013 wives to every 1,000 husbands.

Musalmans.

347. Among Mahomedans polygamy is allowed upto four wives. The husband is enjoined to treat them on an equal footing in all matters with the exception of sexual intercourse. But, as a rule in Gujarat, a Musalman is content to have one wife only, not from any feeling of abhorrence towards this anomalous institution but from his inability to provide for such an expensive luxury. Only a few well-to-do persons are found to have more than one wife. There are only 1,002 wives to every 1,000 husbands. The true proportion is somewhat obscured owing to the habit of Mahomedans to leave their wives at home when they emigrate to other parts, but not so as to disturb the conclusion that the great majority of Mahomedans are monogamous.

POLYANDRY.

Polyandry.

348. The two recognized types of polyandry are: the matriarchal when a woman forms alliances with two or more men, who are not necessarily related to each other and succession is therefore traced through the female; and the fraternal when she becomes the wife of several brothers. Neither of these is to be found within the limits of the State, but traces of the latter remain in the practice of *diyarvatu* or marriage with an elder brother's widow which is prevalent to some extent among some of the lower castes, *viz.*, Koli, Mali, Sathawara, Bhavsar, Darji, Ghanchi, Gola, Kumbhar, Mochi, Salat, Ahir, Bharvad, Rabari, Bhangi, Dhed and Shenva. *Kathi* is the only high caste in which *diyarvatu* is practised. Kathi women are proverbially handsome and, unlike other Hindu females, are treated on a social equality with their husbands. Unmarried and married women, like widows, wear no wrist ornaments. Widow-marriage is allowed but is seldom practised. In such cases the rule is imperative that the younger brother must marry his elder brother's widow. Among the other castes, *diyarvatu* is getting more and more into disrepute. The custom is not looked upon with favour, because in imitation of the higher castes an elder brother's wife is regarded as mother of her husband's younger brothers. A younger brother entitled to marry his brother's widow prefers to forego his right over her on receipt of money equivalent to his diseased brother's marriage expenses from a third party wishing to take her as his wife. It is only when a widow has young children, who are likely to be neglected if she were to marry outside the family, that it is considered advisable for her to marry her *diyar*, provided he is grown up.

HYPERGAMY.

Hypergamy.

349. Hypergamy or the practice of marrying girls in families higher in social rank in the caste than that of their parents, prevails among many Hindu castes, but notably among the Anavala, Audich and Khedaval Brahmans, and the Rajput, Lewa Kanbi, Maratha Kshatriya and Brahma Bhat castes. The different *kuls* or families of the same caste are not treated with equal consideration. Certain families are considered *kulin* or of good birth, either from some honour conferred on their ancestors by the rulers of the land or from the benefits conferred by them on the caste. The *kulins* marry their daughters only in their own circle, but have no objection to take wives from families of inferior rank, provided they get handsome dowries, which range from a few hundred to several thousand rupees. It is always an object of solicitude to the parents of a female child that they should procure her marriage with the scion of a more noble family. To wed her to a bridegroom of inferior rank is considered disgraceful. This feeling, coupled with the heavy expenditure to be incurred at the time of marriage, once led the Jadeja Rajputs of Kutch and Kathiawad and the Kanbis of Gujarat to practise the dreadful crime of female infanticide, which has already been described in the Chapter on Sex (para. 301).

The custom of hypergamy had led to several unusual practices. A father who marries his daughter to a *kulin,* has not only to pay a handsome dowry with his daughter, but also to provide her and her children every year with their wearing apparel. He has to share in the marriage expenses of his daughter's daughters, and to make cash payments to his son-in-law's parents and other relations, when they visit his house and on several other occasions of rejoicing or mourning. He has to take care that his son-in-law or his relations are in no way displeased, for their displeasure may possibly result in his daughter being troubled or discarded. The *kulins* having their own girls as also those from the lower grades in the castes available for marriage, not only do not allow their widows to marry, but also practise polygamy. They are ready to contract a second marriage on the slightest pretext. Caste people quote instances of *kulin* Rajputs, Lewa Kanbis, Anavalas and Audichas in straightened circumstances, having married again and paid off their debts from the dowry received with their second or third wife. On the other hand, there is always a deficiency of brides in the lowest grades of some of these castes and some have actually to remain bachelors for life, or to resort to widow marriage or *sata tekhada, i.e.,* agreeing to give a girl in marriage on condition that a girl from her husband's family shall be given in marriage to one's son or other near relation. Some of the Lewa Kanbis, who give their daughters in marriage to the *kulin* section of their caste in the Charottar, have even to purchase as wives women of unknown origin brought from Kathiawad. They are, however, allowed to give their daughters in marriage to the *kulin* section above them and the latter marry their daughters to the Patidars of the thirteen villages in Charottar, who rank the highest in the caste. Similarly among the Audichas, those who have settled in Vagad, are considered the lowest in the caste owing to their allowing widow-marriage and carrying cooked food to the fields ; and yet they are allowed to give their daughters in marriage to the Audichas of Halawad in Kathiawad, whose daughters marry Dhangadra Audichas and the daughters of Dhangadra Audichas are married to Viramgam, Ahmedabad and Sidhpur Audichas, who, hold the highest social rank in the caste. The custom of hypergamy has ruined several families with many daughters in the castes which practise it. It has forced them to mortgage their lands and to incur other debts beyond their means of repaying. Of late years there has been a change in the attitude of the people towards the *kulins* in their castes. This is partly due to feelings of retaliation brought about by the unreasonable and ever-increasing demands of the *kulins* themselves and partly to western education, which inclines parents to seek educated and well-to-do husbands for their daughters in preference to the mere *kulins,* who are not unfrequently both ignorant and pauper. Hypergamy has already considerably disappeared among Lewa Kanbis, Anavalas and Audichas under the influence of *ekdas* or solemn agreements made by most of their people to eschew the *kulins* and to give and take in marriage only in their own social circle.

ENDOGAMY.

Endogamy.

350. Endogamy or the custom of "marrying in" which forbids the members of a particular social group to marry any one who is not a member of the group, prevails not only among Hindus and Jains, but also among the Animistic tribes. A man must marry not only within his caste but also within his sub-caste, if it is divided into sub-castes. Further restrictions on the selection of brides and bridegrooms are placed in most of the Brahman, Vania and artizan castes by *ekdas* or solemn agreements by which the caste members, residing within a particular area called *gol* or circle, are restricted in giving and taking in marriage to the circumscribed field of their caste-men living within that area. People living in villages are anxious to wed their daughters to dwellers in towns ; while the town people avoid giving their daughters in marriage to those who live in villages. These tendencies lead to uneven results, which the *ekdas* are intended to remedy. Within the last twenty years, the Anavalas, Lewa Kanbis and other castes in which hypergamy prevails are looking towards the *kulins* with feelings of less regard than before, and have in some places resolved to marry their girls only in their own social circle and not to the *kulins*. The result of all these tendencies has been to multiply, even within the limit of a caste, the number of groups within which marriages are restricted. For instance, the Modh Vanias are divided into *Adalja*, from Adalaj, *Goghava* from Gogho and *Mandalia* from Mandal. Each of them is further sub-divided into *Visa*, whole, and *Dasa*, half, a division common to all Vania castes including even Jain Vanias. These again are split into later local sections, Ahmedabadi and Khambhati, with the result that all the sub-divisions dine together, but for purposes of intermarriage, the Modh Vanias have about twelve separate groups. In addition to their local sub-divisions of Vadnagara, Visnagara, Sathodra, etc., each Nagar caste has a *grahastha* or laymen class and a *bhikshuka* or priestly class between which marriages are not allowed. The constant creation of these separate connubial groups has been doing great harm, both moral and physical, to the people by narrowing the circle of selection in marriage. Social reformers are advocating the fusion of sub-castes and the introduction of *roti vyavhar tyan beti vyavhar*, *i.e.*, intermarriage with those with whom one can interdine, *i.e.*, in the whole caste. But though the propriety of the reform is admitted, as yet no action has been taken by any caste to introduce it. I am informed that the Deshaval Brahmans of Patan are carrying on negotiations for intermarriage with the Audich Brahmans ; and so are doing the Visa Khadayata Vanias of Baroda with their Dasa section.

Endogamy among Mahomedans.

351. According to the tenets of the faith, all Mahomedans can interdine as well as intermarry. But though interdining is followed the practice as regards intermarriage is different. Pure Musalmans or those having a foreign strain, *viz.*: Shaikh, Saiyad, Mughal and Pathan, as a rule, do not marry outside their circle or tribe. They are proud of their blood and are averse to form connections which may lower them in the estimation of their people. Among some very exclusive sections like the Saiyads, family trees are examined and every care is taken that the accepted suitor is a Saiyad both on the father's and mother's side. The convert classes observe the same restrictions as regards marriage as Hindus do, and neither give nor take in marriage from any class but their own. The prohibition on intermarriage extends to higher as well as lower castes. A Ghanchi, for instance, must marry none but a Ghanchi. If this rule is transgressed, the offender is hauled up before the Jamat or Caste Panchayat and ejected from the community. The result is that these groups are as strictly endogamous as Hindu castes.

Intermarriage between Mobeds and Behdins.

352. The Parsi community is divided into two classes called Mobed or priests and Behdins or non-priests. The distinction has been handed down from antiquity. The elite were the religious guides and legislators, while the others were common men. It is possible that the two classes sprang from two different peoples. Before the last 50 years intermarriages between the Mobeds and Behdins were unknown. But the Parsis, who are ever progressive and ready to adapt their customs to the times, have given up the restriction and now, except perhaps in a few very orthodox families, intermarriage between the two classes takes place. As Mr. Dalal wrote in his report of the last Census "the Mobeds themselves have spurned the narrow limit of sacerdotal avocations and have zealously entered into all the professions and occupations worth following after discarding the distinctive white turban and dress of Mobeds, and submitting their chins to the razor of the barber; it is now hard to distinguish these from the Behdins and so intermarriages are on the increase every year."

EXOGAMY.

Exogamy.

353. In addition to endogamy, exogamy or the practice of "marrying out" further restricts the circle within which Hindu marriages can be celebrated. It forbids the members of a particular group in a caste, usually supposed to be descended from a common ancestor or associated with a particular locality, to marry any one who is a member of the same group. While endogamy restricts intermarriage in one direction by creating a number of artificially small groups within which people must marry, exogamy brings about the same result by artificially expanding the circle within which they may not marry. The usual rule is that marriages are not allowed among relations on the father's side upto seven degrees, and on the mother's side upto five degrees. In addition to this no two members of the same *gotra* or *shakha* can marry among Brahmans and Bhats. Among Rajputs, members of a clan are forbidden to marry within the clan, as all members of a clan are believed to be the children of one common ancestor. As Sir James Campbell says in the *Bombay Gazetteer* volume on Gujarat Population, p. 124 "the dread of marriage among relations is sometimes carried to a strange extreme. As all Jadavs are in theory of the same stock, members of that great clan, whether Jadejas, Chudasamas or Bhatis, ought not to intermarry. A Jadeja should not marry a Chudasama, although the tribes separated in very early times. When the members of a clan became very numerous and spread over a large extent of country, the practice of naming groups of families mostly after a distinguished common ancestor and sometimes after the place of residence came into vogue. Sometimes surnames are taken from a calling as in the case of *vethias* or carriers of Government property; and at times a mere change in dress is sufficient to create a new surname. The Kachhotias are so called, because their women adopted the practice of passing the robe back between the feet and tucking the end into the waistband. As far as can be ascertained Gujarat Rajputs have one hundred and three surnames. In Surat and Broach most Rajputs have lost all trace of their clan. Some of the sub-clans are so large and so long established that they have the importance of separate clans. Instances have occurred of marriages being annulled when it was found that the clans of the bride and bridegroom were divisions of the same stock." Among Lewa Kanbis, in Charottar, a girl cannot be married to a boy living in the same village; for, although there may be no prohibited relationship between them, all those living in a village, however distant, are believed to be the descendants of a common ancestor, and marriage between children of the same ancestor is considered disgraceful. On the other hand, among Brahmans and Vanias living in towns, it is the custom not to marry girls outside the same place, and it is only when a bridegroom is not locally available that an outsider is considered eligible. This leads to formation of exogamous groups of the local type.

Consanguineous marriages among Mahomedans.

354. Consanguineous marriages are, as a rule, practised among Mahomedans. Within families of the same ancestor, marriages are sometimes arranged by exchange, *i.e.*, a girl is offered for the son, brother or some other relative of the person and his daughter, sister, niece, or some other relation is taken for the son or some other male relation of the person making the offer. When a relation is unable to give a girl in exchange, he is given a girl in marriage on the condition that the first daughter born to him should be given in marriage to some relation of the person who bestows on him the hand of his daughter.

Among Parsis.

355. Consanguineous marriages are also allowed among the Parsis and are very common. They are mainly arranged to save the dowry which would have to be paid if the bridegroom was an outsider. As a general rule, the father of the bride gives a present to the bridegroom and the relatives who accompany him at the marriage. This present which has practically assumed the form of a dowry has much increased in value within the last few years, and the parents of daughters find it difficult to dispose of their girls, if they have not the wherewithal to pay it. The possession of high educational qualifications is a factor which adds greatly to the value of the bridegroom. A Bachelor of Arts, if he is also a bachelor in life, must have from his father-in-law, besides a "wingless nymph" from two to five or even ten thousand rupees in cash.

Looseness of marriage ties.

356. The Animistic tribes are very loose about their marriage relations. Among the Bhils, a woman marries again not only if her husband dies, but if she falls in love with another man and can get him to take her and pay her husband his marriage expenses. The children, if there are any, remain with the father. An unmarried girl is allowed to live with any man she likes without any ceremony either of marriage or betrothal. If after betrothal, a girl goes to live with some other man, her husband has to pay her betrothed the cost of the betrothal ceremony. Among the Koknas and other forest tribes a woman may leave her husband and go to live with another man on his agreeing to pay her husband the amount he spent as bride-price after her. Among the Nayakdas, if a girl reaches the age of sixteen and her parents have not betrothed her, she may go and live with any man she chooses, and if he agrees to pay her parents sixteen rupees, no objection is raised. Again, if a woman deserts her husband and goes to live with another man, he pays her husband sixteen rupees. If the husband consents to give up his wife, he is paid nothing.

Consideration for marriage.

357. The practices of different castes with regard to the consideration for marriage are different. In some castes, such as the Lewa Kanbis, Anavala Brahmans, Rajputs and Marathas, the bride's father has to pay the father of the bridegroom ; in others such as several Brahman, Vania and artizan castes, the bridegroom's father has to pay, and in others again, such as Valmik Kayasth, no money passes. In the lower circles neither bridegroom price nor bride price is paid, but marriage is agreed upon simply on the understanding that a counter marriage will follow. This is called *sata tekhada* or giving a girl in marriage on the agreement that the bridegroom's sister or some other female relative will be given in marriage to the bride's brother or some other near male relation. The practice of the bride's father paying money to the bridegroom is looked upon as a preferable arrangement, while that of the bride's father receiving money from the bridegroom's father, *kanya vikraya*, is looked upon as sinful. But the party who has to pay and the amount he must give, depends generally speaking, on the demand and supply of brides and bridegrooms and this again is determined to a great extent by the existence or otherwise of the custom of hypergamy, widow-marriage and the like. Where girls are paid for, their price depends on their age, and their value rises higher as they approach to maturity. Some parents, especially in Kathiawad, allow their girls to grow up, simply because they may fetch a high price from some grown-up bachelor or rich widower in the matrimonial market. In the functional castes, a widow of

mature age, who is expert in household work and family business, has to be paid for more than a virgin who is younger, but less experienced in household work.

Curious behaviour between husband and wife.

358. Among Hindus a husband does not name his wife nor does a wife utter the name of her husband. If one wants to call the other he or she does not do so by the other's name but uses such expressions as "do you hear," "so and so's mother," naming the child. The belief is that death would be caused or other harm would result if one of the couple calls the other by name. Among most of the castes, the wife does not appear before the husband in the presence of elders or strangers. It is only when they are alone that husband and wife can talk to each other, and as soon as an elder in the family, *e.g.*, an elder brother, father, mother, etc., comes up, the wife covers her face and hurriedly withdraws. A mother or father cannot talk to or even look towards the children in the presence of elders. The idea is that so long as elders are alive, the children are theirs and not of their immediate parents, and it would be want of respect on the part of the latter towards the former to do anything that may signify the contrary.

A great change has taken place within the last thirty years. Old ideas of false decorum are disappearing under the influence of Western education, and parents are táking ever-increasing interest in their own children and husbands in their wives. Twenty or thirty years ago people who left their home for service or business elsewhere, could not take their wives with them. To do so was looked upon as immodest. Wives were left at home and visited only occasionally during the Holi or Diwali holidays. These ideas have now become obsolete, and a man can take away his wife from the family home wherever he likes.

MARRIAGE CUSTOMS AND CEREMONIES.

HINDUS.

Marriage customs and ceremonies among Hindus.

359. The marriage customs and ceremonies of the different Hindu castes differ much from one another, but there are certain essential matters, which are more or less common to all, and they can be briefly described here. Marriages can take place only between members of the same caste, and if it is divided into sub-castes, between members of the same sub-caste. If the caste, or sub-caste is large and spread over a wide area, some territorial limit is fixed beyond which marriages cannot be performed, even within the same caste or sub-caste, without paying such a penalty as may have been fixed. Such an area is called *gol* or circle and the agreement binding the members to restrict their marriage relations within it, is called *ekda*. There are certain families in each caste which are considered *kulin* from the benefits conferred on the caste generally by their ancestors. It is always an object of solicitude to the parents of a female child to procure her marriage with the scion of a more noble family. To wed her to a bridegroom of inferior rank is considered disgraceful. Proposals of marriage emanate from a house of lesser pretension, and the father of a bride who seeks to ally his child to the blue blood of a more distinguished *kul*, must balance the scale with gold. If the families are considered to be on an equality, more money than is customary in the caste is not demanded on either side. The five commonest arrangements are :—(1) the bridegroom receives a portion with the bride ; (2) the bridegroom pays a sum of money to the bride's father ; (3) the bridegroom settles a certain sum on the bride called *pallu*, which becomes a part of her *stridhan* or dower ; (4) no stipulation is made about dowry or portion ; (5) the marriage is agreed on the understanding that a counter-alliance will follow. Of these arrangements, the first is the commonest among Anavala and Audich Brahmans, Lewa Kanbis, Rajputs and Marathas ; the second is found among some Brahman, Vania and other castes among whom there is a scarcity of brides ; the third is common among some high caste Brahmans, artisans and other castes ; the fourth is found among a few castes like Luhanas; and the last, which is called *sata tekhda*,

is adopted to gain brides for men of low family or *kul*, or for those who cannot otherwise secure them. Betrothal generally takes place some years before. When a betrothal is found to be free from any objection, the horoscopes of the bride and bridegroom are consulted, and if the astrologer finds no objection, the girl's father chooses an auspicious day for the betrothal and sends his family priest to the house of the intended husband to make the formal announcement. The priest is fed and is given a rupee or two as a present; and as a sign of joy, the boy's father distributes sugarcandy among his friends and relations. In some castes, the family priest or a relation is sent previous to betrothal to see, by personal interview, that the bride is neither blind nor lame nor afflicted with other bodily defect, and that she is in every respect eligible. Similar inspection is also casually made of the bridegroom. The general rule is that a betrothal cannot be set aside, but the practice of different castes varies. Among some castes such as that of Lad Vanias and Luhanas, a betrothal cannot, under any circumstances, be set aside; among some it may be avoided by the payment of a fine to the caste, while among Nagars and Lewa Kanbis, the offer of a better match is considered a reason enough for breaking the betrothal. Among these differences, one general rule prevails that, if either of the parties to be married becomes maimed or an invalid, the other is freed from the promise. Formerly among some Rajputs, if the betrothed bridegroom died, the girl who should have been his wife was treated as his widow, and considered incapable of entering into the married state. But now a betrothed bride is not so treated and may marry on the death of her affianced.

No rule prevails regarding the length of time between betrothal and marriage. Astrologers are called for to point out the day indicated by the stars as propitious for the marriage. The fixing of the marriage day which must fall between the eleventh of *Kartak Sud* (October-November) and the eleventh of *Ashad Sud*, rests with the girl's father. For marriage purposes every twelfth year, *Sinhastha*, when Jupiter is in the sign of cancer, is altogether avoided. After the day is fixed, great preparations are made on both sides. The house is fresh coloured and white-washed, *papad* and *vadi* (wafer biscuits) are made for use on the marriage days and a booth is built in front of the house. Letters of invitations called *kunkotri* from their being sprinkled with *kunku* (red powder) water are forwarded to the kindred of both bridegroom and bride. About five days before the marriage, Ganpati is installed and worshipped and *mandwa* making ceremony is performed. A hole, about six inches deep is dug in a corner of the booth. The parents of the boy and of the girl with friends and relations sit near the hole and throw into it red powder, milk curds, betelnut and a copper coin. A piece of the *samda* or *khijda* tree (*Prosopis Spicigera*) about a foot long is set up in the hole. One or two days before the marriage day, a ceremony in honour of ancestors and to propitiate the planets, *grahashanti* is performed at the house of the bride and bridegroom. On the marriage day the women of the boy's and of the girl's families go separately to a potter's house with music, worship his wheel with red powder and flowers and bring home earthen pots to be used in the marriage ceremonies. The bride and the bridegroom each at their houses are then rubbed with *pithi*, a mixture of oil, turmeric, camphor and some other fragrant substances. On the marriage day at the bride's house a space, generally in front of the entrance door of the house, about four feet square, is enclosed by four posts one at each of the four corners. At each of the corners, three bamboos are set in the ground leaving between them a space of about eight inches, and round the three bamboos a red string is tied. In the space between the three bamboos, seven decorated earthen pots are piled, the largest at the foot, the smallest at the top. In the square between the four piles of pots, which is called the *chori*, the bride and bridegroom sit and the ceremonies are performed. The bridegroom seated in a palanquin or on horseback is brought to the house of the bride's father. Dholis, drummers, &c., head the procession. Following them come the bridegroom's male relations and friends, then the bridegroom and then the female relations and friends singing songs, bring up the rear. The bridegroom holds seven betelnut leaves, seven betelnuts, a cocoanut and a rupee in the hollow of his hands joined together. To ward off the influence of the evil eye, the sister of the bridegroom sits near him and waves a cup containing salt over his head. When the house of the bride is reached, the procession stops, the bridegroom alights from his horse or palanquin and stands on a wooden stool, just outside of the doorway. Here he is met by the bride's mother who makes a *tilak* on his brow, pulls his nose and shows him a miniature plough, a grinding pestle, a churning stick and an arrow. The object of these ceremonies seems to be to drive away the spirits which may have come into the booth along with the bridegroom. A ball of cowdung ashes is then thrown towards each of the four quarters of heaven. Two small earthen pots full of curds are held mouth to mouth, waved seven times round the bridegroom's body, and set on the ground. The bridegroom puts his right foot on the pots, breaks them to pieces, and enters the marriage hall, *mandva*. He is then led to the square, *chori*, where he sits on a wooden stool, and, with the help of the family-priests, worships Ganpati. The parents of the bride then wash the bridegroom's great toes with milk, curds, honey, sugar and clarified butter. After the worship is over, the bride, dressed in ornaments and clothes, presented to her by her mother's brother, is brought in and placed, by her mother's brother on another stool opposite the bridegroom. A piece of cloth is stretched between the bride and the bridegroom. The Brahmans recite luck-bringing verses, and the family-priests watch the waterclock or timekeeper shouting at intervals of a minute or two *Savadhan* or "Attention," the time is near. When the propitious moment comes, the hands of the bride and bridegroom are joined, the cloth between them is snatched to one side, the hems of their robes are tied together, the marriage garland of cotton threads is thrown over their necks, and the musicians strike up music. Then the relations and friends make presents to the bride and bridegroom. In the middle of the square, *chori*, a sacrificial fire is lighted. The brother of the bride then comes to where the fire is lighted, holding a winnowing fan with barley and sesame, and drops into the hands of the bride and bridegroom four pinches of barley and sesame. Then the bride and bridegroom, throw along with clarified butter the barley and sesame into the fire and again walk round the altar. This is repeated four times. Then the bride and the bridegroom seat themselves on the stools, the bride on the bridegroom's left, and feed each other with four morsels of coarse wheat-flour mixed with clarified butter and sugar prepared by the bride's mother. The bridegroom and bride then worship the constellation of the Great Bear enjoining each other to be as constant as the poles. Then the bride and bridegroom, in front of the family deity inside the house, play at odds and evens each in turn holding some coins in closed hand and the other guessing whether the number of coins is odd or even. Luck in this game is an omen of luck in the game of life. The winner of the game is supposed to be the ruler of the house. If the bride and bridegroom belong to different places, the bridegroom's party stay as guests of the bride's father for two or three days. On an auspicious day after the marriage, the bride is sent away in company with her husband to her new house. The bride's mother worships the carriage sprinkling sandal-dust and flowers on one of the wheels, and laying a cocoanut in front of it as an offering to the carriage that it may bear them safely. When the carriage moves, the mother gathers the pieces of the cocoanut and lays them in her daughter's lap. No one from the bride's house goes with the party. It consists wholly of the bridegroom's friends and relations, the men walking in front of the carriage and the women walking behind singing songs. When the procession reaches the bridegroom's house the bride and bridegroom with the ends of their cloths tied together step out of the carriage and stand in front of the doorway on a wooden stool. The bridegroom's sister keeps the doors closed until she receives money presents from the bridegroom. They are then led into the house by the bridegroom's mother, and taken to bow before the family-deity, and again before the god they play at odds and evens to see which of them is the luckier. This ends the marriage ceremony. Caste dinners are given at the house both of the bride and of the bridegroom on the marriage-day or on some day before or after the marriage. The relations of the bridegroom have a right to dine at the bride's house, but the relations of the bride do not dine at the bridegroom's house.

JAINS.

Marriage ceremonies among the Jains.

360. Like the Hindus marriages are not allowed among the Jains between near relations. The marriage ceremonies of the few Jains in a caste do not differ from those of its Hindu members. But when a whole caste is Jain, as among the Vanias, the ceremonies somewhat differ inasmuch as they discard Brahmanic rites as far as possible. The rules forbidding marriage with any one who does not belong to the same section of the caste are less strict in the case of Jain Vanias than in the case of Hindu Vanias or Meshris as they are called. Among the Meshri Vanias, marriage is forbidden between Dasa and Visa sections of the same caste. A Dasa Shrimali Meshri never marries with a Visa Shrimali and a Dasa Porwad Meshri never marries with a Visa Porwad. But unlike Meshris, members of corresponding minor sub-divisions among Jains sometimes intermarry. A Dasa Shrimali Jain marries a Dasa Porwad and a Dasa Oswal marries a Dasa Porwad and a Dasa Shrimali. The difference of religion is not considered a bar to marriage. A Jain Kanbi marries with a Vaishnav Kanbi and so do Jain and Vaishnav members of other castes. Dasa Shrimali Shravaks marry with Dasa Shrimali Meshris and Dasa and Visa Porwad Shravaks marry with Dasa and Visa Porwad Meshris. With a few exceptions, the Shravak Vania ceremony is the same as that performed by Meshri Vanias. Boys and girls are betrothed sometimes immediately before and sometimes many years before the marriage. The marriage day is fixed by a Brahman astrologer. Five days before the marriage the parents of both the bride and bridegroom worship an image of Ganpati which is painted on the house wall. The women of the bride and bridegroom's families go separately with music to the potter's house, worship his wheel and carry away a store of earthen vessels. At the bride's house a marriage booth is made, one of the pots of which among the Nimas is of *gugal* wood. A *chori* is made in the centre of the booth. No planet pleasing or *grahshanti* ceremony is performed. On the day before the marriage the family goddess is invoked and worshipped. In the evening of the marriage day the bridegroom dressed in rich clothes, with a cocoanut and a rupee in his hands, and with a black silk thread tied to his right ankle to ward off the evil eye, goes on horseback with music to the bride's house, the men of his party walking in front and the women in the rear. Among the Oswals the bridegroom wears a ***mugat***, coronet, and in other castes a turban. An Oswal bridegroom also holds a sword in his hand. The ceremonies of reception at the bride's house and the presenting of miniature plough, arrow, etc., are the same as amongst Hindus. The bridegroom sits on a wooden stool and on his left on another sits the bride who is brought there by her maternal uncle. The bride's parents then formally offer her in marriage to the bridegroom. The maternal uncle lifts the bride and carries her four times round the husband. Brahmans recite *mantras*. The hems of the bride's and bridegroom's clothes are tied together, and they walk four times round a fire which is lit in the *chori*. They then feed each other with coarse wheat flour and worship *Ganpati* and the family goddess.

ANIMISTS.

Marriage customs among the Animistic tribes.

361. The marriage customs of the various animistic tribes are different, but the main features common to all except Dublas are that they pay no respect to Brahmans, and do not make use of their services. The Dublas having come in greater contact with the Hindus, ask Brahmans to fix a lucky day and call them to perform the ceremonies which are almost the same as those practised among Hindus. Among all tribes the bridegroom has to pay bride-price to the bride's father which varies from about 10 to 50 rupees, and among some those who are unable to pay it, serve him for a term of years, as described in para. 365 (6). As amongst Hindus both bride and bridegroom are rubbed with

pithi in all tribes. Among the Bhils a fire is kindled and round it the people dance, the bridegroom taking a few turns with the bride on his shoulder. When the dance is over the bridegroom gives all a drink before they leave. Among the Chodhras, the skirts of the bride and bridegroom are tied by the women of the house and together they walk four times round a pole in the booth. Music, dancing in which the bride and bridegroom join and a feast of rice and pulse complete the ceremony. When the bride leaves for her husband's house, her father gives her a she-buffalo or a money present. Among the Dhodias the bride and her friends go in procession to the bridegroom's house and the bridegroom's mother receives them. The ceremonies are carried on chiefly by women. While the women sing songs, the bride to show her wish to be an obedient wife sweeps the floor, clasps a pillar and declares that empty water pots are full. In front of a lighted lamp four married women tie together the hems of the pair's clothes. As they fasten the knot they sing a song the purport of which is : "Go to market and bring dates and cocoanuts ; eat mutton and fowls together. Have no quarrels. If she runs away give her a kick and bring her back." When the song is finished a Naik unties the knot, strikes together the heads of the pair, and the ceremony is over. Among the Gamits, marriage takes place when the boy can climb a palm tree. The bridegroom wears a sword and he and his party halt under a tree close to the bride's village. The bride's father accompanied by the bride and his friends comes out to meet them and feeds them with *kodri* and *tadi*. They then come to the bride's house when a woman ties the hems of the bride and bridegroom's clothes. The newly married pair dance together in front of the house and their relatives embrace them each paying them about quarter of an anna. Among the Kathodias the bride is brought to the booth by her brother and the skirts of the pair are tied by a Kokna drummer. After a time the knot is loosened, her brother lifts the bride and his uncle lifts the bridegroom and they dance round, the drummers joining them in the dance. Among the Koknas the bride and bridegroom are made to sit on a blanket and their skirts are tied by a woman in front of a lamp. Each says the other's name and the knot is untied. Among the Naayakdas, the bride and bridegroom are seated face to face and two old men who for the occasion are called *pujari* or priests, join their hands and tie their skirts. A sheet is then thrown over their heads and the old men give them some balls of flour and molasses. When each has twice fed the other the cloth is drawn away and the marriage is over.

MAHOMEDANS.

Mahomedan ceremonies.

362. As among the Hindus so among the Musalmans the marriage customs of different communities greatly differ, and a brief description of those in general practice can only be given. Parents of the boy obtain information about a girl likely to make a good match, either through female relations or professional match-makers who are generally females. The women of the boy's family then pay a visit to the girl's house. After seeing her and talking together the guests are offered a glass of sugared water. This they drink if they think well of the girl, but decline to do so, if they do not like her. After drinking, in sign that they ask her in marriage they drop some sugar candy in the girl's mouth. Then they settle what ornaments would be presented on either side and fix the day for the betrothal. In the evening of the betrothal day ornaments and sweetmeats are neatly laid out on trays at the boy's house and are sent generally with music to the girl's house. The bride is decked with the ornaments and covered with a scarf. The party then returns and brings with it trays filled with fresh presents, including a handkerchief, a ring and a *mandil*, gold turban, for the bridegroom. A rich man's betrothal expenses vary on the bridegroom side from Rs. 200 to Rs. 350 and on the bride's from Rs. 50 to Rs. 350 ; for a middle class man on the bridegroom side from Rs. 100 to Rs. 200, and on the bride's from Rs. 50 to Rs. 80 ; for a poor man on the bridegroom's side Rs. 50 to Rs. 90 and on the bride's from Rs. 20 to Rs. 50. The betrothal generally lasts for at least a year. During this time on every holiday gifts pass between the betrothed couple. Eight days

before the marriage the bride keeps to one room and both she and the bridegroom are made to wear yellow clothes. Two or three days before the marriage both at the house of the bridegroom and of the bride earthern pots are arranged in order, food is laid on them and the opening chapter of the Kuran or *fatiha* is repeated with the object of pleasing ancestral spirits. Then the females of the family rub the bride or bridegroom with gram flour mixed with oil and perfumes called *ubatna.* After this a knife, dagger or other sharp iron instrument and a lemon are handed to the bride or bridegroom which he or she is to be careful to keep till the bath on the marriage day. On the evening of the marriage day the bridegroom's party sends to the bride's with a procession of children, called the *bari* or *sachak,* earthen pots painted in gold and green filled with sweetmeats and trays with dresses. In her room the bride is bathed by the women of her family, clothed in new robes and decked in some of the jewels. Then with trays refilled with clothes for the bridegroom with hinna (*mendi*) and with the wife's chattels *jajiz* (cooking utensils, cot, etc.), the company goes back to the bridegroom's. On their return the bridegroom is dressed in his wedding clothes and the furniture of what is to be his honeymoon room is set in order. About 10 p. m. the bridegroom on horse, with music, and followed by his relations and friends starts for the bride's. As he passes under her window, the bride lets fall on the bridegroom some grains of rice. When they arrive at the bride's house, the bridegroom's party sit on one side of the *mandap* and the bride's on the other. In the space between are three seats, one in front of his party for the bridegroom, one in front of the bride's party for her agents, and the third between the two for the Kazi or his deputy. The Kazi asks the bride's agents whether she, with a certain portion, *meher*, accepts so and so as her husband. If told she will have him he takes the attestation of two other witnesses. He then making the bridegroom repeat the creed puts him the same question. The proceedings are recorded and the guests raising hands offer the marriage thanksgiving. The bridegroom is then led to the ladies' quarters in the house and seated on a seat. The bride veiled and arrayed in her wedding garments is seated by his side and a set of ceremonies, such as eating together, are begun. At dawn the bridegroom is for the first time shown his wife's face in a mirror and from a Kuran placed between them the chapter of peace is read. This is the sign that the time has come for the bride to leave her father's house.

Half Hindu, half Musalman ceremonies.

363. As in religion so in marriage ceremonies, Matias, Momnas, Shaikhdas and other converts from Hindus, perform half Musalman and half Hindu rites. They call a Kazi to perform the *nika* or marriage, according to Mahomedan rites, and also a Brahman to perform the Hindu rite of *chori*. Among Ghanchi, Pinjara and Vohoras (peasants) women go singing like the Hindus with the bridegroom to the bride's house and in their feasts, they prepare Hindu dishes of *ladu*, *kansar*, etc.

PARSIS.

Betrothal.

364. When two families desire that their children should marry, they exchange their children's horoscopes, which are sent to an astrologer who settles whether the marriage is likely to be fortunate. If both families approve of the match and the stars are favourable, the marriage is agreed to. Soon after on a lucky day the women of the boy's family go to the girl's to return the horoscope. They take with them a suite of clothes, sugarcandy, curds and fish as emblem of good luck and present the dress to the girl. According to her means, the girl's mother sends her future son-in-law a gold or diamond ring, a suite of clothes and Rs. 5 to 25 in cash. This completes the betrothal, which, though not legally, is practically binding. During the interval between the betrothal and the marriage presents of fish and other articles are exchanged between the two families. Ten to fifteen days before the marriage, comes the turmeric pounding ceremony in which four young married and unwidowed (*sohagan*) females pound turmeric and shake it in a winnowing fan. About eight days before the marriage day, comes

the *mandav* or booth building ceremony. Either before or after the turmeric pounding ceremony, sometimes even on the marriage day, the *adarni* or inviting ceremony is performed. On the *adarni* day, the mother of the boy with relations and friends goes to the bride's and dresses her in clothes and ornaments. The bride's mother entertains the party with sweetmeats and presents the bridegroom's nearest kinswomen with dresses. After they leave, a party of kinswomen and friends set out from the bride's with clothes for the bridegroom, who in return presents the bride's mother with a dress. Next day the bride's mother returns this dress to the bridegroom's mother, accompanying it with a few rupees, as it is thought wrong for the bride's side to receive presents from the bridegroom's side. On the third day before the wedding a suite of clothes and a large silver coin are sent to the bride, who wears the coin round her neck till the marriage ceremonies are over. Towards evening the women of the family seat the bridegroom and bride in front of their respective houses and rub them with the turmeric which was pounded a fortnight before. On the fourth day the marriage ceremony is performed in the evening, after the custom of the Hindus according to the promise given to the Rana of Sanjan by the ancestors of the present Parsis, on their landing at that place. Males dress in *jamas* and *pichhori* and females array themselves in jewellery and dresses of variegated colour, richly ornamented with gold. Shortly before the marriage procession starts, a party of women goes from the bride's to the bridegroom's place with a present of a rich dress and a ring of gold or diamonds, according to her parent's means. All of these are arranged in a rich tray of silver or brass, which is carried by the bride's mother in her right hand. This procession is called *sopara*. They quickly return after executing this errand, and the bridegroom starts in a procession with the guests for the bride's. On reaching the bride's residence the males take their seats among the male guests of the bride's party, and the ladies go inside the house and assume their places with the others. First of all the bride and bridegroom are seated on chairs opposite each other and then a piece of cloth is held between them as a curtain so as to screen them from each other's sight. Under this curtain they are made to hold each other's right hand in their grasp. Then another piece of cloth is placed round so as to encircle them and the ends of the cloth are tied together by a double knot. In the same way raw yarn is taken and wound round the pair seven times by the officiating priests, who during this performance repeat the short prayers of *Yatha Ahu Vairyo*. On completing the seventh round, the twist is tied seven times over the joined hands of the couple, as well as round the double knot of the ends of the cloth previously put about them. When this is over incense is burnt on a fire placed in a flat metallic base, after which the curtain is suddenly dropped down and the bride and bridegroom who have each been provided with a few grains of rice hasten to throw it at one another; whoever is quickest in throwing the rice is supposed to be likely to rule. When the rice throwing is over, the couple sit side by side and two priests stand before them with a witness on each side holding brass plates full of rice. The two priests pronounce *ashirwad* or the marriage blessings, in old Persian and Sanskrit, at each sentence throwing rice on the bride's and bridegroom's heads. At intervals, in the midst of the blessings, the witnesses are asked in Persian, whether the marriage has their consent and the bridegroom and bride are asked if they have chosen each other. They all reply in the affirmative. After these interrogatories and answers, the priests, (*dasturs*) deliver to the couple a short address containing good, sound and practical advice, partly in the Zand and partly in the Sanskrit language. The whole is brought to a conclusion with the recital of *tandurasti, i. e.*, a blessing invoking the bestowal of physical strength, energy and health on the newly married pair. After the conclusion of these ceremonies, the bride and bridegroom sign a marriage certificate, which is afterwards registered at the office of the registrar of the Parsi Marriages. A Parsi marriage is a very costly affair on account of the presents of dresses and ornaments, feasting and other charges, and a poor Parsi can hardly marry his son for less than Rs. 400 and his daughter for Rs. 250. A middle class marriage costs Rs. 800 to Rs. 2,000 and a rich one Rs. 2,000 to 5,000.

SPECIAL MARRIAGE CUSTOMS.

Special marriage customs.

365. There are several curious marriage customs peculiar to particular castes or tribes. The following are some of them collected during the short time at my disposal :—

Periodical marriages among Kadwa Kanbis.

(1) A curious custom of celebrating marriages in the whole caste on one day, once in every nine, ten or eleven years, prevails among the Kadwa Kanbis. Once in every nine, ten or eleven years, certain Brahman priests and astrologers with the two headmen of the caste in the town of Unja in the Kadi District of the State go together to worship *Umiya*, the patron goddess of the caste, who has her temple in the town. Their object is to find out the propitious year for holding marriages. After worship, lots are drawn and, according as the lot falls, the year in which it falls or the following year is declared the proper time. When the year is known, the astrologers name a special day which generally comes in *Vaishakh* (April-May). For the sake of those prevented from sickness or other cause, a second day is chosen about a fortnight later than the first. As soon as the days are fixed, Brahmans start to spread the news in all places where the people of the caste reside. As another period of nine, ten or eleven years must elapse before regular marriages can again take place, every family provides all its unmarried members with suitable matches. Children about a month old and sometimes unborn children are married. It sometimes happens that no suitable husband can be found for the daughter of a house, and as before the next regular marriage day she would reach a marriageable age, some special arrangement is required. To meet this difficulty two practices have been introduced. According to one of these, on the propitious day, the girl is married to a bunch of flowers. The flowers are then thrown in a well or river, the parents of the bride bathe and the girl, now a widow, can, at any time, be married according to the simple *natra* or second marriage form. The other practice is, on the propitious day, to induce some married man for a small money present, to go through the ceremony of the marriage with the girl and to divorce her as soon as the ceremony is over. The girl can then, at any time, be married according to *natra* form. The married bride remains in the house of her father, and when she reaches puberty, the bridegroom goes to his father-in-law's house with a party of his relations to bring her to his house. Caste dinners are given, and this rather than the day of the first ceremony has the character of a marriage day.

How this custom of holding periodic marriages on a certain day in the whole caste arose is shrouded in mystery. It may be due, perhaps, to economy of time and money. The Kadwa Kanbi caste is a busy agricultural community. Periodic marriages save time, and the custom of having them on the same day in the whole caste, dispenses with the necessity of caste-dinners, as in each house there is a marriage, and consequently its own feast. From information obtained from the leaders of the caste at Unja, it appears that during the last hundred years the marriage years were Samvat 1866, 1876, 1886, 1896, 1906, 1916, 1926, 1936, 1946, 1957 and 1966.

Education in the caste has created a feeling against this ancient custom, and the leaders are striving to do away with it and to introduce the custom of holding marriages every year as in other castes. They have succeeded in bringing about a split in the community ; one section adheres to the old and time-honoured custom, while the other and more advanced has resolved for the present to reduce the marriage period to five years, with the object of gradually reducing it still further, so as to make it annual.

Among Bharvads.

(2) Like the Kadwa Kanbis, Bharvads celebrate their marriages only once in twelve, fifteen or twenty-four years on a day in *Vaishakh* (May), and all the Bharvads of the neighbourhood hold their marriages in the same place. The richest Bharvad among those who wish to get their daughters married, buys the ground where the marriages are to be celebrated. This is necessary, because the ground cannot be used a second time for marriages, but is kept a pasture and an ornamental wooden post called the marriage pillar is set up and preserved to show that the ground has been used for marriages. Shortly before the marriage hour, the several brides with their relations and one Brahman priest meet in the booth. At the hour fixed for the marriage all the bridegrooms come to the booth one after the other and are received by the wife of the man who bought the ground and paid for the booth. In receiving each bridegroom, the hostess shows him a miniature plough, arrow and churning stick. Then each bridegroom sits by the side of his bride. The pairs then walk round the post and offer it a cocoanut kernel. They are next taken to the *chori* where the hems of their clothes are tied together, and they walk round the fire which is lighted in the middle. This completes the marriage ceremony. The host feasts the assembled Bharvads for three days and repays himself by levying a fee of Rs. 12½ from the father of each bridegroom.

Among Motala Brahmans.

(3) Among the Motala Brahmans, marriages take place on the same day every fourth year.

Sword Marriage.

(4) Among Rajputs the bridegroom may go personally to the bride's house for marriage or may send his *khandu* or sword as his representative. As by sending the sword, the bridegroom escapes expensive presents to Bhats, Bhavayas and other beggars, the practice has become common. When this practice is to be resorted to, the bridegroom sits in a chariot with a sword and a cocoanut and passes with music and a company of friends and relatives as far as the boundary of his village. There he alights leaving the sword and cocoanut in charge of a maid servant, who takes his place in the chariot. The procession marches to the bride's village and is welcomed at the boundary by the girl's party. After the usual formalities, the maid servant with the sword sits on a stool and the bride sits on another opposite her in the marriage booth, and all the ceremonies are gone through, as if the owner of the sword himself was present for his marriage. Two or three days after the sword marriage, the bride is sent to the bridegroom's house seated in the chariot with the maid who brought the sword. When the bride's party reaches the village boundary, the bridegroom goes to receive the bride and when he reaches her carriage the maid servant leaves her seat and the bridegroom takes his place and escorts his bride home.

Brahma Kshatris.

(5) The marriage customs of Brahma Kshatris differ from those of Brahmans and other high caste Hindus. On the marriage day, in the presence of a company of bride's friends, the bridegroom stands at the central square of the marriage hall and looking down into

a large earthen pan, full of water, touches with the point of his sword four saucers hung over his head from their reflection in the water. This seems to be a relic of the *matsya vedh* or fish test, in accordance with which the suitor of a Kshatriya maiden had, from the reflection in a pond of water, to shoot a fish hung over his head. Unlike other Hindus, the bride is dressed in loose Mahomedan-like trousers and is seated in a closed palanquin or *balai* set in front of the house. The bridegroom walks seven times round the palanquin, the bride's brother at each turn giving him a cut with *karena* (oleander) twig, and the women of the family throwing showers of cakes from the windows. He retires and while mounting his horse, the bride's father comes out, and giving him a present leads him into the marriage hall.

Khandhadiyo or probationer husband.

(6) Among the Animistic tribes, known as Chodhra, Dhodia, Gamit, Kokna, etc., marriage, as a rule, takes place by purchase of the bride and is accompanied by no ceremony worth the name except drinking, eating and dancing. The money to be paid to the father of the bride as bride-price varies from about Rs. 12 to about Rs. 40 in the different tribes. Men with no means of paying even such a moderate price for a wife offer to serve the girl's father for a term of one to five years. Men with means, who do not care to part with their daughters in consideration of the bride-price, admit such impecunious candidates for their daughters as *khandhadiyo* or probationary husband. If the girl does not like the *khandhadiyo*, she refuses to speak to him, and he takes a hint to depart. If she likes him, she not only speaks to him, but also serves him the usual meals. The *khandhadiyo* is allowed to live on intimate terms with her before she is regularly married to him. Many a time the girl conceives and begets children, but this is not considered disgraceful. She and her probationer husband sometimes may not agree and separate even after having lived as man and wife. This event does not come in the way of the girl obtaining a second husband. But the probationer husband can claim payment for his services. When all goes well, the regular marriage ceremony is performed. After marriage, husband and wife may live separate or continue to live in the old house. When the father-in-law is rich, he generally treats his daughter's husband as his son, and gives him a piece of land, called *vavlu*, for his and his wife's maintenance. If the *khandhadiyo* dies before his probationary period is over, *i. e.*, before he is regularly married to the girl for whom he is kept on probation, the girl is made to go through a ceremony of marriage with his dead body. This is done by applying *pithi*, *i.e.*, turmeric powder mixed in oil to the dead body and then making the girl embrace it.

Rajputs and Lewa Kanbis.

(7) Among Rajputs and Lewa Kanbis living in villages, a girl cannot be married with a boy living in the same village. All the caste people living in the same village are looked upon as related to each other as members of a family and marriages must therefore take place with those living outside the village.

Brahmans and Vanias.

(8) Among Brahmans and Vanias living in towns, on the other hand, so far as possible, a girl is married with a boy living in the same town. When she reaches puberty she goes to her husband every day at night time and returns to her parents in the morning. So long as the mother-in-law is alive or she herself has no children, she does not generally stay at her father-in-law's during day-time.

(9) It is unlucky for a man to have married three times, and when a man, who has lost two wives, wants to marry a third one, he goes through a mock marriage with an *akada* bush (*catotropis gigantia*), so that his next wife may be his fourth and not third wife as she otherwise would be. The marriage is called *arkvivaha*. Among the lower classes he simply carries a little doll in his pocket when starting for his new marriage, so that it may represent his third wife and the one that he is going to marry may be the fourth one.

Special customs connected with marriages.

(10) A widower has to present to his new wife a *shokya pagalu*, *i.e.*, a neck ornament with marks to represent the feet of his first wife. This the new wife wears on her neck, so that the spirit of the first wife may not trouble her in life.

A widower has to present a SHOKYA PAGALU.

(11) In castes among which widow marriage is allowed, a bachelor cannot marry a widow. Such a marriage can take place only if the bachelor first marries the ***shami*** tree (*prosopis spicigeru*) and then the widow.

A bachelor cannot marry a widow.

(12) *Kanyadan*, that is giving a girl in marriage, is considered a very meritorious act. Well-to-do people render pecuniary help to poor persons to enable them to celebrate the marriage of their daughters. Some well-to-do childless Hindus celebrate a mock marriage between the image of ***Vishnu*** and the *tulsi* plant. The childless pair, who own the tulsi plant, act as the bride's parents. The image of Vishnu belongs to a friend, who with his wife acts as the bridegroom's parents. On the bright 11th of Kartik or on a day fixed by an astrologer, the image is taken in procession to the basil plant. The male owner of the image, with the image in his hand and the female owner of the plant with the basil pot near her, then go regularly through all the Brahmanic marriage rites. The owner of the plant presents gold and silver ornaments to the image, the owner of which also receives cash presents as the bridegroom's parent.

Mock Marriage of Tulsi and Vishnu.

BIRTH CUSTOMS.

366. A female is considered fit for impregnation on the appearance of the menstrual flow. No ceremonies are performed by Gujarat castes when she first menstruates. *Garbhadhan* or fœtus-bearing ceremony, which according to the Vedas ought to be performed on this occasion and was once performed, is now neglected, and is only nominally performed along with the *simant* ceremony in the seventh, eighth or ninth month of the pregnancy. Among Deccani castes, however, a ceremony called *rutu shanti* or menstruation appeasing, is performed. As soon as a girl first menstruates sugar is distributed among all relations and friends as a sign of joy. The girl is seated in a room specially decorated and friends and relations come and present her with fruits, flowers and sweetmeats. On the fourth day, she is bathed and her lap is filled with five fruits each of the best kinds. Within fifteen days *garbhadhan* or fœtus-bearing ceremony is performed in which the gods are prayed to see that she may conceive and beget a child in due course of time.

Ceremonies on first menstruation.

A woman in menstruation remains impure for three days among the higher Hindu castes. She keeps herself confined in a room and does not show her face to her husband or any elder male relation. She bathes on the fourth day and joins her husband. Lower castes, such as Golas, Kolis, Dheds and Bhangis are not very particular about impurity attaching to this occasion, and among the Animistic tribes no restriction is observed at all.

Barrenness.

367. Barrenness is looked upon with feelings of great uneasiness by females alike among Hindus, Jains, Musalmans and Parsis. A barren woman is called *vanjhani*, which is a term of reproach. A Hindu or Jain woman tries to get rid of her barrenness by a variety of means. If it is believed to be caused by the anger of some god or goddess, she quiets them by prayers and by giving them their pet offerings or taking vows. If the barrenness is due to the unfriendly influence of some planet, she engages a Brahman to repeat prayers in its honour and fasts on the day sacred to it. If the disease is spirit caused, she walks 108 times round the *pipal* tree on a non-moon Monday, pours water at its roots and winds a cotton thread round its trunk. Women are also said to try to get rid of their barrenness by pricking a neighbour's child on a Sunday or Tuesday with the point of a needle or by secretly cutting a tuft of the hair of its head. Some are said to swallow an unclipped betel-nut after keeping it for some time under the cot of a woman in labour or to secretly tear the piece out of the clothes of a pregnant woman or a woman in child-birth—an act which when discovered causes uneasiness to the woman and her relations, as it is believed to cause the child's death or the pregnant woman's miscarriage. Sadhus, Jain priests, Musalman fakirs and others are consulted and charmed water given by them is drunk, or an amulet tied on the left elbow or neck.

Childless Musalman females also resort to various means to obtain children. They obtain charms from saints (pirs) and exorcists (amils). The charm consists of a diagram drawn on a piece of paper. It is to be either washed in rose-water and drunk or worn round the neck. After conception, some talisman is given with the object that the issue may be male. The charm is washed in water, which is drunk immediately or is used for a monthly bath. Some dead saints also have a reputation of giving children. Many childless and spirit possessed Musalman females resort to the grave of saint Miran Datar near Unja in the Kadi District. The leaves of a tree near the grave of the saint are said to favour conception.

Rites during pregnancy: Hindu.

368. The Vedas prescribe 16 *sanskaras* or purifying rites, of which three only, *viz.*, *simant* or pregnancy, *upanayan* or thread-girding and *vivaha* or marriage, are performed by the Brahmans and other high caste Hindus, and only the first and the third by Vanias, Kanbis, Rajputs, artizans and other castes. The first Vedic rite, *garbhadhan* or fœtus-bearing; the second, *pumsavan* or male-making; the third, *anavalobhana* or longing soothing and the fourth, *vishnubali* or guardian pleasing, are performed together at the *simant* or hair-parting ceremony which is performed in the seventh, eighth or ninth month after pregnancy. Among the Animistic tribes, no pregnancy ceremonies are performed. Among the Kanbis, Rajputs, artizans and other lower castes, the *simant* ceremony consists in the *kholobharvo* or lap-filling and the *rakhadi bandhavi* or guard-binding ceremony. On an auspicious day in the seventh month of a first pregnancy, the husband's sister binds round the woman's right wrist a silver ornament called *rakhadi* or guard and receives a money present. The pregnant woman wearing rich clothes sits on a stool and a married woman, who has never lost a child (*akhand sohagan*) drops into her lap five pounds of rice, a cocoanut, five betel leaves, five cloves, five cardamoms, five betel-nuts, five lotus seeds, ten flowers and a rupee. The pregnant woman falls at the feet of her mother-in-law, to whom she hands the articles dropped into her lap. Among Brahman, Vania and some of the artizan castes, like Kansaras, more elaborate ceremonies are performed. The pregnant woman goes to bathe at a relation's, and while coming back walks in the public streets, on cloth specially spread and under a moveable cloth canopy. In front of her husband's house, an altar is made, a fire is lighted and offerings of clarified butter are made with *mantras*. The husband and wife take their seats near the altar and after worshipping *Ganpati*, a *sankalpa* or resolution is made to perform together all pregnancy rites from the *garbhadhan* or fœtus-bearing to the *simantonayan* or

hair-parting. Then the ceremonies are performed one after another. In the *pumsavan* or male-making ceremony a piece of the root of the banian tree (*ficus indica*) or a little *daro* (*cynodondactylon*) is crushed and the juice dropped into the right nostril of the pregnant woman.

Musalman.

Corresponding to these Hindu ceremonies, Musalmans perform the *satmasa*, seven month or *navmasa*, nine month ceremonies. The rite generally begins with the *birat bharna* or pot-filling ceremony. A complete *birat* consists of 125 pots, but sometimes half the number of pots is sent for and sometimes quarter, for which the potter is paid up to 5 rupees. A *sohagan*, married woman who has never lost a child, fills the pots with water, and she and the potter with the pots are brought with music and rejoicings to the pregnant woman's house, in which the pots are arranged in lines in rows of three with a cocoanut at the top. A dinner is cooked and *fatias* are repeated over the pots in the names of dead ancestors, chiefly women of the house who have died childless.

Parsi.

Parsis perform a ceremony called *aghaharani or agarni, i. e.,* sin destroying ceremony, in the seventh month after pregnancy. It is copied from the Hindus and resembles *kholobharvo* ceremony. The pregnant woman's lap is filled with sweet balls, a cocoanut, dried dates, almonds, betel-nuts and betel-leaves mixed with sesame seed and lemon or pomegranate. Carrying these things, she goes to her parent's house and empties them out of her lap into a winnowing fan and with a lamp in one hand and a goblet of water in the other, goes to the lying-in room with the object of driving out evil spirits. She goes round it seven times pouring water all the time. She then returns to her husband's house and comes back to her parents when the time of delivery draws near.

Animistic tribes.

The observances of most of the Animistic tribes resemble those of the Hindus. During pregnancy no ceremony is performed except among the Mangs. Among the Mangs, on a fixed day in the seventh month of a woman's first pregnancy, five women fill her lap with cocoanut kernels and rice or wheat. Friends are fed on rice and pulse, mutton and liquor. On the sixth day after birth, the goddess *chhathi* is worshipped. On the inner walls of the house, lines of *kanku* and turmeric are drawn. Rice is thrown at the drawing, a lamp is lighted before it and a dinner is given. The same day Bhats, who claim to be of Brahman descent and act as their priests, name the child.

Sex divination.

369. Females make guesses about the sex of the baby to be born in a variety of ways. Among Musalmans a few drops of milk are squeezed out from the bosom of the pregnant woman and from its thinness or thickness, the sex of the child is conjectured. If the milk is thin, it is foretold that a boy is to be born. Among Gujarati Hindus, if the face of the pregnant woman is full and blooming, the birth of a female child is predicted. On the other hand, if her face is lean and emaciated a male child is expected. If the pregnant woman gets more than the usual sleep a girl is expected, and if she sleeps less than usual, a boy. If the right side of the abdomen of a pregnant woman appears protruding, a boy is expected, and a girl, if the left side so appears. The objects which appear to a pregnant woman in her dreams are also supposed to furnish an indication of the sex of the child she is to deliver. If they are objects of the male gender, a male child, and if they are of the female gender, a female child is expected.

Seclusion of women at child-birth.

370. A pregnant woman is not allowed to draw water from a well or do any other heavy house-work. She keeps herself confined to the house, and does not appear before the elder male members in the house. When the labour begins, she is taken to a warm room, the windows of which are kept shut. Generally a barber woman acts as midwife. The mother remains secluded for about 40 days among Brahmans, Vanias and other high castes and for a short period varying from 10 to 20 days among the lower classes. As Bharvad children are born when their parents are moving from place to place, no seclusion is observed at all; similarly among most of the nomadic tribes, the mother delivers, puts the child in a basket and moves on without being either sick or sorry. Among Parsis, the mother is kept in the lying-in room up to the fortieth day and is not allowed to move out or touch anything. On the night after the fortieth day, she is bathed and purified.

Prohibited foods before and after-child birth.

371. About two months before delivery, a pregnant woman is not allowed to eat things which cause much of heating in the stomach, *i. e.*, chillies, oil, &c. After delivery, she is not allowed to eat things which are cooling or cause windiness. During the first few days after delivery, she is given a decoction of ginger and oil and such nutritious food as *shira*. Molasses is given in preference to sugar and ghee instead of oil. Drinking water is either boiled or a red hot piece of iron is thrown into it. Such cereals and vegetables as are believed to cause indigestion to the child are avoided. But all this is done in the houses of the well-to-do. Poor people living on *banti-bavto*, or coarse grain, have the same food during confinement as they have ordinarily. Among a few families in Kathiawad, a woman while in confinement eats only fruits and roots or such food as is used on fast days. Among Parsis for five days after a birth, the mother is fed on light food and the child on sugar and water.

Vadhamani.

372. In the Brahman-Vania castes the exact hour of birth is carefully noted with a view to having a horoscope prepared. In the Gola-Ghanchi castes, this is rarely done. If a son is born his feet are smeared with *kanku* and their imprints are taken on a piece of paper which is sent along with the good news to the father and his relations and there is a rejoicing among all the relations and friends. If the child is a girl, there is no rejoicing. For nine nights, the mother is kept in a closed room with her head lightly wrapped with a black cloth. The new-born babe is laid on a wooden stool close to the mother's cot. For two days, the child is given a cotton wick soaked in molasses water to suck and on the third day is put to the mother's breast.

Shasthi Puja or destiny worship.

373. On the sixth night is performed a ceremony called *chhathi* or *shasthi puja*; this is the worship of the goddess sixth. On the same night *Vidhata* (Fate) is supposed to write on the child's forehead, the chief events of its coming life. A wooden stool covered with a white piece of cotton cloth is placed in the mother's room and close to it is set a lamp fed by clarified butter. Six small heaps of wheat or rice are laid on the stool and a betelnut and a copper are set on each heap. A picture of *shasthi* is drawn on the cloth with red powder and near it are laid a reed pen, inkstand and paper for the goddess to write with. The new-born child is laid near the mother's cot and both the child and mother are marked with red powder. On the morning of the seventh, all the articles are removed and given to the family priest, except the cloth which is dyed black and made into a jacket for the child.

Shasthi is also worshipped among the Animistic tribes on the sixth day after a child's birth.

The Parsis also, in imitation of the Hindus, worship *shasthi* on the sixth day after birth.

Among Mahomedans on the fourteenth day after birth, in honour of the mother's recovery, *nao* or boats of grass are with music taken to the nearest water, a lamp is lighted and the boats sent adrift as a thanksgiving to Khaza Khuzr, the water genius.

Couvade.

374. There is a curious caste called Pomla in the City of Baroda which observes the odd rule prevalent among several primitive peoples in different parts of the world requiring that the husband should be doctored while the wife gives birth to a child. This has given rise to the Gujarati saying '*Pomli jane ane Pomlo khaya*'. Immediately after delivery, the female is made to drink the juice of the

bark of the nimb tree and a quantity of oil. She then stirs out of the house and is not allowed to enter it for five days during which time, the husband lies confined and takes the usual medicines. The Pomlas say that they do not lie confined merely to observe a custom, but actually get indisposed during the period and that the indisposition is a mark of favour of their goddess Laxmi Mata. They speak a dialect which resembles Telagu and appear to have come to Gujarat from the South about two or three hundred years ago.

Disposal of dead child's body.

375. A dead child is always buried in the burial ground set apart for the purpose, if it was not more than eighteen months old; if older it is cremated or buried according to the usual practice of the caste.

Treatment of women dying in child birth.

376. If a woman dies within ten days of her delivery, an iron nail is driven into the doorway immediately after her corpse is taken out, so that her spirit may not return and trouble the inmates of the house.

Ear-boring or teething ceremony.

377. No ear-boring or teething ceremony is observed in Gujarat.

Naming ceremony : Hindu.

378. Among Hindus, the *nama karma* or naming ceremony takes place on the 12th day after birth or on some lucky day after the fortieth. The father's sister gives the name which has already been fixed upon. It should begin with one of the letters which is assigned to the sign of the Zodiac in which the moon may be at the time of the child's birth. The child is laid on a white sheet with seven *pipal* (*Ficus Religiosa*) leaves and seven betel-nuts. The four ends of the sheet are raised by four children and the child is rocked four times before which it is named. This ceremony is gradually falling into disuse and the name is now mostly given by the mother without any ceremony. Among Brahmans the *nama karma* ceremony is performed along with *upanayan* or thread-girding ceremony. Among the Animistic tribes, the child is named by the parents or some old woman on the sixth day when *shasthi* is worshipped.

Musalman.

Among Mahomedans, the child is named early in the morning of the sixth day after birth. The father, grandfather or other male relation opens the *Kuran* at a venture and the first letter of the first word of the third line is the initial of the child's name.

Parsi.

Among Parsis on the fifth day or any convenient day, a Brahman or a Parsi astrologer is called and told the hour of the child's birth. He draws chalk marks on a wooden board and gives several suitable names of which one is chosen by the parents.

Both among Hindus and Musalmans, parents who have lost children or whose children do not live, give curious names showing deformity or the most abject humility. *Nathu*, literally nose-bored, is a name which accompanies the actual boring of the nose of the new-born child with the idea of deforming it and thereby making it less liable to spirit attacks. *Bhikho*, beggar, *Ghelo* or *Gando*, mad, *Kachro*, rubbish, and *Bhulo*, forgetful, are also names which are given to mislead evil spirits who attack what is most praised.

Botan or weaning.

379. *Botan* or weaning ceremony which is now performed only in a few Brahman families corresponds to *anna prashan*, the tenth Vedic rite. It is performed in the sixth or eighth month after a birth in the case of a boy and in the fifth or seventh month in the case of a girl. *Khir* or preparation of boiled milk with rice and sugar is laid on a rupee and given to the child to lick by the maternal uncle or some other near relation. This ceremony is also performed among Musalmans when the child is four-and a-half months old. The child's father's sister first offers it some *khir* on a rupee and then a piece of flesh to suck. Though from this time the child takes other food besides milk, it is not actually weaned. Among Hindus, a child continues sucking at its mother's breast till it is from 12 to 18 months old. Among the lower classes, a child is allowed to suck even longer. Among Musalmans, it is not weaned until it is twenty-one months old.

380. Among Parsis, when the child enters on its seventh month, the *besanu* or sitting ceremony is performed. The child is dressed in a new silk frock and cap, its brow is marked with red powder and it is made to sit on a stool placed on lucky chalk marks. As it sits, the child touches a cocoanut which is then broken.

Besana or sitting ceremony among Parsis.

381. *Chaul or chuda karma*, head shaving ceremony, is the eleventh Vedic rite and takes place on some auspicious day either in third or fifth year of the boy or at the time of the *upanayan* or thread-girding. Among Brahman castes, it is generally performed at the time of the *upanayan*. Among Vanias, Kanbis, Kolis and the artizan castes who do not wear the sacred thread, shaving is performed only if a vow is taken to do so, in the temple of the family goddess or some goddess well known in Gujarat such as Bahucharaji, Ambaji, Kalka or Ashapuri. The boy is seated in his mother's lap and the father taking a razor crops off a tuft of the boy's hair. A barber who is in readiness then shaves the head clean. The hair is taken by the father's sister and thrown into a well or river.

Shaving.

Among Jain Vanias when a child is three, five, or seven years old, the boy's head is completely shaved and a tuft of hair is cut from the back of a girl's head; but except that friends and relations are feasted, no ceremonies are performed at the time of hair-cutting. Among Brahma-Kshatris, both boys as well as girls have their hair cut. Among Rajputs hair cutting is performed with most of the marriage ceremonies such as *grahshanti, pithi, varadh bharvi* or bringing earthen pots from the potter's. Among Bhils, a child is shaved when five years old. The child's father's sister receives a cow, a buffalo, or other present for taking the hair in her lap.

382. Shaving rites called *akika* are performed among Mahomedans on the 7th, 14th or 21st day after birth. When the barber passes the razor along the bead of the child its father or some one specially named by him draws a knife across a goat's head saying "I sacrifice this animal for the child named Wali, blood for blood, skin for skin, flesh for flesh, hair for hair." If the child is a girl, one goat is sacrificed, but if it is a boy, two are sacrificed. When the shaving is over the child's hair and nails are laid on a bread and carried away to be thrown into a river.

Hair cutting.

383. Upanayan, literally 'taking before (a preceptor)' is the initiation or thread-girding ceremony among the twice-born Hindus. It was, in olden times, performed before sending a boy to a preceptor for study. After being invested with the thread, a boy became a *brahmachari* or student, left his father's house for that of his preceptor's and did not return before he was from 20 to 25 years old and had finished his studies and his maternal uncle came to him and persuaded him to return under a promise that he would marry him with a suitable bride. Now-a-days the ceremony is performed at any time between the fifth and eleventh year and instead of being looked upon as a preparation for study, is looked upon as conferring fitness for marriage. Some of the early rites such as *jatkarma* or birth rite, *namakarma* or naming, *annaprashan* or food tasting and *chudakarma* or shaving which are neglected to be performed at their proper time, are performed as a formality along with *upanayan*; and after *nishkramana* or house-leaving the maternal uncle brings the boy back to his house, after he has, as a formality, gone away a few yards.

Upanayan.

The cotton thread for the *upanayan* or *janoi*, as it is ordinarily called, is spun by a maiden or a Brahman and is ninety-six times the breadth of four fingers. It is first folded into three and again trebled and the folds are held together by a knot called *brahmagranthi* or Brahma's knot. The *janoi* is thrown over the left shoulder, passed round the right hand and kept suspended.

Many twice-born castes entitled to wear *janoi*, have neglected to do so and now only Brahmans, Bam Nagar Vanias, Prabhus, Mathur Kayasthas, a few Rajputs, Marathas, Brahma Bhats, Bhatias, Khatris, Luhanas, Tragad and Parajia Sonis, Gujjar, Mewada, Pancholi and Vaishya Suthars, Targalas and Garodas do so. Under the preaching of the Arya Samaj, Lewa Kanbis and other Vaishya castes are now introducing the practice among them. Castes who, though entitled to wear the sacred thread, do not ordinarily do so, but put on a strip of cloth to represent it on occasions of *grahashanti* and *shradha* ceremonies.

Instead of the Brahmanic thread, Vanias, Kanbis and other twice-born as well as most of the *shudra* (lower) castes as Kolis, and artizans put on a *kanthi*, rosary of beads, made of the stem of the basil plant. Sometimes, when they are between 7 and 11 years old, both boys and girls are taken to the *guru* (religious preceptor) who binds the rosary round the neck.

Jains wear neither the sacred thread nor a *kanthi*.

Bismillah.

384. The rite of *bismillah*, or taking the name of God, takes place among Musalmans, when a boy or a girl reaches the age of four years, four months and four days. The child is covered with *sahra* or flower sheet and seated on a cushion. Sweetmeats are laid before it and of these two covered with gold paper are given to it. The Mulla or priest repeats the opening chapter of the *Kuran* and the child follows. The priest then invokes blessings on the child and its parents, and the members of the company present say *Amen* at every pause. A procession is then formed and the child is taken to kiss the *dargah* (tomb) of the family guardian saint (Pir). When the procession returns, money presents are made to the child by friends and relations, and the females one by one perform the *balaiya-lena* or the ceremony of taking upon themselves the child's sorrow. In doing it, a woman passes her hands over the child from head to foot and then setting her knuckles or finger tips against her temples presses them till the joints crack.

Navzot.

385. Corresponding to *upanayan* or thread-girding ceremony among Hindus, and the *bismillah* ceremony among Musalmans, is the *navzot* or initiation ceremony among the Parsis. The ceremony consists of clothing the child with a sacred shirt called *sadra* and a sacred cord called *kasti*. *Navzot* means making a new believer and is intended to receive Parsi boys and girls into the Zoroastrian faith. It is performed between the age of seven and nine.

Circumcision.

386. Circumcision or *khatnah* takes place among Musalmans generally when the boy is six or seven years old. Among the Daudi Vohoras, Shiah Mughals and Sunni and Shiah Arabs, it takes place as early as the sixth day after birth. This rite is considered so important by these people that it is performed on girls as well as on boys. The simplest form of circumcision is mere amputation of the prepuce. On the day fixed for the operation, a red cotton cloth, about four feet square, is spread in the room in which it is to be performed. A copper tray, full of soft ashes, is placed in front of it. The boy with only his shirt on and held by a strong male relative is seated on a wooden stool, about a foot high. The barber first introduces into the foreskin a small bamboo chip probably to feel and ascertain that no part of the foreskin adheres to the gland. When he finds that the prepuce is free, he turns up the foreskin, and having cleaned it, lets it go. He then takes a pair of smooth bamboo pincers and holding the ends open, puts them on the lightly drawn-out foreskin; simultaneously with this, he dexterously cuts off with a sharp razor the foreskin close to the pincers. The pincers are then taken out and after drawing up the ends of the foreskin above the gland, a little soft red powder is sprinkled on the wound to staunch the blood. The wound heals up in about two or three days. The recovery of the child is celebrated with great rejoicings. Friends send presents of sugarcandy and sweetmeats. Among Musalmans in the Kadi District circumcision is performed when the boy reaches puberty and is then celebrated with as much pomp as on a marriage.

Superstitions regarding the illness of children. Charms.

387. It is believed both by the Hindus and Musalmans that children are liable to the influence of the evil eye. The two chief guards against it are iron articles and black articles. To turn aside the evil eye, handsome and beloved children also wear a necklace of square copper or silver plates. On these plates numbers are marked whose total when

counted horizontally, vertically or diagonally always comes to the same figure, either 15 or 20. Sometimes the child wears *bajarbatu*, that is lightening guard or a tiger's tooth or claw set in gold and strung through a thread. Whenever a child goes out, a lamp black mark is made on its right cheek or behind the right ear. In order to determine whether a child's sickness is the result of the evil eye or some other cause, live charcoal is put on a bell-metal plate. Seven mustard seeds, seven particles of salt, seven *adad* grains, pinch of clay, a small nail or a needle, a piece of black cloth and some *val* are waved seven times over the child's head and thrown into the plate. On the plate a cup of bell-metal is turned rim down and when it becomes red-hot, the mother prays that the evil eye, whether it belongs to its parents, members of the family, strangers or thieves of the road, the place where four roads meet, the village or its boundary or a mad or unclean woman, a witch or any one else may confine itself within the cup. After muttering this prayer a pot of cowdung and water is waved round the child's head and poured over the cup. If the cup sticks to the plate the evil eye which caused the child's sickness has gone into the cup. If the cup does not stick, the child's illness is believed to be due to some other cause.

Small-pox.

388. Small-pox, including measles (*ori* or *gobru*) and chicken-pox (*achhabda*) is called *sitla* when it is epidemic and *saiad* when it is endemic. Epidemic small-pox is believed by the Hindus to be presided over by a goddess called *Sitla* Mata or small-pox mother, and endemic small-pox by a god called *Saiad Kaka* or *Balia Kaka*, *i.e.*, small-pox uncle or powerful uncle. To protect their children, mothers propitiate *Sitla* Mata once in a year, on the bright or dark seventh of Shravan (August), which is the day sacred to her. As small-pox is believed to be caused by heat, artificial heat is avoided as much as possible on that day and all the members of a family bathe with cold water and eat cold food cooked on the previous day. When a child is actually attacked with small-pox, Balia or Saiad Kaka is propitiated by a visit to his stone image which is kept in a Mahadev or Mata temple or under a nimb, *samdi* or *rukhada* tree. Among Kolis, Bhils and other wild tribes, the small-pox stone is kept near their other objects of worship. One of the most reputed stones of small-pox god in Gujarat is in the village of Por, near Itola in the Baroda Taluka. The small-pox god is visited on the seventh, fifteenth or twenty-first day after the appearance of the disease on a Sunday, Tuesday or Thursday. No medicine is given to the child. The sight of a woman in child-birth or in her monthly sickness, of any person in black and of any unclean person is believed to be very injurious to the child. It is therefore protected from strangers' gaze, and its cot is strewn with nimb leaves to avert the ill-effect produced by the shadow of an unclean person accidently falling on it.

Grinding teeth.

389. If a female child grinds the teeth, it is believed to bring on debts and difficulties to the father; if a male child does so, it is believed to pay off debts and bring on prosperity to the family.

TERMS OF RELATIONSHIP.

Terms of relationship.

390. The Census Commissioner for India directed that inquiries should be made regarding terms of relationship in use among the different people and the result briefly noted in the report. As regards terms of relationship, those in use in the Gujarati language, which is spoken by the Gujarat castes and tribes, are more numerous than in the English language. Many terms of relationship, which are not differentiated in the English language, are differentiated in the local nomenclature, while there are no terms of relationship which are differentiated in English but not in the Vernacular. Whether it is a male or a female who is speaking, a paternal uncle is called *kako*, a maternal uncle, *mamo*, mother's sister's husband, *maso*, and a father's sister's husband *phuvo*; a paternal aunt, *kaki*, a maternal aunt, *mami*, a mother's sister *masi* and a father's sister *phoi*; a brother's son is called *bhatrijo* and his daughter *bhatriji*; a sister's son is called *bhanej* and her daughter *bhaneji*

and a sister's husband, *banevi*. When a man is speaking a brother-in-law is called *salo*, if he is one's wife's brother and *banevi* if he is sister's husband. A sister-in-law is called *sali*, if she is one's wife's sister, *bhabhi* if an elder brother's wife and *bhojai*, if a younger brother's wife. When a woman is speaking, she calls her husband's elder brother *jeth* and his younger brother *diyar* ; she calls the wife of the former *gethani* and that of the latter *derani*. Whether a male or a female is speaking, a father-in-law is called *sasaro* and a mother-in-law *sasu*. A grandfather-in-law is called *vadsasaro* and grandmother-in-law, *vadsasu*.

Terms of relationship used in a classificatory sense.

391. Terms of relationship, while they have a definite connotation, are also used in a classificatory sense, *e. g.*, *bhai*, brother, *kaka*, uncle, *bapa*, father, &c. Those who are equal in age to the speaker are spoken of as brother if males, and as sister, if females ; they are called uncle or aunt if they are of the age of one's father or mother ; and if greater respect or closeness is to be indicated, also as father or mother. Similarly, the words *dikaro* (son), *dikri* (daughter), *bhatrijo* (nephew), and *bhatriji* (niece) are used, as the case may be, by these elders.

Rights and obligations of various relations.

392. It is the privilege of father's sister (*phoi*) to name her brother's children and to get a present for the same. The eldest son of the deceased puts fire into the mouth of the corpse when the funeral fire is lighted. A maternal uncle (*mamo*) is entitled to bring the bride to the *chori* before she is given in marriage by her father. *Diyar* (husband's younger brother) has the right in most of the lower castes to take his elder brother's widow as wife (*vide* para. 348).

Opprobrium attached to some terms of relationship.

393. *Salo* (wife's brother), *sali* (wife's sister), *sasro* (father-in-law), *sasu* (mother-in-law) and *mamo* (mother's brother) are used as terms of abuse. The opprobrium that attaches to these words is due to the fact that to give a girl in marriage implies inferiority. He who is given a bride is believed to be a *kulin* or of a better family than he who gives her. *Banevi* (sister's husband) and *jamai* (son-in-law) are sometimes used in a way which would imply that the party spoken to is *salo*. *sali*, *sasu* or *sasro* as the case may be, of the speaker, *e.g.*, why do you beat your *banevi* or *jamai* ?

SUBSIDIARY TABLE I.—DISTRIBUTION BY CIVIL CONDITION OF 1,000 OF EACH SEX, RELIGION AND MAIN AGE-PERIOD AT EACH OF THE LAST FOUR CENSUSES.

RELIGION, SEX AND AGE.	Unmarried.				Married.				Widowed.			
	1911	1901	1891	1881	1911	1901	1891	1881	1911	1901	1891	1881
1	2	3	4	5	6	7	8	9	10	11	12	13
All Religions.												
MALES.												
0—5	959	973	957	932	39	24	41	65	2	3	2	3
5—10	883	897	879		111	94	117		6	9	4	
10—15	753	730	721	732	236	245	272	260	11	25	7	8
15—20	539	462	488	486	434	481	499	499	27	57	13	15
20—40	163	152	143	156	765	731	814	796	72	117	43	48
40—60	47	65	62	66	764	714	797	795	189	221	141	139
60 and over	49	66	57	66	554	551	618	644	397	383	325	290
FEMALES.												
0—5	915	961	907	846	83	36	92	151	2	3	1	3
5—10	807	836	763		188	154	234		5	10	3	
10—15	464	477	446	453	515	485	542	531	21	38	12	16
15—20	111	127	103	100	856	786	875	868	33	87	22	32
20—40	11	16	14	11	862	786	891	873	127	198	95	116
40—60	5	5	6	3	467	487	530	539	528	508	464	458
60 and over	4	5	3	2	154	250	162	199	842	745	835	799
Hindus.												
MALES.												
0—5	952	972	956	924	45	25	42	73	3	3	2	3
5—10	867	894	871		126	96	125		7	10	4	
10—15	725	716	704	709	263	256	288	281	12	28	8	10
15—20	514	444	471	462	457	492	516	522	29	64	13	16
20—40	159	148	137	151	766	733	821	800	75	119	42	49
40—60	48	68	53	68	758	709	804	792	194	223	143	140
60 and over	52	73	58	70	546	555	616	640	402	372	326	290
FEMALES.												
0—5	902	956	899	826	96	40	100	171	2	4	1	3
5—10	777	826	744		218	162	252		5	12	4	
10—15	405	438	415	412	570	518	572	571	25	44	13	17
15—20	83	106	97	85	882	799	881	882	35	95	22	33
20—40	8	10	13	9	863	784	894	874	129	206	93	117
40—60	3	3	6	3	458	469	533	538	539	528	461	459
60 and over	2	4	4	2	151	221	162	196	847	775	834	802
Jains.												
MALES.												
0—5	992	959	952	990	8	29	47	9·5	...	12	1	0·5
5—10	980	889	942		19	78	57		1	33	1	
10—15	890	750	847	879	107	229	150	119	3	21	3	2
15—20	658	508	569	615	333	455	423	378	9	37	8	7
20—40	269	218	267	265	664	676	689	686	67	106	44	49
40—60	95	96	121	99	677	685	714	740	228	219	165	161
60 and over	75	74	96	71	476	539	542	612	449	387	362	317
FEMALES.												
0—5	989	963	980	973	10	27	19	26	1	10	1	1
5—10	978	871	965		21	112	32		1	17	3	
10—15	739	605	728	668	250	384	265	321	11	11	7	11
15—20	71	111	54	58	880	801	914	891	49	88	32	51
20—40	7	11	10	6	723	738	828	823	270	251	162	171
40—60	3	1	7	2	356	446	421	468	641	553	572	530
60 and over	7	1	...	...	110	217	135	176	883	782	865	824

SUBSIDIARY TABLE I.—Distribution by civil condition of 1,000 of each sex, religion and main age-period at each of the last four Censuses.—*contd.*

Religion, sex and age.	Unmarried.				Married.				Widowed.			
	1911	1901	1891	1881	1911	1901	1891	1881	1911	1901	1891	1881
1	2	3	4	5	6	7	8	9	10	11	12	13
Animists.												
Males.												
0—5	996	997	991	995	4	2·9	9	4·9	...	·1	...	·1
5—10	979	951	984		20	48	16		1	1	...	
10—15	945	834	945	949	54	163	54	50	1	3	1	1
15—20	736	541	641	661	252	439	344	333	12	20	15	6
20—40	119	134	97	132	842	763	870	832	39	103	33	36
40—60	22	22	20	25	863	777	855	866	115	201	125	109
60 and over	36	16	14	26	653	487	698	683	311	497	288	291
Females.												
0—5	998	998	990	993	2	1·8	10	6·8	...	·2	...	·2
5—10	980	929	983		19·9	70·6	17		·1	·4	...	
10—15	850	671	823	865	148	325	176	133	2	4	1	2
15—20	388	226	279	333	604	739	714	653	8	35	7	14
20—40	33	38	30	34	928	836	918	910	39	126	52	56
40—60	9	5	12	5	700	684	652	681	291	311	336	314
60 and over	6	1	6	5	254	445	254	352	740	554	740	643
Musalmans.												
Males.												
0—5	986·8	950	981	964	13	45	19	34	·2	5	...	2
5—10	957	869	937		41	122	61		2	9	2	
10—15	866	752	841	835	128	228	154	159	6	20	5	6
15—20	658	532	645	659	328	427	347	326	14	41	8	15
20—40	205	193	192	211	727	687	766	740	68	120	42	49
40—60	38	71	44	58	785	696	819	801	177	233	137	141
60 and over	31	68	43	43	585	576	642	668	384	356	315	289
Females.												
0—5	969	946	972	925	30	50	27	72	1	4	1	3
5—10	914	822	886		83	166	112		3	12	2	
10—15	635	602	630	625	356	375	364	364	9	23	6	11
15—20	158	197	141	152	814	724	836	815	28	79	23	33
20—40	19	43	20	21	858	760	876	852	123	197	104	127
40—60	12	20	9	8	467	498	497	504	521	482	494	488
60 and over	6	15	7	7	153	283	145	172	841	702	848	821

SUBSIDIARY TABLE I.—Distribution by civil condition of 1,000 of each sex, religion and main age-period at each of the last four Censuses—*contd.*

Religion, sex and Age.	Unmarried.				Married.				Widowed.			
	1911	1901	1891	1881	1911	1901	1891	1881	1911	1901	1891	1881
1	2	3	4	5	6	7	8	9	10	11	12	13
Parsis												
Males.												
0—5	1,000	1,000	983	980	...	...	17	16	...	...	...	4
5—10	995	983	986		5	17	14		...	...	...	
10—15	996	958	932	830	4	40	68	164	...	2	...	6
15—20	951	808	734	416	49	185	254	573	...	7	12	11
20—40	352	241	126	83	622	707	854	813	26	52	20	104
40—60	29	25	8	12	880	814	908	654	91	161	84	334
60 and over	18	13	3	2	691	728	714	426	291	259	283	572
Females.												
0—5	1,000	998	991	943	...	2	9	56	...	...	...	1
5—10	987	975	970		11	25	30		2	...	...	
10—15	954	909	766	617	46	85	234	376	...	6	...	7
15—20	793	389	325	134	200	564	651	863	7	47	24	3
20—40	202	47	38	10	725	849	895	955	73	104	67	35
40—60	71	...	5	...	641	593	682	878	288	407	313	122
60 and over	88	...	...	...	182	224	288	516	730	776	712	484
Christians.												
Males.												
0—5	961	949	1,000	984	37	40	...	16	2	11	...	...
5—10	615	870	963		380	116	37		5	14	...	
10—15	553	612	737	941	413	347	263	59	34	41	...	...
15—20	397	257	911	920	561	683	89	80	42	60	...	...
20—40	103	70	384	666	833	835	607	315	64	95	9	19
40—60	19	19	61	132	824	840	829	750	157	141	110	118
60 and over	18	23	...	167	613	701	1,000	666	369	276	...	167
Females.												
0—5	858	917	970	981	132	67	30	19	10	16	...	...
5—10	462	540	840		418	443	120		120	17	40	
10—15	323	260	937	889	662	692	63	111	15	48	...	...
15—20	304	86	714	333	690	828	286	667	6	86	...	...
20—40	35	13	141	78	900	887	798	875	65	100	61	47
40—60	7	...	...	...	574	505	790	450	419	495	210	550
60 and over	9	109	...	...	195	182	250	...	796	709	750	1,000

SUBSIDIARY TABLE II—Distribution by Civil Condition of 1,000 of each sex,

Religion and Natural Division.	Males.																	
	All ages.			0—5			5—10			10—15			15—40			40 and over.		
	Unmarried.	Married.	Widowed.	Unmarried.	Married.	Widowed.	Unmarried.	Married.	Widowed.	Unmarried.	Married.	Widowed.	Unmarried.	Married.	Widowed.	Unmarried.	Married.	Widowed.
1	2	3	4	5	6	7	8	9	10	11	12	13	14	15	16	17	18	19
Baroda State.																		
All religions	*428*	*496*	*76*	*959*	*39*	*2*	*883*	*111*	*6*	*753*	*236*	*11*	*239*	*698*	*63*	*47*	*727*	*226*
Hindu	418	504	78	952	45	3	867	126	7	725	263	12	231	703	66	721	850	49
Jain	491	421	88	992	8	...	980	19	1	890	107	3	349	596	55	91	640	269
Animist	509	452	39	996	4	...	979	20	1	945	54	1	228	738	34	24	830	146
Musalman	466	461	73	987	13	...	957	41	2	866	128	6	298	645	57	37	746	217
Parsi	574	379	47	1,000	...	...	995	5	...	996	4	...	532	449	19	26	825	149
Christian	340	593	67	961	37	2	615	380	5	553	413	34	175	766	59	19	790	191
Arya Samaj	339	611	50	891	109	...	735	235	30	585	415	...	159	781	60	...	873	127
Brahmo	250	500	250	...	...	...	...	...	...	...	...	...	333	667	...	...	...	1,000
Sikh	407	576	17	1,000	...	...	1,000	...	...	1,000	...	...	263	737	...	...	857	143
Jew	435	565	...	1,000	...	...	1,000	...	...	1,000	...	...	250	750	...	...	1,000	...
Baroda Division.																		
All religions	*416*	*506*	*78*	*983*	*16*	*1*	*928*	*69*	*3*	*734*	*257*	*9*	*227*	*709*	*64*	*60*	*720*	*220*
Hindu	413	506	81	983	16	1	929	69	2	723	268	9	227	706	67	64	710	226
Jain	434	477	89	983	17	...	982	16	2	757	235	8	300	653	47	99	624	277
Animist	457	509	34	987	13	...	937	60	3	853	144	3	124	841	35	8	882	110
Musalman	440	487	73	986	14	...	949	48	3	824	168	8	285	661	54	40	753	207
Parsi	320	667	13	1,000	...	...	1,000	...	...	1,000	...	...	455	545	...	...	970	30
Christian	285	642	73	956	42	2	539	454	7	437	517	46	99	837	64	14	781	205
Kadi Division.																		
All religions	*414*	*504*	*82*	*902*	*75*	*23*	*801*	*186*	*13*	*690*	*292*	*18*	*237*	*690*	*73*	*39*	*723*	*238*
Hindu	407	511	82	915	81	4	785	201	14	669	312	19	229	696	75	37	725	238
Jain	501	411	88	993	7	...	976	23	1	908	91	1	357	584	59	87	650	263
Musalman	471	447	82	980	19	1	948	49	3	872	119	9	305	628	67	32	728	240
Parsi	500	457	43	1,000	...	...	1,000	...	...	1,000	...	...	500	409	91	...	1,000	...
Christian	418	532	50	1,000	...	...	800	200	...	636	364	...	287	657	56	67	800	133
Navsari Division.																		
All religions	*467*	*474*	*59*	*990*	*10*	...	*961*	*38*	*1*	*828*	*169*	*3*	*217*	*739*	*44*	*39*	*752*	*209*
Hindu	438	560	2	985	14	1	946	53	1	769	226	5	186	766	48	43	732	225
Jain	505	401	94	1,000	...	...	994	6	...	913	71	16	366	566	68	101	592	307
Animist	527	432	41	1,000	...	...	996	4	...	969	30	1	265	701	34	29	812	159
Musalman	484	451	65	994	6	...	955	45	...	853	146	1	260	695	45	29	749	222
Parsi	581	371	48	1,000	...	...	995	5	...	996	4	...	508	475	17	23	819	158
Christian	541	459	...	1,000	...	...	1,000	...	...	1,000	...	...	417	583	...	250	750	...
Amreli Division.																		
All religions	*481*	*455*	*64*	*985*	*15*	...	*969*	*30*	*1*	*905*	*93*	*2*	*301*	*656*	*43*	*42*	*742*	*216*
Hindu	473	463	64	984	16	...	966	32	2	897	101	2	294	663	43	42	739	219
Jain	578	358	64	996	4	...	983	17	...	981	19	...	433	530	37	121	647	232
Musalman	529	412	59	990	10	...	986	14	...	949	50	1	339	616	45	38	768	194
Parsi	400	533	67	1,000	...	...	1,000	...	...	...	...	...	500	500	...	...	833	167
Christian	714	143	143	...	...	...	...	...	...	1,000	...	...	1,000	...	...	...	500	500
Baroda City.																		
All religions	*408*	*507*	*85*	*986*	*14*	...	*925*	*74*	*1*	*826*	*170*	*4*	*279*	*659*	*62*	*64*	*709*	*227*
Hindu	398	516	86	983	17	...	911	88	1	804	190	6	264	673	63	68	699	233
Jain	427	466	107	1,000	...	...	980	20	...	933	67	...	307	636	57	60	628	312
Animist	378	530	92	1,000	...	...	1,000	...	...	1,000	...	...	167	712	121	136	728	136
Musalman	435	488	77	994	6	...	976	24	...	898	101	1	317	624	59	45	754	201
Parsi	580	370	50	1,000	...	...	1,000	...	...	1,000	...	...	704	276	20	63	800	137
Christian	619	347	34	1,000	...	...	962	38	...	950	50	...	540	419	41	29	871	100

AT CERTAIN AGES IN EACH RELIGION AND NATURAL DIVISION.

Females.																	
All ages.			0—5			5—10			10—15			15—40			40 and over.		
Unmarried.	Married.	Widowed.	Unmarried.	Married.	Widowed.	Unmarried.	Married.	Widowed.	Unmarried.	Married.	Widowed.	Unmarried.	Married.	Widowed.	Unmarried.	Married.	Widowed.
20	21	22	23	24	25	26	27	28	29	30	31	32	33	34	35	36	37
284	*540*	*176*	*915*	*83*	*2*	*807*	*188*	*5*	*464*	*515*	*21*	*30*	*861*	*109*	*4*	*403*	*593*
268	551	181	902	96	2	777	218	5	405	570	25	22	866	112	3	395	602
296	426	278	989	10	1	978	21	1	739	250	11	19	750	231	4	300	696
452	477	71	998	2	...	980	20	...	850	148	2	865	102	33	8	615	377
320	501	179	969	30	1	914	83	3	635	356	9	45	849	106	11	394	595
450	397	153	1,000	...	...	987	11	2	954	46	...	339	604	57	76	498	426
242	620	138	858	132	10	462	418	120	323	662	15	102	848	50	7	512	481
300	594	106	861	139	...	679	321	...	409	591	...	43	903	54	52	474	474
500	500	...	1,000	...	...	...	...	...	...	...	...	...	1,000	...	...	...	...
516	452	32	1,000	...	...	1,000	...	...	1,000	...	...	143	857	...	...	667	333
588	353	59	1,000	...	...	1,000	...	...	1,000	...	...	625	375	...	...	500	500
255	*569*	*176*	*942*	*57*	*1*	*816*	*178*	*6*	*296*	*687*	*17*	*14*	*892*	*94*	*5*	*417*	*578*
242	576	182	935	64	1	800	195	5	258	724	18	12	891	97	3	412	585
254	468	278	991	(4½) 4·5	(4½) 4·5	976	21	3	502	495	3	8	779	213	4	312	684
405	533	62	995	5	...	966	34	...	587	407	6	12	966	22	1	643	356
288	530	182	968	31	1	868	127	5	467	524	9	22	879	99	19	382	599
471	529	...	1,000	...	...	1,000	...	...	1,000	...	...	250	750	...	...	1,000	...
228	633	139	856	133	11	418	450	132	299	685	16	76	884	40	3	522	475
258	*546*	*196*	*850*	*147*	*3*	*705*	*288*	*7*	*428*	*538*	*34*	*20*	*842*	*138*	*2*	*359*	*639*
252	555	193	840	157	3	681	312	7	395	568	37	19	847	134	2	361	637
294	415	291	987	12	1	984	15	1	776	209	15	20	728	252	3	293	704
319	490	191	947	51	2	909	86	5	654	335	11	42	823	135	8	375	617
452	484	64	1,000	...	...	1,000	...	...	1,000	...	...	313	687	...	...	667	333
224	592	184	720	280	...	778	222	...	167	833	...	45	895	60	88	235	677
373	*508*	*119*	*986*	*14*	...	*924*	*74*	*2*	*625*	*366*	*9*	*78*	*856*	*66*	*10*	*512*	*478*
335	536	129	977	22	1	895	102	3	495	493	12	47	878	75	6	498	496
359	416	225	993	7	...	966	34	...	825	175	...	31	761	208	8	321	671
469	456	75	1,000	...	...	986	14	...	911	88	1	134	829	37	10	606	384
356	482	162	997	3	...	928	72	...	717	277	6	84	831	85	7	424	569
446	394	160	1,000	...	...	987	11	2	951	49	...	325	615	60	81	479	440
522	391	87	1,000	...	...	1,000	...	...	...	...	...	111	778	111	...	667	333
347	*497*	*156*	*984*	*16*	...	*964*	*33*	*3*	*746*	*248*	*6*	*44*	*876*	*80*	*3*	*434*	*563*
342	501	157	984	16	...	961	36	3	731	263	6	42	879	79	2	431	567
395	410	195	992	8	...	979	21	...	877	123	...	29	825	146	...	350	650
378	479	143	991	9	...	983	15	2	826	170	4	58	868	74	4	477	519
429	500	71	...	...	...	1,000	...	..	1,000	...	...	500	500	...	...	800	200
...	1,000	...	...	...	...	...	...	...	...	...	...	...	...	...	...	1,000	...
244	*512*	*244*	*975*	*25*	...	*864*	*133*	*3*	*411*	*568*	*21*	*22*	*839*	*139*	*4*	*304*	*692*
230	515	255	972	28	...	846	151	3	347	629	24	11	838	151	3	291	706
238	466	296	1,000	...	...	925	75	...	537	450	13	12	823	165	9	273	718
300	562	138	1,000	...	...	800	100	100	...	...	...	67	866	67	...	417	583
297	504	199	985	15	...	942	58	...	629	362	9	47	861	92	8	352	640
517	405	78	1,000	...	...	1,000	...	...	1,000	...	...	544	412	44	...	785	215
403	491	106	963	37	...	957	43	...	1,000	...	...	240	711	49	...	561	439

SUBSIDIARY TABLE III.—Distribution by main age-periods and civil condition of 10,000 of each sex and religion.

Religion and Age.	Males.			Females.		
	Unmarried.	Married.	Widowed.	Unmarried.	Married.	Widowed.
1	2	3	4	5	6	7
All Religions	**4,285**	**4,957**	**758**	**2,839**	**5,399**	**1,762**
0—10	2,435	185	10	2,316	329	8
10—15	703	221	11	382	425	18
15—40	1,050	3,068	277	132	3,791	480
40 and over	97	1,483	460	9	854	1,256
Hindus	**4,181**	**5,036**	**783**	**2,676**	**5,516**	**1,808**
0—10	2,383	209	12	2,248	372	8
10—15	674	244	11	328	468	20
15—40	1,024	3,117	291	98	3,830	495
40 and over	100	1,466	469	7	845	1,285
Jains	**4,913**	**4,213**	**874**	**2,960**	**4,261**	**2,779**
0—10	2,278	31	1	2,178	32	2
10—15	912	109	3	690	234	10
15—40	1,509	2,575	240	82	3,231	993
40 and over	214	1,498	630	10	764	1,774
Animist	**5,087**	**4,520**	**393**	**4,520**	**4,766**	**714**
0—10	3,251	35	2	3,305	29	......
10—15	865	49	1	772	135	2
15—40	929	3,004	139	431	3,669	140
40 and over	42	1,432	251	12	933	572
Musalman	**4,656**	**4,609**	**735**	**3,203**	**5,008**	**1,789**
0—10	2,478	64	2	2,439	132	5
10—15	825	122	5	544	305	8
15—40	1,271	2,755	243	196	3,699	459
40 and over	82	1,668	485	24	872	1,317
Parsi	**5,737**	**3,789**	**474**	**4,502**	**3,965**	**1,533**
0—10	2,462	6	......	1,962	11	2
10—15	1,427	6	......	968	46	......
15—40	1,778	1,503	62	1,338	2,384	227
40 and over	70	2,274	412	234	1,524	1,304
Christian	**3,406**	**5,927**	**667**	**2,416**	**6,204**	**1,380**
0—10	1,951	418	8	1,613	645	149
10—15	586	438	36	322	660	15
15—40	835	3,652	280	466	3,847	227
40 and over	34	1,419	343	15	1,052	989
Aryasamaj	**3,386**	**6,116**	**498**	**2,995**	**5,945**	**1,060**
0—10	1,733	340	26	2,304	645	......
10—15	813	580	......	415	599	......
15—40	840	4,120	315	184	3,871	231
40 and over	......	1,076	157	92	830	829
Brahmo	**2,500**	**5,000**	**2,500**	**5,000**	**5,000**	......
0—10	......	......	......	5,000	......	......
10—15	......	......	......	......	......	......
15—40	2,500	5,000	......	......	5,000	......
40 and over	......	......	2,500	......	......	......
Sikh	**4,068**	**5,762**	**170**	**5,161**	**4,516**	**323**
0—10	1,864	......	......	3,548	......	......
10—15	509	......	......	968	......	......
15—40	1,695	4,745	......	645	3,871	......
40 and over	......	1,017	170	......	645	323
Jew	**4,348**	**5,652**	......	**5,883**	**3,529**	**588**
0—10	2,174	......	......	2,941	......	......
10—15	870	......	......	1,177	......	......
15—40	1,304	3,913	......	1,765	2,941	......
40 and over	......	1,739	......	......	588	588

SUBSIDIARY TABLE IV.—Proportion of the sexes by Civil Condition at certain ages for Religions and Natural Divisions.

Natural Division and Religion.	Number of females per 1,000 males.														
	All ages.			0–10			10–15			15–40			40 and over.		
	Unmarried.	Married.	Widowed.	Unmarried.	Married.	Widowed.	Unmarried.	Married.	Widowed.	Unmarried.	Married.	Widowed.	Unmarried.	Married.	Widowed.
1	2	3	4	5	6	7	8	9	10	11	12	13	14	15	16
Baroda State.															
All Religions	*613*	*1,008*	*2,150*	*879*	*1,653*	*712*	*503*	*1,780*	*1,615*	*116*	*1,143*	*1,605*	*90*	*533*	*2,523*
Hindu	588	1,009	2,121	865	1,659	646	448	1,742	1,636	88	1,129	1,951	58	529	2,523
Jain	594	998	3,137	944	1,044	2,500	746	2,109	3,000	53	1,238	4,091	45	503	2,777
Animist	853	1,013	1,745	977	812	125	858	2,643	1,800	445	777	979	277	626	2,185
Musalman	646	1,019	2,285	924	1,914	2,000	619	2,349	1,288	144	1,264	1,778	279	490	2,551
Parsi	1,041	1,387	4,290	1,057	2,500	...	899	10,500	...	998	2,103	4,905	4,416	888	4,191
Christian	616	909	1,799	718	1,341	16,666	478	1,307	357	484	914	704	385	652	2,507
Aryasamaj	564	553	1,310	757	1,077	...	290	591	...	125	535	416	...	434	3,000
Brahmo	1,000	500	...	...	...	...	...	...	...	...	500	...	...	...	...
Sikh	666	412	1,000	1,000	...	...	1,000	...	...	200	428	...	...	333	1,000
Jew	1,000	461	...	1,000	...	...	1,000	...	...	1,030	555	...	...	250	...
Baroda Division.															
All Religions	*534*	*981*	*1,976*	*826*	*2,371*	*1,413*	*301*	*2,004*	*1,365*	*52*	*1,089*	*1,284*	*72*	*529*	*2,399*
Hindu	508	985	1,950	894	2,589	1,093	263	1,994	1,486	45	1,083	1,263	49	535	2,383
Jain	532	891	2,844	947	714	3,000	514	1,633	333	24	1,025	3,891	41	510	2,521
Animist	853	1,010	1,767	1,006	494	...	609	2,487	2,000	98	1,179	659	130	585	2,599
Musalman	566	943	2,170	886	2,244	1,857	425	2,340	843	67	1,143	1,573	412	437	2,491
Parsi	667	360	...	1,250	...	...	2,000	...	...	267	667	...	...	187	...
Christian	764	949	1,794	748	1,322	16,666	692	1,344	357	946	939	714	250	694	241
Kadi Division.															
All Religions	*591*	*1,026*	*2,257*	*854*	*1,516*	*542*	*504*	*1,497*	*1,562*	*82*	*1,171*	*1,797*	*62*	*498*	*26*
Hindu	585	1,024	2,212	846	1,511	524	474	1,464	1,550	78	1,158	1,713	51	499	2,694
Jain	617	1,060	3,489	939	911	2,000	798	2,143	19,000	63	1,376	4,711	43	505	3,000
Musalman	654	1,051	2,259	934	1,942	1,909	657	2,469	1,136	138	1,303	1,765	246	485	3,415
Parsi	609	714	1,000	889	...	...	333	...	...	454	1,222	...	...	333	...
Christian	393	813	2,700	676	3,250	...	143	1,250	...	97	845	667	1,500	333	5,750
Navsari Division.															
All Religions	*787*	*1,052*	*1,975*	*961*	*1,739*	*2,125*	*703*	*2,017*	*2,308*	*362*	*1,174*	*1,521*	*249*	*646*	*2,174*
Hindu	745	1,050	1,910	959	1,738	2,083	588	1,992	2,396	249	1,145	1,534	139	640	2,072
Jain	553	808	1,863	922	6,000	...	795	2,154	...	57	899	2,058	67	451	1,813
Animist	855	1,016	1,744	965	3,261	...	917	2,833	1,500	502	1,172	1,083	296	643	2,080
Musalman	787	1,145	2,665	944	1,337	...	785	177	4,000	385	1,417	2,338	250	619	2,812
Parsi	1,091	1,510	4,739	1,056	2,500	...	919	19,500	...	1,181	2,280	6,125	5,889	959	4,555
Christian	600	539	...	1,571	...	...	...	...	...	100	500	...	...	666	...
Amreli Division.															
All Religions	*678*	*1,027*	*2,294*	*973*	*1,044*	*2,000*	*690*	*2,242*	*2,412*	*133*	*1,233*	*1,706*	*58*	*573*	*2,541*
Hindu	676	1,014	2,274	977	1,045	1,857	677	2,176	2,375	129	1,207	1,477	58	569	2,530
Jain	634	1,064	2,853	1,010	1,400	...	811	5,750	...	58	1,353	3,393	...	516	3,682
Musalman	702	1,144	2,365	933	939	...	752	2,957	3,000	179	1,483	1,741	117	607	2,618
Parsi	1,000	875	1,000	813	...	...	...	...	...	1,000	1,000	...	...	806	1,000
Christian	...	1,000	...	...	...	...	...	...	...	...	...	...	...	1,000	...
Baroda City.															
All Religions	*510*	*860*	*2,467*	*923*	*1,652*	*2,200*	*375*	*2,527*	*3,571*	*62*	*1,006*	*1,765*	*53*	*401*	*2,847*
Hindu	495	857	2,546	919	1,595	2,000	326	2,499	3,400	38	985	1,879	36	397	2,887
Jain	510	916	2,516	885	3,000	...	518	6,000	...	30	110	2,323	167	487	2,570
Animist	533	714	1,000	1,167	...	...	...	...	...	273	830	375	...	312	2,388
Musalman	588	888	2,220	967	2,360	...	578	2,976	6,000	121	1,119	1,252	157	403	2,760
Parsi	676	830	118	1,151	...	...	641	...	...	579	1,119	1,666	...	671	1,077
Christian	282	613	1,333	510	500	...	184	...	...	197	1,024	545	...	377	2,577

SUBSIDIARY TABLE V.—Distribution by civil condition of 1,000 of each sex,

Caste and Locality.	Distribution of 1,000 males of each age by civil condition.																	
	All Ages.			0—5			5—12			12—20			20—40			40 and over.		
	Unmarried.	Married.	Widowed.	Unmarried.	Married.	Widowed.	Unmarried.	Married.	Widowed.	Unmarried.	Married.	Widowed.	Unmarried.	Married.	Widowed.	Unmarried.	Married.	Widowed.
1	2	3	4	5	6	7	8	9	10	11	12	13	14	15	16	17	18	19
Hindu.																		
Ahir	463	468	69	998	2	...	993	7	...	756	234	10	207	726	67	37	754	209
Bahrot	477	404	119	991	9	...	928	71	1	690	292	18	267	619	114	106	579	315
Bava	615	296	89	999	1	...	992	8	...	827	169	4	425	460	115	490	353	157
Bhangi	407	538	55	975	25	...	847	147	6	561	401	38	83	856	61	18	835	147
Bharvad	373	550	77	973	25	2	771	219	10	475	500	25	98	824	78	27	740	233
Bhavsar	388	527	85	997	3	...	883	114	3	431	540	29	113	816	71	39	711	250
Bhoi	397	531	72	990	10	...	872	125	3	533	434	33	119	798	83	19	791	190
Brahman-Anavala	483	412	105	1,000	...	...	960	38	2	645	352	3	252	665	83	165	519	316
,, Audich	465	450	85	992	7	1	975	24	1	764	227	9	239	693	68	64	911	25
,, Desbastha	459	407	134	1,000	...	...	993	7	...	845	151	4	293	634	73	77	573	350
,, Mewada	489	409	102	990	10	...	968	32	...	740	243	17	337	580	83	76	183	741
,, Modh	472	423	105	984	16	...	956	41	3	694	289	17	266	642	92	114	595	291
,, Nagar	475	432	93	978	13	9	978	22	...	730	256	14	370	672	58	92	645	263
,, Tapodhan	455	464	81	975	19	6	920	80	...	618	333	49	212	706	82	41	739	220
Chamar	438	515	47	979	20	1	897	100	3	518	448	34	99	853	48	24	830	146
Darji	429	486	85	988	11	1	895	97	8	567	399	34	126	800	74	42	689	269
Dhed	421	522	57	983	15	2	892	103	5	546	431	23	108	838	54	37	786	177
Garoda	472	474	54	974	26	...	872	126	2	556	420	24	122	819	59	61	753	186
Ghanchi	408	516	76	984	16	...	886	114	...	450	527	23	107	820	73	29	720	251
Gola (Rice-pounders)	296	624	80	930	70	...	479	516	5	227	712	61	56	840	104	33	747	220
Gosain	491	426	83	996	4	...	966	34	...	717	258	25	255	664	81	223	580	197
Hajam	422	492	86	983	14	3	862	130	8	574	382	44	123	789	88	21	746	233
Kachhia	359	515	126	975	23	2	822	176	2	377	555	68	115	754	131	40	662	298
Kanbi-Anjana	409	497	94	963	33	4	831	155	14	521	441	38	162	738	100	43	697	260
,, Kadwa	190	700	110	647	336	17	343	626	31	200	756	44	51	845	104	17	685	298
,, Karadia	500	458	42	1,000	...	...	1,000	...	...	738	262	...	111	849	40	24	811	165
,, Lewa	422	476	102	979	20·5	·5	846	151	3	566	408	26	193	734	73	70	647	283
Koli	450	476	74	986	13	1	907	89	4	696	295	9	130	790	80	32	732	236
Kumbhar	400	522	78	968	30	2	834	157	9	489	460	51	89	826	85	24	759	217
Luhana	470	462	68	988	10	2	961	28	11	691	295	14	185	759	56	29	761	210
Luhar	426	494	180	986	14	...	875	124	1	559	404	37	131	779	90	36	722	242
Machhi	416	511	73	999	1	...	938	60	2	552	432	16	82	855	63	44	726	230
Maratha	441	493	66	995	5	...	978	21	1	803	184	13	190	746	64	43	771	186
Mochi	419	501	80	990	7	3	898	97	5	490	460	50	140	787	73	26	760	214
Rabari	370	544	86	949	49	2	772	220	8	468	492	40	129	780	91	24	755	221
Rajput	475	443	82	989	11	...	956	42	2	717	262	21	251	671	78	59	918	23
Ravalia	399	532	69	969	30	1	859	130	11	505	432	63	94	833	73	31	799	170
Sathawara	411	513	76	974	26	...	859	132	9	547	421	32	104	812	84	11	773	216
Shenva	480	468	52	989	10	1	926	72	2	701	286	13	111	831	58	17	813	170
Soni...	447	457	96	985	14	1	953	46	1	605	352	43	153	760	87	63	673	264
Sutar	419	510	71	985	15	...	915	83	2	549	423	28	128	793	79	24	782	194
Talavia	451	448	101	994	6	...	928	72	...	535	422	43	65	817	118	80	600	320
Targala	420	423	157	994	6	...	977	23	...	572	299	129	84	755	161	46	598	356
Vagher	515	424	61	994	6	...	984	13	3	895	102	3	258	693	49	30	772	198
Vaghari	442	507	51	984·5	15·2	·3	976	22	2	529	453	18	109	840	51	27	805	168
Vania Disaval	442	435	123	986	14	...	962	38	...	709	272	19	268	635	97	100	610	290
,, Lad	44	839	117	996	4	...	954	44	2	534	440	26	213	652	135	115	607	278
,, Shrimali	425	458	117	972	28	...	953	47	...	626	337	37	200	674	126	89	643	268
Jain.																		
Vania Shrimali	480	424	96	996	4	...	971	28	1	701	292	7	185	733	82	60	621	319
Animistic.																		
Bhil	485	480	35	998	2	...	985	14	1	818	166	16	61	909	30	26	847	127
Chodhra	529	423	48	999	1	...	991	9	...	905	89	6	166	787	47	16	803	181
Dhanka	458	506	36	989	11	...	973	24	3	671	323	6	49	923	28	10	852	138
Dhodia	554	394	52	1,000	...	...	989	11	...	880	119	1	160	768	72	26	791	183
Gamit	524	430	46	996	4	...	980	19	1	884	108	8	144	806	50	17	819	164
Nayakda	507	463	30	986	14	...	981	19	...	782	214	4	116	867	17	21	852	127
Musalman.																		
Fakir	476	438	86	981	19	...	889	111	...	691	298	11	262	652	86	175	600	225
Ghanchi	408	518	74	945	55	...	888	112	...	465	510	25	198	733	69	87	705	208
Malek	485	438	77	987	13	...	947	53	...	777	207	16	275	658	67	10	745	245
Memon	465	462	73	997	3	...	978	17	5	670	317	13	103	826	71	26	739	235
Molesalam	420	477	103	974	26	...	882	118	...	640	348	12	226	685	89	41	678	281
Momna	421	494	85	986	14	...	865	128	7	544	436	20	99	821	80	41	657	302
Pathan	465	449	86	990	9	1	955	44	1	810	183	7	273	650	77	18	740	242
Pinjara	415	483	102	998	2	...	821	170	9	539	441	20	126	791	83	35	633	332
Saiyad	484	436	80	986	14	...	970	30	...	809	181	10	254	670	76	65	718	217
Shaikh	453	473	74	989	11	...	975	23	2	785	204	11	305	729	66	20	767	213
Vohora	457	468	75	988	12	...	945	53	2	659	330	11	122	806	72	29	755	216
Parsi.																		
Parsi	574	378	48	1,000	...	...	997	3	...	971	29	...	352	622	26	13	835	152
Christian.																		
Native	341	593	66	961	37	2	629	363	8	422	535	43	102	831	67	18	802	180

AT CERTAIN AGES FOR SELECTED CASTES.

Distribution of 1,000 females of each age by civil condition.																	
All ages.			0—5			5—12			12—20			20—40			40 and over.		
Unmarried.	Married.	Widowed.	Unmarried.	Married.	Widowed.	Unmarried.	Married.	Widowed.	Unmarried.	Married.	Widowed.	Unmarried.	Married.	Widowed.	Unmarried.	Married.	Widowed.
20	21	22	23	24	25	26	27	28	29	30	31	32	33	34	35	36	37
342	504	154	998	2	...	964	36	...	381	619	...	2	935	63	7	404	589
246	471	283	943	54	3	811	175	14	175	743	82	5	724	271	1	358	641
296	610	94	989	11	...	962	38	...	598	383	19	75	843	82	109	693	198
290	553	157	975	25	...	661	334	5	160	803	37	8	849	143	5	423	572
290	572	138	939	61	...	710	285	5	198	780	22	5	921	74	1	464	535
254	512	234	982	18	...	812	182	6	128	821	51	4	780	216	...	351	649
276	536	188	981	19		732	268	...	104	876	20	12	867	121	5	344	651
291	474	235	997	3	...	891	105	4	107	877	16	2	753	145	8	382	610
247	448	305	989	10	1	890	105	5	128	824	48	4	746	250	3	276	721
264	464	272	997	3	...	942	50	8	90	830	80	11	734	255	...	389	611
224	430	346	986	14	...	812	172	16	203	677	120	...	651	349	...	135	765
237	446	317	990	6	4	831	156	13	120	751	129	5	683	312	4	283	713
228	443	329	958	37	5	836	153	11	99	744	157	12	682	306	2	274	724
253	511	236	986	14	...	721	271	8	127	852	21	3	799	198	...	308	692
309	538	153	979	20	1	793	200	7	215	770	15	7	889	104	1	472	527
270	539	191	967	30	3	761	230	9	143	824	33	2	854	144	3	394	603
281	559	160	961	38	1	654	331	15	176	804	20	14	880	106	4	554·6	445
311	520	169	967	33	...	769	228	3	173	794	33	...	874	126	...	362	638
270	533	197	994	5	1	770	226	4	129	813	58	2	855	143	2	368	630
191	607	202	901	99	...	280	702	18	103	831	66	...	820	180	...	376	624
263	520	217	995	5	...	855	142	3	183	726	91	4	866	130	16	375	609
248	556	196	970	29	1	723	266	11	103	864	33	7	820	173	1	399	600
236	571	193	980	20	...	681	315	4	187	789	24	7	880	113	3	449	548
259	512	229	956	40	4	749	244	7	189	762	49	4	809	187	11	311	678
78	720	202	366	625	9	84	894	22	31	922	47	2	823	175	·3	291	708·7
357	483	160	1,000	...	...	952	48	...	400	592	8	...	917	83	...	401	599
263	541	196	976·4	23	·6	790	201	9	146	825	29	5	846	149	2	422	576
287	559	154	959	39	2	800	194	6	254	729	17	13	884	103	·3	518	481·7
275	548	177	967	32	1	722	269	9	146	808	46	25	918	57	10	342	648
340	473	187	996	3	1	950	46	4	221	761	18	5	826	169	...	418	582
274	543	183	959	40	1	751	254	15	157	783	60	24	861	115	12	368	620
300	550	150	985	12	3	766	226	8	100	844	56	9	887	94	3	453	545
265	439	296	994	6	...	894	102	4	118	836	46	12	742	246	17	183	800
284	570	146	980	20	...	751	237	12	145	832	23	3	927	70	...	434	566
291	575	134	942	56	2	739	254	7	223	757	20	8	918	74	3	500	497
264	491	245	975	24	1	828	164	8	230	730	40	9	784	207	3	328	669
299	564	137	966	33	1	744	250	6	190	786	24	14	911	75	2	441	557
257	526	217	965	35	...	699	284	17	75	895	30	3	821	176	...	274	726
343	507	151	978	15	7	893	97	10	257	715	28	2	897	101	...	415	585
269	492	239	984	16	...	837	156	7	145	795	60	2	791	207	...	353	647
261	534	205	984	15	1	754	242	4	148	814	38	5	842	153	1	358	641
332	533	135	987	13	...	887	111	2	804	181	15	16	868	116	14	474	512
207	596	197	940	60	...	910	90	...	260	739	1	4	829	167	...	546	454
330	540	130	991	9	...	970	23	7	512	480	8	7	916	77	...	604	396
343	542	115	985	15	...	794	199	7	251	691	58	10	902	88	3	540	457
243	432	325	986	11	3	921	68	11	114	838	48	6	665	329	3	272	725
245	487	268	1,000	...	...	925	67	8	131	814	55	8	783	259	4	402	594
317	445	238	977	23	...	924	66	10	259	693	48	4	744	252	2	391	607
297	436	267	988	11	1	904	94	2	256	734	10	8	674	318	4	348	643
425	525	50	1,000	...	...	972	27	1	645	352	3	23	957	20	5	706	289
490	437	73	994	6	...	991	9	...	741	256	3	56	899	45	10	620	370
396	534	70	998	2	...	991	8	1	186	807	7	5	970	25	1	604	395
493	427	80	998	2	...	983	17	...	763	233	4	53	901	46	18	585	397
453	470	77	1,000	...	...	986	14	...	672	322	6	43	909	48	7	657	336
449	489	62	999	1	...	982	18	...	547	449	4	22	943	35	17	655	328
324	514	162	977	23	...	889	108	3	342	638	20	16	880	104	...	451	549
285	530	185	953	44	3	764	236	...	286	692	22	10	856	134		428	572
302	484	214	992	6	2	921	77	2	282	691	27	10	822	168	2	365	633
380	491	129	993	6	1	970	28	2	488	499	13	10	886	104	...	607	393
265	526	209	977	21	2	802	198	...	109	843	48	19	811	170	7	407	586
285	564	151	949	49	2	762	223	15	220	753	27	9	894	97	5	448	552
328	464	208	994	6	...	918	80	2	407	575	18	45	804	151	5	351	644
303	529	168	995	5	...	757	230	13	213	764	23	8	880	117	...	443	557
323	474	203	986	14	...	950	50	...	407	562	31	17	805	178	14	396	590
302	508	190	988	12	...	990	10	...	286	690	24	16	856	128	9	290	701
326	528	146	988	12	...	868	130	2	355	628	17	27	876	97	5	518	477
450	397	153	1,000	...	...	989	9	2	853	143	4	202	725	73	76	498	426
236	623	141	854	136	10	434	461	105	292	697	11	32	901	67	5	503	492

Chapter VIII.

EDUCATION.

The meaning of the statistics.

394. In 1881 and 1891, the population was divided in respect of education into three categories—Learning, Literate and Illiterate. It was found, however, that the return of the Learning was vitiated by the omission, at the one end of children who had not long been at school, who were entered as "Illiterate," and at the other, of the more advanced students who were classed as "Literate." There were thus great discrepancies between the Census return of the number of "Learning" or children under instruction and the corresponding statistics of the Education Department. It was therefore decided in 1901 to confine the entry in the enumeration schedules to the two main categories of "Literate" and "Illiterate." The same system has been maintained on the present occasion. The instructions to the enumerators have been slightly altered in the hope of making them clear, but their purport is the same: persons who could "both read and write any language" were to be entered as 'Literate.' In 1901, no general indication was given as to the standard to be taken in applying the rule. On the present occasion, it was laid down in the instructions for the superior Census staff that a person should be regarded as literate if he could write a letter to a friend and read the answer to it, but not otherwise. These more precise instructions have caused some slight variations in the figures as compared with 1901, when those who had studied the first two Vernacular books only and could read or copy from a printed book, were also entered as Literate. While there is a general increase in the total number of literates in all ages above 10, there is actually a decrease from 19 literates in 1901 to 17 in 1911 per mille in the age period 0-10, which can only be attributed to the stricter definition adopted on this occasion. But the number thus excluded from literates being so small and confined only to the first age-period, the comparability of the statistics of the two Censuses is not materially affected.

Literacy in mother-tongue and English only recorded.

395. In 1901 a record was made of the Vernacular languages or scripts in which each person was literate. On the present occasion, the collection of this information was optional, and the Government of His Highness the Maharaja Gaekwad decided that it need not be made. As in 1901, however, record was made of those who were literate in English in addition to their mother tongue.

Reference to statistics.

396. The information thus recorded has been embodied in Imperial Table VIII which shows the number of persons who are literate or illiterate according to age and religion; and in Imperial Table IX, which shows them according to their caste. The number of literate persons who know English is shown in both the tables. Proportional figures illustrating the more important features of the return are, as usual, embodied in Subsidiary Tables which will be found at the end of the Chapter, *viz*:—

Subsidiary Table I.—Education by age, sex and religion.
Subsidiary Table II.—Education by age, sex and locality.
Subsidiary Table III.—Education by religion, sex and locality.
Subsidiary Table IV.—English education by age, sex and locality.
Subsidiary Table V.—Progress of education since 1881.
Subsidiary Table VI.—Education by caste.
Subsidiary Table VII.—Number of institutions and pupils according to the returns of the Education Department.
Subsidiary Table VIII.—Main results of University examinations.
Subsidiary Table IX.—Number and circulation of news-papers, etc.
Subsidiary Table X.—Number of books published in each language.

GENERAL REVIEW.

Extent of literacy.

397. In the total population of the Baroda State, only 10 persons out of a hundred are literate in the limited sense in which this term was used at the Census. Taking the sexes separately, one male in every 6 can read and write and one female in every 50. There would thus appear to be 8 literate males to 1 literate female, but it is possible that there has been some understatement in respect of the latter sex, as amongst some classes of the population, there is a prejudice against admitting that women are literate. Of the total number of literate males, 68 per cent. are over 20 years of age and 4 per cent. are under 10. The remaining 28 per cent. are distributed between the age-periods 10-15 and 15-20. In the case of females, only 43 per cent. of the literate population are over 20, 45 per cent. are between 10 and 20, and 12 per cent. are under 10. The larger proportion of literate females at the lower ages indicates that at the present time the progress of education amongst them is more rapid than amongst males.

Age.	Total Population.		Number of Literates.	
	Male.	Female.	Male.	Female.
0—10	277,732	259,217	6,771	2,477
10—15	98,702	80,601	27,175	5,841
15—20	93,573	79,944	24,189	3,230
20 and over ...	585,928	557,101	126,748	8,516
Total ...	1,055,935	976,863	184,883	20,064

Distribution by locality.

398. The most favoured part of the State from point of view of education is naturally the capital City of Baroda. Here 2 males in every 5 are literate. The Baroda District, which on account of its forward population of Brahmans, Vanias and Lewa Kanbis, was the earliest among the districts to have education facilities, and the Amreli District which was the first to have the boon of compulsory education, come next to Baroda City with 1 male who is literate in every 5.

Diagram showing the number of persons per 1,000 in each Natural Division, who are literate.

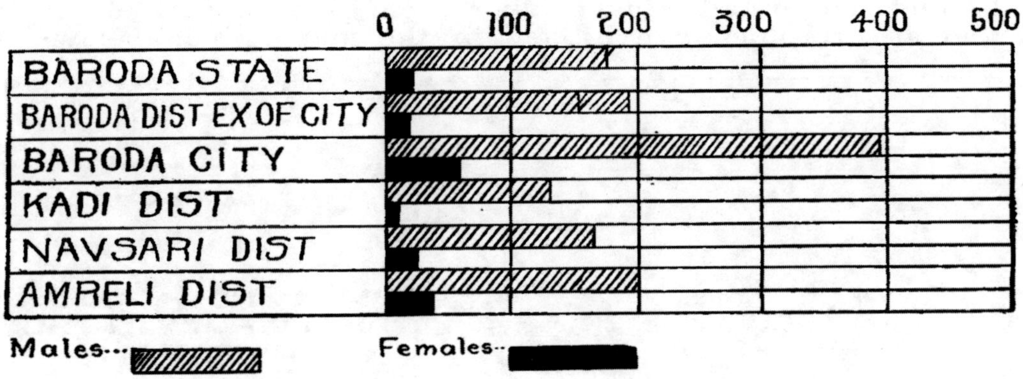

Then follows Navsari District, which though having the Animists as one-fourth of its population, has on an average 1 literate male in every 6, owing to its adventurous Parsis, Vohoras and Anavalas. Kadi having a large Thakarda, Koli and Anjana Kanbi population stands last in the diffusion of the rudiments of learning, having only 1 literate male in every 8. The variations in the proportions of educated females, though on a far lower plane, follow generally those noted above. In the City of Baroda, there is one educated female in every 14. Then comes Amreli with 1 in 28. Then follow Navsari and Baroda Districts with 1 in 40 and 54 respectively. Kadi stands last with only 1 educated female in every 90. The degree of literacy enjoyed by each district (both sexes combined) is shown in the following map :—

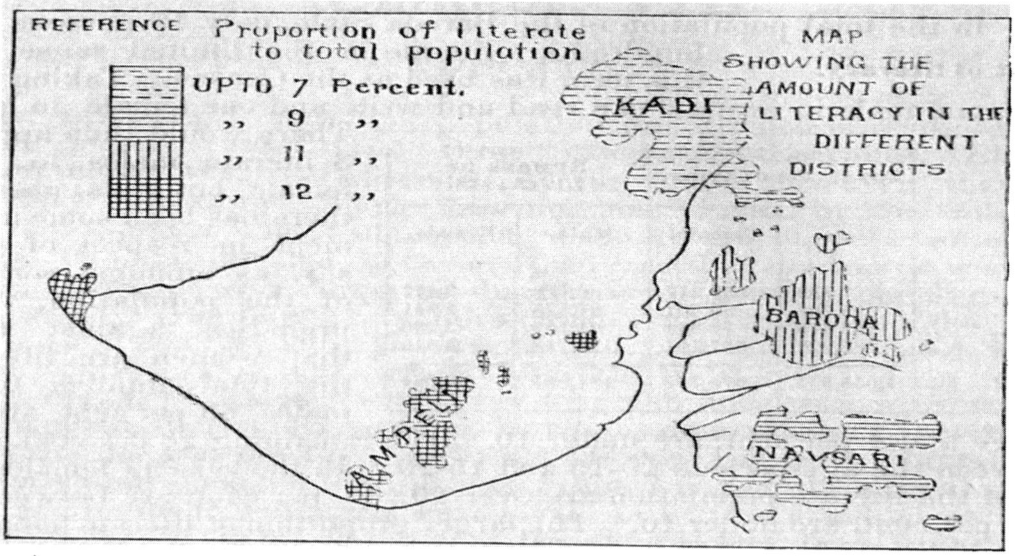

399. In this connection, it should be remembered that the talukas comprised in each district often show very uneven results. For instance, Petlad and Sinore Talukas in the Baroda District have the highest amount of literacy (1 literate person in 6), while Vaghodia and Tilakwada have the least, *viz.* 1 in 16. Visnagar Taluka stands first in literacy (1 in 11) in the Kadi District, while Harij stands last (1 in 28). Navsari Taluka claims the highest number of literates (1 in 5) in the Navsari District, while Songhad (1 in 44), Vyara (1 in 36), Umarpada (1 in 90), and Vakal (1 in 45) show very poor results in education. Even this amount of literacy is mainly due to Government servants and contractors in these backward forest talukas. In the Amreli District, Amreli is the most educated taluka having 1 literate person in every 6, while Khambha and Kodinar are the most backward, having only 1 in every 16. The statistics of education for all talukas have been given separately in Provincial Table II, and are graphically exhibited in the maps given below :—

Education in the Talukas.

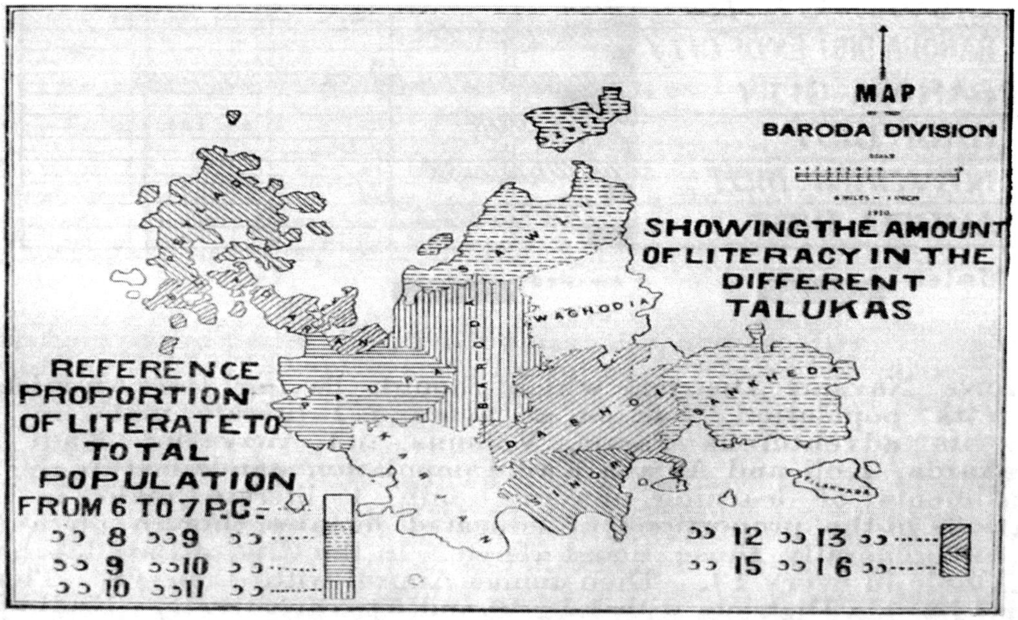

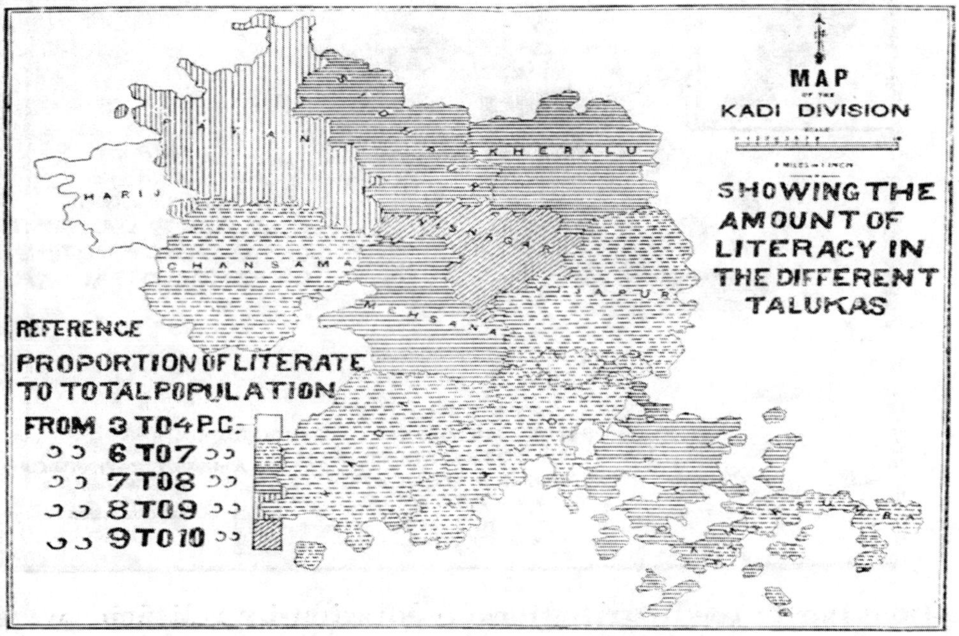
MAP
OF THE
KADI DIVISION
SHOWING THE AMOUNT OF LITERACY IN THE DIFFERENT TALUKAS
HARIJ
CHANSAMA
KHERALU
MEHSANA
REFERENCE
PROPORTION OF LITERATE TO TOTAL POPULATION
FROM 3 TO 4 P.C.
" 6 TO 7 "
" 7 TO 8 "
" 8 TO 9 "
" 9 TO 10 "

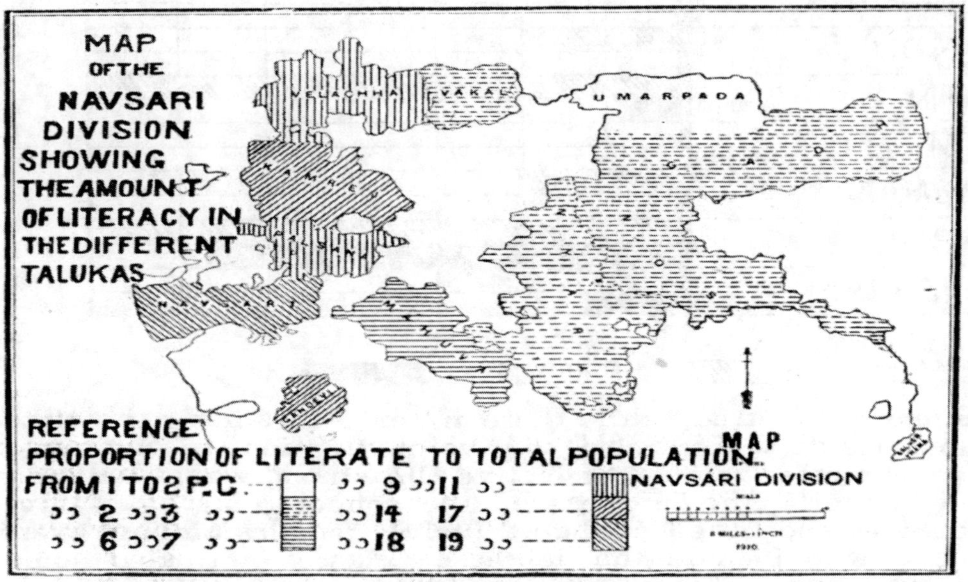
MAP OF THE NAVSARI DIVISION SHOWING THE AMOUNT OF LITERACY IN THE DIFFERENT TALUKAS
VELACHHA
VAKAL
UMARPADA
NAVSARI
REFERENCE
PROPORTION OF LITERATE TO TOTAL POPULATION.
FROM 1 TO 2 P.C.
" 2 " 3 "
" 6 " 7 "
" 9 " 11 "
" 14 17 "
" 18 19 "
MAP
NAVSÁRI DIVISION

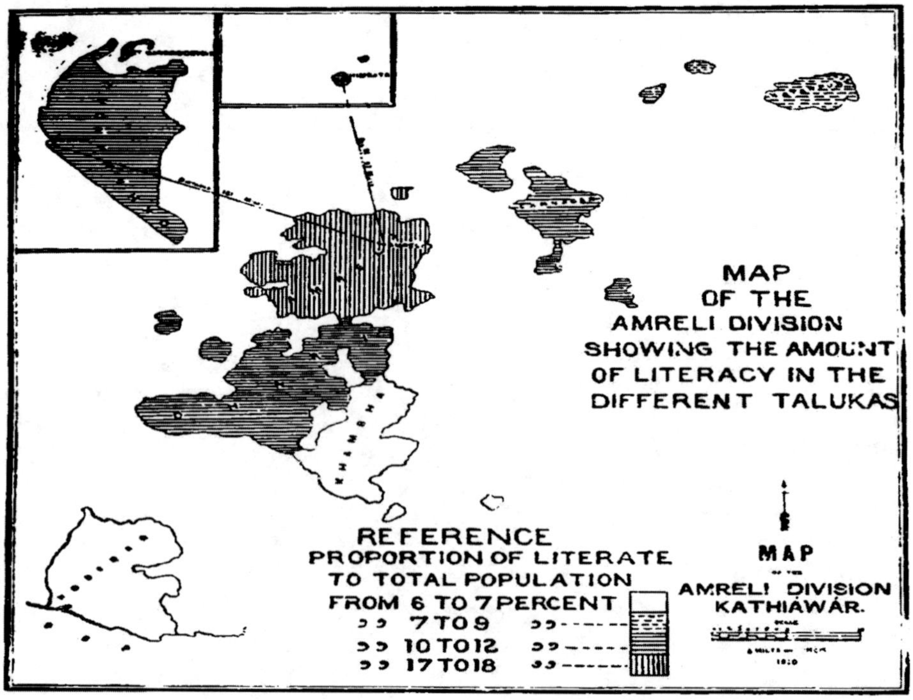

Education by religion.

400. Looking to the distribution of education by religion, we find that the greatest amount of literacy is met with among the Parsis. In every hundred males 69 are literate and in every 100 females 57 are literate. Then follow Jains, who are mainly Vanias, with 69 males and 8 females in every 100 of each sex. Christians have 22 males and 14 females who claim to be literate in every 100 of each sex. A large portion of the literate amongst Christians are foreigners. The native converts are mostly illiterate. Separating the two, we find that among foreign Christians there are 87 literates in every hundred, while there are only 16 among the Native Christians. The Missionaries do their utmost to give instructions to their converts and the proportion of literates among the Native Christians, would have been higher but for the new converts who have passed the school-going age. Musalmans have 21 literate males and little less than 2 literate females among every 100 of each sex. Hindus, who include the depressed classes and also some of the early tribes who have returned themselves as Hindus, have only 17 literate males and 2 literate females in every 100 of each sex. The Animists, as might be expected, come last with only 1 literate male in 100. They have practically no literate females, there being only 1 in 681.

Diagram showing the number of persons per 1,000 in each religion who are literate.

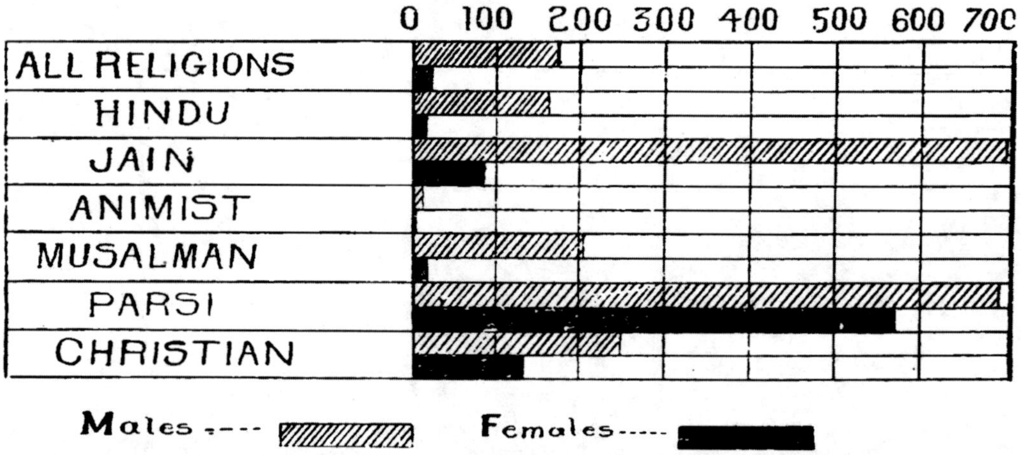

Education by caste: males.

401. One of the most interesting features in connection with the subject of education is the varying extent to which it is diffused amongst the different castes. Subsidiary Table VI gives the leading castes and races of this State, and their number of literates per mille of their population by sexes. Taking first the figures of males, we find that Deshastha, Koknastha and Shenavi Brahmans, Prabhus, and Kapol, Modh, Shrimali and Oswal Vanias stand at the top with 700 or more literate males in 1,000 of their population. Then follow, Anavala, Khedaval, Vadnagara Nagar, Saraswat Brahmans, Brahma-Kshatris, Kayasthas, Disaval, Lad, Khadayata and Nagar Vanias and Parsis with 6 to 7 hundred literates per mille. Among the artizan castes, Bhavsars, Kansaras and Sonis have more than 500 literate males in 1,000 of their population. After them come Lewa Kanbis, Marathas, Sutars, Saiyads, Vohoras, Memons, Khojas, Ghanchis, Khatris and Kachhias with from 300 to 400 literates. Koli, Rabari, Ravalia, Vaghari, Dhed, Bhangi and other low and depressed classes have less than 100 literate males; while Bhil, Chodhra, Gamit, Dubla and other early tribes are the most backward in education, having only from 8 to 20 literate males in 1,000 of their population.

Education by caste: females.

402. Turning next to the figures for females, we find that Parsis stand at the top in female education, having no less than 569 literate females in every 1,000. Then come Shenavis with 478, Prabhus with 277, Nagars with 221, Saraswats with 212, Kayasthas with 210, Modh Vanias with 148, Kapol Vanias with 142, Deshastha Brahmans with 129, Koknastha Brahmans with 130, Oswal Vanias with 117 and Native Christians with 111 literate females in every 1,000 of their community. All the other castes, both high or low, are very backward in female education, having only from 10 to 80 literate females in 1,000. Only 75 Khoja, 61 Maratha, 24 Lewa Kanbi, 10 Rajput, 29 Saiyad, 34 Vohora, 4 Dhed and 2 Bhangi females are literate in 1,000 of their castes. There are practically no literate females among the Animists.

English Education.

District.	No. of literate in English per 10,000.	
	Males.	Females.
State	**90**	**5**
Baroda	64	4
Baroda City	710	57
Kadi	36	·3
Navsari	75	3
Amreli	74	2

403. In the State as a whole, there are 90 persons per 10,000 who stated that they knew English and only 5 females. The ratio is naturally the highest in the City of Baroda (710 males and 57 females per 10,000), not only on account of the larger proportion of English people resident there, but also because it is the centre of higher education and being the capital city, it is there that the educated classes find employment in Government offices. Next to the City comes the Navsari District with 75 males and 3 females literate in English per 10,000, and then stand in order Amreli, Baroda and Kadi Districts. Except in the City of Baroda, where there are some English and Indian ladies literate in English, the proportion of females, who are acquainted with English, is everywhere so small that it may practically be said to be non-existing.

English education by caste.

404. The advantage of English education is taken to the greatest extent by Nagar, Saraswat, Deshastha, Koknastha and Shenavi Brahmans, Prabhus, Brahma-Kshatris, Kayasthas and Parsis, who have from 1,000 to 3,000 of their males literate in English in every 10,000. Anavala and Khedaval Brahmans, Kapol, Lad, Modh, Nagar and Shrimali Vanias and Marathas and Native Christians follow the above castes having from 300 to 500 males literate in English in 10,000 of their population. The rest of the castes are very backward in English education. It is remarkable that the Vania and other trading castes, in spite of their high proportion of persons who are able to read and write some vernacular language, have a low proportion of persons who are literate in English. Parsis and Shenavis, Nagars and Prabhus are the only

communities which give a little English education to their females. English education among females may be said to be non-existing among the other castes, not having even 50 females in 10,000 of the population who know the language.

Comparison with previous Censuses.

405. For the reasons given in paragraph 394 above, it is difficult to institute an effective comparison with the results of the Censuses taken prior to 1901. Some of the persons who would have been shown as learning under the old rule, have been in 1901 and in the present Census classed as literate, while others have been relegated to the category of the illiterate. How many of the learning have been treated as literate and how many as illiterate, it is impossible to say, but it is clear that a great many, who would have been entered as learning under the old rule have been shown as illiterate under the new one. The total number of literate males under 15 years of age was only 29,501 in 1901 and 33,946 in 1911, which is less by 38 and 19 per cent., respectively than the corresponding number returned as learning and literate (combined) in 1891. The best way of instituting comparison appears to be that suggested by the Census Commissioner, *viz.*, to exclude from the comparison persons under 15 years of age and to consider only persons over 15 years of age and to assume that all persons over that age, who were classed as "Learning" in 1881 and 1891 would have been entered as literate, had the present rule been in force at those Censuses. Moreover, the progress in the general spread of education can best be gauged by comparing the proportion of persons of each sex who are literate in the age group 15-20. Comparative figures for the literate over 15 years of age, based on this assumption, will be found in Subsidiary Table V.

406. So far as can be gathered from this comparison, the number of literate males has increased from 87 in 1881 to 109 in 1891 and from 162 in 1901 to 175 in 1911 per 1,000 of the population. The increase in the last decade amounts to 8 per cent. The greatest progress has taken place in the Amreli district where the number of males who can read and write is now greater by 31 per cent. than what it was ten years previously. In the district of Kadi also there has been good progress, the increase being from 113 to 132 per mille, that is about 17 per cent. Baroda City shows an increase of about 7 per cent. in the number of its literate males; but this is 1 per cent. less than for the State as a whole. It is rather disappointing that Baroda and Navsari Districts, instead of showing a good increase as might have been expected, are stationary with regard to the literacy of the male population.

District.	No. of literate males per 1,000 of the male population.			
	1911.	1901.	1891.	1881.
State	**175**	**162**	**109**	**87**
Baroda	195	197	143	112
Baroda City	392	366	282	248
Kadi	132	113	76	59
Navsari	166	168	121	103
Amreli	200	153	122	111

407. Female education has made great strides. In the State as a whole, the number of literate females per mille has risen from 1·4 in 1881 to 4 in 1891 and from 7 in 1901 to 21 in 1911. The increase in the past decade amounts to about 343 per cent. The greatest advance has taken place during the decade in Amreli, where the number is six times as much as it was only 10 years ago. The improvement in the Kadi District is also very nearly the same. In the Baroda District and the Baroda City, the number of

District.	No. of literate females per 1,000 of the female population.			
	1911	1901	1891	1881
State	**21**	**7**	**4**	**1·4**
Baroda	18	6	5	1·4
Baroda City	71	24	18	5
Kadi	11	2	2	1
Navsari	25	20	10	4
Amreli	36	6	3·5	1

literate females has trebled during the decade. Navsari District stands last with an increase of 25 per cent. only in the diffusion of education amongst its females.

408. English education, though yet not widespread, has also made great progress. The number of males knowing English increased from 18 in 1891 to 53 in 1901, and 90 in the present Census per 10,000 of the population. Similarly English education among females increased from 1 in 1891 to 2 in 1901 and 5 in the present Census per 10,000 of the female sex.

Progress in English education.

District.	No. of males literate in English per 10,000 of the population.		
	1911	1901	1891
State ...	**90**	**53**	**18**
Baroda ...	64	38	6
Baroda City	710	441	188
Kadi ...	36	18	6
Navsari ...	75	61	16
Amreli ...	74	31	13

409. The progress made by the Baroda State may not seem very great, but the results are highly satisfactory when compared with India as a whole, and the more important of its provinces and States. Cochin and Travancore were the only States which took rank above it in 1901; all the rest of the Native States and British Provinces were behind it. So far as statistics available up to the date of going to press indicate, not only is the same high position maintained even now, but the actual increase in the amount of literacy in the decade is higher than elsewhere.

Comparison with other Provinces.

Province.	Number per 1,000 who are literate.			
	1911.		1901.	
	Males.	Females.	Males.	Females.
Baroda ...	**175**	**21**	**163**	**8**
Bengal ...	113	8	104	5
Punjab ...	63	6	64	3
Mysore ...	112	13	93	8
Travancore ...	248	50	215	31

Progress of education in Baroda.

410. The high level which Baroda has attained in the education of its people is the result of the care bestowed during the last thirty years. Prior to the accession of the present Maharaja to the *gadi* in 1875, the rulers of Baroda paid practically no attention to the education of their subjects. In 1871, there were only one English and four primary schools in the whole State and the total expenditure on education was only Rs. 13,000 or less than one-hundredth of what it is now. The knowledge of reading and writing was confined to a few persons of those castes whose traditional occupations as priests, traders or government servants necessitated it and who acquired it in private schools maintained by them. The great mass of the people were sunk in the deepest ignorance with few thoughts beyond the provision for themselves and their families of the bare necessities of life. The question of education was taken up in right earnest in 1881, when His Highness the Maharaja Sayajirao Gaekwad assumed the powers of the State. A regular Education Department was created, and schools, both primary and secondary, were opened in all the districts of the State. Their number increased from year to year and there are now in the whole State 2,972 primary schools and 43 secondary schools, including 5 High Schools (of which one is for females), a College which teaches upto the highest examinations of the University of Bombay in Arts and Sciences and a Training College for male teachers and another one for female teachers. In addition to these, there are some special institutions like the *Kala Bhavan* (School of Arts and Industries),

Music schools, Orphanages, Sanskrit schools and Night schools. The children of the depressed castes, in addition to having the ordinary schools open to them, have also special schools established for them. Boarding schools have been opened for them, as also for the children of the aboriginal tribes, in which children of these backward classes are housed, fed and educated. The Maharaja has most at heart the education of his people, and in no department of the administration is the far-sighted liberality of His Highness more conspicuous than in education and in none are the results more real and tangible.

Compulsory education.

411. Baroda is the only State in the whole of India, in which primary education is both compulsory and free. In January 1893, immediately on his return from Europe, His Highness the Maharaja Gaekwad decided to take the bold step of introducing compulsory education in one part of his State, as an experimental measure and selected Amreli Taluka in the Amreli District, for the purpose. The rules framed were that all boys between the ages of 7 and 12 and all girls between the ages of 7 and 10 should attend schools. The guardian of a child of this age absenting for 10 consecutive days or for 15 days in any month, was made liable to a small fine. On these lines, schools were opened in ten villages in November 1893, in ten more villages in May 1895, in ten other villages in December 1897 and in twenty more villages in November 1899. In February 1901 and in July 1904, two more villages were provided with such schools bringing the total to 52 villages. This experiment having proved successful, the idea of extending compulsory education to all the parts of the State, which had for a long time engaged the attention of His Highness, at last took a definite shape and the Amreli rules were embodied in law in 1906. The rules were subsequently revised and the maximum age for girls was raised to 11. Exemption from compulsory attendance is granted to children under certain specified conditions, such as, physical or mental infirmity. The highest standard for study under the compulsory law is the fourth and the parents and guardians of children of the compulsory age are liable to fine in case they fail to send such children to school continuously for six days. In March 1907, as a boon to the public at the time of the celebration of the Silver Jubilee of his reign, His Highness was pleased to make education absolutely free in all the Vernacular schools. A Commission appointed in 1909 to suggest means for improvement and further development of education in the State has led to reforms which are sure to have a far-reaching effect in the further spread of education in the State.

Working of the Compulsory Education Act.

412. The Compulsory Education Act was less than four years in force before the present Census and it is too premature to judge of its success from the Census results of literacy. Most of the children who are now in schools under the law and learning in the first and second standards, are returned as illiterate, according to the Census definition, owing to their inability to read and write a letter, though they could read or copy from their books. The number of such children on the school registers was on the 10th March 1911 147,739 in the whole State. These will no doubt soon come within the definition of Census literacy, and add to the present percentage of literates. Apart from this there can be no doubt that the compulsory law is successfully worked and the proof of this is furnished by a comparison of the number of children at school in March 1911, and of those of the school-going age existing on the Census day. From the annual age-periods we find that in the whole State there were 82,129 girls of the ages from 7 to 11 and 131,501 boys of the ages from 7 to 12. Both of these together form 10·5 per cent. of the total population of the State. From the figures supplied by the Education Department, it appears that there were on the Census day 164,211 pupils of the compulsory ages in the schools. This shows that 49,419 students, who ought to be in schools were not there. But this is accounted for by the fact that out of its 3,096 populated villages, the State has provided only 2,015 with schools. There are about a thousand small villages in which schools yet remain to be provided, and so long as that is not done, enforcement of the compulsory rules is not possible. This, however,

is being done gradually. With regard to some very small villages, there is the difficulty of securing at least 16 children, which is the minimum necessary for opening a school, and with regard to others in jungle and mountainous tracts, there is also the further difficulty of securing teachers. The department of education is vigorously combating against these and other difficulties and it is expected that they will soon be removed and the full operation of the compulsory law will be assured.

413. There is a great correspondence between the percentage of literacy and the statistics of persons under instruction compiled from the school returns. An abstract of the departmental returns will be found in Subsidiary Table VII and the totals for the State are given in the margin. From this it will appear that along with the increase in the number of institutions, the number of scholars has increased and so has also the percentage of literates from Census to Census as mentioned in paras. **406 to 408.**

Class of Institution.	Number of Institutions.			Number of Scholars.		
	1911	1901	1891	1911	1901	1891
English—						
College	1	1	1	329	216	113
High Schools	3	3	2	1,532	886	897
Anglo-Vernacular Schools	25	14	11	3,227	1,401	708
Grant-in-aid Schools	12	4	4	1,583	639	373
Vernacular—						
Vernacular Schools of all grades, Govt.	2,938	1,119	377	173,883	76,986	43,357
Vernacular Schools of all grades, private and aided	34	61	123	2,540	5,524	7,501
General—						
Training and other special schools ...	13	9	3	2,148	817	121

414. The expenditure on education in the State is noted in the margin. It will be noticed that it has gone on increasing from decade to decade and is now 13 times as much more as it was thirty years ago. Roughly speaking it may be said that the State spends more than one-fourteenth part of its gross revenue on education.

Expenditure on education from Government and Local Funds.				Expenditure in 1911.	
1911.	1901.	1891.	1881.	Per 1000 of the Population.	Per 1000 pupils in Public Institutions.
Rs.	Rs.	Rs.	Rs.	Rs.	Rs.
14,06,086	8,55,463	2,86,359	1,06,818	648	7,590

415. The extent of journalistic enterprise affords a good idea of the extent to which people have benefited by the spread of education. There is yet no daily newspaper published in the State, but the number of weekly newspapers has risen from 6 in 1901 to 11 in 1911. Their circulation is estimated to have risen from 4,000 copies in 1900 to 10,000 copies in 1910. Of the eleven weekly newspapers, six are published in Baroda, two in Navsari and three in Amreli. The number of monthly periodicals has risen from 1 in 1900, with an estimated circulation of 300 copies, to 23 in 1910, with an estimated circulation of 7,000 copies. Of the 23 periodicals 13 are published in Baroda Prant, four in Kadi Prant and six in Amreli. The number of printing presses has risen from nine in 1900 to 23 in 1910. Of these thirteen are in Baroda Prant, three in Kadi Prant, three in Navsari Prant and four in Amreli Prant. In addition to the newspapers and periodicals published in the State, a large number of the leading English and Vernacular dailies and weeklies published in Bombay, Poona, Surat and Ahmedabad also find circulation in the principal towns of the State. From inquiries made in the offices of these papers, it appears that their circulation in the State is now more than double of what it was ten years before. The taste for newspaper reading has much increased and there is now hardly any village, even in the remotest corner, where a newspaper of some sort is not to be found.

Extent to which newspapers circulate.

Number of books published.

416. The number of books published by authors from the State population goes on increasing from year to year. The total number of books published in 1901 was 92, while that in 1910 was nearly 200. But these figures are not sufficient to give us an adequate idea of the literary activity which has manifested itself along with the progress in education. Most of the books by authors from the State are printed and published by presses in British territory, notably in Bombay and Ahmedabad, as that secures to them the copyright for the whole of India, which is denied to publications from printing presses within the State. It is roughly calculated that the number of such outside publications is not less than 2 to 3 hundred per annum. Subsidiary Table X at the end of this Chapter gives the number of books published in the various languages spoken in the State during the last decade. It is impossible to make comparison, as statistics for the previous decades are not available. Almost all the books published during the last ten years are in the Gujarati language, which is the most widely spoken language in the State. No books in Urdu and very few in Marathi are published by printing presses in the State.

Libraries and reading rooms.

417. The number of libraries throughout the State in 1901 was only 16, with a total of 21,736 books and 2,214 readers. With the remarkable impetus given to education in the decade, the latter part of that period saw the number of libraries rise to 198, that of books to 75,686 and of readers to 10,079, giving an average of one library for each group of 16 towns and villages and one reader for every 100 in the population. A thorough canvas in the present year of 1911, however, shows a still more phenomenal growth. The number of public libraries now in the State is 275, or one for each group of 11 towns and villages ; the number of books in these libraries is 155,736, an average of 566 books each ; the number of readers frequenting the libraries and reading-rooms has grown to 36,277, an increase of nearly 360 per cent. within the last two or three years.

With a view of giving further impetus to this growing taste for reading, a new department, known as the Central Library Department, has recently been created, with an American expert as its head, under the designation of Director of State Libraries. A Central Library stocked with books in all branches of learning, and with a liberal grant for its further enlargement, has been opened in Baroda—a gift to the State from H. H. the Maharaja Saheb—and a library class has been opened in connection with this library, where pupils may learn modern methods of library administration ; and it is hoped that in the near future the benefits of this school may be extended all over India.

Rules regarding the establishment of new libraries have recently been framed under which villages with a population of 1,000 and above, receive an annual grant of Rs. 50 from the Central Library Department and a like amount from the Panchayat, provided that an equal amount is subscribed by the inhabitants. In villages of 4,000 and over this grant is increased to Rs. 300 and in the District headquarters towns to Rs. 700.

Boxes containing a good supply of books, known as travelling libraries, are forwarded from the Central Library to villages desiring to have them in any part of the State. These libraries remain in the villages three months, after which they are returned to the Central Library and another box of fresh books is forwarded.

These and other beneficent measures are sure to have their good results in due time, and it may be confidently expected that by the time of the next Census, every village of any importance will have its library, and many, if not most, of them will also have an adequate library building.

Signature marks.

418. In connection with the question of literacy, it is interesting to notice the various customs prevailing in the different parts of the State, in respect of the marks affixed to documents in lieu of signature by those who are unable to write. Generally speaking, the person who writes the signature of an illiterate executant of a document,

writes—"Signature of X, in the hand-writing of Y, written at his request." When it is desired to be more exact, the illiterate person is made to make some special mark with his own hand, just near the signature, *e. g.*, that of a glass bangle in the case of females, of a plough in the case of cultivators, etc. A list of such marks is given below :—

Mark as it is made.	Name by which the mark is known.	By whom made.
	*Bangadi* (Bracelet).	Females.
	Hal (Plough).	Cultivators.
	Suraj (Sun).	Females.
	Katar (Dagger)	Girasias.
	Talwar (Sword).	Rajputs, Sepoys, Marathas and Girasias.
	Sathio.	Females.
	Chak (Wheel).	Potters.
	Pingano.	Shoe-makers.
	Kodhi (Hatchet).	Labourers.
	Mâla (Garland of Beads.)	Widows.
	Bandhuk (Gun).	Sepoys.
	Tir (Bow and Arrow.)	Girasias.
	Kâtar (Scissors).	Tailors.

SUBSIDIARY TABLE I.—Education by Age, Sex and Religion.

Religion.	Number per mille who are literate.											Number per mille who are illiterate.			Number per mille who are literate in English.		
	All Ages.			0—10		10—15		15—20		20 and over							
	Total.	Male.	Female.	Male.	Female.	Male.	Female.	Male.	Female.	Male.	Female.	Total.	Male.	Female.	Total.	Male.	Female.
1	2	3	4	5	6	7	8	9	10	11	12	13	14	15	16	17	18
All Religions	**101**	**175**	**21**	**24·3**	**9·6**	275	72	258	**40**	**217**	**16**	**899**	**825**	**979**	**5**	**9**	**·5**
Hindu	94	164	17	23·8	9·2	272	66	247	33	200	11	906	836	983	4·5	8·4	·2
Jain	407	698	85	117	49	776	292	870	163	889	57	593	302	915	11	22	·1
Animist	8	13	1·4	2·7	1	39	4	24	2	14	1·5	992	987	998·6	...	...	..
Musalman	128	208	18	22	7	286	54	313	33	303	14	872	792	982	2	4	·1
Parsi	622	692	569	104	84	633	833	959	860	941	638	378	308	431	106	219	19
Christian	184	225	136	58	43	386	249	373	394	235	103	816	775	864	62	64	59
Native Christian	160	202	111	52	41	374	228	334	345	208	73	840	798	889	33	36	31
Arya Samaj	532	745	157	275	62	906	364	755	250	892	153	468	255	843	100	155	5

SUBSIDIARY TABLE II.—Education by Age, Sex and Locality.

District or Natural Division.	Number per mille who are literate.										
	All Ages.			0—10		10—15		15—20		20 and over.	
	Total.	Male.	Female.	Male.	Female.	Male	Female.	Male.	Female.	Male.	Female.
1	2	3	4	5	6	7	8	9	10	11	12
Baroda State	**101**	**175**	**21**	**24·3**	**9·6**	**275**	**72**	**258**	**40**	**217**	**16**
Baroda Division (Ex. of City) ...	113	195	18	29	12	329	77	305	42	230	11
Baroda City	213	392	71	60	24	486	169	541	151	460	63
Kadi Division	73	132	11	21	8	218	46	176	16	165	7
Navsari Division	96	166	25	13	5	226	51	270	45	219	26
Amreli Division	120	200	36	32	16	362	167	294	71	237	21

SUBSIDIARY TABLE III.—Education by religion, sex and locality.

District or Natural Division.	Number per mille who are literate.											
	Hindu.		Jain.		Animist.		Musalman.		Parsi.		Christian.	
	Male.	Female.	Male.	Female.	Male.	Female.	Male.	Female.	Male.	Female.	Male.	Female.
1	2	3	4	5	6	7	8	9	10	11	12	13
Baroda State	**164**	**17**	**698**	**85**	**13**	**1·4**	**208**	**18**	**692**	**569**	**225**	**136**
Baroda Division (Ex. of City) ...	195	16	688	89	15	2	232	11	880	647	135	101
Baroda City	402	69	611	135	59	12	382	36	887	702	726	567
Kadi Division	108	8	709	72	...	...	187	14	761	710	239	150
Navsari Division	189	14	720	136	13	1	308	16	664	558	568	304
Amreli Division	187	34	675	122	...	...	216	27	867	786	571	1,000

SUBSIDIARY TABLE IV.—English Education by age, sex and locality.

District or Natural Division.	Literate in English per 10,000.													
	1911										1901		1891	
	0—10		10—15		15—20		20 and over		All ages.		All ages.		All ages.	
	Male.	Female.	Male.	Female.	Male.	Female.	Male.	Female.	Male.	Female.	Male.	Female.	Male.	Female.
1	2	3	4	5	6	7	8	9	10	11	12	13	14	15
Baroda State	**1**	**1**	**87**	**9**	**268**	**14**	**109**	**4**	**90**	**5**	**53**	**2**	**18**	**1**
Baroda Division (Ex. of City) ...	·1	1·4	87	16	30	23	55	·9	64	4	33	·1	6	·1
Baroda City	18	8	678	92	1,833	118	76	60	710	57	441	21	188	15
Kadi Division	·1	...	40	·6	8	·3	46	·4	36	·3	18	·3	6	·2
Navsari Division	·2	...	36	2	210	8	102	3	75	3	61	3	16	·6
Amreli Division	...	...	9	4	221	5	80	2	74	2	31	·5	13	·2

SUBSIDIARY TABLE V.—Progress of Education Since 1881.

District or Natural Division.	Number of literate per mille.																			
	All ages.								10—15				15—20				20 and over.			
	Male.				Female.				Male.		Female.		Male.		Female.		Male.		Female.	
	1911	1901	1891	1881	1911	1901	1891	1881	1911	1901	1911	1901	1911	1901	1911	1901	1911	1901	1911	1901
1	2	3	4	5	6	7	8	9	10	11	12	13	14	15	16	17	18	19	20	21
Baroda State	**175**	**162**	**113**	**90**	**21**	**7**	**4**	**1·5**	**275**	**160**	**72**	**12**	**258**	**206**	**40**	**13**	**217**	**208**	**16**	**7**
Baroda Division (Ex. of City) ...	195	197	123	93	18	6	2	1	329	197	77	14	305	216	42	10	230	245	11	5
Baroda City	392	366	310	262	71	24	21	6	486	387	169	47	541	449	151	49	460	430	63	21
Kadi Division	132	113	79	60	11	2	2	1	218	107	46	3	176	142	16	3	165	143	7	2
Navsari Division	166	168	126	105	25	20	9	4	226	186	51	29	270	240	45	38	219	224	26	22
Amreli Division	200	152	125	115	36	6	4	1	362	147	167	11	294	215	71	11	237	194	21	5

SUBSIDIARY TABLE VI.—Education by Caste.

Caste.	Number per 1,000 who are literate.						Number per 10,000 who are literate in English.					
	1911			1901			1911			1901		
	Persons.	Males.	Females.	Persons.	Males	Females.	Persons.	Males.	Females.	Persons.	Males.	Females.
1	2	3	4	5	6	7	8	9	10	11	12	13
Hindu.												
Ahir	31	55	5	15	28	...	14	26	...	...	...	...
Babrot	154	283	17	110	206	6	35	68	...	11	20	...
Bava	294	376	24	127	203	3	25	32	...	3	5	...
Bhangi	16	2·8	2·5	3	6	·3	...	...	...	...	...	...
Bharvad	9	12	5	...	...	...	1	2	...	...	...	...
Bhavsar	271	520	36	194	382	2	39	76	4	17	33	...
Bhoi	38	68	3	31	59	...	9	14	...	...	...	...
Brahman Anavala	365	619	71	370	673	23	276	506	9	80	150	...
Do. Audich	302	552	38	245	471	15	151	286	3	55	110	...
Do. Deshastha	452	727	129	435	723	62	789	1,429	34	451	800	...
Do. Mewada	279	479	36	205	392	11	133	238	5	32	62	...
Do. Modh	319	545	82	226	428	4	163	320	...	51	98	...
Do. Nagar	427	641	221	337	615	67	847	1,679	54	457	885	41
Do. Tapodhan	169	269	30	85	164	1	45	83	...	13	25	...
Chamar	15·5	29	3	3	6	·1	·6	1·3	...	...	...	—
Darji	105	188	29	67	137	·7	14	28	...	4	7	...
Dhed	21·5	38	4	1	12	·1	2·1	3·9	·2	·2	·4	...
Garoda	94	176	13	34	72	·6	3	6	...	5	11	...
Ghanchi	223	418	20	154	294	2	15	29	...	4	8	...
Gola (rice-pounders)	100	193	7	159	323	·3	13	26	...	2	4	...
Gosain	141	244	13	104	173	3	17	31	...	7	11	...
Hajam	78	133	8	27	53	·2	8	17	...	1·2	2·5	...
Kachia	193	348	19	177	344	·8	20	38	...	2	5	...
Kanbi Anjana	70	134	5	27	52	1	13	25	...	...	...	...
Do. Kadwa	74	136	8	41	80	...	14	27	...	4	8	...
Do. Karadia	22	43	1	...	...	...	2	3	...	...	...	...
Do. Lewa	184	311	26	178	316	14	67	122	1	30	56	...
Koli	22	39	3	15	28	1	·6	1	...	·1	·1	...
Kumbhar	44	82	5	27	53	·3	4	9	...	·7	1·5	...
Lubana	314	555	60	224	418	16	111	215	...	32	61	...
Luhar	106	199	16	50	102	2	7	14	...	·5	1	...
Machhi	73	134	6	31	64	...	1·2	2·4	...	...	...	...
Maratha	233	377	61	184	339	8	269	465	35	117	219	2
Mochi	100	174	16	39	72	2	13	26	...	3	7	...
Rabari	9	16	1·5	1·2	2·3	...	·2	·4	...	·3	·5	...
Rajput	80	141	10	77	147	1	12	21	1	13	25	...
Ravalia	14	23	4	1·6	3	...	·9	1·1	...	...	...	...
Sathawara	63	119	9	35	68	1	1·8	3·4	...	6	11	...
Shenva	7	12·5	1	1·3	3	...	1·3	2·5	...	...	...	...
Soni	316	581	53	237	455	8	45	81	...	67	130	...
Sutar	145	259	21	85	164	3	17	33	...	2	4	...
Talavia	8	17	2	2	4	...	...	...	...	...	...	—
Targala	132	285	4	62	132	1	5	10	...	12	25	...
Vagher	15	28	1	6	12	...	2	5	...	...	...	...
Vaghari	7	12	2	1·8	4	...	·3	·7	...	...	...	...
Vania Disaval	367	695	87	313	604	10	241	523	...	63	124	...
Do. Lad	353	628	90	403	756	22	299	602	7	230	434	10
Do. Shrimali	414	704	81	337	618	24	284	526	4	235	446	...
Jain.												
Vania Shrimali	385	700	82	370	710	17	119	242	...	36	71	...
Animistic.												
Bhil	5	8	2									
Chodhra	10	18	2									
Dhanka	9	16	1·4	4	7	·1	...	...	...	·1	·1	...
Dhodia	11	19	2									
Gamit	5	9	·6									
Nayakda	6	10·4	2									
Musalman.												
Fakir	74	131	8	63	166	...	2	4	...	...	...	...
Ghanchi	142	260	14	87	166	2	7	13	...	8	15	...
Malek	84	152	9	57	110	1	4	7·6	...	6	11	...
Memon	112	219	15	110	215	1	7	12	1·4	4	8	...
Molesalam	69	125	4	38	75	1	6	10	...	1	2	...
Momna	103	176	9	50	100	1	4	7	...	2	5	...
Pathan	120	217	10	86	162	2	26	50	...	14	26	...
Pinjara	162	302	13	88	170	1	4	7	...	...	...	...
Saiyad	183	324	29	126	245	6	106	203	...	63	125	...
Shaikh	120	217	14	86	160	4	22	40	·7	13	23	2
Vohora	202	308	34	179	348	21	32	63	8	25	50	2
Parsi.												
Parsi	622	692	569	599	746	483	1,052	2,190	172	1,001	2,142	100
Christian.												
Native	160	203	111	77	115	3	335	356	310	157	259	33

SUBSIDIARY TABLE VII.—Number of Institutions and Pupils according to the returns of the Education Department.

Class of Institutions.	1911.		1901.		1891.	
	Number of		Number of		Number of	
	Institutions.	Scholars.	Institutions.	Scholars.	Institutions.	Scholars.
1	2	3	4	5	6	7
All kinds	**3,026**	**185,242**	**1,211**	**86,419**	**521**	**53,070**
Public Institutions	*2,980*	*181,119*	*1,146*	*80,256*	*394*	*45,196*
Arts College	1	329	1	216	1	113
Secondary Schools	28	4,759	17	2,287	13	1,605
Primary Schools	2,938	173,883	1,119	76,936	377	43,357
Training Schools	2	426	1	26	1	25
Other Special Schools	11	1,722	8	791	2	96
Private Institutions	*46*	*4,123*	*65*	*6,163*	*127*	*7,874*
Advanced	12	1,583	4	639	4	373
Elementary	34	2,540	61	5,524	123	7,501

SUBSIDIARY TABLE VIII.—Main results of University Examinations.

Examination.	1911.		1901.		1891.	
	Candidates.	Passed.	Candidates.	Passed.	Candidates.	Passed.
1	2	3	4	5	6	7
Matriculation (Entrance) ...	141	70	86	37	57	29
F. A. or Intermediate Examination, 1st B. A. or 1st B. Sc....	140	83	128	66	61	26
Degrees in Arts...	30	17	28	23	5	3
Do. Medicine	......	......	......	......	......	......
Do. Law...	......	......	......	......	......	......
Do. Civil Engineering...	......	......	......	......	......	......
Total	*311*	*170*	*242*	*126*	*123*	*58*

SUBSIDIARY TABLE IX.—NUMBER AND CIRCULATION OF NEWSPAPERS, &C.

LANGUAGE.	Class of Newspapers (daily, weekly, &c.).	1911.		1901.		1891.	
		No.	Circulation.	No.	Circulation.	No.	Circulation.
1	2	3	4	5	6	7	8
Gujarati	Weekly ...	9	16,500	Figures not available.			
Do.	Monthly ...	22	14,500				
Total Gujarati ...		*31*	*31,000*				
Gujarati and Marathi combined ...	Monthly ...	1	300	Figures not available.			
Gujarati, Sanskrit and English combined	Do. ...	1	300				
English and Sanskrit combined ...	Quarterly ...	1	300				
Total		*34*	*31,900*				

SUBSIDIARY TABLE X.—NUMBER OF BOOKS PUBLISHED IN EACH LANGUAGE.

LANGUAGE.	NUMBER OF BOOKS PUBLISHED IN.												
	1901.	1902.	1903.	1904.	1905.	1906.	1907.	1908.	1909.	1910.	TOTAL OF DECADE.		
											1901 to 1910.	1891 to 1900.	1881 to 1890.
1	2	3	4	5	6	7	8	9	10	11	12	13	14
Gujarati	77	38	68	37	50	161	161	179	125	127	1,023	Figures not available.	Figures not available.
English	2	1	4	11	11	2	14	20	7	27	99		
Sanskrit	2	...	...	...	1	...	...	4	...	...	7		
Marathi	2	...	2	...	2	...	5	6	1	1	19		
Total ...	*83*	*39*	*74*	*48*	*64*	*163*	*180*	*209*	*133*	*155*	*1,148*		

Chapter IX.

LANGUAGE.

Introductory.

419. The information recorded in the 13th column of the Census Schedule relates to the language which each person ordinarily uses in his own home. The instructions given to the enumerators were as under :—

" Column 13 (Language).—Enter the language which each person ordinarily uses in his own home. In the case of infants and deaf-mutes, the language of the mother should be entered."

The statistics of languages returned as spoken in the State in response to this inquiry, are given in Imperial Table X. The following Subsidiary Tables in which the chief features of the return are presented in a more compendious form, will be found at the end of this chapter :—

(I)—Distribution of the total population by language.

(II)—Distribution by language of the population of each district.

(III)—Comparison of caste and language tables.

(III-a)—Numbers speaking the languages, contrasted with castes and races supposed to speak them.

The accuracy of the return.

420. The answer to the question regarding one's mother-tongue would appear to be very simple, but here also there was a chance of wrong entries mainly owing to the ignorance of the people, about the proper name of the language they speak. For instance, Marathi is often spoken of as Deccani, Urdu as Musalmani, and Hindustani as Pardeshi. These contingencies were foreseen, and a list giving the proper names of the vernaculars to be recorded and the territorial and other names to be avoided, was furnished to the enumerators. It is said that in some parts of India, there is a tendency on the part of Mahomedans to say that their home language is Urdu even when this is not really the case. There was no such intentional wrong return on the part of the people in this State, either with regard to Urdu, or any other language.

Uses of parent tongue statistics.

421. Statistics of the languages spoken by the people are useful for a variety of purposes. They show the philologist what languages are spoken and where and to what extent ; they serve as a guide to the nationality of the people ; and they assist in the solution of administrative questions by showing what languages are most spoken in each area and whether each is increasing or decreasing in popularity, so that orders regarding the languages to be used in courts and schools and by officials and in official papers may be adapted accordingly.

422. No less than 41 languages and dialects have been recorded as the home language of the people living in the Baroda State on the 10th March 1911. Of these, 34 are Vernaculars of India, four languages of other Asiatic countries and three European languages. Of the Vernaculars of India, Gujarati is the old language of the land. Urdu came with the Musalman conquerors of Gujarat and Marathi with the Marathas. These three have the largest number of speakers in the State, and may now be said to be the Vernaculars of the people living in it. The rest of the languages spoken are mostly the languages of immigrants.

Languages spoken.

Name of language.	Speakers.
Gujarati with Bhil dialects related to it ...	1,902,654
Urdu	64,306
Marathi with Bhil dialects related to it ...	36,145
Other languages of India	29,035
Other Asiatic Languages	369
European languages	289

The number of languages spoken in each district.

423. The highest number of languages and dialects spoken is 32 in the Navsari District, then comes Baroda City with 29, then Kadi District with 26, then Baroda District with 22, and Amreli stands last with 20 languages. Excluding Gujarati and the Bhil dialects as being indigenous to the State, we find that the Kadi District comes to the top with 24 foreign languages giving the second place to Baroda City with 22. Then follows Navsari with 21 languages and Baroda and Amreli Districts stand last with only 18 foreign languages.

Linguistic survey of India.

424. The labours of scholars like the late Mr. Beames, Dr. Hoernle, Bishop Caldwel and others have much increased our knowledge of most of the modern Vernaculars of India, but while we know a good deal about some of the languages, our information as to their dialects is, with a few exceptions, most incomplete. There are many languages spoken by the wild tribes of India, of which we know little or nothing except the names. A consideration of these facts led the Government of India to commence a systematic survey of all forms of speech employed in Northern and Eastern India and in the Presidency of Bombay. This has under the able guidance of Dr. Grierson been completed and the results are published in the volumes of the Linguistic Survey of India.

425. There are eight great families of Indian languages, in three of which all the languages spoken in the Baroda State are included. These are the Indo-European, the Dravidian, and the Semetic families. Out of these, the Indo-European family is again split up into two sub-families, the Aryan and the European. The Aryan sub-family has two branches—(1) the Indian and (2) the Iranian. To this Indian branch belong the languages spoken largely by the people of this State. This branch is split up into eight groups, out of which only six, *viz.*, the Western, the Southern, the Eastern, the Northern, the North-Western and the Shinakhowar are found in this State. The languages of the Aryan family are numerically the most important and are spoken by more than 99 per cent. of the total population. The Dravidian family comes next, but its speakers represent only 359 persons, while the Semetic family has less than 50 speakers in the total population of the State.

The family, branches and groups of languages spoken in India.

Family.	No. of languages.	Speakers.
Indo-European	37	2,032,407
Dravidian	3	359
Semetic	1	32

426. Taking a bird's-eye view of the facts stated in Subsidiary Table II, we find that in every 10,000 persons in the population, 8,639 speak the Gujarati language, 720 the Bhil dialects, 171 Marathi, 28 Hindustani, 317 Urdu, 77 Kachhi, 16 Hindi and 32 the rest of the languages. This shows that over 86 per cent. of the population speak the Gujarati language and less than 14 per cent. speak all the other languages. In the Census of 1891 Bhil dialects were included in Gujarati. In the Census of 1901, they were separated from it, but the return was not correct, as a large number of forest tribes, though speaking their tribal dialects, was returned as speaking Gujarati. A greater accuracy in the present Census has reduced the proportion of the speakers of Gujarati to 86 per cent. of the total population against 90 per cent. in 1901 and 93 in 1891. Similarly, the decline in the speakers of Marathi is also due to the exclusion from it of the Bhil dialects connected with it such as Kathodi, Varli, &c. These details account for the large increase in the speakers of the Bhil dialects in

Numbers speaking different languages.

Language.	Speakers per 10,000 of the population.		
	1911	1901	1891
Gujarati	8,639	9,027	9,302
Bhil dialects	720	348	...
Marathi	171	198	214
Hindustani	28	178	375
Urdu	317	174	12
Kachhi	77	56	58
Hindi	16	1	9
Others	32	18	35

the present Census over the figures of 1901. In 1891 and 1901, no clear distinction was made between Urdu and Hindustani and the latter gained at the expense of the former. In the present Census, a clear line was drawn between the two, with the result that both the languages show their true relative proportion. The variations in the speakers of the rest of languages are slight and being mainly due to the greater or less number of foreigners present in the State on the Census day, call for no remarks.

427. Taking the population of a district to be 10,000, the highest number of persons speaking Gujarati, the language of the country, is met with in the Kadi District and the lowest in the City of Baroda. Baroda, Amreli and Navsari Districts rank after Kadi in the order mentioned. The number of persons speaking the Gujarati language in the Navsari District falls to 5,918 in 10,000, owing to a large part of that district being inhabited by forest tribes who speak dialects of their own. The City of Baroda being the capital of the State has a large Marathi-speaking population and also many foreigners in the Military and other services, and it is therefore that it stands at the bottom in the number of persons speaking the Gujarati language.

Diagram showing the number of Gujarati speakers per 10,000 of the population.

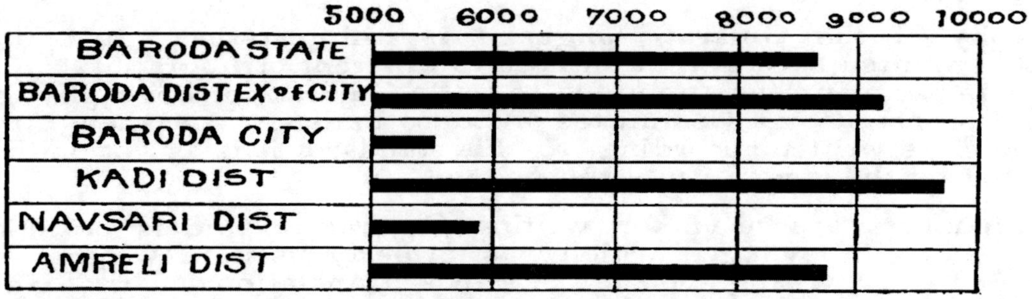

Gujarati language and literature.

428. The Gujarati language is the vernacular not only of the Baroda State, but also of the whole of Gujarat, including Kathiawad. It is also spoken by emigrants from Gujarat in every Province and State in the whole of India. It is the mother-tongue of enterprising Gujarati merchants and Vohoras and is the adopted language of the adventurous Parsis who are to be found all over India. In the Madras Presidency, there is a large colony of silk weavers called Patnulkarans, who centuries ago, migrated from Saurashtra in Gujarat at the invitation of the Nayak Kings of Madura. Many of them still retain the language of their original home, which is known in that Presidency as Patnuli or Khatri, but is really Gujarati.

Modern Gujarati is traced by philologists to its immediate parent, the *Apabhramsha* (meaning corrupt or decayed), which is derived from the *Prakrit* (meaning natural, unartificial), which in its turn is derived from the Sanskrit (meaning purified). It commences with the poetry of Narsinh Mehta, a Vadnagara Nagar Brahman, born at Junagad in 1413 A.D. He has not written any long continuous works, but his fame rests upon his short songs, many of which exhibit considerable elegance. Other poets followed Narsinh Mehta, amongst whom may be mentioned Premanand Bhatt (1681 A. D.), author of *Narsinh Mehta-nu-Mameru*, *Nalakhyana*, *Okhaharan* and several dramas; Vallabha: Pritam ; Ravishanker (translator of the Maha Bharat) ; Muktanand ; Samal Bhatt (author of *Baras Kasturi*, *Mada Pachishi*, *Nand Batrishi*, *Stri Charitra*, *Vikram Charitra*) ; Brahmanand and Dayaram. Among recent poets the names of Dalpatram Dahyabhai and Narmdashanker Lalshanker are noteworthy.

During the last fifty years, western education has enriched the Gujarati language to a considerable extent. Books on a variety of subjects have been written and of these *navalkatha*, or the novel, is a special feature. The novel may be said to be the most flourishing department of modern Gujarati literature. Every year Gujarati novels are published by the score, but like most of the other works, they possess little originality and are mostly translations. Parsi writers are a great auxiliary to Gujarati literature, as the vernacular of these people is Gujarati. Some of them have rendered the language excellent service by writing original social novels and by translating some of the great masterpieces of English fiction. But original novels in Gujarati are very rare. The late Rao Bahadur Nandshanker Tuljashanker Mehta wrote such a one. His *Karan Ghelo*, a historical novel of the *medieval* Gujarat King Karan Ghelo, has already become a classic and is highly prized. *Saraswati Chandra*, a social novel by the late Mr. Govardhanram Tripathi has also become a classical work, and is translated into Marathi and other languages of India. The literary form of the Gujarati language has, during the last thirty years, much developed, and its most marked characteristic is the wholesale adoption of Sanskrit words in the place of old words descended through the Prakrit or obtained from the original non-Aryan inhabitants of the country.

The orthography of the Gujarati language is still unsettled. It is not unusual to find books written by different authors in different orthography. The Bombay Education Department has attempted to settle Gujarati orthography by adopting a standard proposed by a Committee of Educationists. And though the new Gujarati Readers are written according to this standard, it is as yet neither approved nor adopted by the generality of the people.

Gujarati script.

429. Two alphabets are used for writing Gujarati. One is ordinary Devnagri, which was formerly used in Gujarat for writing books. Carey's translation of the New Testament, published at the commencement of the last century, was printed in that alphabet. The other is known as the Gujarati alphabet and is the one in general use. It is based on the same original as Devnagri and closely resembles the ordinary *Kaithi* character employed all over Northern India. In ordinary mercantile correspondence, it is usual to omit vowels except when initials which make the reading of a banker's letter a task of some difficulty. Such a script is called *Bodia* (from *bodu*, clipped or shorn).

Dialects of Gujarati.

430. Except Kathiawadi, and Zalawadi, which were returned by 383 and 94 persons respectively and the Bhili dialects, no other dialects of the Gujarati language were returned in the Census. It is only the Bhili dialects which can be called dialects of Gujarati, as they preserve in inflection, pronunciation and particular words, traces of the original variety of the language not incorporated in the standard language of the country. Kathiawadi, Ahmedabadi, Pattani, Charotari, Kanami and Surati are sometimes loosely spoken of as dialects of the language. According also to the adage current among the people, language (*boli*) "changes" every twelve *gaus*. But these are not dialects in the proper sense of the term. The only true dialectic variation of Gujarati consists in the difference between the speech of the uneducated and the educated. That of the latter is the standard form of the language taught in grammars. That of the former differs from the standard mainly in pronunciation. The differences of pronunciation are nearly all the same over the whole of Gujarat, but, as a rule, though they are the same in kind, they are much less prominent in South Gujarat, and become more and more prominent as we go to the north. Among these may be mentioned a tendency to pronounce *e* for *i*: for instance, *lemdo* for *limdo*, *peplo* for *piplo*, etc.; *ch* and *chh* are pronounced as *s* and as we go north, this becomes the rule. Thus *pons* for *panch*, five; *unso* for *uncho*, high; *sarvu* for *charvu*, to feed cattle; *soru* for *chhoru*, child; *pusvu* for *puchhvu*, to ask and so on. There is often an interchange of consonants in the same word in different parts of the country. Thus *pitvu* for *tipvu*, to beat; *detva* for *devta*, fire; *mag* for *gum*, towards; *nuskan* for *nuksan*, injury. The Parsis and those Musalmans who speak Gujarati generally follow the colloquial Gujarati of their neighbours in pronunciation and inflection. Their Gujarati is sometimes spoken of as a special dialect, but it differs from the ordinary language only in its vocabulary which borrows freely from Persian and Arabic. It is also noticeable for its entire disregard of the distinction between cerebrals and dentals.

431. The Bhils and Nayakdas of Sankheda Taluka and Tilakwada Peta Taluka in the Baroda District and the Gamatda, Chodhra and other aboriginal tribes in the Songhad, Vyara and other Talukas in the Navsari District, speak mixed forms of speech, which are the dialects of Gujarati. They closely resemble each other.

The Bhil Dialects.

Name of Dialect.	Speakers.
Bhili ...	35,111
Banjari	250
Bavachi	336
Chodhari	26,852
Dhodia	18,051
Gamatdi	47,177
Kokani	5,112
Kotwali	1,513
Mavchi	948
Naiki ...	10,118
Kolghi	679
Total ...	146,347

As an illustration, a rendering of the Gujarati sentence, "*Varsad saro thayo chhe; dhan saru pakshe,*" in some of the most important of them is given below :—

Bhili or Vasavi ...	*Varhad hara vaya, anna haru pakayu.*
Chodhari	*Varhat haro hovoha, mal haro pakil.*
Dhodia	*Varhat hajo avno, dana haja pikna.*
Gamatdi	*Pai haro eno, dana haro pakil.*
Kokani	*Rani khub padna, dana besh pakil.*
Naikdi or Naiki ...	*Varsat bhare huna, bhare danyar pikhiyé.*

The Chodhari dialect is purer and more akin to Gujarati than the other forest dialects. Next to it come Gamatdi and Naikdi or Naiki in their purity and affinity to Gujarati. Kokani is a dialect of Marathi rather than of Gujarati and Dhodia, though a dialect of Gujarati is more affected by Marathi words than the other dialects.

The total number of speakers of the Bhili dialects in the present Census is larger than that returned in 1901 by 78,464. But the statistics of language in the Census of 1901 are obviously incorrect, since the total Animistic population returned was 176,250, while the speakers of Bhili dialects numbered 67,883 only, which shows that a large proportion of the speakers of Bhili dialects must have been included in the speakers of Gujarati. In the present Census the Animistic population numbers 115,411 and it is found that 85,566 Animistics have returned themselves as Hindus. These added together give a total of 200,977 real Animists, of whom 146,347 are returned as speakers of Bhili dialects and the rest, *viz.*, 54,630 have abandoned their tribal dialects, and adopted Gujarati as their home-tongue. If such a large number as 108,367 of forest tribes had, as reported in 1901, really adopted Gujarati as their mother-tongue, it is not likely that so many as 53,737 would again have reverted to their tribal tongues and the present Census, in spite of advance in education and greater communication with more civilized people, should return only 54,630 as speakers of Gujarati from among the primitive tribes.

432. Next to Gujarati and its Bhili dialects, Urdu has the largest number of speakers. According to philologists, it is not a language, but a dialect of Western Hindi along with Hindustani, Hindi and Brij, all of which have more or less speakers in the State. Hindustani, the principal dialect of Western Hindi, is not only a local vernacular, but is also spoken over the whole of the north and west of the Continent of India as a *lingua franka*, or second language by every one with any claim to education. It was carried everywhere in India by the lieutenants of the Mughal Empire, and has received considerable literary cultivation at the hands of both Musalmans and Hindus. The former employed the Persian character for recording it and enriched its

Name of language.	Speakers.
Urdu	64,306
Hindustani	5,629
Hindi	3,203
Brij	21

vocabulary with a large stock of Persian and Arabic words. This Persianised form of Hindustani is known as Urdu, a name derived from the *Urdu-e-Maulla* or Royal Military bazar outside Delhi Palace where it took its rise. When employed for poetry, Urdu is called *Rekhta* (scattered or crumbled) from the manner in which Persian words are "scattered" through it. During the first centuries of its existence, Urdu literature was entirely poetical. Prose Urdu owes its origin to the English occupation of India and to the need of text books for the college of Fort William. The Hindi form of Hindustani was invented at the same time by the teachers of that college. It was intended to be a Hindustani for the use of Hindus, and was derived from Urdu by ejecting all words of Arabic and Persian birth and substituting in their place words borrowed or derived from the indigenous Sanskrit. Owing to the popularity of the first book written in it and to its supplying the need for a *lingua franka*, which could be used by the strictest Hindus without their religious prejudices being offended, it became widely adopted and is now the recognised vehicle for writing prose by those inhabitants of Upper India, who do not employ Urdu. Urdu, as becomes its origin, is usually written in a modified form of the Persian character, while Hindi is generally written like Sanskrit in the Devnagari character.

433. The total Musalman population of the State is 160,887, while the speakers of Urdu as returned in the Census number only 64,306 or 40 per cent. of the Musalman population. This shows that 60 per cent. of the Musalmans in the State, who are mainly converts from Hinduism, still adhere to Gujarati even after their conversion centuries ago. The number of Urdu speakers returned in the Census of 1901 was only 34,046. But no clear distinction appears then to have been made between Urdu and Hindustani, as such a large number as 34,769 was returned as speaking Hindustani or *Musulmani*, while in the present Census, the corresponding return is only 5,629. Even, if we include the speakers of Hindustani in those of Urdu, the total in 1901 comes to 68,815, and in the present Census to 69,935. This gives a percentage of 42 and 43 respectively on the total Musalman population in the Censuses of 1901 and 1911. Taking 10,000 as the population of a district, the greatest number of Urdu speakers, 1,315 is naturally found in the City of Baroda. Then comes Baroda District with 338, Amreli with 308, Kadi with 232, and Navsari stands last with only 195 Urdu speakers in 10,000 of its population.

Urdu, not the language of all Musalmans.

District.	Speakers.	Per centage of Urdu speakers to Musalman population.
State	64,306	40
Baroda Dn.(Ex. of City)	19,878	40·5
Baroda City	13,062	76
Kadi Division	19,334	37
Navsari „	6,555	28
Amreli „	5,482	29

434. Next after Urdu, Marathi stands prominent owing to the comparatively larger number of Marathas, Prabhus and Dakshani Brahmans in all the districts of the State. Here also the City stands first, as it being the capital, contains many Maratha Sardar families, Maratha officials, servants and shopkeepers. Navsari comes next after the City, as some of its tracts border on the Deccan districts of Khandesh and Nasik. Then comes the district of Kadi and then Amreli in Kathiawad where comparatively many Maratha families have settled after the abolition of the Contingent and the breaking up of the Manekwada Camp. After Kadi comes the Baroda District. Compared with population, neither of these districts contains a large Marathi-speaking element.

Marathi.

District.	Speakers of Marathi.
State	34,834
Baroda (Ex. of City)	1,596
Baroda City	25,067
Kadi	1,669
Navsari	4,886
Amreli	1,616

Only three dialects of Marathi have been recorded. Of these Kathodi and Varli are spoken by the forest tribes of the Navsari District, and Goanese is spoken by the Goans employed in the State Military Bands.

Dialects of Marathi.

Name.	Speakers.
Kathodi	231
Varli	936
Goanese	144
Total ...	1,311

Gujarati and Marathi compared.

435. The Gujarati language is much simpler than the Marathi. It resembles Persian in the simplicity of its grammar and a disregard for inflexional forms and terminologies; while Marathi is not only richer in expressions and words, but has a very stiff grammar with inflexions for genders, cases and tenses in both numbers, which are difficult to grasp. This is the reason why the Deccanis can speak and write Gujarati, which is the official language in courts and offices, almost as well as the Gujaratis themselves; while the Gujaratis, though they can read and comprehend Marathi fairly well, are unable to talk fluently or write correctly in Marathi.

Mutual effect of Gujarati and Marathi.

436. Marathi and Gujarati have stood together in the Baroda State for more than 150 years, but the two do not appear to have affected each other to any appreciable extent. The two peoples, the Deccanis and Gujaratis have not materially influenced each other in any point. Their language, thier dress, their food, their customs and manners are all entirely exclusive. The languages of both are derived from Sanskrit, and a Gujarati writer, no less than a Marathi one, would look to it for a fresh expression of ideas which cannot be conveyed in the present stock of words in his vernacular. A little mixture of words in the spoken language is however noticeable in the Baroda City, *e. g.*, *kudne*, *haraji*, *ghas* (for *gavat*), *khand* (for *sakar*), etc., from Gujarati into Marathi; and *atopvu*, *adhalavu*, *rangoli*, *binbobhat*, etc., from Marathi into Gujarati.

Effect of English on Vernacular languages.

437. English education and the introduction of new institutions and new ideas like railways, printing presses, factories, etc., have led to the incorporation of many English words in the vernacular languages of the country. Such words as master, class, deputy, rail, director, train, station, ticket, pass, guard, platform, signal, engine, motor, train, conductor, steamer, superintendent, census, newspaper, boat, pantaloon, frock, sale, court, appeal, case, magistrate, barrister, judge, police, bailiff, notice, warrant, doctor, fee, plague, quarantine, transfer, stamp, share, dividend, cupboard, table, type, compose, feet, rule, space, bobbin, gin, press, mill, cricket, ball, wicket, band, bandstand, party, congress, governor, parade, meeting, cornice, etc., are used like ordinary vernacular words. Attempts have been made now and then to eschew these words for new-coined vernacular ones, but they have failed. For instance, court, appeal and notice are preferred to and considered simpler than *nyayadhishi*, *vivad* and *suchana patra*, and *census* is more popular than *vasti gantri* or *khane sumari*.

Sindhi.

438. Among foreign languages Sindhi (821) with its dialect Kachhi (15,268) contributes 16,089 speakers. Kachhi is mainly spoken by the Khojas and Memons in all the Districts, but largely in the Amreli District and Sindhi by the Sindh Sardar and Shilledar families in the City of Baroda and the Kadi District.

Rajasthani.

439. The next foreign language that figures largely is Rajasthani or the language of Rajasthan. It is spoken in Rajputana, which is divided amongst many States and tribes. Each claims to have a language of its own, but all these are really dialects of one and the same form of speech, *viz.*, the Rajasthani. They fall into four main groups, which are called Mewadi, Malvi, Jaipuri and Marwadi. Mewadi, the dialect of Mewar, and its neighbourhood, has only 41 speakers in the State. Jaipuri, the dialect of Eastern Rajputana, and Malvi, the dialect of the Malva country round Indore, have also 38 and 8 speakers respectively. Marwadi,

the most important of the Rajputana dialects, is the language of enterprising merchants and bankers from Marwar, Mewad, Bikaner and Jesalmir and has no less than 3,323 speakers in the State. Sixteen per cent. of the speakers are to be found in the City of Baroda, 31 per cent. in the Baroda District, 40 per cent. in the Kadi District, 12 per cent. in the Navsari District, and less than 1 per cent. in the Amreli District where owing to the presence of local Shylocks, the Kapol Vanias, those from Marwar cannot flourish.

Dravidian languages.

Name of language.	Speakers.
Kanarese	14
Tamil	80
Telugu	265

440. Languages, which are known as Dravidian, form the speech of the south of the Indian Peninsula as contrasted with the Aryan languages of the north. The first language to be mentioned in this group is Kanarese, which contributes the least number of speakers in the State. It is the language spoken in the south-east corner of the Bombay Presidency and in the Mysore State. Then comes Tamil, which is the most cultivated and the best known of the Dravidian forms of speech. Tamil speakers, principally domestic servants, are found in the City of Baroda. The Madras servant is usually without religious prejudices or scruples as to food, headgear or ceremonial. Unlike the North Indian domestic, he can accommodate himself to all circumstances.

The Telugu or Telangi language, which contributes comparatively a large number of speakers in the State population, ranks next to Tamil in respect to culture and copiousness of its vocabulary and exceeds it in euphony. Every word ends in a vowel, and it has therefore been called the Italian of the East.

Other languages.

441. There were 36 persons (13 males and 23 females), who returned Bengali as their mother-tongue, and 12 persons (10 males and 2 females) who returned Naipali as their home-tongue. These were for the most part pilgrims who happened to be in Dwarka or Beyt on the Census day. There were 179 Baloch and 145 Pashto speakers, who were mainly employed in the army and a few were itinerant traders. In addition to these, there were 40 speakers of Multani, who also were, for the most part, traders in the Navsari District or pilgrims in the Amreli District.

Foreign languages.

442. Among languages foreign to India, English alone is worth noticing. It is the home language of 261 persons (132 males and 129 females). Most of them reside in the City of Baroda and the Cantonment and a few are returned from the Railway stations on the lines running through the State. Among the other foreign languages French contributes only 5 speakers, Arabic 32, and Portuguese 23.

The dynamics of language.

443. In India the Aryan languages—the tongues of civilization—are continually superceding the aboriginal languages. Many of the hill tribes in the State, which were formerly speaking a gypsy language of their own, are now speaking mixed tongues which are the main dialects of Gujarati. Recently some of them, like the Dublas, who have come in greater contact with the Ujaliats, have even adopted pure Gujarati as their home-tongue. The reverse however never happens. There is no known case where any community has abandoned an Aryan language and adopted a non-Aryan one. Nor does a community speaking one form of Aryan speech easily give it up in favour of another. The Deccani castes in Baroda continue to speak Marathi, although they have been in Gujarat for about two hundred years. Descendants of Vadnagara Nagars from Gujarat, who migrated to the United Provinces, hundreds of years ago, still speak the Gujarati language in the country of their adoption. Similarly, in the Madras Presidency, there is a colony of silk weavers who, though they emigrated from Gujarat centuries ago, still speak their ancestral language which, from the name of their caste, is known as Patnuli. The Siyalgirs of Midnapur and the Kichaks of Dacca, small isolated communities, who were originally Gujaratis and have settled in the midst of a Bengal population for many years are said to have yet preserved their original Gujarati speech almost unchanged.

Common script for India.

444. There are in India about 147 languages and about 20 different scripts. Most of the languages being Aryan in origin, have many common words and expressions. With the help of a common script, it is possible for people whose mother-tongues are different to read and understand each other's language. A common script, besides opening the treasures of one language to the speakers of the others, would reduce the time and energy now spent in mastering more than one alphabet ; it would also reduce the expenditure of casting types of different kinds. During the decade, the attention of Indians has been drawn to this subject which has been often discussed in committees and conferences. The latest common script conference met at Allahabad in 1910 under the presidentship of the Hon'ble M. V. Krishnaswami Iyer. What the common script should be is yet a disputed point, but the choice lies between the Devnagri and the Roman. So far as the Baroda State is concerned, the question is solved by His Highness the Maharaja Gaikwad's orders to the effect that all the official books, reports, rules and regulations in the vernacular should be printed in the Gujarati language with Devnagri characters. The State Gazette, called the *Adnya Patrika*, is also published in the Gujarati language with Devnagri types. The Devnagri script is taught in all schools and these official publications are therefore read and understood by Marathas, Musalmans, and all other subjects of the State as well as by the Gujaratis themselves.

Caste and language.

445. In Subsidiary Table III and IIIA, the figures of those actually speaking the different important languages have been compared with the total number of castes, tribes and races ordinarily supposed to use them as their mother-tongue. Taking the Gujarati language first, we find from Imperial Table X that 1,756,307 persons speak the language ; whereas by adding up all the true Hindu, Jain, Aryan and other castes and the Parsis, that are known to use Gujarati for their mother-tongue, we find that only 1,628,607 should speak it. Thus so many as 127,700 persons speak the Gujarati language over and above our estimate of those who may be expected to speak it. Where does this excess come from? The reply will be found by comparing the population of the primitive tribes with the speakers of the Bhil dialects and the Musalman population with the speakers of the Urdu, Hindustani, Persian and Arabic languages. There are 146,347 speakers of the Bhil dialects, while the actual population of the people, who may be expected to speak them is 200,977, thereby showing that 54,630 must be speaking the Bhil dialects and must really be Animistics, although they have returned themselves as Hindus. In the same way, although the total Musalman population is 160,887, the speakers of Urdu, Hindustani, Kachhi, Persian, Arabic and other kindred languages together does not exceed 86,627 persons showing thereby that the rest, *viz.*, 74,260, must be speaking the Gujarati language, and they account for the excess of Gujarati speakers over castes and tribes supposed to speak it. And, as a matter of fact, we know that Vohoras, Memons, Pinjaras, Ghanchis, Tais and other Hindu converts to Islam speak their former Gujarati mother-tongue just as converts to Christianity do so. It was neither necessary nor compulsory that converts should change their language also. There is a movement in recent times amongst Mahomedans living in towns towards substituting Urdu for Gujarati ; but during the whole decade the speakers of Urdu and Hindustani together have not increased by more than 1,120 persons or 1 per cent. Similarly there are 34,834 speakers of the Marathi language and its dialects, while the total strength of the Deccani castes and tribes which may be expected to speak that language is 33,243. This shows that there are 1,591 more persons than there ought to be as speakers of the Marathi language. The difference is small, and is mainly contributed by the forest tribes, close to Khandesh, who returned Marathi or some of its dialects as their home-tongue.

SUBSIDIARY TABLE I—Distribution of Total Population by Language.

Language.	Total number of speakers. 1911.	Total number of speakers. 1901.	Number per mille of the population of the State.	Where chiefly spoken.
1	2	3	4	5
Indo-Aryan family—Aryan sub-family.				
Indian Branch: Sanscratic sub-branch.				
(Western Group)				
1. *Gujarati*	1,756,307	1,762,714	864	All the Divisions.
2. *Bhil languages*	146,347	67,883	72	Navsari Division.
3. *Hindustani*	5,629	34,769	3	Baroda City and Kadi Division.
4. *Hindi*	3,208	233	2	Do.
5. *Urdu*	64,306	34,046	31	All the Divisions.
(Southern Group)				
6. *Marathi*	34,834	37,578	17	Baroda City.
7 *Lahanda (Kachhi)*	15,268	10,880	8	Amreli Division.
8 *Others*	6,904	4,589	3	
	2,032,798	1,952,692	1,000	

SUBSIDIARY TABLE II.—Distribution by Language of the Population of each District.

District or Natural Division.	Number per 10,000 of the population speaking: Gujarati.	Bhil Languages.	Urdu.	Marathi.	Hindustani.	Hindi.	Kachhi.	Other Languages.
1	2	3	4	5	6	7	8	9
Baroda State...	**8,639**	**720**	**317**	**171**	**28**	**16**	**77**	**32**
Baroda Division (Ex. of City) ...	9,195	385	338	27	13	9	5	28
Baroda City	5,490	59	1,315	2,523	269	178	30	136
Kadi Division	9,693	...	232	20	16	7	9	23
Navsari Division	5,918	3,667	195	145	15	6	4	50
Amreli Division	8,773	3	308	91	22	8	776	19

SUBSIDIARY TABLE III—Comparison of Caste and Language Tables.

Tribe.	Strength of tribe (Table XIII.)	Number speaking tribal language. (Table X.)
1	2	3
Bhil—		
Hindu	24,755	35,111
Animist	17,081	
	41,836	
Chodhra—		
Hindu	11,709	26,852
Animist	19,657	
	31,366	
Dhanka—		
Hindu	2,033	......
Animist	16,634	
	18,667	
Dhodia—		
Hindu	5,492	18,051
Animist	14,995	
Aryan	3	
	20,490	
Dubla—		
Hindu	37,577	......
Animist	3,399	
	40,976	
Gamit or Gamatda—		
Hindu	27,440	47,177
Animist	22,175	
	49,615	
Kathodia—		
Hindu	128	231
Animist	394	
	522	
Kolgha—		
Hindu	25	679
Animist	667	
	692	
Kokna—		
Hindu	1,906	5,112
Animist	4,545	
	6,451	
Kotvalia—		
Hindu	583	1,513
Animist	1,075	
	1,658	
Marchi—		
Hindu	980	948
Animist	9	
	989	
Nayakda—		
Hindu	3,634	10,118
Animist	6,396	
	10,030	
Talavia—		
Hindu	8,919	......
Animist	728	
	9,647	
Valvi—		
Hindu	565	......
Animist	481	
	1,046	
Vasava—		
Hindu	4,257	......
Animist	6,694	
	10,951	
Varli—		
Hindu	117	936
Animist	481	
	598	

SUBSIDIARY TABLE III—(*a.*)—Numbers speaking the languages contrasted with castes and races supposed to speak them.

Language.	Actual numbers speaking the language.	Castes, tribes and races supposed to speak the language.	Total of estimated speakers.	Excess of actual speakers over estimated	Excess of estimated speakers over actual.
1	2	3	4	5	6
Gujarati	1,756,307	Hindus (1,697,146) except the Animistic population returned as Hindus (85,566); speakers of Marathi (34,834); Hindi (3,203); Rajasthani (3,410); Kanarese and kindred languages (359); *i.e.*, (1,697,146—127,372). Jains (43,462); Arya Samajis (598); Parsi (7,955); Native Christians (6,962—144 Goanese=6,818).	1,628,607	127,700	......
Marathi	34,834	Deshastha, Koknastha, Karhada and other Deccani Brahmans, Marathas (both Kshatriyas and Kanbis); Prabhus, Sonar, Mahar, Gondhali, Kasar and other Deccani castes.	33,243	1,591	......
Hindustani; Urdu, Panjabi; Arabic, Baloch; Pashto; Persian; Sindhi, Kachhi (Memons, etc.).	86,627	Musalman population (a few Hindus speaking Hindustani being neglected).	160,887	......	74,260
Bhil Dialects ...	146,347	Forest tribes (Animistics as also those really Animistics who returned themselves as Hindus).	200,977	......	54,630
Bavchi	536	Bavchas	1,371	......	835
Rajasthani	3,410	Marwari Brahmans, Vanias, etc.	7,000	......	387
Hindi	3,203				
English	261	Europeans and Eurasians	241	20	......
Miscellaneous ...	1,273	Miscellaneous: Goanese, Jews, etc....	472	801	......
	2,032,798		2,032,798	130,112	130,112

Chapter X.

INFIRMITIES.

GENERAL OBSERVATIONS.

The infirmities recorded.

446. The infirmities regarding which information was collected at the Census were the same as on previous occasions, *viz.*, insanity, blindness, corrosive leprosy and deaf-mutism from birth. The instructions given to the enumerators were as follows :—

" *Column 16 Infirmities.*—If any person be blind of both eyes, or insane, or suffering from corrosive leprosy, or deaf and dumb from birth, enter the name of the infirmity in this column."

" Do not enter those who are blind of one eye only or who are suffering from white leprosy or who have become deaf and dumb after birth."

Accuracy of the return.

447. Owing partly to the difficulties in the way of accurate diagnosis and partly to intentional concealment, the statistics of infirmities are generally less reliable than the other Census figures. Persons who, though weak-minded, are not actually insane, are likely to be returned as such. In addition to the persons, who are deaf and dumb from birth, those who have acquired their infirmity by illness or accident after birth are likely to be entered as deaf-mutes. Those whose sight has become dim in old age are likely to be entered as totally blind. Lastly, there is a danger of the entry as lepers of persons who are suffering from some syphilitic taint or leucoderma, *i. e.*, white leprosy. All these contingencies were foreseen and the written instructions given to the enumerators were supplemented by oral ones and the mistakes likely to be committed were fully explained. Most of the enumerators were local men, well acquainted with the people. Their work was fully checked and the correctness of most of the entries made by them was tested by the higher class of Census Officers by actual observation of those enumerated. Patels and Talatis in villages were directed to go over the entries recorded in the infirmity column of the Census schedule and to see that no case within their knowledge was left unrecorded. A few wrong entries, such as *rat-andhalo* (night-blind), *bahero* (deaf only) and *ardh-pangal* (half-mad) were eliminated in the process of tabulation. In the case of those apparently correctly recorded, test inquiries were made through the Taluka Vahivatdars, but in most of the cases the entry was reported to be correct. Under these circumstances, though not recorded by experts, the statistics of infirmities are believed to be fairly accurate.

Reference to statistics.

448. The statistics regarding infirmities will be found in Imperial Tables XII and XII-A. At the end of this Chapter are given Subsidiary Tables, as under :—

Subsidiary Table I.—The number of persons afflicted in each district per 100,000 of the population at each of the last four Censuses.

Subsidiary Table II.—The distribution of the infirm by age per 10,000 of each sex.

Subsidiary Table III.—The number of persons afflicted per 100,000 of the population at each age-period and the number of females afflicted per 1,000 males.

449. The total number of persons suffering from each infirmity at each of the last four enumerations is noted on the next page. The most striking feature of the statistics is the progressive decline in the number of the afflicted upto 1901. This may be ascribed partly to a progressive improvement in the

accuracy of the diagnosis, partly to an improvement in the material condition of the people, better sanitation and (especially in the case of blindness) cure effected with the aid of modern medical and surgical science and partly (in the decade ending 1901) to a relatively high mortality of persons afflicted with infirmities in the famine years. The present Census shows some increase in all infirmities, except deaf-mutism over the figures of 1901. This is partly due to the change of procedure in tabulation adopted in the present Census and partly perhaps to the return to their homes of those infirms who had migrated during the great famine which preceded the Census of 1901. The column for the record of infirmities comes at the end of the schedule and is usually blank. Experience in 1901 showed that there was great danger of entries in this column being overlooked, and in several Provinces, arrangements were accordingly made to have them dealt with separately. On the present occasion, this procedure was adopted in this State also and some increase in the number of infirmities might, therefore, be ascribed to the greater accuracy of tabulation resulting from it.

Infirmity.	1911.	1901.	1891.	1881.
Insane	523	232	845	932
Deaf-mutes...	425	674	918	1,714
Blind	3,361	1,649	4,751	6,501
Lepers	445	277	569	624
Total ...	4,754	2,832	7,083	9,771

INSANITY.

Comparison with previous Censuses.

450. The total number of insane persons disclosed by the last four Censuses in the State as a whole, as also in the four Districts separately, is given in the margin. The proportionate figures per 100,000 of the population are given in Subsidiary Table I at the end of this Chapter. From this it will appear that insanity has gone on decreasing from decade to decade till 1901, but during the present decade, it shows a large increase. There are now 26 insane persons in 100,000 of the population against 12 in 1901. Though a part of the increase may be due to the greater care taken to ensure accuracy on the present occasion, there can be no doubt that there must have been some increase in the causes which contribute to insanity. It is a curious coincidence that the number of lunatics in the Asylum at Baroda at the close of the year 1910 was 28, that is, exactly double the number ten years previously. There has been no change in the principles on which dangerous lunatics are admitted into the Asylum, and the larger number in the Asylum therfore points to an increase in the causes of insanity.

District.	1911.	1901.	1891.	1881.
State	**523**	**232**	**845**	**932**
Baroda	183	93	260	264
Kadi	199	59	403	487
Navsari	123	64	127	149
Amreli	18	16	55	32

Comparison with other Provinces and Countries.

451. In comparison with European countries, mental disease appears to be comparatively rare in India. In England there were in 1901 about 13 persons of unsound mind to 1 in India. This is mainly due to the different conditions of life in the two countries. As observed by Mr. Gait in his Bengal Census Report for 1901 :—" In Europe the competition between man and man is severe and is yearly becoming more so. The mental wear and tear is very great, and the strain on the nervous system deranges many feeble intellects which in the calm and placid East would escape the storm to which they succumb. A crazy craft often plies with safety on inland waters that would not live for a day in the stress of the open sea."

Local distribution of the insane.

452. Compared with population the proportion of insanes to 100,000 persons in the population is 36·6 in Navsari, which is the highest in the State. Then, follows Baroda with 26·6, then Kadi with 24 and Amreli with 10 stands last. This is graphically illustrated in the map on the next page. It is difficult to

find reasons for these local variations. But there seems to be some correspondence between the consumption of liquor and the prevalence of insanity. According to the latest published report of the Abkari Department, the consumption of liquor is the highest in the Navsari District and the least in the Amreli District.

Average consumption of liquor per head in the population.

District.	Gallons.
Baroda	·21
Kadi	·09
Navsari	2·01
Amreli	·05

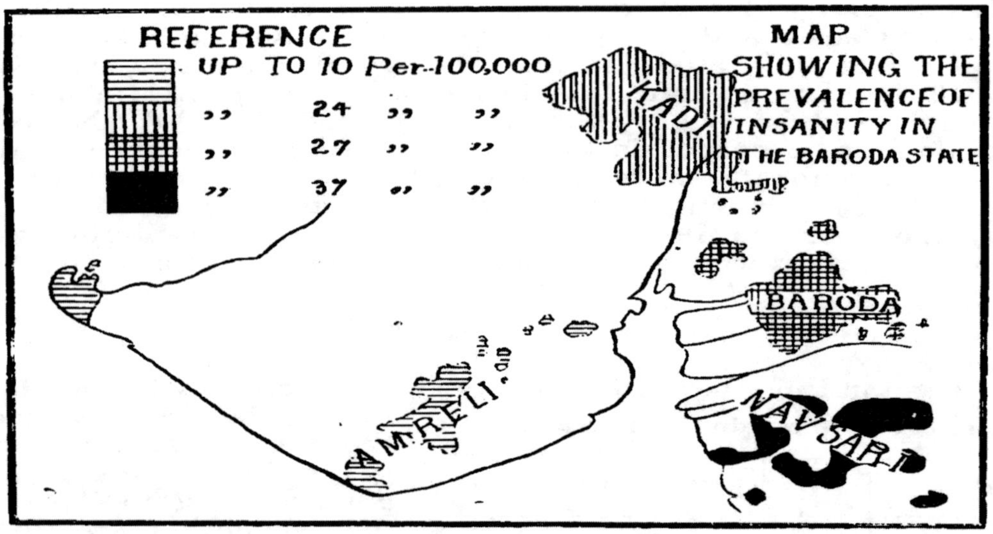

Causes of insanity.

453. Insanity springs mainly from social environments. Though not strictly hereditary, it may be due to that cause also in some cases. To cases of heredity may be added accidental injuries to the head as another extraneous cause. But the vast majority of cases are personal, and depending upon the social habits of a man, are not restricted to any community. They may be ascribed to (1) food and drink, (2) social customs, (3) physical ailments, (4) observances of religion, (5) personal habits, and finally (6) moral causes. Under the first head come the abuse of alcoholic and narcotic drinks, consumption of intoxicating drugs and general intemperance. Among the low classes, country liquor and cheap brandy and other European spirits are consumed on a large scale. Opium-eating which is gradually decreasing, may cloud the intellect temporarily but rarely ends in insanity. On the other hand the preparations of the hemp, *bhang* and *ganja*, are known to lead to produce mental derangement. The finding of the majority in the Hemp Drugs Commission was that the moderate use of *ganja* does no appreciable harm to the brain, although when taken in excess, it may induce insanity. Two members out of seven, were of opinion that the use of this drug is a fertile cause of insanity. Among social customs, enforced widowhood among the Hindus, *zenana* system among high class Hindus and Musalmans, and consanguineous marriages among the Musalmans and Parsis are accountable to a more or less degree for insanity. Uterine disorders, epilepsy and long continuance of diseases may also lead to insanity. The fourth head mentioned above includes fanatics and devotees, who work themselves up to the height of frenzy, particularly on great festivals. They are found both among the Hindus and Musalmans. Sexual excesses and immoral life, and certain dangerous practices in young age are also fruitful causes of insanity. Intense brain work, mental anxiety, losses in trade and disappointment in love and other affairs are some of the moral causes, which along with the increase of civilization in a community tend to foster insanity which often culminates in suicide.

Insanity by religion.

454. In the distribution of insanity by religion, the Parsis head the list. Then follow Mahomedans, Jains, Animistics and Hindus in order. In the Censuses of 1891 and 1901 also Parsis and Mahomedans showed a higher ratio than Jains, Hindus and Animistics. The less prevalence of insanity among the Hindus and Jains may be ascribed to their vegetable diet, abstemiousness from drink and quiet pursuits in life, while animal food, use of spirituous liquors, passionate habits and *parda* system may be the reasons for the higher ratio in the other communities.

Religion.	Insanes per 10,000 of the population.
Parsis	8·9
Mahomedans	4·7
Jains	4·6
Animists...	2·4
Hindus	2·3

Insanity by sex.

455. The number of insane males greatly exceeds that of females. For equal numbers the occurrence of lunacy is 30 per cent. less in the female than in the male sex. This is probably due to women leading a quiet, secluded and abstemious life. They are also restrained from the excesses of various kinds in which men indulge ; their work is lighter and they suffer less from hardship, exposure and anxiety. In the State as a whole, the ratio of insane males to insane females is roughly as 3 to 2. The proportion of insane females to insane males is the highest (5 to 4) in Navsari where insanity is most prevalent and the lowest (8 to 1) in Amreli where it is the least.

Insanity by age.

456. The proportion of sexes varies greatly at the different age-periods. At no age they approach equality except at the age-periods 15-20, 30-35 and 50-55. The figures for both sexes are small in infancy when there is a natural reluctance on the part of the relatives to recognize the existence of the disease, but increase rapidly after the age of 25. Between the ages of 20 and 40 among males and 20 to 35 among females, the proportion of the insane is almost stationary. It then declines upto the age of 60 and then rises higher for the higher ages.

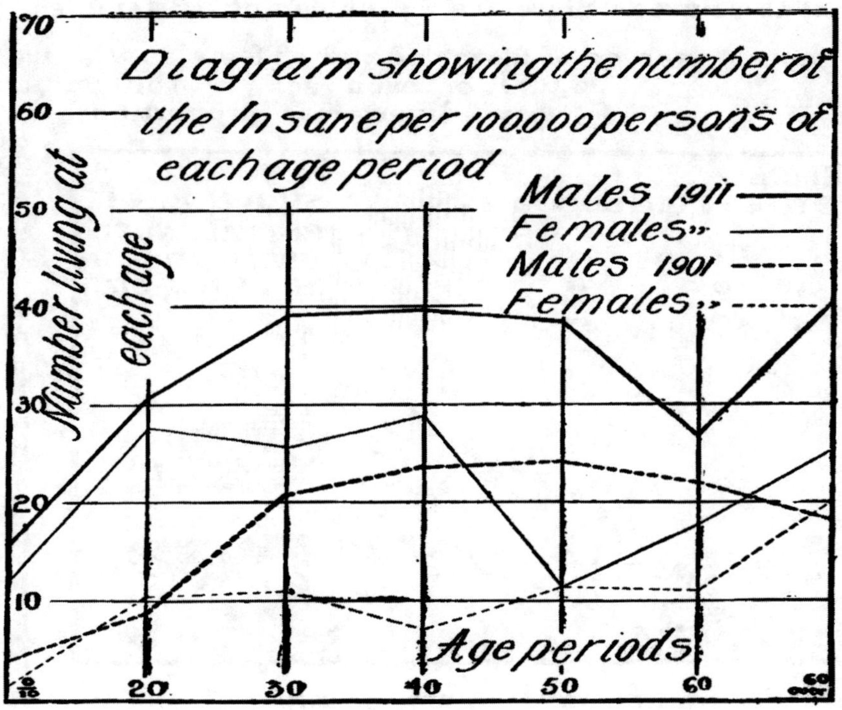

DEAF—MUTISM.

Comparison with previous Censuses.

District.	1911	1901	1891	1881
State	**425**	**674**	**918**	**1,714**
Baroda	137	186	291	495
Kadi	131	209	345	762
Navsari	139	196	202	306
Amreli	18	83	80	151

457. The total number of deaf-mutes in the whole State, given in the margin, shows that the infirmity has declined from Census to Census and is now much less than what it was before. There are now 21 deaf-mutes in 100,000 of the population against 35 in 1901, 38 in 1891, and 79 in 1881. The general decrease in the present Census is shared by all the districts and is due to the accuracy of the return. When a person was afflicted with this infirmity, the enumerators were directed to enter him or her as deaf and dumb ; but sometimes the words "deaf" or "dumb" alone were entered. In the course of tabulation, the entries of 'deaf' were altogether neglected, but persons shown as dumb were assumed to be congenital deaf-mutes. This may possibly have added to the return some persons who had lost their speech by accident or illness, but their number was probably not more than that of genuine deaf-mutes omitted, because shown only as 'deaf' by the enumerators. Deaf-mutism is a congenital defect and deaf-mutes are known to be relatively short-lived. The proportion of deaf-mutes to the total number of persons living at each age-period should show a steady decline and a reference to the diagram given in para. 462 will show that this is, on the whole, the case at the present Census. In 1891 and 1901 on the other hand, the proportion rises rapidly at the higher ages, which shows that on those occasions, many persons returned as deaf-mutes must not be really so, but must have lost the sense of hearing in their old age.

Comparison with other countries.

458. The occurrence of deaf-mutism is said to be somewhat more common in India than in Europe, but the difference is not very marked. In India as a whole, in 1901, 62 males and 42 females were afflicted with this infirmity in a population of 100,000 persons of each sex compared with 60 males and 50 females in England and Wales. The corresponding figures in the present Census of the Baroda State are 29 males and 13 females.

Local distribution.

459. The general average of 29 males and 13 females who are afflicted among 100,000 of each sex in the State, is the resultant of very divergent proportions in the different divisions of the State as illustrated in the map given in the margin. The district in which deaf-mutism is most prevalent is Navsari. Here more than 40 persons in every 100,000 are deaf-mutes. Then follows Baroda with 20 persons, Kadi with 16 persons and Amreli stands last with 10 persons who are deaf-mutes in 100,000 persons of its population.

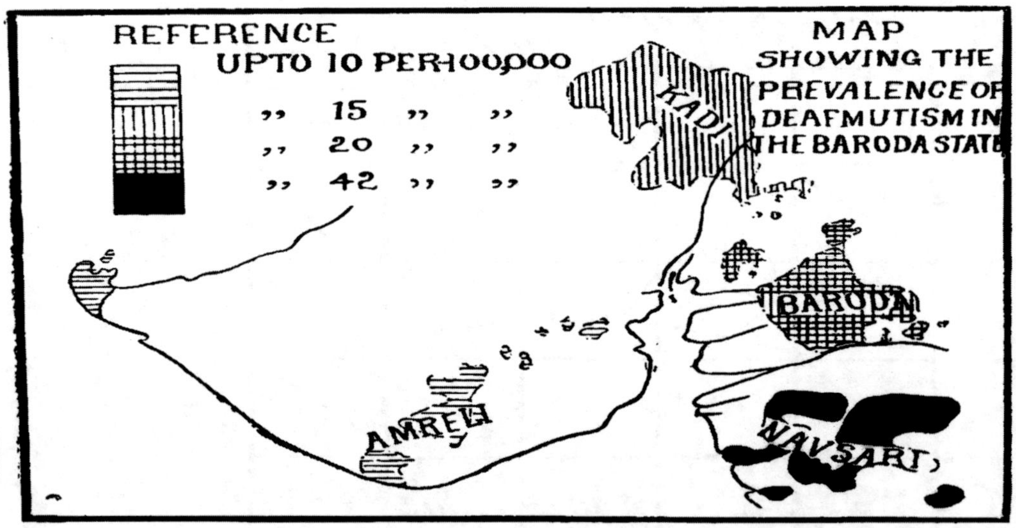

460. The order in which the four districts of the State stand with regard to their figures for insanity remains the same with reference to the figures of deaf-mutism also. Navsari, which enjoys the unenviable reputation of harbouring more insane persons in proportion to its population, has also the highest proportion of deaf-mutes ; and Amreli, which has the lowest proportion of insanes, has also the lowest of deaf-mutes. Insanity and deaf-mutism appear therefore to have some connection between them.

Connection between insanity and deaf-mutism.

461. Distribution of deaf-mutism seems to depend mainly on locality. It has no special predilection for any particular religion or caste. The Parsis and Mahomedans, in spite of their consanguineous marriages are not more prone to the affliction than the Hindus, who eschew such connections. No inference can be drawn from the high or low status of a caste as regards immunity from this infirmity. In those which suffer rather heavily and in those which are comparatively exempt, there are castes both high and low.

Deaf-mutism by religion and caste.

462. As in the case of the insane, so also amongst deaf-mutes, males in all countries suffer more than females. In India, as a whole, they outnumbered them in 1901 in the ratio of 3 to 2. In the present Census, deaf-mute males preponderate over females in this State in the ratio of 5 to 2. In the diagram given in the margin, the proportion of the persons returned as deaf-mutes at each age is compared with the total population of the same age. Parents do not readily admit that a child is deaf and dumb, so long as there is any hope of its acquiring the power of speech and hearing. The number returned at ages under 5 is therefore much below the truth. During the age-periods 5 to 10, the proportion of deaf-mutes steadily increases and from the age of 15 onwards, it steadily declines. This shows that deaf-mutes are short-lived, as compared with persons not so afflicted, and that in the present Census, the figures at the higher ages have not at all been swollen by the inclusion of persons who have merely become deaf in their old age.

Proportion of sex and age distribution.

BLINDNESS.

463. Of all the infirmities recorded at the Census, blindness is the most easy to diagnose and the least likely to be concealed. The Gujarati word *kano* is used in the unambiguous sense of a person suffering from loss of one eye only, and there was thus no possibility of such persons being included among the blind. There is only one word *andhalo* for the blind, but as it is applied also to those who are suffering

Accuracy of statistics.

merely from dimness of sight, due to old age, there was a probability of such persons being entered as blind. But the stress laid upon the subject in the instructions and the increased efficiency of the supervising agency, reduced this source of error to the smallest dimensions. As an extra precaution, a special inquiry was made, through the District Officers, after the Census, for all persons aged 40 and upwards who were entered as blind and only 5 cases of senile glaucoma found to have been wrongly entered, were neglected in the course of tabulation.

464. Statistics of the blind given in the margin show that the infirmity has decreased from decade to decade till 1901 in the State as a whole, as also in all the districts. In 1911, however, there were 1,712 more blind persons than ten years previously. The number of hospitals in the State has increased from 54 in 1901 to 58 in 1911, and, though the number of operations performed for cataract during the decade does not exceed about a hundred, there is no doubt that medical relief is now available in every taluka. Small-pox, which was formerly one of the main causes of blindness, is now not so dangerous, owing to the spread of vaccination throughout the State. There ought, therefore, to be a decrease rather than an increase in the number of the blind in the State. The increase shown by the Census seems to be due to the accuracy of the statistics on the present occasion rather than to any sudden increase in the causes which bring about blindness. The ambiguous wording of the instructions in the past Censuses must have caused the omission of recording as blind those who were not so from birth and the old procedure of copying infirmities on the same slip must have operated to the leaving out of some entries in tabulation.

Comparison with previous enumerations.

District.	1911.	1901.	1891.	1881.
State	**3,361**	**1,649**	**4,751**	**6,501**
Baroda	761	367	1,091	1,635
Kadi	1,688	613	2,718	3,634
Navsari	489	373	515	747
Amreli	423	296	427	485

465. In the State as a whole, there are 166 blind persons per 100,000 of the population. The prevalence of blindness is to a great extent determined by climate. It is most frequent in a hot and dry climate, where there are frequent dust-storms blowing clouds of dust and sand, particles of which continually enter into and irritate the eye. On the other hand, it is comparatively rare in a cool or damp district where there is a comparative absence of dust. The distribution of the blind in the Baroda State is in accordance with what might be expected from the above considerations. Blindness is most common in the Kadi and Amreli Districts, where the temperature is the highest in the State and where frequent dust-storms arise. On the other hand, it is less common in the Baroda and Navsari Districts, where the climate is comparatively cooler and more damp and where dust-storms are scarce.

Local distribution.

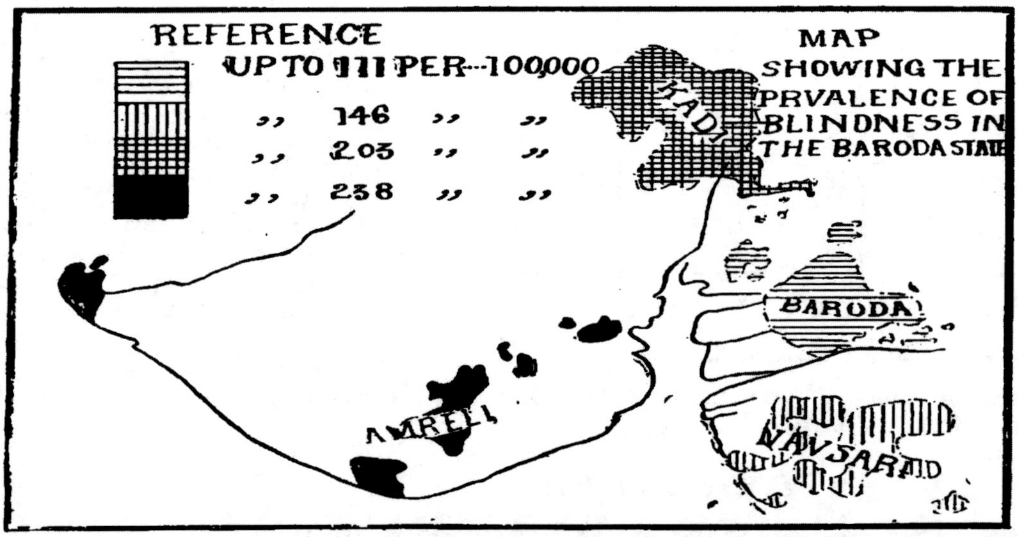

Proportion of the sexes.

466. The domestic arrangements of Hindu houses is a fruitful cause of blindness among the females, except in the case of a few opulent families. The mistress of the house or her daughter-in-law invariably cooks for the household. The cookroom is generally a small dark room wanting in proper passage for the escape of smoke, and the fuel used is of a cheap kind which causes much smoke. Females are generally secluded in the house and are not able to enjoy the green verdure of nature or the delightful and cool breezes in the open air. As a result they suffer in their eyes, as indeed in their general health, and it is no uncommon sight to see women with inflamed eyes unable to bear the glare of the day. It is for this reason that in the number of the blind returned in the Census, females preponderate over males, the excess of blind females being 33 per cent. In 1901 also the number of blind females was in excess over males, though to a smaller extent (21 per cent). In the other Provinces also the blind females are usually more numerous than the males. On a consideration of the proportion of sexes by age-periods, we find that blindness is almost equally prevalent both among males and females upto the age of 20. From 20 onwards females greatly outnumber the males till 60, after which the proportion of blind females is nearly twice as much as that of males.

Distribution by age.

467. While deaf-mutism is congenital and insanity and leprosy are the diseases of early manhood and middle age, blindness usually attacks the old. This is clearly seen from the annexed diagram. Blindness is very rare in youth and goes on increasing as the years advance. After 40, the liability to the disease increases rapidly, mainly owing to cataract. At the earlier ages, the affliction is mainly due to the other causes, chief among which is opacity of the cornea due to neglected conjunctivities in infancy. The proportion of blind persons at the earlier ages is however relatively very small and more than three-fourths of the total number is over 45 years of age.

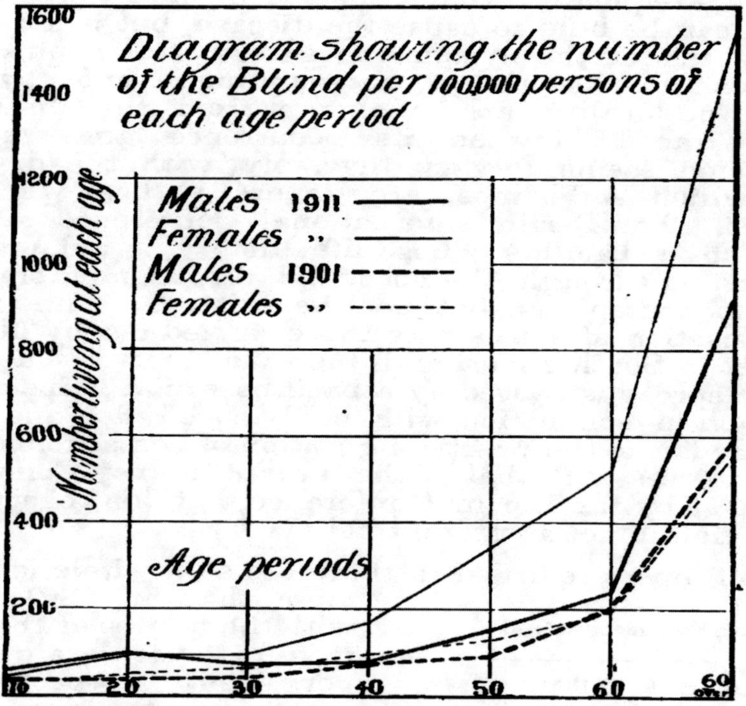

Preventable blindness.

468. There can be no doubt that a large number of cases of blindness is due to ignorance and want of proper and timely treatment. Affections of a delicate and sensitive organ like the eye are either left untreated or are treated by quacks rather than by duly qualified physicians. Every year, Mahomedans from Upper India visit our towns and larger villages and professing to be *unani hakims*, experts in the removal of cataract, attract crowds of patients. Their treatment gives some temporary relief, but in the end most of them cause incurable blindness. An enormous and needless waste of human eyes can be prevented, if such quacks are prohibited by law from treating any affection of the eyes, and a knowledge of

the best methods of prevention and cure is spread among the people as widely as possible. In England and Germany, midwives are expressly prohibited by law from treating any affection of the eyes or eyelids of infants, however slight. On the appearance of the first symptoms, they are required to represent to the parents, or others in charge, that medical assistance is urgently needed, or, if necessary, they are themselves to report to the local authorities and the district doctor. Neglect of these regulations entails liability to punishment. Eleven of the United States of America have enacted laws requiring that, if one or both eyes of an infant should become inflamed, swollen or reddened at any time within two weeks of its birth, it shall be the duty of the midwife or nurse having charge of such infant to report in writing, within six hours, to the health officer or some legally qualified physician, the fact that such inflammation, swelling or redness exists. The penalty for failure to comply is fine or imprisonment.

LEPROSY.

Causes of leprosy.

469. The Leprosy Commission appointed in 1890 to visit India and inquire into the etiology and spread of the disease and the means by which it might be stamped out, reported that the disease has no marked tendency to spread either by hereditary transmission or by contagion, but in the great majority of cases, it originates *de novo*. No race is exempt from the disease, but the poor and destitute are attacked much more frequently than the rich and prosperous. No article of diet, *e. g.*, fish, can be held to cause the disease, but it is possible that some kinds of food may render the system more ready to contract it. The same conclusion applies to insanitary surroundings and syphilis. No geological formation and no locality can be exempt from the disease, and no correspondence can be traced between its occurrence and variations in temperature, but its diffusion seems to vary inversely with the dryness of the climate, and the tracts which suffer most are generally those where endemic cholera is most prevalent. The Berlin International Conference of 1897 held that the disease is caused by a bacillus, whose life history is unknown, but that it probably enters the system through the nose and mucus membrane ; it also held that the disease is contagious, but not hereditary. The most recent investigations into the causation of leprosy are those carried out by Mr. Jonathan Hutchinson, F.R.C.S., first in South Africa and then in India. The conclusion arrived at by him is that leprosy is caused by a bacillus which gains access to the body through the stomach in connection with badly-cured fish and not by the breath or by the skin. So far as the practical question of contagion is concerned, Mr. Hutchinson's theory agrees with that of the Indian Leprosy Commission and differs from that arrived at by the Berlin Conference, but his theory about the disease originating from fish is not at present believed.

Comparison with previous enumerations.

470. The number of lepers returned in the State as a whole is 60 per cent. more than in 1901. Compared with the figures of 1881 and 1891, it is however less by 22 and 29 per cent. respectively. The increase on the present occasion is probably due to the greater accuracy in the present Census and also to the return to their homes of those lepers who in 1901 had migrated elsewhere on account of the famine of 1899-1900. It does not appear that the greater number of lepers now found was due to the inclusion of leucoderma and secondary syphilis, within leprosy.

District.	1911.	1901.	1891.	1881.
State	**445**	**277**	**569**	**624**
Baroda	192	118	255	287
Kadi	25	14	89	123
Navsari	214	129	197	193
Amreli	14	16	28	21

The decline of leprosy in Europe is attributed mainly to improved hygienic habits and surroundings and to increased material prosperity. It may be hoped that the same causes will gradually bring about its disappearance here also.

471. The local distribution of lepers is shown in the sub-joined map. It is of very rare occurrence in the dry districts of Kadi and Amreli. On the other hand, the proportion of lepers is the highest in the Navsari District, which is well-known for its humidity and for the poverty of its people. After Navsari comes Baroda, but the higher proportion of lepers here than in Kadi and Amreli is due to its having the Anusuya Leper Hospital, situated on the bank of the Narbada in the Sinore Taluka. Here is a temple of a goddess called *Anusuya Mata* and the locality has the reputation of curing the lepers by simply rubbing a little of its earth on the afflicted parts. A large number of lepers from all parts of the State, as also from the neighbouring foreign territory, congregates there. To alleviate the sufferings of these miserable beings, the Government of His Highness the Maharaja Gaekwad opened on the 1st August 1890, a leper hospital on the spot. It is in charge of a Sub-Assistant Surgeon, and has attached to it an *Annachhatra* or Boarding House, wherein the lepers are fed and treated. In the Census month, there were 67 lepers (48 males and 19 females) in this institution. Of these 41 (26 males and 15 females) were born in the Baroda District itself, 1 (male) in Kadi, 1 (male) in Amreli and the rest (24) had come from the adjoining British and Native States' territories. Even if the number received from Kadi and Amreli were added to those districts, they show comparatively greater freedom from leprosy than Navsari. No connection between cholera and leprosy can be traced, as suggested by the Leprosy Commission, but according to their other theory, the varying prevalence of the disease in the Districts of Baroda, Kadi and Amreli on one hand and Navsari on the other, can be explained by their comparatively greater prosperity and freedom from humidity of the former than the latter.

Local distribution.

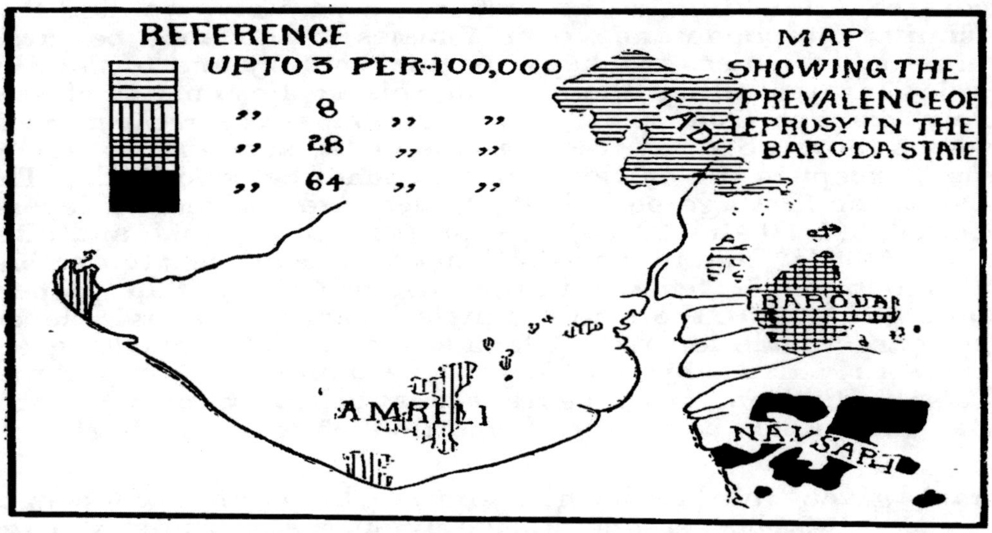

472. In the statistics of lepers by religion, the Animistics show the highest proportion; then come Hindus, Musalmans, and Jains, and Parsis stand last with no lepers at all. This also supports the theory that the poor and destitute are attacked much more frequently than the rich and the prosperous.

Distribution by religion.

473. The general conclusion, which statistics of lepers by castes indicate also supports the above view. The lower castes, which are filthy in their habits and get less nutritious food are most liable to the disease. Dublas and Vasavas appear to be suffering from leprosy to a greater extent than other castes. It is popularly believed that this is due to their eating the flesh of dead animals.

Distribution by Caste.

Caste.	No. per 100,000 who are lepers.
Dubla	1,765
Vasava	1,001
Gamatda	225
Brahman Anavala	40
Vania Shrimali	11
Kanbi	7
Soni	9

Proportion of sexes.

474. Males seem to be more liable to the disease than females. The returns show that in the State as a whole there are 31 male lepers to 12 female lepers in every 100,000 of the population of each sex. Looking to the districts separately, we find that male lepers show a similar preponderance over females. This may be partly due to the seclusion in which females are kept in this country and to the reticence of their male relations regarding them. But this applies only to classes which are comparatively exempt from the disease. Amongst the great mass of the population, the women move about as freely as the males and the existence of a disease like leprosy, except in the earlier stages, cannot be concealed. The age statistics show that at the first age-period (0-5), there are no female lepers; at the next two age-periods (5-10 and 10-15) the proportion is equal, and after that upto the age-period 25-30, it falls to one-half and then continues to decline, until at 40 to 45, males outnumber females in the ratio of 4 to 1. The proportion then again rises and at 55 to 60, there are 2 male lepers to 1 female leper. At "60 and over," there are 9 male lepers to 1 female leper. This result agrees very closely with that arrived at by the Leprosy Commission who found that in the case of small children, both sexes are attacked in nearly equal proportions and that at the higher ages, the proportion of males is higher to that of females.

Age distribution.

475. The diagram given in the margin shows the number of lepers to 100,000 persons of each age-period. Under the age of 15, the proportion of lepers is very small but it soon begins to grow. There is a considerable increase between 15 and 20 and from that age until 45, the rise is uniform and rapid. After 45, there is a decline. A leper's life is a comparatively short one. There is a proverb current among the people which says "*Khai, kharmodo ane pata ae jaya gabadgata*," *i.e.*, those who suffer from consumption, foot and mouth diseases and leprosy die very soon. According to Daniellsen and Boeck, the average duration of life from the date of attack is only nine years and a half for tuberculated, and eighteen years and a half in the case of anethetic leprosy. It follows that the steady increase in the proportion of lepers between the ages 15 and 45 indicates a marked rise in the liability to infection between these ages.

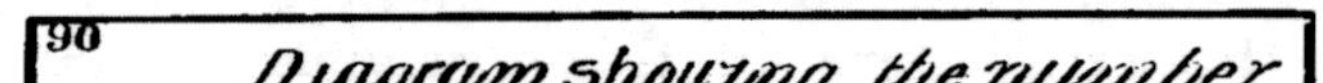

The Lepers' Act.

476. Prior to 1901, it was not unusual to find lepers preparing for sale or selling articles of food, drink or clothing intended for human use. They bathed, washed clothes in or took water from public wells or tanks; they drove or rode in public conveyances plying for hire and exercised such trades or callings as that of a potter, domestic servant, water-carrier, washerman, hotel-keeper, tailor, draper, shoemaker, &c. With a view to check the evils arising from these practices, the Baroda Lepers' Act was passed in November 1910.

It prohibits lepers from preparing or selling articles of food, drink or clothing, bathing or washing in public tanks and conducting or riding in public conveyances. It also authorizes the police to arrest wandering lepers, and, on a medical officer certifying that they are lepers, to forward them to the nearest Leper Asylum. The Act is yet in its infancy, but its beneficial results may be expected in the next Census.

Fight with leprosy in the Philippines.

477. Major Hooton, I.M.S., who attended the recent meetings of the Far Eastern Association of Tropical disease at Manila, submitted a long report to the Government of India dealing with tubercle and leprosy. As regards the latter, he writes:—"The segregation of the lepers is perhaps the most striking of the sanitary reforms that have been inaugurated by the American Government of the Philippines, though great advances have been made in vaccination and other directions. It is now about few years ago that the initial steps were taken. An attempt was first made to explain the etiology of the disease to sufferers and their friends, and prominent Philippinos were induced to assist in the education of their compatriots with this end in view. Then gradually a few lepers were persuaded to take up their residence in the buildings prepared for them in the island of Cubon. Every available means was adopted to make these people contented and comfortable, so that the disinclination of those still at large might be overcome, if possible, without resort to force. As regards the arrangements at the Leper Colony, residents are allowed to write letters and receive visits periodically from their friends, but the letters are disinfected and friends and relations must live in quarters provided for them on an adjacent island. The results of the segregation have more than justified the trouble and expense involved. A Census of lepers in the islands (excepting Mindanao) showed 6,000 at the commencement of the operations, and this number, owing to the large death-rate among the patients and the reduction in infection of healthy persons, has now fallen to 2,300. It is believed that very few lepers remain at large at the present time."

Native remedies for leprosy.

478. Among vaidyas and other native practitioners, leprosy is said to be cured by taking castor-oil and powdered bark of the *nimb* tree. This remedy does not appear to have been tried by any medical practitioner of the western school, but I was assured by a well-known vaidya in Maroli, District Navsari, that some patients have been cured by him by this treatment, continued for a couple of months.

SUBSIDIARY TABLE I.—Number afflicted per 100,000 of the population at each of the last four censuses.

District or Natural Division.	Insane.								Deaf-Mute.							
	Male.				Female.				Male.				Female.			
	1911	1901	1891	1881	1911	1901	1891	1881	1911	1901	1891	1881	1911	1901	1891	1881
1	2	3	4	5	6	7	8	9	10	11	12	13	14	15	16	17
Baroda State	**30**	**15**	**43**	**51**	**21**	**9**	**27**	**34**	**29**	**41**	**45**	**93**	**13**	**28**	**30**	**62**
Baroda Division (with City) ...	33	19	37	45	20	9	26	23	25	36	43	77	14	21	27	51
Kadi Division	26	9	45	56	20	5	28	42	20	28	37	93	10	22	25	60
Navsari Division	40	25	55	57	33	17	24	46	63	77	81	128	19	53	45	84
Amreli Division	17	10	35	34	2	8	25	8	14	57	44	112	5	38	45	92

District or Natural Division.	Blind.								Lepers.							
	Male.				Female.				Male.				Female.			
	1911	1901	1891	1881	1911	1901	1891	1881	1911	1901	1891	1881	1911	1901	1891	1881
1	18	19	20	21	22	23	24	25	26	27	28	29	30	31	32	33
Baroda State	**129**	**75**	**161**	**248**	**204**	**95**	**235**	**351**	**31**	**18**	**32**	**39**	**12**	**10**	**15**	**17**
Baroda Division (with City) ...	91	57	122	189	134	57	147	243	38	21	39	51	16	16	22	22
Kadi Division	158	62	193	305	249	85	304	434	4	2	12	18	1	1	4	6
Navsari Division	114	113	137	210	177	136	186	313	91	59	89	92	36	27	34	41
Amreli Division	169	139	187	250	309	205	291	415	15	13	16	19	...	5	15	8

SUBSIDIARY TABLE II—Distribution of the infirmities by age per 10,000 of each sex.

Age.	Insane. Male. 1911	1901	1891	1881	Insane. Female. 1911	1901	1891	1881	Deaf-Mute. Male. 1911	1901	1891	1881	Deaf-Mute. Female. 1911	1901	1891	1881
1	2	3	4	5	6	7	8	9	10	11	12	13	14	15	16	17
0— 5	94	198	187	244	294	248	32	169	530	289	335	320	407	572	514	231
5—10	1,097	397	599	658	1,030	124	734	904	1,887	994	845	1,025	2,114	1,031	1,329	723
10—15	877	530	1,140	987	932	1,111	766	1,074	1,357	1,211	1,426	958	1,707	1,146	1,429	831
15—20	972	794	1,364	1,265	1,274	1,481	1,809	1,074	1,324	1,236	1,109	921	1,138	954	971	677
20—25	1,191	1,655	1,308	2,286	1,422	1,481	1,002	1,949	1,126	967	1,021	1,381	1,382	1,107	771	1,307
25—30	1,348	1,060	990		1,078	1,111	1,002		1,093	1,012	951		732	726	600	
30—35	1,097	1,457	1,121	2,199	1,470	740	970	1,949	662	791	951	1,419	976	687	829	1,277
35—40	939	994	785		735	493	809		497	606	528		569	954	457	
40—45	846	1,126	879	1,316	490	986	766	1,525	464	1,211	792	1,429	325	687	686	1,415
45—50	533	530	411		148	493	420		397	241	458		407	152	343	
50—55	376	729	599	501	490	618	679	734	166	670	475	1,306	81	648	857	1,708
55—60	158	199	75		98	248	364		166	241	264		81	305	171	
60 and over	472	331	542	544	539	866	647	622	331	531	845	1,241	81	1,031	1,143	1,831

Age.	Blind. Male. 1911	1901	1891	1881	Blind. Female. 1911	1901	1891	1881	Lepers. Male. 1911	1901	1891	1881	Lepers. Female. 1911	1901	1891	1881
1	18	19	20	21	22	23	24	25	26	27	28	29	30	31	32	33
0— 5	491	291	582	286	305	236	326	191	92	165	...	22	...	421	233	57
5—10	688	742	639	547	375	526	398	417	123	385	126	111	254	631	698	344
10—15	756	728	610	513	405	604	351	390	123	549	479	467	254	421	581	747
15—20	606	517	530	545	345	515	446	345	671	440	302	622	762	316	872	862
20—25	556	755	674	1,123	461	537	476	748	854	1,154	1,184	1,755	1,272	210	988	1,495
25—30	547	636	595		461	760	512		915	1,484	1,134		1,357	1,790	1,220	
30—35	526	755	694	1,123	581	705	593	1,114	1,502	1,209	1,007	2,534	1,357	2,527	1,047	2,298
35—40	500	702	600		666	805	497		1,441	1,704	1,033		1,610	1,474	872	
40—45	565	795	744	1,273	771	1,140	856	1,348	1,748	604	1,713	2,266	1,187	210	1,454	1,610
45—50	634	303	496		836	459	457		854	879	982		593	526	465	
50—55	1,078	953	1,002	1,575	1,231	1,174	1,207	1,633	671	934	982	1,357	846	843	698	1,438
55—60	491	517	282		365	302	421		305	219	252		254	105	58	
60 and over	2,562	2,106	2,752	3,015	3,298	2,237	3,460	3,814	701	274	806	866	254	526	814	1,149

SUBSIDIARY TABLE III.—Number afflicted per 100,000 persons of each age-period and number of females afflicted per 1,000 males.

Age.	Number afflicted per 100,000. Insane. Male.	Insane. Female.	Deaf-Mute. Male.	Deaf-Mute. Female.	Blind. Male.	Blind. Female.	Lepers. Male.	Lepers. Female.	Number of females afflicted per 1,000 males. Insane.	Deaf-Mute.	Blind.	Lepers.
1	2	3	4	5	6	7	8	9	10	11	12	13
0— 5	2	4	10	3	42	38	2	...	2,000	312	910	...
5—10	29	20	47	25	77	54	3	3	600	456	591	750
10—15	28	23	42	26	105	100	4	4	678	512	786	750
15—20	33	32	43	18	88	86	23	11	839	350	841	409
20—25	37	29	33	17	75	92	27	15	763	500	1,195	536
25—30	41	22	32	9	73	94	29	16	511	273	1,211	533
30—35	39	34	22	13	80	132	55	18	857	600	1,633	327
35—40	40	23	20	11	90	207	63	29	500	466	1,956	404
40—45	38	15	19	6	111	222	81	20	370	285	1,974	246
45—50	39	8	28	14	195	469	65	19	177	416	1,988	250
50—55	26	22	11	2	316	544	48	22	833	200	1,673	454
55—60	27	13	27	7	372	499	55	20	400	200	1,089	300
60 and over ...	40	25	27	2	928	1,543	61	7	733	100	1,883	130

Chapter XI.

CASTE, TRIBE OR RACE.

Reference to Tables.

479. Five of the Imperial Tables contain statistics bearing upon castes, tribes and races. The chief of these is Table XIII, which gives by sexes the number in each caste, which is found in each district. The others are :—

Table IX.—Education in selected castes.

Table XII A.—Infirmities by selected castes.

Table XIV.—Civil condition by age in selected castes.

Table XVI.—Occupation by selected castes.

Discussions of the statistics in these last four tables will be found in Chapters VIII (Education), X (Infirmities), VII (Civil Condition) and XII (Occupation). The present chapter deals only with the figures in Table XIII.

At the end of this chapter are given two Subsidiary Tables as under :—

Subsidiary Table I.—Castes classified according to their traditional occupations.

Subsidiary Table II.—Variations in caste, tribe, etc., since 1881.

PART I.—DESCRIPTIVE.

Sub-castes recorded.

480. The record of sub-castes was optional in the Imperial Census scheme, but the Government of His Highness the Maharaja Gaekwad having decided that castes as well as sub-castes should be recorded, Table XIII, includes both. The sub-castes have been noted below each caste.

Difficulty of securing a correct return.

481. One of the most difficult tasks in the Census operations is to secure a correct return of castes. The difficulty arises in two ways. In the first place the people themselves have no clear idea as to what caste means, and often give as their caste name, the name of their own occupation, sub-caste, clan or title. In the second place, some people in their present prosperity are ashamed to name their true caste and try to conceal it by assuming some newly-coined name which might give them a higher social status. The enumerators being ordinarily not better informed, are unable to correct the errors which the persons enumerated may commit. Owing to this circumstance, the caste returns in the previous Baroda Censuses have been vitiated by the entry of a large number of persons, not under their true caste name, but under general terms denoting occupation, title, sub-caste, sept, etc. Thus in Table XIII of the last Census, we find 'Achari' entered as a Brahman caste, but it is merely an occupational name, denoting that the person who bears it is a cook. Garasia, Rajput and Thakore are entered as separate castes, but a Garasia is a Rajput, Koli or Kathi holding Giras lands and a Thakore is only an honorific name for a Rajput or a Koli. Sutar (carpenter), Luhar (blacksmith), Soni (goldsmith) and many other occupational names have become true caste names, but there are yet many occupations which are followed by persons of different castes, and in their case, the occupational name is not the caste name. Thus Chudgar (bracelet-maker), Gandhi (grocer), Kagdi (stationer), Khasdar (groom), Maniara (haberdasher), Marwadi (trader from Marwar), Pardeshi (Upper India man), Patwa (silk-thread-maker), and many other similar terms are not true caste names, but only occupational and territorial terms, and yet all these have been returned and tabulated in the past as caste names. The persons who follow these occupations or are known by their territorial names, may belong to several distinct castes. In the same way, the names of several religious mendicants, such as Aghori, Brahmachari, Jangum and Sanyasi, which were

also returned as caste names, are not true caste names, but only general terms denoting religious order or following.

Caste Index.

482. With a view to eliminate all these incorrect names from the caste return and to make it as correct as possible, a Caste Index was prepared on the present occasion. It was divided into two parts—Part A containing a complete list of castes and sub-castes likely to be found in the State ; and Part B containing those terms which are not true caste names but mere local and general terms, occupational names, etc., which were wrongly returned as caste names in the previous Censuses. The Caste Index was first published as a provisional one and circulated among District Officers for opinion and suggestions. The final one was issued after a careful consideration of such suggestions as were received and such further investigation as could be made on the spot during my inspection tour. It was printed in the Gujarati language and copies were freely distributed among the Census staff. Charge Superintendents and District Officers were requested to go over both the lists carefully and to instruct their Supervisors and Enumerators, so that no entry, which was at variance with the names given in the Index, Part A, was made in column 8th of the schedule.

Correctness of return.

483. The number of wrong entries due to ignorance or to deliberate misstatement was thus greatly reduced. If a caste name, not mentioned in the Index, was returned in the course of the preliminary enumeration, the enumerator refused to enter it before making further inquiry. If, in spite of further inquiry, he got a name not mentioned in the Index, he reported the circumstance to his Supervisor, who allowed it to be entered if he was satisfied that, though not mentioned in the Index, it was a true caste name ; and immediately reported the circumstance, through his Charge Superintendent, to my office, where further investigation was made, to make sure that it was really a caste name. A few instances of wrong entries thus prevented may be mentioned. Some people returned such general terms, as Vania, Deccani, Gandhi, etc., as their caste names. The enumerator instead of recording it put such further questions, as, " That is the name of your occupation, or country, but what is your caste name ? What sort of Vania are you ?" and so on. The number of wrong entries, due to ignorance, was thus easily prevented. Those relating to deliberate misstatement were difficult to deal with. A section of Luhars (blacksmiths), known as Panchal Luhars, claimed to be returned as Panchal Brahmans ; some Baria Kolis claimed to be Thakores ; and Kayatia Brahmans wanted to be returned as Acharyas. The idea of raising themselves in the social scale, by adopting new caste names, had occurred also to the Hindu converts to Islam. Those known as Pinjara (cotton carders) wanted to pass themselves off as *Dhunak Pathans* ; and Tais (weavers) wanted to be *Panni* (shuttle cock) Pathans. All these requests, which were not supported by the Caste Index, as also by the orders given on references to higher authorities, were rejected and all the castes were recorded in their true names.

Glossary of castes, tribes and races.

484. The glossary of castes, tribes and races, published as an Appendix at the end of this chapter, gives brief ethnographical notes regarding castes, tribes, etc., included in Imperial Table XIII. The State has not been ethnographically surveyed and the information about the various castes, based as it is on the Bombay Gazetteer Volumes, past Census Reports and the notes made by me in the course of my district tour, is necessarily brief. It was first published provisionally for verification by District Officers and men of light and leading in the different castes. As now finally published, it has been recast and considerably enlarged in the light of suggestions received from them and is believed to be fairly accurate.

The Hindu Caste System.

485. The following extract from an article on Caste in the Encyclopædia of Religion and Ethics, by Mr. Gait, C.I.E., the Census Commissioner for India, shows how class distinction prevailing in Europe and elsewhere is distinguished from the Hindu Caste distinction. " Social distinctions exist amongst all nations, but nowhere are they

so rigidly observed as amongst the Hindus. In modern Europe there are numerous gradations, from the landed aristocracy to the unskilled labourer, and social intercourse is practically confined to persons of approximately the same social standing, but there is no hard and fast boundary between one gradation and the next. The different strata gradually merge, the one into the other; and it is possible for a successful man to raise himself, or at least his children, from the lowest to almost the highest circle of society. Moreover, the spirit of exclusiveness has no external sanction. Each individual is free to decide for himself. He can choose his associates and even his wife from the classes beneath him without any outside interference. People who do not approve of his choice may hold aloof from him, but he incurs no special penalties. The Hindus, on the other hand, are divided into an immense number of entirely separate social groups or castes, the members of which are compelled to abstain from eating with, or marrying, persons belonging to other groups. Their conduct is guided and circumscribed by an infinite number of rules regarding marriage, religious and social ceremonies, eating and drinking, and the like. A man must take his wife from within the caste, or some specified subdivision of it, but she must not belong to his own section of that subdivision, nor must she be within certain prohibited degrees of relationship. He must observe the ceremonies customary amongst his caste-fellows at marriage, on the occurrence of a birth or death in his family, and on other similar occasions. He must abstain from food regarded by his caste-fellows as impure, and from acts which are held to be improper, as, for instance, in many cases, the marriage of widows, or failing to give a girl in marriage before she has attained puberty. He must not take food and drink, or certain kinds of food and drink, from a man of inferior caste, or, as is not infrequently the rule, from a man of any other caste. He must not render certain services to men of low caste. If polluted by their touch, or, it may be, their proximity, he must purify himself; while, if their shadow should fall on his food, he must instantly throw the latter away."

I.—Origin and definition of Caste.

The origin of caste.

486. The question is often asked :—"How is it that the Aryans who migrated to Europe developed into nations, while those who came over to India gave rise to its peculiar caste system ?"

Numerous theories have been put forward by modern students of sociology regarding the origin of the caste system and the manner in which the castes were formed. In the last India Report, Sir Herbert Risley has dealt with the theories propounded by Sir Denzil Ibbetson (Punjab Census Report 1881), Mr. Nesfield (Brief Review of the Caste System of the North-Western Provinces) and M. Senart (Les Castes dans L'Inde), and has given his own conclusion. Summaries of the views of the principal foreign writers on the subject (Senart, Dahlmann, Oldenburg and Bougle) have been circulated by the Census Commissioner for India, for the information of Provincial Superintendents. It is impossible within the compass of this report to review the various theories that have been put forward. But a brief summary of the causes which, in the opinion of most of the savants, gave rise to caste in India may usefully be given here :—

More than four thousand years before Christ, the Sanskrit-speaking people called the Aryans penetrated into India from the North-West. They at first settled in Eastern Kabulistan and along the upper course of the Indus ; and thence they gradually descended the river to the south and spread also to the east in the upper part of the country watered by the five rivers of the Punjab. Unlike other Aryans who migrated elsewhere, the Aryans who came to India had to come into contact with a large aboriginal population differing from them in religion, usages, and physical type and more especially in the conspicuous attribute of colour. Their progress at every step was resisted by these native races which in the Rigveda are designated by the name of Dasyu or Dasa and represented as people of a dark complexion. Those of them who submitted were reduced to slavery and the rest were driven to the fastnesses of mountains. The process was carried on in all the parts of the country to which the Aryans penetrated. When the Aryans entered India from the North-West, they were divided into a number of tribes, each under its own chief. Every householder was a soldier as well as a husbandman, and even the sacerdotal office was not hereditary. Later on, as the society became more complex, the community was divided as in Ancient Persia into several classes. While the Aryans were in the Punjab, there were among them three social grades or ranks. To the first belonged the priests, who composed the Brahmans, *i. e.*, songs or hymns to the gods and knew how to worship them and were therefore called *Brahmans*. Those who acquired political eminence and fought battles belonged to the second grade and were called *Rajans*. All the other Aryans belonged to the third grade and were distinguished by the name of *Visas* or people generally. These three classes formed one community, and such of the aborigines as had yielded to the Aryans were tacked on to it as a fourth grade under the name of *Dasas, i. e.*, slaves or servants. These four classes are mentioned in one of the latest hymns of the Rigveda. But they are designated *varna* (colour) and the word *jati* (caste) was never applied to them. The distinctions involved by them or at least by the first three, were neither so well marked nor so rigid, as those of the modern caste system. There were tribes of Kshatriyas and *gotras* of Brahmans, but no castes. A Kshatriya could become a Brahman or a Brahman a Kshatriya, and although a man was supposed to take his first wife from his own class, there was no binding rule to this effect, while in any case he was free to take a second wife from a lower class. Whenever in the history of the world, one people has subdued another, whether by active invasion or by gradual occupation of their territory, the conquerors have taken the women of the country as concubines or wives, but have given their own daughters in marriage only among themselves. When the two people are of the same race or at any rate of the same colour, this initial stage of hypergamy soon passes away and complete amalgamation takes place. When on the other hand marked distinctions of race and colour intervene and specially if the dominant people are continually recruited by men of their own blood, as was the case in India, the course of evolution runs on different lines. The tendency then is towards the formation of a class of half-breeds like the Eurasians in India, the result of irregular unions between men of the higher race and women of the lower, who marry only among themselves and are to all intents and purposes a caste. There was after a time, amongst the Aryans, a strong feeling that it was desirable, so far as possible, to avoid intermarrying or eating with persons of lower social rank. There was a still stronger feeling amongst this fair race against any sort of social intercourse with the despised black aborigines, a feeling which finds its counterpart at the present day in the attitude of the Boers towards the Kafirs. Some sections of the Aryans came to India with comparatively few women, and these were perforce compelled to take wives from amongst the aborigines. The children of such mixed unions held a lower position than those of pure race, and were, no doubt, divided amongst themselves, like the quadroons and octoroons of America. The rivalry amongst these half-breeds accentuated the already strong sense of racial cleavage. With the progress of Hinduism, social distinctions based on colour and pride of race were complicated by further distinctions based on ceremonial practices, such as the observance or non-observance of certain rules of conduct and of certain restrictions in the matter of food and drink, while some pursuits were regarded as less reputable than others.

The result of the development of the ideas and prejudices enumerated above was that society gradually became divided into a number of well-marked groups. The tendency of the members of each group was to hold aloof from all outsiders, and the belief gradually gained ground that they were descended from a common source. With the growth of this belief in a common origin the tendency would steadily become stronger for each group to regard itself as a separate entity. Marriage and social intercourse between the different groups would thus tend to become more and more unusual; and in a country like India where so much regard is paid to custom, that which is unusual soon comes to be regarded as wrong and unlawful.

The next and crucial stage in the development of the caste system had its origin amongst the functional groups. These groups or guilds gradually organized themselves for craft purposes under *panchayats,* or councils of headmen. The primary duty of the *panchayats* was to settle all questions connected with the craft by which the members of the guild gained their living, and to prevent outsiders from competing with them; but they gradually arrogated greater powers to themselves, first dealing with disputes between members of the guild and afterwards taking cognizance of all breaches of the social rules by which it was thought that the members of the guild ought to be guided.

Intermarriage and commensality were thus in course of time prohibited absolutely, and the idea that each group was an entirely separate entity became stronger than ever. Hence arose amongst the functional castes the rigidity that distinguishes the Indian caste system from other social groupings. The process of development was so slow and gradual that no one ever realized that any change had taken place.

The example set by the functional groups was followed by other groups, not consciously, but merely through the influence which it had in strengthening the already existing sentiments of social exclusiveness and developing the general feeling that any breach of established custom constituted an offence which it was the duty of the community to take cogizance of. Caste in its present form thus became a universal feature of the Hindu social sytem.

Definition of caste.

487. The word "caste" comes from the Portuguese adventurers, who followed Vasco de Gama to the West Coast of India. The word itself is derived from the Latin *castus* and implies purity of blood. In his article on caste on Hobson Jobson, Sir Henry Yule quotes a decree of the Sacred Council of Goa, dated 1567, which recites, how the Gentoos divide themselves into distinct races or castes (*castas*) of greater or less dignity, holding the Christians as of lower degree and keep them so superstitiously that no one of the higher caste can eat or drink with the lower. From that time to this, it has been assumed by some, without further inquiry, that the essential principle of caste is mainly concerned with matters of eating and drinking. But the regulations affecting the food and drink are "comparatively fluid and transitory, while those relating to marriage are remarkably stable and absolute." The most recent as well as the most comprehensive definition of a caste is that given by Sir Herbert Risley in the India Volume of the last Census :—

"A caste may be defined as a collection of families or groups of families, bearing a common name, which usually denotes or is associated with a specific occupation, claiming common descent from a mythical ancestor, human or divine, professing to follow the same professional calling, and regarded by those who are competent to give an opinion as forming a single homogenous community. A caste is almost invariably endogamous in the sense that a member of the large circle denoted by the common name may not marry outside that circle, but within the circle, there are usually a number of smaller circles; each of which is also endogamous. Thus it is not enough to say that a Brahman at the present day cannot marry any woman who is not a Brahman; his wife must not only be a Brahman, she must also belong to the same endogamous division of the Brahman caste."

II.—Caste and Race.

The Kaliparaj.

488. When the Aryans entered Gujarat first by way of Rajputana and Aravali passes from the Punjab and afterwards by the Malwa and Dohad route from Bengal and the North-West, the aborigines who occupied the plains retreated to the mountains, and are still found in their primitive condition, in the hilly and forest tracts of the Navsari and Baroda Districts of the State, as also in the neighbouring

British Districts. They are called *kaliparaj* or the dusky people and are the early tribes called the Dasyus in the Vedas.

Koli.

489. Above the *kaliparaj* come Kolis, who number 370,953, that is, 21·9 per cent. of the Hindu population. They form an intermediate layer between the Kaliparaj and the rest of the population called *ujlivarna* or bright-coloured people. They are half Bhil, half Brahmanical, and have in some parts intermingled with the *ujlivarna*. The earliest traditional kings of Gujarat were Bhils or Kolis. Semi-Rajputs still take their wives from Kolis, and a large section of Kolis of the Kadi District, in which is situated Anhilwad Pattan, the ancient capital of Gujarat, is called *Thakardas* or lordlings. One section of the Kolis, which is looked upon as the most respectable, is called Talbada or Talapada from Sanskrit *sthalodbhava* or soil born and may be the descendants of the *nishadas* of the Ramayan.

Ujlivarna or Aryans.

490. Above the Kaliparaj and Kolis lies the *ujlivarna* which is supposed to represent the Aryans. It consists mainly of the Brahman, Vania, Rajput, Kanbi, bard and craftsman castes. The Ujlivarna classes worship Brahmanical gods, preserve a social fabric based on Brahmanical rituals and customs and generally forbid polygamy and widow-marriage. Many aboriginal customs have, however, crept in among them, and there can be no doubt that a large portion of them must have been recruited from the early people. Besides practising polygamy and widow-marriage, many Ujlivarna castes show a leaning towards element, tree and animal worship, and believe in demonology, sorcery and witchcraft.

Infusion of foreign blood.

491. In addition to this, there has been a great mixture of foreigners with the Aryans in Gujarat. The large sea-board which Gujarat, including Kutch and Kathiawad, possesses, has from very ancient times attracted for purposes of refuge, trade and conquest, a large number of foreigners from Arabia, Persia and Africa. This foreign element received large additions during the centuries before and after the Christian era from hordes of Central Asian Kushans, Hunas and other tribes. The foreigners settled in the Province and their mixture with the Aryans was so great that the Hindu Dharmashastras consider Gujarat a mlechha country and forbid visits to it except on pilgrimage. One of the foreign tribes known as Gujjars passing into India from the north-west, gradually spread as far south as Gujarat, and has given it its name, which is derived from the Prakrit Gujjar-ratta, the Sanskrit of which is Gujjar-rashtra, that is, the country of the Gujjars. The present Gujjars of the Punjab and the United Provinces of Oudh and Agra preserve more of their foreign traits than the Gujjar settlers to the south and the east. In the sixth and seventh centuries, there were three Gujjar kingdoms in Gujarat, which shows that the Gujjar tribe must have settled there in large numbers. The members taking to different callings formed separate castes or joined existing castes as their sub-castes. Several of these Gujjar castes still survive. Among these, are the Gujjar Vanias or traders, Gujjar Sutars or carpenters, Gujjar Sonis or goldsmiths and Gujjar Kumbhars or potters. The Lewa and Kadwa Kanbis, the two leading castes of Gujarat Kanbis, are also of Gujjar origin. The word Kanbi is from the Sanskrit *kutumbin*, that is, one possessing a family or house. From ancient times the title *kutumbin* has been prefixed to the names of cultivators. As cattle-breeding, and not cultivation, was the original, as, it still is the characteristic calling of North India Gujjars, those of the tribe who settled to cultivation came to be known as *kutumbins* or Kanbis.*

The division of Gujarat Kanbis as Lewa and Kadwa corresponds with the division of the Malwa Gujjars into Daha and Karad, with the Lewa origin of the east Khandesh Gujjars, and with the Lawi tribe of the Punjab Gujjars.

Infusion of foreign blood has taken place in all the Aryan classes in Gujarat. The foreigners were either absorbed in the existing classes or formed new castes for themselves. The division of almost all the Vania castes into

* Campbell's History of Gujarat, p. 4.

Visa, full, and *Dasa*, half, and a further division of some into *Pancha*, quarter, shows the proportion of outside intermixture. The Oswal Vanias were originnally Rajputs, who on their conversion to Jainism gave up fighting for trade. About the Anavala Brahmans, there is a tradition that Rama, on his return from the conquest of Ceylon, halted at a place called Patarvada in the hills of Bansda, and failing to find the necessary number of local Brahmans to perform a sacrifice collected eighteen thousand of the hill tribes and made them Brahmans.

The Bhatia and Luhana castes have sprung up from tribes of Turk and Afghan origin and have only recently adopted the leading rules of Hindu life.

The beauty of the Deccan Chambhar, the fairness of Gujarat Dheds and the surnames of Chambhars or leather workers in the Punjab, suggest that these classes have been largely recruited from defeated foreigners.

There has been so much intermixture of blood in Gujarat that, except by the difference in his dress, it would be difficult to distinguish a man of one caste from another. What Mr. Nesfield said for the people of Upper India, fully applies to the people of Gujarat. A stranger walking through the class rooms of the Baroda High School would never dream of supposing that the Hindu students seated before him were distinct one from another in race and blood.

Caste and Anthropometry.

492. The question of race was considered at great length in the last India Census Report (paragraphs 777-809), chiefly on an anthropometrical basis. Scientific anthropometry was introduced into India about thirty years ago in connection with the Ethnographic Survey of Bengal then in progress. Measurements of the head, nose and face occupy a prominent place in anthropometry, and as the result of a large number of such measurements, Sir Herbert Risley made a few interesting deductions :—Three well-known types of feature and physique have long been recognised in the Indian Peninsula, the Aryan or Caucasian chiefly in Upper India, the Mongolian, which is generally believed to be confined to the north-east corner of Bengal, and a Negrito or, as Sir Herbert calls it, a Dravidian type in Central and South India. Excluding the second, which he represents to be so local as to make its elimination a matter of little importance in discussing the ethnology of Indian peoples, Sir H. Risley defines the other two as follows :—

" The Aryan type, as we find it in India at the present day is marked by a relatively long (dolicho-cephalic) head, a straight, finely cut (leptorhine) nose, a long, symmetrically narrow face, a well developed fore-head, regular features, and a high facial angle. In the Dravidian type the form of the head usually inclines to be dolicho-cephalic, but all other characters present a marked contrast to the Aryan. The nose is thick and broad, and the formula expressing its proportionate dimensions is higher than in any known race except the Negro. The facial angle is comparatively low, the lips are thick, the face wide and fleshy, the features course and irregular."

Between these extreme types, which may fairly be regarded as representing two distinct races, we find a large number of intermediate groups, each of which forms, for matrimonial purposes, a sharply defined circle, beyond which none of its members can pass. By applying to the entire series the nasal index or formula of the proportions of the nose, which Professors Flower and Topinard agree in regarding as the best test of race distinctions, some remarkable results are arrived at. Says Sir H. Risley : "Thus, it is scarcely a paradox to lay down as a law of the caste organisation in Eastern India that a man's social status varies in inverse ratio to the width of his nose." As no measurements have been taken of the people in this State, it is not possible for me to say how far the apophthegm that the social status of castes varies inversely with the width of the nose is confirmed or contradicted by actual facts. But so far as mere appearance is concerned, it is usual to find among the Brahman and other high caste people in this state an appreciable section of those who are as flat-faced as the lowest among the Dheds and Chamars. Anthropometry, as a test of race, is now going out of fashion. In his address to the British Association Professor Ridgewey agreed that physical type depends far more on environment than the race ; and it has been shown by Walcher that the head at least depends largely on whether an infant lies on its back or on its side. Moreover, it is now recognised that mere numerical indices are not photography, and the actual contours should be shown. It has been argued by Messrs. O'Donnell Crooke, Enthovan and others that the conclusions drawn from the Indian measurements are not always supported by statistics. Far from its being a law of caste organization in Eastern India, where a large number of such measurements were taken, that a man's social status varies in inverse ratio to the width of his nose, the utmost that can be predicted is that the average nasal index of a large number of the members of any caste, indicates in a very uncertain manner the amount of aboriginal blood amongst its members and thereby indirectly the greater or less respectability of the occupation followed.*

Melanoglossia.

493. From a note on Melanoglossia by Surgeon-Captain F. P. Maynard, I.M.S., circulated by the Census Commissioner for India, it appears that the pigmentation of the tongue varies with the pigmentation of the skin and that pigmented tongues are more frequent among Dravidian tribes than among the Aryans. Dr. R. N. Jadhav, Superintendent, Central Jail, Baroda, who at my request examined 539 prisoners of different castes, reported as under :—

"I came across no case of blue patches amongst children. All that I was able to note was purely in relation to the discolouration of the tongue in the adults as the term Melanoglossia truely implies. The discolouration was of a bluish black type varying in shade from a faint blue tint to a distinct bluish black discolouration, either along the margins of the tongue or more or less confined to the back parts of it towards its base. It was observed in irregularly circular blotches of the size of a two to four-anna piece. Along the margins of the tongue it was in the form of irregular vertical streaks. No discolouration either of the gums, entire surface of the tongue or the roof of the mouth was met with in any case. There seems to be no particular connection between this form of discolouration and malaria, as none of the subjects who had Melanoglossia had enlarged spleen or other evidences of malarial cachexia. It was met with in subjects of all ages, but the majority was of persons between the ages of 25 to 45 years and above all among Hindus belonging to lower castes, such as Kolis, Thakardas, Naikas, etc., who form the lower stratum of civilized society, though there were some cases amongst higher classes but comparatively very few."

Blue patches on children.

494. It is said by Herr Baelz in his article on the "Races of East Asia, with special reference to Japan," summary of which had been circulated by the Census Commissioner for India, that blue patches are found exclusively amongst children of Mongolian race. At my request, some Medical Officers examined a few children under one year of age, brought before them for treatment, but they failed to discover any blue patches on them.

Caste and religion.

495. Caste is a social rather than a religious institution. The Jain religion does not sanction castes, and yet many Jains follow the caste-system like Hindus. So long as a man submits to the various rules and restrictions of his caste, he may believe or disbelieve what he likes in religious matters without in any way injuring his social position. In the present Census, some persons returned themselves as agnostics, atheists, etc., and yet continue to be members of their castes.

Caste and nationality.

496. The general effect of the caste-system has been to sub-divide the people into so many distinct and often antepathetic social groups that vigorous and combined action for any great common object has been rendered difficult. Living always within and for the caste, with little interest beyond it, a Hindu has no idea of Nationality.

* Crooke's Tribes and Castes, Vol. I, p. cxxvii.

Caste and occupation.

497. Considered from the industrial point of view, the occupational castes have played the part of trade guilds and helped the preservation of ancient arts. A caste may be looked upon as a co-operative society in full working order. It forms an effective agency for the suppression of immorality and vice, and is useful in the support and relief of the destitute poor. It has kept alive for ages the doctrine of the dignity of the hereditary priesthood. It has been the efficient practical means of safeguarding Hinduism and maintaining its principles, traditions and customs against religious reformers within its own body and also against the aggressions of alien religions.

Caste and animal food.

498. It is generally supposed that abstinence from meat is an essential condition of Brahmanism. But according to all authorities, the Brahmans and other twice-borns used meat in ancient times.* The flesh of five species of five-clawed animals is permitted to be eaten in the Dharma Sutras and even beef is allowed by Apstamba (1—17, 30, 37). Most of the sacrifices of the old Vedic religion were animal sacrifices, and the animals killed by suffocation for the purpose were goats, sheep, cows or bulls and horses. It is impossible that the idea of offering meat to gods could have originated, unless men themselves liked and used it. But the influence of Buddhism and of Jainism threw discredit on the practice, and those who re-edited Hindu Law in the fourth century of the Christian Era and later, *i.e.*, the writers of the Smritis of Manu and Yajnyavalkya lay down the old permissive precept, but hedge it round with so many restrictions that it amounts almost to prohibition. But in modern times, the Brahmans of Bengal, Mithila, Kashmir and Sindh do use meat, while in countries which were for a long time under the influence of Buddhism and Jainism, such as Gujarat, even the lower castes abstain from it.

New castes.

499. Viewed at a given moment, caste seems fixed and immutable, but great changes have taken place in the past and are still going on. Gujarat is pre-eminently a land of castes. In no part of India are the sub-divisions so minute as in Gujarat. Besides new castes formed by new settlements, one leading influence is the reception of non-Hindu foreigners and aboriginal tribes into the Brahmanic fold. When a new community accepts Brahmanism, it is not absorbed into any section of the old community, but forms itself into a separate caste and sometimes several castes, the separating element being its calling or trade.

Three separating influences—calling, marriage and food—are still at work forming new castes. The cleanliness or dirtiness of the calling, the acceptance of marriage within or without a caste or of widow marriage and strictness in the excluding of forbidden food, not only form new castes but also determine their social status. A few instances are given below :—

(1) A section of Kolis left off their traditional occupation of menial labour and took to the making of bricks. They came to be known as Dalwadi or Talvari, that is cutters, because they dug ponds and made bricks. This new and honourable profession gave them a high social status, and in course of time, they came to be known as a new caste of Kolis. They now call themselves Rajputs and have severed all connection with the other Kolis.

(2) Kandoi is an occupational term, meaning sweetmeat-maker. It is the occupation of a section of Shrimali Vanias, which is looked upon as degraded owing to its following this calling. Till recently, interdining and intermarriage were allowed between them and the other Shrimali Vanias. But, of late, they are looked upon as degraded, and though interdining is allowed, intermarriage is stopped, and the sweetmeat-making Shrimali Vanias have formed a new caste as Kandois.

* Dr. Bhandarkar's "Social History of India," Indian Social Reform, page 14.

(3) Kharvas (salt-carriers) have such surnames as Chohan, Gohil, Jhala, Parmar, Sisodia and Vaghela, and their tradition is that having taken to salt manufacture and sea-faring, they sunk from Rajputs and formed a separate caste.

(4) Modh Ghanchis, a sub-caste of the oil-pressers' caste, were originally Modh Vanias. Owing to their having taken to the degrading profession of oil-pressing, they were looked upon as degraded and came to be regarded as a section of the Ghanchi caste.

(5) Parajia Brahmans belonged to the Audich stock and formerly lived at the village of Ismaliya, whence they migrated to Paraj near Junaghad. They became the priests of Ahirs and Charans and ate with them. They also allowed widow-marriage and were therefore looked upon as a degraded class, with whom no Brahman can have any intercourse.

(6) Gandhraps (musicians) were originally Nagar Brahmans of the Chitroda division. They still wear the sacred thread. Divorce and widow-marriage are not allowed among them. But on account of the degrading profession of acting as fiddlers to songstresses, they were looked upon as degraded and have now no connection whatever with the parent caste. They form a separate caste by themselves and are inferior in the social scale, even to ordinary craftsmen.

(7) Kalal (liquor-sellers) were originally Kanbis or Rajputs. Owing to the degrading nature of their profession, they had to separate themselves from the parent castes, and formed a new caste of their own.

(8) Kachhias (market gardeners) are said to be Kolis who took to the growing of garden produce, and on account of their change of profession, formed a separate caste.

(9) About the Vyas caste, found chiefly in the Kadi and Baroda Districts, it is said that they are the descendants of 108 Brahmans of different castes, who about 400 years ago, conducted the penance ceremony performed by a Brahman jester in the service of a Musalman king of Ahmedabad. The families which took part in these ceremonies were excommunicated and formed a separate caste.

(10) Some Lewa Kanbis, who are the followers of a Kabir Panthi Bhagat, named Uda, have become peculiarly exclusive in their habits and have formed a new caste of Kanbis. They are very exclusive in their habits and do not drink from a brass or copper pot touched even by a Brahman.

(11) Mochis or leather-workers, whom high class Hindus do not touch, are, by leaving their old unclean calling, rising in the social scale. Those of them who have become *Chandlagara* or spangle-makers, *Chitara* or painters, and *Rasania* or electroplaters, are gradually forming distinct castes by stopping social relations with the original leather-workers.

(12) Bhojak, Parajia, Pokarna, Rajgor, Raval and Saraswat are new castes formed by Brahmans, considered degraded on account of dining with their *yajamans*, or serving low castes as priests.

(13) Bhatias and Luhanas, who turned strict vegetarians, separated from their original tribe and formed new castes.

(14) The Lewa and Kadwa Kanbis originally Gujjars, having given up the use of animal food, formed separate castes.

(15) Tapodhans were originally Audich Brahmans, but were looked upon as degraded owing to their practising widow marriage and acting as priests in Shaiva temples, and formed a new caste.

Rising in social status.

500. Some new castes are formed by those who, ashamed of their low caste, in their days of prosperity, gradually conceal it, and assume a better name in its place.

The first stage for a number of people who discover in themselves some quality of social distinction is to refuse to give their women in marriage to other members of the same caste, from which nevertheless they continue to take wives. After a time, when their numbers have increased and they have bred women enough to supply material for a *jus connubii* of their own, they close their ranks, marry only among themselves and pose as a superior sub-caste of the main caste to which they belong. Last of all they break off all connection with the parent stock, assume a new name which ignores or disguises their original affinities and claim general recognition as a distinct caste. The Kadia-Kumbhar caste of Navsari is an illustration of the first stage. Being in better circumstances than their caste-brethren, they first gave up their traditional occupation of pot-making and took to brick-laying or carpentry. After some time they ceased giving their daughters in marriage to the pot-making Kumbhars, but continued to take wives from them. They thus became a superior section of their caste and came to be known as Kadia-Kumbhars or Sutaria Kumbhars. Recently they have broken off all connection with the potter caste and neither intermarry nor eat with its members. The next move will probably be to drop the qualifying term, Kumbhar, and to pass themselves off as simple Kadias or Sutars, and nobody will know that they were originally Kumbhars. The Luhars of the City of Baroda, formerly formed one sub-caste of the Luhar caste. But it has recently split up into two sections, the *Rupaghada* or silversmiths and *Lodhaghada* or ironsmiths. The Rupaghadas having assumed a higher social position on account of their working in silver, refuse to associate with the Lodhaghadas. They interdine, but do not intermarry with them, and form to all intents and purposes a new sub-caste. In the same way some Luhars, who work as carpenters, returned themselves as Luhar-Sutars and not simply as Luhar. They have not yet broken with the ironsmiths, but there should be no wonder, if they do so, as the profession of a Sutar is considered to be of a higher social status than that of a Luhar.

Types of castes.

501. By such processes as those mentioned above and by a variety of complex social influences, whose working cannot be precisely traced, a number of types or varieties of castes have been formed which may be divided into four categories, *viz.*, (1) functional, (2) sectarian, (3) race and (4) mixed castes, *i. e.*, castes derived from the union of persons of different castes.

Functional castes.

502. *The functional type.*—This is so numerous that community of function is ordinarily regarded as the chief factor in the evolution of caste. Almost every caste professes to have a traditional occupation, though many of its members have abandoned it. This type includes the caste of Brahmans or priests, Vanias or traders, and artizans, such as Mochi (shoe-maker), Luhar (blacksmith), Sutar (carpenter), Soni (goldsmith), Darji (tailor), Ghanchi (oil-presser), Machhi (fisherman), &c. There is a separate caste or group of castes for every one of the occupations that were followed in earlier times before the introduction of machinery. The functional castes are not the same all over India. Each of the old important political divisions evolved its own functional groups. The Audich and Modh Brahmans of Gujarat are quite different from the Deshastha and Koknastha Brahmans of the Deccan ; the Lad Vania caste of Baroda and Dabhoi is quite different from the caste of Vanias or Komatis of Southern India. The Mochis, Darjis, Luhars, Goldsmiths and other artizan castes of Gujarat, Deccan, Bengal and other Provinces of India form quite distinct castes, and have nothing in common except the same profession. They all have different customs and are often known by different names.

Sectarian castes.

503. *Sectarian type.*---There are some castes whose existence began as a religious sect. The Atit, Gosai and Jogi castes belong to this category. The Jogis are the descendants of persons who after having been ascetics returned to worldly life and having lost their original caste, found a new caste as Jogis or ascetics.

504. *The tribal type.*—The Rajput, Maratha, Koli, Kanbi, Rabari, Kathi, Vagher and such other castes, which do not owe their origin to function, though they are generally identified with particular trades or occupations, belong to this class. These communities were originally tribes or races, but on entering the fold of Hinduism, they imitated the Hindu social organization and were thus gradually hardened into castes.

Race castes.

505. *The mixed type.*—There are some castes which are formed by crossing, *e. g.*, the Barad Nagar. Those members of the Nagar caste, who could not get brides within their own caste, formed themselves into a new caste known by this name, on account of their excommunication (*bahar karvun*) from the parent caste. The *Khavas* and *Gola* castes have also been formed by the union of persons of different castes serving as personal attendants to Rajput Chiefs. Among the higher castes in the Deccan, it is a common practice to take as maid-servants and concubines, women belonging to the lower clean castes. The offsprings of their maid-servants are known as Kharchya, like the Shagirdpeshas of Bengal. They form a regular caste of the usual type and are divided into endogamous groups with reference to the caste of the male parent, *e.g.*, Sindhe, etc.

Mixed castes.

III.—Origin of sub-castes.

506. The very names of the sub-castes given in Imperial Table XIII show that the differentiation by sub-castes must have arisen partly from residence in different localities, partly from difference in occupation and partly from other causes. The general conclusion that can be drawn from the information collected regarding some twenty typical castes is that sub-castes arise from various causes of which the most common are :—

Origin of sub-castes.

(1) *Residence in a different locality.*—Nearly every caste has territorial sub-castes such as Ghanchi Champaneri, Ghanchi Ahmedabadi, Kumbhar Ajmeri, Kumbhar Khambhati, Sutar Mewada, Soni Mewada, Soni Maru, etc. The Nagar Brahman caste affords an excellent example of sub-castes arising from change of residence. The Nagars are divided into six divisions. The split in the community is attributed to certain Nagars taking *dakshana*, or gift, from Vishaldev, the chief of Visnagar in spite of the orders of their headman to the contrary. The sub-divisions are named after the places of their settlement after the split, *e.g.*, the Vadnagaras from Vadnagar, the Visnagaras from Visnagar, the Prashnoras from Pushkur in Ajmer, the Sathodras from Sathod, the Chitrodas from Chitod and the Krishnoras from Krishnagar.

(2) *The adoption or abandonment of a degrading occupation.*—The Audich Brahmans afford an illustration as to how sub-castes are formed by the adoption of a degrading occupation. They were originally one caste, but were subsequently divided into two subdivisions called *Sahasra* and *Tolakia*, owing to the Sahasras receiving gifts and the Tolakia refusing to do so and therefore claiming superiority. The question of the amount of dishonour that attaches to a Brahman who acts as a family priest to low caste Hindus, also caused a dispute and division among the Audichs. In North Gujarat, the practice is held so degrading that those who follow it have been excommunicated ; in South Gujarat, the practice is tolerated. In the Northern districts, family priests excommunicated for serving low castes have given rise to several sub-castes. Of these, the chief are Hajam Gors, who serve barbers, Koli Gors, who serve Kolis, Mochi Gors, who serve shoe-makers and Gandhrap Gors who serve musicians. These sub-castes are not allowed even the privilege of interdining with the main caste.

Sompura Salats (stone workers) and Sompura Brahmans were originally of one caste. Those who took to stone-working were looked upon as degraded by those who acted as priests and this brought about a division. After the fission, though they never intermarried, Sompura Brahmans and Salats are said for a time to have continued to dine with each other. Sompura Salats wear the Brahmanic thread and observe all the ceremonial practices of Brahmans, but of late, even interdining with them has been stopped by their Brahman brethren.

The Mochi caste illustrates how sub-castes are formed by the abandonment of a degrading occupation. Mochis (shoe-makers) are divided into many sub-castes according to their callings. The chief of these are Mochi (shoe-maker), Chandlagara (maker of lac-spangles), Rasania (electro-plater), Chitara (painter), Minagara (worker in enamel), Panagara (gold and silver foil maker), Angigara (maker of idol ornaments), Pakharia (maker of ornamental horse trappings), Netragara (maker of idol's eyes), Jingar (saddler), and Dhalgar (leather jar maker). Formerly, these different sections ate together and intermarried. But of late the Chandlagara, Chitara and Rasania not only do not eat with other Mochis, but their taking to cleaner callings has in their own estimate so raised them in the social scale that they do not even touch other Mochis.

(3) *Difference of occupation even if neither is degrading.*—Potters who work as brick-layers and agriculturists in the Amreli District, have formed themselves into two sub-castes of potters; the former being known by the name of Kadia-Kumbhar and the latter as Khedu-Kumbhar. Formerly both the sections interdined and intermarried, but of late the Khedu-Kumbhars assuming a social superiority have stopped intermarriage with the Kadia Kumbhars. In the same way, potters in the Navsari District, who work as carpenters, have formed a new sub-caste of potters as Kumbharia Sutar.

(4) *Variation in social practices.*—Formerly the Lewa Kanbis formed only one caste and practised widow marriage. Fifty or sixty years ago, a section of them known in the *Charottar* as Patidars stopped widow marriage and all matrimonial connection with the widow marrying section of their community. Originally Bahrots had no divisions, but divisions arose as they seceded from the Brahman standard of purity. Those who follow all the main Brahman practices, such as wearing the sacred thread, &c., are called Brahma Bhats, while those who do not, are known by other names, either from their calling or their residence. Some sub-castes of Bahrots do and some do not allow widow marriage. In Kutch they dine with Luhanas and Kshatris, but in North Gujarat Brahma Bhats do so neither with the other divisions of Bahrots nor with Vanias and Kanbis.

(5) *Pollution.*—Almost all the Vania castes are divided into *Visa* or twenties and *Dasa* or tens. The Visas are considered superior to the Dasas owing to the purity of their blood. Among some castes, there is a further section called *Pancha* or fives who are regarded as degraded and with whom other Vanias do not dine. All the main castes with their Visa and Dasa sub-divisions eat together but do not intermarry, and the restriction about marriage is in many cases applied to local sections also. Thus among Lad Vanias, the Dasa Lads of Dabhoi do not marry with the Dasa Lads of Baroda. The Visa Deshavals of Baroda do not marry with the Visa Deshavals of Surat.

(6) *Split in the governing body.*—The Chovisa Brahmans are divided into *Mota* (large) and *Nana* (small). One section obeys the jurisdiction of the elder and the other that of the younger branch of the family of the original headman.

(7) *Greater Prosperity.*—When a section of a low caste acquires greater power, wealth and knowledge than the rest, it often tries to dissociate itself from the main body. This is the case with the Dheds. They are divided into several sections, two of which are known as Marwadi or Maru and Surti. The Marwadis who are found chiefly in North Gujarat hold aloof from other Dheds, refuse to eat or drag away dead animals and earn their living as camel drivers. The Surtis by intermixture with Europeans and Parsis have improved in appearance and intelligence. Many of them act as butlers, house-servants and grooms and hold themselves aloof from other Dheds.

(8) *Difference of origin.*—There are numerous instances where the divisions within a caste are due to a real difference of origin. This is especially the case with the functional castes, which are often recruited from different sources. There is a tendency to regard all persons who follow the same profession as belonging to the same caste even though they may originally have come from an entirely different stock. Thus Sonis (goldsmiths) are divided into six main sub-castes, Gujjar, Maru, Mewada, Parajia, Shrimali and Tragad. All these are accretions from different groups. The Gujjars belong to the Gujjar Vania stock and are a trace of the great settlement of Gujjars or Gurjars, who gave its name to Gujarat. Maru Sonis have come into Gujarat from Marwar. Mewada Sonis originally belonged to Mewada or Meywar Vania community. Parajias claim to be Rajputs. They worship fire and their character and physique favour the view that they were formerly a fighting class like the Kathis. Shrimali Sonis originally belonged to the Shrimali Vania caste and were considered as degraded owing to their having taken to goldsmith's profession. Tragads claim Brahman descent, wear the sacred thread and do not eat food cooked by any one who is not a Brahman.

The Sutar (carpenter) caste is divided into four main divisions, Gujjar, Mewada, Pancholi and Vaishya. All the four appear from their names to have different origins. The name Vaishya shows that it must be a trace of the old Hindu division of Vaishya or traders. Gujjars appear to be a section of the Gujjars from the Punjab and Mewada must be immigrants from Meywad. Pancholis who hold the lowest rank are probably so called from *Pancha*, that is half of the *Dasha* or only quarter pure blood. Except that the other three sub-castes eat food cooked by Vanias, none of the four divisions eat together or intermarry. The Vaishya rank the highest. They do not eat food cooked by the other sub-castes because they wear the sacred thread and do not allow their widows to marry. On the other hand, the Pancholis rank the lowest, because they alone prepare oil-presses, build ships and carts and do other work which causes the loss of animal life. But they all form members of the Sutar caste. By the time, these groups of different origin will have completely affiliated themselves, the traces of their different origin will also be obliterated, and they will all join and be one homogeneous caste and claim descent from some fictitious common ancestor like the sub-castes of Luhars who say that they are the descendants of one Pithvo. This imaginary person was so called because he was created by Parvati out of the dust clinging to Shiva's back to prepare weapons in Shiva's wars against the two demons Andhkar and Dhundhkar. When Shiva killed the demons, Pithvo turned their skulls into anvils, their hands into hammers and their lungs into bellows.

Of all the causes of the differentiation of castes into sub-castes, the only one that has always existed is that due to difference of origin. The nature of the others, suggests that they have split off from the parent caste, rather than that they are separate entities as yet imperfectly assimilated.

Rigidity of rules of endogamy and commensality.

507. As a general rule, all the members of a caste including the sub-castes eat together, but intermarriages are permitted only within the limits of the sub-caste. The restrictions on intercourse increase as one goes from the top to the bottom of the caste system. The Brahman, Vania, Rajput and Kanbi castes must marry their girls within their caste or sub-caste, but they can eat together within the large circle of their whole castes and with a few exceptions, even that of the tribes from which their different castes are formed. A Lewa Kanbi will not marry his daughter outside his own group, but he will have no objection to marry his son with the daughter of a Uda Kanbi, if she is well endowered. But the artizan and depressed classes are more strict, both with regard to food and marriage. The Bhavsar caste (dyers) for instance, has three sub-castes which neither eat together nor intermarry. There are eight sub-castes of Darjis, who also neither eat together nor intermarry. Of the six divisions of the Ghanchis, Modhs and Sidhpuris rank highest, the other divisions eating food cooked by them while they do not eat food cooked by the other four. None of the six divisions intermarry. Kansaras belong to four divisions, Champaneri, Maru, Shihora and Visnagara. Except that Visnagaras eat with Champaneris, none of the four divisions eat together or intermarry. The Hajams of the State belong to four main divisions, Bhatia, Limachia, Maru and Masuria or Matakia, of which the Limachias rank the highest. They allow Bhatia Hajams to smoke their *hukka* but will not eat with any other division. None of the divisions intermarry, nor do they eat together except that all will eat food cooked by a Limachia.

Government.

508. No member of any sub-caste can gain admission in to another and each has its own *Panchayat* or administration. A general Panchayat of the whole caste including all its sub-castes meets occasionally for regulating business matters, but so far as social matters are concerned, each sub-caste is quite independent of the rest.

Penalties for breach of the rules which differentiate sub-castes of the same caste.

509. When the members of different sub-castes eat together or smoke from the same *hukka* contrary to the usual practice hardly any notice is taken, except perhaps in the lower castes, and the punishment inflicted if any, is fine only. But if the offence is deemed very serious owing to the low status of one of the sub-castes or want of good understanding between the two sub-castes, the offending party may even be excommunicated till a feast is given to the whole sub-caste. But the punishment of permanent excommunication is never inflicted. When, however, a member of one sub-caste gives his daughter in marriage to, or takes a bride from another sub-caste, excommunication is invariably the result. But, as a general rule, such excommunications are condoned and only a fine is imposed instead, after the delinquent has remained out of caste for some time. If the bride is proved to belong to a sub-caste of the common caste of the parties, she is allowed to remain in the section in which she is married, but if she is of some other caste, the delinquent is readmitted into his caste only on the condition of his abandoning her. Several instances have happened within the last twenty years of Visas of some Vania sub-caste marrying girls from the corresponding Dasa section. Not only they but also their spouses have been retained in the Visa section, on payment of a fine. Khadayata and Deshaval Vanias are trying to amalgamate their Visa and Dasa sub-castes. In the annual caste conferences which are of late held by almost all the castes, for their social amelioration, introduction of intermarriages between the sub-castes which interdine (*jyahan roti vyahvar tyahan beti vyahvar*) forms one of the subjects for discussion and finds favour with a comparatively large majority. Zalavad in Kathiawad is noted for its having grown up brides of the Brahman, Vania and Kanbi castes. Owing to a difficiency of females in their caste some Gujarati Brahmans, Vanias or Kanbis marry Zalavad brides for whom they pay a heavy bride-

price. They are at first excommunicated for so doing, but are readmitted into their caste on payment of a heavy fine and on proof being given that these brides though not of their own sub-caste, belonged to some other sub-caste of the same main caste. Instances have happened within the last few years in which the Zalavad brides were really of Koli, Kumbhar or Kanbi castes and were deceitfully passed off, as belonging to superior castes. Some Vanias who had married them, in the belief that they were of their own caste and had also lived with them for several months were readmitted into the caste on their turning out these girls from their houses and giving a feast to the caste.

Relation between castes and sub-castes.

510. The general conclusion indicated by an examination of the system of sub-castes seems to be that although at any given time, a caste is seen to be split up into numerous separate sub-castes that have often no special connection with each other, the fact that they are included in the same caste holds them together and makes them look upon each other as *biradar* or of the same fraternity. In certain circumstances, different groups coalesce, while in other circumstances fresh sub-castes spring into existence. In any case the restrictions regarding food are very few, while as regards marriage, as noted in para. 509 above, they are often set aside and condoned.

Endogamy as a test of caste.

511. Monsieur Emile Senart in his learned work on "Les castes dans Indie" is of opinion that endogamy is the true test of caste and that the sub-caste ought really to be regarded as the caste, because this is the group which practises endogamy. Where the caste name is a general term, like Vania, Brahman, Kanbi, etc., which are really names of functions or tribes including a number of true castes following the same profession, it is quite right that for the true caste, we must look to the inner groups practising endogamy. For instance, the term Vania is a functional designation and not the name of a caste. It includes all kinds of trading groups, such as Deshaval, Lad, Khadayata, Modh, etc., many of which, not only have no connection with one another, but often are of very different social status. The case is otherwise however when we come to terms like Visa Deshaval and Dasa Deshaval, Visa Khadayata and Dasa Khadayata, Modh Ghanchi and Surati Ghanchi, Dabgar Mochi and Jingar Mochi, Vaishya Sutar and Mewada Sutar and the like. They are the names of sub-castes practising endogamy, but it would be contrary to all hitherto accepted ideas on the subject to treat them as separate castes. In spite of the restrictions on marriage, all the sub-castes of a main caste regard themselves as forming a single community, bound together, not only by the possession of some traditional occupation but also by the belief in a common origin ; they also in many cases worship the same tutelary deity, *e. g.*, Vagheshwari, in the case of the Soni caste, and have the same social and religious observances. Moreover the restrictions on marriage among sub-castes are comparatively lax and as already pointed out, their breaches are often condoned by the imposition of a fine only. While in some places, marriage between two sub-castes is forbidden, in other places, not far distant it is allowed. And some times the restrictions on marriage in the caste of sub-castes apply only to the giving and not to the taking of wives. It often happens in places where the number of members of a particular sub-caste is small that they amalgamate with some other sub-caste of the same main caste. There is far less fixity about a sub-caste than there is about a main caste.

IV.—Caste Government.

Caste Panchayats.

512. With the exception of a few tribal castes such as Rajputs, Kathis and Lewa Kanbis all the functional and other castes have caste *panchayats* or standing Caste committees which deal as a matter of course with all breaches of caste rules and regulations.

Constitution of Caste Panchayat.

513. The primary object of the guild or assembly called caste panchayat, was to regulate matters relating to the calling followed by the caste, but as all the members following an occupation, were generally of one caste, the panchayat gradually assumed the power of regulating caste matters also. In each caste panchayat, there is a headman and two or three leaders or foremen who hold their office by hereditary right. The headmen of the Vanias and other influential castes are called Sheths, and those of the poorer or less influential ones are called Patels. When the regular heir to the dignity is unfit to hold the post from physical or mental weakness, he retains the title, though the actual power is exercised by some other member of his family. Although theoretically all the members of the caste have a right to take part in the deliberations of the caste panchayat along with the headman and the leaders, it is only a few whose personal qualities have gained their influence that actually do so ; and as none of the rest disputes their opinions, caste authority virtually rests with this inner cabinet.

Constitution of Mahajan.

514. Apart from the caste panchayat, there is a general guild for the whole town and including all castes. It is called the Mahajan or town council. Though the Brahman and lower castes are not included in the Mahajan, they are all guided by the orders passed by it. All trade guilds or caste panchayats are subordinate to the Mahajan. The Sheths and Patels of the different occupational castes in a city or town are its members. The president who is called Nagar Sheth is usually a Vania. Theoretically all the occupational castes ought to be represented in the Mahajan but in practice the lower castes such as Luhars, Sutars, Golas, Ghanchis, etc., are ignored and only the Vania and other higher castes form the Mahajan. The Mahajan or town council has jurisdiction not only over the Hindu castes but also over Musalmans and other communities doing business within the town.

Jurisdiction.

515. The jurisdiction of a Nyat Panchayat or caste committee extends over those who belong to that particular caste within a particular area. The members of the caste may all be in one town or may be distributed in different towns or villages, in which case the territorial jurisdiction of the committee extends to all those towns or villages. Generally speaking the territorial limit of a caste committee is limited to the territorial group or circle within which the children of its members are married. It takes cognizance of all matters whether social or professional which concern the caste, *e. g.*, fixing rate of wages, hours of working, holidays, breaking caste rules, giving permission to marry a child outside the limits of the area fixed for contracting marriages, granting divorces, etc. Like the caste panchayat the Mahajan or town council was primarily intended as the highest authority in matters of trade only, but it also arrogated to itself jurisdiction over caste questions and became, as far as Hindu traders are concerned, the supreme authority in matters of caste also. A person dissatisfied with the order of his caste, may appeal against it to the Mahajan and the decision of the Mahajan becomes law both to him and to his caste panchayat. Till recently the Mahajan exercised great influence in State matters. Even now it carries much influence in native states. Orders for *Nagar Ujani*, or feast in the whole town, for strikes and for closing shops on the death of a member of the ruling house or some great man, are given by the Nagar Sheth.

A clear idea of the relative authority of the caste Panchayat and the Mahajan will be formed by the following instance :—

Some years ago, the carpenters' rate of wages was six annas nine pies in the City of Baroda. The carpenters' caste panchayat raised it to 14 annas. The Mahajan interfered and directed the carpenters to keep to the old wages. They would not agree and the Mahajan decided that no one was to employ their services. This lasted for a month when the carpenters had to give in, and the Mahajan fixed their wages at 8½ annas, and the working hours from

8 A. M. to noon and from 2 to 6 P. M. It also prohibited them from working overtime in morning though they were allowed to do so at night.

Servants of the Panchayat.

516. Each caste panchayat has its priest and each Mahajan has a Kotwal or Gumasta, whose duty is to collect the members of the panchayat or Mahajan, as the case may be, when they are wanted. It is only wealthy guilds who employ a Gumasta or a salaried clerk. Ordinarily the work of getting the members together is done by the caste priest or by the village Kotwal. They receive no regular payment but are entitled to certain privileges and gifts on marriage and other occasions. When there is a caste feast the Kotwal is given a dinner. In some places he is paid seven pice by the bride and bridegroom.

Place of meeting.

517. Every caste committee or Mahajan has a place appointed for holding meetings. In former days, the meeting place of the Mahajan was generally the place where the custom duties were collected. Now-a-days, the Mahajan meets at the residence of the Nagar Sheth, while a caste committee ordinarily meets at the residence of the Sheth or Patel (headman). But when the question for decision is important and a large gathering is expected, the meeting place is some temple or *dharmsala*. Poorer classes to whom these places are not available hold their meeting under the shade of some bunyan or mango tree in the open *maidan*.

Procedure.

518. When any one has a complaint, he gives information to the Sheth or Patel of his caste, and the Sheth or Patel after fixing a suitable day and hour sends word through the caste priest to the other caste Panchas, and all the members of the caste to meet him on the appointed day and hour. The party complained against is also given information to be present. All the members of the caste are entitled to be present on the meeting day. But if the question to be decided is not a very important or interesting one, very few attend. The elders under the guidance of the president take evidence, examine witnesses, hear what the accuser and the accused have to say and give such decision as to them may appear proper. The whole proceeding except the final order is oral.

Punishment.

519. The breach of a caste rule is ordinarily punished by a fine. Thus if a mason or a carpenter works overtime or accepts lower wages, against the rules of his guild, he is fined Rs. 51. If he takes up work left unfinished by his fellow craftsman, before his reasonable demands are satisfied by his employer or establishes himself in a village where another member is already settled, all communication with him is stopped till he yields and acts according to the wishes of his guild. Similarly when a marriage is contracted outside the circle marked out by the caste or a bethrothal is broken or any other social act forbidden by the caste is done, the delinquent is fined and if the offence is very serious, such as taking as wife a woman from another caste, he is excommunicated. When this happens nobody can eat, drink or smoke with him. A sentence of excommunication is often commuted to one of fine only, when the offender, unable to bear the excommunication, surrenders himself to the mercy of his caste, promises to behave in a better way in future and gives up the cause which necessitated his excommunication. When the conditions imposed by the panchayat are duly fulfilled, the delinquent is let go with a fine only and is also required to provide a feast for his caste people who by partaking of it in his company, *i.e.*, eating and drinking with him publicly, testify that he is readmitted to the privileges of the community. When a fine is inflicted, it is generally readily paid ; for, refusal to pay it, is generally followed by excommunication. For trifling breaches of caste rules, a humiliating apology, change of the sacred thread or lighting a lamp in a temple, suffices. If the person excommunicated is poor, distribution of *batashas*, sweets, is accepted in place of a caste dinner or he is called to join a dinner party given by some one else.

Newspaper report of the proceedings of a Caste Panchayat.

520. The following extract from a vernacular paper from the Navsari District will serve as an illustration of the working of a caste panchayat :—

"The caste panchayat of the Modh Ghanchis, residing in the 35 villages between Surat and Daman, assembled in the Ashapuri Mata at Navsari on the 13th August 1910. It was called at the instance of one Valabh Ratanji of Abrama, who wanted permission from the caste to marry a second wife in the life-time of the first one who is weak in mind. The expense of lodging and feeding the Panchayat in Navsari, which amounted to about Rs. 600, was borne by the applicant, but the permission solicited by him was not granted as the alleged ground was found, upon inquiry, to be not satisfactory. In this panchayat meeting, the following orders were also passed :—

(1) No female of the caste should offer her services for doing manual labour. If this order of the Panch is transgressed, the delinquent will be fined Rs. 151.

(2) No one should pay more than Rs. 150 as *palla* to the father of the bride. If more is found to have been paid or accepted, both the parties will be fined Rs. 100.

(3) When marriage with a widow is performed, she should be given ornaments worth Rs. 300. If more is demanded, she will be fined Rs. 301.

(4) He who uses liquor on marriage occasions will be fined Rs. 50.

While the assembled caste people were taking their dinner, the Sheth ordered one Dahya Dulabh to get up and help in the service of food. On his refusal to do so, he was fined Rs. 5¼. Another person was ordered by the Sheth to go and fetch some lamps. On his refusing to do so, he was also fined Rs. 5¼." *Navasari Prakash,* dated 14-8-10.)

Appeal.

521. If the caste sentence is unjust or unnecessarily hard, the accused appeals to the Mahajan. In former times, the appellant to the Mahajan would neither eat nor drink nor move from the Mahajan Sheth's house, until his complaint was heard and he was given relief. The Mahajan Sheth follows the same procedure as that of the caste panchayat in calling a meeting of the Mahajan and gives a decision which is binding both to the appellant and his caste. Mahajans usually do not now interfere in caste matters, and their authority in social matters is now a mere matter of history, but in business matters, they still exercise the same control as before.

Communal fund.

522. The artisan classes have generally no sources of revenue except occasional fines for breaches of caste rules. Some castes levy a tax on marriage booths and have other sources of revenue also. The amount of income from fines and other sources is usually spent in a caste dinner, or if it is too little for a dinner, it is put by until enough money has accumulated. Expenses for caste vessels, repairs to caste *wadi* or Dharmshala and such other common objects are also incurred from the balance of the communal fund if any.

The Mahajan in towns and cities, which is generally composed of traders, has many sources of income. In addition to fines imposed for breaches of guild rules, they levy many petty imposts, such as tax on the import and export of the principal articles of trade, sales and mortgages of houses, marriage booths, etc. A considerable income is also derived from the auction sale of the right to keep shops open and do business on holidays. The amounts thus collected as well as the fines go to the upkeep of the local *panjara pole* or home for sick and old animals. In some places, money paid by Shravak Vanias goes to the Panjara Pole and that paid by Meshri Vanias goes to their temples. If the funds are large, a considerable part of them is also spent in *sadavrats*, that is, distribution of food to *sadhus* and other mendicants, *parabs* or places for the supply of drinking water to travellers, *visamas*, or roadside resting places, and other works of charity.

Influence of Panchayat on caste observances.

523. Caste rules are rigidly observed in those functional castes which have standing committees or panchayats, which regulate both caste and trade questions. Kanbis, Kolis, Rajputs and other tribal castes, having no standing committees, are lax in the observance of their caste rules. Among them when an important caste question crops up and its settlement is necessary, the leaders of the community call together a meeting of the whole caste or that section of it with which it has marriage relations, in some central and convenient village or place of pilgrimage and pass such resolutions as may be approved by the general sense of the meeting. But owing to the absence of a standing caste committee and the vast area over which the caste population is spread, such resolutions are never efficaciously carried out. As the village headmen are generally Kanbis, members of this caste are called Patels. The absence of a standing caste committee in the "Patel" caste has grown into a proverb: "*Patel no koi Patel nahi,*" *i. e.*, there can be no headman in the headmen caste. In the same way, Garasias who are generally Rajput land-holders and Kolis who are cultivators, have no standing caste committees. A man is more his own master and less under the control of his neighbours. The result is that there are fewer restraints on marriage, food, etc. Young Patels, who have been lately going to Europe for the prosecution of their studies, quietly rejoin their caste after their return, without anybody calling upon them to make *prayaschit* (penance). No notice is taken of their conduct, even when they openly transgress the caste rules about food. This has given rise to the proverb "*Kanbi nyat baharo nahi ane Garasio gozaro nahi*", *i. e.*, a Kanbi is never an outcaste and a Garasia is never polluted.

V.—Caste control by Hindu Rajas.

Control of the ruling power in caste matters over Marathas.

524. It would be interesting to notice briefly the extent to which the Hindu rulers of the State formerly interfered and still do so in caste matters. It is said that originally there were no weavers in Patan and that king Mulraj invited a few from the south-east of India to settle in his kingdom. The newcomers being strangers to Gujarat, could not intermarry with the members of the other castes and were debarred from every kind of intercourse. Mulraj interfered on their behalf and forced the Lewa Kanbis to associate with them in all matters and to reckon them as of their own caste. From that time the weavers, *i.e.*, the Salvis and Lewa Kanbis belonged to one and the same class, though of late they have separated. The army which Pilajirao Gaekwad brought with him into Gujarat consisted mostly of the Maratha caste. For the disposal of social disputes among these people, a committee (*panch*) composed of two officers from each *paga* was appointed. The committee or Panch Sabha, as it was called, heard the parties near the *jaripatka*, H. H. the Gaekwad's banner, and submitted each case with their opinion for orders to the Maharaja. When the Gaekwad government was firmly established, the committee met regularly in Baroda, before the *jaripatka* and its jurisdiction was extended to Marathas living in the city, though not employed in the army. The committee was provided with a clerk and a peon from the Sarkar and was afterwards given the power of final disposal, the Maharaja retaining to himself only the right of final appeal. A separate panchayat was also established for Maratha Sardars and Shiledars. In Samvat 1945-46 both the panchayats were amalgamated, and one general committee with proper rules of procedure was appointed for all Marathas, whether Sardars or sepoys, under the name of Maratha Panchayat Sabha. It does its work under the general supervision of the Senapati, who is at present a European, and appeals over its decisions lie to the Maharaja.

Control over other castes.

525. Though no jurisdiction is exercised at present over other castes, it appears that formerly the authority of the Maharaja was looked upon as supreme in all social matters. Ordinarily all affairs relating to the castes were dealt with by their

own councils, but there were occasions when the interference of the ruler was sought by the aggrieved party and his orders were looked upon as final. The Maharaja maintained a staff of learned Shastris in connection with the palace, *devaghar* or god-house. The head of the learned body was called Danadhyaksha, or head of the council for the distribution of charities. Those dissatisfied with the rulings of their caste councils appealed to the Maharaja, who in his turn directed the Danadhyaksha to hear the parties and submit the case with his opinion for final orders. The Huzur orders were carried out cheerfully and operated greatly to the relief of persons who were harshly treated by their caste councils. The sentence of excommunication passed by a caste was often mitigated in appeal by the substitution of one of some sort of a penance or a fine. If on a rare occasion, a caste or any section of it did not carry out the orders of the Sarkar, the whole of it was excommunicated, that is, put out of the Mahajan. The result of such an order would be that the washermen, barbers, shop-keepers, graindealers and priests of the State, who hitherto served them, would refuse to do so. Services of barbers, washermen and priests from outside the State could not also be obtained. The recalcitrant caste could not endure this treatment long and had ultimately to give in. This sort of interference has ceased under the present regime, but the following few instances collected from the old Fadnis records may be interesting :—

(1) A Deshastha Brahman had a Maratha concubine. She gave birth to a child who died when about six months old. The Brahman carried the child to the cemetery and buried it. When his caste-people came to know of it, he was excommunicated. He appealed to the Maharaja who in Samvat 1919, after consulting learned Shastris, ordered that he may be restored to the caste on his undergoing certain penances.

(2) A Brahman took with him a Dhobi girl to Kedareshwar, where State charities are distributed among Brahmans and demanded *dakshana* for her. Her appearance having created a suspicion about her being a Brahman, he was asked to say truly who she was, whereupon he replied that she was his sister. For further assurance, he was asked to drink water from her hand, which he did. Subsequently the truth having been found out, he was excommunicated by his caste and he appealed to the Maharaja for mercy. The Maharaja, with the advice of the Court-Pandits, ordered that he might be given *prayaschit* and restored to his caste.

(3) A Kanbi contracted a *natra* marriage with a married woman of his caste, without her having previously obtained release from her husband in the usual way. For this defect, his caste-people objected to recognise her as his wife, upon which he appealed to the Maharaja for redress. It was ordered that the woman, not having obtained release from her first husband, the caste was justified in not recognising her as his wife and that he should abandon her if he cared to be in his caste.

(4) A Khedaval Brahman having been accused of *brahma-hatya* (sin of killing a Brahman) was excommunicated by his caste-people. On appeal to the Maharaja, it was ordered that he should be restored to the caste on his undergoing certain penances and giving four dinners to the caste.

VI.—Caste Restrictions.

Caste restrictions.

526. There are numerous restrictions imposed on the conduct of a man by the unwritten (and now in some cases even written) law of his community. These matters vary greatly not only in different parts of the country but also amongst different social strata. In some respects the higher castes (Brahman-Vania) are more particular than the lower (Gola-Ghanchi), but in others it is not so. Some rules are

only recommended to be observed, while others are mandatory and must be followed, else the result would be fine or even excommunication. The following are some of the principal caste restrictions :—

Marriage.

(1) Marriage must be performed not only within the caste but also within the sub-caste. Almost every caste is divided into a number of smaller groups, who will marry only among themselves, and who will on no account give brides to, or take them from, other groups. Thus among the Nagar Brahmans, in addition to the six sub-castes of Vadnagara, Visnagara, Chitroda, Sathodra, Dungarpura and Prashnora, there is a further professional division among most of these sub-castes into *grahastha* or lay and *bhikshuka* or priestly. Among Vadnagaras again, whether lay or priestly, intermarriage does not ordinarily prevail between Kathiawad and Gujarat nor even between North and South Gujarat. Thus for purposes of intermarriage, the Nagar Brahmans are sub-divided into not less than sixteen separate communities. Among Modh Vanias, there are three sub-castes called Adalja from the village of Adalaj, Goghava, from Gogho, and Mandalia, from Mandal. Each of them is further divided into *Visa* whole, and *Dasa* half, a division common to almost all Vania castes, including even Jain Vanias. These again are split up into local sections called Ahmedabadi and Khambhati, with the result that while all sub-divisions dine together, for purposes of intermarriage, the Modh Vanias have about twelve separate sections. Excommunication would be the result if marriage takes place outside the permissible limits. It may be condoned and a fine only may be imposed at the discretion of the caste, if only territorial limit is transgressed, but excommunication is sure if the limit of the caste or sub-caste is set aside.

Widow marriage.

(2) As a general rule, widow marriage is not allowed in the Brahman-Vania class, but it is performed among the lower classes of Sonis, Sutars, Kanbis, Marathas, Luhanas, Bhats and Rajputs. Such of the Brahmans and Vanias, as allow widow marriage in spite of caste prohibition, are held to be degraded and excommunicated. The low position of Cutch Audich, Bhojak, Jethimal-Modh, Rajgor and Tapodhan Brahmans and of Lata or Pancha Oswal Vanias of Cutch is due to their allowing widow marriage. Among the Ghanchi-Gola class, widow marriage is, as a general rule, allowed and performed, but even among them, the higher class of families abstain from it. The widow of a man sometimes marries his younger brother. The practice which is called *diyarvatun* is fast falling into disuse, and is now followed only among the Mochi, Salat, Gola, Darji, Rabari, Koli and such other castes. When her deceased husband's brother has a first claim upon a widow, she may either marry him or have the expenses of her first husband's marriage paid to her by any other man whom she marries.

Early marriage.

(3) Early marriages are practised, but there is no binding rule to the effect that they must be performed. The question is fully treated in the chapter on Civil Condition.

Food.

(4) A man must eat food cooked in water by a person of his own caste or a caste which is considered to be higher than his, but he cannot eat food cooked by a member of a lower caste. Thus a Vania can eat food cooked by a Vania or a Brahman, but if he eats food cooked by a Kanbi, a Koli or a member of any other caste

socially inferior to him, he loses his caste. Some Brahmans, *e.g.*, the Nagars do not eat food cooked even by other Brahmans. If they do, they lose their caste. But food cooked in *ghee*, *e.g.*, *sukhadi* or in milk, *e.g.*, *dashami* by the member of a lower caste, may be eaten by the member of a higher caste without any defilement.

(5) **Water.** The members of all castes except the untouchable may draw water from the same well either in metal or earthen pots without causing any defilement. Even Musalmans may draw water from the same well. But the untouchable castes, that is, Dheds, Bhangis and Chamars are not allowed to draw water from the same well with other castes. There are in each village separate wells for these people, and where none exists they have to wait at a distance from the village well and take such water as may generously be poured from a distance into their vessels by people of the clean castes. A new and unused earthen pot may be used for bringing water for Brahman and other high caste people. But if it is once used by the member of a caste it is fit to be used only for his caste, and for all others who may eat food cooked by him in water. A metal pot, however, even though used by a man of one caste may be used for another of the higher caste, after being cleansed with a little earth and water. High caste Hindus are not particular in Gujarat about the caste of the person fetching their water. They use water fetched by even Kumbhars or Kolis. In villages, Brahmans drink water from a leather *mote* and in some of the Shravak Vania castes in Patan, water is supplied to householders by *pakhalis* in leather *masaks*.

(6) **Occupation.** In theory each caste has a distinctive traditional occupation, but it is not necessary that it should be practised by its members. The traditional occupation of the Brahmans is priesthood, but in practice they follow all sorts of callings. Many are clerks or cooks, while some are soldiers, shop-keepers, agriculturists and even day-labourers, but they remain Brahmans all the same. Even in ancient times, the occupations of Brahmans were as diverse as they are at the present day. In the list of Brahmans given by Manu (Laws of Manu 111, 151, 166) whom a pious householder should not entertain at a Shradha, we find physicians, temple-priests, sellers of meat, shop-keepers, usurers, cow-herds, actors, singers, oil-men, keepers of gambling houses, sellers of spices, makers of bows and arrows, trainers of elephants, oxen, horses or camels, astrologers, bird fanciers, fencing masters, architects, breeders of sporting dogs, falconers, cultivators, shepherds and carriers of dead bodies. Some occupations are considered socially degrading, but a man who chooses to follow them does not thereby lose his caste, unless it is not reconcilable with the present practices of his caste with regard to food, *e.g.*, a Brahman or a Vania following the profession of a butcher. Many Brahmans and Vanias now follow even the degrading professions of the Dhobi and the Mochi, under their modern names of Washing and Dyeing Companies and Boot and Shoe Supplying Companies. So long as an occupation does not cause pollution, it may be, in these days, followed by the members of any caste, however low it may be.

(7) **Sacred thread.** The Brahman-Vania class wear the sacred thread habitually or at least on ceremonial occasions. The sacred thread is habitually worn by all Brahmans, Agarval and Bam Nagar Vanias, Bhatias,

Luhanas, some classes of Sonis, Maru Kansaras, Vaishya and Mewada Sutars, Sompura Salats, Brahma Bhats, Khatris (weavers) and Garodas or Dhed priests. The result of not wearing the thread in those castes which habitually wear it, would be excommunication.

(8) The influence of Jainism has rendered most of the Gujarat castes quite vegetarian. Only a few of the higher castes, such as Rajputs and Marathas and some of the lowest castes, such as Kolis, Dheds and Bhangis eat the flesh of goats, sheep or fowls, and fishes of all kinds. The eating of animal food in castes in which it is prohibited, would result in excommunication. Cows and peacocks are considered holy and slaughtering or shooting them is resented even by the flesh-eating Hindus.

Flesh-eating.

(9) As a rule the Brahman-Vania class indulge in no distilled or fermented drinks. To this there are two exceptions, a class of orthodox Hindus known as Shakta or Vammargi, who drink country-made liquor, and a class of innovators, who drink European wines and spirits. Among the youths of high caste Hindu families, the practice of drinking European wines and spirits has of late spread so rapidly that twenty or thirty years ago, what would have caused excommunication, is now passed unnoticed. Still a certain dishonour attaches both to the orthodox and to the innovating liquor drinkers. Among the Ghanchi-Gola castes, liquor drinking is allowed. But among them also, some castes do not drink at all, and some have recently passed rules imposing fines on those who do.

Fermented and distilled drinks.

(10) Except a few Brahmans, men of all classes smoke tobacco. It is also chewed and taken in the form of snuff. There is no prohibition against smoking tobacco, except among the Brahmans and even among them its violation is not noticed.

Tobacco.

(11) Ideas regarding pollution are not so developed in Gujarat as they are in the South of India. Mere proximity of a Dhed or Bhangi causes no pollution, though his touch does. Even as regards touch, the rule varies according to the necessity of the case. Cloth woven by a Dhed is considered touchable, so long as it is not washed, after sprinkling a little water or throwing a pinch of dust on it. Defilement caused by the touch of a Dhed or Bhangi is deemed to be removed, without undergoing the purification of a bath, merely by the sprinkling of a few drops of water touched with gold or even by simply touching a Musalman.

Pollution by touch.

527. When a man is excommunicated his fellow-castemen sever their connection with him so completely that—

Nature of the penalty of exclusion from caste.

(*a*) nobody eats, drinks or smokes with him,
(*b*) he is not invited to any caste-dinner,
(*c*) he cannot obtain brides or bride-grooms for his children,
(*d*) even his own married daughters cannot visit him,
(*e*) he is not helped even at the funeral of a member of his household,
(*f*) the caste-priest and even his own barber and washerman refuse to serve him, and
(*g*) in some cases he is debarred access to public temples.

528. It is obvious that when each caste is exclusive with regard to food and drink, there can be very little social intercourse between the members of the different castes. A man who wants to entertain his friends must call a Brahman cook, and if

Social intercourse.

one of the party happens to be a Nagar Brahman, none but a Nagar cook would do. Even with the proper arrangement for a cook, the food must be eaten by each guest sitting apart. A person of a lower caste would have to sit at a distance which would be quite humiliating, and if a non-Hindu is in the party, he would not only have to sit apart at a great distance, but he would be served from other dishes specially kept apart, so as not to cause pollution. For these reasons, there are very few mixed parties, and social intercourse between persons of different castes may be said to be practically non-existing. When such is the case with the Hindus themselves, social intercourse with Europeans is quite out of question. Apart from the difficulties due to caste, the mode of living is quite different among both. Squatting on the ground and eating of only vegetable dishes without knives and forks would be a feat which few Europeans would care to perform. But of late tea parties and garden parties are occasionally given in the City of Baroda, in which Hindus readily join their Musalman and Christian friends.

Caste dinners.

529. Gujarati Hindus are very fond of giving caste dinners in honour of some family event. Though the feasting of caste-fellows is not enjoined by religion, custom in Gujarat has made such entertainments rather compulsory on some occasions, such as, a wife's first pregnancy, an investiture with the sacred thread, a marriage and a death. In addition to these, there are some optional feasts, given either to the whole caste or to relatives, friends and acquaintances, such as on the anniversary of a death (*shradh* and *samvatsari*); on finishing a new house (*vastushanti* or home-peace feast) to atone for the loss of life caused in its building; on performing a vow; on coming back from a pilgrimage; on completing some religious observance or *vrat*; on recovering from a serious illness; on a birth-day; on the birth of a son; on naming a son; on first shaving his head; and on first sending him to school.

Caste dinners are also given from the income from fines for breaches of caste discipline, from the income of funds dedicated for the purpose by some rich member, or from a sum raised by special subscription. Special caste dinners are given by rich men anxious either to gain or keep up a name for liberality.

On the morning of the day fixed for the dinner, the family priest or some ladies of the family are sent round from house to house to ask the guests. Among the Brahma-Kshatris, a Bhat and among Rajputs and Kolis, a barber invites the guests. All except those who on account of old age or mourning do not appear in public, attend a caste dinner. Each guest brings his own drinking pot and cup. They are dressed in their best and are decked with ornaments either borrowed or their own. In the towns, most of the higher castes, have a *wadi* or caste dining hall, built at the cost of some one of their members or from funds raised by subscription. Elsewhere the dinner is given near the house of the host, and the guests sit in the open space near it or on the public road. Dinner is served on leaf plates except among the Jains, who use brass pots.

The expenses of a caste-dinner vary according to the nature of the occasion and the number of caste-people invited. Ordinarily a marriage or death-dinner costs from Rs.100 to Rs.2,000. Many people lead a frugal life, stinting themselves even of the ordinary comforts, with a view to lay by a sufficient amount for a caste-dinner. Those who have no money, borrow it at a high rate of interest on the security of their ornaments, houses, lands and other property and ruin their own and their children's prospects in life.

Modern disintegrating tendencies.

530. Within the last twenty or thirty years education and contact with foreigners have brought about many changes in some of the minor caste restrictions. The change is most perceptible in the distinctive caste dress. *Peherans* and *angerkhas* have yielded place to European fashioned shirts and coats; and the *payadi* or head dress to skull caps, *fentos* and even sola hats. Collars and ties have come into fashion among the educated and half-educated

of the new generation. The practice of shaving the head and keeping a small tuft of hair on the crown of the head (*shendi*), which was the distinctive sign of a Hindu, has been discarded and the practice of having close cropped hair has been the fashion of the day. Formerly one could at a glance guess the caste of a Hindu from his peculiar dress, but now the change in his exterior has been so great that it becomes difficult to find out not only his caste, but also whether he is a Hindu, Parsi or Musalman. Caste restrictions regarding food and pollution by touch are also being broken down owing to the spread of western ideas and the improved means of communication. Promiscuous travelling now prevails throughout the country, and Brahmans and other twice-borns sit and take refreshment in contact with *shudras*, outcastes and *mlechhas* on the levelling benches of the railway cars, conveniently closing their eyes to the contamination which such contiguity involves. Like the railways, public hospitals, jails, law courts and such other institutions ignore the claims of castes within their walls. In the public schools and colleges persons of all castes, except the lowest, sit together in the same class-room, join in the same games on the play-ground and often reside and eat meals together in boarding houses attached to some of them.

Twenty years ago, Nagar and Shrimali Brahmans could not eat food which was not cooked by a member of their own caste. Now many of them employ in their houses cooks from the Khedaval, Modh, Audich and other Brahman castes. Though this is not unknown to others, it passes unnoticed. Ten years ago, Deshastha, Koknastha and other Deccani Brahmans would not drink tea or water, when members of other non-Brahman castes were sitting on the same carpet with them ; now most of them do so without any hesitation. Every year hundreds of Indians visit Europe for purposes of study or trade or for mere pleasure. While there, they set aside the restrictions of the caste system in which they have been reared. When they return home, they are re-admitted into their caste on performing a nominal penance and in some castes even without performing any. And, although, they make an appearance of observing their caste, it is really never with them what it once was. In the garden and other parties which are now-a-days becoming common in towns, Brahmans, Vanias and Shudras partake of refreshments from the same buffet. Drinking of ærated waters prepared by non-Hindus has become fashionable, and it is a matter of everyday observation that tea or coffee from the Goanese refreshment-room-keepers at railway stations is preferred to the inferior stuff hawked by Brahmans. Biscuits manufactured by Huntly and Palmer and other western manufactures are freely partaken, and when doctors advise, there is no hesitation even in taking chicken soup or egg-mixture. There are many educated Hindus who deliberately break through the rules of caste when it suits them to do so, and many apparently orthodox Hindus enjoy in convenient European hotels in Bombay, Baroda, Ahmedabad and elsewhere and in the houses of their European, Parsi or Mahomedan friends, a hearty meal of forbidden food cooked and served by even Mahomedans.

But in their own homes the fear of giving offence to their more orthodox caste-fellows and the female members of the family lead them to observe the established rules and proprieties. So long as they do this their laxity elsewhere is condoned. Brought up in seclusion and without much education, the females in a family are tenacious of the old observances and restrictions and regard any departure from them with disfavour. There have recently, however, been signs of a great change in the treatment of Hindu ladies of high caste. Following the example of other advanced communities, Hindu gentlemen are now becoming anxious to give their daughters a good education. It is now only a matter of time for females of the educated classes to appear freely in public, and when they do so, the restrictions of the caste system, so far as ordinary social intercourse is concerned, are doomed. The uneducated masses, however, are far more conservative than the educated few, and it may be doubted whether they will quickly imitate their example in these matters. In some places, however, even amongst them, there is a slow but steady change. But the preservation of the caste system depends more upon the strict observance of its marriage rules than upon the rules limiting the persons with whom food may be partaken. No change is apparent in this important matter except in the gradual raising of the marriageable age and the condonement of marriages between sub-castes with fines only. There have been no marriages out of the limit of the caste. No one has shown the courage to face excommunication which would be the result of such a course. The State has passed a Civil Marriage Act on the lines of India Act III of 1872. It legalizes marriage under contractual form and except consanguinity, allows no bar against the contraction of marriages. But nobody has yet taken advantage of this provision of law. Instead of widening, the area for the selection of brides and bridegrooms has much decreased. Within the last 15 years, owing to the formation of groups or circles, girls cannot be married, even to members of the same caste, outside the groups without paying a high penalty. Educated Hindus sympathise with the hard lot of the widows of their community. A movement to support widow marriage has come into existence, but the conservative opposition to it is so strong that the results upto the present may be said to be insignificant. The remarriage of a Hindu widow is permitted by the law of the State, but the attitude of the people has rendered it a deadletter. Under the auspices of the Widow Remarriage Associations in Bombay and Ahmedabad, a few widows and widowers from the State remarried, but they suffered so much persecution at the hands of their relations and their caste, that their fate has been a warning to others rather than a good example to be followed. Instead of widow marriage being encouraged, prohibitions against it are getting strong and castes, which formerly allowed it, no longer do so, under the belief that by so doing, they raise themselves socially. The activity already started in favour of widow marriage may, in due course of time, achieve its aim, and widow marriage, between persons of the same caste may come about at least in those castes which have a scarcity of girls. But the limitations with respect to the sphere within which marriage may be contracted, the most essential feature of the caste system, has been, and will be, more enduring.

Attitude towards the depressed classes.

531. The attitude of the educated section of the higher castes towards the depressed classes has, within the decade, undergone a remarkable change. Theosophists, Brahmo Samajists, Arya Samajists, Prarthana Samajists, high class Hindus and Christian missionaries are all taking an active interest in their welfare. The work of the depressed-class mission in Bombay and other parts of Western India is progressing. The untouchables are being touched. The stigma is being removed. The first step has been taken and there is no doubt that the movement now going on for their elevation is bound to succeed. In the Baroda State, His Highness the Maharaja Sayajirao Gaekwad is a keen sympathiser with the lot of these poor people. Schools and Boarding Houses have been opened for their education. Dheds, Bhangis and Chamars can now enter the precincts of courts and government offices, like other castes, and even the public service is thrown open to them. As His Highness pointed out in one of his most eloquent speeches, it is now being recognised that " A Government within easy reach of the latest thought, with unlimited moral and material resources, such as there is in India, should not remain content with simply asserting the equality of man under the common law and maintaining order, but must sympathetically see from time to time that the different sections of its subjects are provided with ample means of progress."

VII.—Caste among Jains.

Caste among Jains.

532. The Jain religion does not sanction castes. But the Jains in Gujarat follow the caste system just in the same way as the Hindus. The bond of caste is to them even stronger than that of religion. When Jainism was first propagated, it was not insisted that the converts to its doctrines should give up their castes. There are certain castes, such as the Agarval, Oswal, Porwad and Shrimali Vanias, some of whose members are Hindus while others are Jains. The Hindu Vanias

are called Meshri while the Jain section is called Shravak. When one section of a caste is Jain and another Hindu, intermarriage takes place between them, *e.g.*, between Dasa Shrimali Meshris and Dasa Shrimali Jains or between Meshri and Jain Porwads. Individual members of a caste who accept Jainism as their religion continue to be its members along with those who follow Hinduism. Thus some members of the Lewa Kanbi, Bhavsar, Anjana Kanbi and such other castes, who have adopted Jainism as their religion, continue to be the members of their castes. A Vaishnav girl married into a Jain family attends the Jain temple (*apasara*) when at her husband's house and worships the old Brahmanical gods when she visits her parents. In spite of their religious differences, the social customs of Shravaks and Meshris are much alike. The religious classes of the Jains—Gorji and Sadhu—are ascetics and take no part in birth, marriage or death ceremonies. These social ceremonies are therefore performed with the help of Brahmans who do not suffer in social position because they act as priests to Shravaks.

VIII.—Caste among Mahomedans.

The two classes.

533. The Mahomedan religion does not allow the differentiation of its followers by castes. All Mahomedans can eat together, and though generally marriages among them are restricted among members of certain groups and tribes only, there is nothing like outcasting or excommunication for marrying beyond these limits. The main distinction between Mahomedans is that founded on their being foreigners or indigenous. The foreigners are those who have themselves come from beyond India or are the descendants of those who have migrated into India and settled there. The others are converts to Islam from the masses of the people of India. It is remarkable that, though professing the same religion, the two have never mingled and have remained apart for centuries. Those with a foreign strain are divided into four main sections—Saiyad, Shaikh, Mughal and Pathan, all of whom claim superiority over the local converts.

Saiyads.

534. The *Saiyads* claim descent from Fatimah and Ali, the daughter and son-in-law of the Prophet. They are the representatives of the Saiyads, who during the period of Musalman rule in Gujarat came as religious teachers, soldiers and adventurers from Turkey, Arabia and Central Asia. They mark their high birth by using among males, the title *Saiyad* or *Mir* before or *Shah* after and among females, the title *Begam* after their names. They take wives from any of the four regular Musalman classes, but marry their daughters only among themselves. Among some exclusive classes of Saiyads family trees are examined and every care is taken to make sure that the accepted suitor is a Saiyad, both on the father's and mother's side. Saiyads follow all professions. But most of them, as the descendants of saints, are *pirs* or spiritual guides to other Musalmans.

Shaikhs.

535. The title *Shaikh* (meaning elder) belongs strictly only to three branches of the Khuraish family to which the Prophet himself belonged. On the strength of the Prophet's tradition (hadith) that "all converts to my faith are of me and my tribe," the term is now indiscriminately applied to local Hindu and other converts, as well as to foreigners. This has given rise to the saying: "A Brahman without a caste is an Audich and a Musalman of no family is a Shaikh." There is a class of Hindu converts called Shaikh or Shaikhda. They are quite distinct from the regular Shaikhs with whom they have no marriage relations.

Mughals.

536. The term *Mughal* includes two distinct classes, the Persian and Indian Mughals. The Persian Mughals are the descendants of Persian political refugees and merchants and are Shiah in religion. The Indian Mughals are the descendants of the Mughal conquerors of India, and are Sunnis in religion. Both place the title *Mirza* (born of a great man) before and add *Beg* (lord) after their names

among males and add *Khanam* to the female names. Local Mughals differ in no way from the great body of the Sunni Musalman population.

Pathans.

537. *Pathans* are of Afghan origin. The men add *Khan* to their names and the women *Khanam* or *Khatu* to theirs. Their ancestors came to Gujarat as soldiers and merchants; and like the representatives of other foreign Musalmans, they have in most cases lost their peculiarities of feature and character by intermixture with other classes.

Mixed marriages how far allowed.

538. The pride of blood among Musalmans claiming foreign descent is considerable. They are very conservative and the general tendency is for a Saiyad to marry a Saiyad, a Pathan, to a Pathan, and so forth. So long as both parties belong to the section with a foreign blood, no slur attaches to mixed marriages and they generally do take place. But intermarriages between persons of the higher classes and the local converts are not approved.

Castes among local converts.

539. The divisions among the local converts are still more marked. The Vohora, Khoja, Memon, Shaikh, Molesalam Ghanchi, Pinjara, Darji, Dhobi, Kasai, Makawana, Matia and other groups formed by local converts follow their traditional caste occupations and adhere to their old Hindu caste notions. Some of them like the Matia Kanbis and the Shaikhdas are more Hindu than Musalman in their dress, names and observances. All of them constitute regular castes of the Hindu pattern. There are fewer restrictions in eating with members of other groups than there are amongst the Hindus. But the rule that a man may not marry outside the limits of his own group or pass from one group to another is equally rigid. There is however this marked difference that though a Tai cannot become a Pinjara or a Pinjara, a Kasbati, there is no great difficulty in the way of a member of any of these groups, who rises in life in joining the ranks of the Shaikhs, Mughals or Pathans. A well-to-do man of the functional group will often drop the functional name and call himself a Shaikh or Pathan, and by dint of hospitality secure for himself a circle of friends from the poorer members of the upper class. He will then marry into some upper class family, possibly of doubtful status and his son will be unquestionably a true Shaikh or Pathan.

Jamat.

540. A closer bond than religion of either sameness of descent or of calling, unites the members of each group of local converts who form a *jamat* (union) with, as a rule, a headman called Mukhi or Patel. Each union has its rules, generally social but sometimes connected with their calling. Amongst the social offences of which Jamats take cognizance are adultery, divorcing a wife without proper cause and marrying persons not belonging to the group. Breaches of rules and regulations are enforced by fines and from this and other sources is formed a fund chiefly spent in yearly public feasts, building or repairing mosques and also, at times, helping distressed and destitute members.

IX.—Caste in proverbs and popular sayings.

Caste in proverbs.

541. Many proverbs are current in Gujarati about the various castes which go to illustrate their traits and to give an estimate of the opinion in which they are held by the general public. A few of them, for the more important and numerous castes, are as under :—

Barber.

If a cat can keep in its belly rice-pudding, a barber can keep a secret. (Refers to his inherent nature of disclosing the secret of others.)

Bava.

By putting on a cap, *i. e.*, by becoming a Bava, you have three advantages—no taxes to pay, no compulsory labour to undergo, and all will call you a Bava (*i. e.*, father), and you will easily support yourself. (Refers to the utter freedom of the ascetic, from the troubles which beset a householder.)

Bharvad. If you have not seen a *bhut*, see a Bharvad. (Refers to his frightening appearance.)

Bhat. A Bhat is always garrulous. (Refers to his speaking certain things unnecessarily.)

Bhats, Tentas (Garasias) and sickles are always bent. (Refers to their crooked nature and behaviour.)

Bhathela. A Bhathela's mouth was opened with a hatchet. (Refers to his fondness to use foul language.)

He is a donkey's son who trusts a *bhut* a Bhathela or a tailless serpent. (They are so treacherous.)

Brahmans. A Brahman, a he-buffalo and a dog—these three are always jealous.

Food cooked by a Brahman can be eaten by a Brahman or a buffalo. (It is so badly cooked.)

If one *Tilva* (Brahman) is killed, a hundred *Tilvas* (Brahmans) can be fed. (Refers to the hatred in which the lower castes hold them.)

The abode of Brahmans is known by people moving about with short digogies and pits in their stomach. (Refers to their scanty clothing and half-starved appearance.)

Brahman-Audich. The Audich caste is a veritable sea. (Refers to its being so large that one can easily pretend to be one of the caste.)

Brahman-Mewada. Foolish is the tribe of Mewadas, they earn little but dress like beaux.

Brahman-Modh. A Modh, a Mewada and a black ant will destroy their own kind.

A Modh, even when on death-bed will try to kill a Shrimali. (Refers to the animosity between the two castes.)

Better to have white leprosy on your forehead than a Modh Brahman in your neighbourhood.

Brahman-Nagar. A Nagar will never speak the truth. If he does, his *guru* must be a fool.

A Nagar bride is open for inspection (before selection). (Refers to her unquestionable beauty.)

Nagars, crows and cocks are discreet. (સુગત)

You must have a jarful of money before you can get a Nagar bride.

Dhed. Among quadrupeds, a Kolo is a rogue and among bipeds a Dhed (Refers to the roguery of Dheds.)

Ghanchi Soni. A Ghanchi is the Satan's bedstead.

Goldsmith. If you have not seen a thief, see a Soni. (Refers to his tact of filching gold and silver even though keenly watched).

Jat. It is not advisable to irritate a Jat in a forest, fire in summer, a Turk (Musalman) in a Kasba, and a Bakal (Vania) in a bazar. (Refers to their strength in the respective places.)

Kachhia. A Kachhia has cheated even god. (Refers to his cunningness.)

Kanbis. A Kanbi is the supporter of scores of people, but himself is supported by none. (Refers to his power of producing staple corn which is essential to sustain life.)

There is no giver like Kanbis. (Refers to their generosity.)

Matias, Anjanas and Marus are a little better than Dheds. (Refers to their mean living and behaviour.)

Kathi. One Kathi is equal to a hundred Vanias. (Refers to their valorous nature.)

Koli. Holi holidays have arrived and the Koli has nothing with him. (Refers to his living from hand to mouth and utter disregard for the future.)

Luhar. Where five Luhars meet, everything is spoiled. (Refers to their uncompromising nature.)

Parsi. A Parsi breaks his word in no time.

Prabhu. To-day of a Prabhu means a week, to-morrow twenty days, and the day after to-morrow twenty-five. (Refers to his delay in paying debts).

Rajput. Even if a cord (string) is burnt, the twists remain. (Refers to the feeling of vengeance burning in the heart of a Rajput even though fallen.)

Thakors are gone and Thags have taken their place. (Refers to the disappearance of the old good Rajputs and the existence of the present mean ones.)

Where five Rajputs assemble, they make the matter strong. (Refers to their inherent strength of character, body and mind.)

Tailors, Goldsmiths, etc. A tailor, a goldsmith and a weaver are birds of the same feather. (Refers to their similarity in dexterous filching.)

A tailor's to-night and shoe-maker's to-morrow. (Refers to their procrastinating habits.)

Even God cannot detect a tailor, goldsmith and a weaver. (Refers to their dexterous filching.)

Vania-Lad. A Lad is a dried up tree and Dave is a sharp axe. (Refers to hard-heartedness and stinginess of Lad Vanias and Khedaval Brahmans respectively.)

Vanias in general. A Vania is foresighted.

A Vania will not call a spade a spade. (Refers to his timidity and cunningness.)

Damn the face of a Baj, a Lad and a Khedaval. (Refers to their dissociable nature).

Vanias are liberal-hearted in spending after marriage processions.

Even god has no anxiety for a Vania and an ass. (He is able to take care of himself.)

Vohoras. A sickle has no scabbard and a Vohora has no knowledge. (Refers to his want of sense.)

Vohoras are the refuse of society, as *buru* (husks) are the refuse of *Juwar*.

PART II.—STATISTICAL.

Classification of castes.

542. In 1891 the classification of castes was based on considerations "partly ethnological, partly historical and partly again functional." In 1901, Sir Herbert Risley while pointing out the disadvantages of this scheme said:—"Judged by its results the scheme seems to me to be open to criticism in many respects. It accords neither with native tradition and practice nor with any theory of caste that has ever been propounded by students of the subject. In different parts, it proceeds on different principles with the result that on one hand, it separates groups which are really allied and on the other, includes in the same category groups of widely different origin and status. It is in fact a patch-work classification in which occupation predominates, varied here and there by considerations of caste, history, tradition, ethnical affinity and geographical position." (page 312 of the India Administrative Volume, 1901.) He therefore prescribed in its stead a classification by social precedence. The inquiries which were made to this end yielded a great deal of interesting information which is embodied in Chapter VIII of the 1901 Report. It is doubtful whether after so short an interval as ten years, much fresh information on this subject would be forthcoming. Moreover, the discussion which took place in 1901 aroused a

great deal of ill-feeling which has hardly yet been assuaged, and it would be inadvisable "to stir up the embers of the various controversies," which then took place. It was therefore decided by the Census Commissioner for India that on the present occasion the question of social precedence should not be re-opened, and that the castes should be grouped according to their traditional occupations which were the main bases of classification adopted in 1891. This has been done in Subsidiary Table I at the end of this Chapter. In Imperial Table XIII, the various castes are arranged alphabetically. Where more than one religion is returned by the members of a caste, separate figures have been given for each.

Distribution and Variation since 1872.

543. In India as a whole there are over two thousand castes. No less than 352 main castes and 195 sub-castes have been returned at the Census in this State alone. The number is so large that it is impossible to discuss in detail the distribution and the variation in the strength of each compared with previous Censuses. Only the important castes have been dealt with in Subsidiary Table II at the end of this chapter and the reader is referred to Imperial Table XIII of the present and previous censuses for the rest.

Castes and Sub-castes.

	Castes.	Sub-Castes.
Hindu	231	174
Jain	35	16
Animist	16	......
Musalman	70	5
Total ...	352	195

Percentages of main castes.

544. Taking all castes together, Brahmans of all kinds number 113,237 (including 104 Arya Samajists) or nearly 7 per cent. of the Hindu population. Kanbis of all kinds number 402,657 (including 1,456 Jains and 284 Arya Samajists) or 24 per cent. of the Hindu population and nearly 20 per cent. of the total population. Kolis of all kinds number 370,953 (including 7 Jains and 3 Arya Samajists) or 22 per cent. of the Hindu population and 18·2 of the total population, and Vanias of all kinds, including both Meshris (38,951 Hindus and 14 Arya Samajists) and Shravaks (39,657) number 78,622 or nearly 4 per cent. of the State population. The total number of Jains is 43,462 of which 39,657 are Vanias and 3,805 are members of other castes. The total number of all the untouchable castes together is 173,194 or 10 per cent. of the Hindu and about 8 per cent. of the State population. The Animistic tribes number 199,038 or nearly 10 per cent. of the total population of the State.

545. The relative strength of Hindu castes having a population of 10,000 and above is exhibited in the diagram in the margin. It will be noticed that the Lewa Kanbi caste which claims 183,289 persons (exclusive of 1,333 Jains and 188 Arya Samajists) or 9 per cent. of the total population of the State, takes the first number in numerical strength. After it comes the Kadwa Kanbi caste and then follow in order Thakarda Kolis, Dheds and Talbada Kolis.

Diagram showing the relative strength of Hindu Castes.

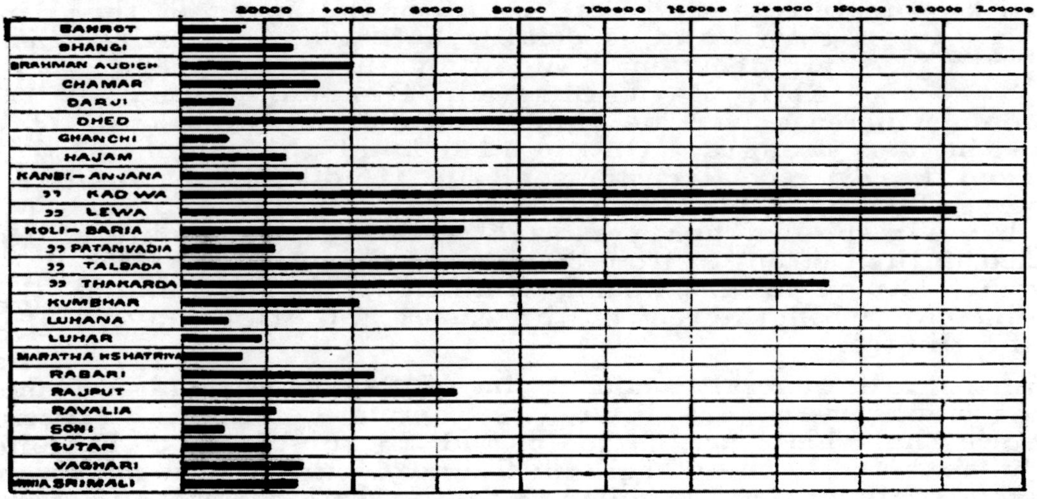

546. Among the Animistic tribes (returned as Animists) the Gamit tribe, which has 22,175 persons, is numerically the strongest. After it come the Chodhra, Bhil, Dhanka and Dhodia tribes in order of their population.

Diagram showing the relative strength of Animists.

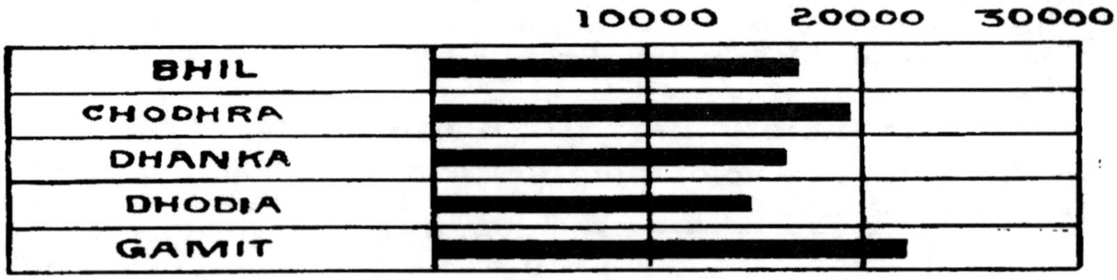

547. Among Musalmans the largest number has returned themselves as Shaikhs. After Shaikhs come Vohoras (both traders and peasants together) and then Pathans and Memons in order.

Diagram showing the relative strength of Musalman Castes.

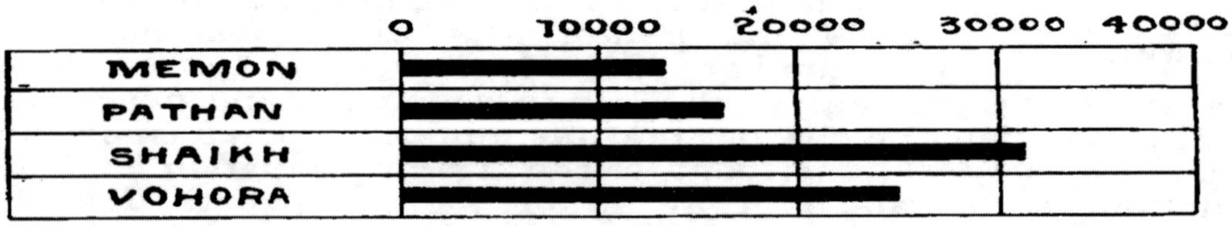

Variations in the strength of castes.

548. We shall now group the castes according to their traditional occupations and briefly glance at the variations in their number from census to census.

Hindus and Jain Castes.

Most of the high castes decadent.

549. One striking feature of the caste return is that most of the Hindu castes, and especially the higher and artizan castes, are decadent. A few of the lower castes, such as Ahir, Bava, Bharvad, Ghanchi, Sathawara and Shenva show some net increase over the figures of 1881, but almost all of the rest have declined in their strength. On the other hand the Animistic tribes, which are free from the evil social customs of the Hindus, have wonderfully grown in number. Dhodia, Dubla, Gamit, Nayakda, Vasava and such other primitive tribes have, in spite of heavy mortality during the famine of 1899-1900, all increased in their strength from 30 to more than 100 per cent. during the last thirty years. Amongst Musalmans, Ghanchis, Memons and Pathans only show some increase while the rest of the castes and tribes have declined in number like the Hindus.

550. Brahmans are generally said to be of 84 castes, and a feast in which Brahmans of all castes are invited is therefore called a *Chorashi*. The Census shows that there are 64 main and 28 sub-castes of Brahmans in the State. The six noted in the margin on the next page are the most important. The Anavala Brahmans are peculiar to the Navsari District and those of their number who are found in other districts have emigrated for search of employment. Of the Nagars, the most numerous is the Visnagara section

whose strength is the greatest in the Kadi District. Deshastha Brahmans are immigrants from the Deccan and are mainly to be found in the City of Baroda. Like other higher castes, Brahman castes are also decadent. Audich Brahmans who are even now the most numerous among the Brahman castes have lost on the whole nearly 15 per cent. of their population during the last 30 years. Similarly Mewadas have lost 28 per cent., Modhs 24 per cent. and Nagars 20 per cent. The Deshastha Brahmans have increased by 13 per cent. during the decade, but still they are now less numerous than what they were 30 years ago by about 32 per cent. Most of them were dependant upon the State service or State charities ; and as the latter became less accessible to them on the gradual introduction of reform in their distribution, their number gradually decreased.

Priests.

Name.	Baroda.	Kadi.	Navsari.	Amreli.	Total.
Brahman—					
1. Anavala	283	64	9,559	10	9,916
2. Audich	10,602	23,506	2,061	4,510	40,679
3. Deshastha	4,715	662	723	364	6,464
4. Mewada	1,445	3,008	235	136	4,824
5. Modh	2,417	3,975	1,696	712	8,800
6. Nagar	1,803	5,771	79	337	7,990
Others	19,152	7,773	1,414	6,225	34,564
Total ...	40,417	44,759	15,767	12,294	113,237

551. Vanias who are followers of the Vallabhachari sect are called Meshri Vanias, while those who follow Jainism are called Shravak Vanias. The latter are a little more numerous (by 692 persons only) than the former in this State. There are 21 castes of Meshri Vanias, with a total strength of 38,965 (including 14 Arya Samajists) persons, or 2·3 per cent. of the total Hindu population. They are all traders and so are also members of the Bhatia and Luhana castes, who together number 12,149. The most numerous among the Vanias are Disaval, Khadayata, Lad, Modh, Nagar and Shrimali, who are to be found in all the Districts ; Kapol and Sorathia Vanias are peculiar to the Amreli District; Luhanas are the most numerous in the Amreli District, but are also to be found in Baroda and Kadi Districts. Bhatias are to be found mainly in Amreli and Kadi Districts.

Traders—Hindu.

Name.	Baroda.	Kadi.	Navsari.	Amreli.	Total.
Vania—					
Agarval	116	109	57	2	384
Baj	96	......	105	......	201
Disaval	1,740	4,010	56	14	5,820
Gujjar	32	75	3	3	113
Jharola	1,451	569	9	......	2,029
Kapol	54	8	154	2,286	2,503
Khadayata	1,795	800	156	24	2,775
Lad	6,066	436	1,571	23	8,096
Mewada	684	195	77	......	956
Modh	1,698	391	360	1,104	3,558
Nagar	624	2,978	46	9	3,657
Oswal	155	39	6	......	200
Porwad	750	846	36	48	1,680
Shrimali	2,829	1,340	136	747	5,052
Sorathia	2	13	22	388	425
Umad	142	1	...	3	146
Vayada	365	374	1	......	740
Others	181	543	2	10	736
Total ...	18,780	12,727	2,797	4,661	38,965
Bhatia	87	293	6	225	561
Luhana	2,311	1,455	21	7,801	11,588
Total ...	2,346	1,748	27	8,026	12,149
Grand Total ...	21,128	14,475	2,824	12,687	51,114

The Vania castes seem to be decadent. Most of them have more or less decreased in number. The greatest loss has been suffered by the Disavals, who lost 25 per cent. of their population in the Census of 1901 and 18 per cent. in the present Census. Their number is now 37 per cent. less than what it was in 1881. Similarly the Lads are now 17 per cent. less numerous than what they were thirty years ago.

552. Of the Jain or Shravak traders, Oswal, Porwad and Shrimali castes are the most numerous. More than 60 per cent. of the Jain Vanias are to be found in the Kadi District. Their number in the Baroda District is only one-third of that in Kadi. The only important Jain Vania caste in the Amreli District is that of Shrimalis. Jain element is the lowest in the Navsari District. Its Jain Vania population is only one-sixteenth of the total Jain Vania population in the State.

Traders—Jain.

Name.	Baroda.	Kadi.	Navsari.	Amreli.	Total.
Vania—					
Agarval	......	19	......	......	19
Disaval	......	325	......	......	325
Jharola	25	......	......	......	25
Lad	248	150	6	......	404
Mewada	732	4	......	......	736
Modh	4	......	3	......	7
Nema	108	2	......	......	110
Oswal	581	1,594	520	49	2,744
Porwad	746	4,718	1,467	3	6,933
Shrimali	5,526	18,065	330	2,992	26,913
Sorathia	......	......	......	28	28
Umad	555	772	64	......	1,391
Others	16	1	5	......	22
Total ...	8,541	25,650	2,395	3,071	39,657

553. The five castes, noted in the margin, are looked upon as Kshatriyas or warrior castes. They form 5 per cent. of the Hindu population of the State. The Rajput caste is found in the largest number in the Kadi District. The Rajputs in the State are now 8 per cent. more than what they were in 1901, but compared with their population in the past, they have decreased by nearly 20 per cent. from what they were in 1881. Marathas are mostly found in the Baroda District, and Kathis, Vaghers and Vadhels only in the Amreli District. The number of Marathas has declined by 24 per cent. from what it was in 1881, owing mainly to the gradual reduction in the irregular army of the State, and the retinue of the sirdars.

Warrior classes.

Name.	Baroda.	Kadi.	Navsari.	Amreli.	Total.
Rajput	24,088	31,833	4,914	3,393	64,228
Maratha	11,863	756	889	1,277	14,785
Kathi	13	......	......	3,460	3,473
Vagher	4	1	......	4,272	4,277
Vadhel	......	......	......	69	69
Total ...	35,968	32,590	5,803	12,471	86,832

554. Though a large proportion of the people in the State, either partly or entirely, depend upon agriculture for their maintenance, the number of professional husbandmen is small. It includes the castes mentioned in the margin, with a total strength of 420,881 or nearly 25 per cent. of the Hindu population. Sagars are peculiar to the Amreli District and Sathawaras to the Kadi District, while Kachhias, though largely found in the Baroda District, are also to be found in Kadi and Navsari. The Anjana Kanbis are to be found mainly in the Kadi District. The Kadwa Kanbis, though found in all the districts, have their largest number in the Kadi District; and similarly the Lewas have their greatest strength in the Baroda District. Matias are peculiar to the Navsari District, and are those who having been once converted to Islam, subsequently reverted to their ancestral religion.

Husbandmen.

Name.	Baroda.	Kadi.	Navsari.	Amreli.	Total.
Kachhia	5,763	759	1,491	16	8,029
Kanbi	123,024	216,042	18,507	45,084	402,657
Anjana	308	29,714	887	11	30,920
Kadwa	6,173	160,226	4,093	2,364	172,856
Lewa	112,235	25,809	10,049	36,717	184,810
Matia	5	......	398	......	408
Others	4,303	293	3,080	5,992	13,668
Mali	884	1,660	162	77	2,783
Sagar	18	......	......	1,564	1,582
Sathawara	194	5,160	......	476	5,830
Total ...	129,883	223,631	20,160	47,217	420,881

555. The sixteen castes noted in the margin constitute the Hindu craftsmen of the State. Their total strength is 147,321 persons or nearly 9 per cent. of the total Hindu population. It is noteworthy that in Navsari the number of Luhars is smaller than that of Sonis, while elsewhere Luhars are more numerous than Sonis. Salvi is a weaving caste peculiar to the Kadi District, similarly the Vanza caste is peculiar to Amreli. Khatris are more numerous in Navsari than in other districts of the State. Compared with previous Censuses almost all the principal craftsman castes seem to have decreased in their strength. As compared with 1881, Bhavsar population is now less by 36 per cent., Darji by 11 per cent., Kumbhar by 4 per cent., Mochi by 3 per cent., Soni by 18 per cent., and Sutar by 14 per cent. Golas have kept up their number, while the net increase in the strength of the Ghanchis has only been 3 per cent. during the last 30 years. The decline in the castes which have decreased in number took place mainly in the decade 1891-1901 and was due to the great famine and the consequent emigration to other parts of India and to Africa in search of employment.

Craftsmen.

Name.	Baroda.	Kadi.	Navsari.	Amreli.	Total.
Bhavsar	1,315	3,504	800	70	5,689
Chhipa	341	54	100	7	502
Darji (including 39 Shimpis) ...	2,712	6,987	1,758	1,864	13,316
Galiara	63	......	1	......	64
Ghanchi (including 39 Telis) ...	2,525	7,303	2,068	15	11,906
Gola	3,694	217	1,299	......	5,210
Kansara	567	987	332	178	2,064
Khatri	1,045	435	1,130	785	3,395
Kumbhar	7,291	22,073	4,452	7,877	41,693
Luhar	5,119	11,487	789	1,817	19,212
Mochi	2,714	2,473	1,467	2,061	8,715
Salat	597	489	47	43	1,176
Salvi	4	89	1	......	94
Soni (including 539 Sonars)... ...	4,425	3,382	1,412	1,440	10,659
Sutar (including 116 Kharadis, 1,328 Kumbhar Sutars and 72 Sutar Luhars)	6,036	11,187	3,160	1,902	22,235
Vanza	......	......	......	1,391	1,391
Total ...	38,448	70,617	18,806	19,450	147,321

556. Under the head bards and actors come five castes noted in the margin, with a strength of 22,216 persons or 1·3 per cent. of the total Hindu population. Two-thirds of their number are to be found in the Kadi District, in which is situated Patan, the ancient capital of Gujarat, in the time of its Rajput rulers. Their occupation is not now so flourishing as it was before, and most of them have taken to agriculture or trade. Their number is gradually declining. Bhats are now 31 per cent. less than what they were in 1881; and Targalas, though they have increased by about 2 per cent. in the present Census, are now less numerous than in 1881 by about 28 per cent.

Bards and Actors.

Name.	Baroda.	Kadi.	Navsari.	Amreli.	Total.
Bhat	4,929	9,268	271	188	14,656
Charan	464	834	7	654	1,959
Gandhrap	15	70	......	......	85
Targala	409	3,983	28	48	4,468
Turi	20	979	......	49	1,048
Total ...	5,837	15,134	306	939	22,216

557. Dhobi, Hajam and Khavas are castes whose traditional occupation is personal service. They form 1·6 per cent. of the total Hindu population. Their number is naturally larger in Kadi and Baroda Districts than in Amreli and Navsari. Khavas are mainly confined to the Amreli District where they find employment in Kathi households.

Personal servants.

Name.	Baroda.	Kadi.	Navsari.	Amreli.	Total.
Dhobi	1,099	501	400	438	2,438
Hajam	8,986	12,493	1,421	1,938	24,838
Khavas	1	14	...	236	251
Total ...	10,086	13,008	1,821	2,612	27,527

558. Kolis have a total strength of 370,953 or 21·9 per cent. of the Hindu population of the State. They are the most numerous in the Baroda and Kadi Districts. Of the several Koli castes, Baria, Patanvadia and Talbada are the most numerous in the Baroda District, and Thakarda in the Kadi District. Gedia is a Koli caste peculiar to the Amreli District. Kolis have increased in the present Census by 14 per cent. and in the decade 1881-1891 by 10 per cent. But 31 per cent. of their number perished in the great famine which preceded the Census of 1901, and the Koli population in the whole State is now about 14 per cent. less than what it was in 1881.

Koli.

Name.	Baroda.	Kadi.	Navsari.	Amreli.	Total.
Baria	62,160	2,957	1,028	110	66,255
Bhallia	2,737	......	555	6	3,298
Chunvalia	1,727	1,324	147	4,509	7,707
Dalvadi	847	......	205	......	1,052
Gedia	......	......	......	3,716	3,716
Khant	27	1,432	171	1,118	2,748
Patanvadia	17,957	3,975	331	......	22,263
Makvana	......	2,015	......	......	2,015
Talbada	67,798	1,364	17,414	4,951	91,527
Thakarda	926	151,817	510	8	153,261
Unspecified	179	10,950	4,822	1,165	17,116
Total ...	154,358	175,834	25,183	15,578	370,953

559. Under herdsmen come Ahir, Bharvad and Rabari castes with a strength of 58,587 or 3·5 per cent. of the total Hindu population. Ahirs, the Abhirs or cowherds of ancient Hindu writings, are found chiefly in the Amreli District. They are said to have come there from Mathura with Shri Krishna. Bharvads are found in all districts, but their number in the Navsari and Amreli Districts is larger than in Kadi and Baroda. Rabaris are found in all districts, but their number is the largest in the Kadi District, where by breaking fences and grazing their cattle on standing crops, they cause great loss and annoyance to the cultivators.

Herdsmen.

Name.	Baroda.	Kadi.	Navsari.	Amreli.	Total.
Ahir	224	23	58	4,877	5,182
Bharvad	1,238	1,800	3,110	2,341	8,489
Rabari	6,351	35,473	410	2,682	44,916
Total ...	7,813	36,796	3,578	10,400	58,587

560. Bhangi, Dhed, Garoda, Chamar and Shenva are the five important castes which are known as the depressed, or as Hindus hold them, unclean castes. Their total strength is 173,194 or 10 per cent. of the whole Hindu population. Except Shenvas, who are found only in Baroda and Kadi, the other castes are well distributed in all the districts. Among high class Hindus, the degree of aversion for people of these castes depends on the kind of work by which they live. Chamars (tanners) rank below Dheds, and both of them are above Bhangis or sweepers. Still, all of them are Hindus and cleaner than the *mlechhas, i.e.*, Musalman, etc. Educated Indians are now beginning to realize that the disabilities under which the Antyajas or the depressed classes, as they are called, are labouring, can hardly be defended. It is gratifying to observe that there has been a gradual reversion of feeling of late in their favour, and the efforts of the Arya Samaj bid fair to secure some

The depressed classes.

Name.	Baroda.	Kadi.	Navsari.	Amreli.	Total.
Bhangi	15,102	8,561	982	1,752	26,397
Dhed	33,579	40,386	14,540	11,293	99,798
Garoda	1,702	4,204	230	145	6,281
Chamar	10,480	19,129	1,843	808	32,210
Shenva	374	7,207	4	2	7,587
Burud	70	16	54	10	150
Holar	51	...	...	...	51
Mahar	642	20	39	...	701
Others	19	...	...	...	19
Total ...	61,969	79,523	17,692	14,010	173,194

recognition of their status. His Highness the Maharaja Gaekwad, with his usual high sense of justice and mercy, has often evinced his great desire to secure full measure of justice for these poor people at the hands of his subjects. Numerous schools have been opened in the State for the boys and girls of the *antyaja* classes. Educated Antyajas find employment in the public service and are allowed free access to public buildings, such as schools and law courts. It is recognised that they are chips of the same block from which the rest have emanated and are entitled to equal rights and privileges.

Animistic tribes.

561. Under the term Animistic tribes are included all the primitive people who, at one time holding the plain country were, by the Kolis, cultivating Brahmans, Kanbis, Rajputs and other waves of northern settlers ousted from their strongholds and driven to the hills and forests that border Gujarat on the east. This section of the people includes several tribes, of which the 16 noted in the margin are found in this State. Their distribution shows that these tribes are found in the Baroda and Navsari Districts along the whole length of the eastern border. Except a few Bhils, Animistic tribes are not found in the Kadi and Amreli Districts. It is difficult to estimate the exact growth of the Animistic tribes, for many of them have not been correctly returned in the past. There can, however, be no doubt that most of the tribes have considerably increased in number from Census to Census except in 1901. Bhils alone show a large decline of 26 per cent. from their strength in 1881, but this is due to the heavy mortality among them during the great famine of 1899-1900. The Animistic tribes taken together number 199,038 and form nearly 10 per cent. of the total population of the State.

Animistic Tribes.

Name.	Baroda.	Kadi.	Navsari.	Amreli.	Total.
Bhil	26,697	1,666	13,392	81	41,836
Chodhra	12	1	31,353	...	31,366
Dhanka	18,663	...	4	...	18,667
Dhodia	19	...	20,471	...	20,490
Dubla	6	...	3,393	...	3,399
Gamit or Gamta ...	3	...	49,612	...	49,615
Kathodia	...	...	522	...	523
Kolgha	...	...	692	...	692
Kokna	21	...	6,430	...	6,451
Kotvalia	39	5	1,614	...	1,658
Mavchi	...	2	987	...	989
Nayakda	2,811	74	7,145	...	10,030
Talavia	712	...	16	...	728
Valvi	334	...	712	...	1,046
Varli	...	...	598	...	598
Vasava	1,486	...	9,465	...	10,951
Total ...	50,803	1,748	146,406	81	199,038

Musalmans.

562. The Musalmans with a foreign strain number 57,643 or 36 per cent. of the total Musalman population. Shaikhs are naturally the most numerous as they include many descendants of local converts also. After Shaikhs come Pathans and then Saiyads and Mughals in their numerical strength. Nearly 50 per cent. of these four superior classes of Mahomedans are in the Baroda District, 33 per cent. in the Kadi District and the rest are distributed in the districts of Navsari and Amreli. All the classes, except Mughals, show abnormal increase during the decade (Pathan 43 per cent., Saiyad 20 per cent. and Shaikh 40 per cent.), which is probably due to local converts trying to raise their social status by passing themselves off as Shaikhs, Saiyads or Pathans. As I have mentioned elsewhere, some Pinjaras were actually detected in passing themselves off as Dhunak Pathans, and some Tais, as Panni Pathans. But doubtless many others must have passed unnoticed.

Partly foreign Musalmans.

Name.	Baroda.	Kadi.	Navsari.	Amreli.	Total.
Shaikh	13,741	10,221	5,813	1,736	31,510
Saiyad	3,949	2,966	803	1,054	8,772
Mughal	441	379	171	63	1,054
Pathan	8,189	5,868	1,354	896	16,307
Total ...	26,320	19,434	8,140	3,749	57,643

563. The Musalmans of almost entirely Hindu descent are divided into several communities or classes, of which the principal ones found in the State are enumerated in the margin. Their total strength is 103,244 or 64 per cent. of the total Musalman population. The most numerous class is that of Memons whose principal home is Kathiawad. In the Gujarat Districts they are mainly immigrants for trade purposes. Next to Memons in numerical strength are the Vohora traders, who were originally converts from the trading classes, and are still mainly traders. They are to be found in the largest number in the Kadi District in which the town of Sidhpur is their head-quarters. A different kind of Vohoras, called Vohora peasants, who were mainly converted from the agricultural classes, are found only in the Baroda and Navsari Districts, and are still mainly agriculturists. A large number of these people has of late taken to trade, and migrated to Burma or South Africa. Maleks, Molesalams, Momnas, Ghanchis, Tais, Pinjaras and similar other castes, who still keep up many of their Hindu customs and practices, are to be found in all districts, but they are more numerous in Baroda and Kadi than in Navsari and Amreli. Among local converts, Ghanchis and Memons have remarkably increased in number during the last thirty years. To their number in 1881, Ghanchis have added 22 per cent. and Memons 147 per cent. During the last ten years, Momnas have decreased by 43 per cent. The Pinjaras have added 28 per cent. to their strength in 1901, but their loss in the great famine was heavy, and they have not yet regained their numerical strength in 1881. Maleks, Molesalams and Vohoras show some decrease during this Census as well as that of 1901, which is probably due to migration.

Local converts.

Name.	Baroda.	Kadi.	Navsari	Amreli.	Total.
Vohora (traders) ...	2,806	5,026	4,388	957	13,177
Vohora (peasants) ...	6,147	...	5,711	...	11,858
Ghanchi	1,912	1,006	583	1,113	4,614
Fakir	2,223	1,646	385	395	4,639
Khoja	28	134	...	1,799	1,961
Kasbati	1,813	4,126	227	157	6,323
Malek	5,117	1,512	834	56	7,519
Molesalam	7,982	792	173	19	8,966
Momna	2,913	4,268	2	...	7,183
Memon	1,087	6,873	506	5,074	13,540
Pinjara	2,075	2,442	320	571	5,408
Tai	1,407	283	1,084	156	2,930
Sindhi	1,516	1,187	23	792	3,548
Others	2,822	3,858	831	4,067	11,578
Total ...	39,868	33,153	15,067	15,156	103,244

Changes in material condition.

564. The material condition of the people of all castes generally has undergone during the last quarter of a century considerable change, particularly in respect of their mode of living, style of dwelling and nature of furniture. Western ideas are gaining ever firmer hold upon the upper and middle classes. The strong durable brass lamps called *samais*, which were once universally used, have yielded place to English or German lamps with fragile globes and glass chimneys. Castor seed oil has yielded place to kerosine oil, and in lieu of the *gadi takia* of the old style, most houses have now a few chairs and a sofa of western pattern ; and a writing desk in place of the old *bajat* or *chaurang*. Holders and steel pens have displaced the old fashioned *kalams* and the rough but strong Ahmedabadi paper has been displaced by the smooth and white but less durable paper of foreign manufacture. The old-fashioned cloth bags (*joranas*) have been displaced by steel trunks and *rajais* by rugs. *Angarkhas* have been displaced by coats and big and heavy turbans are either reduced in bulk or exchanged for skull caps and *fentas*. Native shoes made of red-coloured country leather and ornamented with brass eyelets and a long beak-like projection in the front are being rapidly displaced by black or tan western shaped boots and shoes. The old practice of keeping only a tuft of hair on the crown of the head and shaving the rest clean is fast disappearing and the western fashion of wearing close cut hair over the whole head is coming into vogue.

The change in female dress, though not much, is well marked. Heavy, durable and cheap country-made *sallas* have, to some extent, yielded place to costly and foreign made silk *saris* or Manchester *gavans*. Costly country-made *saris* of *kinkhap* or cloth of gold, once universally used and lasting for generations, are fastly disappearing. The *kapada* (bodice) is being replaced by more decent looking but costly *cholis* and *polkas*.

Heavy ivory and wooden *chudas* (bracelets) are being replaced by machine-polished gold bangles and light and fragile glass bangles. Silver *kallans*, and *sanklas* (anklets of various shapes) have either disappeared or are being displaced by lighter and finer ones. Most Hindu women are yet to be seen walking barefooted in the streets, but a few living in towns and cities have taken to putting on slippers and even boots and shoes.

The joint family system is gradually disappearing, the general tendency being for brothers and cousins to live separate. In a few families, harmony is preserved, and brothers manage to live amicably under one roof so long as their parents are living. But when they are no more, friction often arises and the influence of the womenfolk and western education impels the brothers to live separate. Thirty years ago, those who left their native place for some other place, either for business or service, could not dream of taking their wives with them, however exalted their position might be. Now even a petty clerk can take away his wife from the family home and live with her in the place of his business.

SUBSIDIARY TABLE I.—Castes classified according to their traditional Occupations.

Group and Caste.	Strength.
1	2
Land-holders and Cultivators ...	526,335 259
Brahman-Anavala	9,916
Kachhia	8,029
Kanbi-Anjana	30,920
„ Kadwa	172,856
„ Karadia	5,974
„ Lewa	184,810
Kasbati	6,323
Malek	7,519
Molesalam	8,966
Memna	7,183
Pathan	16,307
Sathawara	5,830
Shaikh	31,510
Sindhi	3,548
Vohora (peasants)	11,858
Others	14,786
Military and Dominant	86,835 43
Maratha	14,788
Rajput	64,228
Vagher	4,277
Others	3,542
Labourers	426,691 210
Gola (rice-pounders)	5,210
Koli-Baria	66,255
„ Chunvalia	7,707
Dubla (Hindus)	37,577
Koli-Patanvadia	22,263
„ Talbada	91,527
„ Thakarda	153,261
„ Unspecified	17,116
Talavia	8,919
Others	16,856
Forest and Hill Tribes	199,038 98
Bhil	41,836
Chodhra	31,366
Dhanka	18,667
Dhodia	20,490
Gamit	49,615
Kokna	6,451
Nayakda	10,030
Vasava	10,951
Others	9,632
Graziers and dairymen	59,428 29
Ahir	5,182
Bharvad	8,489
Rabari	44,916
Others	841
Fishermen, boatmen and palki bearers.	13,545 7
Bhoi	4,079
Dhimar	5,410
Others	4,056
Hunters and fowlers	28,129 14
Vaghari	28,129
Priests and devotees	134,667 66
Bava	9,718
Brahman-Audich	40,679
„ Deshastha	6,464
„ Mewada	4,824
„ Modh	8,800
„ Nagar	7,990
Fakir	4,639
Garoda	6,281
Gosain	6,363
Saiyad	8,772
Others	30,137
Temple-servants	5,014 2
Brahman Tapodhan	4,465
Others	549
Genealogists, Bards and Astrologers..	16,703 8
Bahrot	14,656
Others	2,047
Writers	4,541 2
Writers (Prabhu, Brahma-Kshatri and others)	4,541

The number below the total strength of each group indicates the proportion per mille to the total population.

SUBSIDIARY TABLE I.—Castes classified according to their traditional occupations—*continued.*

Group and Caste.	Strength.
1	2
Musicians, Singers, Dancers, Mimes, Jugglers and Drummers	*32,430* *16*
Ravalia	22,484
Targala	4,468
Others	5,478
Traders and pedlers	*119,572* *59*
Luhana	11,588
Memon	13,540
Vania-Disaval	6,145
,, Lad	8,500
,, Porwad	8,613
,, Shrimali	31,965
Vohora (traders)	13,177
Others	26,044
Carriers by pack animals	*644* *0*
Barbers	*25,787* *13*
Hajam	24,838
Others	949
Washermen	*2,676* *1*
Weavers, Carders and Dyers ...	*119,968* *59*
Bhavsar	5,689
Dhed	99,798
Pinjara	5,408
Others	9,073
Tailors	*13,323* *7*
Darji	13,277
Others	46
Carpenters	*22,306* *11*
Sutar	20,719
Others	1,587
Masons	*1,239* *1*
Potters	*42,360* *21*
Kumbhar	41,693
Others	667

Group and Caste.	Strength.
1	2
Glass and lac workers	*78* *0*
Blacksmiths	*19,523* *10*
Luhar	19,169
Others	354
Goldsmiths and silversmiths	*10,702* *5*
Soni	10,120
Others	582
Brass and coppersmiths	*2,111* *1*
Confectioners and grain parchers ...	*491* *0*
Oil pressers	*16,520* *8*
Ghanchi (H. 11,867, and M. 4,614) .	16,481
Others	39
Toddy drawers and distillers ...	*1,649* *1*
Butchers	*380* *0*
Leather workers	*42,432* *21*
Chamar	32,210
Mochi	8,715
Others	1,507
Basket and net makers	*325* *0*
Earth, salt, &c., workers and quarriers	*1,639* *1*
Domestic servants	*251* *0*
Village watchmen and menials ...	*9,695* *5*
Shenva	7,587
Others	2,108
Sweepers	*27,109* *13*
Bhangi	26,397
Others	712
Others	*18,662* *9*
Christians	7,203
Parsis	7,955
Others	3,504

The number below the total strength of each group indicates the proportion per mille to the total population.

SUBSIDIARY TABLE II.—Variation in Caste, Tribe, &c., since 1881.

Caste, tribe or race.	Persons.				Percentage of Variation Increase (+) Decrease (—).			Net Variation 1881-1911.	
	1911.	1901.	1891.	1881.	1901 to 1911.	1891 to 1901.	1881 to 1891.	Net.	Percentage.
1	2	3	4	5	6	7	8	9	10
Hindus, &c.									
Ahir	5,182	4,316	5,214	4,714	+ 20·07	— 17·22	+ 10·61	+ 468	+ 9·93
Hindu	5,181	4,316	5,214	4,714	...	...	...	...	...
Aryasamaj	1	...	...	...	...	...	..	...	...
Bahrot	14,656	16,052	21,432	21,280	— 8·70	— 25·10	+ ·71	— 6,624	— 31·13
Hindu	14,653	16,034	21,432	21,280	...	...	...	...	...
Jain	...	18	...	...	...	...	...	...	...
Aryasamaj	3	...	...	...	...	...	...	...	...
Bava	9,718	9,425	7,570	5,631	+ 3·11	+ 24·55	+ 34·43	+ 4,087	+ 72·58
Bhangi	26,397	24,011	30,965	30,881	+ 9·93	— 22·44	+ ·26	— 4,484	— 14·52
Hindu	26,397	23,978	30,965	30,881	...	...	...	...	...
Jain	...	33	...	...	...	...	...	...	...
Bharvad	8,489	7,077	9,589	7,401	+ 19·95	— 26·19	+ 29·56	+ 1,088	+ 14·70
Bhavsar	5,689	7,378	9,083	8,956	— 22·89	— 18·77	+ 1·42	— 3,267	— 36·48
Hindu	4,581	6,066	7,750	7,911	...	...	...	...	...
Jain	1,105	1,312	1,333	1,045	...	...	...	...	...
Aryasamaj	3	...	...	...	...	...	...	...	...
Bhil	41,836	37,650	59,541	56,690	+ 11·12	— 36·76	+ 5·03	— 14,854	— 26·20
Hindu	24,755	...	38,920	24,913	...	...	...	...	...
Animist	17,081	37,650	20,621	31,777	...	...	...	...	...
Bhoi	4,079	4,127	4,531	4,070	— 1·16	— 8·91	+ 11·32	+ 9	+ ·22
Brahman Anavala	9,916	10,862	11,148	10,335	— 8·71	— 2·56	+ 7·87	— 419	— 4·05
Hindu	9,893	10,862	11,148	10,335	...	...	...	...	...
Aryasamaj	23	...	...	...	...	...	...	...	...
Brahman Audich	40,679	41,497	49,460	47,774	— 1·97	— 16·1	+ 3·53	— 7,095	— 14·87
Hindu	40,628	41,497	49,460	47,774	...	...	...	...	...
Aryasamaj	51	...	...	...	...	...	...	...	...
Brahman Deshastha	6,464	5,694	8,273	9,514	+ 13·52	— 31·17	— 13·04	— 3,050	— 32·06
Hindu	6,460	5,694	8,273	9,514	...	...	...	...	...
Aryasamaj	4	...	...	...	...	...	...	...	...
Brahman Mewada	4,824	5,383	7,014	6,719	— 10·38	— 23·25	+ 4·39	— 1,895	— 28·20
Hindu	4,823	5,383	7,014	6,719	...	...	...	...	...
Aryasamaj	1	...	...	...	...	...	...	...	...
Brahman Modh	8,800	9,578	12,129	11,588	— 8·12	— 21·03	+ 4·67	— 2,788	— 24·06
Hindu	8,795	9,578	12,129	11,588	...	...	...	...	...
Aryasamaj	5	...	...	...	...	...	...	...	...
Brahman Nagar	7,990	8,144	9,505	9,937	— 1·89	— 14·32	— 4·35	— 1,947	— 19·59
Hindu	7,987	8,144	9,505	9,937	...	...	...	...	...
Aryasamaj	3	...	...	...	...	...	...	...	...
Brahman Tapodhan	4,465	4,740	5,451	5,187	— 5·80	— 13·04	+ 5·09	— 722	— 13·92
Chamar or Khalpa	32,210	29,746	37,7!7	31,913	+ 8·29	— 21·13	+ 18·19	+ 297	+ ·93
Chodhra	31,366	23,324	29,496	32,217	+ 34·48	— 20·92	— 8·45	— 851	— 2·64
Hindu	11,709	...	26,646	5,527	...	...	...	...	...
Animist	19,657	23,324	2,850	26,690	...	...	...	...	...
Darji	13,277	14,023	16,308	14,973	— 5·32	— 14·01	+ 8·92	— 1,696	— 11·33
Hindu	13,261	14,015	16,308	14,973	...	...	...	...	...
Jain	12	8	...	...	...	...	...	...	...
Aryasamaj	4	...	...	...	...	...	...	...	...
Dhanka	18,667	5,524	27,999	20,324	+ 237·93	— 80·27	+ 37·76	— 1,657	— 8·15
Hindu	2,033	...	27,840	20,291	...	...	...	...	...
Animist	16,634	5,524	159	33	...	..	...	...	...
Dhed	99,798	94,388	124,324	110,040	+ 5·73	— 24·08	+ 12·98	— 10,242	— 9·31
Hindu	99,727	94,376	124,324	110,040	...	...	...	..	...
Jain	...	12	...	...	...	...	...	...	...
Aryasamaj	71	...	...	...	...	...	...	..	...
Dhimar	5,410	...	...	...	...	...	..	...	...

SUBSIDIARY TABLE II.—Variation in Caste, Tribe, &c., since 1881—*contd.*

Caste, tribe or race.	Persons. 1911.	1901.	1891.	1881.	Percentage of variation Increase (+) Decrease (—). 1901 to 1911.	1891 to 1901.	1881 to 1891.	Net variation 1881-1911. Net.	Percentage.
1	2	3	4	5	6	7	8	9	10
Hindus, &c.—*contd.*									
Dhodia	20,490	15,861	15,961	13,485	+ 29·18	— ·63	+ 18·36	+ 7,005	+ 51·95
Hindu	5,492	...	15,951	12,570	...	...	...	...	...
Aryasamaj	3	...	...	...	...	...	...	...	...
Animist	14,995	15,861	10	915	...	...	...	...	...
Dubla	40,976	28,492	32,185	20,706	+ 43·82	— 11·48	+ 55·44	+ 20,270	+ 97·89
Hindu	37,577	...	32,170	20,186	...	...	...	...	...
Animist	3,399	28,492	15	520	...	...	...	...	...
Gamit	49,615	38,169	41,615	31,141	+ 29·98	— 8·28	+ 33·63	+ 18,474	+ 59·32
Hindu	27,440	...	38,237	510	...	...	...	...	...
Animist	22,175	38,169	3,378	30,631	...	...	...	...	...
Garoda	6,281	5,919	7,453	7,719	+ 6·12	— 20·58	— 3·45	— 1,438	— 18·63
Hindu	6,277	5,919	7,453	7,719	...	...	...	...	...
Aryasamaj	4	...	...	...	...	...	...	...	...
Ghanchi	11,867	12,211	14,052	11,425	— 2·82	— 13·11	+ 22·99	+ 442	+ 3·87
Hindu	11,862	12,182	14,043	11,425	...	-	...	...	...
Aryasamaj	5	29	9	......	...	...	...	...	...
Gola (rice-pounders)	5,210	5,660	5,984	5,223	— 7·95	— 5·41	+ 14·57	— 13	— ·25
Gosain	6,363	5,672	10,221	10,014	— 12·18	— 44·9	+ 2·07	— 3,651	— 36·42
Hajam	24,838	24,878	31,557	29,388	— ·16	— 21·17	+ 7·38	— 4,550	— 15·48
Hindu	24,832	24,856	31,557	29,388	...	...	...	...	...
Jain	6	22	...	...	...	...	...	...	...
Kachhia	8,029	8,192	8,912	9,857	— 1·99	— 8·08	— 9·59	— 1,828	— 18·54
Hindu	8,027	8,190	8,912	9,857	...	...	...	...	...
Jain	2	2	...	...	...	...	...	...	...
Kanbi-Anjana	30,920	32,532	31,488	30,402	— 4·95	+ 3·31	+ 3·57	+ 518	+ 1·74
Hindu	30,918	32,514	31,488	30,402	...	...	...	...	...
Jain	2	18	...	...	...	...	...	...	...
Kanbi-Kadwa	172,856	175,664	200,058	175,264	— 1·59	— 12·19	+ 14·14	— 2,408	— 1·34
Hindu	172,641	175,570	200,058	175,264	...	...	...	...	...
Jain	121	94	...	...	...	...	...	...	...
Aryasamaj	94	...	...	...	...	...	...	...	...
Kanbi Karadia	5,974	6,456	...	...	— 7·47	...	...	— 482	— 7·46
Kanbi Lewa	184,810	171,223	199,917	185,637	+ 7·93	— 14·35	+ 7·69	— 827	— ·45
Hindu	183,289	170,390	199,169	185,364	...	...	...	...	...
Jain	1,333	825	748	273	...	...	...	...	...
Aryasamaj	188	8	...	...	...	...	...	...	...
Kokna	6,451	3,646	5,613	3,800	+ 76·94	— 35·04	+ 47·71	+ 2,651	+ 69·76
Hindu	1,906	...	5,590	414	...	...	...	...	...
Animist	4,545	3,646	23	3,386	...	...	...	...	...
Koli	370,953	324,554	471,762	429,688	+ 14·29	— 31·20	+ 9·79	— 58,735	— 13·67
Hindu	370,943	324,527	471,762	429,688	...	...	...	...	...
Jain	7	27	...	...	...	...	...	...	...
Aryasamaj	3	...	...	...	...	...	...	...	...
Kumbhar	41,693	41,395	49,860	43,560	+ ·72	— 16·98	+ 14·46	— 1,867	— 4·28
Hindu	41,692	41,375	49,853	43,560	...	...	...	...	...
Jain	...	20	7	...	...	...	...	...	...
Aryasamaj	1	...	...	...	...	...	...	...	...
Luhana	11,588	10,461	11,099	8,832	+ 10·77	— 5·75	+ 25·67	+ 2,756	+ 31·20
Hindu	11,561	10,447	11,099	8,832	...	...	...	...	...
Jain	...	8	...	...	...	...	...	...	...
Aryasamaj	27	6	...	...	...	...	...	...	...
Luhar	19,212	19,052	24,186	22,019	+ ·84	— 21·23	+ 9·84	— 2,807	— 12·75
Hindu	19,208	19,045	24,186	22,019	...	...	...	...	...
Jain	4	7	...	...	...	...	...	...	...
Maratha	14,785	17,392	19,943	19,413	— 14·99	— 12·79	+ 2·75	— 4,628	— 23·84
Hindu	14,782	17,386	19,943	19,413	...	...	...	...	...
Jain	2	6	...	...	...	...	...	...	...
Aryasamaj	1	...	...	...	...	...	...	...	...

SUBSIDIARY TABLE II.—Variation in Caste, Tribe, &c., since 1881—*concld.*

Caste, tribe or race.	Persons.				Percentage of variation Increase (+) Decrease (—)			Net variation 1881-1911.	
	1911.	1901.	1891.	1881	1901 to 1911.	1891 to 1901.	1881 to 1891.	Net.	Percentage.
1	2	3	4	5	6	7	8	9	10
Hindus, &c.—*concld.*									
Mochi	8,715	8,593	9,599	9,008	+ 1·42	— 10·48	+ 6·56	— 293	— 3·25
Nayakda	10,030	6,970	8,616	7,244	+ 43·90	— 19·10	+ 18·94	+ 2,786	+ 38·46
Hindu	3,634	...	6,454	6,728	...	...	...	...	...
Animist	6,396	6,970	2,162	516	...	...	...	...	...
Rabari	44,916	39,593	58,087	54,508	+ 13·45	— 31·84	+ 6·57	— 9,592	— 17·59
Rajput	64,228	59,414	97,713	79,853	+ 8·10	— 39·18	+ 22·37	— 15,625	— 19·57
Hindu	64,202	59,410	97,713	79,853	...	...	...	...	...
Jain	3	4	...	...	...	...	...	...	...
Aryasamaj	23	...	...	...	...	...	...	...	...
Ravalia...	22,484	19,672	28,785	25,894	+ 14·29	— 31·66	+ 11·17	— 3,410	— 13·17
Hindu	22,482	19,672	28,785	25,894	...	...	...	...	...
Jain...	2	...	...	...	...	...	...	...	...
Sathawara	5,830	5,362	6,606	5,633	+ 8·73	— 18·83	+ 17·28	+ 197	+ 3·50
Shenva	7,587	5,209	7,587	6,718	+ 45·65	— 31·34	+ 12·94	+ 869	+ 12·95
Soni	10,120	11,098	12,267	12,332	— 8·81	— 9·53	— ·53	— 2,212	— 17·94
Hindu	10,112	11,080	12,251	12,332	...	...	...	...	...
Jain...	3	18	16	...	...	...	...	...	...
Aryasamaj...	5	...	...	...	...	...	...	...	...
Sutar	20,719	22,585	25,312	24,031	— 8·26	— 10·77	+ 5·33	— 3,312	— 13·78
Hindu	20,719	22,554	25,312	24,031	...	...	...	...	...
Jain	...	31	...	...	...	...	...	...	...
Talavia	9,647	12,551	16,700	21,494	— 23·14	— 24·85	— 22·30	— 11,847	— 55·12
Hindu	8,919	12,551	16,699	21,421	...	...	...	...	...
Animist	728	...	1	73	...	...	...	...	...
Targala...	4,468	4,367	4,747	6,228	+ 2·31	— 8·006	— 23·78	— 1,760	— 28·26
Vaghari	28,129	23,264	34,442	29,785	+ 20·91	— 32·45	+ 15·63	— 1,656	— 5·56
Vagher	4,277	4,306	4,349	3,360	— ·67	— ·99	+ 29·43	+ 917	+ 27·29
Vania-Disaval	6,145	7,461	10,014	9,646	— 17·64	— 25·49	+ 3·82	— 3,501	— 37·33
Hindu	5,817	7,290	9,903	9,556	...	...	...	...	...
Jain...	325	171	111	90	...	...	...	...	...
Aryasamaj	3	...	...	...	...	...	...	...	...
Vania-Lad	8,500	8,556	8,974	10,308	— ·66	— 4·66	— 12·94	— 1,808	— 17·54
Hindu	8,096	8,381	8,943	10,306	...	...	...	...	...
Jain...	404	175	31	2	...	...	...	...	...
Vania-Porwad	8,613	9,500	11,920	11,504	— 9·34	— 20·30	+ 3·62	— 2,891	— 25·13
Hindu	1,680	1,640	1,685	1,462	...	...	...	...	...
Jain...	6,933	7,860	10,235	10,042	...	...	...	...	...
Vania Shrimali	31,965	27,415	32,879	33,214	+ 16·59	— 16·62	— 1·01	— 1,249	— 3·76
Hindu	5,044	4,123	4,767	4,422	...	...	...	...	...
Jain...	26,913	23,292	28,112	28,792	...	...	...	...	...
Aryasamaj	8	...	...	...	...	...	...	...	...
Vasava	10,951	2,383	...	...	+ 359·55	...	...	...	...
Hindu	4,257	...	...	...	...	...	...	...	...
Animist	6,694	2,383	...	...	...	...	...	...	...
Musalmans.									
Fakir	4,639	4,725	7,089	5,957	— 1·82	— 33·35	+ 19·01	— 1,318	— 22·13
Ghanchi	4,614	3,989	5,117	3,775	+ 15·67	— 22·04	+ 35·55	+ 839	+ 22·23
Kasbati...	6,323	...	...	...	...	...	...	...	...
Malek	7,519	8,988	12,079	10,576	— 16·34	— 25·59	+ 14·21	— 3,057	— 28·91
Memon	13,540	7,607	6,621	5,462	+ 78·01	+ 14·89	+ 21·22	+ 8,078	+ 147·89
Molesalam	8,966	9,778	16,072	14,759	— 8·31	— 34·16	+ 8·89	— 5,793	— 39·25
Momna	7,183	12,153	13,854	11,297	— 40·89	— 12·28	+ 22·63	— 4,114	— 36·42
Pathan	16,307	11,402	17,976	14,235	+ 43·02	— 36·57	+ 26·28	+ 2,072	+ 14·56
Pinjara	5,408	4,217	5,499	5,514	+ 28·24	— 23·31	— 0·27	— 106	— 1·92
Saiyad	8,772	7,295	9,326	8,954	+ 20·25	— 21·67	+ 4·16	— 182	— 2·03
Shaikh	31,510	22,416	29,324	36,001	+ 40·57	— 23·55	— 18·54	— 4,491	— 12·47
Vohora	25,035	25,372	26,078	30,004	— 1·33	— 2·71	— 13·1	— 4,969	— 16·56
Christians	7,203	7,691	646	771	— 6·35	+1,090·56	— 16·21	+ 6,432	+ 834·24
Parsis...	7,955	8,409	8,206	8,118	— 4·21	+ 2·47	+ 1·08	— 163	— 2

APPENDIX TO CHAPTER XI.

GLOSSARY OF CASTES, TRIBES & RACES.

(Those included in Imperial Table XIII).

Note:—(1) Names printed in Heavy type as **Aboti** are those of the main castes, and names printed in Small Capital type are those of sub-castes, the distribution of which by districts is given in Table XIII. The figures entered in brackets after each name show the total strength of the caste or sub-caste.

(2) When there are Musalman castes like those of Hindus, they are shown separately below the Hindu caste names and are marked with an asterisk; but when there are only a few Musalmans or Hindus following a particular trade, their number only is shown separately in brackets after the name of the Hindu or Musalman main caste, *e.g.*, Bhangi (H. 26,397 ; M. 9).

(3) The sub-castes noted are only those found in the State. Outside the State, some castes have additional sub-castes also.

Aboti (452).—A caste of Brahmans, found mainly in the Okhamandal Taluka of the Amreli district. They trace their origin to the younger son of sage Valmiki. Other Brahmans do not eat food cooked by them. As a class, they are poor and live as temple servants, beggars, confectioners and cultivators.

ACHARYA.—A term used by Kâyatiâ Brahmans as their caste name. They feel ashamed to call themselves Kâyatiâ (performers of after-death rites), which is looked upon as a term of reproach and try to pass themselves off by the name of Achârya or preceptor.

ADALJA (76).—A sub-caste of Modh Vania.

Afghan (113).—Also called Kabuli. The word Afghan means the free. The tradition regarding its origin is that the mother of the great ancestor of the Afghans gave him the name Afghan because on passing through the pangs of delivery, she joyfully exclaimed *Afghânâ*, that is, I am free. They are immigrants from Kabul. Most of them are traders dealing in horses, warm clothing and dry fruits. Of late, they have taken to lending money on high rates of interest to Dheds, Bhangis and other low castes. They never resort to Courts and often take the law in their own hand for recovering their dues. They are also called Pathans, but are quite distinct from local Musalmans known by that appellation.

Agarval (303).—A Vania caste. It takes its name from the town of Agar, about forty miles north-east of Ujjain. Agarvals are divided into Visa (154) and Dasa (96). Their family priests are the Agarval Brahmans. They wear the sacred thread. The Hindu proverb illustrative of their character is *Agarvale sub Thakrale* (among Agarvals, each individual is a chief).

AGIARASANA (1,171).—A sub-caste of Modh Brahman.

Ahir (5,182).—Cattle-breeders; found chiefly in Kathiawad. According to Manu, they are sprung from a Brahman and an *Ambastha* or *Vaidya* woman; according to the Brahma Puran, from a Kshatriya father and a Vaishya mother; according to the Bhagavat Puran, from Vaishya parents, and according to an old tradition, from a Rajput slave girl and a Vaishya slave. They claim to be Vaishyas but are regarded by others as Shudras. They were once a ruling class and like the Ahirs of the United Provinces claim Krishna's birth place, Mathura, as their first seat. Some of their surnames are the same as Rajput tribe names, *e.g.*, Chavda, Chudasama, Gohel, Goria, Pithia, Ravalia, Sisodia, &c. The men wear a black and white headdress like the Mers, a shortpuckered jacket and light ankled trousers of hard woven cotton like Bharvads. The women are easily known by their coarse free hanging blanket shawls, pink cotton skirt and smooth flattened anklets. They have given up cattle breeding and except a few who are carpenters live as husbandmen. They reverence *Tulsishyam* (Lakshmi and Krishna) and a number of local goddesses. Their ordinary food is like that of Vanias and Kanbis, millet bread, pulse, milk and vegetable, but they can eat mutton, venison and other game but not beef. Children are betrothed at any age and married between twelve and fifteen. Like Rabaris, they celebrate their marriages every year on one fixed day. Among them it is usual for the younger brother to marry his elder brother's widow. The caste has a headman who, with a committee of the caste, settles all disputes. Breaches of caste rules are punished with fine and eating with forbidden persons by excommunication.

AJVALIA (5,236).—A sub-caste of Kachhia.

ALIA (664).—A section of trading Vohoras.

Anavala (9,916).—A Brahman caste from Anaval, a village in the Mahuva Taluka of the Navsari district, found in that district and in the neighbouring Surat district. It is said that when Shri Ramchandra performed a sacrifice near Unai, he wanted Brahmans to officiate at the same and so converted the Naikas, Vasavas and Chodhras into Brahmans. These people said that they would not bathe with cold water and so the Unai hot springs were created for them; they would not accept *dakshina* and so lands were settled upon them. The Brahmans thus created became the Naiks, Vasis and Desais of the Anavala caste. They are also known as *Mastans* and

Bhathelas. Mastan may be a corruption of *mahasthan* (great place), a name of some former settlement of the tribe or it may simply mean a community, as such phrases as Soni Mastan (the goldsmith community), Khadayata Mastan, &c., are in common local use. The present Brahmans of Orrisa are also called *Mastans.* Bhathela is a corruption of *bhrasthela* or fallen and was probably the name given by some of the later Brahman settlers from North India. It is looked upon as a term of disrespect and is not liked by the community. The Anavala Brahmans are the earliest settlers in South Gujarat, and it was under their management that it was redeemed from forest and brought under cultivation.

Anavala Brahmans are *gruhasthas.* There are no priests or mendicants among them. Socially they are divided into an upper or *Desai* class, the revenue farmers, and a lower or Bhathela class, the ordinary cultivators. The Desais eat with Bhathelas, but object to marry their daughters into any except Desai families. On the other hand Bhathelas, anxious to improve their social position, try hard to marry their daughters into Desai families. This rivalry for the hands for men of good family has, as among the Patidars of Charottar, led to some unusual practices. Polygamy is not uncommon. A Desai who finds himself in difficulty marries another wife and receives from his bride's father money to pay off his debts. Expenses consequent upon marriages, such as dowry, sending the bride to her husband's house, pregnancy, birth of a child, &c., are incurred not by the husband but by the wife's father. Even the expenses incurred by the mother of the bridegroom at the time of her delivery have to be paid by the father of the bride at the time of marriage. Some Desai families with many daughters have fallen into debts and have been forced to mortgage their lands. During the last twenty years reforms in marriage customs have been inaugurated by the educated in the community, which have resulted in the reduction of marriage expenses, stopping polygamy and marrying of girls without reference to *kul* or family.

ANDHARIA.—(1,328).—A sub-caste of Kachhia.

Anglo-Indian (82).—A new name given to those who were known in previous Censuses as Eurasians. It includes all persons of mixed blood and is not confined to those of British origin.

Anjana (30,920).—A caste of Kanbis mainly found in the Kadi District. They are more like Rajputs than Kanbis. Like Rajputs some of their names end in *sing* as Dansing, Harising, &c. There are among them 23 clans who eat together and intermarry. Some of these clan names are Rathod, Solanki, Chohan and Parmar. Unlike other Kanbis, Anjanas eat flesh of sheep and goats and of the wild boar and hare. They eat opium and drink liquor. Most of the males wear flowing whiskers divided by a narrow parting down the chin. Anjanas are conjectured to be originally of the same stock as the Animistic Chodhras of the Navsari District. Some members of this tribe were employed as carriers by the Rajput Kings of North Gujarat, and the Anjanas are supposed to be their descendants. Even now they style themselves as Chodhra. They celebrate the birth of a child just as the Animistic Chodhras do. They give to female mourners cooked wheat or *juwar*, just as the Animistic Chodhras give *val* or *mag*. By occupation they are cultivators. Their women help them in the field work. In religion they are Ramanuji, Shaiva and Swaminarayan. Their priests are Audich, Mewada, Modh and Visnagara Nagar Brahmans. Girls are married before 11 years old. Widow marriage and divorce are allowed. They have their headman, who in consultation with a few respectable castemen, settles divorce cases and caste disputes.

Arab (316).—Immigrants from Arabia, mostly found in Baroda, where they were formerly employed as mercenaries, but now serve as peons, guards, &c. Newcomers are called *wilatis* and country-borns *muwallads.* Their home language is Hindustani, guttural in tone and with some letters oddly changed. The chief peculiarities are *sh* instead of *s*; the guttural *ain* for the Hindustani *a*; *b* for *p* and *g* instead of the Arabic *k* or *qu*. The rich among them keep to the original Arab dress. But poor Arabs dress like ordinary Gujarat Musalmans, with the exception that the dirk, *jamaia*, is stuck in a cloth wound round the waist and the trousers are shorter. They have a great zeal for their faith and are careful in discharging their religious duties. As a rule no initiation, *bismillah* ceremony, is performed, and marriage is generally in the *nika* form. In obedience to the order of the Prophet, a death is followed by no signs of mourning. They marry freely with other Sunni Musalmans and have no special social or religious organization.

ATIT.—Same as Gosain.

Audich (40,679).—A Brahman caste so called, because they entered Gujarat from the North (*Udicha*). According to their caste tradition, they were invited to Gujarat by King Mulraj (*A. D.* 961-996) from the north, to help him in holding a sacrifice. When the sacrifice was over, the King offered them money and grants of land to induce them to stay in his country. About a thousand (*sahasra*), who readily agreed, came to be known as *Audich Sahasra* (36,754), while the rest who formed a *toli* (band) and refused till they were persuaded by further grants, came to be known as *Audich Tolakia* (3,925). The *Sahasras* are superior in social rank to the *Tolakias.* The *Sahasras* are again divided into *Sihoras* and *Sidhpurias* from the towns of Sihor in the Bhavnagar State and Sidhpur in the Baroda State, which are said to have been bestowed on their ancestors.

Audich Brahmans live on alms; a few are cultivators, the rest are cooks or family or village priests. Those of them who are priests of Darjis (tailors), Gandhraps (musicians), Hajams (barbers), Kolis and Mochis (shoemakers) are looked upon as degraded. Excommunications for serving low caste people have given rise to several sub-divisions, such as Darjigor who serve tailors, Hajamgor who serve barbers, Gandhrapgor who serve Gandraps or musicians, Koligor who serve Kolis, Mochigor who serve shoemakers, etc. Those Audichas who have settled in Vagad are held degraded and are treated as outcastes, because they smoke the *huka*, allow widow marriage and carry cooked food to the fields. They are, however, allowed to give their daughters in marriage to Audichas of Halawad in Kathiawad, whose daughters marry Dhangadra Audichas and the daughters of Dhangadra Audichas are married to Viramgam, Ahmedabad and Sidhpur Audichas, who hold the highest social rank in the caste. The Sidhpuria Audichas are regarded as superior to other Audichas, and it is considered honourable to give a daughter in marriage to a Sidhpuria Audich. It is this competition for bridegrooms from Sidhpur which has given rise to polygamy in the caste. Rodhval, Napal, Borsada and Harsola Brahman castes have emanated from the Audich Brahmans owing to some members of them emigrating from their home to other places; and Koligor, Rajgor, Kayatia, Kriyagor, Vyas and Targala castes have emanated from the same original caste owing to their taking to degrading occupations.

Avartia—A section of Kathis.

Babar (479).—Also called Babaria. They have their settlement in Babariavad in Kathiawad. In spite of their small number, the Babaria clan has no less than 72 divisions of which the three principal are Kotila, Dhankda and Varu. They marry their daughters to Kathis and take in marriage the daughters of Ahirs. They are not restricted to the number of wives, marrying as many as they are able to maintain.

Badva—A name given to Bhil *bhagats* or exorcists.

Bahrot or **Bhat** (14,656).—Bards and heralds; they are found in large numbers in the Kadi and Baroda Districts and in small numbers in the Amreli and Navsari Districts. Local inquiries seem to show that Gujarat Bhats were originally Brahmans from Allahabad and Marwar, who settled in Kadi and its neighbourhood. That some at least came from North India appears from the existence of Kanojia Bhats, both in Kathiawad and Cutch. There are eleven Bhat settlements in North Gujarat. Of these four are in British Ahmedabad District, five in Baroda Kadi District, two in Kaira and one in Cambay. Traces of their Brahman origin survive in their wearing the Brahmanic thread and in their having such clans or *shakhas* as *Harmani*, *Kashiani* and *Parvatani*. Like Brahmans, Bhats of the same shâkhâ do not intermarry. In central Gujarat Brahman (Brahma) Bhats are found in large numbers. In North Gujarat and Kathiawad, besides Brahma Bhat (13,345), there are six subcastes, *viz*., Dashnami (161), Kankali (232), Kanojia (6), Nagari (9), Pakhia (2) and Vahivancha (513). Though the members of these sub-divisions neither interdine nor intermarry, all eat food cooked by Vanias and Kanbis. Brahma Bhats hold a higher place than any of the six divisions. Their marriage ceremonies do not differ from those of Kanbis. A man may divorce his wife, but the wife is not allowed to divorce her husband. Some sub-castes allow widow remarriage, but Brahma Bhats and those among others who are considered *kulins* or of good family forbid it. A *kulia* eats with an *akulia*, but does not give him his daughter in marriage. Female infanticide was formerly practised among the *kulias*. Gujarat Bhats are vegetarians living on food-grains.

The honorific title of Rao or Gadhvi is applied to all Bahrots. Their main occupation is repeating verses of their own composition or selections from Hindu legends. They chant verses in a style peculiar to themselves and not unpleasant to a stranger, as the modulation of the voice and an energetic graceful action give effect to the poetry which is either to praise some renowned warrior, commemorate a victory, record a tragic event or panegyrise a present object. The chief patrons of the Bhats are Rajputs, but Kanbis, Kolis and Luhanas also have their Bhats who visit their patrons' house. The Bhat is the geneologist, bard and historian of his patron's family. His *vahi* or book is a record of authority by which questions of consanguinity are determined when a marriage or right to ancestral property is in dispute. An interesting feature in the history of the Bhats was their use as securities. They became guarantees for treaties between rival princes and for the performance of bonds by individuals. No security was deemed so binding or sacred as that of a Bhat; for the reason that on failure he had at his command means of extorting compliance with his demands which were seldom used in vain. These were the rites of *traga* and *dharna*. Traga consisted in shedding his own blood or the blood of some member of his family and in calling down the vengeance of heaven upon the offender whose obstinacy necessitated the sacrifice. Dharna consisted in placing round the dwelling of the recusant a cordon of bards who fasted and compelled the inhabitants of the house to fast until their demands were complied with. For these services, the Bhats received an annual stipend from the district, village or individual they guaranteed. Under the establishment of British supremacy in Gujarat, these rites became impossible and the custom of employing Bhats as securities fell into disuse. Many Bhats have abandoned their hereditary calling and become husbandmen. Some are well-to-do bankers, money-lenders and traders. Some are grocers and village shop-keepers and some are day-labourers, domestic servants and messengers. A few live by begging. While moving from house to house, the Nagari Bhats beat a *tokri* or drum, the Kankali carry a trident and the Palimanga, a knife.

In religion, Bhats are Ramanuji, Shaiva and Vaishnava and worshippers of Amba, Bahucharaji and Kalika. Their priests are Audich, Modh or Shrimali Brahmans.

Bhats have no hereditary headman. Social disputes are settled by a few respectable castemen.

Baj (201).—A caste of Vanias, formed by some members of the Lad Vania caste, who were excommunicated for some fault. Baj appears to be a corruption of *bahya*.

Bajania (2,532).—A wandering and labouring caste. They are rope-dancers and derive their name from *bajavavu*, to play upon a drum. They are also called *Dholis* or drummers. They are divided into Parmars and Naghors who eat, drink and smoke together and intermarry, the members of each branch being forbidden to marry among themselves. They eat flesh of all kinds except that of the pig and the cow and drink liquor. They eat food cooked by almost all classes including Musalmans, but will not touch food prepared by Dheds, Chamadias and other depressed classes. They also refuse meat prepared by Darjis (tailors), because at their weddings, Darjis offer their god the image of a cow made of *gol* or mollasses. They hold one Sambhai Naik in special veneration as he is said to have lost his life in performing a wonderful athletic feat. They call no Brahman to officiate at any of their ceremonies. The uncle of the bride or an elder member of her family presides on the day of marriage. The bridegroom's father pays twelve rupees to the bride's father of which four are spent in purchasing clothes for the bride. They bury their dead. No ceremonies are performed at a woman's first pregnancy. The widow marries the younger brother of the deceased husband and divorce is allowed. Caste disputes are settled by five leading men.

Baloch (951).—Descendants of Baluchi immigrants. They are of many clans. But the clan distinction is of little consequence, as they intermarry and together form one sub-division of the Pathans. They speak Hindustani much mixed up with Gujarati and both men and women dress like ordinary Musalmans. Their wives are generally natives of Gujarat, sometimes Jhala or Jadeja Rajputs from Kathiawad or Vagad.

BANDA (6).—A sub-caste of Kumbhar.

Bandhara (60).—Silk folders. Originally a sub-division of Bhavsars; now a separate caste on account of its having taken to a superior occupation. They have a special way of washing, cleaning and glazing silk clothes, so as not to spoil the texture or softness.

***Bandhara** (16).—Silk folders. They are descendants of converts to Islam from the Hindu caste of the same name. Their home speech is Urdu. Women wear Hindu dress and males dress like ordinary Musalmans. They are Sunni in faith. They marry only among themselves and have a caste government by elders but no headman.

BARAD.—A term applied to those members of a caste who marry girls from an inferior class, and are therefore outcasted, *e. g.*, Barad Nagar, Barad Kanbi, etc.

Barad Kanbi (1306).—A section of those Kanbis who not finding brides in their own caste took girls from inferior castes, such as Koli, Mali, &c., and being therefore excommunicated, formed a new caste.

Bardai (78).—A Brahman caste found in Kathiawad; so called from their being the residents of Barda, a tract of country belonging to the Porbandar State in Kathiawad.

Baria (66,255).—A caste of Kolis. They are found chiefly in the Baroda District. Their own account makes Baria in Rewakantha their original home, from which towards the close of the 15th century they were expelled by the Chohan Rajputs, who in turn had been driven out of Champaner by the Mahomedans under Mahmud Begada (A. D. 1484).

Bava (9,718).—Religious mendicants, also called Veragi or Sadhu. They are generally celibates.

Bavcha (1,371).—An early tribe mostly found in the Songhad Taluka of the Navsari District. They accompanied the Gaekwads as grooms, and have settled in Baroda, Patan and other places. Their women still dress like the women of the early tribes. They are occupied as grooms, grass-sellers, bricklayers and day-labourers.

Behlim (492).—The yare converted Rajputs of the Behlim tribe and are chiefly found in the Kadi District. They intermarry with other Musalmans.

Bhadbhunja (319).—Grain parchers. Literally parchers at the *bhad* or fireplace. They are immigrants from Northern India.

***Bhadbhunja** (8).—Musalman grain parchers. They are also immigrants from Upper India. They marry among themselves and also with the local Musalmans.

Bhadela (1,109).—A name given to Musalman sailors known as lascars, found in Amreli District.

Bhallia (3,298).—A caste of Kolis. They are immigrants from Bhâl near Dholka, and are found chiefly in the Petlad and Savli Talukas of the Baroda State.

Bhand (H. 5, M. 128).—Jesters. They derive their name from the Sanskrit word *bhand*, a jest. The majority of Bhands are Mahomedans and only a few are Hindus. Their main occupation is dancing, acting and singing. They resemble Bhavaiyas in all their social customs.

Bhandari (205).—An immigrant caste from the Konkan. Their main occupation is toddy drawing in the Navsari District.

Bhangi or **Bhangia** (H. 26,397; M. 9).—Scavengers. They are so-called because they split bamboos for making them into baskets. They are also called Olgana from their living on scrape-meat. They are said to be the descendants of a Brahman sage who carried away and buried a dog that died in a Brahman assembly. They have for their surnames such names as Chohan, Chudasama, Dafada, Jethva, Makvana, Solanki, Vaghela, Vadher and Vadhiya, which point to a Rajput origin. They have also Dhevda, Maru, Purbiya and such other names as surnames which suggest a mixture of castes. They are scavengers and night-soil carriers and are viewed with kindlier feelings than Dheds. The cloth that covers the dead and the pot in which fire is carried before the corpse are given to the Bhangis. Presents of grain, clothes and money are made to Bhangis on an eclipse day, as Rahu the "tormentor and eclipser" of the Sun and Moon, is a Bhangia and by pleasing them, he is pacified. Like Dheds, Bhangis are religious and honour all Brahman divinities. As they are not allowed to enter Hindu temples, they bow to the idol from a distance. They are worshippers of Hanuman, Meldi, Sikotri and the basil plant. Many Bhangis are followers of the sects of Kabir, Ramanand and Nanak. Polygamy, divorce and widow remarriage are allowed. A younger brother generally marries the widow of his elder brother. Priests of their own castes or Garodas (Dhed Brahmans) officiate at all their ceremonies. They eat flesh of every kind except in Surat, where the flesh of animals which die a natural death is not taken. They eat food cooked by Musalmans. Caste disputes are settled by the headman of the caste either alone or with the help of some elders. Breaches of caste rules are punished by forbidding the offenders the use of water or fire, and they are re-admitted into the caste on paying a fine.

Bhansali (10).—A caste found in Kathiawad. They are husbandmen, shopkeepers and traders. Their family goddess is Hingalaj in Sindh. Their family priests are Saraswat Brahmans who eat with them. Widows are allowed to marry. Animal food is allowed, but those following the Vaishnav sect are strict vegetarians.

BHARDA.—A contemptuous term used for the caste of Tapodhan Brahmans.

Bhargava (352).—A Brahman caste, found mostly in the Kamrej Taluka of the Navsari District. They take their name from the great Rishi Bhrigu, the founder of Broach, where also there are many Brahmans of this name. They are said at one time to have been very powerful in Broach, and a trace of their influence remains in the practice of all castes in Broach, including the Parsis in paying a fixed sum to the Bhargav community on marriage occasions. In addition to the ordinary Brahmanic distinctions between *bhikshuk* (priests) and *gruhastha* (the lay), Bhargavas are divided into *Visa* and *Dasa*. Between these divisions, intermarriage is forbidden. Many of the Kamrej Bhargavas are peasants and labourers and are therefore looked upon by the Broach Bhargavas as their inferiors in social rank.

Bharthari (265)—A class of itinerant beggars, who dress as Gosain or Ravlia and move about playing on their fiddle and singing moral odes from Bhartruhari.

Bharvad (8,489).—A caste of shepherds. They claim Gokul Brindavan as their original home and to be of the same Meher caste to which Krishna's foster-father Nand Meher belonged. From Gokul, they are said to have moved to Meywar and from Meywar to have spread into Gujarat, Kathiawad and Cutch. They are closely related to Rabaris with whom they eat but do not intermarry.

They live on milk and bread, but can also eat the flesh of sheep and goats. They sell goat and ewes' milk and weave and sell woollen blankets. Except a few who are Ramanandi, Bharvads are followers of *Mata*. Like Kadwa Kanbis, Bharvads in Kathiawad and North Gujarat celebrate their marriages only once in twelve, fifteen or twenty-five years, on a day in the month of *Vaishakh*, and all the Bharvads of the neighbourhood hold their marriages in the same place. The richest Bharvad among those who wish to get their daughters married, buys the ground where the marriages are to be celebrated. This is necessary because the ground cannot be used a second time for the same purpose. It is kept as pasture and an ornamental wooden post, called the marriage pillar, is set up on it and preserved to show that the ground has been used for marriages. Among the Bharvads of Central and South Gujarat, marriages are performed with little or no ceremony. A Brahman or a Darji, or in their absence, one of the members of the bride's family officiates at the marriage. Polygamy and widow marriage are allowed. A younger brother of the deceased husband has the first claim on his widow. Divorce is allowed. In some places the mother is not held impure after child-birth and does her household work from the day of delivery; in other places, she remains impure for fifteen days. Bharvads burn the dead. *Shradha* ceremony is performed with the help of a Kayatia Brahman. Caste people are feasted on the 12th day. Caste disputes are settled at a meeting of the adult castemen. Elopement is punished with excommunication and other breaches of caste rules by fine.

***Bhat** (88).—Converts to Islam from the Bahrot caste.

BHATHELA.—A contemptuous term for an Anavala Brahman.

Bhathiara (164).—An occupational term used as a caste name by Musalman bakers.

Bhatia (561).—Found all over the State. More than half their number is in the Kadi and Amreli Districts, and the rest are distributed in the other districts. They were originally Bhati Rajputs of the Yadava stock, who under the name of Bhati are the ruling tribe of Jesalmir in North Rajputana, and who as Musalman Bhatis are found in large numbers in Lahore and Multan divisions of the Punjab, and to a small extent in the North-Western Provinces. It was probably by the later Musalman invaders that the Bhatias were driven south into Sindh, where they still continue to eat fish and drink spirits. From Sindh they settled in Cutch and Kathiawad and gradually spread over the whole of Gujarat and especially established themselves in

Bha.-Bhi.

Bombay. Gujarat Bhatias are Vaishnavas, and after their conversion to Vaishnavism have become strict vegetarians. They neither eat nor marry with Sindh Bhatias. They have two main divisions, Halai from Halar in Kathiawad and Katchhi from Cutch, who eat together and intermarry. Over and above their two main divisions into Halai and Katchhi, there is a third division called Gujarati Bhatias, who are to be found in Baroda, Surat and other places. Halai and Katchhi Bhatias speak the Kachhi dialect; Gujarati Bhatias speak only the Gujarati and know nothing of Kachhi. Like Vanias, they are also divided into *Visa* and *Dasa*. The Visa, while taking Dasa girls, rarely give them their daughters in marriage. Besides *gotras* or family stocks, the Bhatias have eighty-four *nukhs* which correspond to clan titles. Marriage in the same *gotra* and *nukh* is forbidden. The excessive want of girls in this caste led some of them during this decade to find out a new field at Hardwar for getting wives. Those who married Hardwar Bhatia girls are not held in much respect by their fellow castemen. Bhatias, as a class, are prosperous and well-to-do. This is due to the broad views of the caste in allowing them to undertake distant sea voyages. In religion they are Vaishnava of the Vallabhachari sect and hold in great reverence the Vaishnava Maharajas called Gosaiji. Some were once so devout in their reverence to their spiritual teachers as to allow them the *jus primus noctis*. After their return from a pilgrimage some of the religiously-minded become *marjadi*, that is, over-scrupulous in the observance of ceremonial purity and do not eat food cooked by any one except a *marjadi*.

Girls are married between nine and twelve. The supply of marriageable girls being short of demand, the bridegroom has to pay from 4 to 5 thousand rupees as purchase money and many have to remain unmarried. Widows are not allowed to marry and divorce is not granted. Polygamy is allowed when the first wife is barren. Disparity between the ages of husband and wife is common. There is no headman in the caste. Caste disputes are settled by a few respectable men with the consent of the majority of the caste people. Breaches of caste rules are punished with fine and in grave cases with excommunication. The fines are credited to the caste fund. The caste also levies fixed contributions on the occasions of birth, marriage and death. The accumulated fund is used in making or repairing caste vessels, in making donations to the spiritual heads and in other charitable works.

BHAT NAGAR (10).—A sub-caste of Kayastha.

BHAVAIYA.—Same as Targala.

Bhavsar (5,689).—A caste of calico printers. Bhâvsars are found chiefly in cities and large towns. According to their story they were originally Kshatriyas, who during Parshuram's persecution hid themselves in a Mata's temple and for this act of *bhav* or confidence in the goddess, came to be known as Bhavsar. They have such tribal surnames as Bhatte, Chohan, Gohel, Parmar and Rathod, which support their claim of Rajput descent. The original home of their ancestors was Brij Mathura in North India from which they moved to Marwar and thence to Champaner and the country bordering the Mahi and the Narbada. From Central Gujarat some went to Kathiawad and Cutch in the north and some to Surat in the south. Ahmedabadi, Harsolia, Jamnagri, Mesania, Moderia, Prantia, Visnagara and other local surnames bear witness to their early settlements. Their family goddesses are Ambaji and Hingalaj. Besides being divided into Meshri and Jain Bhavsars, who eat together but do not intermarry, Bhavsars have three sub-divisions—Rewakanthia (319), living on the banks of the Mahi and the Narbada, Ramdeshis (383), living in Pali and Pratapgad, and Talabda (2,849) living in North Gujarat. The members of these three divisions neither eat together nor intermarry. But Ramdeshis and Rewakanthias eat food cooked by Talabdas. Of the three sub-divisions, the Talabdas alone live on vegetable diet; Ramdeshis and Rewakanthias, except those who are Jains, have no scruple in eating animal food in South Gujarat. Many Bhavsars have given up calico printing and have become confectioners, tailors, washermen and sellers of cloth and pretty brass-ware. By religion some are Jain and the rest belong to the Kabirpanthi, Radhavallabhi, Ramanandi, Santrampanthi, Swaminarayan and Vallabhachari sects. In their marriage rites they do not differ from Vanias and Shravaks. Girls are married before they are eleven and boys at any time after ten. Marriage is not allowed between people of the same surname. Divorce is allowed and a widow sometimes remarries the younger brother of her deceased husband. They burn their dead, the Jain Bhavsars with the full Shravak Vania rituals, and the Meshri Bhavsars with Meshri Vania rites. Each community has its headman who settles caste disputes at a meeting of all the members of the caste.

Bhil (41,836).—An aboriginal tribe, generally very dark in colour and very wild in appearance. The men are muscular, well built and of a medium height. The women are well made, but have coarse irregular features. Among the men, the hair of the head is, as a rule, worn long. The women fasten their hair in braids or plaits brought low down near each temple. Formerly they used to live in huts in their own fields. But now-a-days they live in groups of houses on the village site.

The Bhil's usual dress is a cloth wound round the loin and a long strip twisted round the head. The women commonly dress in a large *ghagra* (petticoat), a bodice, and a *sari* wrapped round the body and brought over the head. They tattoo their faces and pierce their ears and noses for wearing ornaments. Bracelets of tin or brass cover the arm from the wrist to the elbow. Glass and lac bangles are also worn.

Bhils eat all animals except the ass, horse, camel, rat, snake and monkey. Formerly they were always changing their houses and lands, but now most of them have settled in villages and till regularly, though roughly, the same fields. Fifty years ago there were almost daily complaints of their daring robberies. And though they are even now considered a criminal class, most of them are gradually becoming quiet and law-abiding cultivators. Though not considered one of the classes whose touch defiles, Bhils hold a very low place in the social scale and no high caste Hindu will take water from their hands. **Bhi.-Bra.**

They worship *Mata* or *Devi*, reverence the moon and believe in witches. Their chief objects of worship are spirits and ghosts. To these they offer clay horses, jars and beehive-shaped vessels.

As a rule, marriage seldom takes place before a boy is twenty and a girl fifteen. A man may marry a second or third wife in the life-time of the first. A woman marries again not only when her husband dies, but even when she gets tired of him. Her new husband pays her old husband his marriage expenses. The children, if any, stay with their father.

The dead are burnt. As soon as the deceased's family can raise enough money, the anniversary day is held, when much liquor is drunk. If the deceased was a man of importance, a year or two after his death his relations go to a stone mason and make him cut on a stone slab the figure of a man on horse-back with a spear in his hand. The stone is washed and taken to the village *devasthan* or spirit-yard. There, a goat is killed, its blood sprinkled on the stone and its flesh cooked and eaten with as much liquor as the party can afford.

Among the Bhils, there are many tribes or clans. Some of them claim a Rajput descent and bear such names as Makvana, Rathod and Parmar. Each clan has its own *tadvadi* or headman. Disputes are settled by *panchayats*. They generally relate to caste marriage rules. The offender is generally punished with a fine or put out of caste. When one is put out of caste, the other Bhils do not eat, drink or smoke with him. If he begs for pardon, the leading Bhils of the village call two or three men of a class called Vasâvâ and cause him to give them a present of from 5 to 10 rupees. If the Vasâvâs allow him to drink or smoke with him, the offender is taken back into the caste.

Bhisti (143).—Musalman water-carriers.

Bhoi (4,079).—Water-carriers and palanquin-bearers. They make nets and practise fishing also. According to them they are Rajputs from Lucknow. They have nine sub-divisions—Bakoria, Bathava, Gadhedia, Gudia, Kahar, Machhi or Dhimar, Mali, Meta and Purbia. Of these, Mali and Bakoria eat together and intermarry; Mali, Gudia and Kahar eat with one another but do not intermarry; the rest neither eat together nor intermarry. They are strongly built and dark like Kolis. Except the Purbia, whose home speech is Hindustani, they speak Gujarati. Palanquins are now used only on marriage occasions and in carrying about high caste *parda* ladies or idols. Bhois now also till lands, tend sheep or goats, grow water chestnuts, or work as field labourers. They employ Audich or Modh Brahmans as their priests. Widows are allowed to marry and divorce is easy. They worship *Mehaldi Mata*; but some of them are Bijmargi, Ramanandi, Shaiva or Vallabhachari.

***Bhoi** (86).—Converts to Islam from Hindu class of the same name.

Bhojak (373).—Said to have originated from Shrimali Brahmans who having adopted the Jain faith for a living and dined with Oswal Vanias were called *bhojak* or eaters and formed a separate caste. In Visnagar and Mehsana in the Kadi District, they interdine and intermarry with Targalas, but in Patan, though there is interdining, there is no intermarriage between the two.

Borsada (362).—A Brahman caste which takes its name from the town of Borsad in the British Kaira District. A tradition about the origin of the Borsada and Napal Brahmans runs as follows :—

In old times, there ruled in Gujarat a king who offered to give handsome presents to those learned Brahmans who would settle in his territories with their wives. Two Audich Brahman youths, hearing of this, set out for the capital of the king; but being unaccompanied by their wives, they took with them two girls of other castes and passed them off as their wives. The king bestowed upon one the village of Napa and upon the other that of Borsad as gifts. Then they thought of giving up the girls; but being in their turn threatened by them, with exposure, they continued them as their wives and settled in the said villages. They and their descendants have thence forward been known as Napal and Borsada Brahmans.

Borsadas are found chiefly in the Baroda District. Their calling as husbandmen and their position as village headmen mark them as one of the early Brahman colony.

BRAHMABHAT (13,345).—A sub-caste of Bahrot.

Brahma-Kshatri (865).—They are so called from their being the descendants of Kshatriya women who, at the time of Parshuram's massacre, were saved by passing as Brahman women. Besides the main body of Brahma-Kshatri, there are two minor divisions, *Dasa* and *Panchs*, said to be the offspring of a Brahma-Kshatri and a woman of another caste. The members of these divisions neither dine together nor intermarry.

Brahma-Kshatris are said to be of the same stock as the Kshatris of the Punjab and to have migrated from the Punjab and settled first at Champaner and then moved to Ahmedabad and other places. Their priest or *purohits* are Saraswat Brahmans, who are considered degraded for eating with them. They speak Gujarati with a few Hindustani words as *roti* for bread, *chacha* for uncle, *bua* for *phoi*, father's sister, *barat* for marriage procession, *nana* for mother's father, &c.,

Each household has its *kuldevi* who is held in high respect. They keep the rules laid down for Brahmans, such as wearing silk robe at dinner time, etc. The family goddess is worshipped on the hair-cutting, pregnancy and marriage ceremonies. On these occasions, the priest slits the right ear of a black male kid and touches with its blood the forehead of the child, its parents and other members of the family. Their marriage customs differ in some particulars from those of other high caste Hindus. The bride is dressed in loose Musalman-like trousers and is seated in a closed palanquin or *valai* set near the house. The bridegroom walks seven times round the palanquin, the bride's brother at each turn giving him a cut with a *karena*. (oleander) twig. Pregnancy ceremony lasts for eight days instead of for one or two as among other castes. They have no headman.

Burud (150).—Deccani bamboo splitters.

CHAMADIA.—Same as Khalpa.

CHAMAR.—Same as Khalpa or Chamadia.

CHANDRASENIYA KAYASTHA (3,013).— A sub-caste of Prabhus.

Charan (1,959).—Found in Baroda, Kadi and Amreli Districts. According to a bardic account, Charans are the descendants of a son born to an unmarried girl of the Dhadhi clan of the Rajputs. To hide her shame, the girl threw the boy as soon as he was born behind a *gadh* (fortress). The boy was saved and called Gadhvi, by which name Charans are still known in Gujarat. Gujarat Charans include four distinct sections :—Gujjar (876), Kachhela or Kachh Charan, also called Parajia or outsiders (57), Maru or Marwar Charan (678), and Tumer (313), probably from Sindh. The Kachhelas are the largest division of Gujarat Charans. Besides Cutch, they are found all over Kathiawad and form the bulk of the Charan population, both in North and Central Gujarat. Kachhela Charans are closely allied to the Kathis and the Ahirs, who are their great patrons.

Charans follow various callings ; some are bards keeping geneologies of Kathis and Rajputs and reciting their praises and the exploits of their forefathers ; some hold grants of lands, some are cultivators, some are traders and some are beggars receiving presents at feasts and marriages. Most of them, especially of the Kachhela division, are graziers, cattle-sellers and pack carriers. Formerly like Bhats, they used to stand security and enforce the obligations for which they had guaranteed by practising *traga*, which generally did not go further than a cut on the arm with the *kutar*.

Unlike Bhats, Charans do not put on the sacred thread. Most of them are Shaiva and are devotees of the consort of Shiva under many names, such as Amba, Bhavani, Parvati, etc. Girls are married between ten and twenty. Their marriage customs do not differ from those of Kanbis. Widow remarriage is allowed.

Chhipa (502).—Calenderers and printers. Originally a sub-division of Bhavsar, they have now grown into a separate caste. Unlike Bhavsars, they eat fish and drink liquor. They polish and dress by beating with heavy wooden mallets, black cloth for export to Africa and other places. On account of the decline in the demand for this cloth, many Chhipas have given up their former occupation, and now earn a living as labourers and brick-layers. They allow widow marriage and have a caste *panchayat* for settling social disputes.

* **Chhipa** (308).—Musalman calico printers. They are Hindu converts who follow their old occupation. They are Sunni in religion. In all their settlements, they have a well-managed union or *jamat* with a headman chosen by the members.

CHITPAVAN.—Same as Koknastha. Immigrants from the Deccan.

Chodhra (31,366).—A tribe found chiefly in the Rani Mahals of the Navsari District. It has several divisions of which only two,—Chokapuri (8,572) and Valvada (3,137)—have been recorded. Of these, the highest in social rank are the Chokapuris, who are also called Pavagadia. They claim partly to be of Rajput descent and to have lived as carriers in the Rajput kingdoms of North Gujarat and fled south on their overthrow by the Musalmans. This appears very probable, as the Anjana Kanbis of Kheralu are very similar to them in their appearance, manners and customs and may be the descendants of those of them who remained in North Gujarat. The men are stronger and fairer and the women are better looking than those of the other early tribes. The men dress in a turban, coat and waist cloth. The women keep their hair very tidy and wear a coloured cloth over the head, a bodice and a cloth round the waist. The men's ornaments are silver, brass and tin ear and finger rings, and if well-to-do, bands of silver at the elbow and wrist. Women wear round the neck coils of white glass beads and, if well-to-do, a silver necklace, brass brooch on the arm and tin brass anklets. Except the cow, buffalo, horse, donkey, jackal, rat, snake, dog and cat, they eat most animals. Their chief worship is paid to the spirits of their forefathers. They set apart near each village a plot of ground as the *devasthan* or spirit-yard. They honour Rama, but the objects of their special worship are *palio* and *simadio devs* (boundary-gods and village guardians). They pay no special respect to Brahmans and never make use of their services. On the 6th day after a birth, they worship the goddess *chhatthi*, feasting their friends on liquor and *val*. A boy is considered fit to marry after 18, and a girl after 16. A man anxious to marry his son, goes to the girl's house, and if the father is willing, entertains her parents and relations with liquor. One or two days before marriage, the bride and bridegroom are rubbed with yellow powder. On the marriage day, the bridegroom goes to the girl's house, and after the boy's father has paid the girl's father Rs. 32½ as dowry, and presented the bride with a *sala*, a bodice and a silver necklace worth about Rs. 13, the bride and the bridegroom are seated in the marriage-booth. Their skirts are tied by the women of the house and together they walk four times round the pole of the booth. Dancing, in which the bride and the bride-groom join and a feast of rice and pulse, complete the ceremony. When the bride leaves her father's house, the father according to his means, gives a few buffaloes or a little money as present. The practice of winning a bride by taking service with her father, *khandhadio*, is common among the Chodhras. Their dead are burned. Before lighting the funeral pyre, Chodhras place cooked rice and pulse in the corpse's mouth and consider it lucky, if a crow comes and takes it away. On the fourth day, after a death, a spirit medium (*bahadar havria*), accompanied by the friends of the deceased, takes a stone and groaning and shaking, as if possessed, sets it in the spirit yard. He kills a fowl, letting some of the blood fall on the stone. Next, he adds butter, grain and liquor and making the stone red, consecrates it to the spirit of the deceased. Near the stone, the friends place a small clay cow or she-buffalo for a woman or a horse for a man. Three times a year on *Akhatrij*, *Divaso* and *Divali*, Chodhras in a body visit these shrines. They offer fowls, goats and sheep, drink freely and men and women dance together and close the feast. The Chodhras have no headman, and there is an entire want of caste organization in them.

Chovisa (793).—Literally "of the twenty-four"; a Brahman caste mostly found in the Baroda City and in every taluka of the Baroda District. Their great number is in Sinore. They are supposed to be originally Nandoras. The story goes that a Nandora Brahman confined a newly-married Nandora Vania pair in the temple of *Nanda Ananda Mata* for the sake of exacting from them the customary fee of Rs. 125; that while so confined, the bridegroom was bitten by a snake and died, whereupon the bride became *sati* and cursed the Nandora Brahmans; and that upon this, 24 of them gave up the priesthood of Nandora Vanias and avoided the curse. They and their descendants were thenceforth called Chovisa. They are divided into two sections called *Mota* or large (452) and *Nana* or small (228). The sub-castes were formed owing to a small section having separated itself from the main body on account of differences in caste government. They interdine but do not intermarry.

Chunvalia (7,707).—A caste of Kolis. They take their name from Chunval, a tract of country near Kadi, so called from its originally containing *chunvalis* or 44 villages. They are mostly found in the Kadi District. Fifty years ago, they were the terror of North Gujarat. Led by their chiefs or *Thakardas* of partly Rajput descent, they lived in villages protected by impassable thorn fences and levied contributions from the districts round, planning, if refused regular night attacks and dividing the booty according to recognised rules, under which live-stock and coin belonged to the chief, and cloth, grain and such articles belonged to the captors. There are still among them men of criminal habits, but as a class they have settled as cultivators and labourers. They have twenty-one principal sub-divisions: Abasania, Adhgama, Baroga, Basukia, Dabhi, Dhamodia, Dhandhukia, Gohel, Jandaria, Jhenjuwadia, Kanaja, Lilapara, Makvana, Palegia, Parmar, Piplia, Babaria, Sadria, Solanki, Vadhlakhia and Vaghela. They intermarry among their own class alone, but not among members of the same sub-division.

Dabgar (549).—A caste of leather jar makers. They say that they were Vanias, who having taken to this work, were looked upon as degraded and therefore formed a separate caste. Even now, they are called *Adhiya Vania*. Properly speaking, they are a sub-caste of Mochis and are considered unclean on account of the raw leather used by them in the manufacture of leather jars.

Dadhich (36).—A Brahman caste. It is a small community and is found in the City of Baroda and the Baroda District. Dadhichs say that they belonged originally to the Audich Sahasra stock and got the present name by settling in the village of Dehvan near Vijapur, where there is an *ashram* or hermitage belonging to the Dadhich Rishi. Most of them are money-lenders and cultivators.

Dalvadi (1,052).—A caste of Kolis. They are generally brickmakers, and owing to their better calling, look upon themselves as of a higher social status than ordinary Kolis, with whom they neither eat nor intermarry.

Darji (13,277).—They are also called Merai or Sui, from *sui*, a needle, and live chiefly in towns and large villages. They are of twelve divisions, Dhandhaya (29), Doshi (114), Dungarpuri (101), Gujjar (3,545), Maru (387), Ramdeshi (11), Champaneri (1,695), Charotaria (1,657). Kathiawadi (46), Pepavanshi (4,916), Surati (448) and Vakalia (169), none of whom either eat together or intermarry. The Pepavanshi or Rajkali, who are found in the Kadi and Baroda Districts, seem to be of Rajput origin of which a trace remains in the surnames Chavda, Chohan, Gohel, Dabhi, Makvana, Parmar, Rathod, Solanki and Sonora. The Ramdeshis, who are found in the Baroda District, were originally Marwadi Girasias. Darjis hold a middle position in society. In South Gujarat in the absence of Brahmans, a Darji officiates at Bharvad marriage. Besides tailoring, Darjis blow trumpets at marriage and other processions. Now-a days they look upon this occupation as humiliating and in most places have resolved not to perform it. In religion they belong to the Madhvachari, Parnamipanthi, Radha-Vallabhi, Ramanandi, Swaminarayan and Vallabhachari sects. Their widows are allowed to remarry. Husband and wife are free to divorce each other in some places, and in others like Kadi, a husband can divorce his wife but a wife cannot divorce her husband. Caste disputes are settled by a few leading men at a caste meeting.

***Darji** (7).—Converts to Islam from the Darji caste.

DAUDI (7,008).—A section of trading Vohoras.

Deshastha (6,464).—Immigrant Mahrashtra Brahmans from the Deccan, mainly for State service. It is said that a Maharashtra King who wanted to perform a sacrifice invited them to the Deccan from the North. After the ceremony was completed, he gave them rich gifts and settled them there. Hence they were known as Deshastha, *i. e.*, those settled in the country (*desh*).

Deshaval or Disaval (134).—A Brahman caste found chiefly in the Kadi and Baroda districts. It derives its name from the town of Deesa near Palanpur. Disaval Brahmans are the priests of Disaval Vanias.

Deshaval or Disaval (6,145).—A Vania caste found mainly in the Kadi and Baroda Districts. Disavals are found in large numbers in Kalol, Kadi, Patan and Sidhpur Talukas. They take their name from Deesa, an ancient town near the military station of the same name. They are divided into Visa (1,956), Dasa (4,025) and Pancha (161). Dasas are further subdivided into Ahmedabadi, Surati and Ghoghari. Both Visa and Dasa eat together but do not intermarry. The Panchas form a separate community. Bride and bridegroom go round the *chori* eight times among the Deshavals instead of seven times as in other Vania castes. Their family priests are Deshaval Brahmans and they are followers of the Vallabhachari sect.

Devrukha (553).—A Brahman caste; immigrants from the Deccan. About their origin the tradition is as under :—There lived a Chitpavan Brahman by name Vasudev Chitale. He thought of digging a well, as a charitable act, for the public on a high road. He prevailed upon the passers-by to assist him in his work. While the work was in progress, some Karhada Brahmans from Devrukha happened to come that way and were astonished to see a number of Brahmans engaged in digging earth. Thereupon they asked Chitale the reason of it ; he told them what he wanted and requested them also to lend a hand. But on their refusing to enter into such humble work, he cursed them saying that for all future time they would be known contemptuously as Devrukhas, and would suffer from poverty and meanness.

Dhadhi (468).—Same as Mir. They are musicians and beggars.

DHALGAR (5).—A section of the Mochi caste, so called from their occupation of making *dhals* or shields.

Dhangar (502).—A caste of Deccani shepherds found all over the State, but mainly in the Baroda District. They follow like the Bharvads and Ahirs of Gujarat, the occupation of cattle grazing.

Dhanka (18,667).—Literally one who taps the palm tree. It is a general term applied to all members of the forest tribe, but in the present census many have returned the term as their caste name.

DHEBRA.—Same as Dhimar.

Dhed (H. 99,798 : M. 8).—Said to be the descendants of Kshatris who during Parshuram's persecution, passed themselves off as belonging to the impure castes. Chavda, Chohan, Chudasma, Dabhi, Gohel, Makvana, Parmar, Rathod, Solanki, Vaghela and other surnames which they have, show that they must have Rajput blood in them.

Dheds from Marwad are called Marvadi or Maru and those from the Konkan and the Deccan are called Mahar. Besides these, there are ten local divisions named either from the tract of the country in which they live or from their callings. Patania (of Patan), Bhalia (of Cambay), Charotaria or Talabda (of Petlad and Kaira), Chorasia or Mahikanthia, (of Baroda and Mahikantha), Kahanamia (of Kahanam tract in Baroda and Broach) and Surtis (of Surat) are the six place-names. Hadias (bone-men), Megwans (rain-men) and Vankers (weavers) are the three craft names. Only one, Gujjar, is race-name and is adopted by the Dheds of Broach. None of these divisions intermarry but all except the Marus dine with each other. They live chiefly on grains, but have no scruple about eating flesh. They have their own priests called *Garodas*. They worship *Hanuman*, *Ganpati* and *Mata*. Many belong to Bijmargi, Ramanandi, Kabirpanthi and Swaminarayan sects. Some of them have recently embraced Christianity. Polygamy, divorce and widow remarriage are allowed. The widow of a man generally marries his younger brother. Except a few, who are well-to-do, Dheds bury their dead. Death pollution is observed for 11 days. *Shradha* ceremony is performed by the chief mourner on the twelfth day or four days from the tenth to the thirteenth. Dheds believe that a high future is in store for their tribe. A king will marry a Dhed woman and will raise the whole caste to the position of Brahmans. Each village has its headman called *Mehtar* in North Gujarat, and *Patel* in South Gujarat. Along with three or four other members of the caste, he settles all caste and other social disputes. Dheds are strict in punishing breaches of caste rules and show more respect than other artisan castes to the opinion of their headman.

Dhimar (5,410).—Deccani fishermen who settled in South Gujarat. They have the peculiar North Konkan custom of naming their children from the week-day of their birth, *e.g.*, Mangli (born on Tuesday), Budhio (born on Wednesday), &c. A Brahman officiates at their marriage.

Dhobi (2,438).—A washerman, from *dhovun* to wash ; found in every town and city and in large villages. Though in the Navsari District some eat fish and drink liquor, the Dhobi's ordinary food consists of grain and vegetables.

They allow divorce and widow marriage. Dhobis generally wear their employers' clothes, which has given rise to the proverb *dhobina panch parayan*. (The Dhobi's five, *i.e.*, cap, jacket, coat, waistcoat and *khes* belong to others). In religion they are Kabirpanthi, Ramanuji, and Vallabhachari. Though they respect Hindu gods, they have no house gods and do not go to temples.

Caste disputes are settled by a headman in consultation with the men of the caste assembled at a special meeting.

***Dhobi** (238).—Hindu converts to Islam, who follow their old profession of washerman. They marry only among themselves and have their own *jamat*.

Dhodia (20,490).—An early tribe found in the Navsari District. Man's ornaments are ear-rings and armlets of brass, tin or silver. The females put on solid rings of brass over the whole of the leg upto the knee and also on the arm from the wrist to the elbow. These ornaments weigh from 18 to 20 lbs. Dhodias hold a higher social position than the other early tribes, all of which except Chodhras eat food cooked by them. But a Dhodia dines with no one who is not of his own tribe. Among the Dhodias, there are many *kula, i. e.*, families whose status depends upon the villages inhabited by them and the occupations followed by them. They do not allow marriage within the same *kula*. Dhodias of higher families contract early marriages. A bride is purchased by the payment of about Rs. 25 to her father. Men with no means of paying the dowry, offer to serve the girl's father for a term of one to five years. During this time, the suitor receives food and clothing, but his earnings go to his master. If he proves idle or gluttonous, he may at any time be sent off. Even when the three years are over, the girl may refuse him, but then he can claim payment for his services. When all goes well, the regular marriage ceremony is performed. But it is not necessary to allow the pair to live as husband and wife. This is called *khandhadia* or bride-purchase system. In certain rare cases, Dhodias purchase a girl for their boy and allow the pair to live as husband and wife without making them go through any ceremony.

They do not use Brahmans as priests. Divorce and remarriage are allowed. A wife has to pay Rs. 5 only to be released from her husband. Corpses are taken in a procession with music playing to the burning ground. On the bier are placed a scythe, a *tansala* (brass bowl) and a *lota* (water jug.) A *khatrun* (memorial stone) is erected in honour of the deceased. When the husband dies, the wife throws into the pyre her ornaments of solid rings of brass which she is wearing. When the wife dies, the husband throws one of his chief ornament in the same way. In most Dhodia villages, one family has the hereditary right of headmanship. The Naik, as he is called, is treated with respect, but most of the social disputes are decided by a mass meeting of the tribe at one of the big funeral feasts. Breaches of caste rules are punished by fine, or if the offence is heinous by turning the culprit out of caste.

Dhuldhoya (24).—Literally dust washers. They are said to be converted Hindus of the Khatri caste. They buy dust and other rubbish from the house of goldsmiths, wash and shift it and carefully pick out the particles of gold or silver found in the refuse. They marry only among themselves and form a separate body with a headman of their own.

Dodi.—A contemptuous term applied to the Koli caste on account of its members living on the sprouts and leaves of a creeper called *dodi*.

Dubla (40,976).—Derived from Sankrit *durbala* (weak); an early tribe found in the Navsari District. They have come into closer contact with the civilised castes and do not much differ in appearace from Kolis. They have eight sub-divisions, Bava, Damani, Narda, Palia or Khodia, Sarvia, Talavia, Vasava and Voharia. The members of these clans seldom eat together and never intermarry. They claim a strain of Rajput blood and call themselves Rathod. Females wear the *kanchali*, and do not move about with open breasts like Gamits and other early tribes. They are peasants and labourers. Most of them are *halis* or the hereditary servants of Bhathelas, Kanbis and other better classes of cultivators. They are entirely dependent on their masters for food and clothing. They treat Brahmans with respect and make use of their services on marriage and other occasions. Boys are married between 10 and 20 and girls between 10 and 18. Widow marriage is allowed, but polygamy is not allowed. The dead are burned. Caste disputes are settled by a few hereditary leaders or *patels*.

Dudhvala (293).—They are the descendants of Hindu converts to Islam from Sabalia and Gauli castes and are found mainly in Baroda City. They sell milk and hire out carts. Women milk and look after the cows and buffaloes. They are Sunni in name knowing very little of the Koran and are not careful to say their prayers. They speak Gujarati. As among the Hindus, women join in the marriage procession, singing Gujarati songs. Like Hindu women, they also beat the breast at deaths. They add *ji* to their name as Ismailji. They marry among themselves and form a separate community with a headman.

Eka.-Gha.

EKADASIA BRAHMANS.—Same as Kayatia Brahmans.

Fakir (4,639).—Musalman religious beggars. (See Chapter IV, para. 263, for a description of their main divisions).

Gadaria (31).—Same as Bharvad.

Galiara (64).—A sub-division of Bhavsars, who by taking to the new profession of indigo-dyeing, has become a separate caste as Galiara or indigo-dyers. From the decline of their craft, they have fallen into a low state, and find other means of earning their livelihood, such as agriculture, shop-keeping, labour, etc.

* **Galiara** (84).—Musalman indigo-dyers. They are partly descendants of foreign immigrants and partly of converted Hindus. Their customs are those of ordinary Musalmans and they generally marry among themselves.

GAMATDA.—Same as Gamit.

Gamit (49,615).—Also called Gamtâ or Gamatdâ ; an early tribe found in the Navsari District. They eat sheep. goat, rabbit and fowl, but will not touch the flesh of a cow nor of any animal found dead. They are peasants and wood-cutters. They worship *Vaghdev*, *Samladev* and *Devli Mata*. They never make use of a Brahman's services nor pay him any respect. Men of their own caste act as their priests. Among Gamtas marriage takes place when a boy can climb a palm tree, *i. e.*, generally after he is 12 years of age. *Khandhadia* system prevails. Polygamy and divorce are allowed. Remarriage is also allowed but only between the widowed of both the sexes. A widowed person of either sex is not allowed to take as a partner the unmarried of the opposite sex. The dead are burned. Caste disputes are referred to a few hereditary leaders or *patels*.

GAMTA.—Same as Gamit.

GANCHA.—Same as Vansfoda.

Gandhrap (85).—A caste of musicians from "Gandharva", the mythological musician of the gods. They are found in Kadi and Baroda Prants. They have entered the province from the north and say that they were originally Chitroda Nagar Brahmans. Traces of a northern origin remain in the men's long and flowing turbans and in the coverlets with which the women swathe themselves when they go out of doors. They play on various musical instruments and accompany dancing girls in all their performances. They wear the Brahmanic thread and their priests are Audich Brahmans. They are vegetarians. Divorce and widow marriage are not allowed, but owing to the smallness of their number, marriage among the children of brothers and sisters is allowed and practised. Some of them are Shaiva and others Vaishnav. They have no headman and all social disputes are settled at a mass meeting of the male members of the caste.

* **Gandhrap** (159).—Singers, converts from the Hindu caste of the same name. They are Sunnis in religion. In the dry season, they move about the country and in the rainy months, return to their homes and cultivate. As their girls become professional dancers and prostitutes, the men never marry in their own caste. They seek wives from among the poor Musalmans and sometimes Kolis. The parents live on their daughter's earnings. They have a union and headman and during the rainy season generally meet together at marriages.

Garoda (6,281).—Priests of the unclean castes, including Bhangis in Central Gujarat, but except Bhangis in South Gujarat. Their surnames—Dave, Joshi and Shukal—point to a Brahman origin, but a few bear Rajput surnames such as Gohel, Parmar, &c. They keep the Brahman fasts and holidays, understand Sanskrit and recite hymns and passages from the Purans. They are called Brahmans by Dheds, Bhangis, Chamars, etc., and officiate at their marriages and deaths. As among Brahmans, a few men, called Shukals act as priests of Garoda. They draw up and use horoscopes. Some Garodas till, others weave and a few act as tailors and barbers to Dheds. Their dead are buried and they perform *shradhas*. Divorce and widow marriage are allowed. They have no headman but a council of their caste punishes breaches of caste rules by fines or expulsion.

Gauda (502).—A section of Brahmans from Upper India.

Gauli (15).—An immigrant caste from the Deccan, mostly found in the Baroda City. In the Deccan, they follow the same occupation as Rabaris and Bharvads do in Gujarat. But in this State, they do not follow the traditional profession of their caste. They are either agriculturists or menial servants.

Gayaval (26).—A Brahman caste found only in the City of Baroda. They are an offshoot from the mendicant Brahmans of Gaya and are mainly immigrants in the State for service.

Gedia (3,716).—A caste of Kolis found in the Amreli District. They are so called from Ged, the name of the tract between Porebunder and Madhavpur, in which they originally lived.

Ghadsi (10).—Immigrants from the Deccan. They are musicians and ballad singers.

Ghanchi (11.867).—Oilmen, found chiefly in towns and large villages. They are of 8 divisions:—Ahmedabadi (652), Champaneria (145), Modh (8,909), Patani (168), Sidhpuria (164), Surati (58), Khambhati (?) and Pancholi (210). They have Rajput tribal surnames such as Gohel, Jhala, Parmar and Solanki. Of the eight divisions, the Modhs and Sidhpurias rank highest, the other divisions eating food cooked by them, while they do not eat food cooked by the other six. None of the eight divisions intermarry. Though they hold almost as good a position as Bhavsars and Sutars, the common Gujarati expression Ghanchi-Gola is used in the sense of low caste Hindus, just as Brahman-Vania is used for high caste Hindus. Ghanchis are fairly religious and belong to Kabirpanthi, Ramanandi, Swaminarayan, and Vallabhachari sects. They are also great worshippers of the *Kalka* and *Behechara Matas*. Marriage ceremonies do not differ from those performed by Kanbis, except in the fact that *Hanuman* is worshipped by the bride and bridegroom immediately after marriage. Polygamy and widow remarriage are allowed, but divorce is rarely granted. The widow of a man sometimes marries his younger brother. Each sub-caste has its own headman who settles caste disputes at a meeting of all the men of the caste.

***Ghanchi** (4,614).—Musalman oilmen. They are also called Ghanchi-Vohora. They are the descendants of Hindus of the Pinjara and Ghanchi castes. In their houses, they speak the Gujarati language. Their females dress like Hindu and have such Hindu names as Dhanbai, Jivi, Mankor, &c. Males put on Hindu-like turbans. At marriage, their women go singing like the Hindus with the bridegroom to the bride's house, and in their feasts they have Hindu dishes of *ladu*, *kansar*, etc. At death women wail and beat the breast. They are Sunni in faith. They marry only among themselves and the Pinjaras. They have a *jamat*, with a headman chosen by the members.

Girnara (70).—A Brahman caste found chiefly in the Amreli District, deriving its name from Girnar. They have a tradition that they were settled at Girnar by Krishna after he rose from the *Damodar* reservoir in the bed of the Sonarekha river at Junaghad. They are considered specially sacred and have the monopoly of the office of priests to pilgrims visiting Girnar and Somnath Pattan. They have four sub-divisions, Ajakia, Bardai, Chorvadya and Panai. By profession, they are Vaishnava temple priests, beggars, traders, money-lenders, cooks and husbandmen.

Gola—Rice-pounders—(H. 5210; M. 10).—Found in most of the towns. According to their story, they were originally Rajputs of Chitor in Mevad who called themselves slaves or *golas* to protect themselves from the persecution of Parshuram. In token of Rajput strain, the word *Rana* is always added to the name Gola. Their tribal surnames are Chohan, Chodhavada, Daladia, Divadia, Hirvana, Katakia, Manhora, Nagaretha, Panchshahdia, Pat, Parmar, Pasia, Samalia, Sitpuri, Solanki, Takoria, Vaghela, Vaghmar, Varaskia and Vehiriji. They eat besides coarse food-grains, fish, fowl and the flesh of the goat, deer, hare and antelope. They drink liquor to excess especially at their feasts and caste dinners. This leads to abusing each other and sometimes coming to blows, and has passed into a proverb. A quarrel ending in abuse with a certain amount of gentle slapping is called *gola laahat* or Gola brawl. When employed in pounding rice, they have to be closely watched as they frequently carry rice away. Some Golas have given up rice-pounding and work as sawyers, *gumastas* to grocers and cloth-dealers, as sellers of salt and carriers of goods either on their shoulders or on donkey-back. The Gola is held in little respect. A slovenly Vania is called a Gola in contempt. The Golas and Ghanchis are the first on the other side of the boundary line between high and low caste Hindus. As a class they are religious and are either Bijpanthi, Kabirpanthi, Ramanandi or Swaminarayan. Some belong to the Pirana sect, who, while they worship their saint's tomb, also respect Hindu gods. Marriages are not allowed among near relations or between people bearing the same surname. Except that they are less detailed, their marriage ceremonies do not differ from those performed by Kanbis. Widow remarriage is allowed, the widow sometimes marrying a younger brother of her deceased husband. Caste disputes are settled by a headman with the help of five leading men.

GOLA (KHAVAS)—A class of personal attendants. They are the offsprings of female slaves called *chhokris*, *vadharans* or *poris* in Rajput families. They are quite distinct from *golas* or rice-pounders —*See* Khavas.

Golak (4).—A caste of degraded Brahmans from the Deccan. They are said to be the descendants of a Brahman of the Chitpavan caste and a widow.

Gomtival (55).—A Brahman caste found mostly in the Kadi District, said to take its name from Gautam Rishi. A more likely origin is from the old city Gomti, among the Barda hills in South-west of Kathiawad. They are mostly beggars, and live on alms.

Gondhali (46).—Immigrants from the Deccan. They resemble the Gujarati Bhavaiyas in their occupation. They are found mainly in the City of Baroda owing to the Deccani element in the population. They perform what is called a *gondhal*,—performance which consists in singing songs or ballads in honour of some goddess. In several Deccani Hindu families, it is customary to perform *gondhal*, after marriage or *munj* ceremony.

Gorji (38).—Jain ascetics. Any Shravak may leave his family and become a Gorji. At present, most Gorjis are the sons of low caste Hindus or are illegitimate children who are bought or brought up by Gorjis. The Gorji, like the Sadhu, wears only two clothes, a waist and a shoulder cloth. He differs from the Sadhu by wearing white instead of red ochre robes. Gorjis grow the moustaches and the hair of the head. They beg cooked food or *bhiksha* from the Shravaks, and where there are no Shravaks, from other Hindus, except the low castes. They practise sorcery and magic and prescribe medicines.

Gosain (6,363).—Also called Atit. They are divided into two classes, *mathdhari* (celibates, and *gharbari* (householders), of which the latter is the larger class. They are all Shaivas and belong to ten sects,—Gir, Parbat, Sagar, Puri, Bharathi, Van, Aram, Saraswati, Tirth and Ashram. They add the clan name to the personal name as Karangar, Hirapuri, Chanchalbharathi, &c. All of these clans have some of their members householders (Gharbaris) and others monks (Mathdharis). Among the Mathdharis, the *Guru Shishya Sampradaya* or succession from preceptor to disciple obtains. The appointment of a *chela* is made by tonsure (*mundan*) and covering him with *chadar*, which ceremony is followed by a feast to the members of the caste, which is called *bhandaro*. Gosains are either entirely or partly clad in brown. Most of them are professional beggars. But among them some are bankers, merchants, state servants and soldiers. They do not wear the sacred thread and allow widow marriage.

Gugali (1,580).—A Brahman caste, so called from *gugal*, aloe incense. Another derivation is from Gokul, the birthplace of Shri Krishna, and appears more likely as connecting Shri Krishna with Kathiawad. They are numerous in Beyt and Dwarka where they are Vaishnav temple *pujari* or priests; they act as *purohit* and pilgrim conductors, and are also shopkeepers. They are not much respected by other Brahmans. Though not returned in the Census, there is a small sub-caste called *Bodha* among the Gugalis. Bodhas are neither allowed to intermarry nor interdine with other Gugalis. The cause of the split is said to be due to a gentleman of the caste inviting all the individuals of the caste to attend a sacrificial ceremony and saying that those who did not come in time would be excommunicated. It so happened that some nephews of the man happened to come late. He was naturally angry and called them *bodha, i.e.,* fools, and excommunicated them.

Gujjar (113).—A Vania caste found chiefly in the Kadi and Baroda Districts. These Vanias were originally Gujjars and settled in Gujarat before other Vanias. Formerly they were divided into *Dasa* and *Visa*. Lately the Visas finding themselves diminishing joined the Dasas. Their family priests are the Shrimali Brahmans and they are followers of the Vallabhachari sect.

Gurav (176).—Immigrants from the Deccan. They were originally Brahmans, but were degraded and now form a separate caste. About their origin, it is said that when Buddhism prevailed, the ministrants in temples were called *guru* or preceptors, *guravah* being the honorific plural of the term. After the triumph of Brahmanism over Buddhism, the old worshippers in temples naturally lost the popular esteem and respect they once commanded, but as their successors retained their old occupation of worship, they also retained their name as Gurav. They were naturally regarded as being lower in status than the Brahmans. In the Deccan and especially in Konkan, Guravs are generally worshippers in temples. In the Baroda territory, their main occupation is that of playing music. In the *kirtans* of *Haridas* or *Buva*, the man who plays on the "*mridung*" is generally a Gurav. Another occupation followed by Guravs is that of preparing leaf-plates or *patravala* used by Hindus for placing food on at the time of meals.

Hajam (24,838)—Barbers. They are found in every town and village in Gujarat. The word Hajam is derived from Arabic *hajam*, to cup, and refers to his doing cupping operations in olden times. A Hajam is also called *valand* from his cutting the hair or *val*; a *gainzo* from his old operation of dressing wounds or *gha*; a *rat* from his carrying a torch at night-time or *rat*, and a *matko* from an earthen pot on which barber boys are taught to shave. There are seven main divisions of Hajams:—Limachia (21,450), Bhatia (825), Maru (1,578), Masuria (642), Pardeshi (8) and Dakshani (115). Of these divisions, the Limachia rank the highest. They allow Bhatia Hajams to smoke out of their pipes, but do not eat with any other division. None of the divisions intermarry or interdine, but all except the Pardeshi and Dakshani eat food cooked by a Limachia Hajam The Limachias claim descent from a band of Rajputs, who after some defeat fled for protection to their goddess Limacha in Patan. From Patan they went to Champaner and from Champaner they spread over Gujarat. Among the Limachia surnames are Bhati, Chavda, Chohan, Dabhi, Gohel, Parmar, Rathod, &c. Except the Masurias of South Gujarat, who eat goat's flesh and drink liquor, and also work as *dholis*, or drum-beaters on marriage occasions, Hajams live on ordinary food-grains. Their ordinary profession is shaving, but in villages they also cultivate land. Their women act as midwives. High caste Hindus do not allow Hajams to touch drinking pots. Among Kanbis and low caste Hindus, a barber touches the drinking pots and cleanses the cooking pots and vessels. Hajams' priests are Audich, Rayakval, Borsada and Shrigaud Brahmans, who by way of slight are called Hajamgors. By religion, Hajams are Bijpanthi, Kabirpanthi, Ramanandi and Vallabhachari. Divorce and widow remarriage are allowed. The widow of a man sometimes marries his younger brother. Hajams are proverbially talkative, boastful and pretentious. A fool or an unlettered person is commonly called Hajam and a country barber is called a *bhens mudo* (buffallo shaver) or a *kumbhar* (potter).

Caste disputes are settled sometimes by a headman in consultation with the caste people and sometimes by a few respectable men of the caste.

***Hajam Turki** (949).—Musalman barbers. They are said to be partly the descendants of immigrants and partly of converted Hindu barbers. They have two sections: *Jokhari* (leechmen) and *Hajam* (barbers). In Navsari they speak Hindustani, but in Baroda and Kadi their home-tongue is Gujarati. They marry only among their two sections and have a union of their own under a headman.

Hijda (H. 144 ; M. 2).—Eunuchs. They are also called Fatda or Pavaya. They are found in small numbers in towns. They are recruited from Hindus and Musalmans who consider themselves the creatures of *Behecharaji Mata*, who has her temple in the Chansma Taluka of the Baroda State. Except that they do not dine together, Musalman and Hindu Hijdas are closely alike. According to their tradition, a king of Champaner got a son through the favour of Behecharaji. He was named Jetho and was impotent from birth. The king set him apart for the service of the goddess through whose favour he got him. The goddess appeared to him in dream and told him to cut off his private parts and dress himself as a woman. Jetho obeyed the goddess and the practice has been kept up by those who follow the class. Impotence is the indispensable qualification for admission into the class. When an impotent man wants to be admitted into the class, he goes to a Hijda and makes the request. His ears are bored with a needle, a solemn oath is given to him for not stealing and never acting as a pimp to a woman. The novice is admitted on probation from 6 to 12 months, during which period his conduct is carefully watched, and his impotence tested by prostitutes. When impotency is established, the next ceremony is the cutting off of the genital parts. The operation is performed on a day approved by the goddess. The lopping is performed by the person himself without any assistance. After the operation, the patient lies on his back on a cot for three days, sesame oil is poured on the part lopped off. Till the wound is healed, it is washed with a decoction of *bordi* (*Ziziphus Jujuba*) and *baval* (*Acacia Arabica*) bark. The operation is held to correspond to a birth ceremony which makes the patient a member of the caste. The new Hijda is given a female name which generally ends in *de*, such as Dhanade, Ladude, &c. Since 1880, emasculation is prohibited by H. H. the Gaekwad's Government and is not now practised in Baroda. But impotent persons with female tendencies continue to join the caste. Hijdas live as beggars, singing the praises of their patron goddess Behecharaji. They beg in bands within certain beats and receive fixed yearly dues from shopkeepers, carpenters, tailors, shoemakers, goldsmiths, blacksmiths, Dheds, Sathawaras and Charans. They also receive fees from Kanbis on the birth and marriage of their sons. They live on coarse grain, but have no objection to eat fish and flesh of sheep and goats. Hijdas bury their dead. As they are neither males nor females, they do not touch the coffin, which is carried by Musalmans, the companions of the dead standing by mourning. On the *dasa* or the tenth day and on the *chalisa* or fortieth day after a death, the companions of the deceased feed the caste people and the Musalman bier-bearers.

Social disputes are settled by a *panch* of four or five leading members of the caste. Any member who has been found guilty of committing theft or acting as a pimp is excommunicated, but is re-admitted on paying a penalty.

Holar (51).—A Deccani untouchable caste. They are musicians and ballad singers. Immigrants from the Deccan.

JAFFRI (2,824).—Also called Patani, a section of trading Vohoras.

Jambu (2,670).—A Brahman caste, also called Jambusaria, found in the Baroda District. They derive their name from the town of Jambusar in the Broach District. They are said to be descended from the sage Yajnavalkya and according to tradition were the first colonists of the town of Jambusar. Copperplate grants show that they were settled there as early as the beginning of the fourth century. They were once a large and learned community, but are now mostly family priests in villages and cultivators.

Jat (H. 259 ; M. 3).—A warlike tribe from the Punjab. They claim to be Yadavas. Though in Rajputana, there are many Jats and a few Jat-ruled States, the superiority of the Rajput over the Jat is admitted. In the Punjab, where the later Gujjar has freely mixed with the elder Jat, no line divides the Jat from the Rajput.

JETHIMAL (48).—A sub-caste of Modh Brahmans.

Jew (40).—Members of the Beni-Israel community. A tradition current in the community says that the earliest representatives of the race in India were shipwrecked near the village of Navgaon, Kolaba District, and adopted the calling of oil-pressing and agriculture. Many gradually forsook their hereditary occupations in favour of the medical, legal and clerical professions. In the early portion of the nineteenth century, the ordinary dress of a Beni-Israel consisted of a turban, a long coat of Hindu pattern, trousers or *dhotar* and Indian shoes. The turban was gradually replaced firstly by the Turkish or Persian cap and secondly by the English hat or cap, which is now generally worn. Similarly the women, who formerly wore the Brahman or Prabhu *sari* and *choli*, now dress in Parsi fashion and a few have adopted European dress. Their home tongue is Marathi. Most of the Jews in the State are employed in the State service.

Jharola (2,054).—A Vania caste found chiefly in Baroda and Kadi Districts. Jharolas are found in large numbers in the Dabhoi and Sankheda Talukas. They take their name from Jhalor in Marwar and are divided into Dasa (923), Visa (958) and Pancha (91). The Visa and Dasa dine together but do not intermarry. The Panchas form a separate community. Their family priests are Jharola Brahmans and they are Vallabhachari Vaishnava.

Jharola (225).—A Brahman caste found in Kadi and Baroda Districts. They take their name from Jhalor in Marwar, whence they immigrated to Gujarat. Most of them act as family priests to Jharola Vanias.

JINGAR (5,264).—A sub-caste of Mochi.

JOGI.—Same as Ravalia, q. v. They cannot trace their descent from any single caste, as they are a conglomeration of the descendants of such *Atits* or ascetics who have returned to secular life and formed a new caste.

KABULI.—Afghan settlers and itinerant traders from Kabul. They are a muscular well-made race. A Kabuli wears a country scarf, *dupatta*, wound round the head, a loose shirt of white cloth, a second scarf thrown round the shoulders, a pair of striped or white cotton trousers, very loose above and gathered at the instep, and native shoes. Most of them are traders dealing in horses, fruit, asafœtida, shawls, etc.

Kachhia (8,029).—The caste of market growers, from *katchha*, a vegetable garden. They are said to be originally Kanbi or Koli cultivators who took to the growing of garden produce and formed a separate caste. They are of three divisions in North Gujarat and four divisions in South Gujarat. The three North Gujarat divisions are Ajvalia (5,236), Andharia (1,328) and Khambhati (63), of which the Andharias are the lowest in social rank. Ajvalia and Khambhati eat together, but do not intermarry. The four South Gujarat divisions are Ahmedabadi (497), Khambhar (776), Khatri (3) and Mali (1), of which Ahmedabadi rank the highest. The four divisions neither eat together nor intermarry. In addition to growing garden produce, Kachhias are also bricklayers, hand-loom weavers, carpenters, sawyers and shop-keepers. In religion, they are Bijpanthi, Swaminarayan or Vallabhachari. The Andharia and Khatri Kachhias are like the Matia Kanbis, followers of Imam Shah and observe half-Hindu, half-Mahomedan rites. They fast on *Ramjan* and visit Pirana instead of Hindu places of pilgrimage. Children are married before they are ten years old. Marriage ceremonies do not differ from those of Lewa Kanbis. Marriages are not allowed among relations on father or mother side. Widow marriage and divorce are allowed. The dead are burnt and *shradha* ceremonies are performed. They have a *patel* who settles caste disputes in a meeting of the caste.

KADIA.—It is an occupational name sometimes wrongly returned as a caste name by bricklayers who belong to Kachhia, Gola, Chhipa, Sathawara, Kanbi, Koli and other castes.

Kadia-Kumbhar (45).—Those Kumbhars who having taken to the work of bricklaying, consider themselves to be superior to the pot-making Kumbhars, and have formed a separate caste in Amreli.

Kadwa Kanbi (172,856).—A caste of cultivators. They are found in all the districts of the State but are most numerous in the Kadi District, which is their original home. They dine but do not intermarry with Lewa Kanbis. About their origin it is said that when Shankar went to perform austerities on Mount Kailasa, his consort Parvati to beguile the tedium of solitude, thought of creating some human beings. She thereupon created 52 males and females from the perspiration on her waist. Shiva being apprised of this by the sage Narad, returned from Kailasa and seeing these human beings enquired of Parvati as to how they came to be there. She told him plainly what she had done. This pleased Shiva so much that he allowed these beings to go to the earth and settle there under the name of Kadwa, as they had been created from the perspiration of the *ked* or waist. At the same time he gave them *kana*, grain and *bij*, seeds to maintain themselves; and so they came to be called Kadwa Kanbis. There is a temple of their patron goddess *Umia Mata* at Unja in the Kadi District. A curious marriage custom prevails among the Kadwa Kanbis. Once in every 9, 10 or 11 years, priests and astrologers connected with the temple of Umia Mata, fix a day on which marriages take place in the whole caste. Children about a year old and even unborn children are married. In the latter case the pregnant women walk round the *chori* on an understanding that, if their children are a boy and a girl, the couple will marry. If a suitable husband cannot be secured for a girl, she is married to a bunch of flowers. The flowers are afterwards thrown into a well or a river, and the girl, now a widow, can at any time be married according to the simple *natra* form. Sometimes a married man is induced, for a money consideration, to go through the form of marriage with a girl, and to divorce her as soon as the ceremony is over. The girl can then be married according to the *natra* form.

Widows marry, but not necessarily to the brother of the deceased husband. A husband can divorce his wife, but a wife cannot divorce her husband without his consent or after she has become a mother. Certain families of good birth hold the position of *shethia* or *patel*, which is a hereditary distinction and manage the affairs of the caste.

Kalal (1338).—Liquor sellers. Most of them were originally Kanbis or Rajputs, who were looked upon as degraded owing to their taking to this new profession and formed a separate caste.

* **Kalal** (106).—Descendants of converts from the Hindu class of the same name.

Kamalia (90).—They are worshippers of Behecharaji Mata in the Kadi District. They were originally Kanojia Brahmans, who were converted by Emperor Ala-ud-Din (A.D. 1297). Their name is derived from *kamal*, meaning perfect, the title given to their headmen when converted to Islam. They do not circumcise and except that they brand a dead man's breast and bury him, their ceremonies are Hindu. They marry and have children.

Kampani (6).—A Vania caste, from *kampan*, meaning a pair of scales, found only in the Kadi District. The name Kampani is said to have thus originated :—Years ago there were no correct scales in the province fit for the weighing of costly exciseable articles. Some enterprising parties, who set up accurate scales then obtained the exclusive right of weighing taxable goods. The monopoly continued till very lately and was done away with on the introduction of revised custom arrangements. Though originally an occupational term, the monopolists and their descendants came to be regarded as a separate caste as Kampani. **Kan.-Kas.**

Kanbi-Maratha (1,362).—A division of Marathas.

KANDOI.—An occupational name, meaning maker of sweetmeats. A Kandoi may be a Brahman, Vania or of any other clean caste. Though not a caste name, it is often returned as such by these people.

Kandolia (334).—A Brahman caste which takes its name from the village of Kandol near Than in Jhalavad. They act as family priests to Kapol and Sorathia Vanias and serve as cooks. Their family goddess is Samudri Mata.

KANKALI (232).—A sub-caste of Bahrot.

Kanojia or **Kanyakubja** (1042).—A caste of Brahmans from Upper India. They are a section of Sarvaria Brahmans, who came to be looked upon as degraded from their having accepted gifts.

Kansara (2,064).—Copper-smiths ; derive their name from *kansu* (bell-metal). They are found in most of the large towns except Sidhpur in the Kadi District, where there are no copper-smiths. The saying is "Copper will not melt in Sidhpur." They say that their original home was Pavaghad, twenty-nine miles east of Baroda. According to their story, five brothers lived at Pavaghad and were warm devotees of *Kalika Mata*, whom they worshipped by beating bell-metal cymbols. The goddess was so pleased with their devotion that she told them to make a living by "beating" metal. From beating brass they advanced to making brass, copper and bell-metal vessels. Their surnames are Bagaya, Barmeya, Bhatti, Gohel, Karkasariya, Parmar and Solanki. The tribal surnames of Bhatti, Gohel and Parmar show that Kansaras have some strain of Rajput blood. Kansaras belong to five divisions :—Champaneri (445), Maru (206), Shihora (20), Ahmedabadi (221) and Visnagara (1,101). None of the five divisions eat together or intermarry. Of the five divisions, the Maru or Marwari wear the sacred thread. In their look, dress and speech, Kansaras do not differ from Vanias and Kanbis. Kansaras hold a respectable position like Vanias and call themselves *Mahajan*. In religion they are Ramanandi, Shaiva and Vallabhachari, but hold their family goddess Kalika Mata in high reverence. Their great holiday is the bright ninth of *Aso*, on which day they perform in some of their settlements a sacrifice and at midnight dance and leap, holding a wreath of *karena* (oleander) flowers in one hand and a lighted torch in the other, and shouting *Palai ! Palai ! Palai !* One of the revellers, inspired by the goddess, professes to cut off his tongue with a sword. They visit the shrines of Ambaji, Behecharaji and Kalika. Their priests belong to many divisions of Brahmans--Audich, Mewada, Shrigod and Shrimali. Except among Visnagaras, widow remarriage is allowed. They have their own trade guild. In South Gujarat, an outsider who sets up a coppersmith's shop, pays Rs. 7 to the guild fund, Rs. 11, if he starts a pedler's business and Rs. 150 if he wishes to work in brass.

Kapil (12).—A caste of Brahmans. They say that they take their name from the Rishi Kapil, but are probably so called on account of their being originally residents of a village named Kavi in the Broach District where they are mainly found. In Baroda there are only a few Kapil families. They are chiefly cultivators.

Kapol (2,502).—A Vania caste. It traces its origin to Junaghad or Girnar. Kapols are chiefly found in the Amreli and Dhari Talukas of the Amreli District. They are not divided into Dasa and Visa. But they have divisions called Delvadia and Ghoghari, who interdine but do not intermarry. Their family priests are Kandolia Brahmans who take their name from Kandol near Than in Kathiawad. Their family goddess is *Samudri Mata*, whose chief shrine is at Samudri, a Dhangadra village, twenty miles from Than. Some of their families have settled in Bombay, where they hold a high place as merchants. They are Vaishnava Vallabhachari in religion.

Karadia (5,974).—A caste of Kanbi cultivators found in the Kodinar Taluka of the Amreli District. They are said to be originally Rajputs, and have such surnames as Zala, Vaghela, Rathod, Chohan, Parmar, Jadhav, &c. They have acquired their present name from their having paid *kar* or taxes to Government. They are agriculturists. Their females appear in public. They dine with Rajputs but marry among themselves. Widow marriage is allowed.

Karhada (1,265).—A caste of Brahmans from the Deccan. They are so called from their originally settling in the Karhat country, *i. e.*, the tract between Ratnagiri and Savantwadi State, called *Karahatta desh*. There is also another tradition about their origin, *viz.*, that they were made by Parashuram from camel's bones. The Karhadas were until recently supposed to be human sacrificers and even now, there are people, especially some Tailangi Brahmans who have scruples to take their meals at the house of a Karhada. Karhadas are invariably Rigvedi.

Kasai (380).—Butchers. They are of two classes, Gayakasai or beef-butchers and Bakkar-kasai or mutton-butchers. Both of them believe themselves to be of Rajput origin. Cow-killing butchers do not intermarry with goat-killing butchers. Their home tongue is Urdu in cities and Gujarati in villages. They marry only among themselves. They have a headman and a well-managed union with a common fund spent on mosques, feeding travellers and the poor. They are not held in good esteem. The proverb says "*na dekha ho bag, to dekho belai, na dekha ho thag, to dekho Kasai.*"

Kasar (78).—Deccani bangle sellers.

Kas.-Kha.

Kasbati (6,323).—Literally dwellers in towns. Some of them are the descendants of Baloch or Pathan mercenaries and others of Rajput converts. Their home language is Urdu mixed with Gujarati or Urdu only. Some of them hold grants of land and the rest are agriculturists or employed in Government service as sepoys, police constables, &c. Their women do not appear in public. They are Sunni in faith. The males have Pathan names as Jaferkhan, Sirdarkhan; and the females have such names as Laduibibi or Dulubibi. They give their daughters only to Musalmans but occasionally marry Hindu wives of the Rajput or Koli castes. At such marriages, the brides' friends occasionally call in a Brahman. In other cases the ceremony is entirely Musalman. They have no headman and do not form a distinct community.

Kathi (3,473).—A curious and interesting race found in Kathiawad. The cradle of this race is unknown, but it appears to have come from Central Asia, driven by the tide of Mahomedan invasion, through Sindh and Cutch in the 14th century. A party of them, under the leadership of Umro, came to Dhank, ruled by a Vala Rajput. Umro had a beautiful daughter named Umarbai with whom the Dhank chieftain Dhan Vala fell in love. Umro agreed to marry her with him on the condition that they should eat together. To this Dhan agreed, but his brethren considering him degraded, drove him out. He became the leader of the Kathis, and had by her three sons, Vala, Khuman and Khachar whose descendants bear their names and are considered the three noble tribes of Kathis. They are called Shakhayats, while the descendants of the original Kathis are called Avartias or inferior.

Kathis worship the Sun and use it as a symbol on all their documents. Owing to contact with Hindus, they worship Hindu gods and respect Brahmans. At funeral ceremonies, instead of feeding crows, they feed plovers and have a strong friendly feeling for them. They have adopted the Hindu feeling about the sacredness of the cow. They eat food cooked by any Hindu except the unclean ones and drink liquor. Widow marriage is allowed, but is seldom practised, except in the case of the deceased husband having a younger brother. In such a case, the rule is peremptory that he should marry his widow. They do not observe *sutak* like Hindus. Similarly women are not segregated as among the Hindus at particular seasons.

Kathodia (522).—An early tribe found in the Navsari District. It has four sub-divisions: Helam, Jadu, Pawar and Sindhi. The Kathodias found in the State belong to the last class and are the most degraded. They are black in colour and go about almost naked. They are labourers and catechu makers. They worship the Bhil *Dev*. They pay no respect to Brahmans and never make use of their services. Boys and girls generally marry after they are fifteen years old. *Khandhadiya* system prevails. Polygamy and widow marriage are allowed and practised. The dead are burned. A funeral feast is given by those who can afford to do so. They raise no tomb-stone and no other ceremonies in honour of the dead. They have a headman and a caste committee.

Kayastha (523).—A caste having its headquarters in Surat. Most of them found in the State are immigrants for service. Gujarat Kayasthas claim descent from Chandra Gupta and appear to be of the same stock as the Kayasthas of Bengal. Of the twelve branches of Bengal Kayasthas, only three, Valmiki, Mathur and Bhat Nagar, are found in Gujarat. The three divisions neither dine together nor intermarry in Gujarat, but they are said to do so in Bengal.

Valmiki Kayastha (432) much resemble the better class Brahmans, such as Nagars. They are strict vegetarians. Owing to their fondness for show and pleasure, they are called *lalaji* or *lala lok*. They belong to the Vallabhachari sect. Early marriage was formerly the rule, but now boys are not married before 18 and girls before 14. There is no headman in the caste. Social disputes are settled at a general meeting of the community.

Mathur Kayastha (19) are found in Baroda and Navsari Districts. They are so called from Mathura, their original home. They came to Gujarat with the Mughal Viceroys as their clerks and interpreters. Thirty or forty years ago, they spoke the Hindustani language in their houses, but now speak Gujarati. In religion, they are Ramanuji, Vallabhachari or Shaiva. Clerkship is the hereditary calling of the class, but some are now landlords. They look like ordinary Vanias. They have no headman. Social disputes are settled by the majority of the caste present at a meeting.

Bhat Nagar Kayastha (10) are found in Baroda like the other Kayasthas. They came originally from North India where they are still found in large numbers. They have two subdivisions called *Visa* and *Dasa*, of which Visa ranks higher. Visas formerly refused to eat food cooked by Dasas. They take Dasa girls in marriage, but do not give their girls to Dasa. They are Vallabhachari in religion. They have no headman. Caste disputes are settled by the majority of men present at a special caste meeting.

Kayatia (282).—A caste of degraded Brahmans. They are found all over Gujarat. They take their name from *kaltu* or *kayatu*, the eleventh day funeral ceremony which they alone conduct. In addition to their special duties, they act as family priests for such castes as Machhi, Mochi, etc.

Khadayata (39).—A Brahman caste, which like the Khadayata Vania caste, takes its name from Khadat, a village near Vijapur in the Kadi District. They act as priests of Khadayata Vanias.

Khadayata (2,777).—A Vania caste which takes its name from Khadat, a village near Vijapur. Khadayatas are found chiefly in Baroda and Kadi Districts. They are numerous in the Savli and Vaghodia Talukas. They are divided into Visa (1,232) and Dasa (1,543). Their family priests are Khadayata Brahmans and their family deity is *Kotyarkeshvar* of Khadat Mahudi near Vijapur in the Kadi District. They are Vallabhachari Vaishnava and have to pay large sums for marriageable girls. **Kha.**

Khalpa (32,210).—The name is derived from *khal*, outer skin. They are also known as Chamars or Chamadias from *charm*, skin. They are tanners and skin-dressers and are found all over Gujarat. They bear Rajput surnames and appear to be descendants of Rajputs degraded for following their unclean profession. In Northern Gujarat they rank below and in Southern Gujarat above Dheds. Their work is the tanning and colouring of leather, the making of leather buckets, bags and ropes, and the repairing of old shoes. The leather is chiefly made from the skins of buffaloes, bullocks and cows. With goat and sheep skins they have nothing to do. They bury their dead. They eat coarse grain, but have no scruples to eat flesh. Their priests are Garodas. They have a headman or *patel* in each village and settle all caste disputes by calling together five of their own body.

KHAMBHAR (776).—A sub-caste of Kachhias peculiar to the Kadi District. Their main occupation is that of selling vegetables.

Khant (2,743).—A caste of Kolis chiefly found in the Kadi and Amreli Districts.

Kharadi (116).—Turners. Found chiefly in the Baroda and Kadi Districts.

Kharva (2,073).—The name is derived from *kshâr vâha*, salt carriers. They are found mainly in the Baroda and Amreli Districts and are immigrants from Cambay. They claim Rajput descent and have such surnames as Chohan, Parmar, Jhala, Gohel, &c. Their tradition is that having taken to salt manufacture and seafaring, they were looked upon as degraded and were called Khârvâ. Besides Kharvas of Rajput descent there are those, especially in south Kathiawad, who have a strong infusion of Koli blood and have Talagia, Shihali and other Koli surnames.

Gujarat Kharvas have three sub-castes, called Surati, Hansoti and Khambhati. The Khambhatis rank the highest, and while marrying with Suratis and Hansotis, they do not give their own girls in marriage to them. Except those who belong to the Swaminarayan sect, all Kharvas eat fish and flesh and drink liquor. After the closing of salt works on the introduction of the Imperial salt duty in 1878, Cambay Kharvas have taken to house building, tile-turning and labour. They also make coir cords, brooms and mats. Except some Khambhati families, all Kharvas allow polygamy and widow marriage, especially with the deceased husband's brother (*diyarvatu*). *Shradhas* are performed.

KHARVA (2,128).—A sub-caste of Machhis. They eat together with Dhimar Machhis but do not intermarry.

* **Kharva** (240).—Hindu converts from the Bhoi and Kharva castes. They are also known as Machhis. They form two divisions, inland and coast Machhis. Both speak Hindustani and dress like ordinary Musalmans. The inland Machhis are fresh water fishers. The coast Machhis make long sea voyages. Each division marries only among its own members and has a union and headman.

Khatki (670).—They are Musalman tanners. They belong to the same class as Kasai and intermarry with them. They tan sheep and goat skins and in country places sell mutton. A section of them, like a section of Hindu Mochis, is called *Dhalgars*, shield-makers.

Khatri (3,395).—The caste of weavers ; found chiefly in all districts. They say that they belong to the Brahma-Kshatri stock and came into Gujarat from Sindh in the 16th and 17th centuries, tempted by the strong European demand for their cloth. Their regular features and fair complexion and the fact that they wear the sacred thread favour their claim to be of Brahma-Kshatri origin. The great veneration in which they hold the temple of *Hingalaj Mata* on the western border of Sindh, also points to some early connection with that province. Except that their widows remarry, their customs differ little from those of Vanias. Many in South Gujarat eat fish and drink liquor. By religion they are Vaishnava. Each community has its headman and settles its social disputes at a meeting of all the men of the caste.

* **Khatri** (121).—Descendants of converts to Islam from Hindu weavers of the same name. They marry only among themselves and have a union and headman.

Khavas (251).—Personal attendants. They are household servants in the families of Rajput, chiefs and landholders. They are also called Golas (Kathiawad), Hajuris (Rewakantha), Vajirs (Palanpur) and Lundas (Gujarat in general). In the Baroda State they are mostly found in the Amreli Prant. A Khavas may be of a Rajput, Koli, Musalman or Dhanka origin. They eat and marry with their caste people. In Cutch and Kathiawad, Khavas form a distinct community recruited from people of all castes. Originally Khavas and Golas were on the same footing, but the necessity of men of position for having around them a trusty set of servants led to the gradual elevation of the Khavas over the Golas and a Girasia may even take a Khavas girl in marriage if well dowered. Corresponding to male servants are Khavasans and Golis, who are also called Vadharans or Chhokris. Khavasans have an independence which is denied to Golis. They and their parents decide whether they are to take service and whether they will accompany their young mistresses, on their marriage into other families. The Golis are generally girls of illegitimate birth or are purchased from destitute parents. They are seldom married and are generally sent with their young mistresses as a portion of their dowry. Their intrigues with males swell the rank of Golas and Golis who in process of time rise to the rank of Khavas or Khavasans.

Khedaval (3,548).—A Brahman caste which takes its name from Kheda or Kaira, the headquarters of the British Kaira District. Their chief settlements are at Umreth in the Kaira District and Sojitra in the Baroda District. According to their tradition they are descended from a band of *Tripravari* and *Panchpravari* Brahmans who under the leadership of Shankar Joshi and Dave came from Shrirangapattam in Mysore and settled in Kaira during the reign of a certain Mordhvaj, a Rajput of the lunar stock. The truth of the story is supported by the fact that Khedavals are still connected with Shrirangapattam. Their females wear a necklace called *chitak* and ear-rings called *kap* of the same shape as those worn by Deccani Brahman women and like them their widows dress in white. Many Khedavals, some from Sojitra in the Baroda District and others from towns in the Kaira District, have settled in Madras, Bengal, the Central and the United Provinces. Most of them are jewellers and traders.

They are divided into *Baj* "outsiders" (2,493) and *Bhitra* "insiders" (798). It is said that the Kaira chief, anxious to have a son, once offered them cows of gold as gift. The greater number refusing the gift secretly scaled the walls of the city, and came therefore to be known as *bahya*, corrupted into *baj*. Those who accepted the gift remained within the walls and came to be called as *bhitra* or insiders. Even to this day, the Baj Khedavals look upon the non-acceptance of gifts by their ancestors with feelings of pride.

Khoja (1,961).—Literally meaning "honourable converts" are the descendants of Luhanas who were converted to Islam by the preachings of a Shiah preacher called Nur Satagur or Nur-ud-Din in the 12th century. Nur Satagur is said to have made a number of converts in Gujarat by ordering the idols of a Hindu temple to speak and bear testimony to the truth of his mission. In addition to adopting the name of Nur Satagur (teacher of pure light) he practised the Hindu abstraction or *samadhi*, which shows the process by which the first Ismalia preachers succeeded in converting the Hindus. The Luhanas were the first to be converted, and they who when Kshatriyas were called Thakkar, were called *Khavaja* (lord) after their conversion. A later element of strength in the Khoja community was the conversion of a race of Sun worshippers called *Chak* and other tribes in the Punjab and Kashmir. One of Nur Satagur's successor Rande, originally a Tuwar Rajput, sowed the seed of Ismalia faith in Cutch and Kathiawad.

On their first settlement in the towns of Gujarat, the Khojas were parched grain-sellers, fuel sellers and bricklayers. They now enjoy powerful position in all the trades. They are scattered all over Gujarat and are to be found in all important trade centres within and outside of India.

Khojas have many observances and customs differing from those of regular Musalmans. They observe the *chhathi* or sixth day ceremony after birth. Their marriage keeps a relic of the marriage by purchase, which they believe once obtained among them. The father of the bridegroom pays Rs. 5½ to the father of the bride which he hands over to the *jamat*. Like Hindus, they follow the Hindu law of inheritance.

The religion of the Khojas is "Shiah Ismailism." In order to present the Ismalia faith in an inviting form to the *Shakti* worshipping Luhanas, the first Ismalia missionary made some modifications in its doctrines. The *Mahdi* or unrevealed Imam of Alamut was preached to the Shaktipanthis as they looked for the tenth incarnation, the *Nikalanki* or stainless *avatâr*. The five Pandavas were the first five Ismailia pontiffs. The first Ismailia missionary Nur Satagur (A. D. 1163) was the incarnation of Brahma that appeared on earth next after Budhha. Among the Matapanthis, each of the four Yugas has its own preacher or *bhakta*. To the first epoch is assigned as *bhakta* Pralhad, to the second, Harischandra and to the third, Udhishthir. Instead of the fourth Balibhadra, Pir Sadruddin, the third Khoja missionary, added his own name. The four sacrifices of the four Yugas were confirmed, as were also confirmed the Ghat-Path Mantra or prayer and ritual of the Shaktipanthis. Instead of Shaktipanth, Sadruddin adopted the name of Satpanth or "True Doctrine" for his new faith. Sadruddin was not connected with the family of Aga Khan, the present religious head of the Khoja community by lineal descent, but is alleged to have been a disciple of his ancestor Shah Nazir. He said to Shah Nazir that on his return to India, he would declare Hazarat Ali, the first Imam to be *Nikalanki* or the tenth *avatar* and Shah Nazir his descendant. When Aga Khan's ancestors came and settled in India, the Khojas transferred their allegiance to them, they being believed to be the proper religious heads of their community and discarded the descendants of Saiyad Sadruddin Shah.

Originally the Khojas were a single body. But since about twenty years, they have split up into two factions called Panjaibhai and Pirai. The Panjaibhai section is the most orthodox body and look upon the Aga Khan as the representative of the Prophet or the incarnation of God himself. The Pirai, which is a very small division, consider Agha Khan merely a *pir* or religious head of their community and nothing more.

A Khoja has to pay his Imam the *dassonth* or tithe and the *petondh*, a smaller contribution and about sixteen other minor contributions, varying from a few annas to Rs. 1,000. Besides this when pressed for money, the Imam sends the *jholi* demanding an extraordinary levy of the *dassonth* and *petondh*. The regular dassonth, tenth part of income, is levied on each new moon day, each Khoja dropping in the *jholi*, kept in the *jamatkhana* for the purpose, as much as he is inclined to pay.

Khokhar (240).—Converted Rajputs of the Khokhar tribe. They claim Afghan extraction and are said to derive their name from *koh*, mountain, and *gir*, taker, because they once took an impregnable mountain fortress. They are landholders in Patan. As far as possible, they intermarry among themselves, but do not object to matrimonial connections with Babis, Lohanis and other Pathans. **Kho -Kol.**

KOHADA.—Same as Patanvadia Koli.

Kokani (1,666).—A Maratha Kanbi caste ; immigrants from Konkan.

Koknastha (3,214)—Also called Chitpavan. A Brahman caste, the members of which have immigrated from the Deccan mainly for the purpose of State service. The tradition about their origin is as under :—

When Parshuram, the sixth incarnation of Vishnu, had destroyed the Kshatriyas, he, to atone for that sin, granted the whole earth to the Brahmans in gift and brought out a strip of land for his own use from the sea. Having settled there, he once wanted to have some Brahmans for the performance of a *shradha* and a sacrifice, and sent emissaries in search of them ; but none came. This enraged him so much that he wished to create new Brahmans. With this idea uppermost in his mind, he went to the sea-shore for his morning bath and there found some fishermen standing near a funeral pyre (*chita*). He asked them who they were ; they replied they were *kaivartas* and lived on fishing. On this he granted them Brahmanhood and said that they would be known to the world as the Chitpavan Brahmans, since they had been purified near a funeral pyre.

They are also supposed by some to have migrated from the north-west of India, or from Egypt, and this supposition is based upon their colour. The celebrated family of the Peshwas belonged to this caste. Koknastha Brahmans are among the Maharashtra Brahmans what the Nagars are among the Gujarati Brahmans. Koknasthas are either *Rigvedi* or *Apasthamba*.

Kolgha (692).—They are one of the lowest of the early tribes, found in the Navsari District. Though reckoned impure, they neither eat with nor touch a Bhangi. The men's dress is a cap or scanty turban, a waist cloth and a loin cloth. The women wear two clothes, one thrown over the head and shoulders, the other wound round the waist. Of ornaments they have earrings, two or three solid brass bands on each arm and one or two coils of glass beads round the neck. Anklets are not worn. As a class they are very poor and at times live on roots or fast for two or three days together. They pay no respect to Brahmans and have no priests of their own class. On the sixth day after a birth, the goddess *chhathi* is worshipped. On marriage occasions the boy's father gives the girl's father Rs. 3 as dowry. Polygamy and widow marriage are allowed and practised. They have no headman. Social disputes are settled by the whole caste.

Koli (370,953).—A term applied to tribes that differ widely from each other. Some writers speak of them as aboriginals of the plain or civilized Bhils ; others find them so little unlike Rajputs as to lead to the conclusion that Kolis and Rajputs are in the main of the same stock. Bhils and Kolis of Eastern Gujarat are as hard to distinguish as are the Kolis and Rajputs of Western Gujarat. According to the author of the Bombay Gazetteer volume on Gujarat population, the explanation of this difference seems to be that the Mihiras or Gujjars, coming into Gujarat from the west, north-west and north-east, found the plain country held by Bhils. In central parts, the newcomers so dominated the earlier race that the result was a Koli hardly to be known from a Rajput. In the eastern parts, on the other hand, the newcome element was small and intermixture produced a Koli or half-blood who can hardly be known from a Bhil. Similarly the Kolis in the south had a later element so weak as to have but little affected the Dubla, Dhodia and other stocks with whom it mixed. Again in the north and west, when the struggles with the Musalmans set in, newcomers, classed under the general head of Rajputs, joining with the earlier settlements of Kolis, were in some cases absorbed by them and in others succeeded in raising the Kolis to their own level. Even now intermarriage goes on between the daughters of Talbada Kolis and the sons of Rajputs and the distinction between a Rajput and a Koli is one of rank than of race. Kolis are divided into several divisions, the principal of which are Chunvalia (7,707), Talbada (91,527), Baria (66,255), Patanvadia (22,263) and Thakarda (153,261). These classes are distinct and, as a rule, do not intermarry. Each class is divided into a number of sub-divisions or families and members of the same sub-division or family do not intermarry. Kolis used to live as robbers. Though they have now taken to husbandry and other callings, the love of thieving has not disappeared and they contribute the largest number of convicts in the State Jails. As husbandmen, they are inferior only to Kanbis. Kolis eat fish and flesh, but owing to poverty they are generally vegetarians. They worship all Hindu gods and goddesses, but specially *Khodiyar*, *Meladi* and *Verai Matas*. The Mahikantha Kolis regard the Mahi river as their family goddess. Some Kolis in the Navsari Taluka are *Matia, i. e.,* followers of the Pirana sect. Many Kolis are followers of Bijpanth and some follow the sects of Swaminarayan, Kabir and Ramsanehi. At the beginning of the present century, the Swaminarayan Acharyas are said to have reclaimed many Kolis from lives of violence and crime. Brahmans are respected by them and also used as priests. Their priests mostly belong to Shrimali or Audich castes of Brahmans. Kolis are superstitious and have a firm belief in spirits and spirit possession. They employ a *bhuvo* to exercise spirits.

Boys and girls are married after their twelfth year. The Rajput practice of marrying out of the clan is closely followed. Polygamy and widow marriage are allowed. Preference is given by a widow to her deceased husband's younger brother. A Koli can divorce his wife merely by a formal declaration to that effect in writing. A Koli woman can also abandon her husband, but in that case, she must return the *palla* or dowry settled on her at the time of marriage. As a rule, Kolis burn their dead, but children under eighteen months are buried. All questions relating to marriage are settled by a *panch* or committee of *agevans* or leaders of the caste.

Komti (3).—An immigrant Deccani caste preparing sacred threads and necklaces of beads.

Kokana (6,451).—An early tribe found in the Navsari District. They speak a mixed dialect of Marathi and Gujarati, and from their name seem to have passed into Gujarat from Konkan. They are labourers and cultivators. Some who from want of bullocks themselves drag the plough are called *hathodia* or hand-ploughmen. They worship *Brahm* and *Vaghdev*. Brahm, a stone placed near a *samdi* tree, is supplied with a clay horse, lampstand and flag. Vagh, a wooden pillar, with a tiger cut on it, is generally covered with *sindur*. Kokanas show no respect to Brahmans and never make use of their services as priests. The age for marriage is 16 to 20 for boys and 15 to 18 for girls.

The practice of *khandhadio* prevails. Polygamy is allowed and practised and widows marry again. A woman may leave her husband and go to live with another man on his agreeing to pay her husband the amount he spent as her dowry. The dead are cremated. Kokanas have a well-organised caste system. When a man suspects his wife of adultery, he calls a meeting of the tribe. The *panchayat* hears the charge, and, if proved, fines the adulterer. Part of the fine is spent in liquor and the rest is made over to the complainant as compensation.

Kotwalia (1,658).—An early tribe found in the Navsari District. They are dark in colour. The males put on a small *dhotar* and a turban only; the females cover their lower limbs with a small piece of cloth, and their head with another like piece. They put on a bodice only when they have to go to a large town. They put on bracelets of brass, anklets of tin, and necklaces of beads. Marriages among them take place by mutual selection and choice. When a boy and a girl have agreed to join in matrimony after their meetings on the roads or in the fields, the parents of the boy visit those of the girl and contract to pay from Rs. 4½ to 10 as her dowry, and fix a day for the marriage. On the day so fixed, the girl and her parents go to the boy's house, and there dance, eat and drink. At this time ornaments are given to the girl by her future husband, excepting anklets, which are given to her by her father. The next morning the girl and the boy are severally placed on the shoulders of two men who dance about, and then their hands are joined. This finishes their marriage. After this, all join in drinking liquor and toddy, and the girl's parents then depart to their house. Marriages with the children of a maternal uncle or a paternal aunt are legal with these people, but it is otherwise with the children of a mother's sister and of a brother.

In spite of this choice marriage, if the husband does not like his wife, he sends her away from his house; and if the contrary is the case, the wife returns the dowry paid to her and leaves him. This is the easy way of divorce with them. Remarriage is also prevalent among them.

The *khandhadio* system obtains among them. The Kotwalias either burn or bury their dead; but before doing so they place a small quantity of *kodri* and a pice in the mouth of the corpse. After disposing of the dead body, they drink and then separate; at the end of a year they place a *khatrun* in the spirit yard and worship it every year.

They have no other ceremonies; but 5 days after the birth of a child, they cowdung the house, drink liquor and toddy, and name the newly-born babe.

Kshatriya Maratha (14,785).—A section of Marathas.

Kumbhar (41,693).—Potters; the name is derived from *kumbhakar* (*kumbh*, a water pot and *kar*, maker); they are generally found in all cities and villages. In some places, they are called Ojhas and jocularly *prajapatis* (creaters). Some of them have Rajput surnames, such as Chavda, Rathod, Gohel, Solanki, &c., and show the usual pretensions to Rajput descent. They are divided into nine sub-castes as follows:—Gujjar (32,706), Lad (2,753), Maru (1,369), Ajmeri (291), Banda (6), Khambhati (830), Sami (165), Varia (2,096), and Vatalia (1,261). Besides working as potters, many of this caste are employed in villages as domestic servants and in towns have become carpenters or bricklayers. Those who have taken to carpentry or bricklaying, call themselves Sutar-Kumbhar or Kadia-Kumbhar and claim superiority over others. Marriage between near relations is prohibited. Widows remarry, the younger brother of a deceased husband has no particular claim. They live mostly on vegetable food, but some in south Gujarat take liquor and even eat flesh. Brahmans officiate at their ceremonies, and are treated on equal terms by other Brahmans. They burn their dead and perform *shradha*. Each division has its headman and settles social disputes at the meeting of all the men of the caste.

***Kumbhar** (667)—Descendants of Hindu converts from the Kumbhar caste. They are also called Karatia. They speak Gujarati. The men dress like poor Musalmans and women like Hindus, except that they wear silver bracelets of the Musalman pattern. They sell but do not make pots. The men work as labourers and servants. They marry among themselves and with Kathiaras or wood-cutters. With the Kathiaras, they form a *jamat*, union, and have a headman to settle disputes.

Kumbhar-Sutharia (1,328).—These are those Kumbhars who, having taken to carpenters' work, consider themselves to be superior to pot-making Kumbhars, and have formed a separate caste. **Kum.-Luh.**

Lad (8,500).—A Vania caste ; next to Shrimalis and Porwads, Lads are the most numerous in the Vania population of the State. They are found chiefly in Baroda and Dabhoi. They take their name from *Lat-desh*, the old name of South Gujarat, that is the country south of the Mahi river. They are divided into Visa (4,414) and Dasa (4,086). Their family priests are Khedaval Brahmans and their family deity is *Ashapuri Mata* near Petlad. Their old names ended in *rai* and *pal* instead of in *das* or *lal* as at present, as Kalianrai, Dhanpal, &c. They are Vallabhachari Vaishnav.

LAD (2,753).—A sub-caste of Kumbhars.

Lewa Kanbi (184,810).—A caste of landlords and cultivators. They are found all over the State, but are most numerous in the Baroda District. Kanbi is a descriptive term for the big functional group of husbandmen. Gujarat Kanbis claim to be of Kshatriya stock. There is now no doubt that they are Gujjars and came from the Punjab. Socially they are divided into Patidars or shareholders in the village lands and Kanbis or cultivators. As a general rule, Kanbis allow widow marriage, but Patidars, in imitation of the Brahmans and Vanias, do not allow it. Patidars eat with Kanbis and even take their daughters in marriage, if endowed with a good dowry. Patidars of 13 villages in the Charottar (7 under Baroda, 5 under Kaira and 1 under Cambay) are considered *kulin* and are hypergamous to the rest. They do not give their girls in marriage outide these villages, but take as wives girls from any village. They not only exact large dowries from other Patidars wishing to give them their daughters in marriage but also practise polygamy. Within the last twenty years, there has been a change in the general attitude of the caste towards kulin Patidars, and in most of the villages *ekda* or solemn agreements have been made to eschew the kulins and to give and take in marriage only in their own social circle. There is no headman and no caste government, except among the Kanbis and Lewa Patidars of some villages.

LIMACHIA (21,450).—A sub-caste of Hajams.

Lingayat Vania (32).—Immigrants from the Deccan. A section of the Lingayats, who after relinquishing the caste system have again reverted to it.

Lodh (4).—Cultivators and labourers found in the Baroda City and Kadi and Amreli Districts.

Lonia (49).—A caste of labourers from Upper India.

Luhana (11,588).—A corruption of Lohana. They are said to derive their name from Lohanpur or Lohokat in Multan and were originally Rathod Rajputs. They were driven by the Musalmans from the Punjab into Sindh and afterwards, in the 13th century, found their way to Cutch, Kathiawad and Gujarat. In Sindh they eat flesh, are addicted to spirituous liquors, do not object to eat fish and onions and drink water from the hands of their inferiors as well as superiors in caste. Tod (Annals of Rajasthan, 292) says :—" Of the Lohanas tbe proverb runs—' Except cats and cows they will eat anything.' " In Cutch they still use animal food, but in Kathiawad and Gujarat they neither eat flesh nor drink spirits. Gujarat and Kathiawad Luhanas do not therefore regard those of Cutch and Sindh as belonging to their caste. Luhanas are Vaishnava of Vallabhachari and Ramanuji sects. Their family goddess is *Randel Mata*, and they are devout worshippers of Darya Pir, the spirit of the Indus, who is said to have saved them when they fled from Multan. They wear the sacred thread and allow polygamy and widow marriage. Their customs do not differ from those of the Bhatias. Their family priests are Saraswat Brahmans. They have a headman (*patel*) but give him no personal authority. Social disputes are settled according to the opinion of the majority of the members.

Luhar or **Lavar** (19,212).—Blacksmiths, from Sanskrit *lohkar*. They are found in cities and large villages. According to their account they are the descendants of one Pithvo, who was created by Parvati out of the dust clinging to Shiva's back, to prepare weapons in Shiva's war against the demons Andhkar and Dhundhakar. They have such surnames as Chavda, Chohan, Dodia, Sirohia, etc., which show that some Rajputs also must have taken to their calling. There are 13 main divisions in this caste, who neither eat together nor intermarry. They are Gujjar (12,177), Bhavnagari (266), Panchal (1,173), Sirohia (107), Surati (176), Chokia (51), Dali (30), Khambhati (1,350), Lodhaghada (47), Rupaghada (43), Pithva (2,910) and Parajia (332). Panchal Luhars claim to be Brahmans, who were degraded owing to their taking to the blacksmiths' profession, and in the present Census some returned themselves as Panchal Brahmans. Luhars are strict vegetarians, except in South Gujarat where they privately eat flesh and fish and drink liquor. In blowing the bellows and in the lighter part of the work, the Luhar is helped by the women of his family. The competition of European ironware has forced Luhars to give up their original calling and become silversmiths, carpenters, watch repairers, etc., and in some cases field-labourers. In return for mending field tools, the villagers pay a Luhar in grain at harvest time. Marriage between near relations is avoided. Divorce and remarriage are allowed. Luhars belong to many religious sects, such as Kabirpanthi, Swaminarayan, Ramanadi, etc. Their priests, belong to many divisions of Brahmans, who are known as *Luhar Gors* and are despised by other Brahmans.

* **Luhar** (46).—Musalman blacksmiths. They are mostly immigrants from Sindh. The men dress like Memons with a Musalman turban, coat and trousers. The women dress like

Hindus. They make knives, nut-crackers, spear-heads and daggers. They are Sunnis in religion. They marry with other Musalmans and have no separate headman or union.

Machhi (2,542).—The caste of fishers. They are found chiefly in sea-board towns and villages. They appear to be Kolis, deriving their present name from their occupation of catching and living by the sale of *machha*, from Sanskrit, *matsya*, a fish. They have two divisions, Machhi proper and Koli Machhi, who eat together but do not intermarry. In the Navsari District, there is also a colony of Deccani fishermen called Dhebras or Dhimars (Sanskrit *dhivar*, a fisherman) who dine with the Machhi sub-divisions. Machhis eat fish and flesh, but eschew beef and pork. Besides catching fish, they ply boats for hire, sell vegetables, turn tiles, cultivate and work as labourers. Koli Machhis are very enterprising and serve as *malams* (navigators) and *nakhudas* (captains) on country crafts and steamboats. The fisherman's favourite goddesses are *Shikotri* and *Hinglaj*. They employ Brahman priests, who as Machhi Gors are looked upon as degraded. They have a headman in each village. Caste disputes are settled according to the opinion of the community assembled in a meeting.

* **Machhi** (79).—Musalman fishers found in the Amreli District.

Mahar (703).—Deccani Dheds.

Maithil (2).—A caste of Brahmans from the Province of Maithil.

Makarani (566).—Foreigners from Makran coast. They wear the hair very long and tie them in a knot at the top of the head. They part the beard, and tie the ends behind the head. Their women are generally of Gujarati descent. They speak mixed Hindustani and Gujarati. They are brave and serve as watchmen. Their women do not appear in public. In religion, they are Sunnis. They have no community or headman.

Makvan (2,015).—A caste of Kolis. From being landlords, they have fallen to be servants and peasant proprietors.

* **Makvana** (79).—Converts from the Makvana tribe of Rajputs or Kolis, who are found in the Kadi District. They wear the hair long and keep the beard parted from the middle and tie it behind the ears. Their home language is Hindustani. Their females do not appear in public. They are Sunnis in faith. Their sons marry either into Musalman, Makwana or Koli families; and their daughters into Musalman families of the Makvana, Babi or Pathan tribes. They employ a Brahman priest at their weddings. They have no headman and no caste organization.

Mali (H. 2,783; M. 3).—A caste of gardeners resembling Kanbis in appearance and dress. They are gardeners and flower sellers. In the Kadi District, they are ministrants in Jain temples and domestic servants. They are vegetarians. In religion, they are Kabirpanthi, Ramanuji, Vallabhachari, Swaminarayan or Jain. Their birth, marriage, pregnancy and death customs do not differ from those of Kanbis. Marriage between near relations is forbidden. Widows are allowed to remarry. The widow of the elder brother marries his younger brother. Divorce is granted. Mali women are of easy virtue. Social disputes are settled by a few of the elders of the caste.

Malik or Malek (7,519).—They are converted Hindus. Their home tongue is Gujarati in North Gujarat and Hindustani in South Gujarat. They are landlords, cultivators and constables. In their marriage and other customs, they do not differ from other converted Rajputs.

Mang (122).—A wandering criminal tribe, found mainly in the Baroda and Navsari Districts. They make baskets and winnowing fans. Socially they are the lowest. They never make use of a Brahman's services nor pay him any respect. Among them, is a class of men called *Bhats* who claim to be of Brahman descent and act as their priests. Except the dog, cat and ass, they eat all animals. Polygamy and widow marriage are allowed and practised. The Mangs bury the dead. A silver image of the dead is kept in the house and in front of the image, every seven or eight days, a lamp is lighted. Some men with the title of *patel* are chosen to settle social disputes. A man guilty of breaking caste rules is fined and the money spent in drink.

Maratha (16,147).—An immigrant caste from the Deccan. It has two divisions, Maratha Kshatriya (14,785) and Maratha Kanbi (1,362), of which the former is hypergamous to the latter, but was not originally distinct. Maratha Kshatriyas support their claim to social superiority over Maratha Kanbis, by favouring infant marriages, forbidding the remarriage of widows and wearing the sacred thread. The Kanbi on the other hand does not claim to be a Kshatriya, allows both adult marriages and the remarriages of widows and wears no thread to indicate the twice-born status. The dividing line between the Kanbi and the Maratha is not of the nature of a permanent barrier, such, for instance, as that which exists between the Shenavi and Deshastha Brahmans. The Marathas proper are allowed to marry the daughters of the Kanbis. The latter would not ordinarily secure a daughter in marriage from their social superiors. The difficulty however is frequently surmounted by a well-to-do Kanbi, who rises to the higher rank as his means increase, and if common report is to be believed, adopts the title of Kshatriya with the sacred thread and its restrictions on adult and widow marriage. The superior division is supposed to consist of ninety-six families or *kula*, such as Surve, Bhonsle, Ghorpade, Salunke, Sitole, Chavan, etc. The bearers of the best name among the ninety Kulas are undoubtedly of Rajput origin. In 1836, the Raja of Satara sent a Shastri to the Rana of Udaipur to make inquiries regarding the origin of the Bhonsles, a leading Maratha family. The Rana sent a word that the

Bhonsles and his family were one and despatched with a messenger, Raghunathsing Zale, a letter to the same effect written by Raja Shahu in A. D. 1726 to Vaghaji Sisode of Pimple in Mewar (Udaipur). Raghunathsing is reported to have satisfied himself by inquiry at Satara of the purity of blood of certain Maratha families, *viz.,* Bhonsle, Savant, Khanvilkar, Ghorpade, Chavan, Mohite, Nimbalkar, Shirke, Salunke, Mane, Jadhav, and several others. At the same time, it has to be borne in mind that several Maratha families have *kuldevak* or totems which cannot be reconciled with a pure Rajput origin. Sun flower, *kadam* tree, the mango, the conch shell and the peacock's feather are examples of these totems which are rapidly falling into oblivion but are still worshipped on the occasion of marriages and when a new house is occupied for the first time. (Bombay Census Report, p. 183).

Maru (456).—A caste of Kanbis. Originally Malis, who after taking to agriculture assumed the name of Kanbi Maru.

Mathur (19).—A sub-caste of Kayasthas.

Matia (403).—A caste of Kanbis mostly found in the Baroda and Navsari Districts. They were originally Lewa Kanbis, who came to be called *Matia*, because they followed the *mat* or doctrine of the *Pir*. About 300 years ago, a company of Lewa Kanbis on their way to Benares, put up at Pirana, where the saint Imamshah prevailed upon them to abstain from the hardships of a journey saying that he would show Benares to them there. This miracle he is said to have performed, and then these Kanbis looked upon him and accepted him as their holy saint. They thus acquired many Musalman customs and observances and had to separate from the Lewa Kanbis. They are strict vegetarians eating neither fish nor flesh and drinking no spirits. They also do not use asafœtida, garlic, and onions. They follow the Atharva Veda and call themselves *Satpanthi*. They worship the tombs of Musalman saints whose mausoleums are at Pirana, Navsari, Ahmedabad and Burhanpur. Their sacred book is a collection of religious precepts called *Shiksha Patri* made by Imamshah, the saint of Pirana. Some of them learn this book by heart and are called *Kaka* or devotee. A family of the *Kakas* officiates at a temple at Kukas in the Sinore Taluka. Matias have three religious divisions, *Panchia* or followers of Surabhai's mausoleum, originally managed by five devotees; *Satia* or followers of Baba Mahomed's mausoleum, originally managed by seven devotees; and *Athia* or followers of Bakr Ali's mausoleum, originally managed by eight devotees. Except in being called by different saints, these divisions do not differ in belief or in practice. Matias keep *Ramjan* fast and observe as holiday the *Uras* or saint's day. Besides Musalman holidays, they observe as days of fasting, *Holi*, *Akhatrij*, *Divaso*, *Balev* and *Divali*. Their chief places of pilgrimage are Navsari, Vemar, Pirana and Burhanpur. Widow marriage is allowed, the widow of a man marrying his younger brother. Divorce is lawful. A bachelor cannot marry a widow or a divorced woman without first undergoing a mock marriage with the *shami* tree (*Prosopis Spicigera*). Matias bury their dead. They have no headman. Caste disputes are settled by the leading men. Fines inflicted on the offenders, are used in purchasing vessels for the caste's use or are sent as presents to the saint's shrines.

From 1880 there has been a split among the Matias. Through the preaching of an ascetic called Nirmaldas, who told them of their Lewa Kanbi origin, some 200 families calling themselves Vaishnava Matias formed themselves into a separate caste as distinguished from the Pirana Matias. The seceding or Vaishnava Matias have joined the Ramanandi and Dadupanthi sects. They worship images of *Ranchhodji* or *Dwarkanathaji* and go on pilgrimage to Benares, Mathura, etc. Vaishnav and Pirana Matias do not eat together. The Vaishnav Matias have abandoned all Musalman customs, call Brahmans to officiate on marriage and other occasions and in all respects live like Lewa Kanbis. But Lewa Kanbis do not dine with them.

Mavchi (989).—A forest tribe found in the Navsari District. Those who came to Baroda as grooms are known as Bavcha.

Meghwal.—Same as Shenva.

Meher or **Mer** (9).—From Sanskrit, *mihir*, fish, are the fish-bannered race found chiefly in the Porbunder State in Kathiawad. They claim to be Rajputs and are divided into five clans who intermarry. They allow widow remarriage, but in other respects follow Rajput customs. Generally speaking, their faces are refined and pleasing. They dress after the fashion of Bharvads. They are abstemious in their habits and live on millet bread and curds. They seldom eat meat. Their disputes are settled by a meeting of elders.

Memon (13,540).—A corruption of *muamin* or believers, a name given to the descendants of Musalman converts from the Hindu castes of Luhanas and Kachhias. The conversion first took place in the middle of the 15th century in Sindh under the persuasion of one Saiyad Eusuf-ud-Din Kadri, a descendant of a saint in Bagdad. At that time, Manekji, the head of the eighty-four *nukhs* of the Luhana community, was in favour at Nagar-thatha in the court of a Samma ruler named Markat Khan. Markat Khan became a follower of the Saiyad and Manekji, his two sons and 700 other Luhana families followed their ruler's example. On conversion, the saint changed the name of the community to Muamin or believers. Before leaving Sindh, he blessed his people,—a blessing to which the Memons trace their fruitfulness and success in trade. From Sindh, the Memons spread to Cutch and Kathiawad and are now to be found in all important towns in India and also in Burma, Siam, Singapur, Java and East Africa. They wear the moustaches short, according to the *sunnat* (practice) of the Prophet and the beard about six inches long at the most. Most of them shave the head. Both males and females blacken their eyelids with collyrium. Memon women redden their palms, fingers and finger nails and their soles and toes with henna. Memons are fond of costly clothes. The men are fond of gold embroidery and the women of gay colours. They are great eaters and fond of good cheer. They have two divisions, Kachhi and Halai. The Kachhis are the descendants of market gardening Luhanas of Sindh and the Halai from Halar. From Halai, there have been three offshoots called *Dhoka* (belonging to Dholka), *Bhavnagari* (from Bhavnagar) and *Veravda* (from Veraval). The Halai Memons are darker and smaller than the Kachhi Memons, with whom they never intermarry. In spite of the Sindh strain in the Kachhi and the Kathiawadi strain in the Halai, the speech of both the divisions is fundamentally the same. Contact with Urdu-speaking Musalmans has given all Memons colloquial knowledge of Urdu. Both are Sunnis of the Hanafi School. As a class, they are religious, though some of them, especially the Kachhi, keep to their former non-Islamic social usages. The most notable of these is their refusal to allow their daughters and widows any inheritance. They are very fond of performing pilgrimage to Mecca and about 50 per cent. of them have the honourable prefix of *Haji* or pilgrim. They believe in astrology and consult astrologers, a practice condemned by the Prophet. The religious head of the Kachhi Memons lives at Mundra in Cutch. He pays his followers a yearly or two yearly visit when a money subscription called *kheda*, from Rs. 2 to Rs. 200, is gathered from every Memon family and is paid to the *Pir*. Besides having a high priest in Sarhind in the Punjab, who visits his Gujarat followers every five years, the Halai Memons have a provincial head or Mukhi at Dhoraji in Kathiawad. He hears and passes orders in marriage and divorce matters and sometimes in inheritance cases.

MESHRI.—A general term applied to Vanias of Vaishnava persuasion.

Mewada (1,692).—A Vania caste found chiefly in Baroda, Kadi and Navsari Districts in this State and also in Kaira and Surat in British Gujarat. Mewada Vanias are said to have come from Mewar and are divided into Visa (1,162) and Dasa (493). They are partly Vallabhachari Vaishnava and partly Jains. Their priests are Mewada Brahmans.

Mewada (4,824).—A Brahman caste which, as its name indicates, originally came from Mewad in Rajputana. Mewadas are divided into three classes, Bhat (1,560), Chorasi (851), and Trivedi (2,275). These three interdine, but do not intermarry. They are mostly beggars, family priests and peasants. There is a curious custom among the Trivedi Mewadas. Before marriage, the bridegroom reposes on a cot and the bride applies molasses to his navel. After this, the bridegroom goes to the marriage hall.

Mir or **Merasi** (310).—Literally lords, also called Langha (singers), Dholi (drum-players), Dadhi and Dom, are found chiefly in the Kadi District. In the rainy season, they work as cultivators. In the fair season, the men move about begging, singing and telling tales and playing on the drum, the fiddle, and the tambourine. Their women, who dress like Hindus, stay at home and under the name of Domni and Langha, attend Mahomedan houses at marriage and other feasts and play and sing before the women. They marry only among themselves and with their Saiyad as their head form a well managed community.

Mochi (H. 8,715; M. 239).—Leather workers. They are found in towns and in most of the villages. According to their own account, they were Rajputs living near Champaner, who got their present name, because one of them made a pair of stockings or *moju* out of a tiger's skin. Traces of their Rajput descent appear in their tribal surnames: Chohan, Chudasma, Dabhi, Gohel, Jhala, Makvana, Maru, Parmar, Rathod, Solanki and Vaghela. Their local divisions are Ahmedabadi, Khambhati, and Surati, who eat together but do not intermarry. Besides being divided according to their settlements, they have split up into many sections, according to their callings. The chief of these craft sections are Chandlagara or makers of lac spangles (1,568), Rasania or electro-platers (123), Chitara or painters (77), Minagara or workers in enamel (391), Panagara or gold and silver foil-makers (250), Pakhari or makers of ornamental horse hangings (41), Netragara or makers or idols' eyes (50), Jingara or saddlers (5,264), Dhalgar or shield makers (5) and Sikligara or grinders (18). The different sub-divisions eat together, but those Mochis who have left off working on leather, and especially the Chandlagaras, Chitaras and Rasanias have, of late, separated into separate castes and raised themselves to the level of bricklayers, carpenters, masons and other artisans. The Mochi holds a low position in social scale, and though he does not touch Khalpas, Dheds or other depressed classes, a high caste Hindu considers the touch of a Mochi a pollution. Mochis used to eat fish and flesh, but of late years, owing to many of them becoming followers of Swaminarayan, the use of flesh and liquor has grown less and in some places has ceased.

In all their ceremonies, they employ Brahman priests, who are called Mochi Gors and are despised by other Brahmans. Girls are married before ten and boys at any age after eight. Polygamy is allowed and divorce is granted. Widow remarriage is allowed. The offputting of a Mochi has passed into a proverb "*Saini sanj ane Mochinu vahanu*" (the tailor's to-night and the shoe-makers's to-morrow morning). As a caste, Mochis are generally unambitious. The proverb "*Mel karrata Mochina Mochi*". (Even if sawn in two, a Mochi remains a Mochi) illustrates that they are quite satisfied with their lot. The proverb has its origin in the following tradition:—It is said to have been the belief in olden times, that if a man got himself sawn in two at Benares, he would get the position he wishes at his next birth. Accordingly a Mochi went to Benares and desired to be sawn in two. The person in charge of the sacred saw asked him what caste he would like to have at his next birth. He pondered for a while and came to the conclusion that the caste of Mochi was preferable to all others, and openly declared "*Mel Karvat Mochina Mochi.*" The moral usually deduced from this is that each generally likes his own caste.

Each sub-division of the caste has its headman. Social disputes are settled at a meeting of all men of the caste.

Modh (8,800).—A Brahman caste, so called from Modhera, once an important place in the Chansma Taluka, Kadi District. They are divided into five classes—Agiarasana (1,171), Chaturvedi (6,394), Dhinoja (759), Jethimal (48), and Trivedi (70). These neither interdine nor intermarry. There is a great difficulty in obtaining wives in this caste, in consequence of the large amount to be paid to the bride's father. All the five sub-divisions are to be found in the State, the Chaturvedi who are proficient in the four Vedas, the Trivedi, who know three, the Jethi who are wrestlers, the Dhinoja, who live at Dhinoj in the Chansma Taluka and the Agiarasana, who are found in Baroda and Amreli Districts. The Dhinojas were till the last century, professional thieves and murderers and their depredations spread far and wide.

Modh (3,560).—A Vania caste which derives its name from Modhera in the Chansma Taluka of the Kadi District. Modh Vanias form an important element in the Vania community and are found in all the Districts. They are also found in Malwa, where some of them seem to have, emigrated from Modhera, while others migrated to Adalaj, Gogha and other places in Gujarat, when Ala-ud-Din's army invaded Gujarat in 1298 A. D. Modh Vanias are divided into six different sub-castes, each of which keeps itself aloof from the rest, and illustrates how castes are sub-divided in Gujarat. The main divisions are *Adalja* (76), from Adalaj near Ahmedabad; *Goghava* from Gogha and *Mandaliya*, from Mandal, formerly a place of consequence about 48 miles north-west of Ahmedabad. All the divisions are sub-divided into Visa (1,109) and Dasa (2,203). Goghava and Adalja intermarry in Kathiawad and Cutch, but not in Gujarat proper. At the wedding of Modh Vanias, a sword and a flywhisk are used which suggest a Rajput origin. But no trace of tribal surnames remains. They are Vallabhachari Vaishnavas. Malwa Modhs used to allow widow remarriage so late as in the 17th century. They appear to have however given it up in imitation of the Deccani Brahmans, who accompanied the Maratha invaders and settled in Malwa.

The large class of oilmen, known in Gujarat as Modh Ghanchi, were originally Modh Vanias, who by taking to making and selling oil were considered as degraded and now form a separate caste.

Molesalam (8,966).—Converts to Islam, made from among the Rajputs, chiefly in the reign of Mahmad Begada (A. D. 1459-1513). The name is derived from *Maula-Islam*, meaning masters in Islam. When an infidel was converted to Islam, it was the custom to call him *Maula*. Molesalams dine with other Musalmans, and though they sometimes take flesh, ordinarily they eat vegetables like Hindus. A Molesalam will marry his daughter to a Shaikh, Sayad, Mughal or Babi, but not, as a rule, to Musalmans of the lower order. The son of a chief may get a Rajput girl in marriage. But other Molesalams marry either among their own people or the poorer classes of Musalmans. They employ *kazis* and *maulvis*, but also maintain their old Brahman family priests and support Bhats and Charans.

Momna (7,183).—From *momin* (believers) they are the descendants of Hindus of many castes converted to the Shiah form of the faith by different members of the Ismaliya Saiyads, of whom Imamshah of Pirana was the most distinguished. Most of them on Palanpur side shave the head and wear the beard, but those on the Ahmedabad side, keep the *choti*, shave the face and look like Kanbis. They put on their old Kanbi turbans. Their females dress like Hindus. Almost all eat flesh, but those living in the Kanam tract of the Baroda District are strict vegetarians. Instead of the *Koran*, they read Imamshah's book of religious rules and also worship Hindu gods. Circumcision is practised and the dead are buried. Both males and females have Hindu names. In addition to Musalman marriage, the Kanam Momnas call in a Brahman and go through the Hindu ceremony. Like Hindus, women wail and beat the breast at deaths. Palanpur and Baroda Momnas do not intermarry. Each settlement has its union, headman and code of rules, which are generally well kept.

Motala (30).—A caste of Brahmans. It takes its name from Mota, a village about 16 miles south-east of Surat. The Motala, Jambu and Kapil Brahmans are said to have come to Gujarat from the Deccan about the same time. About a century ago, intermarriages took place between the Motala and Jambu Brahmans. In addition to their appearance, their practice in four points is the same as that of Deccani Brahmans and supports the tradition that the Motala Brahmans came from the Deccan. Their *kuldevi* is the Kolhapur Maha Lakshmi. At the time of marriage and four days after, the bride keeps her head uncovered and fastens the end of her *sadi* from left to right. The marriage wrist cord is made of wool instead of cotton thread. They belong to the *Kanva Shakha*. In the last three points, the practice of the Jambu and Kapil Brahmans is also the same. One peculiar custom among the Motala Brahmans is that marriages take place on the same day every fourth year. They are very intelligent and are chiefly engaged as clerks in Government and private offices.

Mughal (1,054).—They are of two distinct classes, the Persian and the Indian Mughals. Persian Mughals are the descendants of Persian political refugees and merchants. They form a distinct community and generally marry among themselves. They are chiefly found in cities.

The second or Indian Mughals are the descendants of the Mughal conquerors of India and are found in all parts of the State. Like the Persian Mughals, the men place the title of *Mirza* (born of a great man) before their names and add *Beg* (lord) after them, as Mirza Mahomed Beg. The women add *Khanam* to their names, as Hussaini Khanam. In appearance they do not differ from ordinary Musalmans. In religion, they are Sunnis. They are occupied as cultivators, constables and sepoys.

Multani (49).—Musalman immigrants from Multan. They were originally Hindus who left the Punjab during the early Mahomedan invasions and settled in Gujarat. They are said to have been converted in the reign of Mahmad Begada (A. D. 1459-1513). They add Khan to their names and are soldiers, tailors, shoe-makers or servants. As far as possible, they marry among themselves and hold a low position among Musalmans.

Nagar (7,990).—A caste of Brahmans. They claim to be the highest among the Brahman castes of Gujarat. As a rule Gujarati Brahmans do not intermarry, but they have no objection to interdine, except with those Brahmans who are considered as degraded. But Nagars neither intermarry nor interdine with other Brahmans. They rank themselves above all other Brahmans and are undoubtedly a shrewd and intelligent people. They have an engaging address and their women are comely. By their tact, skill and intelligence, they always advance themselves into power in Government service, which is their main occupation. Their motto is "*Kalam, kadchhi ane barchhi*" (pen, laddle and spear) which means that writing, cooking or fighting is the only work which a Nagar will do.

There are several traditions current among the Nagars about their origin. One tradition says that they were created to officiate at Shiva's marriage. According to another they were created to officiate at Shiva's-sacrifice. A third tradition is that they are the descendants of a Nag, who pursued by some enraged snake charmers, assumed the form of a Brahman, fled to Vadnagar, married a Brahman girl and had several children by her, who came to be known as Nagars. Vadnagar was no doubt the place of their original settlement, and has given to them the name Vadnagara Nagars. Nagar is a Sanskrit word meaning belonging to or residing in a *nagar* or city. Nagars were probably so called either from their residence in the city or from their descent from the Nag tribe of people, who appear to have followed the Indo-Scythian king Kanaksen, intermarried with local Brahmans and settled in Vadnagar. Even at the present day Nagars say that their women are Nag *kanyas* or Nag maidens.

There are seven main sub-divisions of Nagars.—Vadnagara (2,368), Chitroda (85), Krashnora, Prashnora (157), Sathodra (223), Dungarpura and Visnagara (4,963). None of the divisions intermarry or dine together except that food cooked by Vadnagaras or Dungarpuras is eaten by all other classes except Prashnoras. The split in the community is attributed to Shiva's wrath whose temple (Hatkeshwar) was excluded from Vadnagar when the town wall was built. It is said that from that day Nagars commenced leaving Vadnagar and the town now contains but one Vadnagara Nagar family. Another tradition attributes the Nagar migration to certain Nagars taking presents from Vishaldev, the Chohan king of Patan. When Vishaldev founded Visnagar, he caused a sacrifice to be made at which he invited many Vadnagara Nagar Brahmans and offered them *dakshina*, but they refused to accept it. The king then wrote upon pieces of paper the grant of certain villages and wrapped them in betel leaves which the unsuspecting Brahmans accepted. The grantees however were excommunicated by their caste men, who had remained behind at Vadnagar; whereupon they went and settled in the villages granted to them, and formed a separate caste as Vishalnagara Nagars. In addition to the seven main divisions, there is an eighth sub-division of Nagars called Barad among the Visnagaras and Sathodras. They are those who, unable to have wives from their own community, married girls from other castes and lived apart. The rest of the sub-divisions are named after the places of their settlements subsequent to the split into Vadnagaras and Visnagaras. The Chitrodas take their name from the town of Chitrod, which is believed to be near Bhavnagar. They are a small body and are found in Bhavnagar and Baroda. The Sathodras take their name from Sathod, a village near Dabhoi. They are found in Dabhoi, in this State and in Nadiad, Ahmedabad and other places in British Gujarat. The Prashnoras take their name from Pushkar near Ajmer and are found mainly in Baroda District and Kathiawad. They are *vaidyas* and readers of *Purans*. The Krashnoras take their name from Krishnanagar or Krishnasagar. They are found in Gujarat.

Of the seven divisions, Vadnagara, Visnagara and Sathodra are again sub-divided in *grahastha* (laymen) and *bhikshuka* (priests). There are no intermarriages between the Grahastha and Bhikshuka sections among the Vadnagara Nagars.

Among Nagars marriage is a very expensive thing. The bridegroom has to present to the bride money for gold and silver ornaments and this has given rise to the proverb: *Rupiya hoya gagardi, to male Nagardi* (a Nagar can marry if he has a potful of rupees).

Nagar (3,657).—A caste of Vanias. Like Nagar Brahmans, it claims Vadnagar as its original seat. Nagar Vanias are found in considerable number in the Kadi Prant, more especially in Vadnagar, Visnagar and Vijapur. They are divided into Dasa (1,156), Visa (2,356) and Pancha (97). Like the Brahmans of the same name, they are shrewd and intelligent and are mainly employed in trade or Government service. In religion they are Vallabhachari Vaishnava. A small sub-division called Bam Nagars wear the sacred thread and are Shaiva. They are strict observers of religious ceremonials and do not eat with other Vanias.

Naghori (105).—Musalman cart-drivers. Before railway, they brought people from Malwa to Gujarat. Now they go only on short distances. They marry among themselves and form a separate community with a headman chosen by the people.

NAGHOSHI.—Same as **Rotis**, a section of trading **Vohoras**.

NAIDA.—A general term applied to all the members of the early tribes in the Navsari District.

Naika or **Nayakda** (10,030).—An early tribe found in the Navsari and Baroda Districts. It has four sub-divisions—Cholival, Nicha, Gabad and Kadhad—of which the first two eat together but not with the last two. None of them intermarry. This tribe once held the place of leaders among the Dhodias, who look upon them with respect, and at marriage and other ceremonies treat them as Brahmans. Like Dhodias, they are peasants and cultivators. At betrothal and marriage, men and women dance both singly and in pairs. The dead are cremated. A year after a death, a memorial stone (*khatrun*), is set up. It is rubbed with red lead, a hen is killed and its blood sprinkled on it. After the ceremony is over, the hen is roasted and eaten by the party. Every year at *Holi* time, a hen is offered to the memorial stone. Hereditary headmen settle caste disputes.

Nair (9).—Immigrants from Madras side.

Nandora (16).—A caste of Vanias. It takes its name from Nandod, the capital of Rajpipla. Nandoras are found chiefly in the Baroda City. They are not divided into Dasa and Visa. Their family priests are Nandora Brahmans; their family deity is *Nandikeshwar Mahadeo* and they are Vallabhachari Vaishnavas in religion.

Nandora (1,039).—A caste of Brahmans, found mainly in the Baroda District and especially in the Baroda, Karjan and Sinore Talukas. Nandora Brahmans, like Nandora Vanias, take their name from Nandod, the capital of Rajpipla. To this class belong the family priests of the Rajas of Nandod and Dharampur. The rest are cultivators or priests of the Kanbis or beggars.

Napal (28).—A Brahman caste; derives its name from Napa, a village in the Borsad Taluka, Kaira District. They are chiefly peasants, and say that originally they belonged to the Audich stock.

Nat (63).—Rope dancers and acrobats. They derive their name from the word *nrit*, to dance.

* **Nat** (4).—Musalman tumblers, found in small numbers, are converts from the Hindu tribe of the same name. Besides Hindustani and Gujarati, they speak a gypsy dialect of their own. In the rainy season, fifty to hundred families meet together in some central town, settle disputes and hold marriage and death feasts. After the beginning of the fair season, they start in bands of eight to ten with their donkeys, sheep, goats, dogs and fowls and perform acrobatic feats. In this, the females take the chief part and are called *kabutari*, *machhli*, &c. Except that they circumcise their boys, bury their dead and eat animal food, they are Musalman in name. They honour Hindu gods and perform Hindu ceremonies at their births and marriages. When a Nat dies, a small spot is burnt in the head. This is called *dagh dena* or branding.

Nima or Nema (135).—A Vania caste. It is said to have entered Gujarat from Marwar about 200 years ago. They are divided into Visa (121) and Dasa (7), who neither eat together nor intermarry. The Visa are both Vaishnava and Jain and the Dasa are only Vallabhachari Vaishnava. Their family deity is *Shamlaji* near Idar.

Ode (1,639).—Earth diggers. They were originally brought by Sidharaj Jesing to dig the Sahasraling tank at Patan. They are now earth-diggers, bricklayers and day-labourers.

OLGANA.—Same as Bhangi.

Oswal (2,944).—A caste of Vanias. According to Tod (Western India, 465), they are descendants of the Solanki Kings of Anhilwada (A. D. 942-1240), who gave up the sword for the till. They have such surnames as Chaudhri, Jhala, etc., which supports the theory of their Rajput origin. They are divided into three sub-castes, Visa (1,253), Dasa (1,422) and Pancha or Leta. The last sub-division is found in Cutch and ranks the lowest. They allow widow remarriage and few Shravak or Meshri Vanias eat with them. Dasa Oswal marry Dasa Shrimali and Dasa Porwad, but Dasa and Visa Oswals, though they eat together, do not intermarry. The family goddess of all Oswals is *Osia* in Marwar. Their priests are mostly Audich Brahmans.

Otara (47).—Brass founders. They are found in the Navsari District.

PAGI.—A sub-division of Talbada Kolis.

Pakhali (23).—Water carriers.

PAKHARIA (41).—A sub-caste of Mochis.

PAKHIA (2).—A sub-caste of Bahrots.

Palival (27).—A Brahman caste chiefly found in the Baroda City as well as in the Kadi and Amreli Districts. They belong to the Kanyakubja division of Brahmans and take their name from Pali, a chief trade-centre in Marwar.

PANAGARA (250).—A sub-caste of Mochis.

PANCHAL (1,173).—A sub-caste of Luhars.

PANCHOLI (210).—A sub-caste of Ghanchis.

PANCHOLI (2,711).—A sub-caste of Sutars.

Pan.-Pin.

Panjnigara (52).—Musalman cotton thread starchers. They are converts from the Hindu caste of the same name. Both males and females wear the ordinary Musalman dress. They marry only among themselves. They have a well-managed union with separate headman.

PARAJIA (332).—A sub-caste of Luhars.

PARAJIA (1,250).—A sub-caste of Sonis.

Parashar (10).—A caste of Brahmans so called from the name of their *gotra*.

Parmar (91).—They are Musalman converts from the Parmar clan of Rajputs. They intermarry among the converted Rajput classes and are either land owners, cultivators or servants.

Parsi (7,955).—The name means the people of Pars or Fars, the south-west province of Persia, the capital of which is now Shiraz. The present Parsis of India are the descendants of those who were forced out of their country more than 1,280 years ago by the Arabs, who conquered and well-nigh annihilated them. They landed first at Diu, then at Cambay and subsequently near Sanjan, a little to the north of modern Daman, where they kindled the sacred fire called Iranshah which now burns at Udwada, in thanksgiving of their safe arrival; but the traditional belief is that they brought it unextinguished from Persia. The Hindu king of Sanjan allowed them free liberty to follow their own religion, while they had to import certain ceremonies and customs of the Hindus. Very little is known of them for over 800 years after this settlement. But they still follow their own religion in laborious rituals, which have been handed down to the present day. Among the Parsis, there is a sort of hierarchy, though not on the rigid method of the Hindus, but there are no castes. The Mobeds are to them what the Brahmans are to the Hindus. The stronghold of Mobeds is the Baroda town of Navsari, because the Parsis migrated to it from Sanjan and Bahrot and have thrived and flourished there ever since. No religious ceremony can be performed, no marriage tie can be knit, no prayers after the dead be recited and no funeral services can be held except by the Mobeds. When a child is seven years old, the ceremony of investing it with the *kasti* or sacred thread is performed. The Kasti is made by the intertwinings of 72 strong threads, spun out of wool and woven in a special way on a sort of loom. It is sufficiently long to go thrice round the waist and to allow of its being knotted up in certain ways, which every child is taught to do. Mobed (priests) and Behdin (laymen) could not intermarry 50 years before. But the restriction is not now much observed.

Parsis are divided into two divisions, called Shehenshahi and Kadami. This division arose in A. D. 1745 from a dispute regarding the reckoning of the year. Shehenshahis are those who kept to the Indian reckoning and the Kadamis those who adopted the Persian practice. Formerly intermarriage was shunned but it is now common. Conversions from one division into another are rare.

Parsis speak the Gujarati language and put on a head-dress peculiar to them. The priests dress wholly in white. Parsi women wind a white piece of muslin round the head.

Fire is the chief object of Parsi veneration and the Fire temple is the public place of Parsi worship. Besides the leading rites and ceremonies called *jashan*, *gambhar* and *muktad*, Parsis have many minor practices and observances to which more or less a religious sanction is attached. A Parsi must always keep his head and feet covered, he must never be without the sacred shirt and cord, must never smoke and must wash his hands, if he puts his fingers in his mouth. After shaving his face, a Parsi bathes before touching anything.

Parsis followed many of the practices and beliefs of Hindus and Musalmans. They made offerings to the Hindu *Holi*, offered vows and sacrificed goats and fowls to *Shitala Devi*, and some offered oil to *Hanuman*. They offered vows and made presents to *Tabuts* and at the tombs of Musalman *Pirs*. Their women had great faith in amulets which they bought from sorcerers and wore round their neck or in their hair to win the favour of their husbands. Most of these superstitious practices have now died out of the community as a whole on account of the spread of education.

Pasi (15).—A caste of labourers from Central India.

Patanvadia (22,263).—A caste of Kolis, so called from Patan, their original home. They are also called Kohoda. They freely partake of animal food and are the only class of Kolis who eat the flesh of the buffalo. They are lower in social rank to other Kolis. Most of them have Rajput surnames such as Chavda, Dabhi, Vaghela, etc.

Pathan (16,307).—One of the four classes into which the regular Musalmans are divided. They are of Afghan origin. The men add *Khan* to their names and women *Khatun* or *Khatu*.

PATHARE (140).—A sub-caste of Prabhus.

PATIDAR.—A term applied to superior class of Lewa Kanbis from their being sharers in the village lands.

PEPAVANSHI (4,916).—A sub-caste of Darji.

Pindhara (203).—A Musalman caste chiefly found in the Kadi District. They are labourers and petty traders.

Pinjara (5,408).—Cotton-cleaners. A term applied to Hindu converts who follow the profession of cotton cleaning. A Pinjara is a cotton scutcher, who striking a bow with a heavy wooden plectrum uses the vibrations of the bow-string to separate the fibres of the cotton, to arrange them side by side and to part them from dirt and other impurities. Some of them have left their traditional occupation after the introduction of cotton mills and are now shopkeepers, bricklayers, pedlars, oil-pressers, &c. They are ashamed of their old name of Pinjara and call themselves Vohora or Dhunak Pathans. In villages they put on Kanbi-like turbans and in towns *fentas*. Their women dress like Hindu females.

PITHVA (2,910).—A sub-caste of Luhars.

Poladi (44).—The descendants of Afghans, who came to Gujarat with the army of Alla-ud-Din Khilji. They came to be known as *Poladi*, from *polad*, steel on account of the dexterity displayed by them in breaking the hard stones of the *Rudramala* temple at Sidhpur in the Kadi District. Poladis are now mostly agriculturists or serve as peons and constables. They are mainly found in the Sidhpur Taluka. They marry only among themselves and with Khureshi, Behlim and other *Ashraf* tribes. Their women do not appear in public. They dress like ordinary Musalmans.

Pomla (44).—A curious caste found in the City of Baroda. Its members speak a dialect which resembles the Telugu. Both males and females have Gujarati names, such as, Haribhai, Narsi, Jamni, Kashi, etc. They live upon making and selling toys, brooms and baskets of palm leaves and seem to have migrated into Gujarat from the Madras Presidency about two hundred years ago. They have the custom known under the name of *la couvade*, that is, the odd rule prevalent among several primitive peoples in different parts of the world, requiring that the husband should be doctored while the wife gives birth to a child. This has given rise to the proverb :—"*Pomli jane ane Pomlo khâya*" which is applied when one enjoys the fruit while another undergoes the labour for earning it. Immediately after delivery the female is made to drink the juice of the bark of the *nimb* tree, and a quantity of oil. She then stirs out of the house and is not allowed to enter it for five days during which time the male lies confined and takes the usual medicines. The Pomlas say that they do not lie confined merely to observe a custom; that they actually feel indisposed during the period and the indisposition is but a mark of favour of the Mata or goddess, and that immoral ones among them being outside the Mata's protection are not allowed by the Mata to lie confined. They have small settlements in Nadiad, Ahmedabad, Broach and Surat also. At every twelve years, a gathering of this caste takes place at Dumral Bhagol in Nadiad in honour of the Mata, when those who are specially favoured of the goddess perform various miraculous feats, such as walking on fire, etc.

Remarriage is not common among the Pomlas, the belief being that their tutelary goddess *Lakshmi Mata* does not favour those who perform it.

Porwad (8,613).—A Vania caste said to take its name from Porwad, a suburb of Shrimâl or Bhinmâl, the old capital of south Marwar. They are divided into Visa (2,852) and Dasa (5,694) who interdine but do not intermarry. Among Visa Porwads, there are both Jains and Vaishnavas. Their family priests are the Shrimali Brahmans and their family deity is the *Shri* or *Mahalakshmi* of Shrimal. They are partly Vaishnavas and partly Jains.

Prabhu (3,153).—A caste of the Kshatriya class, originally immigrants from the Deccan. Prabhus are found in all the divisions of the State. Their main occupation is government service. They are divided into Chandraseni Kayastha (3,013) and Pathare (140), who neither interdine nor intermarry. There are no sub-divisions among them. At one time, "Dawne Prabhus" were considered a sub-division of Chandraseni Kayastha Prabhus, who took food with them, but did not allow marriage relations. It being proved that Dawne Prabhus were true Chandraseni Kayastha Prabhus and were so called simply on account of their residence in the District of Daman and that 'Damne' was changed into 'Dawne'. Marriages are also allowed and the two sections are now treated as one without any distinction.

PRASHNORA (157).—A sub-caste of Nagar Brahmans.

Pushkarna or **Pokarna** (68).—A Brahman caste found mainly in the Kadi and Amreli Districts. They take their name from Pushkar or Pokar lake about eight miles north-west of Ajmer. They act as family priests to Bhatias and are also engaged as husbandmen, confectioners and clerks. They are enterprising and travel to various parts of India, and also visit Zanzibar and Arabia. They are followers of Vallabhacharya and their family goddesses are *Laxmiji* and *Chamunda* in Marwar. They sometimes wear the sacred thread at some place of pilgrimage. Gujarat Brahmans do not dine with Pokarnas who eat cakes and balls cooked by Bhatias. On the sixth day after a birth the women of the family, singing as at marriage, bring a clay horse from the house of the mother's father to her husband's house. On marriage occasions, men dance in procession and women sing immodest songs.

Rabari (44,916).—Herdsmen. They claim to be Rajputs, who instead of marrying Rajput women, married celestial damsels (*apsaras*) that is perhaps Charan women or daughters of god (*devputris*) as they style themselves and were therefore called Rahâ-bahâri, that is going out of path. Their original home is said to be the United Provinces from which they moved to Marwar, and from thence to Gujarat, Kathiawad and Cutch. Some of their surnames are the same as Rajput tribe names, *e. g.*, Chohan, Dodiya, Gohel, Jadav, etc. Except in Kathiawad, Rabaris have no sub-castes. In Kathiawad, there are six sub-divisions which interdine but do not intermarry. They take flesh and drink spirits and in Kathiawad eat with Musalmans. They are quarrelsome people and by breaking fences, and grazing their cattle on crops cause great loss and annoyance to cultivators. In religion they belong to Bijmargi, Ramanandi, and Pirânâ sects. Their priests are Audich and Sompura Brahmans. Among them all marriages take place on the same day. The Rabaris of one or more villages who wish to have their daughters married meet in a temple. A Brahman is called and he fixes the marriage day. Marriage among near relations is avoided. Widow marriage and divorce are allowed. The younger brother of the deceased husband has the first claim upon his widow. The dead are buried. *Shradhas* are performed, and caste people are feasted on the eleventh and twelfth day after a death. Rabaris have a headman but he has little authority and caste disputes are settled at meetings of the men of the caste.

Rajgor (1,016).—A caste of Brahmans; so called because they are the priests of chiefs, and are found mainly in the Amreli and Kadi Districts. They were originally Audich Brahmans, but were looked upon as degraded, owing to their allowing widow marriage and eating with Vanias and Kanbis. They are the priests of Rajputs, Kathi chiefs and Oswal Shravaks.

Rajput (64,228).—A Kshatriya caste found in all the parts of the State but principally in the Kadi Prant, as Anhilwad Patan in that district was, for many centuries, the capital of the Rajput kings of Gujarat. The chief social peculiarity of the Rajputs is their division into clans. The following is a list of the 103 Rajput clan names in use in Gujarat:—

Ada, Avera, Balater, Barod, Bhati, Bihola, Solanki, Biya, Bodav, Chamarpa, Chandavrat, Chavada, Chavad, Chochu, Chiod, Chohan, Chudavat, Dabhi, Dagh, Daima, Dairja, Devchand, Devda, Dhandhu, Dod, Dodiya, Duval, Ed, Galecha, Ghelot, Gohel, Golter, Gor, Gujjar, Hadial, Harashi, Hatha, Humad, Jadav, Jadeja, Jhala, Jiriya, Jodha Rathod, Joja, Jut, Kaba, Kachhotia, Kalam, Karadia, Kher, Khod, Khula, Kukan, Lakam, Mahida, Makvana, Mal, Masani, Mer, Mohal, Mori, Narvan, Padhra, Padhiar, Palonia, Parmar, Pesrau, Puravia Chohan, Rana, Ranrathod, Rathod, Raval, Ravar-Solanki, Rehevar, Revod, Sedhal, Sisodia, Sodha, Sodria, or Sadria, Sojatria, Solanki, Songad, Surcha, Suvar, Tank, Tantol, Thokiya, Tuar, Vadhel, Vadvasia, Vaghela Vaish, Vaja, Vala, Vamla, Vanol, Vantia, Varam, Vejola, Vethia, Vezania, Virpura Solanki, Udvat and Uma.

All clans eat together and intermarry, but the members of a clan are forbidden to marry within the clan, as they are believed to be the children of one common ancestor. The Dagh, Karadia and Padhra clans allow widow remarriage and let their women appear in public. They are therefore looked upon as degraded. The Daghs are found in Cutch, Karadias are scattered all over Gujarat and Kathiawad; and Padhras are found only in the Surat and Navsari districts. Of the other clans only Chavada, Chohan, Daima, Gohel, Gori, Jadeja, Jhala, Parmar, Rathod, Rehevar, Sarvaiya, Sisodia, Solanki and Vaghelas have retained their importance. The rest have sunk into insignificance.

Rajputs are by birth soldiers and land holders. Some of them are even now chiefs, *Girasias* or land holders and holders of service lands. But their service as soldiers is not in demand; and by their indolence, habits of extravagant expenditure and opium taking, most of the land-holders have lost their patrimony and dwindled into peasant proprietors. A great many of them are forced to take service as peons and constables and even as personal attendants and field labourers.

Except among their lower classes, Rajputs have no headman. Caste disputes are usually settled by a jury of four or five respectable persons of the clan who have the power to fine or expel from the caste.

Rangrej (48).—They are dyers of Hindu origin and are said to be converts from the Khatri or weaver caste. Their home tongue is Urdu. Their women appear in public and knot cloth for calico printing. Except that in marriages the bridegroom walks instead of riding, they have no particular customs. They form a distinct community and have a union and headman. They marry only among themselves.

Rathod (59).—They are Musalman converts from the Rathod tribe of Rajputs. They are Sunni in name, neither learning the Koran nor saying the prayers. Their ceremonies are in many respects Hindu. They keep to the Rajput custom of sending a *khandu* to the bride's village. When the bride is a Hindu, both Hindu and Musalman ceremonies are performed. At deaths women wail and beat the breast like Hindus. Some of them reverence the *Acharya* of the Swaminarayan sect. They have no headmen and do not form a separate community.

Raval (41).—A caste of Brahmans. It takes its name from Raval, a village in Kathiawad. Ravals are found mainly in the Baroda and Kadi Districts. They say they are a branch of the Valam Brahmans who in consequence of some dispute formed a separate community. Some Kathiawad and Cutch Ravals have been degraded for eating and intermarrying with Charans.

Ravalia (22,484).—Also called Jogi. They appear to be of Rajput origin and are subdivided into Sakhia (clansmen) and Vahalia (carriers). Sakhias are divided into Joshi Raval, Maru Raval and Pataï Raval. Both Sakhias and Vahalias eat together and intermarry. Surat Ravals are divided into Khambhati, Rajbhari and Surati; and Ahmedabad Ravals into Baria, Bhallia, Bhoinia, Makvana and Udlia. The five Ahmedabad sub-divisions eat together, but do not intermarry. Ravals eat fish, mutton and fowl and drink liquor. They keep sheep and asses and work as carriers and labourers; some weave bed tapes and a few cultivate lands. They also beg and it is considered pious to give cooked food to a Raval especially when there has been some death in the family. Widow remarriage and divorce are allowed; younger brother has the choice of marrying his elder brother's widow. They have caste councils and headmen in large villages.

Rayakval (155). A Brahman caste, found mainly in the Baroda District. It takes its name from Raika near Dhandhuka. Rayakval Brahmans are divided into two classes, *Mota* or great (24) and *Nana* or small. The members of the small community are looked upon as degraded and in many respects correspond with Kanbis. The cause of degradation was the remarriage of a widow and a Rayakval marrying a Bharvad's daughter. **Ray.-Sar.**

Rayakval (5).—A Vania caste; derives its name from Raika, near Ahmedabad. They are not divided into Visa and Dasa. Their priests are Rayakval Brahmans and they are Vallabhachari Vaishnava in religion.

REWAKANTHIA (319).—A sub-caste of Bhavsar.

ROTIA (12).—Also called *Naghoshi*, from their being vegetarians. A section of trading Vohoras.

RUPAGHADA (43).—A sub-caste of Luhar.

Sachora (210).—A Brahman caste; takes its name from Sachora in the south of Marwar. They are divided into Visa (91) and Dasa (106) and do not eat food cooked by other Brahmans. Some of them act as *mukhiajis* in Vallabhachari temples and others are either cooks or peasants.

SADHU.—A general term applied to the Hindu ascetic class.

Sagar or **Sagaria** (1,582).—A caste peculiar to Kathiawad and much resembling Kolis. Some of the caste work as carpenters, some are agriculturists, some are brick-layers and the rest are labourers.

SAHASRA (36,754).—A sub-caste of Audich Brahmans.

Sajodra (27).—A Brahman caste which takes its name from Sajod, a village in Ankleshwar taluka of the Broach District. They are found mainly in the Navsari District. Agriculture is their chief occupation and they resemble the Anavalas in their manners and customs. Both appear originally to belong to the same stock.

Salat (1,176).—Derived from *salya*, a stone; they are stone-workers and are found all over the State, but chiefly in the City of Baroda and some large towns such as Patan, Vadnagar, Visnagar, etc. The leading and the only true class of Salats are the Sompura Salats who are found in North Gujarat, Kathiawad and Cutch. Others calling themselves Salats, are Kumbhars or Talbada Kolis who have taken to stone-cutting and have formed separate castes from other Kumbhars and other Talbada Kolis. According to their own story, the Sompura Salats were originally Brahmans and took to stone-cutting at the desire of *Somnath Mahadeo*. Those of their original caste who remained Brahmans acted as their priests. After this division though they never intermarried, Sompura Brahmans and Sompura Salats are said for a time to have continued to dine with each other. Though Kumbhars and Talbada Koli Salats have formed separate castes they are, except in their calling, in every respect like other Kumbhars and Kolis. Sompura Salats put on Brahmanic thread and are strict vegetarians. They do not allow divorce, but their widows remarry. The widow of a man marries his younger brother. In religion, they are generally Swaminarayan or Shaiva. Their priests are Audich and Sompura Brahmans. Caste disputes are settled by the headman in some places, and in others by five or six leading men.

* **Salat** (18).—They are masons said to be converts to Islam from the Hindu caste of the same name. They speak Urdu and both men and women dress like Mahomedans. They are Sunni in religion. They intermarry with other Musalmans, but have a separate union and a headman of their own.

Salvi (94).—From *sal*, a loom, is a small class of hand-loom weavers of silk mostly found in the Kadi District. It is said that there were originally no weavers of this class in Patan and that Mulraj invited a few from the south-east of India to settle in his kingdom. The new-comers being strangers to Gujarat could not intermarry with other castes and were debarred from every other kind of intercourse. Mulraj interfered on their behalf and forced the Lewa Kanbis to associate with them in all matters, and to reckon them as of their own caste. From that time, the Salvis and those Lewa Kanbis who associated with them, formed a separate caste.

Sanadya or **Sanadia** (35).—A caste of Brahmans; so called from *san*, sin and *adya*, first. It is said that when Râma entered Ayodhya after his victory over Ravan, he performed a sacrifice for the atonement of his sin in his having killed a number of Rakshasas. The Adi Gauda Brahmans were employed to officiate as priests. On the completion of the sacrifice, Rama offered them gifts which some accepted and some did not. Those who accepted came to be known as Sanadia.

SANGHADIA.—Same as Kharadi.

Saraniya (H. 294; M. 14).—Knife grinders. A section of Vagharis who separated themselves from the main body on account of their taking to this new calling and formed a new caste.

Saraswat (404).—A very ancient Brahman tribe which still inhabits a tract in the north-west of India beyond Delhi, once watered by the famous Saraswati river. It is said that they are the descendents of Saraswat Muni. They came from the Punjab to Gujarat by way of Sindh and Cutch with their *yajmans*, patrons, the Luhanas, Bhansalis and Bhatias. In religion they are Shaiva and also worship the goddess Saraswati whose temple is in the Punjab on the river of the same name. They are also the priests of the Brahma Kshatris of Surat, Broach and Ahmedabad and of the Parajia Sonis of Kathiawad. They are divided into two branches, Sorathia and Sindhia, of which the former dines with their patrons, while the latter does not. In Kathiawad and Cutch, they allow widow remarriage.

Sarvaria (740).—A Brahman caste immigrant from the north. It seems to have originated from the caste of Saraswat Brahmans. It is said that two Saraswat brothers by name Kanya and Kubja went to the great sacrifice performed by king Rama in Oudh for the atonement of his sins. There the younger brother Kubja declined to accept gifts and went with his followers to the bank of the river Saryu; they were consequently known as Sarvaria Brahmans. The elder brother and his followers accepted gifts and settled in Kanoja, and were therefore known as Kanojia.

Sathawara (5,830).—A caste peculiar to the Kadi and Amreli Districts where its members follow agricultural operations in villages but are bricklayers in towns.

Saiyad (8,772).—One of the four classes into which the Musalmans with a foreign strain are divided. They claim descent from Fatima and Ali, the daughter and son-in-law of the Prophet and are the descendants of those who came during the period of Musalman rule in Gujarat, as religious teachers, soldiers and adventurers. They mark their high birth by placing the title *Saiyad* or *Mir* before, or *Shah* after male names, and *Begam* after female names. They marry their daughters only among themselves but take wives from other Musalmans. Some of them are *pirs* or spiritual guides and the rest follow all callings.

Setpal (9).—A Brahman caste, immigrant from Upper India.

Shaikh (31,510).—Properly speaking one of the four classes into which the Musalmans with a foreign strain are divided. But the term "Shaikh" which means *elder* is applied to descendants of local converts as well as of foreigners. The men have the title *Shaikh* or *Mahomed* placed before their names and women *Bibi* after theirs. They follow all callings and are found in every grade of life.

Shaikh or **Shaikhada** (51).—They are found chiefly in the Baroda District. Originally Hindus, they are converts to Islam worshipping the shrine of Bala Mahomed Shah, one of the minor Pirana saints. In their ways, they are similar to the Matia Kanbis. They bury their dead, but otherwise follow Hindu customs. They are not circumcised and do not eat with Musalmans. They make *tila* and many of them have lately been following the tenets of the Swaminarayan sect, and have returned themselves as Hindus in the present Census. At the time of marriage, both a Hindu and Mahomedan priest attends. Nika is performed by a Fakir and afterwards the Hindu rite of *chori* is performed by a Brahman. They form a distinct community and marry only among themselves.

Shenva (7,587).—Also called Sindhva from plaiting the leaves of *shendi* or wild date and Tirgar from making *tir* or arrows. They bear such Rajput names as Rathod, Solanki, Vaghela and Makvana. Most of them earn their livelihood by making mats and brooms from date trees and ropes of *bhendi* fibre. A few also serve as village servants. They rank between Dheds and Bhangis. Dheds do not touch them and they do not touch Bhangis. Their priests are Garodas. Their food is coarse grain, but they also eat flesh when they can get it. They are Bijmargi, Ramanandi and worshippers of *Ramde Pir* and *Bhildi Mata*. They observe the ordinary Hindu fasts and feasts, but the followers of *Ramde Pir* fast on new moon days and do not work on Fridays. Some of them go on pilgrimage to Ambaji, Behecharaji, Dakor and Dwarka. They do not enter the temple, but worship standing near the door. Among them divorce and widow-marriage are allowed. The widow of a man marries his younger brother. Social disputes are settled by a few of the elders.

Shenavi (68).—A Brahman caste, immigrant from the Deccan. About its origin, there is a tradition that Parshuram invited 64 families of Gauda Saraswat Brahmans to Konkan and settled them in the country about Goa. After a lapse of time, king Shikhivarma granted to them 96 villages in gift. From that time they were known as the *Shannava*, meaning ninety-six Brahmans. Shenavi is a corruption of that term.

Shimpi (39).—Deccani Darji found chiefly in the City of Baroda.

SHRAVAK.—A general term applied to members of Jain Vania castes as opposed to Meshri or Vaishnava Vanias.

Shravan (9).—A Brahman caste, immigrant from Upper India.

Shrigod (1,982).—Those Gauda Brahmans who migrated to Shrinagar in Kashmir, became known as Shrigod. They are divided into Malvi (375) and Derola. Once when the country suffered from a severe famine, those who migrated to Malva, became known as Malviya or Malvi. The Malvi Shrigod are sub-divided into Juna (257) and Nava (173), *i. e.*, those who came first, and those who came afterwards. Nava Malvi Shrigod are further sub-divided into Kharola and Kharsodia from the names of the villages where they settled. Those who were compelled to take for wives, girls from the lower castes were called Derola.

Shrimali (31,965).—A Vania caste. Like Shrimali Brahmans they are settlers from Marwar. They are sub-divided into Visa (11,621), Dasa (20,130) and the Ladva (70). Visa and Dasa Shrimalis eat together but do not intermarry; neither of them eat with the Ladvas. The Visa Shrimalis are mostly Jains. The Dasas are either Jains or Vaishnavas. Jains and Vaishnava Shrimali Vanias do not dine together in South Gujarat. Vaishnava Shrimalis are pretty equally distributed in the Kadi and Baroda Districts and in the Baroda City. The Shrimali Sonis originally belonged to the Shrimali Vania class, but now form a new caste owing to their change of occupation.

Shrimali (1,829).—A Brahman caste; derives its name from Shrimal or Bhinmal, about fifty miles west of Mount Abu, which from the 6th to the 9th century was the capital of the Gujjar kingdom. In the Baroda State they are found mainly in the Kadi District, and act as family priests to Jains of the Oswal and Porwad Vania castes and to Shrimali Sonis and Vanias. Among the Shrimalis a serpent named *Karkotak Nag* is worshipped at the time of marriage or at any anniversary. A picture of the Nag is drawn and worshipped. The Shrimalis are often called Astamangli. The bridegroom has among them to go round the marriage *homa* or sacrificial fire, eight times with his bride, while the other Brahmans go round only four or seven times. The word Astamangli is used as a nickname indicative of shrewdness and means that it is not easy to deceive Shrimalis.

Siddi (133).—Literally masters, also called Habshis, are chiefly found in the Amreli District and the towns of Dabhoi, Sidhpur, Amreli, Kodinar, etc. They are the descendants of African negroes, chiefly from the Somali coast brought to India as slaves. New arrivals are called *wilati* and country borns *muvalad*. They speak among themselves a Somali dialect and with others a broken Hindustani. They are poor and live by service and begging. They are much given to dancing and singing and have a talent for imitation. They are Suni in faith, but their chief object of worship is *Baba Ghor*, an Abysinian saint, whose tomb stands on a hill near Ratanpur in Western Rajpipla.

SIKALIGAR (18).—A sub-caste of Mochis.

Sindhi (3,548).—A tribe of Musalman immigrants from Sindh. They are chiefly found in Baroda, Kadi and Amreli Districts.

SINDHVA.—Same as Shenva.

Sipahi (780).—Literally soldiers. They are found in the Navsari and Amreli Districts only, and seem to be of mixed origin, partly descendants of immigrants and partly of Rajput converts, as their surnames Chohan, Rathod and Parmar show. Their home-tongue is Urdu in some places and Gujarati in others. They marry with other Musalmans and form no very distinct community, though they have a union and a headman. They are husbandmen and day-labourers, and are also employed in government service as *chaprasis* and constables. Their females, except in the case of the poor, do not appear in public.

Sompura (57).—A Brahman caste. They receive their name from the celebrated temple of Somnath in Kathiawar. Sompuras are mentioned in an inscription of Sidhraj on a pillar at Somnath. The inscription bears date equivalent to A. D. 1115. They are the descendants of the priests that used to minister in that temple. They are now scattered and depend for their living on alms. A few Sompura Brahmans are considered degraded as they follow the occupation of sculptors.

Sonar (539).—Deccani Soni found chiefly in the City of Baroda and the Navsari District. They settled there during the Maratha rule, but they have not mixed with the Gujarati Sonis. Their home speech is Marathi and their dress, habits and customs are the same as those of the other Dakshanis.

Soni (10,120).—Gold and silversmiths. They are found in towns and large villages. They are of eight main divisions:—Gujjar (792), Maru (660), Mewada (21), Parajia (1,250), Shrimali (5,829), Tragad (1,334), Kathiawadi (26) and Khandeshi (58). The Tragad or Mastan community has two divisions, called *nanu* (small) and *motu* (large) and claims descent from a Vania father and a Brahman mother. In token of their partly Brahman origin, they wear the Brahmanic thread and do not eat food cooked by any one, other than a Brahman. The Parajias called after the village of Paraj near Junaghad, claim to be Rajputs. They are of two branches, Garana and Patni. Gango, the founder of the Garana branch, established himself at Girnar and his descendants are found in Halar and Sorath. Nando, the founder of the Patni branch, went to Patan during the reign of Sidhraj Jayasing (A. D. 1094-1143) and established himself there. The Patnis and Garanas eat together but do not intermarry. The four other sub-divisions, Gujjar, Maru, Mewada and Shrimali claim to have once been Vanias. The Shrimali Sonis, who originally belonged to the Shrimali Vania community, are divided into Ahmedabadi and Charotaria. They eat together. The Ahmedabadis take Charotaria wives, but never give their daughters to a Charotaria in marriage. Mewada Sonis originally belonged to Mewada Vania community; the Maru or Marwari Sonis have come into Gujarat from Marwar; and the Gujjar belong to the Gujjar Vania stock and are a trace of the great settlement of Gujjars who gave its name to Gujarat.

Arranged according to their work, *Sonis* are goldsmiths or workers of gold ornaments, *Jadias* or tracers of designs on ornaments and *Panchigars* or diamond and precious stone setters.

Like Vanias Sonis live on grain and smoke tobacco. They have a bad name for filching gold and for mixing metal. The saying is:—"A Soni takes gold even out of his sister's ornaments." Socially Sonis hold a high position, ranking next to Vanias. Some of them are Shaiva, some Vallabhachari, and some Swaminarayana. Their family priests are Audich, Saraswat and Shrimali Brahmans. The Maru, Parajia and Charotaria Shrimali Sonis practise polygamy and allow widow remarriage. Among Charotaria Shrimalis alone, the wife is free to divorce her husband. Each community has its headman or *patel* who, in consultation with four or five leading men, settles caste disputes at a meeting of all the men of the caste.

Sorathia (60).—A Brahman caste, found chiefly in Kathiawad. They eat with clothes on and do not observe the Brahman rules of purity. They are therefore looked upon as degraded Brahmans. They are labourers, water-bearers and servants.

Sorathia (453).—A Vania caste, found chiefly in the Amreli District. They take their name from Sorath, the south coast of Kathiawad. They are divided into Visa (136) and Dasa (289), and are remarkable for their commercial enterprise. Their family priests are the Kandolia Brahmans and their family deity is *Samudri*, whose shrine is at Sundri in Dhrangadra. They are followers of the Vallabhachari sect.

SULEMANI (992).—A section of trading Vohoras.

Sutar (H. 20,719 : M. 71).—Carpenters from the Sanskrit word *sutradhar* (*sutra, i. e.*, the thread with which the course of the saw is marked). They are pretty evenly distributed over the whole State. They belong to six divisions, Pithva (73), Gujjar (8,513), Mewada (1,285), Pancholi (2,711), Marwadi (164) and Vaishya (7,845). Of these, the Pancholis and Vaishyas are found only in Gujarat proper, the Gujjars and Marwadis in Gujarat, Kathiawad and Cutch and the Pithvas in Kadi. The Gujjar, Mewada, Pancholi and Vaishya claim to be the descendants of Vishvakarma, the divine world-builder. Both Marwadis and Pithvas claim to be Rajputs who took to carpentry when Parshuram résolved to destroy the Kshatriyas. Except that the other five divisions eat food cooked by Vaishyas, none of the six divisions eat together or intermarry. The Vaishyas rank highest, because they do not eat food cooked by the other divisions, wear the sacred thread and do not allow their widows to marry. The Pancholis rank lowest, because they alone prepare oil-presses and do other woodwork which causes the loss of animal life. Besides the regular carpenters, some Darjis, Kolis, Kumbhars and Tapodhans have taken to carpentry.

In look and dress, Sutars do not differ from Vanias. All the six divisions of Sutars are thrifty and sober. In religion they are Parnamipanthi, Ramanandi, Shaiva, Swaminarayan and Vallabhachari. Of the six divisions of Sutars, the Vaishya and Mewada in North Gujarat wear the Brahmanic thread. The Sutars' marriage customs do not differ from those of Vanias and Kanbis. Among the Vaishya and the Mewada, widow remarriage, polygamy and divorce are not allowed; among the rest widows are allowed to marry, divorce is granted and polygamy practised. Caste disputes among the several divisions are settled either by a headman or a few leading men at the meeting of all the men of the caste. No fee is levied from an outsider who takes to carpentry. Carpenters who do not observe as a close day the dark fifteenth of every Hindu month, or the day on which a death has taken place in the caste in a town or village, are fined; and those who work as shoemakers are excommunicated.

Sutar—Luhar (72).—A section of Luhars who do carpenters' work and considering themselves thereby exalted, have separated from the main caste and formed a new one.

Tadvi (24).—One of the early tribes found in the Baroda and Kadi Districts.

Tai (2,930).—Weavers found chiefly in Dabhoi Taluka of the Baroda District and also in the Navsari District. They claim descent from Hatim Tai, but appear to be a mixed class of foreigners and converted Hindus. Some of them speak Hindustani and others, Gujarati. They wear cotton robes and turbans. Like Hindus, they give caste dinners on pregnancy, marriage and death occasions. They marry only among themselves and form a separate *jamat* with a headman of their own.

Tailangu (83).—A caste of Brahmans; immigrants from the South.

Talajia (5).—A caste of Brahmans found in the Baroda District. It is said about their origin that Rama, the king of Ayodhya, on his way to Prabhas Patan, halted near the temple of the goddess *Rutamba* (now Rahapuri Mata in Bhavnagar) and there performed a *homa* in her honour. At its completion, he commenced to offer *dakshina* (money presents). Some fishermen came to receive *dakshina* in the disguise of Brahmans. Rama was enraged with them; but at the intercession of the goddess, they were allowed to depart in the garb they had assumed and to settle in a village named Tuljapur (now Talaja); they were thenceforth known as Talajia Brahmans.

Talavia (9,647).—Originally a sub-caste of Dublas now grown into an independent caste. Talavias seldom eat with other Dublas and never intermarry with them. They are chiefly found in the Navsari and Baroda Districts.

Talbada (91,527).—A caste of Kolis; also called Dharala or swordsmen. The name Talbada is derived from *sthalpada*, meaning local. Talbadas consider themselves superior to other Kolis and do not dine with them. They intermarry and observe the Rajput rule of avoiding marriages between members of the same clan. They are divided into six main classes, namely, Baria, Dabhi, Jalia, Khant, Kotwal and Pagi. Baria, Dabhi and Khant are considered *kulin*. They receive *gunju* or dowries for giving their sons in marriage. Kotwals and Pagis serve as guards and village trackers.

Tamboli (524).—Betel leaf sellers. They derive their name from the Sanskrit word *tambul*, a betel leaf. It is both a caste name and an occupational term. It is the caste name of those Sathawaras (green grocers) who have taken to betel leaf growing and selling and the occupational name of persons of different castes who follow the profession of selling betel leaves. In the town of Kadi, there are Pardeshi Tambolis who have no connection whatsoever with Sathawaras. These people originally came from the Deccan where they wear the sacred thread.

Tapodhan (4,465).—A Brahman caste also contemptuously called Bharda. It is found in all the districts of the State. Tapodhans are *pujaris* of Mahadev, Mata and Shravak temples. Those who are not engaged in temple service are husbandmen, labourers and bricklayers. They are considered degraded as they accept food and other articles offered to Mahadev and allow widow marriage. **Tap.-Uda.**

Targala (4,468).—Also called Bhavaiya, that is performers of *bhavai* or comedy. They are found mostly in the Kadi Prant. The word *bhavai* is derived from the Sanskrit word *bhav* which is a name of the god Shiva and is so called from that deity being personated in acting. Bhavaiyas are said to be the descendants of one Asit, an Audich Brahman of Unja in the Kadi District. Asit was excommunicated by other Audich Brahmans for dining with a Kanbi girl. He was a good songster and supported himself by singing and dancing. His descendants followed his profession and formed a new caste. The Targalas have two divisions, the Vyas and the Bhavaiyas who neither eat together nor intermarry. Both consider that they have the right to wear the Brahmanic thread, but are not very careful about wearing it. The Vyas do not eat with other castes lower than Kanbis, while some Bhavaiyas eat with Kolis. The latter are called Bhil Bhavaiyas with whom other Bhavaiyas neither eat nor intermarry. They travel during the fair season in companies of 15 to 30 and return to their homes and cultivate their fields during the rains. Each company or *toli* has its *naik*. They have no theatres and perform in open places in the outskirts of towns and villages. The high class performers now-a-days take service as actors in dramatic companies in Bombay and other places. Their marriage and death ceremonies do not differ from those of Kanbis. Marriages are not allowed among the descendants of collateral males on the father's side, but they are allowed among the descendants on the mother's side, when they are from three to seven degrees removed. Widow remarriage is allowed, but the widow of a man does not marry his younger brother. Divorce is granted on the ground of disagreement, the offending party having to pay a fine of Rs. 12. They have a headman in Ahmedabad who exercises little control. Social disputes are settled by a majority of the caste people. Targalas are Shaiva and keep in their houses, images of *Umia Mata* and *Mahadev*. No band starts on its cold weather acting tour without first performing before the Behecharaji Mata.

Teli (39).—Deccani oil-pressers, chiefly found in the Songhad taluka of the Navsari District. They press out oil only from *tal* (sesamum) and consider themselves degraded, if they press it out from castor seeds.

Thakarda (153,261).—A caste of Kolis mainly found in the Kadi District. They are so called from their half Rajput descent.

THAKKAR.—A term applied to Luhanas.

Thakor-Pardeshi (313).—A caste formed by those Thakors from Upper India who have settled in Gujarat.

Thelari (72).—Pack drivers from the Deccan.

Thori (49).—A wandering tribe living upon the sale of *katharot* (wooden plates), *chatva* (wooden laddles) and plaited reed baskets. They are divided into Garasia and Makwana who differ in no way except that intermarriage is not allowed. They appear to be of Rajput descent, but are looked upon as untouchable like Dheds, etc. They are reputed to be cattlelifters. Their head-quarters are in Kapadvanj under Kaira and Mandva near Chandod, where they stay during the monsoon. During the rest of the year they travel from place to place in bands of ten to fifteen for the sale of their wares. Their home language is Gujarati but they understand Hindustani also. All social disputes are settled by a *panch* whose decision is final. Widow marriage is allowed. Those dying of small-pox, or without ever having small-pox, are buried. All others are burnt. Flesh of any kind except pork and beef is eaten. Brahmans are not employed.

TOLAKIA (3,925).—A sub-caste of Audich Brahmans.

TRAGAD (1,334).—A sub-caste of Soni.

TUMBR (313).—A sub-caste of Charan.

Turi (1,048).—A caste found chiefly in the Kadi District. They take their name from *tur* (drum). They are said to be the descendants of a Bhangi and Musalman dancing girl. According to their own story they are the descendants of a Bhat. They are probably degraded Rajputs as among their surnames are Dabhi, Makvana and Parmar. In appearance, dress and language, they do not differ from Dheds. In position they rank between Dheds and Bhangis. Besides grain of all kinds, they eat fish and flesh of animals that die a natural death. They eat the flesh of goats, sheep, fowls, deer, bears, hares and porcupines, but do not eat dogs, cats, horses, asses, jackals, camels, cows, vultures, owls, serpents, cranes or iguanas. They cultivate during the rains and wander about in the fair season playing on *tur* and singing tales, half prose, half verse to the accompaniment of a *sarangi*. Widow remarriage and divorce are allowed. The younger brother of the deceased husband has the first claim to his widow. The dead are buried. They have a headman who with the majority of the men present at a caste meeting, settles all disputes. Breaches of caste rules are punished with fines which are spent in caste feasts.

Uda (2,897).—A caste formed by some dissenters from Lewa Kanbis. They are so called from their being the followers of a *bhagat* called *Udo*. They are peculiarly exclusive in their habits and would not drink from a brass or copper pot touched even by a Brahman. They are generally Kabirpanthis.

Udambar (11).—A Brahman caste; takes its name from the sage Udambar. They are family priests, beggars and peasants and are found chiefly in the City of Baroda.

Umad (1,537).—A Vania caste: said to have entered Gujarat from Marwar about ten centuries ago. They are partly Vaishnava and partly Jain and are found mainly in the Kadi and Baroda Districts. They are divided into Visa (882) and Dasa (650) who eat together but do not intermarry.

Uneval (1,353).—A Brahman caste found chiefly in the Baroda and Amreli Districts and said to take its name from Una, a village in Kathiawad. They are either peasants or beggars.

Vadadra (186).—A Brahman caste; takes its name from Vadad, about fourteen miles north-east of Ahmedabad. At present their chief head-quarter is Mehmedabad near Kaira. They are sooth-sayers and jugglers. Starting from home in the cold season, they move on a begging expedition from town to town and go as far as Bombay and Malwa. When a Vadadra visits a street, he gathers the people together by calling on his deities the *Behechara* and *Amba Mata* to protect the inhabitants. Then he begins a course of sooth-saying and foretelling the evils of the coming year. When this is over he performs as a juggler taking from his mouth large quantities of *kanku* (red powder), cocoanut and *chunddi* (silk sari).

Vadhel (69).—A caste peculiar to the Amreli District. They were originally Rathods from Marwar. Under one Umedsing Rathod, their ancestors came from Marwar, slew the Choras and took possession of Beyt, whence the tribe is called Vadhel or Badhel, from *vadha* a massacre. Vadhels originally belonged to Okhamandal, but are now found in Dhari and Amreli talukas also.

Vadi (511).—Jugglers and snake charmers. They are so called from the word *vad*, to play on a musical instrument. They generally play upon *morli*, a sort of flute. They work as cultivators and day labourers also.

VADNAGARA (368).—A sub-caste of Nagar Brahmans.

Vaghari (28,129).—A caste deriving its name from Sanscrit, *wagura*, meaning a net and means tribe of netters. In appearance and occupation, they seem associated with fowlers and birdcatchers known as Pardhis. Vagharis are superior to Dheds but inferior to Kolis. According to their own account they are Chohan Rajputs. Their surnames, however, do not favour a separate tribal origin. Chavan, Charan, and Koli suggest a mixed people, descendants of men of higher classes who either in time of famine or from a passion for a girl of the tribe or from some breach of caste rule, sank to be Vagharis.

Vagharis are divided into four main sub-castes:—Chunaras or lime-burners, who are also cultivators and fowlers (2,973); Datanias who sell *datan* or tooth brushes (9,253); Vedu who grow and sell *aria*, a species of gourd, and live in towns (632), and Patani who trade in wood and bamboos and sell chickens (3,087). The names of the other sub-divisions are Talbada (4,717), Champta, Kankodia, Marwadi, Saraniya (27), etc. The Talbadas neither eat nor drink with the other divisions. The other divisions are of a lower grade and eat and drink together but do not intermarry.

Except the owl and the jackal, they eat all animals including the pig. Their favourite food is the flesh of the iguana or *gho* and *sandha* (a reptile of the lizard species). They generally keep goats and fowls, sell eggs, catch birds, and go as *shikaris*. They need no Brahmans for betrothal, marriage or death ceremonies. They believe in spirits and lucky and unlucky days. They worship goddesses, the chief among whom are *Behcharaji*, *Kalka*, *Khodiar*, *Meldi*, *Hadkai* and *Vihat*. Children are married when 10 or 15 years old. They burn or bury their dead. Widow marriage and divorce are allowed. They have their headmen or *patels*, but all caste disputes are decided by the council of the caste.

Vagher (4,277).—They are partly Hindus and partly Musalmans and are found in Okhamandal of which they claim to be the earliest inhabitants. The name Vagher is partly derived from *vai*, without, and *gher*, smell, meaning a tiger devoid of the sense of smell. In time the term was applied to the Kala tribe who were as criminal and sanguinary as tigers. Another legend is that vaghers were so called because they cooled the gods on a visit to hot Okhamandal by *gher* (enclosing) of *va*, or wind and this refreshed them.

Vaghers are a fine looking race, strong, sturdy and enterprising. Like Rajputs, Rabaris and Charans, they part the beard in the middle curling the ends behind the ears. Their women are well-built and hard-working. The mother-tongue of the vaghers is a currupt form of the Kachhi dialect. By nature they are restless, turbulent, impatient of control and have predatory leanings. They rose four times between 1816 and 1873 against the constituted authority. By occupation, they were first fishermen, then pirates and freebooters and are now land-holders, fishermen and sailors. By religion, Musalman converts are Sunni. Those who are Hindus hold Dwarkadhish in great veneration. All vaghers come to Dwarka on the *Bhim Agiaras* day (11th of the bright half of Jeth), bathe in the Gomti and worship Ranchhodji. Hindu vaghers do not eat food cooked by Musalmans, but give their daughters in marriage to those Musalmans who can pay for them.

VAHIVANCHA (513).—A sub-caste of Bahrot.

VAISHYA (7,845).—A sub-caste of Sutar.

VAKALIA (159).—A sub-caste of Darji.

Valam (740).—A Brahman caste found chiefly in the Baroda District. They are the priests of Patidars, a section of Lewa Kanbis. They take their name from Valam, a village in the Visnagar taluka of the Kadi District. Most of them are beggars, priests or cultivators. They are said to have settled in Valla in the 14th century as the priests of Kayasthas. Owing to disputes with their patrons, they were driven from that place to Dhandhuka, Vaso, Sojitra, Pihij and other places in the Charottar.

VALARI.—Same as Varli.

VALMIK (432).—A sub-caste of Kayastha.

VALVADA (3,137).—A sub-caste of Chodhra.

Valvi (1,046).—A forest tribe found in the Baroda and Navsari Districts.

Vansfoda (9).—Found in the Baroda City. So called from their occupation of splitting bamboos and making baskets, *chiks*, etc. They are also called Ghancha.

Vanza (1,391).—A caste of weavers in the Amreli District. They are distinct from Salvis and regard themselves superior to them. They have gradually left off weaving and taken to other occupations, such as tailoring, calico-printing, etc.

Vanza Gor (6).—The priests of the Vanza caste. They are looked upon as degraded on account of their serving the Vanzas.

Vanzara (572).—Derived from two Hindustani words, *banaj*, trade, and *hara*, doer, and literally meaning traders. They are also called Banjara. They are a wandering tribe, moving backwards and forwards between Malwa and Gujarat. They come from four Rajput tribes, Rathods, Burtias, Chohans and Parmars. The men wear the hair long and beard of average length. The women draw the *sadi* over the head and raise the robe into a high peaked head-dress by setting inside it an upright stick about nine inches long. Besides the robe, they wear a loose unbacked bodice, a long full petticoat and peaked shoes. They carry from Marwar wool and blankets, taking back grain, salt, cocoanuts and tobacco. The women drive the bullocks. They circumcise, bury the dead and are married in Musalman form. They bear Hindu names, believe in Hindu gods and do not eat beef. Each horde (*tanda*) has a separate headman, called Naik, whose authority extends as far as the levy of fines, from Rs. 5 to 7 in civil disputes. In the present decay of their carrying trade, they have taken to no new industries and are said to be dying out.

VARIA (2,096).—A sub-caste of Kumbhar.

Varli (598).—An early tribe found in the Navsari District. They seem to have come from North Konkan where they are found in large numbers. The name is said to be derived from *varal*, a patch of cultivated ground. The men shave the head and do not wear the beard. The women wear the hair oiled and plaited. They do not eat the flesh of a cow or of a dead animal. They are fond of smoking and drinking. They cultivate land and also rear fowls. On the sixth day after a birth, the goddess *chhathi* is worshipped. Children are married at any time after they are twelve years old. The practice of serving for a wife, *khandadio*, prevails. Widow marriage is allowed but polygamy is not practised. The dead are burned. Brahmans do not officiate on any ceremonial occasions. A headman who holds office during the pleasure of the community decides all caste questions.

Vasava (10,951).—An early tribe, also called Vasavda, found in the Baroda and Navsari Districts. Their males put on *dhotee* or *payjama*, a jacket and a turban. But one of their peculiarities is worth noting. Whenever a new garment is brought for the wife, the husband tears off a piece from it sufficient to cover his nakedness. This piece is kept hanging from the thread on his waist at day time and is made to cover up his loins at night. The females wrap a piece of cloth round about their lower limbs and put another on the head. They begin to put on a bodice only when they go to their husbands'. They wear necklaces of white stones and two anklets of brass on each leg. When a boy has attained puberty, his parents and relations go out in search of a wife for him and take him along with them. If the boy likes the girl shown to him by his parents, they send for toddy from the market and drink it with the girl's parents. The boy's father agrees to pay from Rs. 22 to 30, and settles a day for the marriage and returns home. A day previous to that fixed for the performance of the ceremony, the boy and his parents, relations and others come to the village where the girl and her parents reside and put up for the night outside the village and dance there the whole night. Next morning they go to the bride's house, where a bamboo is held lengthwise between the bride's and bridegroom's parties and dancing commences. After a time when a bottle of wine and two pice are given to the girl's party by that of the boy, the bamboo is removed and both parties dance together. Then, a new garment in one of the corners of which are tied a rupee and 4 pice is given to the bride by the bridegroom. Both are then anointed with oil and turmeric powder and are placed on the shoulders of two men; the boy with a sword and the girl with its sheath. Both of these men dance away with the human burden on their shoulders for a time and then put them down. After that, they sit down to dinner; which when over, the boy and party return home with the new bride. When nine days have passed after this auspicious event, the leading men of the village of the bride's parents go to her husband's house and dance in front of it without speaking, until a bottle of wine and a rupee are given to them by the boy's father. Then they speak with him, dine at his house and return with the girl to their village. The system of *khandhadio*, as well as remarriage and divorce, obtain among these people.

No sooner a Vasava dies, a match-lock is fired. The dead body is then placed on a bedstead and carried in procession with music playing and matchlocks firing to the burning ground. Then the pyre is erected, around which the dead body with the bedstead is taken seven times and is afterwards placed on the pyre. Food is placed in the mouth of the dead body and his usual implements and weapons are placed by his side. The body is then burned and the mourners bathe and go home. In the evening they again assemble, drink and eat together. This being over, a relative of the deceased gets up and pierces an adjacent tree with an arrow to mark the completion of the funeral ceremonies.

They do not perform menstruation and pregnancy ceremonies at all, but give a small feast on the fifth day after the birth of a child and then give a name to it.

VATALIA (1,261).—A sub-caste of Kumbhar.

Vayada (4).—A Brahman caste; found in a small number in the Kadi District. They are priests of the Vayada Vanias and like their patrons take their name from Vayad, a village near Patan.

Vayada (740).—A Vania caste. Like Vayada Brahmans it takes its name from Vayad, a village near Patan. They are divided into Dasa (523) and Visa (153) who eat together but do not intermarry. The Visas are further divided into Ahmedabadi and Surati who eat together and intermarry. Most of the Vayadas are Vallabhachari and few are Shaiva. A curious marriage custom obtains among these people. Unlike other Vanias, the bridegroom goes to the bride's house in a bullock cart with his head covered with a piece of cloth and the marriage ceremony takes place at high night. On his way to the bride's house the bridegroom performs the *chakla* or cross-road worship. In the middle of the square, a sweet-ball is placed on a *khaju* or fried cake and at each corner an earthen pot with a sweet-ball and a copper coin on it. After the worship is over the corner pots are given to four unmarried boys as a lucky present to ensure speedy marriage. A sweet-ball is then set on the ground and on it a waist cloth is spread. On the cloth a sword is placed and the bridegroom's cart is made to pass over the sword. If the edge of the sword is broken, it is considered a bad omen. The bride also performs the cross-road ceremony in company of her friends and relatives.

VEDU (632).—A sub-caste of Vaghari.

VERAGI.—Same as Bava.

Vidur (16).—Immigrants from the Deccan. They are degraded Brahmans.

VISNAGARA (4,963).—A sub-caste of Nagar Brahmans.

VOHORA.—A general term derived from the Gujarati word *vohorvun*, to trade, and applied to converts to Islam from the Hindu castes belonging to the unarmed or non-fighting classes. Such names as Molesalam, Malik, Sepahi, etc., were coined for converts from the Rajput, Koli and other fighting classes, but the general term Vohora was applied to the rest. Vohoras are divided into two main classes, Vohora traders and Vohora peasants. Both are quite distinct from each other in their manners, customs and religious beliefs.

Vohora-peasants (11,858).—Are the descendants of the Kanbi and other cultivating castes, who adopted Islam at the close of the fourteenth and during the fifteenth centuries. They are found mainly in the Baroda and Navsari Districts. Their language is Gujarati and their ordinary food is rice, millet-bread and pulse. They eat fish or flesh but never drink liquor. Except in towns where they have lately adopted Musalman fashions, peasant Vohoras, both males and females, dress like ordinary Hindus, males in *dhoti, bandi* and *fenta* and women in *sallo, ghagro* and *kapdu*. Their ornaments, are peculiar, very massive and heavy and in make partly Hindu, partly Musalman. They marry only among themselves. But a few rich men in towns have begun to marry with regular Musalmans. Those who claim high class descent, *i.e.*, from Brahmans, Vanias, or Kanbis, take wives from, but refuse to give their daughters in marriage to those who are descended from Kolis, Ravalias, Dheds and other low castes. Almost all are landholders or peasants, but some go to Burma or East Africa for trade or labour. Their home language is Gujarati, but a change is going on from Gujarati to Urdu. They are Sunnis in faith and have their Pirzadahs or spiritual guides whom they treat with great respect. Most of the peasant Vohoras still keep some Hindu practices. Some of their males have Hindu names, as Akhuji, Bajibhai, &c., others have oddly changed Musalman names, Ibru or Ibla for Ibrahim and Ipsu or Isap for Yusuf; among women, Khaja for Khatija and Fatudi for Fatima. At death, their women beat their breast and wail like Hindus. They celebrate marriage, pregnancy and death by giving caste dinners in which *ladu*, *kansar* and such other vegetable Hindu dishes alone are prepared. When a caste dinner is to be given, the village barber is sent round to ask the guests. Each village has its headman of the community and caste disputes are settled in a meeting of the community in some central place.

Vohora-traders (13,177)—Are mostly descendants of Hindu converts to the teaching of Ismalian missionaries, who came to Gujarat in the 11th century. Even now, they have such surnames as Dave, Travadi, Mehta, &c., pointing to their Brahman or Vania origin. A few Vohoras claim descent from Egyptian and Arab refugees. They are the richest and most prosperous class of Musalmans in the State. Trading Vohoras are divided into five sections—Daudi, Sulemani, Alia, Jaffri and Naghoshi or Rotia. The last four were formed by schisms from the main body.

Daudi Vohoras (7,008)—Are the most numerous among the Vohoras in the State. They are also the richest and the most widely spread class in India. They are to be found in Aden,

Zanzibar, Rangoon, Siam, China, and other places, where they have migrated for trade. Boys' names end in *ji* or *ali*, as Ismailji, Yusafali, &c. A few girls have Hindu names, but the rest have oddly changed Musalman names such as Khatli for Khatija, Fatudi for Fatima and Ahli for Ayeshah. They shave their head, wear long thin beards and cut the hair on the upper lip close. Their women pencil their eyelids with collyrium, blacken their teeth with *missi* and redden the palms of their hands and the soles of their feet with henna. Their home-tongue is Gujarati marked by some peculiarities in pronunciation, such as the irregular use of the dental and palatal *d* and *t* and of *kh* for *qu*. Daudi Vohoras are noted for their fondness for living in large and airy houses and for their love of display in house ornaments and furniture. Their chief occupation is trade. Some Daudis in Sidhpur have large trade dealings in Bombay, Madras and Africa. Others are local traders and shopkeepers selling hardware, stationery, &c. Their women do house work and weave cotton turbans. Daudis are Shiahs of the Mustalian division of the great Ismaili sect. They are fond of pilgrimages to Mecca and Karbala. They abstain from music and dancing and from using or dealing in tobacco and intoxicating drinks or drugs. Of late, they have made a few converts chiefly of their servants and Hindu women taken in marriage. Their leader, both in things religious and social, is their Mullah who has headquarters at Surat. The Daudi Vohoras in Kadi have their Mullah there who decides all religious and social disputes. Appeals against his decision lie to the Miya Saheb who resides in Ahmedabad and appeal against the decisions of the latter lie to the Bhai Saheb who also resides in Ahmedabad. The final appeal lies to the Bava Saheb who resides in Surat. On both religious and civil questions, his authority is final. Discipline is enforced in religious matters by fine and in cases of adultery and drunkenness, by fine and excommunication. Every important settlement of Daudi Vohoras has its Mullah or Deputy of the head Mullah. Appeal from him lies to the head Mullah.

Sulemani Vohoras (992) though not so numerous as Daudi Vohoras, are an influential division of the trading Vohoras. The origin of the Sulemani sect was during the sixteenth century, when a Surat Vohora sent as a missionary to Arabia, succeeded in making a considerable number of converts. These, besides by the regular name of Ismail, became known as Biazi Vohoras, from the priest's title of Biazi, the fair. For a time, they considered the Gujarat high priest as their head. But about the close of the sixteenth century upon the death of Daud bin Ajabshah, the high priest of Gujarat Vohoras, the Gujarat Vohoras chose as his successor one Daud bin Kutabshah. Meanwhile one of the Yaman priesthood, Suleman by name, was accepted by the people of Yaman as the successor. He came over to Gujarat, but finding his claim rejected by all, returned to Arabia. Such of the Gujarat Vohoras as upheld his claim were called Sulemani. In look, belief and customs, the Sulemanis do not differ from the Daudi Vohoras, with whom they associate but do not marry. They are a small class. They have given up the Gujarat Vohora dress and turban. Their home language is both Gujarati and Hindustani and they have begun to marry with regular Musalmans.

Alia Vohoras (664) are so called from Ali, the founder, one of the sons of Shaikh Adam, the head Mullah, who passing over his sons, appointed one Shaikh Tayyib as his successor. Tayyib had very few followers. Like Sulemanis, Alias do not intermarry with Daudis but do not differ from them in appearance or customs.

Jaffri Vohoras (2,824) are a section of the trading Vohoras, who became Sunni on the advent of Muzaffar I, as Governor of Gujarat in A. D. 1391. They kept up their marriage relations with the Daudi section until their connection was severed by a saint named *Sayad Jaafari Shiraji* from whose name, they are called Jaffri. They are also called *Patani* from Patan, their headquarters. Because they are Sunnis, they are also known as *badi jamat*, the large body, and as *char yari* or believers in the Prophet's four companions, *as-habs*. In appearance they differ somewhat from Daudis, and from ordinary Musalmans by their round narrow-rimmed brown or black turban. Their occupation is trade and keeping of hardware, glass, cloth and stationery shops. Among them, males have such names as Umar, Usman and Ali, preceded by Mian and followed by Bhai. Female names are like those of Daudi women. They marry only among themselves. Each settlement has its headman and forms a fairly organised body.

Naghoshi or Rotia (12) literally, means bread-eater. They form a very small section founded in A. D. 1789 by a member who held certain peculiar doctrines prominent among which was that to eat animal food was sin. From this, his followers came to be called *Naghoshi*, non-flesh-eating or *Rotia*, bread-eaters. They intermarry with Alia but not with Daudi Vohoras.

Vyas (558).—A Brahman caste found in Kadi and Baroda Districts. They are the descendants of 108 Brahmans of several sub-divisions who conducted a penance ceremony performed by a Brahman jester in the employ of one of the Musalman kings of Ahmedabad. The families who took part in this ceremony were excommunicated and formed a separate caste. Vyas allow widow marriage and in appearance and dress resemble Rajputs and Kanbis. They are husbandmen, clothsellers, moneylenders and beggars. Shortly after the formation of the Vyas Brahman caste, some members of it began to act as Bhavaiyas or strolling players and were looked upon as degraded. They formed a separate caste with the Targalas or Bhavaiyas.

Yajurvedi (504).—A caste of Deccani Brahmans, so called on account of its members being followers of the *Yajurveda*. A Yajurvedi often styles himself a *Deshastha* in contradiction to *Koknastha* and it is not improbable that in the number of Deshasthas recorded in the Census, several Yajurvedis were included.

LIST OF ILLUSTRATIONS OF TYPICAL CASTES, TRIBES AND RACES.

(*For descriptive matter, see each name in the General Glossary.*)

Hindu Castes.

Animistic Tribes.

Musalman Castes and Tribes.

HINDU CASTES.

ANJANA KANBI.

BARIA KOLI.

BHADBHUNJA (*Grain-parcher*).

BHANGI (*Sweeper*).

CHAMAR.

HINDU CASTES—*contd.*

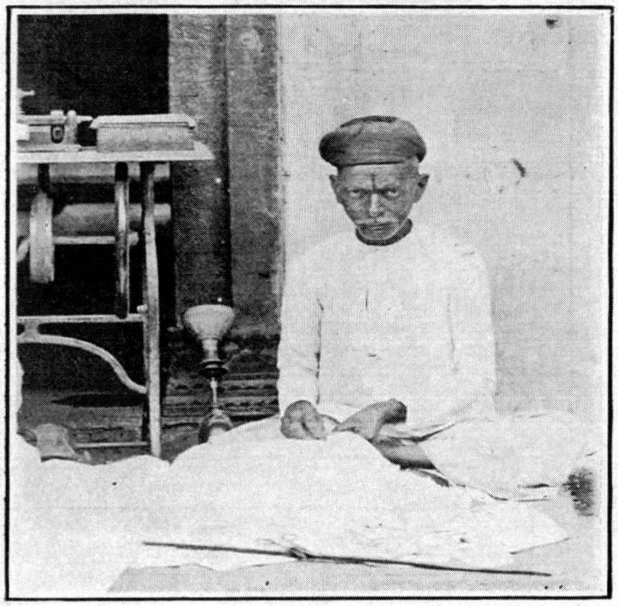

DARJI (*Tailor*).

DESHASTHA BRAHMAN.

DHED.

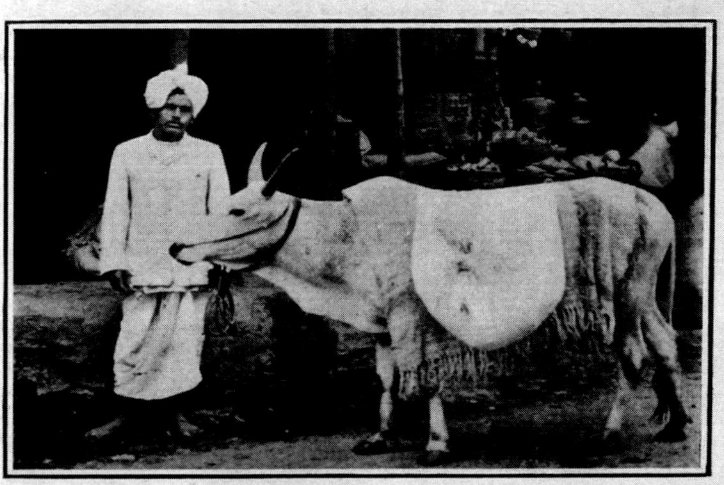

DHOBI (*Washerman*).

HINDU CASTES—*contd.*

GARODA.

GHANCHI (*Oil-presser*).

GOLA (*Rice-pounder*).

GUGALI BRAHMAN.

HINDU CASTES—*contd.*

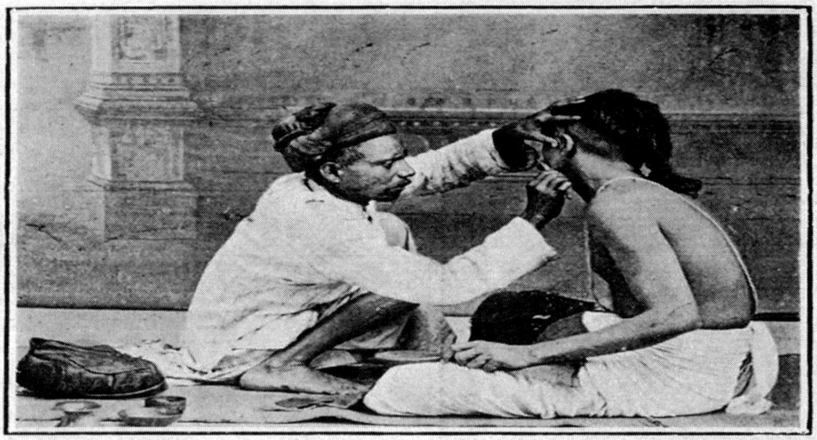

HAJAM (*Barber*).

KADWA KANBI.

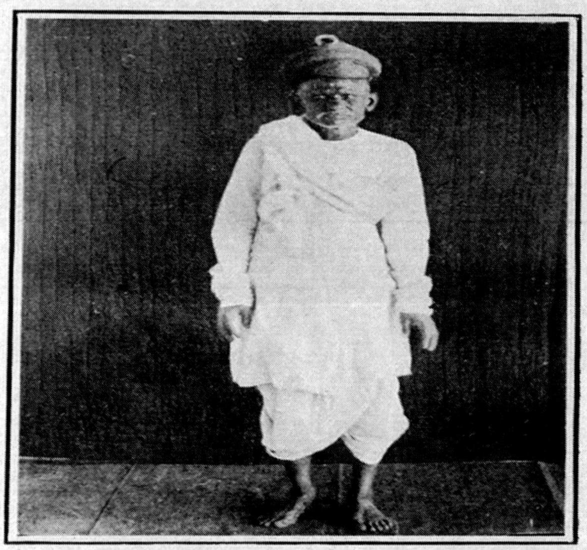

KANDOLIA BRAHMAN.

KANSARA.

KAPOL VANIA.

HINDU CASTES—*contd.*

KATHI.

KHARADI (*Turner*).

KHARVA.

KHATRI (*Weaver*).

KUMBHAR (*Potter*).

HINDU CASTES—*contd.*

LAD VANIA.

LEWA KANBI.

LUHANA.

LUHAR (*Blacksmith*).

HINDU CASTES—*contd.*

MARATHA.

MOCHI (*Shoe-maker*).

MODH BRAHMAN.

RABARI.

HINDU CASTES—*contd.*

RAVALIA.

SALAT.

SONI (*Goldsmith*).

SUTAR (*Carpenter*).

TARGALA.

HINDU CASTES.—*contd.*

THAKARDA KOLI.

VADHEL.

VAGHARI.

VAGHER.

ANIMISTIC TRIBES.

BHIL.

DHODIA.

DUBLA.

GAMIT.

ANIMISTIC TRIBES.—*contd.*

KATHODIA.

KOTWALIA.

MAVCHI.

NAYAKDA.

VARLI.

MUSALMAN CASTES AND TRIBES.

KHOJA.

MEMON.

PINJARA.

SHAIKH.

VOHORA (*Trader*).

Chapter XII.

OCCUPATION.

Reference to statistics.

565. The statistics regarding occupations will be found in Tables XV and XVI. The former table is divided into five parts, *viz* :—

A.—General summary showing the number of persons for the whole State, the Districts and the City of Baroda, following each occupation in the classified scheme to be presently referred to.

B.—The subsidiary occupations of the actual workers among the agriculturists only.

C.—Showing for certain mixed occupations the number of persons who returned each as their (*a*) principal and (*b*) subsidiary means of livelihood.

D.—Distribution of occupations by religion.

E.—Information regarding factories collected in a special industrial schedule filled up by the owners or agents of factories, mills, etc., in which at least twenty persons were employed on the 10th March 1911.

In Table XVI occupation is combined with caste. Only the more numerous castes are dealt with and for each of these, the actual workers are distributed to the sub-classes or main divisions in the general occupation scheme. 7 of the sub-classes are sub-divided, so as to bring out more clearly the character of the occupations which are followed by the members of the selected castes.

At the end of this chapter will be found the following Subsidiary Tables in which the more important features of the statistics are presented in a more readable form by means of proportional figures :—

Subsidiary Table I.—General distribution by occupation.

Subsidiary Table II.—Distribution by occupation in Natural Divisions.

Subsidiary Table III.—Distribution of the agricultural, industrial, commercial and professional population in Natural Divisions and Districts.

Subsidiary Table IV.—Occupations combined with agriculture (where agriculture is the subsidiary occupation).

Subsidiary Table V.—Occupations combined with agriculture (where agriculture is the principal occupation).

Subsidiary Table VI.—Occupation of females by sub-classes and selected orders and groups.

Subsidiary Table VII.—Selected occupations, 1911 and 1901.

Subsidiary Table VIII.—Occupations of selected castes.

The nature of the information collected.

566. In 1891 the information regarding occupations was collected in a single column of the schedule headed "Occupation or means of subsistence." In 1901, as also in the present Census, three columns were provided as noted in the margin, two for the principal and subsidiary occupations respectively, of actual workers and the third for the means of subsistence of dependants or persons supported by the labour of others.

Occupation or means of subsistence of actual workers.		Means of subsistence of dependants on actual workers.
Principal.	Subsidiary.	
9	10	11

Instructions to the enumerators.

567. The instructions given to the enumerators were as under :—

"**Column 9 (Principal occupation of actual workers).**—Enter the principal means of livelihood of all persons who actually do work or carry on business, whether personally or by means of servants, or who live on *house-rent, pension*, etc. Enter the exact occupation and avoid vague terms such as 'service' or 'writing' or 'labour.' For example, in the case of labour, say whether in the fields, or in a ginning factory, or cotton mill, or on earthwork, etc. In the case of agriculture, distinguish between persons who receive rent (Jamindars) and those who pay rent (cultivators). If a person makes the articles he sells, he should be entered as 'maker and seller' of them. Women and children who work at any occupation, which helps to augment the family income, must be entered in column 9 under that occupation and not in column 11. Column 9 will be blank for dependants.

Column 10 (Subsidiary occupation of actual workers).—Enter here any occupation which actual workers pursue at any time of the year in addition to their principal occupations. Thus, if a person lives principally by his earnings as a boatman, but partly also by fishing, the word 'boatman' will be entered in column 9 and 'fisherman' in column 10. If an actual worker has no additional occupation, enter in column 10 the word 'none.' This column will be blank for dependants.

Column 11 (Means of subsistence of dependants).—For children and women and old or infirm persons, who do not work, either personally or by means of servants, enter the *principal* occupation of the person who supports them. This column will be blank for actual workers."

In the instructions to Supervisors these rules were thus amplified :—

"(1). The entry of occupation in columns 9 to 11 of the schedule is another matter requiring special care. Only those women and children will be shown as workers who help to augment the family income. A woman who looks after her house and cooks the food is not a worker but a dependant. But a woman who collects and sells firewood or cowdung is thereby adding to the family income, and should be shown as a worker. So also a woman who regularly assists her husband in his work (*e.g.*, the wife of a potter, who fetches the clay from which he makes his pots,) but not one who merely renders a little occasional help. A boy who sometimes looks after his father's cattle is a dependant, but one who is a regular cowherd should be recorded as such in column 9. Boys at school or college should be entered as dependants. Dependants on a joint family, the members of which follow different avocations, should be entered in column 11 under the occupation of the principal working member. Domestic servants must be entered as cook, *bhisti*, etc., in column 9, and not in column 11 as dependants on their master's occupation. Persons temporarily out of employ should be shown as following their previous occupation.

(2). Where a man has two occupations, the principal one is that on which he relies mainly for his support and from which he gets the major part of his income. A subsidiary occupation should be entered, if followed at any time of the year. *Only one subsidiary occupation (the most important one) should be entered in column* 10; this must be impressed upon the enumerators.

(3). In column 9 do not use general or indefinite terms, such as 'service,' 'shop-keeping,' 'writing,' 'labour,' etc. Find out and state the exact kind of service, the goods sold, the class of writing or labour.

If a man says his occupation is 'service,' distinguish (1) government service, (2) railway service, (3) municipal service, (4) village service, (5) service in a shop or office, and (6) domestic service, stating his rank and the nature of his work.

In the case of domestic service, state precisely the kind of service rendered, *e.g.*, cook, water-carrier, *khidmatgar*, etc.

Show pensioners as military or civil, as the case may be.

Show persons who live on the rent of lands or buildings in towns separately from persons who derive their income from agricultural land.

In the case of persons living on agriculture, distinguish rent-receivers and rent-payers. The term rent-receiver includes jamindars, and tenure-holders, such as Inamdars, Ijardars, and others who receive rent from ryots. The term rent-payer includes all ryots and under-ryots, whether paying cash or produce rent. Where a person cultivates part of his land and sublets part, he should be shown in column 9 as a rent-payer and in column 10 as a rent-receiver, if he gets the greater part of his income from the land which he cultivates himself, and *vice versa*.

Show gardeners and growers of special products, such as tea, betel, etc., separately.

In the case of labourers, distinguish agricultural labourers, earthworkers, labourers in mines, and operatives in mills, etc., stating the kind of mill or factory, such as cotton mills, ginning factories, etc.

In the case of clerks, show the occupation of the clerk's employer (*e.g.*, lawyer's clerk).

In the case of traders, specify carefully the kind of trade, (*e.g.*, grain dealers).

In the case of large manufactures, show the proprietor as a manufacturer, and specify the branch of manufacture, as cotton manufacturer, etc. For minor industries, state precisely the nature of the work done; for example, whether a weaver weaves cotton, silk, carpets, etc."

568. In spite of the care taken to ensure accuracy, vague entries, such as *nokri* (service), *majuri* (labour), *dukan* (shop), *bhikshavriti* (mendicancy), *karigar* (artizan), *karkun* (clerk), *kantract* (contract), etc., were by no means uncommon. A clue to the precise occupation was often furnished by the place of birth, caste, sex and other entries on the slips relating to these persons, and they were assigned to the right group in the occupation scheme. But in a large number of cases, even such guessing could not be made, and they had to be relegated to the order "General terms which do not indicate a definite occupation."

Accuracy of the return.

Errors in compilation may occur owing to careless copying and sorting, misposting of entries in the sorters' tickets and compilation registers and wrong classification. It is believed, however, that on the present occasion such mistakes were minimised by the minute instructions which were laid down in the Code, and the close supervision that was exercised. Moreover the simplicity of the scheme of classification adopted and the alphabetical list of all possible occupations properly classified which was printed in the vernacular from the one in English, supplied by the Census Commissioner, hardly left any room for errors due to misunderstanding or wrong interpretation of instructions.

CLASSIFICATION OF OCCUPATIONS.

569. The scheme for the classification of occupations adopted in India in 1901 was based on that devised by Mr. Baines in 1891. It divided all occupations into eight main classes. These classes were sub-divided into twenty-four orders and seventy-nine sub-orders; and the sub-orders were further divided into 520 groups. The main objection to this scheme is its extreme elaboration and want of scientific precision. The entries in the schedules are not sufficiently precise to enable an accurate detailed classification to be made. The question was fully discussed in the last India Census Report, and it was also proposed by most of the Provincial Superintendents that in the present Census a simple scheme of classification should be introduced. The general question of the classification of occupations has, in recent years, been the subject of much discussion by European statisticians and great stress has been laid on the importance of introducing general uniformity between the occupation schemes of different countries so as to make it possible to institute an international comparison. The Census Commissioner for India drew up, therefore, on the present occasion, a new scheme of classification based on that of Dr. Jasques Bertillon, Chef des Travaux Statistiques de la ville de Paris, a prominent European statistician.

System of classification.

570. According to the scheme of M. Bertillon, all occupations are first divided into four grand classes:—(A) Production of Raw Materials; (B) Transformation and Employment of Raw Materials; (C) Public Administration and Liberal Arts; and (D) Miscellaneous. These main classes are so logical that there is scarcely any need to justify them. Each of the main classes is then divided into sub-classes:—(A) Raw Materials necessary for every occupation are produced either by working upon the soil (I. Agriculture) or by working under the soil; (II. Extraction of Minerals). (B) These raw materials are then changed by the arts and manufactures (III. Manufactures); carried to the place where they are needed (IV Transport); and distributed among consumers by trade (V Trade). (C) To keep good order and guard the welfare of the preceding occupations, every country has an army and a public force (VI); and a public administration (VII). The liberal professions (VIII) and persons living upon their income (IX) naturally follow the occupations just reviewed. (D) Finally, it is expedient to establish a division for domestic service (X); insufficiently described occupations (XI); and unproductive (XII). This classification gives us 4 classes and 12 sub-classes. The sub-classes may be further divided into orders and the orders may be divided into groups; and the groups, if desired, may also be further divided.

General principles of M. Bertillon's classification.

The new classification as adopted for India.

571. M. Bertillon's system has the great merit of elasticity, and so long as his first classification (by orders) is adhered to, the classification adopted in individual countries may be as detailed or as simple as desired without interfering with the comparability of the statistics. As modified for India by the Census Commissioner, the classes, sub-classes and with a few exceptions the orders of M. Bertillon's scheme have been maintained unchanged, but the sub-division of the orders into groups has been carried out with reference to local conditions. As revised and finally adopted the new scheme of classification contains 4 classes, 12 sub-classes, 55 orders and 169 groups. The reduction would have been still greater, but for the fact that it was necessary to sub-divide some of the old groups in order to preserve throughout the scheme, the distinction between industry and trade. Persons, who make any article, are in all cases classed under "Industry" whether they sell the articles made by them to middlemen or direct to the consumer, while persons who sell only and do not make, are classified under "Trade."

Principles underlying the new classification.

572. The information collected in the general schedules was the same as in 1901, but in tabulating the results more attention was paid on the present occasion to the entries in column 10. At the last Census the only use generally made of this column was to ascertain the number of persons who follow agriculture as an accessory to some other occupation. On the present occasion the information regarding the dependence of the population on agriculture has been completed by tabulating also the subsidiary occupation of persons whose main occupation is agriculture (Table XV-B). An attempt has also been made (Table XV-C) to obtain information regarding the more important dual occupations, such as boatmen and fishermen, shepherds and blanket-weavers, cattle-breeders and milkmen, grain-dealers and money-lenders, &c. The attempt made at the last Census to distinguish in the general schedule between workers in factories and those engaged in home industries and to sub-divide the latter between "owners, managers and superior staff" and "operatives" was unsuccessful and was not repeated. The information which it was thus sought to collect was obtained on the present occasion (Table XV-E) by means of a special schedule to be filled in by the managers of factories, workshops and the like, in which at least 20 persons were employed.

A few words may be said in explanation of the general principles underlying the new system of classification. A person is classed in Table XV-A according to his principal occupation; the number of persons in each group, who are partly dependant on agriculture, is given, but otherwise subsidiary occupations are not dealt with in this part of the table, but in parts B and C. Only those government servants are shown in sub-class VII who are engaged in the general administration including the administration of justice. Members of the medical, irrigation, opium, post office and other similar services are classed under the special heads provided for these occupations. What is looked to is the actual occupation and not the source from which the salary comes, or the ultimate object which it serves. A different principle has however been followed in Table XV-E which is based on the special industrial schedule. Here the industry is looked to and not the actual occupation of the individual employed in it. A carpenter in a brewery, for instance, is merged in the general head of brewery employees. In the general occupation table on the other hand, only persons directly concerned with the industry or trade, including clerks and menials are classed under it and not those with distinctive occupations of their own. Persons temporarily out of employ are shown under the occupation, previously followed by them.

Classified scheme of occupation.

573. The classes, sub-classes and orders of the new scheme are transcribed below, in order to make the matter of this chapter intelligible and to show the general reader how all the occupations are grouped under certain main heads. For facility of reference and economy of space, the total number

of persons returned in the Census as supported by each division is given after it in brackets :—

Class.	Sub-class.	Order.
A.—Production of raw materials (1,332,881).	I.—Exploitation of the surface of the earth (1,332,756).	1. Pasture and Agriculture (1,332,961). (*a*) Ordinary cultivation (1,284,365). (*b*) Growers of special products and market gardening (2,536). (*c*) Forestry (810). (*d*) Raising of farm stock (42,239). (*e*) Raising of small animals (11). 2. Fishing and hunting (2,795).
	II.—Extraction of minerals (125).	3. Mines (125). 4. Quarries of hard rocks. 5. Salt, etc.
B.—Preparation and supply of material substances (396,588).	III.—Industry (250,050) ...	6. Textiles (52,435). 7. Hides, skins and hard materials from the animal kingdom (16,032). 8. Wood (26,275). 9. Metals (16,150). 10. Ceramics (26,743). 11. Chemical products properly so called and analogous (10,953). 12. Food industries (11,314). 13. Industries of dress and the toilet (45,632) 14. Furniture industries (142). 15. Building industries (12,931). 16. Construction of means of transport (247). 17. Production and transmission of physical forces (heat, light, electricity, motive power, &c.) (101). 18. Industries of luxury and those pertaining to literature and the arts and sciences (11,507). 19. Industries concerned with refuse matter (19,590).
	IV.—Transport (16,638) ...	20. Transport by water (1,861). 21. Transport by road (5,960). 22. Transport by rail (6,458). 23. Post Office, Telegraph and Telephone services (2,359).
	V.—Trade (129,900). ...	24. Banks, establishments of credit, exchange and insurance (17,600). 25. Brokerage, commission and export (1,200) 26. Trade in textiles (11,131). 27. Trade in skins, leather and furs (1,688). 28. Trade in wood (930). 29. Trade in metals (954). 30. Trade in pottery (94) 31. Trade in chemical products (256). 32. Hotels, cafes, restaurants, &c. (3,390). 33. Other trade in food-stuffs (54,718). 34. Trade in clothing and toilet articles (1,425). 35. Trade in furniture (523). 36. Trade in building materials (489). 37. Trade in means of transport (1,754) 38. Trade in fuel (1581). 39. Trade in articles of luxury and those pertaining to letters and the arts and sciences (2,670). 40. Trade in refuse matter (97). 41. Trade of other sorts (29,400).
	VI.—Public force (26,904) ...	42. Army (11,560). 43. Navy (...) 44. Police (15,344)
	VII.—Public Administration (38,217).	45. Public Administration (38,217).
	VIII.—Professions and liberal arts (74,692).	46. Religion (51,985). 47. Law (1,670). 48. Medicine (3,079). 49. Instruction (9,399). 50. Letters and arts and sciences (8,559)
	IX.—Persons living on their income (8,462).	51. Persons living principally on their income (8,462).
	X.—Domestic service (3,510) ...	52. Domestic service (3,510).
	XI.—Insufficiently described occupations (142,285).	53. General terms which do not indicate a definite occupation (142,285).
	XII.—Unproductive (9,259) ...	54. Inmates of jails, asylums and hospitals (802). 55. Beggars, vagrants, prostitutes (8,457).

GENERAL FEATURES OF THE RETURN.

Population supported by each class of occupation.

574. Before dealing with the minor heads of the occupation scheme, it will be desirable to view the results from a more general point of view and to note the functional distribution of the people according to the larger divisions. The most striking feature of the return is the immense preponderance of agricultural pursuits. Nearly two-thirds of the total population (65·6 per cent.) are engaged in the exploitation of the surface of the earth for the production of raw materials. There is no extraction of minerals in the State worth the name. Nearly 19·5 per cent. of the population are maintained by the preparation and supply of material substances. Public administration and liberal arts are the principal means of support of 7·3 per cent. of the population ; and miscellaneous occupations like domestic service, and unproductive and unsufficiently described occupations support 7·6 per cent. of the population.

Diagram showing the general distribution of the population by occupation (sub-classes).

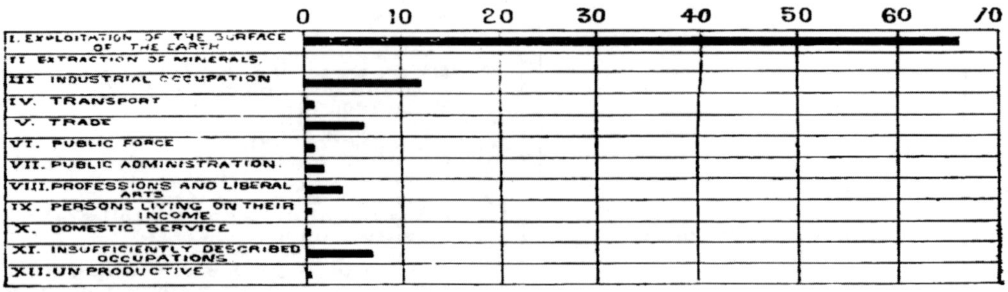

General proportion in the natural divisions.

575. The foregoing remarks refer to the main distribution of occupations in the State as a whole. The diagram in the margin has been prepared to indicate for the natural divisions, the number of persons who are chiefly supported by Agriculture (Sub-class I, Groups 1 to 6) ; Industries (Sub-class III), Commerce (Sub-class IV and V); Professions (Sub-class VIII) and all "other" means of subsistence. The proportion of persons dependant on agriculture is the highest in the Navsari Division. After it comes the Baroda Division. Then follow Kadi and Amreli in order, while Baroda City stands last in agrestic pursuits with only 34 persons in a 1,000. Industries naturally support the largest relative number of persons in the Baroda City while among the Districts, Amreli stands first and

Diagram showing the distribution of the population by occupation (classes) in the divisions.

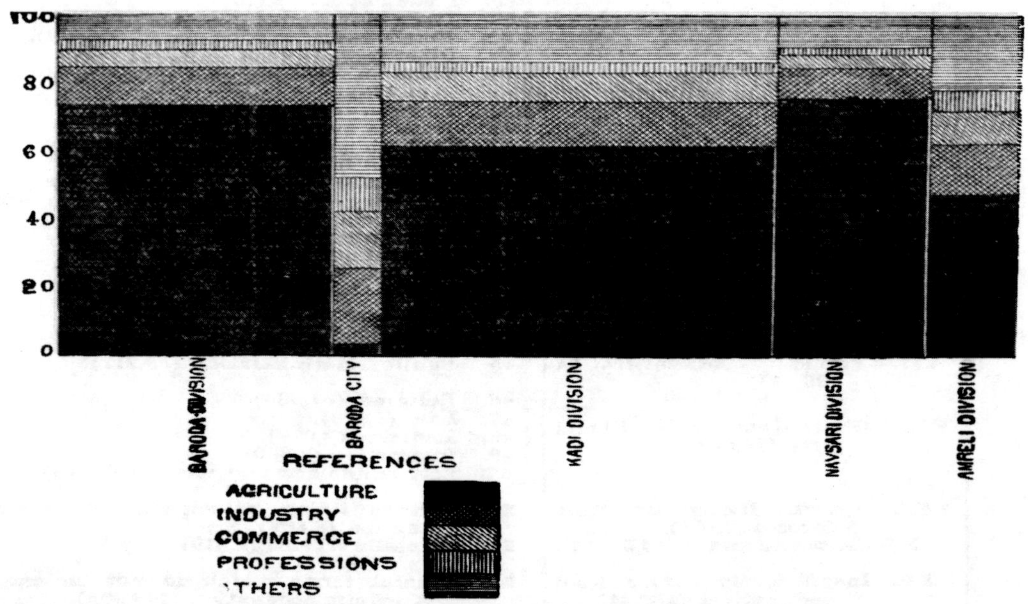

then follow Kadi, Baroda and Navsari in order. Kathiawadi carpenters, blacksmiths, tailors, shoe-makers and other artizans are to be found everywhere in the State, and their earnings support a large number of their families in their native country. The commercial and professional classes form 16 and 10 per cent. respectively of the population in the City, but elsewhere they form but a very small portion of the population. The head "others" which includes government and domestic service, persons living on their own means and indefinite and unproductive occupations, supports nearly one-half of the population in the City of Baroda.

RURAL OCCUPATIONS.

576. **Village industries.** Another method of viewing the occupation statistics from a general standpoint is, as was done in the last India Census Report, by picking out the occupations commonly followed in every village, *i.e.*, those which, taken together, meet all the requirements of ordinary rural life. The number per 10,000 of the population, who subsist by these primitive occupations in the State as a whole, is noted below :—

Occupation.	Groups included.	No. per 10,000 of total population.
Landlords and tenants	1, 2, 6	4,788
Labourers.		
Agricultural labourers	4	1,542
General labourers	98, 104, 168	572
Stock-owners, milkmen and herdsmen	9, 10, 12, 61	200
Cotton workers (not in mills)	21, 22	20
Goldsmiths and blacksmiths	41, 89	108
Brass, copper and bell metal workers	42	11
Carpenters	8, 36	82
Fishermen and boatmen	14, 60, 97, 116	26
Oil-pressers	58, 118	72
Barbers	72	97
Washermen	71	15
Toddy-drawers and sellers	65, 114	12
Grain-parchers	58	2
Leather-workers	32, 108, 109	142
Basket-makers, scavengers and drummers	37, 93, 160	135
Priests	137, 145, 151	220
Potters	47, 48, 112	133
Mendicants	149, 169	75
Village quacks and midwives	155	5
Grocers and confectioners	63, 117, 119	30
Grain-dealers and money-lenders	106, 121	125
Tailors	68	68
Vegetable and fruit sellers	120	16
Other shopkeepers	135	138
Makers and sellers of bangles	45, 90, 132	5
Silk-worm rearers and silk-weavers	13, 27	6
Total ...	....	8,645

In the State as a whole, nine persons out of ten are supported by simple village occupations here referred to. A peculiar feature of Indian rural life is the way in which each village is provided with a complete equipment of artizans and menials and until the recent introduction of western commodities, such as machine-made cloth, kerosine oil, umbrellas and the like, it was wholly self-supporting and independent. Most of the village occupations are hereditary. The potter's son becomes a potter, the barber's son, a barber, the shoe-maker's son, a shoe-maker and the like. The affairs of each functional caste are regulated, as pointed in the chapter on Caste, by its own *panchayat*. The village barber, potter, blacksmith, carpenter, washerman, *purohit*, etc., each has his defined circle of customers (*gharaks*) within which he works and no one else can attempt to deprive him of his customers without severe punishment at the hands of the caste panchayat. The duties and remuneration of each group are fixed by custom and the caste rules prohibit a man from entering into competition with another of the same caste. The method of payment for professional services rendered by barbers, potters, etc., consists in their taking a recognised share of grain, when the crop has been reaped and brought to the thrashing floor. In addition to this, small cash payments or presents of clothes, etc., are made on particular occasions, *e. g.*, to the barber and *purohit* on marriage and death occasions. Cooked food is also occasionally given, especially on occasions of caste-dinners to the barbers, potters and others whose caste rules allow them to eat it and *sidha* (flour, ghee, rice, pulse, etc.) to the *purohit* and others.

OCCUPATIONS IN THE CITY OF BARODA.

Scope of statistics.

577. In 1891 the occupations of all persons living in towns as defined for Census purposes were tabulated separately. The object in view was to ascertain how far the occupations of the urban community differed from those of people living in rural areas. The result was obscured by the large extent to which the smaller towns, such as those in this State, partake of the nature of overgrown villages. In 1901, therefore, it was thought better to take as the basis of the urban statistics the figures for cities alone. In this State, we have only one City and the figures for it are shown separately in Table XV and the proportional figures are given in the Subsidiary Tables.

General features of the statistics.

578. The main distribution of occupations in the City differs totally from that in the State as a whole. Whereas in the latter 63 per cent. of the population are dependent on the land, in the City the proportion falls to only 3 per cent. Moreover, while the rent-payers in the whole State outnumber the rent-receivers in the ratio of 36 to 1, in the City they are in the ratio of 5 to 1 only. Actual cultivators are more numerous in villages, while landlords are numerous in towns. The most common avocations of the residents in the cities are those connected with the preparation and supply of material substances, especially food industries, textile industries, and industries of dress and toilet. The persons engaged in public force, public administration, the learned professions and domestic and personal services are relatively far more numerous in the City than elsewhere.

Occupation.	Number supported per 1,000 in the	
	State.	Baroda City.
Public force	13	139
Public Administration	19	118
Domestic service	1	11
Agriculture	633	34
Pasture	21	2
Textile industry	26	56
Food industries	5	24
Industry of dress and toilet	22	37
Profession and liberal arts	87	103
Persons living on their own income	4	36

WORKERS AND DEPENDANTS.

Workers and dependants.

579. In every 100 persons, there are 47 workers and 53 dependants in the State as a whole. Taking the districts separately, we find that the corresponding proportion of workers and dependants for the districts are 48 and 52 in the Baroda, 46 and 54 in the City, 44 and 56 in Kadi, 54 and 46 in Navsari and 41 and 59 in Amreli. It was laid down in the instructions to the enumerators that women and children who work at any occupation of any kind, not being an amusement or of a purely domestic character, such as cooking, must be entered as actual workers. Only those persons were to be returned as dependants who did not in any way add to the earnings of the family. But amongst some classes in the community it is not considered respectable that a woman should help to augment the family income and the return of actual workers was perhaps vitiated in consequence to a certain extent.

Orders in which workers are the most or the least numerous.

580. The proportion of workers and dependants in agriculture, the most common occupation in the State, is equal to the average for the whole State, *viz.*, 47 workers and 53 dependants in 100. In every 100 persons supported by industries, there is one less worker and one more dependant, and in trade, there are 10 less workers and 10 more dependants as compared with agriculture. The proportion returned as workers is higher as compared with dependants in Order 10.—Ceramics, Order 12.—Food industries, Order 17.—Production and transmission of physical forces, Order 19.—Industries concerned with refuse matter, Order 23.—Post, telegraph and telephone services, Order 28.—Trade in wood, Order 40.—Trade in refuse matter, Order 52.—Domestic service, Sub-class XI.—Insufficiently described occupations and Sub-class XII.—Unproductive occupations. On the other hand, the proportion of workers to dependants is smaller in occupations connected with Transport (Sub-class IV), Public administration (Sub-class VII), and professions and liberal arts (Sub-class VIII).

Female Occupations.

581. In the State as a whole, amongst 100 actual workers more than two-thirds (70 per cent.) are males and a little less than one-third (30 per cent.) are females. The proportion of female to male workers is the highest in the Navsari District and the least in the Amreli District. This is mainly to be explained by the higher proportion of agriculturists in the former district, and that

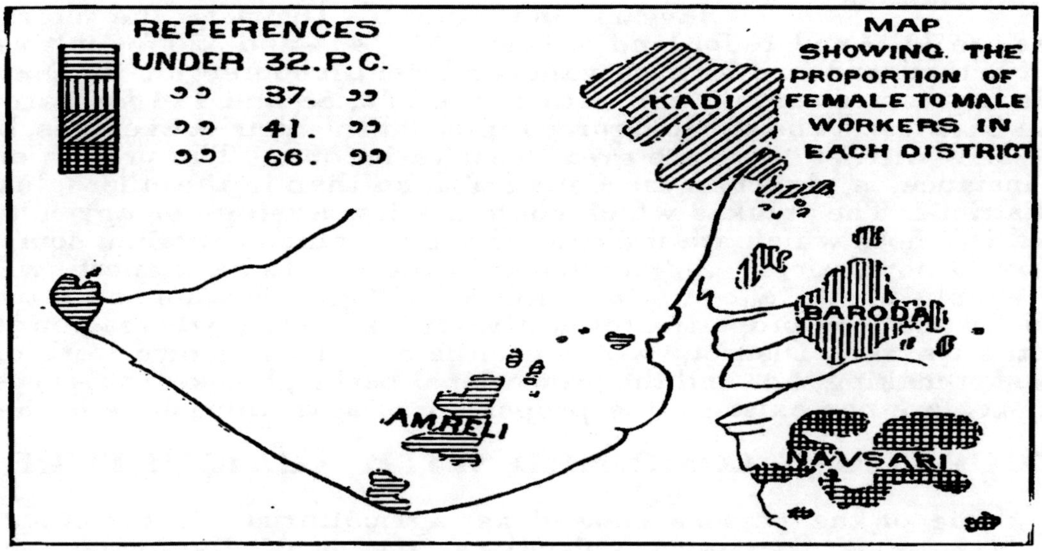

of artizans in the latter one. A more interesting feature of the return is the light which it throws upon the occupations of females. There are certain occupations which are practically monopolised by females. Among the pursuits which are mainly in the hands of women may be mentioned rope-making, basket-making, rice-pounding and flour-grinding, cap-making, toy-making, ghee-making, field labour and trade in refuse matter. The occupations in which females are engaged may be grouped into three classes—those which are followed by them independently without reference to the work of their male relations, such as flour-grinding, sewing, leaf-plate-making, midwifery, domestic service, etc.; those which are supplementary to their husbands' occupations, such as cotton spinning, selling of fruits, vegetables, milk and fish, dairy-making; and lastly those in which both the sexes work together, such as basket-making, field-labour, pot-making, sewing, etc. The occupations which females follow either independently or as supplementary to some kindred employment of their male relatives are generally distinguished by their simplicity and the small amount of physical labour they involve.

AGRICULTURAL OCCUPATIONS.

582. The detailed figures in the table of occupation may now be reviewed briefly. "Exploitation of the surface of the earth," the first sub-class in the occupation scheme is divided into (1) Agriculture (groups 1 to 6); Pasture (groups 9 to 12); fishing and hunting (groups 14—15) and "others" (groups 7—8 and 12). The groups included in Agriculture with the number of persons per 1,000 supported by them are given in the margin. As mentioned before, of the total population of the State, nearly two-thirds returned some form of Agriculture as their principal means of subsistence. Out of a thousand persons, 13 returned themselves as rent-receivers (landlords); 465 as rent-payers (ordinary cultivators), 154 as farm servants and field labourers and only 1 as fruit, flower or vegetable grower.

Sub-class I-Agriculture. Order I (a) and (b), Groups 1 to 6.

No.	Occupation.	Number supported per mille.
	(a) ORDINARY CULTIVATION.	
1	Income from rent of agricultural land (rent-receivers)...	13
2	Ordinary cultivators (rent-payers)	465
3	Agents and managers of landed estates (not planters, clerks, rent-collectors, etc.)	......
4	Farm servants and field labourers	154
5	Tea, coffee and indigo plantations	......
6	Fruit, flower, vegetable, betel, vine, areca nut, etc., growers	1

Local distribution.

583. Baroda Division claims the highest proportion per mille of landlords (21) and cultivators (541), while in the Kadi, Navsari and Amreli Districts the corresponding proportions are 11, 4 and 18 for landlords and 517, 414 and 320 for cultivators. 39 persons in a thousand are farm servants and field labourers in the Navsari District, while the corresponding proportions are 172, 88 and 144 for Baroda, Kadi and Amreli Districts. The above figures represent the district averages, but within the limits of a district there are great local variations. The proportion of landlords, for instance, is higher in the Petlad Taluka than in the other talukas of the Baroda District. The talukas which contain a low average of agriculturists are not necessarily those which are infertile, but those which contain a comparatively large industrial population. As mentioned in the last India Report, where each village is supplied with a complete outfit of village servants and artizans as in the Amreli District, the proportion of cultivators is lower; whereas in the Rani Mahals of the Navsari District, where each family does its own work of plough-making, basket-making, &c., and the professional barber, blacksmith, carpenter and scavenger, &c., are non-existent, the proportion of agriculturists is higher.

OCCUPATIONS COMBINED WITH AGRICULTURE.

Occupations combined with agriculture.

584. Some of the persons classed as agriculturists follow other pursuits as a subsidiary means of livelihood. Similarly, some persons who have been classed under some non-agricultural head, because that was returned as their main occupation, are also partially dependant on agriculture. In other words, the return of the agricultural population has, on the one hand, been swollen by the inclusion of persons whose means of subsistence are mainly, though not wholly, agricultural, while, on the other, it has been reduced by the total exclusion of those who practise agriculture as a subsidiary form of employment.

(i) Where agriculture is the subsidiary occupation.

585. The number (actual workers only) of those who returned agriculture as a subsidiary means of subsistence is shown in the columns (9, 10 ; 15, 16 ; 21, 22 ; 27, 28 ; 33, 34 ; 39, 40) against each non-agricultural head of occupation in Table XV. We may assume that the proportion of persons with dual occupations, which is found to exist among workers, applies equally to the whole population, including dependants, and, if so, in the State as a whole, in addition to the 465 persons per mille who are wholly or mainly dependant on

agriculture, there are also 19* per mille who depend on it as a secondary means of subsistence. The proportion of such persons is the largest (23 per mille) in the Kadi District. Then follow Navsari, Amreli and Baroda Districts in order with 22, 18 and 13 per mille, respectively.

The proportion of persons who are partially agriculturists is the highest in the case of occupations falling under Group 12—Herdsmen, shepherds and goat-herds where one person in 8 depends on some agricultural pursuit as a subsidiary means of support. One person in 12 of those engaged in "Public force" and one in 20 of those engaged in Sub-class VII—Public Administration—have returned some form of agriculture as a subsidiary employment. It would be tedious to recite the proportions in further detail, as they are all available in Subsidiary Table IV at the end of this Chapter, but attention may be drawn to the close connection indicated by the figures for Sub-class 3—Industry—where one in every 14 persons engaged in the preparation and supply of material substances, such as potters, blacksmiths, etc., is also partially agriculturist. Those engaged in trade and the professions and liberal arts, such as bankers, pleaders, priests, etc., are also dependant to some extent on agriculture for their maintenance.

(ii) Where agriculture is the main occupation.

In Table XV-B, details have been given under a few main heads of the subsidiary occupations followed by those whose principal means of support is agriculture. These statistics are reduced to proportionate figures in Subsidiary Table V and have been so arranged as to enable us to distinguish the non-agricultural occupations of zamindars or rent-receivers from those of cultivators or rent-payers and agricultural labourers. Of the rent-receivers with subsidiary occupations one in 119 is a government servant, one in 147 is a money-lender, one in 86 is a trader and one in 435 is a school-master ; one in 417 is an artizan, one in 666 is a priest, one in 3,333 is a lawyer and one in 2,000 is a medical practitioner. Of the cultivators or rent-payers who returned a second occupation, one in 250 is a government employe of all kinds ; one in 86 is a shop-keeper, one in 455 is a potter, one in 666 is a village watchman, one in 1,111 is a barber and one in 5,000 is a fisherman or boatman. Amongst agricultural labourers with some other employment, one in 625 is a village watchman, one in 1,666 is a herdsman, one in 769 is a weaver and one in 10,000 is an oil-presser.

Comparison with 1901.

586. The proportion of persons maintained by agriculture at the present Census is 634 per mille compared with only 519 in 1901. The Census of 1901 was preceded by the great famine which led many to relinquish agriculture and to turn to other means of subsistence. The large increase of 115 per mille in those dependant on agriculture shows a return to agriculture on the part of those who abandoned it ten years previously. We have now 155 farm servants and field labourers against 191 per mille in the last Census which indicates that 36 per mille of the landless labourers have now become cultivators. In 1901, the cultivated land in the whole State was 5,815,095 bighas. In 1911 it was 6,074,321, showing an increase in the decade of 259,226 bighas or 4·5 per cent. Large tracts of jungle and grass lands in the Sankheda, Vaghodia and Savli Talukas of the Baroda District and the Rani Mahals of the Navsari District have been brought under the plough. Hundreds of bighas of land in the Kadi, Dehgam and Patan Talukas, which were relinquished during the famine, have again been taken up. All these have naturally brought about a very large increase in the number of actual cultivators and a reduction in the number of field labourers.

Effect on agricultural labour.

587. In addition to extension of cultivation, growth of factories in the State as also in the foreign territory on the boundary has brought about a considerable reduction in the number of field labourers. The wages of agricultural labour have risen by more than a hundred per cent. within the last few years. Ten years ago, a labourer for weeding or cutting could be had for a

* This ratio refers to the total population. If we exclude those who are mainly agriculturists and base our calculation on the number whose principal occupation was non-agricultural, the proportion rises to 56 per mille.

noon-day meal of bread and pulse and an anna and a half in cash. Now it is difficult to secure his services for less than a similar meal and four or five annas in cash. The condition of agricultural labourers and of labourers of all kinds has consequently much improved within the decade.

588. Pasture or the provision and care of animals maintains 21 per mille in the whole State. The proportion maintained by this occupation in 1901, was almost the same (21·6 per mille). Looking to the districts, we find that the largest proportion dependant on pasture (32 per mille) is in the Kadi District. Then follows Amreli with 29 per mille, and Baroda and Navsari stand last with only 10 per mille, who are dependant on this class of occupation.

Sub-Class I—Order 1 : Groups 9 to 12, pasture.

Group No.	Occupation.	No. supported per 1,000.
9	Cattle and buffalo-breeders and keepers	12
10	Sheep, goat and pig-breeders	5
11	Breeders of other animals, horses, mules, etc.	1
12	Herdsmen, goat herds and shepherds	3

NON-AGRICULTURAL OCCUPATIONS.

Sub-Class I—Order 2 ; Fishing and hunting.

589. Fishing and hunting support only one person in a thousand in the whole State. 5 per mille in the Baroda City, 7 per mille in the Navsari District and 2 per mille in the Amreli District are maintained by fishing and hunting. In the Kadi and Baroda Districts there is no fishing and hunting industry worth the name.

Sub-Class II—Mines.

590. There is practically no mining industry in the State. Only 41 males and three females have returned "mines and metallic minerals" (Group No. 17) as their occupation ; and the majority of these (26 males) are in the Amreli District. In 1893 a Geological Survey of the State was made by Mr. R. B. Foote, of the Geological Survey of India. But the question of Economic Geology was not thoroughly investigated then with the result that the Baroda Government remained in ignorance as to the hidden resources of the State. A new Geological Survey was therefore conducted in 1909 from an economic point of view by obtaining a loan of the services of Mr. V. S. Sambashiv Iyer, an expert from the Mysore Government. The result of his investigations has just been published in a detailed report which deals principally with ceramic materials, materials for glass-making and cement. The subject is under the consideration of the newly organised Department of Commerce and Industries, and a considerable development of mining industry in the State may confidently be expected in the near future.

591. Next to Sub-class I, Sub-class III is numerically the most important in the whole occupation scheme and goes to support 123 per thousand or nearly one-eighth of the total population. It comprises no less than 14 orders which are further sub-divided into 73 groups in Table XV. The number per 1,000 supported by each of the main industries is noted in the margin, from which it will appear that textiles alone include more than one-fifth of the total population supported by all industries together. 36 per mille are supported by textiles in Baroda City, 35 in the Amreli District, 29 in the Kadi District and 20 in the Baroda District. Textile fabrics and dress together supported 34 per mille in 1901. Adding up the number supported by order 6 (textiles) and order 13

Sub-Class III—Industry.

Order.	Name of industries.	No. supported per 1,000.
6	Textiles	26
7	Hides, skins and hard materials from the animal kingdom	8
8	Wood	13
9	Metals	8
10	Ceramics	13
11	Chemical products	5
12	Food industries	6
13	Industries of dress and the toilet ...	22
15	Building industries	6
18	Industries of luxury and literature, arts and sciences	6
19	Industries concerned with refuse matter.	10

(industries of dress, etc.), we find that the two together now support 48 per mille showing an increase of 14 per mille supported by these industries. The improvement is mainly due to impetus given to hand and power-loom weaving in the decade and there is yet a bright future for this old and important industry. The weaving industry of Navsari District is of ancient repute. Fine *dhoti, sari, basta,* and *bafta* made in Navsari and Gandevi were in great demand at the Portuguese, Dutch and English factories in Surat in the seventeenth and eighteenth centuries for export to Europe, and in 1788, Dr. Hove, a European traveller visited Gandevi, to learn the art from Parsi weavers. The industry practically died out early in the nineteenth century, but Parsi women still manufacture quantities of *kasti,* the sacred thread worn by Parsi men and women, and are skilful in making ornamental borders of *saris.* In Baroda District, there is considerable weaving industry at Dabhoi where fine turbans are manufactured. Cloth, superior to the common coarse cloth of the lower classes, is produced at Petlad, Vaso and some other places. In the Kadi District, Patan, the old capital of Gujarat (from the 8th to the 14th century) was famous for its weaving industry. A great part of the trade was transplanted to Ahmedabad, when that place was chosen as the capital, but the decayed weaving community of Patan still turn out a superior quality of cloth which has a fair sale. Silks, however, are the speciality of Patan, and the silk *patola* of this town is largely in demand in all parts of Gujarat. The rise of Ahmedabad diverted a part of the silk as well as the cotton weaving from Patan which has never flourished since.

Order 7—Hides, skins, etc.

592. Industries relating to hides, skins and hard materials from the animal kingdom supports 16,032 persons or nearly 8 per mille of the population. The number of actual workers is only 5,760 males and 694 females ; the rest are dependants. Most of these who are tanners, curriers and leather dressers belong to the Chamar caste and those who make trunks, scales, water-bags, etc., belong to the Dabgar caste. Shoe-makers are treated separately in group No. 69 of Order 13—" Industries of dress and the toilet." The tanning and curing work done by Chamars is the most primitive. For three or four weeks the skin is allowed to soak in lime-water till it is divested of hair. It is then saturated several times with a solution of *baval* (*acacia arabica*) bark. After being rubbed with salt and dried, the skin is handed over to the shoemaker who blackens it with *hirakashi,* sulphate of iron. The butcher tans the goat-skins in a different manner. To divest it of hair he places it in salt for a fortnight, then rubs lac into it to give it a red colour and finally soaks it in a solution of *garmala* (*cassica fistula*) to make it pliant. Hides and skins thus cured, and bones are exported in large quantities from all the districts and are again re-imported as finished articles. There is a good scope for the establishment of leather, button and other industries on modern methods.

Order 8—Wood Industry.

593. 26,275 persons or nearly 13 per mille are supported by wood industries. This order includes sawyers, carpenters, turners and joiners and also basket-makers and other industries of woody materials, including leaves. The occupation of sawyers and carpenters mainly concerns buildings. A carpenter in this State is not only a house-builder, but also a plough-maker, furniture-maker and a carriage builder. Turners are mostly of the Kharadi or Sanghadia caste, who employ the lathe in turning bed posts, children's cradles and the bracelets of blackwood or ivory worn by Hindu women. They are found in all towns but those of Patan, Vadnagar, Dabhoi and Navsari are well-known. The art of ornamental wood-carving was formerly very common and a few specimens of carving on the doors and verandahs of the houses, are still to be seen in Vaso, Sojitra, Petlad and other places. Owing to consideration of cheapness, wood-carving in house construction is growing out of fashion.

Basket-making and other industries of woody materials, including leaves, support no less than 5,306 persons, of which 1,533 males and 1,632 are actual workers. This is one of the few industries in which female workers preponderate over males. Basket-making is the main occupation of Vansfodas and Buruds and the subsidiary occupation of Bhangis (scavengers). There is a large industry in *datan* or tooth-sticks, which are made by cutting tender branches of *babul* trees and *aval* and *kamboi* shrubs and are used by most of the people in cleansing their teeth. Making of leaf-plates is also a flourishing industry. In all Hindu caste dinners, food is served in leaf-plates and leaf-cups made of *palash*, *vad* or *mahuda* leaves.

Order 9—Metals.

594. Industries relating to metals include forging and rolling of iron and other metals (group 38), plough and agricultural implement makers (group 39), makers of arms, guns, etc. (group 40), other workers in iron (group 41), workers in brass, copper and bell metal (group 42), workers in tin, zinc, lead and quicksilver (group 43), and workers in mints and die-sinkers (group 44). Goldsmiths, jewel-setters, enamellers, etc., are classed separately under order 18—Industries of luxury. The total population supported is 16,150 persons or 8 in 1,000. Of those, 6,405 males and 335 females are actual workers and the rest are dependants. There are no returns under groups 38 and 39, because forging and rolling, etc., are not a separate industry but are included in groups 41, 42 and 43. Making of arms, guns, etc., has practically ceased to be an industry, the 6 persons who are returned being only repairers of arms. There are 5,851 males and 326 females who work in iron. The females engaged in this industry blow the bellows, while the hard work is done by the males. Most of the iron workers belong to the Luhar caste. The village blacksmiths make and mend the rude agricultural implements in use. 954 males and 7 females, who are actual workers in brass, copper and bell-metal, support 2,195 persons in all. Most of these people belong to the Kansara caste. Brass and copper sheets imported from Europe are used in the manufacture. In the Kadi District, the brass ware of Visnagar is much prized, and much of it is exported to Ahmedadad and Kathiawad. Coppersmiths are to be found in most of the large towns except Sidhpur. The tradition is that copper will not melt in Sidhpur, and that is the reason why coppersmiths have not settled there. Most of the workers in tin, zinc., etc., are Vohoras or Musalmans and are to be found in the larger towns.

Order 10—Ceramics.

595. The most important industry in this order is pottery and brick and tile-making. Pottery is naturally an extensive industry in a country where the mass of the people use earthenware for storing drinking water, cooking and other purposes. It supports 25,633 persons. Next to it is the brick and tile-making industry. Ordinary potters make bricks and tiles, in addition to pots, and it is only the *Dalwadis* who confine themselves to only brick-making. The number of persons supported by these two industries together is 26,472 or 13 per cent. of the population. Only 77 males and 21 females have returned the making of glass and crystal ware as their occupation, and there have been no entries under the heads "makers of porcelain and crockery" and "other (mosaic, talc, mica, etc.,) workers." The recent Geological Survey has brought to light valuable information regarding places in the State where materials for a variety of modern clay and glass industries are available, and we may with confidence look forward to their development in due course of time.

Order 11.—Chemical products properly so called and analogous.

596. Order 11 includes those engaged in the manufacture of matches and explosive materials, ærated and mineral waters, makers of dies, paint and ink, soap, candle and lac, perfumes, paper and vegetable and mineral oils. The total number supported by these industries is 10,953 persons or a little more than 5 per mille and the actual workers are 3,403 males and 786 females. Manufacture and refining of vegetable oils are the only important industries in this order; the rest together have only 153 workers and support only 312 persons. The oil pressers belong to the Ghanchi caste and are both Hindus and Musalmans. The country *ghani* or mill is of rude construction. In a solid wooden frame is firmly fixed at a depth of five feet a round block of wood, of which the centre is hollowed out; into this mortar is introduced another block of wood which almost fits into it and to the latter is attached a long handle which is made to revolve horizontally by a bullock. The seed is crushed between

the two blocks of wood. Oil mills of western model have lately been erected at Baroda, Petlad, Kadi and Sidhpur, where manufacture of oil from castor, sesame, rape, cotton and other oil-seeds is carried on a large scale, but as yet, they are not known to have been a commercial success except in a few cases. Castor-seed oil was formerly solely used as an illuminant but within the last thirty years, the introduction of kerosine-oil, even into villages, has considerably reduced its manufacture. Sesame oil is used in frying vegetables and making pickles, and is largely manufactured. Rape, castor and other oil-seeds are largely exported to Europe, and cotton seeds are used as fodder for cattle. Owing to decline in their business, Ghanchis are gradually taking to other pursuits, such as shop-keeping, milk selling, general labour, etc.

Order 12.—Food industries.

597. Food industries include rice-pounding and flour-grinding, bakers, biscuit-makers, grain-parchers, butchers, fish-curers, butter and ghee makers, makers of sugar and molasses, sweetmeat makers, brewers and distillers, toddy drawers and manufacturers of tobacco, opium and ganja. They together maintain 11,314 persons or about 6 per mille, of which 2,565 males and 277 females are workers and the rest are dependants. Food-stuffs are generally sold by those who manufacture them, and if we add to this the number of 54,718 persons returned under trade in Order 33, we get a total of 66,032 or 3·2 per cent. of the population, who are supported by other manufacture and trade. Of all industries connected with food, rice-pounding and grinding are the most important and support nearly one-half of the persons returned under this Order. Golas are generally professional rice-pounders and huskers, but in most of the families this work is done by the females in the house. There are only a few bakers in the whole State, and they are confined to the City of Baroda. There are no consumers of ready-made bread elsewhere. Grain-parchers mostly from Upper India and sweetmeat sellers, mostly Shrimali Vanias, are to be found in most of the towns and together support 1,848 persons. In the whole State, there are only 683 males and 42 females who work as butchers. Fish-curers have not been returned separately from fish-dealers, who under Order 33, Group 116, number 510 males and 137 females. The small number of butchers and fish-dealers shows the very limited extent to which meat-eating enters into the diet of the people. Even those who are not precluded from eating it by religious scruples, cannot afford it owing to poverty. There are only 132 brewers and distillers who are confined to the city of Baroda, where the State Central Distillery is situated and only 884 toddy drawers, who are confined to the Navsari District, where juice yielding palms grow. Makers of molasses and *gur* are generally those who grow sugar plantations and they having been returned as agriculturists, no more than 3 persons have been returned under this head in this Order. Sugarcane is largely grown in the Navsari and Gandevi talukas of the Navsari District, and Kodinar and some other parts of the Amreli District. The sugarcane mill or *koholu* is of the same primitive construction as the oil pressing *ghani*. It is composed of two cylinders of wood which revolve in opposite directions but in close proximity. The cane introduced between the two is drawn in, crushed and cast out. The juice collected in an earthen vessel below is removed to a boiler close by and converted in molasses. Recently iron roller mills for crushing sugarcane have come into use in Amreli. There is a sugar mill at Gandevi, but on the Census day, it was not in working order.

Ghee and butter are made by females of agriculturists and herdsmen, as a subsidiary occupation. It is, therefore, that the manufacturers of these articles have not been returned separately. Professional ghee, butter and milk-sellers are included in Order 33, Group 118.

Manufacture of tobacco, opium and ganja is returned as supporting 1,328 persons only. The growers of these special products are included under agriculture and their sellers, who with their dependants number 17,814, under trade (Order 27, Group 122). Opium manufacture is confined to the Government factory at Sidhpur, while tobacco manufacture consists mainly in making snuff. In every large town, snuff is manufactured, but the snuff of Petlad, Vadnagar and Kadi is considered the best and is largely exported. Manufacturing tobacco into cigars and cigarettes is capable of becoming a very paying industry in the Petlad taluka where the *paddas* prepared at present fetch only 4 or 5 rupees per maund.

Order 13—Industries of dress and toilet.

598. Industries of dress and toilet support 45,632 persons or 22 per mille of the population. They include 13,801 maintained by tailoring, 8,266 by shoe-making, 3,000 by washing and 19,798 by shaving and hair-cutting.

Order 14—Furniture industries.

599. Furniture industries support only 142 persons mainly in Baroda and Navsari. Furniture is generally made by those who sell it, and if we include those returned under trade in Order 35, we get a total of 665 who are supported by making and selling furniture. Very little furniture is used by the people in this country, and a few tables, chairs and cots of the most ordinary kind, as are required, are made by the common carpenters. Under the patronage of His Highness the Maharaja Saheb, a Furniture Factory has lately been started in Baroda and is likely to both create and supply a demand in artistic furniture.

Order 15.—Building industries.

600. 12,931 persons or 6 per mille are supported by building industries, such as lime-burners, masons and bricklayers, building contractors, house-painters, tilers, etc. Carpenters and sawyers are classed separately under Order 8—Wood industries. The number of actual workers in building industries is 5,593 and 7,388 are dependants. The number of actual workers and dependants is probably much larger than returned under this order. Most of the Kadias or bricklayers belong to the Kachhia, Sathawara, Koli, Kanbi and other castes, and as they combine agriculture with this occupation, they must have returned agriculture as their principal occupation. The art of sculpture was once very flourishing in the State. Splendid specimens of stone carving still exist in different parts of the State which prove how great was once the excellence attained in this direction. In the Baroda District, Dabhoi stands pre-eminent with its side gates, the Diamond gate and the temple adjoining it. Base-reliefs, and figures of superior workmanship may also be found in Padra, Sinore and Petlad. The Kadi District is naturally the richest in such remains of ancient skill in sculpture and architecture. The artistic riches of Patan, Sidhpur, Modhera and many other places, which still survive the bigotry of the Musalman invaders, may some day yet serve to excite the emulation of the people. Though the decay of the art has been enormous, the stone masons of the State, especially those from Patan, Visnagar and Vadnagar, are in good repute and find employment in Bombay, Ahmedabad and other centres of industry. Wages of bricklayers have of late risen by more than 10 per cent. Throughout the State, those who are able to afford are replacing structures of mud and other less durable materials by houses of brick and the building industry is apparently very thriving.

Order 16—Construction of means of transport.

601. There is practically no entry under this order. Only 122 workers and 125 dependants have been returned in the whole State. Ordinary carts and carriages are manufactured for their customers by the village carpenters who are included in 'wood workers.' Ready-made carts and carriages are made by those who sell them and their number with their dependants is included under trade in Order 37, Group 129. Horse carriages are made and sold only in the City of Baroda, and bullock carts and carriages are made and sold in Vyara, Petlad and other towns. Boats and country crafts are built at Bilimora and Dwarka, where there are a few persons maintained by this industry.

Order 17—Production and transmission of physical forces.

602. The only industry coming under Order 17 is the Electric Power House at Baroda which illuminates the palace and a part of the City, and supports 101 persons, of whom 61 are workers.

Order 18—Industries of luxury.

603. Industries of luxury include (1) printing, engravers and litho-graphers, who number 337 and support 624 persons, (2) news-paper managers and editors who with their dependants number only 22, (3) 27 book-binders, (4) 21 musical instrument makers, (5) 148 watch and clock makers, (6) 13 bangle makers, (7) 441 supported by kite and toy making and (8) 10,158 persons supported by workers in precious stones and metals. The last group is the most important and includes Sonis (goldsmiths), who are to be found in most of the villages, Jadias (tracers of designs on ornaments) and Panchigars (precious stone setters), who are to be found in most of the towns. Females in this country are very fond of ornaments. Whatever their position in life may be, they must have some ornaments of gold or silver for the adornment of their body. Some ornaments have come to be regarded as symbolical of married life and must always be worn by a female whose husband is alive. The goldsmiths have, therefore, a thriving business. They have a bad name in Gujarat for filching gold and for mixing metal. The saying is "A goldsmith steals gold even out of his sister's ornaments."

Order 19—Industries concerned with refuse matter.

604. Order 19—Industries concerned with refuse matter, includes sweepers, scavengers and dust and sweeping contractors. They support 19,590 persons or nearly 10 per mille, of which 56 per cent. (7,337 males and 8,671 females) are workers and 8,582 or 54 per cent. dependants. Most of the sweepers engaged in refuse matter are Government or Municipal servants and receive as pay from 2 to 4 rupees a month. This income is supplemented by grain or food allowance from private people near whose houses they work and who are looked upon by them as their customers.

STATISTICS OF INDUSTRIES IN FACTORIES.

Statistics of factories specially collected.

605. We have hitherto been considering industries without distinction as to whether they are conducted by individuals at home or in factories. In 1901 an attempt was made to distinguish between workers in factories and those engaged in home industries and also to distinguish between owners, managers and supervision staff and operatives, but the entries in the schedules were far too vague to permit of accurate information on these points being obtained. In the present Census, therefore, in addition to the general and household schedule, a special schedule was prescribed for persons working in factories. It was filled up by the owners, managers or agents of factories, mills, &c., in which at least 20 persons were employed on the 10th March 1911. The information thus collected is given in Table XV-E and throws great light on recent industrial developments.

Development of industries.

606. Before 1901-02, the record of trades and industries in the State was a poor one. The old industries were on the decline, while those under new methods had not achieved any notable success. There were only 44 cotton ginning factories and one cotton spinning mill in the whole State. This state of things was mainly attributable to the backwardness of the people and their lack of enterprise and want of adaptability to new circumstances. During the present decade, the Government of Baroda set themselves seriously to the difficult task of stimulating industries within their territory. The only mill then existing had been established by the State in 1883-84 at a capital expenditure of Rs. 6,35,000 with a view to encourage local manufacture and to foster private enterprise. The mill worked for over 20 years, but failed to stimulate private enterprise. Believing that the transfer of the concern to private hands would be an encouragement to private enterprise and that one mill successfully worked by private owners would lead other capitalists to follow the example, His Highness the Maharaja sanctioned the sale of the mill to a private company in 1905. The expectations of Government were fully realised and the successful management of the first cotton mill in Baroda by private owners resulted in the erection of three others within the last few years. With a view to develop arts and industries in the State, a Technical Institute called 'Kala Bhavan,' literally 'the house of arts,'

had been established in the State so early as in 1890. Over and above the technical education provided in Baroda, a large number of students are being sent up every year, to foreign countries for being trained up at State expense in agriculture, architecture, cabinet-making, textile industries, watch-making and the science of commerce. The co-operative movement started in British India soon reached Baroda and in the year 1904-05 an Act on the lines of the British Indian Co-operative Credit Societies was passed by the Baroda Government and arrangements were made to explain to the people the advantages of co-operation. Twenty-four societies were organised in the first year of the movement and there are now no less than 98 registered societies. Agricultural banks were established in 1899-1900 and 1900-01 at Songhad and Vyara in the Navsari District and Harij in the Kadi District with a small capital to help the backward population of these talukas and, though joint stock in name are practically financed and managed by the State. The banks make advances in cash and kind for all purposes to *bona fide* cultivators. Recoveries are made by the staff, but in cases of obstructiveness on the part of the borrowers, recourse is had to civil courts. The most important event in connection with the development of industries in the State was the creation in 1905 of the office of an Economic Adviser who visited the principal towns of the State and recommended the establishment of a bank, as economic development generally depends in the first place upon the organisation of joint stock banking. The Bank of Baroda, Ltd., an institution subsidised by the State, was therefore started on the 19th July 1908, with an authorised capital of 20 lacs. It provides adequate banking facilities of the modern type in the State for the development of commerce and industry. The Economic Adviser then diverted his attention to cotton-seed oil industry, tanning and fibre industries, improvement of the cotton staple, dyeing and other industries. A large number of duties which hampered trade were abolished in 1904 and finally, with a view to further stimulate trade and industries, custom duties of every kind were abolished in 1909 at a considerable sacrifice to revenue. All these activities have resulted in a wonderful development of industries within the short space of a few years in the present decade. The total number of factories in the State has arisen from one cotton spinning mill and 44 ginning factories and presses in 1901 to 86 factories of all kinds in 1911. Of these, 39 are in the Baroda District, 17 in Baroda City, 7 in the Kadi District, 16 in Navsari and 7 in Amreli. Kadi, though it has the largest area and population of all the districts, has shown the least industrial development. There is yet a great scope for further development, and with the continuance of the present liberal policy of its Government there is every hope that Baroda will in the near future take its legitimate place as a centre of manufacture in Western India.

Classification of factories.

607. Of the 86 factories, 48 are cotton ginning factories, seven are cotton presses, four cotton spinning and weaving mills, one silk factory, one brush factory, four dyeing factories, one leather factory, one saw mill, three brick factories, three oil mills, one chemical works, one rice mill, one sugar factory, one water works, one opium factory, one furniture factory, one tramway, one railway bridge work, one electric light works and four printing presses.

Classification of power employed.

76 factories are worked by steam, two by oil, one by electricity and the rest by manual power.

Ownership of factories.

Of 62 important factories, ten are owned by companies and 52 by private owners. All the directors of the factories, owned by companies, are Indians, while one Brahman, one Brahma-Kshatri, twenty-two Vanias, eleven Lewa Kanbis, four Kadwa Kanbis, one Sutar, four Mahomedans, and eleven Parsis are the owners of private factories.

Classification of persons employed in factories.

The total number employed in all the factories is 9,421 persons or 5 per mille of the population. Of these, about three-fourths are males and the rest females. Five Europeans and Anglo-Indians and 732 Indians are engaged in direction, supervision and clerical work; fourteen Europeans and Anglo-Indians and 1,779 Indians are employed as skilled workmen and 5,643 persons aged fourteen and over and 1,250 under fourteen are employed as unskilled labourers.

Caste or race of the managers of factories.

Of the 48 cotton ginning factories, one is managed by a Brahman, one by a Brahma-Kshatri, 19 by Vanias, eleven by Lewa Kanbis, two by Kadwa Kanbis, one by a Sutar, five by Musalmans and eight by Parsis. Of the seven cotton presses, two are managed by Vanias, three by Lewa Kanbis and two by Parsis. All the four cotton spinning and weaving mills are managed by Vanias. Two of the four dyeing factories are managed by Vanias and two by Lewa Kanbis. Vanias, Lewa Kanbis and Parsis thus appear to have the largest share in the management of factories.

State of business in factories.

All factories, except those connected with cotton presses, reported their business to be much brisker than usual. Cotton ginning, pressing and spinning and weaving factories reported their business to be slacker than usual.

Sub-class IV—Transport.

608. Sub-class IV relates to transport which includes the Orders : (1) Transport by water, (2) Transport by road, (3) Transport by rail, and (4) Transport by post and telegraph. The total number of persons supported under this head is 16,638 or a little more than 8 per mille, of which 43 per cent. are workers and 57 per cent. dependants. Transport by water is mainly conducted in this State by boats in rivers and on the sea-coast by 655 boatmen who are found in the largest number in the Navsari District (404), and who together with their dependants number only 1,816. Transport by road is conducted by means of carts, hackney carriages, pack bullocks, donkeys and porters, and gives maintenance to 5,960 persons. The first thing to attract the notice of a visitor to Baroda City as he steps out from the B. B. & C. I. Railway Station would be perhaps the tram cars and the row of hackney carriages waiting in the open space to the left. The main roads are covered by the tramway line which has come to be recognised as a public conveyance of great value to the city. Besides its intrinsic value, the necessity developed by it for widening some narrow roads which have conduced alike to the convenience of the people and the beauty of the town, is an advantage that may be set down to its credit. In addition to the tram car service, there are about 200 public conveyances in the shape of horse *shigrams*, of which those with rubber tyres are classed first and those without them second.

Transport by rail gives employment to 2,730 persons who with their dependants number 6,226 or a little more than 3 per mille. According to the information specially collected in connection with the present Census through the Railway Department, of those employed on the railways, 11 Europeans and Anglo-Indians and 968 Indians were directly employed in the Traffic Department and 265 Indians, including contractors and coolies, were indirectly employed. Similarly four Europeans and 1,976 Indians were directly employed in the Engineering Department and 651 Indians were indirectly employed. Three Europeans and 211 Indians were directly employed in the Locomotive Department and 44 Indians were indirectly employed. One European and 287 Indians were directly employed and 1,608 persons, including Contractors' coolies, etc., were indirectly employed on Railway construction works.

Post and Telegraph Offices employ 1,277 persons who with their dependants number 2,359 persons or a little more than 1 per mille. According to the information specially collected through the Postal Department, amongst the postal employés in the State, there are 7 supervising officers, 81 postmasters, 335 miscellaneous agents, 85 clerks, 757 postmen and other servants, 11 railway mail sorters, and 9 signallers in combined offices.

Sub-class V.—Trade.

609. Trade supports 129,900 persons or 64 per mille. Of these, 37 per cent. are actual workers and 63 per cent. dependants. This sub-class is divided into 18 Orders (Nos. 24 to 41), which are further sub-divided into 33 groups (Nos. 106 to 138). The division of labour into making and selling of articles is not fully carried out in this country, where most of the industries are still in a primitive condition and

most of the artizans sell to their customers the articles they make without a trader as middleman. The potter sells the pots he makes, the sweetmeat-maker sells the sweetmeats he makes, and the fisherman sells the fish he catches. Although, according to the new scheme of classification adopted in the present Census, those who both make and sell things are to be classed under industry, and those who only sell them are to be classed under trade, it is likely that such a clear distinction did not appear in the original return between the two as to ensure a correct classification. In order to gain a full idea of the persons engaged in any industry, we must look both to Sub-class III and Sub-class V. Most of the traders are either shop-keepers, who sell cloth, grain, grocery, hardware and other miscellaneous articles, or money-lenders and belong mostly to the Vania and Vohora castes. The most important groups under the head of trade are money-lending, which supports 17,600 persons, brokerage which supports 1,200 persons, trade in piece-goods which supports 11,131 persons, hotels, cafés, restaurants and liquor shops which support 3,390 persons, and sale of grocery, vegetables, sweetmeats, milk, ghee, betel-leaves, tobacco and other food stuffs, which altogether support 54,718 persons or 27 per mille of the population. The money-lender is often a piece-goods dealer or a general merchant, and he also trades in grain. Females carry on this business through their *gumastas* or *munims*. In villages money-lenders are well-to-do cultivators. Money changing and testing supported 10,479 persons in 1901, but owing to demonetization of the *babashai* and *shikkai* coins, this business has ceased to exist, and a large number of persons in the Kadi and Baroda Districts has turned to other avocations. The Bank of Baroda, Ltd., has branches in Navsari, Mehsana and other places and provides adequate banking facilities of the modern type for the development of commerce and industry in the State. Branches of two Bombay Banks have also been lately opened in Baroda. One noticeable feature of the present decade is the large increase in the number of *vishis* (hotels) and tea shops. In 1901 there were only four tea shops in the City of Baroda. The number has now increased to more than a hundred. Tea was formerly a luxury which only the rich could afford. Now even coolies, cart-drivers, sweepers and even beggars cannot do without it.

Sub-class VI.—Public force.

610. Those engaged in the Imperial and State army, the police and village watchmen together form Sub-class VI—Public force—and number according to the Census returns 12,276 and with their dependants contribute 26,904 persons or 13 per mille of the population. The Census return of those employed in the army and the police is fairly accurate and corresponds with those actually in service. But the return of village watchmen (2,573) is much under the real strength. It would seem that many of them whose subsidiary occupation is agriculture or labour must have returned themselves under those heads. Village watchmen are paid a poor pittance of Rs. 2 to 4, which is barely sufficient for their maintenance, and in most villages it is difficult to find men to fill up vacancies.

Sub-class VII.—Public administration.

611. Public administration includes State and foreign services, municipal and other local services and village officials and servants other than watchmen. They together number 14,137 persons and with their dependants make a total of 38,217 persons or 19 per mille of the population. Other servants of the State, *e.g.*, those employed in Education, Medical, Public Works, Army and the Police are grouped under separate heads in the present classification scheme. If all of these, who are mainly in the employ of the State, were added together those in the employ of the State would number about 32,123 and with their dependants form a total of 79,122 persons or 39 per mille, who are supported by State service.

Sub-class VIII.—Professions and liberal arts.

612. Occupations connected with the professions and liberal arts include those engaged in religion, law, medicine, instruction and letters, arts and sciences. Altogether 74,692 persons or nearly 37 per mille are supported in this sub-class. Of these, 46 per cent. are actual workers and 54 per cent. are dependants. Religion supports 25 per mille and includes 39,101 persons supported

as priests and ministers, 7,137 persons as religious mendicants and inmates of monasteries, 922 in church and mission service and 4,825 persons maintained in temple, burial or burning ground service, and as pilgrim conductors and circumcisers. Law supports 1,670 persons or barely 1 per mille and includes lawyers and their clerks, *kazis, mukhtyars* and petition writers. Medicine supports 3,079 persons or 1·5 per mille of the population. This includes 721 medical practitioners of all kinds, such as doctors, *vaidyas, hakims*, etc., and their families, and 276 males and 185 females returned as vaccinators, compounders and midwives and their families. 4,147 males and 179 females returned themselves as professors and teachers and clerks and servants connected with education, and with their families number 9,399 persons or 4·6 per mille, who are supported under the head of education. 972 engineers, surveyors, architects and their employés, 188 photographers, botanists and astronomers and 2,259 singers, actors and dancers who together with their families number 8,559 or 4·2 per mille are returned as being supported by letters, arts and sciences.

Sub-class IX.—Persons living on their own income.

613. The 9th sub-class includes those persons who do not work for their livelihood but live on their income from property other than agricultural land, and on cash allowances of various kinds, such as *nemnuks*, pensions and scholarships. The total number of persons maintained from this source is in the whole State 8,462 or 4 in 1,000. The largest of their number is naturally to be found in the capital city of Baroda, where most of the *nemnukdars*, pensioners and scholars reside. The number per mille of the total population supported from this source is 36 in the city of Baroda, three each in Kadi and Baroda Districts, two in Navsari and barely one in Amreli.

Sub-class X.—Domestic service.

614. The number of persons solely dependent on personal and domestic service is 3,510 or less than 2 per mille. This shows that only a small proportion of the people can afford the luxury of engaging personal servants and the large majority have to depend upon the members of their household, and the family barbers and upon the casual services of *purohits* and others in domestic matters. In most of the well-to-do families grinding and pounding work is done by those who maintain themselves by doing such work; the barber washes clothes and cleanses pots ; the Kumbhar or Bhoi fetches water ; and the *purohit* purchases vegetables, oil, sugar, etc., from the bazaar for his patron. This also explains why the number of those who returned themselves as domestic servants is so small. Looking to the districts individually, we find that out of one thousand in the population, eleven persons in Baroda City, two in the Kadi District and one each in Baroda, Navsari and Amreli Districts serve as domestic servants. Domestic service seems to be very unpopular. It is very easy to secure the services of a clerk or a peon on Rs. 8 or 10, but very difficult to get a cook or servant for the same wages.

615. 7 per cent. of the people are supported by occupations which were returned in general terms not indicating a definite occupation and had therefore to be relegated to Sub-class XI—Insufficiently described occupations. Nearly one-fifth of these were returned as cashiers, accountants, book-keepers, clerks and other employés in unspecified offices, warehouses and shops ; and four-fifths as labourers and workmen otherwise unspecified. The highest proportion, 156 per mille, of insufficiently described occupations was returned from Baroda City. The corresponding proportions for the districts are Baroda 43, Kadi 72, Navsari 53 and Amreli 135 per mille.

Sub-class XI.—Insufficiently described occupations.

Group No.	Name of Occupations returned.	Total workers and dependants.
165	Cashiers, accountants, book-keepers, clerks, &c.... ...	28,354
166	Mechanics, otherwise unspecified	118
167	Labourers and workmen, otherwise unspecified ...	115,813

Sub-class XII.—Unproductive occupations.

Group No.	Number of persons supported.
168	802
169	8,457
Total ...	9,259

616. Inmates of jails, asylums and hospitals (Group No. 168) and beggars, vagrants, procurers, prostitutes, receivers of stolen property and cattle poisoners (Group No. 169) are included in Sub-class XII—Unproductive occupations. Those in Group No. 168 are correctly recorded, but those in Group No. 169 do not seem to have shown their full strength. Instead of returning a disreputable occupation, many real beggars, vagrants, prostitutes and criminals must have passed them selves off as agriculturists, labourers and the like. Religious mendicants are entered under a separate head (Group No. 149), but the distinction between them and beggars is so uncertain and hazy that many real beggars must have passed as religious mendicants. Their number (7,137) added to those returned under Group No. 169 makes a total of 15,594 or 8 per 1,000 of the population who are practically living upon the earnings of others. Compared with 1901 (241 beggars, prostitutes, etc., and 2,656 religious mendicants), there appears to have been a very large increase, nearly five-fold, in the number of people living upon other's income. But probably the return of 1901 was not so accurate as on the present occasion and the increase is therefore only apparent. With the spread of education, the hold which the so-called ascetics and begging fraternities have on the imagination of the people is getting weaker and their number must be on the decline.

OCCUPATION BY RELIGION.

Occupation by religion.

617. Table XV-D shows the distribution of occupations by religions. The prominent features of this branch of occupation statistics are clearly illustrated in Subsidiary Table VI at the end of this Chapter and the diagram given in the margin. In this part of the occupation return, no distinction has been made between workers and dependants, and the figures both in the table and the discussion which follows refer not merely to the actual workers, but to the total number of persons supported by each occupation, whether they personally work it or not.

Diagram showing the main distribution by occupation (classes) for religions.

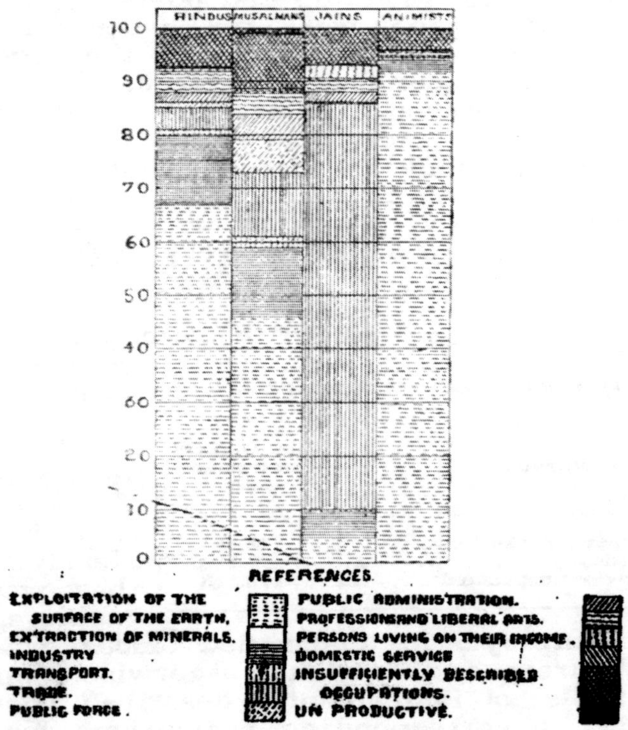

618. As the Hindus represent about four-fifths of the total population, their distribution by occupation does not differ materially from that in the State as a whole. 67 per cent. of their number are supported by agriculture, 13 per cent. by industry, 4 per cent. by trade, 3 per cent. by service in the public force and public administration together, and 4 per cent. in the professions and liberal arts. 1 in 400 lives upon his own income and 4 in a 1,000 are either beggars or vagrants.

Hindus.

619. 46 per cent. of the Musalmans in the State are engaged in agriculture, 13 per cent. in industry and 12 per cent. in trade. Compared with Hindus, Musalmans are more numerous both in the public force and public administration. This is due to the large number of their people employed as constables or sepoys. In the professions and liberal arts, Musalmans are only a little behind the Hindus, their proportion being 37·6 in 1,000 as against 39 in the same number of Hindus. The proportion of Musalmans following disreputable professions, such as beggars, vagrants, and prostitutes, is the highest amongst all the religions, being 13 in 1,000.

Mahomedans.

620. Trade is the principal occupation of Jains, both in the city and the districts. 76 per cent. of them are employed as traders of various kinds, such as bankers, money lenders, jewellers, brokers, grocers, grain dealers and miscellaneous shopkeepers. Only 4·5 of their number—mostly Kanbis, Bhavsars, and others—are engaged in agriculture either as landlords or cultivators and nearly 5 per cent. in public service and liberal arts. To their great credit, Jains have in their whole community no more than 19 beggars, vagrants and others following disreputable occupations.

Jains.

621. The Animistic tribes depend chiefly upon agricultural pursuits for their maintenance. 92 per cent. of them are cultivators and field labourers and the rest are herdsmen, wood-cutters, basket-makers, toddy-drawers, cart-drivers, village watchmen and general labourers. Only 192 Animists are employed in the public administration, including 74 village officials and servants, other than watchmen. Their number in the professions and the liberal arts is only 141, including 51 religious priests and 70 teachers and clerks connected with education. Only 63 were returned in the whole State as following disreputable occupations, compared with 6,262 Hindus and 1,964 Mahomedans entered under this head.

Animists.

622. The Parsis are found in the greatest number in the Navsari District, where nearly one-third of their number is engaged in agriculture, either as landlords or cultivators and the rest are traders, shop-keepers, government and railway servants and priests. Most of the Parsis in the other districts and in the City of Baroda are either contractors, shop-keepers or Government or Railway servants.

Parsis.

623. Owing to the large number of native converts drawn principally from the Dhed and other low castes, nearly one-half of the Christians in the districts are cultivators and field labourers and of the rest, a great majority (2,925) are engaged in textile industries, such as cotton spinning, sizing and weaving and the rest are employed on railways. Most of the Europeans reside in the Baroda City or Cantonment and are employed in the army, public administration and the professions and liberal arts.

Christians.

OCCUPATION BY CASTE.

624. The most interesting feature in connection with the occupation statistics is the return of occupation by castes. Imperial Table XVI contains details for most of the important castes and Subsidiary Table VIII at the end of this chapter gives proportionate figures for some of them. In theory, each caste has a distinctive occupation, but it is not practised by all its members. Looking to the statistics,

Occupation by caste.

we find that most of the castes have abandoned the narrow limit of the special occupations laid down for them by *Shastra* and tradition. Only 5 per cent. of the Ahirs follow their traditional occupation of cattle-breeders or graziers and the rest are either agriculturists or field labourers. Only 8 per cent. of Bahrots are now bards and geneologists and the rest are cultivators, traders or labourers. The traditional profession of the Brahmans is priesthood, but in practice they follow all manner of pursuits. Many are clerks or cooks, while some are soldiers, lawyers, shop-keepers and even day-labourers. Anavala and Jambu Brahmans are mostly agriculturists. Audich, Deshastha, Koknastha, Khedaval, Mewada, Modh, Nagar, Tapodhan and other Brahman castes have a small proportion following their traditional occupation of priests, but most of them follow other occupations, such as agriculture, trade, government service, domestic service, and general labour. Disaval, Kapol, Khadayata, Lad and other Vania castes mostly follow their traditional occupation of trade, but some of them have taken to other pursuits and are employed as clerks in private and government offices, and as lawyers, doctors and teachers. 35 per cent. of Kanbis and 18 per cent. of Kolis are engaged in their traditional occupation of agriculture and agricultural labour, but the rest, *viz.*, 65 and 82 per cent. respectively follow other occupations, such as industry, trade, labour and service. Less than 30 per cent. of Bhavsars follow their traditional occupation as calenderers and dyers and the rest are traders, cultivators and general labourers. Only 20 per cent. of the workers among Ghanchis are oil-pressers and the rest are shop-keepers, milk-sellers and labourers. Darji, Dhobi, Hajam, Kumbhar and other artisans are more faithful to their traditional profession, but it is not uncommon to find a few of their number engaged in trade, agriculture or public and private service. The Animistic tribes are still engaged in their primitive occupation of agriculture and forest labour, but they are now-a-days turning to other occupations also, and a few of their number are now cattle-breeders, artisans and government servants. More than half the number of Dheds are still following their old occupation of weaving and field and general labour; but some have now-a-days become cultivators, traders and teachers. The decline of the weaving and cotton carding industries has been gradually diverting Khatris, Vanzas, Pinjaras and Tais to trade, labour and other pursuits. An economic revolution is going on and the people are adjusting themselves to the altered conditions of life. There is yet a feeling of false pride which makes some members of the high castes prefer to starve rather than accept manual occupations. The dignity of honest labour is not yet thoroughly recognised. A great change has, however, already taken place, and in the struggle for existence, there is a growing tendency to set aside old ideas and yield to necessity.

SUBSIDIARY TABLE I.—General distribution by occupation.

Class, Sub-class and Order.	Number per 10,000 of total population		Percentage in each Class, Sub-class and Order of		Percentage of actual workers employed		Percentage of dependents to actual workers	
	Persons Supported.	Actual Workers.	Actual Workers.	Dependents.	In cities.	In rural areas.	In cities.	In rural areas.
1	2	3	4	5	6	7	8	9
BARODA STATE	10,000	4,657	47	53	5	95	119	114
A.—Production of raw materials	6,557	3,098	47	53	......	100	131	112
I.—Exploitation of Surface of the Earth	*6,556*	*3,097*	*47*	*53*	......	*100*	*131*	*112*
1. Pasture and agriculture	6,542	3,091	47	53	......	100	120	111
2. Fishing and hunting	14	6	45	55	2	98	1,005	110
II.—Extraction of Minerals	*1*	*1*	*35*	*65*	......	*100*	......	*184*
3. Mines	1	1	35	65	......	100	......	184
4. Quarries of hard rocks	......	......	......	......	......	......	......	......
5. Salt, etc.	......	......	......	......	......	......	......	......
B.—Preparation and supply of material substances	1,951	847	43	57	10	90	119	137
III.—Industry	*1,230*	*573*	*46*	*54*	*9*	*91*	*103*	*122*
6. Textiles	258	127	49	51	8	92	67	106
7. Hides, skins and hard materials from the animal kingdom	79	34	43	57	1	99	193	133
8. Wood	129	54	42	58	9	91	110	142
9. Metals	79	33	42	58	6	94	142	139
10. Ceramics	131	68	51	49	4	96	66	96
11. Chemical production	54	21	39	61	8	92	139	154
12. Food Industries	56	32	57	43	19	81	93	69
13. Industries of dress	225	101	45	55	9	91	91	125
14. Furniture industries	1	......	33	67	38	62	366	100
15. Building industries	63	27	43	57	25	75	137	132
16. Construction of means of transport	1	1	49	51	1	99	......	103
17. Production and transmission of physical forces	1	......	60	40	100	......	65	......
18. Industries of luxury and those pertaining to literature and the arts and sciences	57	21	36	64	20	80	180	173
19. Industries concerned with refuse matter.	96	54	56	44	8	92	78	78
IV.—Transport	*82*	*35*	*43*	*57*	*19*	*81*	*151*	*129*
20. Transport by water	9	3	36	64	2	98	207	176
21. Transport by road	29	12	41	59	23	77	167	136
22. Transport by rail	32	14	42	58	21	79	156	131
23. Post, Telegraph and Telephone services	12	6	54	46	17	83	94	33
V.—Trade	*639*	*239*	*37*	*63*	*10*	*80*	*150*	*169*
24. Banks, establishments of credit exchange and insurance	86	28	33	67	7	93	225	204
25. Brokerage, commission and export	6	3	44	56	7	93	150	125
26. Trade in textiles	55	19	34	66	11	89	208	191
27. Trade in skins, leather and furs	8	4	44	56	1	99	112	126
28. Trade in wood	5	3	55	45	7	98	85	81
29. Trade in metals	5	1	21	79	19	81	269	385
30. Trade in pottery	1	......	35	65	21	79	100	208
31. Trade in chemical products	1	......	26	74	45	55	260	300
32. Hotels, cafès, restaurants, etc.	16	6	33	67	17	83	184	198
33. Other trade in food stuffs	269	114	42	58	11	89	113	144
34. Trade in clothing and toilet articles	7	2	34	66	30	70	169	197
35. Trade in furniture	3	1	38	62	43	57	242	95
36. Trade in building materials	2	1	38	62	73	27	136	246
37. Trade in means of transport	9	4	50	50	1	99	316	98
38. Trade in fuel	8	3	44	56	14	86	187	115
39. Trade in articles of luxury and those pertaining to letters and arts and sciences.	13	4	33	67	42	58	186	208
40. Trade in refuse matter	5	......	67	33	72	28	68	......
41. Trade of other sorts	145	46	32	68	5	95	169	221
C.—Public administration and liberal arts	729	314	43	57	24	76	149	127
VI.—Public force	*132*	*60*	*46*	*54*	*48*	*52*	*114*	*124*
42. Army	57	28	49	51	84	16	104	94
43. Navy	......	......	......	......	......	......	......	......
44. Police	75	32	43	57	16	84	161	129
VII.—Public administration	*188*	*69*	*37*	*63*	*26*	*74*	*218*	*154*
45. Public administration	188	69	37	63	26	74	218	154
VIII.—Professions and liberal arts	*367*	*169*	*46*	*54*	*12*	*88*	*146*	*114*
46. Religion	256	122	48	52	8	92	89	111
47. Law	8	3	26	74	31	69	362	242
48. Medicine	15	6	38	62	25	75	329	137
49. Instruction	46	21	46	54	19	81	194	99
50. Letters and arts and sciences	42	17	40	60	25	75	174	142
IX.—Persons living on their income.								
51. Persons living on their income	42	16	38	62	49	51	122	196
D.—Miscellaneous	763	398	52	48	13	87	70	95
X.—Domestic Service.								
52. Domestic Service	17	9	52	48	38	62	54	114
XI.—Insufficiently described occupations.								
53. General terms which do not indicate a definite occupation	700	365	52	48	12	88	71	94
XII.—Unproductive	*46*	*24*	*53*	*47*	*20*	*80*	*45*	*100*
54. Inmates of jails, asylums and hospitals	4	3	84	16	77	23	16	31
55. Beggars, vagrants and prostitutes.	42	21	50	50	11	89	77	102

SUBSIDIARY TABLE II.—Distribution by occupation in Natural Divisions.

Occupation	Number per mille of total population supported in					
	Baroda State.	Baroda Division.	Baroda City.	Kadi Division.	Navsari Division.	Amreli Division.
1	2	3	4	5.	6.	7
TOTAL...	1,000	1,000	1,000	1,000	1,000	1,000
I.—Exploitation of the surface of the earth	*656*	*745*	*42*	*648*	*774*	*514*
1.-(a) *Agriculture*	*633*	*734*	*35*	*616*	*757*	*482*
(1). Income from rent of Agricultural land.	13	21	5	10	4	13
(2). Ordinary cultivators	465	540	25	516	414	320
(3). Agents, Managers of landed estates (not planters) clerks, rent collectors, etc.	......	......	1	......	......	......
(4). Farm servants and field labourers	154	172	3	88	339	144
(5). Tea, coffee and cinchona plantation	......	......	......	......	......	......
(6). Fruit, flower, vegetable, betel, vine, areca nut, etc., growers	1	1	1	2	......	......
(b) *Pasture*	*21*	*11*	*3*	*32*	*10*	*30*
(9). Cattle and buffalo breeders and keepers...	12	8	2	17	3	29
(10). Sheep, goat and pig breeders	5	2	......	9	3	......
(11). Breeders of other animals (horses, mules, camels, etc.)	1	......	......	2	3	......
(12). Herdsmen, shepherds, goatherds, etc.	3	1	1	4	4	1
(13). Birds, bees, silkworms, etc.	......	......	......	......	......	......
2. Fishing and hunting	1	......	2	......	6	2
Others	1	......	2	......	1	......
II.—Extraction of Minerals	......	......	......	......	......	......
III.—Industry	*123*	*108*	*225*	*131*	*89*	*144*
6. Textile Industries	24	20	36	29	22	35
8. Wood Industries	13	12	20	13	12	14
9. Metal Industries	8	5	10	9	7	9
12. Food Industries	5	4	24	8	8	9
13. Industries of dress and toilet	22	21	37	23	13	36
Other Industries	49	46	98	54	27	41
IV.—Transport	*8*	*4*	*34*	*8*	*7*	*11*
V.—Trade	*64*	*43*	*130*	*77*	*35*	*85*
26. Trade in Textiles	5	5	1	4	5	10
32. Trade in food stuffs	1	1	......	1	4	1
33. Other trade in food stuffs	17	21	56	29	11	42
Other trade	41	16	73	43	15	32
VI.—Public force	*13*	*5*	*126*	*7*	*6*	*18*
VII.—Public administration	*19*	*13*	*118*	*13*	*12*	*27*
VIII.—Professions and liberal arts	*37*	*32*	*103*	*32*	*20*	*67*
IX.—Persons living on their income.	*4*	*2*	*36*	*3*	*2*	*1*
X.—Domestic Service	*1*	*1*	*11*	*2*	*1*	*1*
XI.—Insufficiently described occupations	*70*	*44*	*161*	*72*	*53*	*131*
XII.—Unproductive	*4*	*3*	*14*	*7*	*1*	*1*

SUBSIDIARY TABLE III.—Distribution of the Agricultural, Industrial, Commercial and Professional Population in Natural Divisions or Districts.

District or Natural Division.	Agriculture.				Industry (including Mines.)			
	Population supported by Agriculture.	Proportion of Agricultural Population per 1,000 of District Population.	Percentage on Agricultural Population of		Population supported by Industry.	Proportion of Industrial Population per 1,000 of District Population.	Percentage on Industrial Population of	
			Actual Workers.	Dependants.			Actual Workers.	Dependants.
1	2	3	4	5	6	7	8	9
Baroda State	1,286,901	633	47	53	250,175	123	46	54
Baroda Division	431,219	734	48	52	63,325	108	47	53
Baroda City	3,402	35	45	55	23,333	236	49	51
Kadi Division	512,414	616	43	57	108,903	131	46	54
Navsari Division	253,950	757	55	45	29,885	89	53	47
Amreli Division	55,916	482	46	54	25,729	144	39	61

District or Natural Division.	Commerce.				Professions.				Other Occupations.			
	Population supported by Commerce.	Proportion of Commercial Population per 1,000 of District Population.	Percentage on Commercial Population of		Populations supported by Professions.	Proportion of Professional population per 1,000 of District Population.	Percentage on Professional Population of		Population supported by other Occupations.	Proportion of other Occupation Followers per 1,000 of District Population.	Percentage on other Occupation Followers of	
			Actual Workers.	Dependants.			Actual Workers.	Dependants.			Actual Workers.	Dependants.
1	10	11	12	13	14	15	16	17	18	19	20	21
Baroda State	146,538	72	37	63	74,692	37	46	54	274,492	135	48	52
Baroda Division	28,024	47	41	59	18,889	32	46	54	46,148	79	52	48
Baroda City	16,324	164	40	60	10,225	103	41	59	47,061	473	47	53
Kadi Division	70,928	85	38	62	27,031	32	50	50	112,886	136	48	52
Navsari Division	14,168	42	40	60	6,619	20	45	55	30,845	92	46	54
Amreli Division	17,094	96	29	71	11,978	67	42	58	37,552	211	35	65

SUBSIDIARY TABLE IV.—Occupations combined with Agriculture, where Agriculture is the subsidiary occupation.

Occupation.	Number per mille who are partially Agriculturists.					
	Baroda State.	Baroda Division.	Baroda City.	Kadi Division.	Navsari Division.	Amreli Division.
1	2	3	4	5	6	7
TOTAL ...	19	13	7	23	22	18
I.—Exploitation of the surface of the earth ...	*1*	*·6*	......	*2*	*·7*	*·2*
1.—(a) Agriculture—						
(1) Income from rent of agricultural land ...	......	......	......	......	......	......
(2) Ordinary cultivators ...	......	......	......	......	......	......
(3) Agents, managers of landed estates (not planters), clerks, rent collectors, etc. ...	62	......	......	136	......	......
(4) Farm servants and field-labourers ...	......	......	......	......	......	......
(5) Tea, coffee and cinchona plantations ...	......	......	......	......	......	......
(6) Fruit, flower, vegetable, betel, wine, areca nut-growers ...	53	123	......	7	433	......
(b) Pasture ...	*37*	*34*	......	*45*	*22*	*6*
(9) Cattle and buffalo breeders and keepers ...	26	43	......	26	31	6
(10) Sheep, goat and pig breeders ...	5	4	......	1	34	......
(11) Breeders of other animals (horses, mules, camels, asses, etc.) ...	7	......	......	7	......	......
(12) Herdsmen, shepherds, goat-herds, etc. ...	129	21	......	271	13	......
(13) Birds, bees, silkworms, etc.	300	......	......	1,000	......	......
2. Fishing and hunting ...	5	......	......	......	6	......
(Others) groups 7-8 ...	42	17	......	......	87	......
II.—Extraction of Minerals ...	......	......	......	......	......	......
III.—Industry ...	*70*	*105*	......	*79*	*15*	*26*
6. Textile industries ...	92	15	......	54	275	36
8. Wood industries ...	72	61	......	86	12	30
9. Metal industries ...	69	83	......	101	29	19
12. Food industries ...	44	4	......	30	140	......
13. Industries of dress and toilet.	72	114	......	76	68	24
Other industries ...	59	47	......	55	156	28
IV.—Transport ...	*41*	*6*	......	60	*84*	*10*
V.—Trade ...	*64*	*37*	......	*94*	*75*	*22*
26. Trade in textiles ...	37	19	......	76	49	13
32. Hotels, cafe servants, etc. ...	71	78	......	134	57	24
33. Trade in food-stuffs ...	60	25	1	97	59	20
Other trades ...	72	53	......	91	96	19
VI.—Public Force ...	*80*	*106*	*58*	*116*	*203*	*7*
VII.—Public Administration ...	*53*	*53*	*1*	*88*	*103*	32
VIII.—Professions and liberal arts ...	*51*	*44*	......	*70*	*135*	*9*
IX.—Persons living on their income ...	*9*	*14*	......	*20*	*21*	*14*
X.—Domestic service ...	*27*	*3*	*3*	*78*	*43*	......
XI.—Insufficiently described occupations ...	*28*	*35*	*1*	*14*	*23*	......
XII.—Unproductive ...	*5·4*	*13*	......	*6*	......	......

SUBSIDIARY TABLE V—Occupations combined with Agriculture (where Agriculture is the principal occupation).

Landlords (Rent-receivers).		Cultivators (Rent-payers).		Farm Servants—Field-labourers.	
Subsidiary Occupation.	Number per 10,000 who follow it.	Subsidiary Occupation.	Number per 10,000 who follow it.	Subsidiary Occupation.	Number per 10,000 who follow it.
1	2	3	4	5	6
Rent-payers	409	Rent-receivers...	18	Rent-receivers	6
Agricultural labourers ...	32	Agricultural labourers ...	65	Rent-payers	26
Government employès of all kinds	84	General labourers	29	General labourers	20
Money-lenders and grain-dealers	68	Government employês of all kinds	40	Village watchmen	16
Other traders of all kinds ...	116	Money-lenders and grain-dealers	11	Cattle-breeders and milkmen.	6
Priests	15	Other traders of all kinds ...	116	Mill-hands	2
Clerks of all kinds (not Government)	25	Fishermen and boatmen ...	2	Fishermen and boatmen ...	·05
School Masters	23	Cattle-breeders and milkmen.	13	Rice-pounders...	·05
Lawyers	3	Village watchmen	15	Traders of all kinds	2
Estate Agents and Managers.	3	Weavers	5	Oil-pressers	1
Medical Practitioners ...	5	Barbers...	9	Weavers	13
Artisans	24	Oil-pressers	3	Potters	2
Others	105	Washermen	4	Leather-workers	3
		Potters	22	Blacksmiths and carpenters.	1
		Blacksmiths	20	Washermen	......
		Others	87	Others	32

SUBSIDIARY TABLE VI.—Occupations of females by sub-classes, and selected orders and groups.

Group. No.	OCCUPATION.	Number of Actual Workers.		Number of Females per 1000 Males.
		Males.	Females.	
1	2	3	4	5
	BARODA STATE	661,522	285,247	431
	I.—Exploitation of the Surface of the Earth	*428,474*	*201,129*	*469*
	1. Pasture and Agriculture	*427,679*	*200,884*	*469*
1	Income from rent of Agricultural land	7,984	1,935	242
2	Ordinary cultivators	310,548	86,686	279
3	Agents, Managers of landed estates (not planters), clerks, rent collectors, etc.	93	4	43
4	Farm servants and field labourers	93,656	107,568	1,148
6	Fruit, flower, vegetable, betel, vine, areca nut, etc., growers ...	942	332	352
8	Wood cutters, fire wood, lac, catechu, rubber, etc., collectors and charcoal burners	105	24	228
9	Cattle and buffalo breeders and keepers	8,571	2,138	249
10	Sheep, goat and pig breeders	2,098	1,659	790
11	Breeders of other animals (horses, mules, camels, asses, etc.) ...	931	16	17
12	Herdsmen, shepherds, goat-herds, etc.	2,467	322	130
	2. Fishing and hunting			
14	Fishing	792	445	561
	II.—Extraction of Minerals	*41*	*3*	*73*
	3. Mines	*41*	*3*	*73*
17	Mines and metallic minerals (gold, iron, manganese, etc.)... ...	41	3	73
	III.—Industry	*85,547*	*31,013*	*362*
	6. Textiles	*16,351*	*9,477*	*579*
21	Cotton ginning, cleaning and pressing	3,551	1,860	523
22	Cotton spinning, sizing and weaving	10,667	5,540	519
23	Jute spinning, pressing and weaving	10	7	700
24	Rope, twine and string	97	175	1,804
25	Other fibres (cocoanut, aloes, palm-leaf, flax, hemp, straw, etc.) ...	......	277	......
27	Silk spinners and weavers	364	205	563
30	Dyeing, bleaching, printing, preparation and sponging of textiles.	1,378	663	482
31	Other textile industries	249	750	3,012
	7. Hides, Skins and hard materials from animal kingdom ...	*5,760*	*1,105*	*191*
32	Tanners, carriers, leather dressers, etc.	5,439	1,063	195
33	Makers of leather articles such as trunks, water bags, etc.... ...	307	42	136
	8. Wood	*9,045*	*1,944*	*214*
36	Sawyers, carpenters, turners and joiners, etc.	7,512	312	41
37	Basket makers and other industries of woody material including leaves	1,533	1,632	1,064
	9. Metals	*6,405*	*335*	*52*
41	Other workers in iron and makers of implements and tools principally or exclusively of iron	5,851	326	60
	10. Ceramics	*8,599*	*5,137*	*597*
45	Makers of glass and crystal ware	77	21	272
47	Potters and earthen pipe and bowl makers	8,365	4,929	589
48	Brick and tile makers	157	207	1,318
	11. Chemical Products properly so called	*3,551*	*799*	*225*
53	Manufacture and refining of vegetable and mineral oils	3,408	786	201
	12. Food industries			
56	Rice pounders and huskers and flour grinders	956	2,398	2,508
58	Grain parchers, etc.	124	33	266
59	Butchers	698	42	60
63	Sweetmeat makers, preparers of jam and condiments, etc.... ...	674	54	80
66	Manufacturers of tobacco, opium and ganja	657	38	57

SUBSIDIARY TABLE VI.—Occupations of females by sub-classes, and selected orders and groups—*contd.*

Group. No.	OCCUPATION.	Number of Actual Workers. Males.	Number of Actual Workers. Females.	Number of Females per 1,000 Males.
1	2	3	4	5
	13. Industries of dress and the toilet	*15,536*	*5,043*	*324*
67	Hat, cap and turban makers	86	210	2,441
68	Tailors, milliners, dress makers and darners, embroiderers on linen	4,451	3,252	730
69	Shoe, boot and sandal makers...	2,744	794	289
70	Other industries pertaining to dress-gloves, &c.	37	16	432
71	Washing, cleaning and dyeing	1,064	585	549
72	Barbers, hair dressers and wig makers	7,154	186	26
	15. Building industries	*4,908*	*635*	*129*
76	Lime burners, cement workers	103	49	475
77	Excavators, plinth builders and well sinkers	394	80	203
78	Stone and marble workers, masons and brick layers	3,641	492	135
79	Others (thatchers, building contractors, house painters, tilers, plumbers, locksmiths, &c.)	770	14	18
	18. Industries of luxury and those pertaining to literature and the arts and sciences	*3,887*	*281*	*72*
89	Workers in precious stones and metals, enamellers, imitation jewellery makers, gilders, etc.	3,419	155	45
91	Toy, kite, cage, fishing, fishing tackle, etc., makers, taxidermists, etc.	14	125	8,928
	19. Industries connected with refuse matter	*7,337*	*3,671*	*500*
93	Sweepers, scavengers, dust and sweeping contractors	7,337	3,671	500
	IV.—Transport	*6,773*	*345*	*50*
	21. Transport by road	*2,266*	*183*	*80*
98	Persons employed on the construction and maintenance of road and bridges	117	44	376
99	Cart-owners and drivers, coachmen, stable boys, tramway, mail carriage, etc., managers and employès (excluding private servants)	1,809	106	58
101	Pack elephant, camel, mule, ass and bullock owners and drivers...	235	17	72
102	Porters and messengers	99	16	161
	22. Transport by rail	*2,570*	*159*	*618*
103	Railway employès of all kinds other than construction coolies ...	2,551	145	56
104	Labourers employed on railway construction	19	14	736
106	*24. Bank managers, money-lenders, exchange and insurance agents, money changers and brokers and their employes* ...	*967*	*785*	*158*
108	*26. Trade in piece-goods, wool, cotton, silk, hair and other textiles.*	*3,617*	*183*	*50*
109	*27. Trade in skins, leather, furs, feathers, horns, etc.*	*1,054*	*92*	*87*
110	*28. Trade in wood (not fire-wood), cork, bark, etc.*	*384*	*129*	*335*
	32. Hotels, cafes, restaurants, etc.	*1,054*	*92*	*87*
114	Vendors of wine, liquors, aërated waters, etc.	814	78	93
115	Owners and managers of hotels, cookshops, sarais, etc., and their employès	240	14	58
	33. Other Trade in foodstuffs	*17,332*	*5,804*	*327*
116	Fish dealers	510	137	268
117	Grocers and sellers of vegetable oil, salt and other condiments ...	1,659	44	26
118	Sellers of milk, butter, ghee, poultry, eggs, etc.	811	602	742
119	Sellers of sweetmeats, sugar, *gur* and molasses	158	56	326
120	Cardamom, betel-leaf, vegetables, fruit and areca nut sellers ...	5,438	3,963	728
121	Grain and pulse dealers	7,607	820	107
122	Tobacco, opium, ganja, etc., sellers	740	52	70
123	Dealers in sheep, goats and pigs	233	......	.....
124	Dealers in hay, grass and fodder	171	130	760
125	*34. Trade in ready-made clothing and the toilet articles, etc.* ...	*460*	*33*	71

SUBSIDIARY TABLE VI.—Occupations of females by sub-classes, and selected orders and groups—*concld.*

Group No.	OCCUPATION.	Number of actual Workers. Males.	Females.	Number of Females per 1,000 Males.
1	2	3	4	5
	35. Trade in furniture ...	*132*	*70*	*530*
126	Trade in furniture, carpets, curtains and bedding ...	73	70	95
129	*37. Trade in means of transport* ...	*321*	*556*	*1,732*
130	*38. Trade in fuel (firewood, charcoal, coal, cowdung, etc.)* ...	*535*	*168*	*314*
131	Dealers in precious stones, jewellery (real and imitation), clock, optical instruments, etc. ...	475	19	40
132	Dealers in common bangles, bead necklaces, fans and small articles, toys, hunting and fishing tackle, flowers, etc. ...	197	128	649
133	Publishers, booksellers, stationers, dealers in music pictures, musical instruments and curiosities...	63	12	190
134	*40. Trade in refuse matter* ...	*16*	*49*	*3,062*
	41. Trade of other sorts ...	*7,934*	*1,329*	*161*
135	Shopkeepers otherwise unspecified ...	7,398	1,282	173
137	Conjurors, acrobats, fortunetellers, reciters, exhibitors of curiosities and wild animals...	389	22	56
138	Other trades (including farmers of pounds, tolls and markets) ...	85	25	294
	VI.—Public Force ...	*12,276*	......	......
	VII.—Public Administration ...	*13,853*	*284*	*20*
144	Service of the State ...	11,622	233	20
145	Service of Native and Foreign States ...	85	7	82
146	Municipal and other local (not village) service ...	689	39	56
147	Village officials and servants other than watchmen ...	1,457	5	3
	VIII.—Professions and liberal arts ...	*28,734*	*5,523*	*192*
	46. Religion ...	*20,004*	*4,886*	*244*
148	Priests, ministers, etc. ...	14,968	4,212	274
149	Religious mendicants, inmates of monasteries, etc ...	2,328	385	165
150	Catechists, readers, church and mission service ...	339	26	76
	48. Medicine ...	*978*	*204*	*208*
154	Medical practitioners of all kinds, including dentists, oculists and veterinary surgeons ...	702	19	27
155	Midwives, vaccinaters, compounders, nurses, masseurs, etc. ...	276	185	666
156	*49. Instruction (professors and teachers of all kinds)* ...	*4,147*	*179*	*43*
	50. Letters and arts and sciences ...	*3,165*	*254*	*80*
159	Others (authors, photographers, artists, etc.)...	177	11	62
160	Music composers and masters, players on all kinds of musical instruments (not military), singers, actors and dancers ...	2,021	238	117
161	IX.—51.—Persons living on their income ...	*1,943*	*1,277*	*657*
	X.—Domestic Service ...	*1,237*	*595*	*481*
	52. Domestic Service ...	*1,237*	*595*	*481*
	XI.—Insufficiently described occupations ...	......	......	......
162	Cooks, water-carriers, door-keepers, watchmen and indoor servants ...	1,197	564	471
163	Private grooms, coachmen, dog boys, etc. ...	40	31	775
	53. General terms which do not indicate a definite occupation ...	*40,235*	*33,727*	*838*
165	Cashiers, accountants, book-keepers, clerks, etc. ...	1,051	876	834
167	Labourers and workmen otherwise unspecified ...	33,590	35,099	1,044
	XII.—Unproductive ...	*3,379*	*1,532*	*453*
168	*54. Inmates of jails, asylums, and hospitals* ...	*576*	*97*	*171*
169	*55. Beggars, vagrants, prostitutes, etc.* ...	*2,803*	*1,435*	*512*

SUBSIDIARY TABLE VII.—SELECTED OCCUPATIONS.

Group Number.	Occupation.	Population supported in 1911.	Population supported in 1901.	Percentage of variation.
1	2	3	4	5
	A.—Production of raw materials	1,332,881	1,061,632	+ 25·55
	I.—EXPLOITATION OF THE SURFACE OF THE EARTH.	1,332,756	1,061,321	+ 25·6
	1 Pasture and agriculture	1,329,961	1,059,674	+ 25·5
1	Income from rent of Agricultural land	25,681	78,569	— 67·3
2	Ordinary cultivators	944,994	556,119	— 69·9
3	Agents, managers of landed estates (not planters), clerks, rent collectors, etc.	211	1,950	— 89·2
4	Farm servants and field labourers	313,479	372,964	— 15·9
5	Tea, coffee, cinchona and indigo plantations...	...	85	— 100
6	Fruit, flowers, vegetable, betel, vine, areca nut, etc., growers ...	2,536	4,942	— 48·6
8	Wood-cutters, firewood, lac, catechu, rubber, etc., collectors and charcoal burners.	281	1,845	— 84·8
9	Cattle and buffalo breeders and keepers	25,330	8,542	+ 196·5
10	Sheep, goat and pig breeders	9,740	7,698	+ 26·5
11	Breeders of other animals (horses, mules, camels, asses, etc.) ...	1,536	831	+ 84·8
12	Herdsmen, shepherds, goat-herds, etc.	5,633	25,820	— 78·2
	2. Fishing and hunting...	2,795	1,647	+ 69·7
14	Fishing	2,783	1,330	+ 109·2
15	Hunting	12	317	— 96·2
	II—EXTRACTION OF MINERALS	125	311	— 59·8
	B.—Preparation and supply of material substances ...	396,588	386,644	+ 2·6
	III.—INDUSTRY	250,050	234,840	+ 6·5
	6. Textiles...	52,433	44,935	+ 16·7
21	Cotton ginning, cleaning and pressing	10,635	4,415	+ 140·9
22	Cotton spinning, sizing and weaving	33,802	35,128	— 3·8
23	Jute spinning, pressing and weaving	46	92	— 50
24	Rope, twine and string	491	958	— 48·7
26	Wool carders and spinners, weavers of woollen blankets, carpets, etc.	92	535	— 82·8
27	Silk spinners and weavers	1,191	138	+ 763
30	Dyeing, bleaching, printing, preparation and sponging of textiles.	3,966	3,555	+ 11·6
	7. Hides, skins and hard materials from the animal kingdom ...	16,032	19,390	— 16·5
32	Tanners, curriers, leather dressers and dyers, etc.	14,967	18,111	— 17·4
33	Makers of leather articles, such as trunks, water bags, etc.... ...	1,035	1,250	— 17·2
35	Bone, ivory, horn, shell, etc., workers	30	29	+ 3·1
	8. Wood	26,275	16,256	+ 61·6
36	Sawyers, carpenters, turners and joiners, etc....	20,969	12,561	+ 66·9
37	Basket-makers and other industries of woody material, including leaves.	5,306	3,695	+ 43·6
	9. Metals	16,150	10,758	+ 50·1
38	Forging and rolling of iron and other metals	......	102	— 100
40	Makers of arms, guns, etc.	20	45	— 55·6
42	Workers in brass, copper and bell metal	2,195	405	+ 441·98
43	Workers in other metals (tin, zinc, lead, quick-silver, etc.)	277	576	— 51·9
	10.—Ceramics	26,743	24,446	+ 9·4
48	Brick and tile makers	809	1,642	— 50·7
	11.—Chemical products properly so called and analogous	10,953	10,191	+ 7·5
54	Manufacture of paper, card-board and papier mache	3	103	— 97·1

SUBSIDIARY TABLE VII.—SELECTED OCCUPATIONS—(*contd.*)

Group Number.	Occupation.	Population supported in 1911.	Population supported in 1901.	Percentage of variation.
1	2	3	4	5
	12.—Food industries ...	*11,314*	*12,069*	*— 6·25*
57	Bakers and biscuit makers ...	**12**	**347**	**— 96·5**
58	Grain parchers, etc. ...	**310**	**918**	**— 66·2**
59	Butchers ...	**1,641**	**1,317**	**+ 24·6**
60	Fish curers ...	......	**330**	**— 100**
61	Butter, cheese and ghee makers ...	......	**177**	**— 100**
63	Sweetmeat makers, preparers of jam and condiments, etc. ...	**1,538**	**868**	**+ 77·2**
64	Brewers and distillers ...	**248**	**731**	**— 66·1**
65	Toddy drawers ...	**884**	**54**	**+1,537·0**
66	Manufacturers of tobacco, opium and ganja...	**1,328**	**179**	**+ 645·9**
	13.—Industries of dress and the toilet ...	*45,632*	*47,034*	*— 2·98*
69	Shoe, boot and sandal-makers ...	**8,266**	**9,504**	**— 13**
70	Other industries pertaining to dress—gloves, socks, gaiters, belts, buttons, umbrellas, canes, etc.	**127**	**238**	**— 46·6**
72	Barbers, hairdressers and wig-makers ...	**19,787**	**19,837**	**— 0·25**
73	Other industries connected with the toilet (tattooers, shampooers, bath houses, etc.)	......	**219**	**— 100**
	15.—Building industries ...	*12,931*	*15,327*	*— 15·6*
77	Excavators, plinth builders and well sinkers ...	**1,222**	**4,070**	**— 70**
78	Stone and marble workers, masons and bricklayers ...	**9,253**	**9,091**	**+ 1·8**
	18.—Industries of luxury and those pertaining to literature and the arts and sciences.	*11,507*	*13,741*	*— 15·5*
89	Workers in precious stones and metals, enamellers, imitation jewellery makers, gilders, etc.	**10,158**	**8,813**	**+ 15·3**
90	Makers of bangles, rosaries, bead and other necklaces, spangles, lingams and sacred threads.	**13**	**2,669**	**— 99·5**
93	*19.—Industries concerned with refuse matter, sweepers, scavengers, dust and sweeping contractors.*	*19,590*	*18,300*	*+ 7·05*
	IV.—TRANSPORT ...	*16,638*	*8,742*	*+ 90·1*
	20.—Transport by water ...	*1,861*	*4,344*	*— 57·2*
95	Ship owners and their employes, ship brokers, ships' officers, engineers, mariners and firemen.	......	**587**	**— 100**
96	Persons employed on the maintenance of streams, rivers and canals (including construction).	**41**	**3,509**	**— 98·8**
97	Boat owners, boatmen and tow men. ...	**1,816**	**240**	**+ 656·7**
	21.—Transport by road ...	*5,960*	*1,704*	*+ 249·8*
99	Cart owners and drivers, coachmen, stable boys, tramway, mail carriage, etc., managers and employes (excluding private servants).	**4,534**	**818**	**+ 454·3**
100	Palki, etc., bearers and owners ...	**12**	**160**	**— 92·5**
101	Pack elephant, camel, mule, ass and bullock owners and drivers...	**850**	**320**	**+ 165·6**
102	Porters and messengers ...	**236**	**406**	**— 41·9**
	22.—Transport by rail ...	*6,458*	*2,129*	*+ 203·3*
103	Railway employes of all kinds other than construction coolies ...	**6,226**	**2,129**	**+ 192·4**
104	Labourers employed on railway construction ...	**232**	......	......
105	*23.—Post Office, Telegraph and Telephone services* ...	*2,359*	*565*	*+ 317·5*
	V.—TRADE ...	*129,900*	*143,062*	*— 9·2*
106	*24.—Banks, establishments of credit, exchange and insurance, Bank managers, money lenders, exchange and insurance agents, money changers and brokers and their employes.*	*17,600*	*16,582*	*+ 6·1*
107	*25—Brokerage, commission and export. Brokers, commission agents, commercial travellers, warehouse owners and employes.*	*1,200*	*1,852*	*— 35·2*
108	*26—Trade in textiles, piece-goods, wool, cotton, silk, hair and other textiles.*	*11,131*	*9,892*	*+ 12·5*
109	*27—Trade in skins, leather, furs, feathers, horn, etc.* ...	*1,688*	*1,742*	*— 7·7*

SUBSIDIARY TABLE VII.—SELECTED OCCUPATIONS—(*contd.*)

Group Number.	Occupation.	Population supported in 1911.	Population supported in 1901.	Percentage of variation.
1	2	3	4	5
110	28—*Trade in wood (not firewood), cork, bark, etc.*	*930*	*319*	+ *191·5*
111	29—*Trade in metals, machinery, knife, tool, etc., sellers*	*954*	*31*	+ *29,77·4*
112	30—*Trade in pottery*	*94*	*2,595*	— *96·4*
113	31—*Trade in chemical products (drugs, dyes, paints, petroleum, explosives, etc.*	*256*	*947*	— *73*
	32—*Hotels, cafes, restaurants, etc*	*3,390*	*2,297*	+ *47·6*
114	Vendors of wine, liquors, ærated waters, etc.	**2,779**	**2,090**	+ **32·97**
115	Owners and managers of hotels, cook-shops, serais, etc., and their employes.	**611**	**207**	+ **195·2**
	33—*Other trade in food stuffs*	*54,718*	*53,534*	+ *2·2*
116	Fish dealers	**1,696**	**1,844**	— **8**
117	Grocers and sellers of vegetable oil, salt and other condiments ...	**4,556**	**7,456**	— **38·9**
118	Sellers of milk, butter, ghee, poultry, eggs, etc.	**3,249**	**2,794**	+ **15·2**
119	Sellers of sweetmeats, sugar, gur and molasses	**637**	**1,067**	— **40·3**
120	Cardamom, betel-leaf, vegetables, fruit and areca nut sellers ...	**17,814**	**13,372**	+ **33·2**
121	Grain and pulse dealers	**23,864**	**19,341**	+ **23·4**
122	Tobacco, opium, ganja, etc., sellers	**1,811**	**1,624**	+ **11·5**
123	Dealers in sheep, goats and pigs	**541**	**2,054**	— **73·7**
124	Dealers in hay, grass and fodder	**550**	**3,982**	— **86·2**
125	34—*Trade in clothing and toilet articles, ready-made clothing and other articles of dress and the toilet (hats, umbrellas, socks, ready-made shoes, perfumes, etc.)*	*1,425*	*3,950*	— *63·9*
	35—*Trade in furniture*	*523*	*2,240*	— *76·65*
126	Trade in furniture, carpets, curtains and bedding	**404**	**405**	— **0·25**
128	36.—*Trade in building materials (stones, bricks, plaster, cement, sand, tiles, thatch, etc.)*	*489*	*955*	— *48·8*
129	37.—*Trade in means of transport, dealers and hirers of elephants, camels, horses, cattle, asses, mules, etc.; sellers (not makers) of carriages, saddlery, etc.*	*1,754*	*9,051*	— *80·6*
130	38.—*Trade in fuel (firewood, charcoal, coal, cowdung, etc.)* ...	*1,581*	*3,997*	— *60·4*
	39.—*Trade in articles of luxury and those pertaining to letters and the arts and sciences.*	*2,670*	*5,068*	— *47·3*
131	Dealers in precious stones, jewellery (real and imitation), clocks, optical instruments, etc.	**1,759**	**161**	+ **992·5**
132	Dealers in common bangles, bead necklaces, fans, small articles, toys, hunting and fishing tackle, flowers, etc.	**709**	**4,484**	— **84·2**
133	Publishers, booksellers, stationers, dealers in music, pictures, musical instruments and curiosities.	**202**	**423**	— **52·2**
134	40.—*Trade in refuse matter (rags, stable refuse, etc.)*	*97*	......	......
	41.—*Trade of other sorts*	*29,400*	*28,010*	+ *4·96*
136	Itinerant traders, pedlars, hawkers, etc.	**279**	**1,488**	— **81·25**
	C.—Public administration and liberal arts ...	**148,275**	**127,179**	+ **16·6**
	VI—PUBLIC FORCE...	*26,904*	*4,249*	+ *533·2*
	42.—*Army...*	*11,560*	*3,470*	+ *233·1*
139	Army (Baroda State)	**10,551**	**3,199**	+ **229·8**
140	Army (Imperial)	**1,009**	**271**	+ **272·3**
141	43.—*Navy*	......	......	......
	44.—*Police...*	*15,344*	*779*	+ *1,869·7*
143	Village watchmen...	**5,425**	**22**	+**24,557·1**

SUBSIDIARY TABLE VII.—Selected Occupations—(concld.)

Group Number.	Occupation.	Population supported in 1911.	Population supported in 1901.	Percentage of variation.
1	2	3	4	5
	VII.—45—PUBLIC ADMINISTRATION	*38,217*	*63,698*	— *40·*
144	Service of the State	**33,318**	**38,685**	— **13·9**
145	Service of Native and Foreign States	**376**	**1,905**	— **80·3**
146	Municipal and other local (not village) service	**1,959**	**5,565**	— **64·8**
147	Village officials and servants other than watchmen	**2,564**	**17,543**	— **85·4**
	VIII.—PROFESSIONS AND LIBERAL ARTS	*74,692*	*47,999*	+ *55·6*
	46.—Religion	*51,985*	*34,863*	+ *49·1*
148	Priests, ministers, etc.	**39,101**	**25,732**	+ **51·9**
149	Religious mendicants, inmates of monasteries, etc.	**7,137**	**2,656**	+ **168·7**
150	Catechists, readers, church and mission service	**922**	**3,333**	— **72·3**
151	Temple, burial or burning ground service, pilgrim conductors, circumcisers.	**4,825**	**3,142**	+ **53·6**
	47.—Law	*1,670*	*1,460*	+ *14·4*
152	Lawyers of all kinds, including Kazis, law agents and mukhtiars .	**1,212**	**1,297**	— **6·55**
153	Lawyers' clerks, petition writers, etc.	**458**	**163**	+ **181·**
	48.—Medicine	*3,079*	*2,603*	+ *18·3*
154	Medical practitioners, of all kinds, including dentists, oculists and veterinary surgeons.	**1,950**	**2,001**	— **2·5**
155	Midwives, vaccinators, compounders, nurses, masseurs, etc. ...	**1,129**	**602**	+ **87·5**
156	*49.—Instruction (professors and teachers of all kinds, and clerks and servants connected with education).*	*9,399*	*5,500*	+ *70·9*
	50.—Letters and arts and sciences	*8,559*	*3,573*	+ *139·5*
157	Public scribes, stenographers, etc.	......	**62**	— **100**
160	Music composers and masters, players on all kinds of musical instruments (not military), singers, actors and dancers.	**5,607**	**1,278**	+ **338·7**
161	*IX.—51.—PERSONS LIVING ON THEIR INCOME.—PROPRIETORS (OTHER THAN OF AGRICULTURAL LAND), FUND AND SCHOLARSHIP HOLDERS AND PENSIONERS.*	*8,462*	*11,233*	— *24·7*
	D.—Miscellaneous	**155,054**	**377,237**	— **58·9**
	X.—52.—DOMESTIC SERVICE	*3,510*	*52,267*	— *93·3*
162	Cooks, water-carriers, door-keepers, watchmen and other indoor servants.	**3,349**	**50,578**	— **93·4**
163	Private grooms, coachmen, dog boys, etc.	**161**	**1,689**	— **90·5**
	XI.—53.—INSUFFICIENTLY DESCRIBED OCCUPATIONS (GENERAL TERMS WHICH DO NOT INDICATE A DEFINITE OCCUPATION).	*142,285*	*280,225*	— *49·2*
164	Manufacturers, business men and contractors, otherwise unspecified.	......	**430**	— **100·**
165	Cashiers, accountants, book-keepers, clerks and other employes in unspecified offices, warehouses and shops.	**26,354**	**31,240**	— **15·6**
166	Mechanics, otherwise unspecified	**118**	......	......
	XII.—UNPRODUCTIVE	*9,259*	*44,745*	— *79·3*
168	*54.—Inmates of jails, asylums and hospitals*	*802*	*3,227*	— *75·1*
169	*55.—Beggars, vagrants, procurers, prostitutes, receivers of stolen goods and cattle poisoners.*	*8,457*	*41,518*	— *79·6*

SUBSIDIARY TABLE VIII.—Occupations of Selected Castes.

Caste and Occupation.	Number per 1,000 workers engaged on each occupation.	Number of female workers per 100 males.
1	2	3
HINDUS.		
Ahir—Cattle breeders and graziers ...	*100*	*10*
Cultivators ...	482	11
Field labourers, &c. ...	268	194
Labourers unspecified ...	51	60
Others ...	99	7
Bahrot—Bards and geneologists.	*160*	*21*
Cultivators ...	432	14
Trade ...	71	42
Labourers unspecified ...	103	164
Others ...	234	31
Bava—Devotees ...	*886*	*32*
Cultivators ...	100	6
Labourers unspecified ...	4	93
Beggars, &c. ...	3	0
Others ...	7	32
Bhangi—Scavengers ...	*504*	*45*
Cultivators ...	84	7
Field labourers, &c. ...	258	160
Labourers unspecified ...	133	94
Others ...	21	49
Bharvad—Cattle breeders and graziers ...	*803*	*26*
Cultivators ...	33	34
Field labourers, &c. ...	90	528
Labourers unspecified ...	45	376
Others ...	29	61
Bhavsar—Calenderers and dyers.	*540*	*67*
Industries ...	46	34
Trade ...	215	21
Labourers unspecified ...	111	162
Others ...	88	21
Bhoi—Fishermen and palki-bearers ...	*146*	*35*
Cultivators ...	184	11
Field labourers ...	150	70
Labourers unspecified ...	284	49
Others ...	286	24
Brahman—Anavala—cultivators.	*784*	*9*
Trade ...	23	4
Public administration ...	65	0
Arts and professions ...	61	7
Others ...	67	29
Brahman—Audich—Priests ...	*331*	*24*
Cultivators... ...	180	20
Arts and professions ...	129	7
Labourers unspecified ...	110	90
Others ...	250	15
Brahman—Deshastha—Priests ...	*129*	*18*
Public administration ...	424	0
Arts and professions ...	121	9
Persons living on their income ...	73	9
Others ...	253	33
Brahman—Mewada—Priests ...	*242*	*22*
Cultivators	296	28
Arts and professions ...	100	23
Labourers unspecified ...	101	9
Others ...	261	56
Brahman—Modh—Priests ...	*290*	*22*
Cultivators ...	214	18
Arts and professions ...	135	14
Labourers unspecified ...	77	152
Others ...	284	33
Brahman—Nagar—Priests ...	*263*	*46*
Income from rent of land ...	167	12
Public administration ...	176	1
Arts and professions ...	143	10
Others ...	251	17
Brahman—Tapodhan—Temple servants ...	*208*	*40*
Cultivators... ...	311	9
Industries	121	3
Arts and professions ...	79	10
Others ...	281	42
Chamar—Tanners ...	*511*	*27*
Cultivators... ...	112	39
Field labourers, &c. ...	231	178
Labourers unspecified ...	127	111
Others ...	19	45
Darji—Tailors ...	*955*	*67*
Cultivators... ...	10	30
Raisers of livestock, milkmen, herdsmen, &c. ...	6	100
Transport	3	0
Others ...	26	159
Dhed—Weavers ...	*280*	*40*
Cultivators... ...	151	13
Field labourers, &c. ...	389	141
Labourers unspecified ...	134	107
Others ...	46	39
Ghanchi—Oil-Pressers ...	*603*	*27*
Cultivators... ...	35	20
Trade ...	126	19
Labourers unspecified ...	171	94
Others ...	65	34
Garoda—Priests ...	*659*	*37*
Field Labourers, &c. ...	106	326
Labourers unspecified ...	70	209
Beggars, &c. ...	98	14
Others ...	67	23
Gola—Rice-Pounders ...	*556*	*82*
Cultivators... ...	16	17
Trade ...	62	83
Labourers unspecified ...	386	158
Others ...	30	4

SUBSIDIARY TABLE VIII.—Occupations of Selected Castes—*contd.*

Caste and Occupation.	Number per 1,000 workers engaged on each occupation.	Number of female workers per 100 males.
1	2	3
HINDUS—*contd.*		
Gosain—Devotees	*545*	*22*
Cultivators	284	15
Field labourers, &c.	55	178
Beggars, &c.	24	13
Others	92	39
Hajam—Barbers	*732*	*1*
Cultivators	97	42
Public administration	20	0
Arts and Professions	11	66
Others	140	597
Kachhia—Cultivators and vegetable sellers	*608*	*25*
Field labourers, etc.	58	424
Industries	189	24
Labourers unspecified	58	450
Others	87	10
Kanbi-Anjana—Cultivators ...	*837*	*31*
Income from rent of land ...	12	42
Field labourers, &c.	118	269
Labourers unspecified	13	148
Others	20	21
Kanbi-Kadwa—Cultivators ...	*852*	*30*
Income from rent of land ...	9	42
Field labourers, &c.	97	287
Labourers unspecified	17	218
Others	25	19
Kanbi-Karadia—Cultivators ...	*684*	*6*
Field labourers, &c.	257	173
Public administration	9	......
Labourers unspecified ...	29	11
Others	31	19
Kanbi-Lewa—Cultivators... ...	*754*	*14*
Income from rent of land ...	41	11
Field labourers	77	78
Contractors, clerks, &c.	68	1
Others	60	28
Koli—Agricultural labourers ...	*357*	*109*
Cultivators	497	15
Industries	7	18
Labourers unspecified	91	105
Others	48	14
Kumbhar—Potters	*675*	*48*
Cultivators...	148	33
Field labourers, &c.	96	121
Labourers unspecified	64	154
Others	17	21
Luhana—Traders	678	*11*
Cultivators	95	4
Field labourers, &c.	41	130
Labourers unspecified	65	124
Others	121	17
Luhar—Blacksmiths	*597*	*10*
Cultivators	156	40
Field labourers, &c.	81	354
Industries	76	11
Others	90	65
Machhi—Fishermen	*440*	*25*
Cultivators	155	21
Field labourers, &c.	177	303
Labourers unspecified	166	278
Others	62	93
Maratha-Kshatriya—Military and dominant	*69*	......
Public force	283	......
Public administration	198	2
Labourers unspecified	180	285
Others	270	25
Mochi—Shoe-makers	*781*	*23*
Cultivators	33	37
Field labourers, &c.	83	306
Labourers unspecified	56	233
Others	47	53
Rabari—Graziers and cattle breeders	*518*	*24*
Cultivators, &c.	355	25
Field labourers, &c.	64	158
Labourers unspecified ...	44	123
Others	19	109
Rajput—Military and dominant...	*34*	......
Income from rent of land ...	64	21
Cultivators...	634	17
Field labourers, &c.	97	132
Others	171	36
Ravalia—Tape weavers and drummers	*343*	*63*
Field labourers, &c.	73	83
Trade	186	90
Labourers unspecified	253	41
Others	195	52
Sathawara—Vegetable growers and sellers	*250*	*194*
Cultivators	310	15
Industries	204	3
Labourers unspecified	126	167
Others	110	58
Shenwa—Village watchmen ...	*62*	*6*
Cultivators...	220	20
Field labourers, &c.	338	62
Labourers unspecified	244	90
Others	86	27
Soni—Goldsmiths	*867*	*3*
Industries	13	95
Trade	10	85
Public administration	8	......
Others	103	344

SUBSIDIARY TABLE VIII.—Occupations of Selected Castes—*contd.*

Caste and Occupation.	Number per 1,000 workers engaged on each occupation.	Number of female workers per 100 males.
1	2	3
HINDUS—*contd.*		
Sutar—Carpenters	*778*	*2*
Cultivators	80	49
Industries	12	5
Trade	4	58
Others	126	541
Talavia—Agricultural labourers.	*713*	*53*
Cultivators	124	130
Industries	10	......
Labourers, unspecified	104	41
Others	19	98
Targala—Actors, dancers, singers, &c.	*405*	*7*
Cultivators	234	32
Field labourers, &c.	58	330
Labourers, unspecified	213	122
Others	90	27
Vagher—Military and dominant.	*808*	*5*
Field labourers	80	24
Public administration	37	......
Labourers, unspecified	47	48
Others	38	32
Vaghari—Hunters and fowlers...	*52*	*12*
Cultivators...	158	26
Field Labourers, &c.	230	64
Labourers, unspecified	331	70
Others	229	65
Vania—Disaval—Traders	*608*	*12*
Public administration	61	......
Persons living on their income ...	80	101
Labourers, unspecified	155	134
Others	96	32
Vania—Lad—Traders	*488*	*3*
Trade	88	66
Public administration	78	......
Contractors, clerks, &c.	146	3
Labourers, unspecified	59	136
Others	150	38
Vania Shrimali—Traders	*397*	*11*
Public administration	59	......
Contractors, clerks, &c.	257	10
Labourers, unspecified	60	180
Others	227	23
JAINS.		
Vania—Shrimali—Traders ...	*688*	*5*
Trade	24	101
Cultivators...	19	10
Contractors, clerks, &c.	152	26
Labourers, unspecified	46	115
Others	71	36
ANIMISTS.		
Bhil—Cultivators and Agricultural Labourers	*871*	*78*
Industries	10	......
Public administration ...	8	......
Labourers, unspecified	85	74
Others	26	17
Chodhra—Cultivators and Agricultural Labourers	*961*	*75*
Field Labourers	11	12
Raisers of livestock, milkmen and herdsmen	1	13
Public administration	1	......
Labourers, unspecified	19	47
Others	7	20
Dhanka—Cultivators and Agricultural Labourers	*923*	*81*
Industries	7	......
Transport	6	......
Labourers, unspecified	41	48
Others	23	17
Dhodia—Cultivators and Agricultural labourers	*824*	*116*
Field labourers, &c.	125	......
Raisers of livestock, milkmen and herdsmen	3	17
Industries	3	......
Labourers, unspecified	33	15
Others	12	31
Gamit—Cultivators and Agricultural labourers	*943*	*84*
Field labourers	11	1
Raisers of livestock, milkmen and herdsmen	7	25
Transport	4	2
Labourers, unspecified	26	72
Others	9	2
Nayakda—Cultivators and Agricultural labourers	*757*	*141*
Field labourers, &c.	149	......
Raisers of livestock, milkmen and herdsmen	12	......
Public administration	7	......
Labourers, unspecified	40	46
Others	35	58
MUSALMANS.		
Fakir—Mendicants	*756*	*25*
Cultivators	119	21
Field labourers, &c.	28	111
Labourers, unspecified	29	307
Others	68	37
Ghanchi—Oil-pressers	*540*	*12*
Cultivators...	146	36
Field labourers, &c.	84	182
Trade	76	48
Others	145	41

SUBSIDIARY TABLE VIII.—OCCUPATIONS OF SELECTED CASTES—*concld.*

CASTE AND OCCUPATION.	Number per 1,000 workers engaged on each occupation.	Number of female workers per 100 males.
1	2	3
MUSALMANS—*contd.*		
MALEK—CULTIVATORS	*520*	*14*
Field labourers, &c.	107	184
Public force	67	......
Labourers, unspecified	120	61
Others	186	16
MEMON—TRADERS AND PEDLARS ...	*314*	*13*
Cultivators...	475	5
Field labourers, &c.	44	261
Labourers, unspecified	72	103
Others	95	57
MOLESALAM—CULTIVATORS	*712*	*13*
Field labourers, &c.	128	147
Industries	16	9
Labourers, unspecified	77	55
Others	67	10
MOMNA—CULTIVATORS	*767*	*16*
Field labourers, &c.	111	224
Industries	62	32
Labourers, unspecified	33	511
Others	27	11
PATHANS—CULTIVATORS	*318*	*14*
Public force	123	......
Public administration	119	...
Labourers, unspecified	157	63
Others	283	43
PINJARA—COTTON CARDERS	*270*	*35*
Cultivators	142	23
Trade	247	26
Labourers, unspecified	133	97
Others	208	38
SAIYAD—PRIESTS	*178*	*19*
Cultivators	199	7
Public administration	105	......
Labourers, unspecified	127	79
Others	391	19
SHAIKH—CULTIVATORS	*284*	*20*
Field labourers, &c.	85	130
Industries	104	40
Labourers, unspecified	197	64
Others	330	7
VOHORA—TRADERS, PEDLARS AND CULTIVATORS	*305*	*9*
Cultivators...	404	28
Field labourers, &c.	83	193
Labourers, unspecified	38	49
Others	170	85
PARSIS.		
PARSI—TRADERS	*390*	*4*
Cultivators	129	20
Industries	247	289
Arts and Professions	58	14
Others	176	15
CHRISTIANS.		
NATIVE CHRISTIANS—CULTIVATORS .	*270*	*36*
Field labourers	193	49
Industries	376	58
Labourers, unspecified	67	35
Others	94	36

INDEX.

[*The reference is to the number of paras.*]

For the glossary of caste names, see pages 281 *to* 321.